14/18 – Rupture or Continuity
Belgian Art around World War I

14/18 – Rupture or Continuity

Belgian Art around World War I

Edited by
Inga Rossi-Schrimpf
in collaboration with
Laura Kollwelter

Leuven University Press

ISBN 978 94 6270 136 6
D / 2018/ 1869 / 26
NUR: 654

Layout: Friedemann Vervoort
Cover design: Piet Bodyn & Vladimir Tanghe

GPRC Guaranteed Peer Reviewed Content www.gprc.be

TABLE OF CONTENTS

Préface

MICHEL DRAGUET

Dans le cadre des commémorations de la Grande Guerre, les Musées royaux des Beaux-Arts de Belgique ont consacré un projet de deux ans à la question de l'évolution de l'art belge à l'époque de la Première Guerre mondiale, sous le titre : « 14/18 – Avant et après, Rupture ou continuité? L'art belge au temps de la Grande Guerre ». Mené sous la direction d'Inga Rossi-Schrimpf, chef de travaux et conservatrice, et avec le concours de Laura Kollwelter, chercheuse, l'objectif était de répondre à un manque dans l'histoire de l'art belge, à savoir son évolution globale entre 1910 et 1925. L'idée de départ était de lier l'avant et l'après de la Grande Guerre plutôt que de la considérer comme un point final ou un point de départ. À la différence des scènes artistiques en France ou aux Pays-Bas, celle en Belgique a fortement subi les conséquences d'une invasion, puis occupation et d'un départ en exil d'un bon nombre d'artistes. Les échanges qui s'ensuivirent, ont souvent eu l'effet catalyseur pour de jeunes artistes. L'avant-garde proprement dite doit cependant être confrontée à l'ensemble de la création artistique belge de l'époque afin de mieux la situer.

Ce projet comprenait trois volets, à savoir une recherche menée dans les collections des Musées royaux depuis avril 2016, une exposition-focus en 2016/17 ainsi qu'un colloque international de deux jours en novembre 2016. En réunissant les travaux de recherches d'experts belges et internationaux aux recherches menées par les Musées royaux des Beaux-Arts eux-mêmes, nous espérons stimuler des recherches futures sur cette période continue allant de la fin-de-siècle aux années 1920/30. Cette publication est le résultat de ces efforts.

Encadrant le colloque international, l'exposition focus '14-18 – Rupture or Continuity' montrait une sélection d'œuvres de la période 1910 à 1925 issues des riches collections des Musées royaux des Beaux-Arts. Elle faisait également écho à l'exposition 'Power of the avant-garde' montrée au même moment à Bozar et qui se concentrait sur l'art international. Les différents sujets abordés dans la salle consacrée à cette présentation faisaient écho aux thématiques qui étaient abordées lors du colloque international. Le programme final avait privilégié cinq thèmes principaux : les artistes en guerre, échange interculturel et occupation, influence de la guerre sur le marché de l'art et les stratégies d'exposition, l'art politisé, l'art belge et l'avant-garde international des années 1920. L'intensité des transferts culturels en temps de guerre semble être le constat le plus frappant. L'internationalisation de l'art s'opérant notamment à travers ce temps d'exil et d'occupation. Les sujets ayant attraits aux échanges et transferts entre le milieu belge et le milieu germanique sont ainsi nombreux et ouvre la voie à un autre terrain de recherche encore peu exploité en histoire de l'art belge.

Enfin, le projet permettait également de travailler sur certaines parties des collections des MRBAB, et notamment au récolement des œuvres sur papier de la période concernée et au dépouillement des Archives d'Art Contemporain en Belgique, ici tout d'abord du Fonds De Graaf. Ce récolement a permis la mise en ligne de cette partie de la collection des œuvres sur papier, et de planifier celle de la correspondance du Fonds De Graaf. Ce travail permet d'ores et déjà un accès plus facile aux données de cette collection ce qui contribuera à stimuler la recherche.

Nous tenons à remercier amicalement Inga Rossi-Schrimpf, promoteur du projet, et Laura Kollwelter, qui a pu être engagé comme chercheuse supplémentaire grâce à Belspo, pour l'organisation du colloque, pour le commissariat de l'exposition et de l'outil digital, sans oublier l'important travail d'édition. Elles ont été soutenues pour le colloque par le comité scientifique composé de Véronique Cardon (MRBAB | KMSKB), Christina Kott (Université Panthéon-Assas Paris 2 | Institut d'histoire du temps présent IHTP), Hubert Roland (Université Catholique de Louvain | FNRS), Lara Schrijver (Universiteit Antwerpen), Axel Tixhon (Facultés Universitaires de Namur), Rudi Van Doorslaer (CEGESOMA | Universiteit Gent), Michèle Van Kalck (MRBAB | KMSKB), Francisca Vandepitte (MRBAB | KMSKB), Caterina Verdickt (Universiteit Antwerpen). Ma gratitude va également aux auteurs qui ont participé à ce colloque aussi bien à des scientifiques expérimentés qu'à des jeunes chercheurs ou des amateurs d'art. Aux auteurs repris ici, je souhaiterais associer ceux qui, tout en prenant part au colloque, n'ont pu transposer en texte rédigé leur contribution. Leurs réflexions ont toutefois nourri le texte général sur le projet.

L'organisation du colloque et l'édition de cette publication qui s'inscrivent dans la dynamique de valorisation du patrimoine artistique belge, n'aurait pas été possible sans le précieux soutien financier de la Politique Scientifique fédérale et de la Région Bruxelles-Capitale/Visit Brussels, du Fonds de la Recherche Scientifique (FNRS) et notre partenaire l'Université Catholique de Louvain (UCL). Et nous nous réjouissons de la collaboration avec Leuven University Press.

Le succès du colloque et de l'exposition, confirmé par le nombre de visiteurs et la couverture médiatique, témoigne du vif intérêt porté à ce sujet tant par le milieu scientifique que par le grand public. Nous espérons que la lecture de cet ouvrage permettra de mesurer l'impact de la Grande Guerre sur l'art belge, mais aussi la valeur de cet art belge dans le contexte international des années 1910 à 1925.

Before and After? Rupture or Continuity? Belgian Art around the First World War An Introduction

Inga Rossi-Schrimpf

The centenary of the First World War has internationally triggered a large variety of events and projects. In Belgium, regional and national initiatives were manifold, emphasising different aspects and pursuing different objectives.[1] The intensification and renewal of the study of this war are part of it. This publication is the result of a threefold flourish of activities: an international symposium, a focus exhibition on the collections of the Royal Museums of Fine Arts of Belgium, and a research project. With the objective of encouraging exchange between researchers in different countries, as well as new research on this still too neglected field of Belgian art history, it also wants to provide a missing link between knowledge and literature, on the one hand, on Belgium's fin-de-siècle and, on the other hand, on modernism or surrealism.

With regard to the First World War and art at the beginning of the 20th century, rapid associations are made on the rise of the avant-garde, the reaction to war by artists, between silence and the depiction of horror, and of course the impact of the war on art, generally described as a rupture or turning point. One would naturally think of Futurism, Expressionism and Dadaism. The names of artists who depicted the horrors, such as Otto Dix, as well as of those who perished in the war such as Umberto Boccioni and Franz Marc, are commonly remembered. Not surprisingly, recent exhibition projects such as *1914! La Vanguardia y la Gran Guerra* (Madrid, 2008/09) and *1914. Die Avantgarden im Kampf* (Bonn, 2014) focused on international, mostly vanguard courants, and the First World War as the turning point that led to the rise of the avant-garde. Belgian art was generally lacking although we could find one Belgian artist included in both, respectively: Constant Permeke and Frans Masereel. The 1917 survey (*1917*, Metz, 2013), being more general, also included a painting by Achille Van Sassenbrouck, a member of the *Section artistique de l'armée belge en campagne* [Artistic Section of the Belgian Army in the Field], but also works by Jules Schmalzigaug, Georges Vantongerloo and again Frans Masereel. Parallel to our project, the Brussels Bozar Centre showed another exhibition focusing on the avant-garde: *The Power of the Avantgarde* (Brussels, 2016). Due to the collaboration between the museum and Bozar, a small section was dedicated to Belgian avant-garde: artists including Marthe Donas, Prosper de Troyer, Paul Joostens, Jozef Peeters and Oscar Jespers. However, initially it did not include Belgian artists of the young generation emerging around 1914/18, underpinning the statement that Belgian avant-garde of the early 20th century is still largely unknown outside the country's borders. Interestingly, contemporary artists who were asked to participate in this exhibition by choosing a tandem from the historical avant-garde did choose Belgian artists from the former generations, namely James Ensor and Léon Spilliaert. Both are individual figures in Belgian art history. The first is recognised as a figurehead of Belgian art of the late 19th century and a precursor of 20th-century modernism, the second is mainly associated with late symbolism and pre-surrealism. All of this raised the question of a, at least, perceived gap in artistic relevance between the high point of international recognition of Belgian fin-de-siècle art, and the nowadays international presence of Belgian surrealism. This might be the famous rupture brought about by the war.

However, how true is the assertion that the First World War was THE turning point in the arts and catalyst of the historical avant-garde? Is there really a long 19th century that vanished with the outbreak of the war? What about, for example, the young expressionist movements born around 1905 or the impact of Futurism on interwar art? Finally, how could all of this apply (or not) to the specific case of Belgian art and the Belgian art scene? When it comes to Belgian art, the Great War has been considered either in exhibitions on the artist-soldiers organised since 1916 in the *Section artistique de l'armée belge en campagne* (several exh.), or on the history of artistic exile (exh. Ghent/ Heino/ Cardiff 2002).[2] In our own permanent display, we created, under the title Fin de Siècle – Museum, a section going from 1868 to 1914, ending with Léon Spilliaert but not including our large collection of Rik Wouters, and one could question why Spilliaert ends a long 19th century and Wouters starts a short 20th. Another question is the position of abstract art in Belgian art history. For a long time, art historians judged avant-gardism to be marginal in Belgian art, focusing on the so-called Flemish Expressionism or more conservative movements such as the artists' groups of the school of Sint-Martens-Latem in Flanders or Nervia in Wallonia. After a first exhibition in 1992 on Belgian avant-garde between 1917 and 1929 (Brussels/ Antwerp), it is just in recent years that overviews (Modernism, Ghent 2013) and several monographic exhibitions on artists such as Victor Servranckx,

Jozef Peeters, Karel Maes, Marthe Donas and Jules Schmalzigaug have highlighted this aspect of Belgian art history. Nevertheless, 14/18 has generally been considered as a point of rupture. With few exceptions, art historians were either speaking of a long 19th century ending in 1914 with the outbreak of the war but also with the last exhibition of *La Libre Esthétique*, or of a new avant-garde breaking through as from 1917. In discussions with colleagues inside and outside the Royal Museums of Fine Arts, it became clear that there was a need and a wish to approach Belgian art history and the question of the impact of World War I on it with a larger vision.

This publication aims to give a first overview on the question of the situation of Belgian art, artists and the art scene around the years of war, occupation and exile. It proposes to juxtapose the standard claim of a turning point or rupture with the specific cultural context of Belgian art at the dawn of the 20th century. Nevertheless, it does not in any way pretend to be exhaustive. How could it be! Our dearest wish is to give a basis and important impulse for further research as well as to trigger different viewpoints and associations from those commonly made.

Definition of the topic

The chosen subject is defined by its guiding question on continuities or ruptures around the First World War and by its geographical extensions, its time frame and the more detailed subject of study. The title already outlines the topic quite well:

"14/18" indicates a time frame that is enlarged through the subtitle "around World War I".[3] Indeed, one could not define ruptures and/or continuities without taking into account a certain period before and after the war years. Apart from the fact that dates of political history should not be unquestioned in art historical research, our topic requested a before/after dichotomy to structure the subject and address the question of during. The perspective backwards from the 1920s was even more important to answer our main question. The extent of the before and of the after still had to be defined. Former projects could give inspiration with the time frames of 1917 to 1929, 1912 to 1930, or 1900 to 1930.[4] We emphasised a time frame from ca. 1910 to 1925, from the rise of a new, though timid impulse around 1910/11 with artists like Rik Wouters and Jules Schmalzigaug to the near end of abstraction. The year 1916 appeared as a watershed in several respects and served as a reference point. That said, the research focused not only on those relatively young artists who launched their artistic careers around 1910, and who had developed a personal body of work by around 1920. The question of continuities does not solely apply to rather new or vanguard movements, but also to those artists at the end or in the middle of their careers. The experience of the First World War – particularly of exile or, more broadly speaking, of artistic migration and isolation – led to a certain upheaval in the artistic milieu, but also formed part of a long-standing process of change which should not be overlooked. Thus, to answer the question of continuities clearly it is justified to keep in mind 1900 to 1930 as a broader time frame. Around 1900, Belgian art was highly recognised throughout Europe as a modern force and Brussels was a crossroads for European artists. In the first two decennia of the 20th century it lost its position as an important centre of modernity and renewal. With its own form of Post-Impressionism and fading Symbolism, Belgian art seemed to come to a dead end, while at the same time its protagonists of the 1890s influenced a younger generation in their search for renewal. Several figureheads of the 1890s – including James Ensor, Fernand Khnopff, George Minne, Jean Delville, Constant Montald and Henry van de Velde – continued working and, for some, teaching after the war. Certain of them experienced a sort of comeback at the end of the 1920s. We think of Ensor's itinerary exhibition organised by *Kunst van Heden/ L'Art Contemporain* or the acquisition of several works by Minne for the RMFAB to dedicate a whole room to this artist or the founding of the *La Cambre* art school by van de Velde. By keeping the late 1920s in mind, we were reminded of the importance of figurative tendencies and the phenomenon of the "return to order". It makes clear that certain ruptures were of a temporary nature.

"Belgian art" in the title defines a national framework for the topic, rather than a geographical one. One could of course question this national approach. But national in the case of Belgium at that time is inherently transnational, too. Except for perhaps the contributions of Sandrine Smets and Werner Adriaenssens, there is virtually no contribution that does not in a way transgress national limits. The particularity of being an art scene in relative decline and delayed in respect to the vanguard movements of the two first decades of the 20th century, on the one hand, and being an art scene under occupation or in exile, on the other, makes the Belgian case a fascinating and rich (research) subject. The intellectual benefits of researching Belgian First World War experiences have already been pointed out by Sophie De Schaepdrijver in a half-term account of Belgian commemorations.[5] There is of course the particularity of the Belgian case as a most densely populated country, as a country with two cultures and a country in the centre and at the margin of the conflict. It was also the only country with an art scene that burst between exile and occupation. The Belgian heritage and memory of this war is influenced by this even today. For our topic, we remember that Belgian art is thus not art in Belgium, but art made by Belgians or the image, perception and use of Belgian art.

Within this chronological and national framework, the selection of contributions and of exhibition sections was defined by the central research question: "Rupture or Continuity?". According to this we emphasised reasons for a possible rupture and post-war phenomena which could confirm or refute the assertion of the First World War as a breaking point. The keynote of Sophie De Schaepdrijver gives a general overview of the function and power of images during war, and particularly of occupation as the liminal space in which most of Belgium and the majority of its population experienced the war. In ten images she draws the setting in which Belgian art evolved at least within Belgian territory. The culture of images is of course not restricted to art works and this introduction shows the force of images in a more general way. The following contributions concentrate then according to the main scope of our project on art works and artists. Further, in order to understand the main issues of what happened to Belgian art and its art scene around the years 1914 to 1918, it seemed pertinent to us to focus as a first step on fine arts, and foremost on the context of artistic production. The aim was not to produce a history of what artists did during the four years of war, nor a Belgian iconography of the First World War. According to the main scope of the collections of the Royal Museums of Fine Arts, comprising painting, sculpture and graphic arts from that period, as well as in response to the large majority of proposals, we favoured contributions related to these art forms. In this way the exhibition based on the research project on the collection and archives of the RMFAB accorded with the sections of the symposium. This allowed the dissemination of the scientific topics studied by the experts to a large public through the exhibition and educative tools, the touch table "Digital experience" and a special guided visit linking the Fin de Siècle-Museum and the 14/18-Focus exhibition. As a consequence, several aspects are lacking and would perhaps have slightly changed the conclusions of this project. It is evident that in a second step these conclusions should be confronted and completed with studies in the field of photography and film, architecture and decorative arts.[6]

After a brief survey on the evolution of Belgian art from 1910 to 1925 in the focus exhibition and in the text by Inga Rossi-Schrimpf and Laura Kollwelter, the contributions from the symposium go deeper in its context and background. On the one hand, we looked into the specific situation of Belgian art and the art scene due to invasion and occupation. In the context of propaganda and censorship, occupied territories and trenches, the breakdown of the art market and temporary lock-down of museums and exhibition spaces, the significance of administration and specific war measures, as well of the exiled Belgian as the occupying German government, how did Belgian artists and its art scene react? This included the now disturbed and difficult relationship with Germany and the German-speaking world as well as the politicisation of art through ideas of Community art as through Flemish activism. Isolation was but one aspect of life in exile and under occupation, which also happened to be a particularly rich period in terms of cultural transfer. This opens regional studies to international aspects. With occupation and exile, a new dynamic took hold on the Belgian art scene. The notion of "forced interculturality" is an important factor here. The symposium thus addressed in a second part the question on the position of Belgian art within the international art scene in general and for certain artists in particular. We looked into the search for a new world and a new humanity and the interrelationship between Belgian art and innovative movements.

The situation of Belgian art and its art scene 1900 to 1914

Around 1900, Belgian contemporary artists were present around Europe in exhibitions, galleries and collections. Since the 1880s, and definitely with the founding of the artists' association *Les XX* (1883-1893), Belgium, and especially Brussels, moved from artistic periphery to the centre. Even if one should nuance the characterisation of Brussels as a cultural crossroads of the end of the 19th century, it is true that the exhibitions of *Les XX* and subsequently *La Libre Esthétique,* with their joint programme of concerts and lectures, contributed to the rise of modernity not just in Belgium but in Europe. If the image of Belgian artistic life was then and is still now dominated by this enterprise largely led by the Brussels impresario, Octave Maus, other initiatives should be mentioned as well regarding niche associations or initiatives, such as in Brussels *Pour l'art* and slightly later the *Salon de l'idéalisme* by Jean Delville or more traditional groups like *Als ik kan* in Antwerp. Bruges as a place of pilgrimage for those international artists and writers in search of authenticity, as it was attributed to the primitivism of the Middle Ages, and the success of all kind of neo-styles like neo-Gothic, was another facet of this modernity that made Belgium an important factor in art and literature for almost a whole generation. In 1902, a major exhibition on Flemish primitives was organised that attracted a great number of visitors many of whom were artists. Next to Symbolism and Idealism, the revival of medieval primitivism and neo-styles, Belgian art nouveau in architecture and design was the main feature of what characterised Belgian art at that time. The spectrum of artistic creation was astonishing for such a small country, as was its economic strength. The big industries and the coal mines brought wealth but also social upheaval. It is of consequence that another feature of Belgian art that marked its image was "social art". Of course, there are those artists like Eugène Laermans who depicted workers, peasants, strikes and emigration, but then there were also initiatives to make art accessible to everyone through artistic design in everyday life or through education. The initiatives of the *Maison du Peuple* are the most evident. Last but not least, we should mention in this question the Flemish Movement, that if linked to the emancipation of a language and a culture was also social, as many workers in Wallonia were Flemish. Although Flemish was far from having the same rights as the French language in Belgium, the duality of its culture and its Flemish roots were perhaps even the most important aspect in the identity of writers and, to a lesser extent, artists, though many of them spoke and wrote in French.

In the years just after 1900, the influence of this creation abroad can be observed from the Netherlands to Italy, from the Viennese Secession to the *Brücke* in Dresden, but less west of the country's borders. Sculpture and decorative arts were the most influential. The largest contemporary collections of Meunier and Minne could be found abroad, respectively in Denmark, Germany and Austria. Henry van de Velde, Georges Lemmen and Théo Van Rysselberghe contributed to the diffusion of the "Belgian style" in interior design and typography. Finally, the influence of artists like Félicien Rops and James Ensor on the establishment of print techniques as self-standing and equal works of art refers to an important overall phenomenon: the slow disappearance of the limits between the arts. From fine arts and print, it was just one step to poster design and typography, and some more to other applied arts and architecture. The importance of graphic arts during and just after the First World War grew out of this change in the late 19th century.[7] Photography as a new medium influenced fine arts. It was, for example, also introduced for educational purposes at the Brussels Academy of Arts, where the mayor of the city of Brussels at the time, Charles Buls, as well as Charles van der Stappen, the director, contributed to this new openness.

Although while internationally the reputation of Belgian art of the 1890s reached a high point in the first decade of the 20th century, especially in the German-speaking art scene, the contemporary Belgian creation reached a halt. In the early years of the 20th century symbolism was outdated even in the eyes of some of its own ambassadors. Luminism, the Belgian version of post-impressionism, was widespread, and young artists relocated to the Flemish countryside to be able to work near its utmost representative, Emile Claus. The question was what comes next? Around 1910, we can discern some older artists experiencing a creative crisis and several young artists such as Léon Spilliaert, Rik Wouters, Ferdinand Schirren, Auguste Oleffe and Jules Schmalzigaug, searching for a renewal. The first and the last are quite singular figures, one re-interpreting symbolism with a modernist note, and the other adapting futurist aesthetics. The others built on the overall present impressionist legacy as well as on an admiration of Ensor's early works and were inspired by Cézanne more then by French Fauvism which they could have seen in Brussels in 1906 at *La Libre Esthétique*. If their use of colour and the construction of the composition are modern, their iconography and their fidelity to nature are not. Nevertheless, when new actors such as *Kunst van Heden,* Salon des Indépendants and the George Giroux Gallery showed French Cubism, Italian Futurism and German Expressionism in exhibitions between 1911 and 1913, an immediate impact on Belgian artists was not measurable. In 1914, the so-called "Bleus", the young artists around Wouters and Oleffe, were consecrated in exhibitions as well as at the long-established *La Libre Esthétique* and at the newly opened Giroux Gallery.

After1918 Belgian art did not look completely different. Apart from the example of the symbolist Jean Delville who emphasised his idealism in patriotism, the artists of the first generation of Sint-Martens-Latem continued or transformed their formal language and iconography from before 1914. They were also the so-called "fathers" of the second generation which is commonly classified under Flemish Expressionism. Others like the Jesper brothers can be assimilated with this tendency. Next to this story of transformation and continuity, not rupture, the deaths of Jules Schmalzigaug and Rik Wouters stopped two promising careers abruptly. The Futurist adventure of Schmalzigaug nevertheless is reflected in his influence on Georges Vantongerloo, and in the influence of Futurism and Dadaism on a young generation which started its careers only after 1910. Their formal language – abstraction – is the most visible rupture to pre-war Belgian art. However, as can be shown through the contributions of Hans Vandevoorde, Sergio Servellón and Eva Francioli, there was no complete rejection of tradition, and even several links to ideas of the two preceding generations. The "return to order" in the second half of the 1920s of even such radical artists like Paul Joostens inscribes itself in a larger, not only Belgian, but European movement. The Surrealist Avant-garde around René Magritte and E.L.T. Mesens now took over. Although it was being born out of Dadaism, their purpose was rather reconstructing art than destroying it.[8] In this respect, Surrealism participated in a return to order based on the *Pittura metafisica*.

The specific impact of the First World War on (the) Belgian art (scene)

The situation of Belgian artists and the art scene throughout the decennia between 1910 and 1920 differs substantially from the art scenes of the French, British and Germans, but also those of Austro-Hungarians, Italians and Russians. Albeit that modern life and war affected all of them, revolution, the decline of old orders and the creation of new states and new orders significantly changed the art scenes in central and Eastern Europe, but not those in the West. Socialist ideas on art, as well as an entanglement of Flemish Nationalism and art, prevailed in young vanguard movements just after the war in Belgium, too. This united Belgian artists to international currents, especially North and East of its borders. However, the designated goal of Belgium and Belgians (in their majority) was to re-establish the Belgian state, and thus the "old order". The Belgian art scene as a whole was more affected by the experience of occupation and exile due to a violation of its neutrality. The ensuing image of Belgium as a Martyr led to many actions of charity, among them numerous art exhibitions. It also influenced the Belgian iconography of the war. The Belgian artistic community was forcefully dispersed in 1914 with the invasion and occupation of the vast majority of Belgian territory by German troops. (fig. 1.1) The front line and the trenches occupied the remaining Belgian territory. Consequently, Belgian artists experienced the four years of war in three distinct ways: as soldiers at the front, in exile or under occupation where they needed to define their attitude towards the occupier. This might be the most visible rupture in Belgium's art scene due to war: no common experience to unite them during and after the war. Consequently, the need to reconstruct the (artistic) community might be one of its biggest challenges. The evolution of Belgian art in the years between 1910 and 1925 cannot be understood without this background of occupation and exile. The experience of the front and combat seemed in retrospective less influential on Belgian artistic creation.

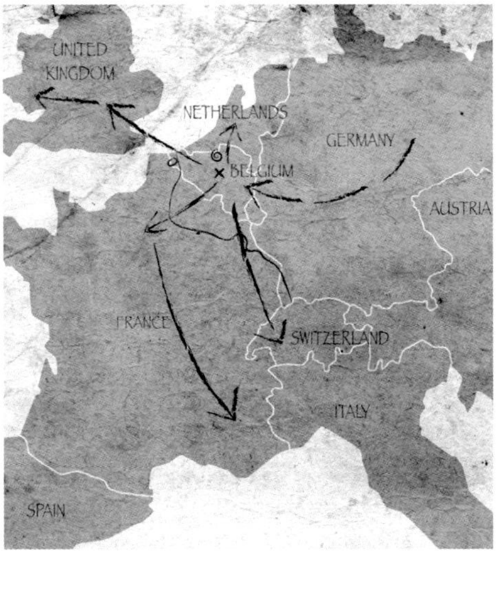

1.1. Map of migrations of Belgian artists. Royal Museums of Fine Arts of Belgium.

Iconography: to show or not to show the war in all its facets

With the invasion by the German army of Belgian territory on 4 August, several measures concerning the art world were taken and museums and exhibitions closed. Art works that were circulating in international exhibitions were kept in place. Of course, artists were also enrolled as they were among those civilians that fled the German army. Direct belligerent action could be witnessed by many, and the experience of utmost violence, the so-called "rape of Belgium" and the propagandistic enforcement of an already horrible reality influenced the Belgian collective memory and its image of the neighbouring country dramatically. A general process of violence and brutalisation of life was one of the consequences of this long and gruelling war. It makes sense that artists involved in or witnessing those actions would try to make sense of them through images. At the symposium itself, Pierre Dejemeppe introduced the first panel with the interesting question on the pictorial reaction of (Belgian) painters facing the horrors of the First World War. He asked, as did Philippe Dagen in his book "Le silence des peintres", how to explain the rather general absence of a depiction of these horrors.[9] He opposed the lack of visual images of wounded and dead soldiers, of fear and of atrocities to the quite explicit written testimonials of artists. Was it easier to express in words rather than in forms and pictures what they saw and experienced? Dagen proposed the loss of the tradition of heroic war paintings as a major explication for the lack of images of this war in art history.[10] However, it is not true that there are no or many fewer images of this war than of former wars. But they are different, in iconography and purpose, as well as the different artistic nations depicted a different war which is in my opinion due to the nature of this first modern warfare. So, would the more appropriate question not rather be what did the artists indeed show of this war, why and what does it tell us about this war?

Recent years have seen an abundance of literature and exhibitions on the First World war in art, mainly regarding French, British or German art.[11] The specific Belgian case was addressed in few exhibitions, but without a comparative approach.[12] Although deeper studies must still be carried out, we can assume some first conclusions from the conference and the following discussion. In Belgian depictions of the war, the most common symbol of the suffering of one belligerent and the barbarism of the other is ruins. There is however a difference in the official works executed during the years of war and those produced in its aftermath. The images almost exclusively of ruins and of healthy and strong soldiers during war gave way to monuments showing dying, dead or hurt soldiers emphasising through this iconographic shift sacrifice and the martyr of Belgium. In both cases, reality is suppressed in favour of propagandistic goals.

The images executed by German artists, often in retrospect, show a wider range of iconography from idyllic land- or cityscapes to horrific scenes in the trenches. Many of them date to the experiences at the front in Belgium and Northern France, where now famous artists, such as Max Beckmann, Otto Dix and Erich Heckel served. Already during the war, several artists challenged the slaughter, especially from 1916 on. We would mention among others Willy Jaeckel's "Memento 1914/15", Max Pechstein's "Somme 1916" and Heinrich Ehmsen's "Gefallener I", 1919. But the most critical works were executed in the aftermath of the war. The same type of representations of the horror of the trenches or the hideous character of occupation are rarely dealt with in Belgian or in British and French art, although they are not completely absent. An exception is the pacifist artist Frans Masereel who denounced the violence of war in similar pictures when in exile in Switzerland in his series "Debouts les morts".

If we keep it with the comparison of the Belgian and the German cases, several reasons for a difference in the depictions of the war can be put forward. The pathos of German Expressionism led, even before the war, to apocalyptic scenes. Most German artists entered the war with an enthusiastic belief in its purifying action. The war and its horrors then became a sort of nourishment for their art, as we can presume of quotations such as the one by Max Beckmann who assures us that drawing protects against danger and death or by Heinrich Nauen who presumes that if ever he were to depict the war, this work would be absolutely different from everything else.[13] Finally, the shock of reality led to a general deception that must have even deepened the face of reality. With the end of the war and the change of order, the war itself became a historical phenomenon and its horrors were depicted by Otto Dix in his famous graphic series.[14] Others like Käthe Kollwitz concentrated on the suffering of those left at home ("Der Krieg", 1921). For Belgium, on the contrary, those preliminary expressionist ideas did not exist, and the heroic soldier or patriotic martyr is the prevalent narrative that did not need to be interrupted after the armistice. Germany was defeated, whilest Belgium won the war in the end after its territory had been violently invaded. The trauma of the invasion and of occupation, but also of the heroism of the Belgian soldier, with as figurehead the "roi-soldat" Albert Ier, remained prevalent in the Belgian imagery of the Great War.

However, during war, a shift in the depiction of the war can be observed as from 1916 for both camps. For Germany, there is the example of the replacement of the *Kriegszeit* revue (1914-1915) by the *Bildermann* (1916), both edited by the gallerist Paul Cassirer and always containing a series of engravings by artists of his gallery, the first being supportive to the war, the second delivering, due to censorship, a subtle critique on it. In Belgium, the creation of the *Section artistique de l'armée belge en campagne* in 1916 to document the war is an example of the need to change the propaganda strategy of "Poor little Belgium" to a different, more heroic image. Sandrine Smets explains that painting was considered more capable of transmitting emotions than for example photography. This might explain why next to the new media with the *Service photographique de l'Armée Belge* which was then incorporated in the *Service Cinématographique de l'Armée Belge*[15] the Belgian government and army relied on fine-arts in their propaganda policy. The iconography of these paintings and drawings thus had as a goal the transmission of the image of a non-aggressive but strong and healthy Belgian soldier, pointing the blame at the attacking enemy and assuring people of a strong army that is holding up well. The only horrors that were depicted were those accentuating the barbarism of the enemy. By considering the iconography of war in Belgian art, we should not forget either that under occupation and German censorship, depictions of the effects of the war were prohibited, which might also partly explain the lack of images accusing the war. Religious themes could sometimes be a derived way of accusing. However, it is not correct that there are no depictions of the horrors of the war from Belgian artists at all. Often, they were created by artists who did not experience the front themselves, but based their works on published photographs, for example Jules De Bruycker and Henry De Groux.[16] De Groux expresses the violence and foremost the sorrow generated by this war still in a quite stylised manner. However, it is clear that this kind of work depends on propaganda, too, and is thus partial. Also, after the war, Belgian art and depictions of the war kept being overall linked to (official) propaganda. There was no place for other images in the reconstruction of Belgian society and self-image. This seems to us another explanation why critical and even cruel depictions are absent in Belgian art even in the interwar years. On the contrary, the graphic series of Otto Dix appeared to the Belgian painter Pierre-Louis Flouquet as a nihilist poem rather than a political pamphlet.[17]

Exile: Belgian art and artists on the move

Many artists who are still prominently present in Belgian art history today did not experience the front. Exceptions are Rik Wouters and Constant Permeke, but both ended up in exile where Wouters died and Permeke found his artistic language. *The stranger* of 1916 (fig. 1.2) is a sort of turning point in his career and is one of the strongest Belgian images on the experience of exile. It was executed in Great Britain where a great number of Belgian artists arrived as from the end of 1914. As Caterina Verdickt explains in her contribution, the Belgian colony in Great Britain was quite active and exchange with the local population varied. The Belgian ministry of Science and the Arts had been installed during the war in London, and most of the activities were indeed proposed and carried out against the background of propaganda and charity. Similar to the creation of the Artistic Section of the Belgian Army, these events thus did not propagate artistic renewal but emphasised conservative positions. This makes sense if one wants to underpin national identity and tradition in art. It was also one very important feature in Belgian self-image as we will see in other contributions. Linked to government's expectations and the main goal of maintaining British support, there are other reasons that pushed Paul Lambotte, the director of Fine Arts at the ministry at that time and organiser behind this policy, to such a choice: his own aesthetic preferences, the rejection of any artists with clear former artistic or commercial links to Germany and the goal of keeping the conservative British public well-disposed to Belgian refugees. For his politics and choices, he was accused by many artists of desertion and partiality. The sustaining of Belgian post-impressionism or late Symbolism in Great Britain, and more in general the action and position of Paul Lambotte, later found its prolongation in Belgian cultural policy in the interwar period. Emphasising rootedness and tradition this "return to order" accentuates again national specificities as they were declared outdated by international avant-garde in the direct aftermath of the war.

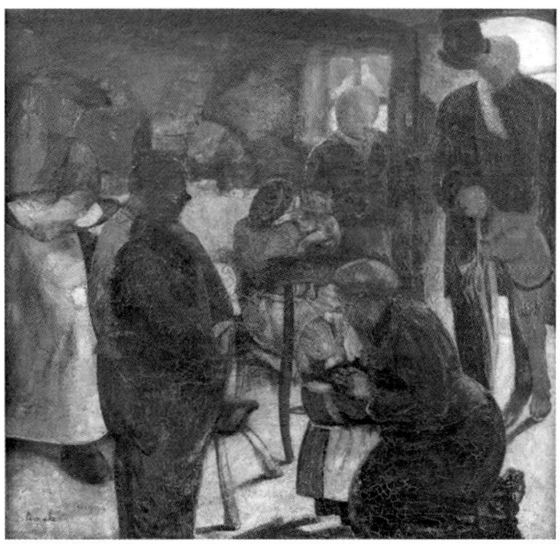

1.2. Constant Permeke, *The Stranger*, 1916. Oil on canvas, 173 x 180 cm. Brussels, Royal Museums of Fine Arts of Belgium, Inv. 4655.

The exhibitions organised by Lambotte were not at last commercial, often "au profit des réfugiés belges" and Belgian artists in exile in France or the Netherlands could equally send works for these exhibitions. The different Belgian communities in exile were thus in contact, and similar activities were organised in France and in the Netherlands. The network concerned conservative artists. For example, in London Jean Delville[18] was a main figure, and in the Netherlands the painters Isidore Opsomer and Robert Wytsman were the main figures of a committee set up to make Belgian art known in the Netherlands. Here again, preference was given to conservative positions and, for example, the painters Gustave De Smet and Frits Van den Berghe did not participate. The fact that there was an active exhibitions policy for Belgian art in France, Great Britain and the Netherlands, or even Scandinavia, however did not mean that Belgian artists did not need to care for their financial survival and had easily found an alternative art market. This was less than true for all those artists who had been pushed aside by the official apparatus. As with Gustave De Smet and Frits Van den Berghe in the Netherlands, these were mostly artists of the School of Sint-Martens-Latem in Great Britain, among them George Minne, Gustave Van de Woestyne and Gustave's brother, Léon De Smet.

Alternatives had to be found by those artists. In Aberystwyth and Llandiloes in Wales there were the Davies sisters who became Maecenas for the Belgian artists. They had in mind a stimulation of culture and arts for Wales due to this foreign impulse. Yet, their action stopped with the return of the Belgian refugees to their home country in 1918/19, whereas a long-lasting relationship between artists and Maecenas grew when Gustave Van de Woestyne, Léon de Smet and Edgard Tytgat met the London-based Dutch businessman Jacob De Graaf. The analysis of the correspondence between De Graaf and ten artists by Laura Kollwelter shows an all-pervading network of mutual support. De Graaf remained loyal to "his" Belgian artists throughout the 1920s when they returned to Belgium. The relationship with their Maecenas changed with this move. De Graaf benefitted then from the knowledge and network of these former exiled artists to acquire an important collection of French art next to his Belgian collection. The new dynamic of the Belgian art scene and art market with new galleries such as *Sélection* and *Le Centaure* and others renewing their action like the *Galerie Georges Giroux*, thus equally benefitted collectors and artists. So-called *Flemish Expressionism* and similar movements, still pushed aside by political apparatus during the war, now became acknowledged also by official circles as the contemporary national style.

Great Britain was only one of several host countries for Belgian refugees during the First World War. Its conservatism and the presence of the Belgian administration of Fine Arts in exile did not leave much space for renewing tendencies. Constant Permeke was an exception, and this was not least due to his contact with fellow artists in the Netherlands. The environment and ambiance in the Netherlands were quite different. Two aspects are interesting for our main question, but also regarding the question of cultural transfers, as will be discussed below. First, the fact that Amsterdam and The Hague at that time saw a young avant-garde emerging. The founding of the group *De Stijl* around Theo van Doesburg is the most obvious sign of the new leading role that Dutch modernism was to take after having looked at what their Southern neighbours did throughout the 19th century. Second, the fact that the

Netherlands were neutral and not overrun by a hostile army. Unlike in Great Britain, there was consequently neither anti-German resentment nor a rather rapid disinterest in the Belgian cause in favour of more national concerns such as the course of the war and the fate of English soldiers at the front. Belgian artists in the Netherlands therefore not only got more visibility throughout the four years of war in exhibitions of Dutch artistic associations, they could also stay informed on new international movements in France, Russia and Germany. If we also quickly look at the Belgian artists' colony in Le Havre, France, during the war, it becomes clear that artistic exile was not the same experience for everyone. Four very individual cases may underpin this statement and the complexity of the experiences of exile: her itinerant exile and encounter with Alexander Archipenko was a springboard for the career of Antwerp artist Marthe Donas (see Peter Pauwels's contribution); his involvement in Pacifism brought Frans Masereel to neutral Switzerland while Henry van de Velde arrived there only in 1917 to escape house arrest as an enemy alien in Germany, that same year, Jules Schmalzigaug ended his own life and at the same time his suffering from artistic isolation in his Dutch exile.

There were already tensions among Belgian artists in exile between conservative, progressive and individual circuits and groups, but Belgium's artistic community was also split between those who left and those who stayed. Sophie De Schapedrijver emphasised the very specific and disturbing experience, for the occupied as well as for the occupier, in the liminal space[19] of occupation. This confusing experience for both occupied and occupier might even be the most specific feature of Belgian memory of the Great war. The "emmurés"[20], as Octave Maus, former secretary of *Les XX* and impresario of *La Libre Esthétique*, called those Belgians who experienced military occupation throughout more than four years, despised the exiles for their lack of suffering. In fact, artists in Belgium acted quite differently under occupation. Jakob Smits for example completely stopped his artistic production for the four years and worked for the *Comité voor hulpverlening en voedselvoorziening van het kanton Mol* to help the suffering population of his region. James Ensor also stayed in Belgium throughout the war and welcomed a number of German artists to his studio. He was also arrested by the occupier because of a caricature he made, depicting Kaiser Wilhelm II as a vulture and was released only after the successful intervention of several German artists. Though he did not stop creating, his production diminished. Not all artists of the village of Sint-Martens-Latem left their homes either. One of the few who stayed was Albert Servaes who had regular contact with German intellectuals, members of the occupation administration, such as Hermann Nohl.[21] In fact, these examples stand for others that show how difficult it was to continue artistic work under occupation – for practical and moral reasons, as well as the various contacts with the occupying power. In addition to these difficulties, there was also the isolation from the art scenes outside Belgium as everything passed German censorship. Belgian artists often relied on those German publications like *Die weissen Blätter*, *Die Aktion* or *Der Sturm*, which passed censorship. Even the development of Belgian artists in exile was largely unknown to the occupied as, for example, we can presume through the arguments and selection in the 1918 text on Expressionism in Flanders by Paul van Ostaijen.[22] In consequence, after armistice, the quite different experiences of the Belgians according to where they had lived during the conflict and the lack of mutual understanding revealed a yawning chasm in Belgian mentality between the two groups.[23]

Though the conditions had changed dramatically, artistic life in Belgium was not at a standstill. The counterpart of Belgian cultural policy in exile was German cultural policy in occupation in which intellectuals, writers and artists were equally involved. During war a rich cultural life in German and for Germans can be observed.[24] Two important aspects of this policy are addressed in the contribution by Hubert Roland and Christina Kott. The main goal of this policy was the consolidation of the German hegemony over Belgium also after the expected peace.[25] It was therefore in itself a long-term policy. Cultural policy was strongly linked to the so-called "Flamenpolitik", a pro-Flemish policy of German authorities based on the narrative of a Germanic brotherhood and the claims of the Flemish movement. Its influence on Flemish and Belgian cultural life at that time may be exemplified by the contributions by Sergio Servellón and Erik Buelinckx, and is still tangible today. On the German side, initiatives such as those described by Hubert Roland and Christina Kott were at least ambiguous. Often carried out by intellectuals, writers or artists who were involved in Belgian art long before the war, they were on the one hand well-intentioned as they took on the other hand part in cultural propaganda and nationalist policy. In the long run, the disastrous cultural policy of the National socialists during the second German occupation of the countries was a consequence, as is the lively German interest in Flemish and Belgian literature and art still today.

Werner Adriaenssens discusses a less studied aspect of artistic life under occupation. With the invasion of Belgium, precautions were taken, and museums as well as exhibitions and galleries closed their doors.[26] There was no talk of reopening, as leisure and amusement were not patriotic, but in December the German "Verwaltungschef" ordered the re-opening of the museums. They thus opened successively in 1915. The museums continued their work as normally as possible, although acquisitions were difficult. Indeed, the most tangible changes for the museums can be detected as from 1917 within the framework of the so-called "Flamenpolitik". Several exhibitions were also organised in the rooms of the Royal museum in Brussels, either with a clear prospect of charity for Belgian artists, imposed by the German occupier or at least with an activist background. The exhibition of the *Doe Stil Voort* group was the last manifestation in this series. But besides these official initiatives, galleries equally reopened their doors. Charity was not the main object. Art works were apparently sold because they were considered a safe investment. The occupier had less influence on this choice. The emphasis on painting was then certainly due to the war and the shortage of material. This shortage affected not only the art market, but also creation. The sculptor George Minne, for example, had no opportunity to sculpt in exile, but brought back about 400 charcoal drawings. Although there were exhibitions and sales in public and private galleries throughout the war in Brussels and elsewhere, the dynamic that had been started just before the war with exhibitions on renewing Belgian art as well as on international avant garde was interrupted. Not only had the exhibitions to suit the occupier, but it seems even more that the idyllic depictions shown, responded to a need for people to escape the sombre reality of occupation. With these new insights and the knowledge on German cultural life in Belgium from 1915 to 1918, we can state that cultural activities did not come to a halt. The relation of the two spheres of cultural life during the war, that of the occupier and that of the Belgian, needs to be analysed further. One interesting aspect in this is, for example, the role of German art dealers and collectors as the German market was a key market for Belgian art before the hostilities.

Cultural transfers in time of war

Cultural transfer as defined in the 1980s by Michel Espagne et Michael Werner[27] for the French-German field has been equally in the focus in the last decennia regarding Belgian culture, both as the receiving and the giving culture. The question of cultural transfers is also inherent in several contributions to this volume and specifically addressed in those of Hubert Roland/ Christina Kott and Inga Rossi-Schrimpf. Both contributions look into the Belgo-German case or in a broader perspective the transfer between Belgian- and German-speaking culture, although this might appear paradoxical in times of war and occupation opposing both nations or both cultural territories. One would at least expect a story of clear rupture in 1914. But Hans-Jürgen Lüsebrink brought forward the thesis of times of war as particularly intense periods of cultural transfer.[28] This applies, according to us, especially to the Belgian case around 1914-18 with its forced interculturality through exile and occupation. In relation to transfers, the Flemish Movement and the decline of Brussels as a cultural hotspot of the turn of the century are of particular interest in our case, on the one hand, and the strength of Belgian heritage, e.g. Flemish Primitivism, and of the social movement, on the other. Further, there was the very strong identity as a dual culture between the Roman and the Germanic as emphasised especially by Flemish French-speaking writers at the end of the 19th century which was also fertile soil for cultural encounters and transfers. For the arts, we should especially mention the existing links between French and Belgian Impressionism and Neo-impressionism, between the English Arts-and-Crafts Movement and Belgian Art Nouveau and neo-Gothic movements, or Belgian symbolism and German-Austrian expressionism. The two decennia just before the war could even be qualified as the high-point of German-Belgian cultural encounters and transfers, also in the arts.[29] Contrary to expectation, cultural transfer was not broken by the war, not even that between German and Belgian culture. What significantly changed for those who stayed in Belgium was that the prevalent link to Paris was more or less cut off due to the front and occupation. The now exiled Belgian artists went less often to France and, if they did, they stayed in the province nearby the exiled government. England and Wales, the Netherlands and, not as paradoxically as it might seem, German-occupied Belgium are thus the cultural territories for transfers or encounters throughout the conflict. The triangle Belgium – Netherlands – Germany should be emphasised in this respect as it remained an important component in the aftermath of the war.[30]

An entire volume could be dedicated to the question of cultural transfers between Belgian culture and those of the hosting as well as occupying countries. The exhibition *Art in Exile. Flanders, Wales and the First World War* (Ghent, 2002) already addressed this question for the Belgian-British case. Other publications focused on Belgian artists in the Netherlands.[31] And a workshop in Lille paralleled the situation in Northern France and Belgium. Special attention was paid to the artists' colony in Le Havre.[32] But in matters of art, in contrast to literature and cultural politics, a similar history of Belgium and Germany still has to be written. The Belgian-German case as exemplified here is very specific and must be understood not only through the actual situation of occupation, but also against the background of several aforementioned pre-war themes and the often called "Nordic" form of modernism in which British Preraphaelism and Arts & Crafts became allied. By extension, Belgian art and its rootedness attracted largely German art critics and art historians in search of a national German art tempering the French domination in the arts. Medieval art and Germanic roots were common factors in this imagined brotherhood of nations. German art historians were not least among the most erudite experts on Flemish primitivism. But modern Belgium equally inspired German intellectuals and artists for its socialist movement and seemingly rebellious character in social questions. This discourse of the end of the 19th century had a major influence on the cultural politics or individual interests of the occupier during the war and explains the harsh reactions, at least in the beginning of invasion and occupation, regarding the Germans, now perceived from a Belgian point of view as barbaric.

Two initially nationalistic and expansionist enterprises are in focus because of their long-term trans-national repercussions. The *Flämische Serie*, a book series of German translations of Flemish, but not just Flemish-speaking literature, was not only a result of the "Flamenpolitik" of the German administration in occupied Belgium, but, as Hubert Roland points out, is part of a longer tradition dating back to the 19th century. A rapprochement and an interest in Flemish literature had already been encouraged through several members of the Flemish movement, and we think for example of Pol de Mont. But it will also be long-lasting. The actual series continued through the 1930s, but the interest in Flemish literature persists in Germany even today. Regarding art and culture in a more general way, the efforts of the German administration as well as of individuals in occupied Belgium stand in the direct tradition of the 19th century. First, there is the pan-Germanic idea. Then there is the revival of medieval primitivism and the rediscovery of the baroque. Though the establishment of a first national photographic inventory of Belgian heritage by the German occupier was used mainly for propaganda and preparation of reconstruction after the war, the focus on the Middle Ages, Renaissance and Baroque definitely framed historical interest on Belgium within existing German art history. Several of the 30 German art historians involved in the inventory had published on Belgian art before. As Christina Kott explains and the exhibition on the *German Negatives* in 2017[33] showed to a large public, the 10.000 or so photographs are of a high quality and, still today, prove very useful for the study and preservation of Belgian heritage. The fact that one of the photographers was Richard Hamann, the later founder of the prestigious *Bildarchiv Foto Marburg*, is also an example of transfer of methodology. Further, after the dispute about the ownership of this inventory just after the war, it became the base of the Belgian Royal Institute for artistic heritage. Nevertheless, it took nearly 100 years and the funding of the national commemorations before this rich collection was studied in depth and even led to new photographic missions throughout Belgium.

The image and self-image of the rootedness in the Middle Ages and the dual character of Belgian culture and identity remained prevalent in the 1920s, as Inga Rossi-Schrimpf shows through German written texts of the interwar period. Flagships of Belgian art had been welcomed very positively in German and Austrian circles since before 1900 and influenced several outstanding artists. When German artists came as soldiers to Belgium, more precisely to Flanders and Brussels, they came also with this background. The visits to Ensor by the now famous Erich Heckel and Max Beckmann are just the most obvious examples of this transfer.[34] The post-war example of the Swiss architect Hannes Meyer shows not only that several main "images" of before the war stay prevalent in its aftermath but recalls also a kind of "histoire croisée" or entanglement and the larger, synchronic mobilisation after 1918, with communitarian aspects and "sovietisation" in which next to East-European, Dutch and French avant-gardes, the German Novembergruppe, Dadaists and the Bauhaus as well as the Belgian avant-garde around the Flemish *Het Overzicht* and the Brussels, French-speaking *7Arts* took part. As emerges also in the contributions of Erik Buelinckx and Sergio Servellón, cultural transfer between (former) occupied and occupier was particularly intense through aspects of political art, rebellion and the belief in a new world to create after the end of the war. In this respect movements and names like the *Clarté*-Pacificism and Paul Colin, the magazine *Résurrection,* Clément Pansaers and Paul van Ostaijen and Flemish activism should be mentioned among others and bring up another important aspect of Belgian artistic life during and just after the war.

Rebellion and propaganda – politicisation of art

The political instrumentalisation of art through propaganda is one aspect of Belgian art in and around the First World War. The work of the Artistic Section of the Belgian Army somehow found its prolongation in the commission and production of a multitude of war memorials. They had to confirm the image of "brave little Belgium". In this sense, the theses in this volume should be confronted with those on war memorials.[35] It seems probable that the conclusions on this matter in fine arts would coincide with those on Belgian cinema around the Great War as established by Leen Engelen: that the fight of the "during" went on in the "after" and the fierce image of the enemy continued to be opposed to that of an idealised Belgian nation.[36] The evolution of art and particularly of graphic art up to and during the First World War shows how Belgian art equally became an instrument of propaganda and a medium of political messages. At the same time, evolution from the late 19th century and a typical feature of the years around the war, this politicised art is both a national and an international phenomenon. In this publication, the question of propaganda and political use of art is introduced in the keynote and addressed through the subjects such as the Artistic Section of the Belgian army or the cultural politics of the occupier and of the Belgian government in exile. We however concentrated in one panel on more leftist positions, on the one hand, and the tension of humanitarian internationalism and Flemish Nationalism, on the other hand. Other subjects would shed other lights on this question, for example, the circles around other art magazines such as *L'Art libre*, *Ça ira!*, *Het Overzicht* and *Résurrection* as well as other personalities like Paul Colin, Frans Masereel and Roger Avermaete. But the main question would stay the same: what could and should be the role of art in society?

One of the photographs that Sophie De Schaepdrijver used in her keynote on the images of occupied Belgium is that of young male students of the Flemish university of Ghent, founded by the German occupier. This defying image is a strong introduction to one aspect of Belgian art around World War I, or more specifically of the period ca. 1917 to 1925: a rebellion of young men and artists against the establishment. It is the amalgam of Communitaurism and Humanitarian Expressionism, thus socialism, and Flemish Nationalism. Indeed, many young men in occupied Belgium lived in a sort of vacuum. What would they do to find a place in society when they did not try illegally to join the Belgian army which actually, in proportion, quite few did. In a more general way, passive resistance as well as complete rejection of German culture faded with the duration of the war. And under certain circumstances the occupier has even been seen as a means of getting closer to one's own claims. This was true for a part of the Flemish movement, but also in a more general rebellion for certain young intellectuals.[37] For this generation that Hans Vandevoorde defined as the generation of 1920, one way to define themselves in Belgian World War I society was rebellion against the bourgeois heritage of their parents and, in the case of the Flemish, a rapprochement with Flemish Nationalism. One important event for this young Flemish artistic avant-garde was the foundation of the *Doe Stil Voort* artists' association and its first exhibition in 1918 showing works of the pioneers of abstract art in Flanders. We will find the same artists names later around the magazine *Het Overzicht* or the *Kring voor moderne kunst* association in Antwerp. Being supported by the *Raad van Vlaanderen* (Council of Flanders), an institution founded under the Germans in order to promote the segregation of Flanders, this initiative cannot deny a political dimension, as Sergio Servellón pointed out. Indeed, activism and new art forms entangle in these last years of war with the magazine *Ruimte* as an important platform for the exchange of ideas. It is here also that we read for the first time in Belgian art theory the notion of "community art" (*gemeenschapskunst*). As aforementioned, here lie links to German avant-garde of the direct aftermath and a quite astonishing exchange takes place as from the last days of war between these movements in the two enemy countries. But Flemish avant-garde was just one, albeit important, aspect of this movement in Belgium, and as Eva Francioli argues for Brussels-based, French-speaking *7Arts* in their idea of a social or socialist community art, equally lie links to the past.[38] The case of the multifaceted figure of Albert Dhaenens brought to life in Erik Buelinckx's essay shows the complexity of politicised art in Belgium around the First World War. The Walloon writer and artist and, next to Joostens, sole Belgian Dadaist Clément Pansaers and his journal *Résurrection* added another aspect.[39] However, and despite the single position of a personality such as Albert Dhaenens and the adventure of the pre- and the post-war series of the magazine *Haro!*, an argument by Hans Vandevoorde might underline that we are nevertheless observing, in the case of community art and abstraction, a rupture in Belgian art history due to the First World War: he states that there is no direct precursor for abstraction in the former generation of artists, which he calls a "lost generation" for abstraction. It is right that Belgians had to be influenced by external factors and examples and developed very late into expressionist and abstract movements, either as political or formal movements. But the lack of a direct precursor must not shadow the various links and preliminary movements in Belgian art since around 1900.

So what seems most important to us is that, although abstraction has its sources in pre-war movements, for Belgium this is the most obvious artistic and aesthetic rupture with the situation of Belgian art in 1913/14, Jules Schmalzigaug being an exception. Quite rebellious in terms of Belgian art at that time, he altered Futurism in a sole aesthetic matter as he was not interested in the political and social dimensions of it. Rebellion and the creation of a new world needed new forms and re-defining of the role of art in society. The impulses given by Dutch artists through *De Stijl* as part of the intense cultural transfer during this disturbing period, and the reading of art magazines such as *Die Aktion* or *Der Sturm* accepted by the censorship or later the knowledge of German initiatives taken by artists in the days of the so-called "Novemberrevolution" contributed to this evolution. It goes without saying that this utopian vision did not last long and that with the decline of the belief in this new world artistic positions soon changed as well.

Internationalism, Avant-garde and a "new" generation

In a time when nationalism(s), prevalent also in art historical discourse since the 19th century, had just led to the first total war, internationalist movements became important as counter-movements. The very example of the Flemish avant-garde shows that Nationalism and Internationalism must not exclude each other. Speaking of community art, it occurs to one that such a vision cannot be an individual undertaking. Although, the art world always functioned through networks and connections, and although these had been international for centuries, the synchronisation between different cultures through the socialisation of art and the belief in the creation of a new world (against philistines) gave international networks and collaboration a new quality. National and international did not exclude each other. But this idea was at the beginning of the 1920s not totally new either. It was already being discussed within the *Van Nu en Straks* movement founded in 1893.[40]

Nevertheless, Hans Vandevoorde distinguishes a generation of 1920 from that of 1910, which he calls a "lost generation" in equivalence to that generation "lost" due to a totalitarian state and again a war just two decennia later. For this generation of 1920, which I would label as a "new generation", the central question became what place was there for art in society? And the answer for a certain number of young artists, architects and art critics was that art is one means of protesting against the existing world and creating a new one. No more individual and subjective art but an ethical or social art in a community. In short, art has to have a social connotation and needs to dedicate itself to social commitment. In this respect, in Belgium, it is also political. This art is different in style as well. It puts forward interdisciplinarity and concords with the evolution of the international avant-garde. The articles on and of international vanguard artists from France and the Netherlands, but also largely from Germany, Hungary, Poland, Switzerland and so on easily confirm the international orientation of the Belgian avant-garde.

In recent years the importance of abstraction and early 1920s avant-garde in Belgium has finally been emphasised and recognised. The modernist movements as analysed in the 2013 exhibition on Belgian Modernism and its international ties are one aspect of the very internationalist avant-garde in the aftermath of the war.[41] The example of the *Section d'or* and the individual case of Marthe Donas, as exposed by Françoise Lucebert and Peter Pauwels, are others. The post-war *Section d'or* shows a certain decline in French or even Parisian dominance in the aftermath of the war. Unlike the modernist circles, it did not promote a common style but was more about giving artists exhibition and sales opportunities in a more and more competitive art world that still struggled with the consequences of the war. The exhibition of the *Section d'or*, but also the participation of international artists in Belgian exhibitions and vice versa show that Belgium was directly integrated in international art after occupation and exile ended. This was not least due to contacts laid down during the years of war. Also, the international avant-garde was led by the wish for reconciliation between people. This was for example the major message propagated by the magazine *L'Art libre*, edited by Paul Colin. As we could observe throughout the symposium and the research on the RMFAB collection, Belgian art of that time evolved between the traditional and the novel. The contributions of Laura Kollwelter, Caterina Verdickt and Ole Fischer give an insight into the other pole of Belgian art and the real impact of this "new" generation and the success of the "new world". As Ole Fischer's case-study on Henry van de Velde shows, Belgian protagonists of turn of the century avant-garde ran already through an artistic crisis in the beginning of the second decennium of the century. From an artistic point of view, they did not contribute with their later art works to a renewal in art. Nevertheless, their former works and art theory had major influence on the younger generation and the avant-garde of the 1920s. One may think of Henry van de Velde and especially his Werkbund theatre, of course, but also of George Minne or James Ensor. Eva Francioli rightly pointed out the links between ideas on social art at the end of the 19th century in *Art moderne* or *L'art social* or the activities of *La Maison du Peuple* and those propagated in the 1920s by the modernists around the art magazine *7 Arts* who claimed Victor Horta and Henry van de Velde among others as their precursors. In the same manner, the ideas on community art in the Flemish magazine *Ruimte* were rooted in similar ideas expressed by John Ruskin and William Morris in the past century. Consequently, the "new" generation and the "new" art were no rupture but a transformation and still rooted in traditions. This is also true for the next generation, the Surrealists.

Next to the avant-garde, there existed a generation of moderate artists more evidently rooted in Belgian tradition and promoted as a national school. This national movement participated also in international contacts, parallel or sometimes interwoven with the first. The network around the Dutch Maecenas De Graaf is one example, the official networks around Paul Lambotte and Ernest Verlant are others. This "other" generation emphasised heritage rather than renewal. Flemish Expressionism, Animism or other figurative tendencies were promoted by official instances quite on the contrary to abstraction and modernism. At the end of the 1920s, it became prevalent. In a way, Flemish expressionism, Belgian Surrealism, Dutch Magic Realism and German New Objectivity are in the end individual parts of a general evolution based largely on a "return to order" or at least on a revision.[42]

Caesura or no caesura – conclusions on Belgian art around the First World War

Of course, this volume does not pretend to exhaustively answer the question on the evolution of Belgian art and the art scene around the First World War. Many topics are still to be studied and discussed in order to confirm this general outline of the situation of Belgian art and artists around World War I.

On the basis of the symposium and our own research we can however conclude that, at least in painting, sculpture and graphic arts, the main rupture and challenge was not so much new forms, iconography or content. It was the bursting of the art scene due to exile and occupation and the necessary reconstruction of it after armistice which affected the Belgian art scene as a whole. Migration can be seen certainly as one important factor in the becoming of the avant-garde.[43] The image of "re-crystallization" as Sophie de Schaepdrijver used it for Belgian culture in a broader sense seems most appropriate also regarding artistic creation and theory. Rather than breaking up pre-war traditions, it transformed them. With the forced step outside their comfort zone, Belgian artists tackled the road to renewal more determinedly. Their art was more affected by the forced confrontation with other art scenes and other issues outside the country's borders than by the encounter with the newest artistic trends from Paris, Italy or Germany in Belgium right before the war. Nevertheless, the changes did not come out of the blue. They had built up slowly since around 1910. The exchange as well as the rivalry between the two generations (of 1910 and 1920) underlines that not rupture or continuity but transformation would be the more appropriate term to describe the evolution of Belgian art and art scene in those disturbing years around the First World War.

The image of continuity was already stressed in the 1920s by official art discourse where abstraction and community art were completely missing. It emphasised, through acquisition policy as well as official exhibitions, moderate art movements relying on a Belgian or even more specifically Flemish figurative tradition. In the interwar period abstraction seemed to be an interlude, which did not significantly shake up Belgian art in the longer run. It is only after the next World War that Belgian art took up on this generation. It is also the war of 1939-1945 and not 14/18 which in European art history is a clear breaking point. Even more than for the First World War, artists were now confronted with the question of what images they could still take away with them after such horror.

It was not just artistic creation but also cultural life that was affected by the war and underwent changes. Though we can state that cultural life took up again under occupation, it differed in many ways from before 1914. Exhibitions had to respond to the criteria of propaganda, charity or escapism. Belgian artists lost a great part of their market, and not least the German-Austrian one. The invasion somehow ended the high point of German-Belgian cultural relations bringing on a major identity crisis of Belgian literates and intellectuals. Propaganda and Censorship affected artistic creation but also the influences and inspiration, as available sources depended on them. In this context we can mention the idea of forced interculturality: transnational transfer between the culture of the occupier and the occupied was intensified through censure and through occupation politics, in the case of Belgium this resumed essentially in "Flamenpolitik" and the limited accessibility of sources on contemporary art other than those accepted by German census. The important action of cultural policy through exhibitions was pursued after the war through organisations such as the *Ligue Belge d'expansion artistique* or the government itself. Numerous Belgian, politically motivated exhibitions travelled foremost to France and the Netherlands, but also to Switzerland, Scandinavia and, as from the second half of the 1920s, again to Germany. The touring exhibitions of Flemish art organised by the DeVlAG in the 1940s lie in a certain continuity of the "Flamenpolitik".

To conclude and change the initial question in an affirmation, we thus propose a slight but consequent change in the title of our project "Rupture or Continuity?": instead of OR, we propose to put AND.

Notes

1 Cf. the special issue "DEBATE – DÉBAT. Les commémorations du centenaire de la Première Guerre mondiale: réflexion à mi-terme," *Revue belge d'Histoire contemporaine* XLVI, 3/4 (2016).

2 Cf. Bibliography for these exhibition catalogues and the following catalogues mentioned below.

3 In 2013, there had been a symposium on the year 1914 as watershed, emphasising a shift between before and after the outbreak of the war, and thus taking a quite different perspective: Marine Branland, ed., *1914 – Guerre et avant-gardes* (Paris: Presses universitaires Paris Ouest, 2016).

4 Eliane de Wilde et al., eds., *Avant-garde in België: 1917-1929* (Brussels: Gemeentekrediet, 1992); Johan de Smet, ed., *Modernisme: L'art abstrait belge et l'Europe* (Brussels, Gent: Fonds Mercator; Museum voor Schone Kunsten Gent, 2013); Robert Hoozee and Piet Boyens, *Vlaams expressionisme in Europese context, 1900-1930* (Gent: Snoeck-Ducaju; Ludion, 1990).

5 Sophie de Schaepdrijver, "New Research on First World War Belgium," *Revue belge d'Histoire contemporaine* XLVI, 3/4 (2016), 206-210.

6 Possible subjects for a second volume could be the continuities and ruptures in the use of photography and photographic techniques by artists or those between Art Nouveau architecture and decorative arts with Modernism, but also in the idea of the equivalence between the arts, design and the artisanal work linked to that of the 'Gesamtkunstwerk'.

7 Marine Branland studied the use of graphic arts during the war intensively in her dissertation: *La gravure en Grande Guerre: donner corps à son experience (France, Belgique, Angleterre)*, sous la direction de Thierry Dufrêne et Anette Becker, Paris X Nanterre, soutenue le 28.10.2013. See also Martin Hopkins, "Belgian Prints in Britain during World War I," *Print Quarterly* XXXIII, no. 4 (2016), 416-427.

8 Kylikki Zacharias proposed an interesting parallel between Surrealism and Objectivity: Kylikki Zacharias, "Surreale Sachlichkeit," in *Surreale Sachlichkeit: Werke der 1920er- und 1930er Jahre aus der Nationalgalerie*, ed. Kylikki Zacharias (Berlin, Dresden: Neue Nationalgalerie – Staatliche Museen zu Berlin; Sandstein Verlag, 2016), 8-23.

9 Philippe Dagen, *Le silence des peintres: Les artistes face à la Grande Guerre* (Paris: editions Hazan, 2012), 16. Dagen questioned a more general quantitative lack of images.

10 *Ibid.*

11 For example Claire Maingon, *L'art face à la guerre* (Vincennes: éd. PUV, 2015); Gerhard Finckh, ed., *Das Menschenschlachthaus: Der Erste Weltkrieg in der französischen und deutschen Kunst* (Wuppertal: von der Heydt-Museum, 2014); Sean Rainbird, ed., *Kollwitz – Beckmann – Dix – Grosz: Kriegszeit* (Tübingen/ Berlin: Ernst Wasmuth Verlag, 2011); Bernd Küster, ed., *Der Erste Weltkrieg und die Kunst: Von der Propaganda zum Widerstand* (Gifkendorf: Merlin Verlag, 2008); Richard Cork, *A Bitter Truth: Avant-Garde Art and the Great War* (New Haven et al.: Yale University Press, 1994). Emma Chambers, ed., *Aftermath. Art in the Wake of World War One* (London: Tate Publishing, 2018).

12 Jean Lorette, ed., *14-18: Kunstenaarsvisie* (Brussels: Koninklijk Museum van het Leger en van Krijgsgeschiedenis, 1993); Sébastien Clerbois, ed., *Artistes belges en 1914-18: 80ème anniversaire de l'Armistice du 11 novembre* (La Louvière: Musée Ianchelevici, 1998).

13 Cf. Exh. Cat. *1914. Avantgarden im Kampf*, 304 and 317.

14 See on the idea that World War I impacted on art most when it became a historical phenomenon: Stephen C. Foster, "World War I: The Grand Illusion, the Avant-Garde and the Formal Revolution" in Rumold, Rainer; Werckmeister, Otto Karl, eds, *The Ideological crisis of expressionism. The literary and artistic German War colony in Belgium 1914-1918* (Columbia: Camden House, 1990), 284.

15 See on Belgian Film and the Great War: Leen Engelen, "Film/ Cinéma (Belgium)," *1914-1918-online. International Encyclopedia of the First World War*, no. 85 (2017), accessed 15-10-17, doi:10.15463/ie1418.10320.

16 Parallel to the 14/18 exhibition the RMFAB showed a selection of works on the First World War by Henry De Groux of the collection of the Print Room of the Royal Library in the Fin-de-Siècle Museum. Cf. on De Groux's works on the First World War: Jan Dewilde and Thomas Schlesser, *Henry De Groux. Oorlogsgetuige/ Témoin de guerre 1866-1930* (Ieper: In Flanders Fields Museum vzw, 2008).

17 "Réaliste avant tout, Dix ne commente aucune théorie politique. Sa série 'La Guerre' est moins un pamphlet qu'un poème au néant, [...]". Pierre Flouquet "Cabinet graphique: Otto Dix. Série: 'La Guerre'", *7 Arts*, 3 (1924/25), 14 (5.02.).

18 See on Jean Delville Hubert Roland, "Jean Delville et la Première Guerre Mondiale," in *Jean Delville (1867-1953): Maître de l'idéal*, Denis Laoureux, ed. (Paris: Somogy Editions, 2014), 96-102.

19 See for the visual representations of occupation in Belgium and France also François Robichon, ed., *La France et la Belgique occupées (1914-1918): Regards croisés*, Cahiers de l'IRHiS n° 7, Lille, 2009.

20 Letter from Octave Maus to Paul Lambotte, Lausanne, 30 March 1919, Brussels, Bibliothèque Royale de Belgique, Section des Manuscrits, MS.7133/597-609. I thank Noémie Goldman for informing me about this letter.

21 On Nohl's contacts with Belgian artists, cf. Herman Nohl, *Ein Landsturmmann im Himmel: Flandern und der Erste Weltkrieg in den Briefen von Herman Nohl an seine Frau*, ed. Walter Thys (Leipzig: Leipziger Univ.-Verl., 2005).

22 See this conclusion in Gerrit Borgers, *Paul Van Ostaijen: Een documentatie*, 2nd ed. (Amsterdam: Uitgeverij Bert Bakker, 1996).

23 This opposition between occupied and exiled Belgians was a more general phenomenon during the First World War, cf. Michaël Amara, *Des Belges à l'épreuve de l'exil: Les réfugiés de la Première guerre mondiale: France, Grande-Bretagne, Pays-Bas. 1914-1918*, 2nd ed. (Brussels, Paris, Le Plessis-Pâté: Éditions de l'Université de Bruxelles, 2014). See also the letter by Octave Maus to Paul Lambotte, as footnote 20.

24 Cf. Ulrich Tiedau, "De Duitse cultuurpolitiek in België Tijdens de Eerste Wereldoorlog," *Cahiers d'Histoire du Temps présent*, no. 11 (2003), 21-45.

25 See on these matters Christina Kott, *Préserver l'art de l'ennemi? Le patrimoine artistique en Belgique et en France occupées, 1914-1918,* Comparatisme et société No. 4 (Brussels, Bern, Berlin, Frankfurt am Main, New York, Oxford, Wien: PIE Lang, 2006) and Tiedau, "De Duitse cultuurpolitiek in België Tijdens de Eerste Wereldoorlog".

26 Anneleen Arnout, "Archimedes achterna: De Belgische musea tijdens de Eerste Wereldoorlog," *Bijdragen tot de Eigentijdse Geschiedenis* 22 (2010), 55-92.

27 Michel Espagne and Michael Werner, *Transferts et relations interculturelles dans l'espace Franco-Allemand [18. et 19 siècle]* (Paris: Ed. Recherche sur les Civilisations, 1988).

28 Cf. the contribution by Christina Kott and Hubert Roland on p. 174, footnote 2.

29 Several aspects have already been emphasised, but a specific study of German-Belgian transfers in the arts is still outstanding and a research focus of the author.

30 Nathalie Toussaint, "Interconnexions des avant-gardes picturales entre la Belgique, l'Allemagne et les Pays-Bas de 1914 à 1924: Une exemplification" (Thèse présentée en vue de l'obtention du grade de docteur en Philologie et Lettres (Archéologie et Histoire de l'Art), Philosophie et Lettres (Archéologie et Histoire de l'Art), Université Catholique de Louvain, 2000). I thank Nathalie Toussaint for the possibility to consult her thesis.

31 Oliver Fairclough and Robert Hoozee, eds., *Art in Exile: Flanders, Wales and the First World War* (Antwerp: Petraco-Pandora, 2002); Piet Boyens, *De Passage: Vlaamse kunstenaars in Nederland 1914-1922,* Kranenburgh Cahiers 10 (Bergen: Museum Kranenburgh, 2000); Adriaan Venema, *De ballingen: Frits van den Berghe, Gustave De Smet en Rik Wouters in Nerderland 1914-1921* (Baarn: Het Wereldvenster, 1979).

32 Cf. *La France et la Belgique occupées (1914-1918): Regards croisés,* especially the contribution of Céline De Potter.

33 *Les clichés allemands (1917-1918). Le patrimoine artistique belge à travers l'objectif de l'occupant / De Duitse negatieven (1917-1918). Het Belgisch artistiek erfgoed door de lens van de bezetter*, Parc de Bruxelles, Brussels, 15.06.2017-17.09.2017, organised by KIK-IRPA.

34 Paul Hadermann was the first to emphasise the links of German art to Belgium around World War I, expanding by this the well-studied question of such transfers in literature. Cf. Paul Hadermann, "Echanges belgo-berlinois de l'Art Nouveau aux années vingt," in *Expressionisme à Berlin, 1910-1920: Palais des beaux-arts, Bruxelles, 22 septembre-4 novembre 1984* (Brussels: Société des expositions du Palais des beaux-arts de Bruxelles, 1984), 33-37, and Paul Hadermann, "Belgo-German Relations in the Arts, 1890-1918," in *The Ideological crisis of expressionism: The literary and artistic German War colony in Belgium 1914-1918,* ed. Rainer Rumold and Otto K. Werckmeister, Studies in German literature, linguistics, and culture 51 (Columbia, SC: Camden House, 1990), 19-39.

35 For example, Stéphanie Claisse, *Du soldat inconnu aux monuments commémoratifs belges de la guerre 14-18,* Mémoire de la classe des lettres et des sciences morales et politiques 1 (Brussels: Académie Royale des Sciences, 2013).

36 Engelen, "Film/ Cinéma (Belgium)," here conclusions.

37 Cf. here for example the study of An Paenhuysen, *De nieuwe wereld: De wonderjaren van de Belgische avant-garde (1918-1939)* (Antwerpen: Meulenhoff/Manteau, 2010).

38 Cf. next to the contribution of Eva Francioli also Erik Buelinckx, "Henry Van de Velde, Art Nouveau and Intellectual Anarchism," *Uncommon Culture* 4, 7/8 (Art Nouveau) (2013), 33-43.

39 Cf. on Clément Pansaers Hubert Roland, "*Résurrection*, Clément Pansaers et Carl Sternheim : 'comment rendre une revue intéressante'," *Les Lettres romanes* (XLVIII, 3-4, 1994), 259-275.

40 Auguste Vermeylen, "Vlaamsche en Europese Beweging," *Van Nu en Straks* (new series 4, 5/6, November 1900), 310.

41 De Smet, *Modernisme*.

42 Virginie Devillez, *Le retour à l'ordre: Art et politique en Belgique 1918-1945* (Brussels: Dexia, 2003) and Virginie Devillez, "Les arts en crise: la Belgique dans le contexte européen (1918-1940)," *Textyles. Revue des lettres belges de langue française* 24 (2004), 52-62.

43 Another factor is urbanisation. And indeed, the young Belgian generation discovered the topic of the city equally during the war years. Cf. Music-Hall (1916) by Paul van Ostaijen.

Shaping the Experience of Military Occupation: Ten Images

Sophie De Schaepdrijver

Introduction

When we refer to "the cultural history of the First World War," we tend to think of masterpieces, such as Picasso's monumental overture curtain for the epoch-making 1917 ballet *Parade*.[1] What does such a work of art say about the war – or, rather, what does it *not* say?[2]

However, "the cultural history of the First World War" also refers to rather less high-brow and less avant-garde expressions of art.

Many men on the Western Front, for instance, would have seen (and possibly cherished) images generated by a popular devotion that gained extraordinary heights during the war – that to the French nun Thérèse de Lisieux (who had died in 1897 and would be canonised in 1925).[3] Those images often represented her as the only force standing between the troops and destruction. The wider point to be made is that "art" in the First World War needs to be defined in the widest possible sense, including popular arts and crafts, traditional or reactionary art forms, advertising, and so on.

To go even further: "the cultural history of the First World War" need not even refer to "art" in the accepted sense at all.

As John Horne, the pre-eminent cultural historian of the First World War, points out, as the "fronts" in the First World War formed, they had to be acknowledged. Participants had to realise that they were not fighting the mobile Napoleonic war they had been raised to expect.

> "The drama [therefore] was one of cognition and imagination since it entailed slowly and painfully replacing understandings of war inherited from an earlier era with those that addressed industrial siege warfare. The 'front,' therefore, did not just happen. It had to be conceived and imagined."[4]

That too is cultural history in the sense of defining "culture" broadly; "culture" as the sets of beliefs and representations and habits and customs that allow humans to make sense of what is happening to them, that allows them to interact.[5] The cultural history of the First World War, then, aims to retrace the ways in which those who lived through the war made sense of their experience both during and after the conflict.

This approach is particularly fruitful with regard to military occupation. During the First World War, occupied Europe formed a liminal space, neither "front" nor "home front". Military occupation was a confusing experience, both for the occupied and for the occupiers. The cultural-history question of how contemporaries made sense of their war experience – or at least attempted to make sense of it – is of especial interest.

In what follows, I will pursue this question with regard to the German occupation of Belgium in "14-18". I will look at this both from the perspective of the occupied civilians and from the perspective of members of the occupying administration and army. For heuristic purposes, I will do so by presenting and analysing ten images which, each in its own way, shed light on the way in which those who lived through occupation sought to give shape to the experience – both for themselves and for others.

Giving shape to experience was a particularly arduous endeavour, because the occupation was a disorienting experience. Including for the occupiers: the great German sociologist Max Weber, looking at the effort of occupying Belgium, called the whole project "gespenstisch", nightmarish.[6] And we know from the work of Hubert Roland how members of the occupation administration created a separate and almost unreal world for themselves.[7] As for the occupied civilians, they lacked means of communication and they felt trapped; one diarist compared life under occupation to "the murky, mind-numbing regimen of the prison cell",[8] an existence without markers, without a clear direction.

It is precisely the effort to formulate a clear direction for the occupied civilians that provides me with my first image.

Image 1: Mercier, patriotisme et endurance

As many of you may know, the primate of the Catholic Church of Belgium, Cardinal Mercier, in his pastoral letter for the New Year 1915 defined what he saw as the task that confronted the occupied civilians: that is to say, to show solidarity and fight the material misery that was threatening to drown ever more people; show themselves worthy of the soldiers at the front and stop complaining; and, vis-à-vis the German army, to refrain from armed action because that would endanger fellow citizens, but at the same time to deny the new occupation regime all legitimacy: Mercier stated forcefully that an occupation regime by definition would not last:

> "The Power which has invaded our soil and temporarily occupies most of it ... is not a legitimate authority. In your heart of hearts you owe it neither respect, nor loyalty, nor obedience."[9]

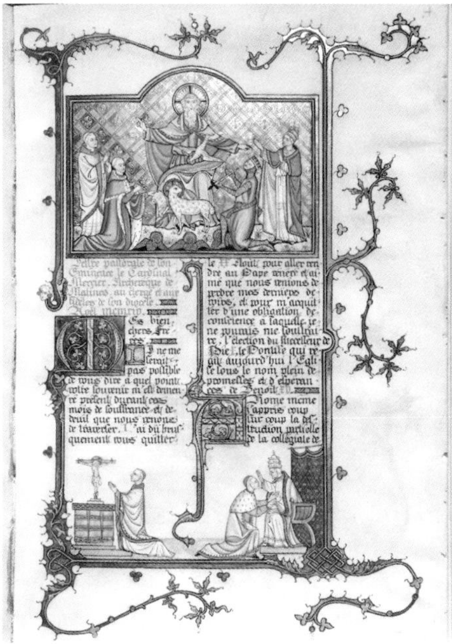

2.1. Cardinal Mercier, Pastoral letter, Patriotisme et endurance, Illuminated manuscript, 1915, Benedictine cloister Maredret (Namur). 13 leaves, bound: vellum, ill., 150x110mm. Pierpont Morgan Library, New York.

This was a major statement which made a great deal of impact, not just among Catholics. Its impact was increased because it became a forbidden text – which, of course, strengthened its message that the occupation regime was not legitimate. The ban on the text also, paradoxically, made it more present in a material way: given the risks of printing it, entire monastic communities set about transcribing it by hand. Some modes of transmission were especially fanciful: this image is a rendering of the text in the manner of a medieval manuscript, done by the Benedictine Sisters at the Convent of Maredret near Namur, which specialised in neo-medieval illuminations. The choice of medium is very telling. The Cardinal's message becomes a sacred text. In addition, the medium deliberately slows down time: the highly labour-intensive rendering sets the timelessness of Mercier's message of ultimate justice against the merely temporary imposition of a regime. The very medium expresses the duty of "endurance" that Mercier urged on civilians.

Image 2: The underground press

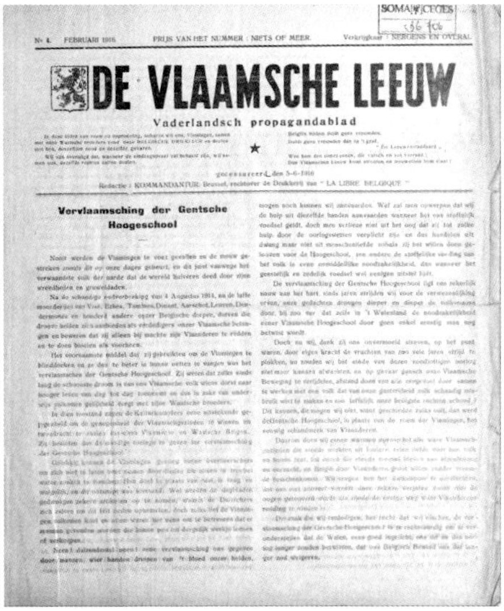

N° 4. FEBRUARI 1916 PRIJS VAN HET NUMMER : NIETS OF MEER. Verkrijgbaar : NERGENS EN OVERAL

DE VLAAMSCHE LEEUW

Vaderlandsch propagandablad

Redactie : KOMMANDANTUR Brussel, rechtover de Drukkerij van " LA LIBRE BELGIQUE "

Vervlaamsching der Gentsche Hoogeschool

2.2. Front page of clandestine newspaper *De Vlaamsche Leeuw*, February 1916.

Mercier's Pastoral Letter, a forbidden text, launched an entire underground press. This second image refers to the existence of that underground press in occupied Belgium – the most lively resistance press in all of occupied Europe during the First World War. Its main task was to urge civilians to remember that the regime would disappear; and, in the meantime, to endure, to help each other, and to refuse any compliance with the regime. This clandestine press was a collective effort made by communities of citizens, which in turn created an entire subculture of its own, made up of people with a secret. Studying these networks and their clandestine production reveals a great deal about the occupied population's ever renewed effort to draw clear lines in the sand, to praise and to criticise, to define civilians' duty. But studying this clandestine press also shows this effort over time: at its height in 1915, it flagged greatly in 1916, and hit its lowest point in 1917, a year of enormous doubt across Europe. [10]

Image 3: Solidarity... and exhaustion

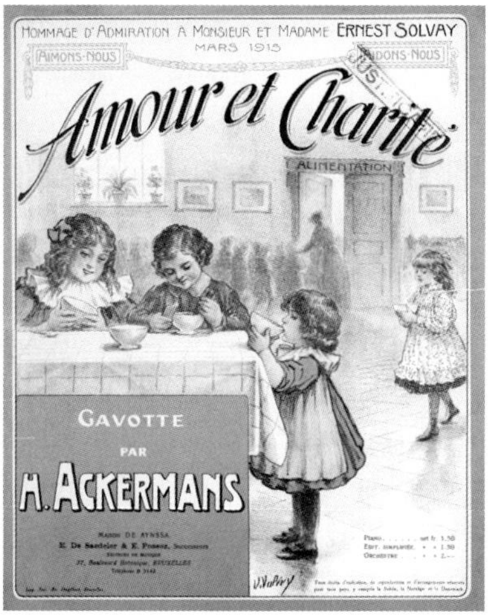

2.3a. Sheet-music and lyrics from 1915, *Amour et charité: aimons-nous - aidons-nous* (Gavotte). Hippolyte Ackermans, Brussels: E. De Saedeler & E. Possoz, 1915, 8 p.

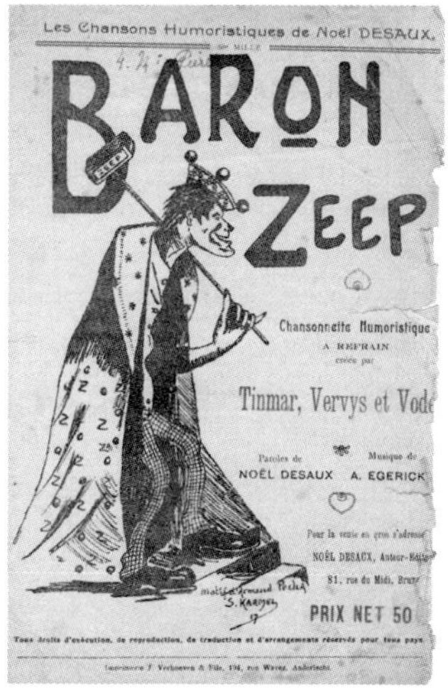

2.3b. Sheet-music and lyrics from 1917, *Baron zeep* (satirical). Lyrics: Noël Desaux, music: Aug. Egerickx, Brussels: Noël Desaux, [s.d.], 3 p.

Patriotic culture defined solidarity as a central duty of civilians. The sheet-music image from 1915 is indicative of an entire culture that sprang up around this central tenet of the patriotic message. Charity efforts generated a great deal of artistic and semi-artistic output – fancy-fairs, charity performances, art-work produced to boost charities' profile.[11]

The well-known Symbolist painter Fernand Khnopff (1858-1921), for instance, was one of several Belgian artists who made creations to benefit the charity organisation *L'Assistance Discrète*, which specialised in helping out the impoverished petite bourgeoisie.[12] It bears pointing out that the emphasis on class differences was part and parcel of war culture.

Like the clandestine press, the collective effort of charity showed signs of exhaustion by 1917. The satirical image which dates from that year forms, in a way, a pendant to the 1915 charity image: in public depictions, the image of unity made way for an image of discord. As it did in private depictions: personal diaries testify to this shift.[13]

Before returning to the exhaustion of patriotic culture, to its inherent tensions and paradoxes, it is important to draw attention to another one of its elements: it defined the soldiers at the front as the ultimate criterion of sacrifice. It behoved civilians to show themselves worthy of the soldiers.

Image 4: Soldiers' sacrifice

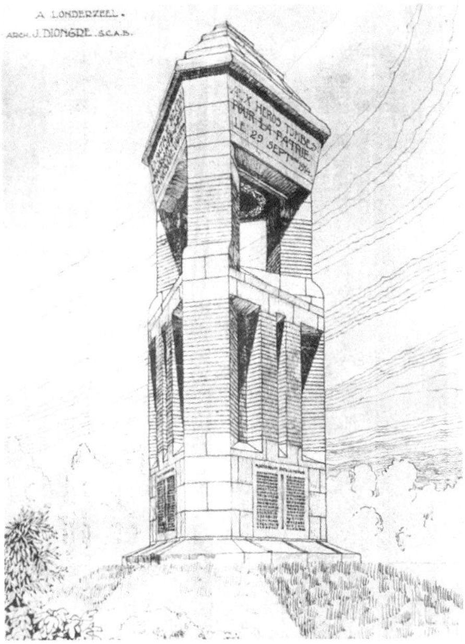

2.4. Wartime sketch for a war memorial at Londerzeel (Brabant) by the architect Joseph Diongre. Algemeen Rijksarchief, Brussel, Fonds Jeanne Orianne.

Although occupied Belgium was not allowed any contact with Belgium at the front, "the front" was an enduring presence. It made for a continuous soundscape: the guns on the Yser and at Ypres could be heard very clearly as far as Brussels and even beyond. Under occupation, civilians could not engage in concrete work for the soldiers. But at least patriots could take care of the remains of those men who had died during the first phase of the fighting and who lay buried across the now occupied country. These were largely individual initiatives. The most successful example hails from Brabant province: it is that of Jeanne Orianne, an officer's daughter from Londerzeel with some independent means and a great deal of resolve. Among the major artists she contacted to raise money for her reburial enterprise was Joseph Diongre (1878-1963),who would go on to become one of Belgium's most famous Art Deco architects in the 1920s and 1930s. Diongre contributed an architect's sketch for a memorial, which Orianne sold as a postcard to raise funds.

The point to be made here is that the soldier dying on the battlefield was the ultimate emblem of duty – impossible for a civilian to emulate, to be sure, but nevertheless indicating standards of self-abnegation.

One element of civilians' duty was to keep a proper distance from the occupier.

Image 5: Keeping the occupier at arm's length

Keeping one's "patriotic distance" from the occupier was a means of underscoring the essential illegitimacy of the occupation regime.[14] Bourgeois respectability demanded it: Belgium's elites, especially, were supposed to keep their distance from the occupiers. But "patriotic distance" also had its vernacular side. One Brussels cartoon, presumably from 1915, clearly expresses the gist of this message. It represents a street urchin making fun of a German guard standing behind a fruit-cart. The guard's spike-helmeted face appears above a cart in such a manner that it resembles a large pear. The setup aims to put the occupier in his place. Instead of dominating the urban context, the soldier is dragged into it. His weapons are essentially taken away: the bayonet sticks ludicrously out of the mass of fruit; the spike-helmet reinforces the pear simile. The cartoon takes the threat out of the occupiers' presence by ridiculing it. It is, in fact, a kind of charivari: a traditional, unsophisticated form of expression that aims at the restoration of normality and order.[15] More in general, much of clandestine patriotic discourse was fundamentally conservative. While protesting at the authorities in place, it did not define itself as rebellious; rather, it strove for the return to a (presumably) natural order of things, and its moral reasoning hinged on the notion of immanent justice – the belief that iniquities *would* be punished and that usurped authority was by definition temporary.

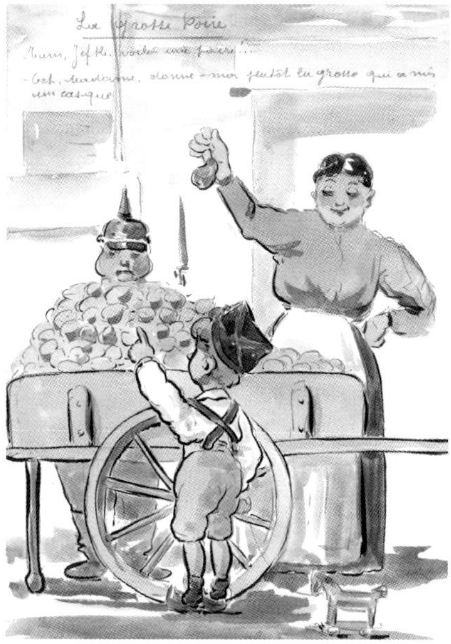

2.5. Satirical image "La Grosse Poire," signed René [possibly René De Pauw, 1887-1946], n.d. [1915?]. Brussels City Archives, Fonds Keym 59/64.

But the culture of "patriotic endurance" carried its internal contradictions. This brief essay will point out only two of them: the ravages of time and the impossible situation of young people.

Image 6: The ravages of time

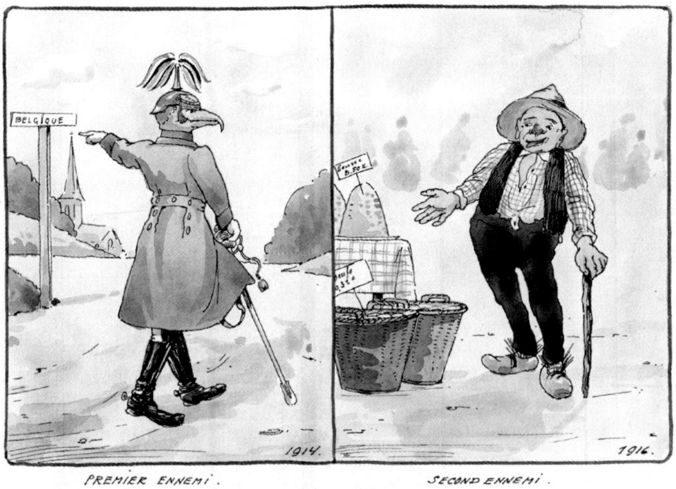

2.6. Brussels caricature "L'ennemi de 1914 – l'ennemi de 1916." Brussels City Archives, Fonds Keym.

As mentioned above, the credo that justice *would* prevail in the long run was key to patriotic belief. Patriotism, therefore, meant sitting out the occupation in a spirit of hope, and refusing offers of advancement that would benefit the conquering power. But in the meantime, misery arose. The long run meant little to people facing destitution, and, worse, forced to witness their children going hungry in the knowledge that malnutrition would forever stunt their growth. "Endurance" made sense as a collective project, but was too harsh a proposition in the context of individual lives. The nation might emerge vindicated; but the damage to individual lives would be beyond repair.

Even those not starving felt impoverished; by and by, bourgeois tables too felt the pinch and many people of rank looked ever shabbier. This contrasted with the allurements of breaking "patriotic distance" and establishing lucrative links to the occupying regime and army. Recruits of the German counterespionage bureaus treated themselves to pastries, now a rare pleasure; the newly rich found their way to the first great Belgian fashion-house, *Maison Norine*, which opened during the war.[16] Breaking the rule to keep "patriotic distance"might also mean tending to one's fame for fear of seeing it damaged beyond repair by a self-imposed silence. The novelist Georges Eekhoud, for one, fretted about losing his literary celebrity. His famous confrères Émile Verhaeren and Maurice Maeterlinck spent the war in exile and could put their literary fame to use for the national cause, in the process increasing their fame, whereas Eekhoud, under occupation, was supposed to refrain from publishing in protest against German censorship – another choice imposed by patriotic culture, with which Eekhoud eventually broke by signing a contract with a German publisher; tellingly, he spent part of his advance on having all of his oeuvre bound in fine leather.[17]

The ravages of time, then, could sap the bases for patriotic endurance. This is not to say that this endurance crumbled. Civilians kept hoping for liberation; only a very small minority completely threw in their lot with the occupier. Complaints about the population's naïveté by the occupying authorities and those who worked with them attest to this stubborn hope. Yet, among the occupied, more and more people came to see the war as a parenthesis in their actual lives. As war's end seemed further and further away, more and more civilians turned towards their own interests – family, social life, career, politics, survival. They no longer had the stomach for the great confrontations that had marked the year 1915, such as the forbidden celebration of the national holiday that year. People no longer ostentatiously covered their ears to German army bands. Would-be army volunteers now had to come up with their own money to bribe guards to help them cross the border. And the German secret police could recruit ever further into the urban middle classes.[18]

Image 7: No country for young men

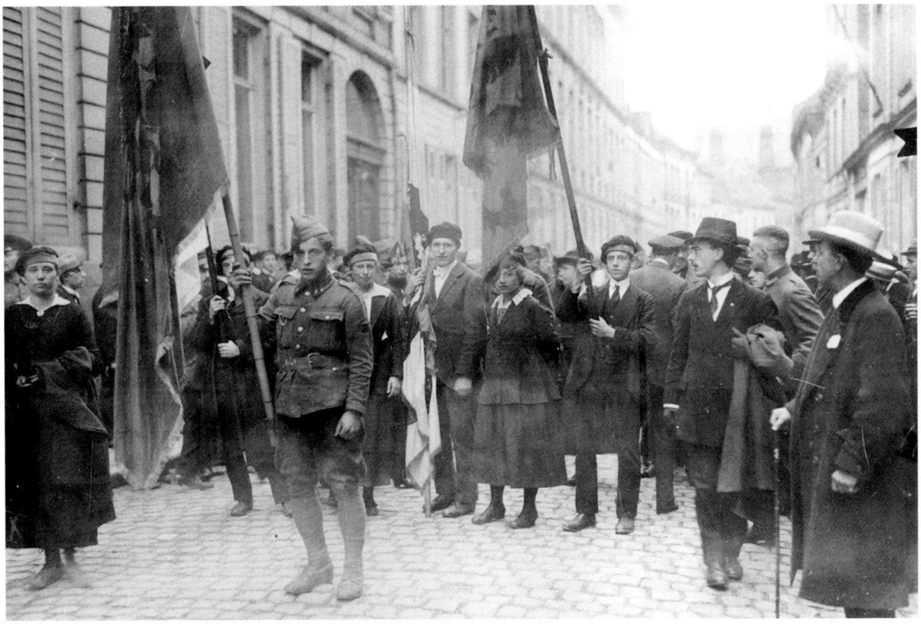

2.7. Parade of students of the wartime university at Ghent Ghent n.d. [early summer] 1918. Private collection Daniel Vanacker, Ghent.

Patriotic culture under occupation stressed the specific dignity of the civilian, who did not take up arms, yet confronted an armed invader in his own way. But at the same time, patriotic culture had no space for the army-aged young men who remained in the occupied country. Patriots, especially those with sons or husbands at the front, resented their very presence. Such young men were expected to make themselves invisible. Those who enjoyed themselves in public – going out, playing tennis, dancing – were viciously criticised. One patriotically-minded Brussels physician, whose sons were at the front, in his diary gave way to a vengeful fantasy: young "fops" ought to be branded with a hot iron after the war, as an indelible mark of their wartime cowardice.[19] This impossible situation led some educated young men to accept the occupation regime's attractive offers. Several dynamics came into play here – expectations of professional and personal fulfilment, flattering personal contacts with high-ranking members of the occupation regime, even a sense of cultural innovation.[20]

This image of a 1918 parade refers to the decision made by a few hundred young men (and, significantly, some young women) to enrol at the wartime University of Ghent, which was opened under the auspices of the occupation regime. Patriots called it the "Von-Bissing University" (after the German Governor-General of occupied Belgium) and defined enrolment as the ultimate transgression of norms. First, because the university, an all-Flemish institution, was created by the occupation regime to garner legitimacy; second, because taking up one's studies in wartime was held to show a lack of solidarity with those young men who were at the front and also with the working-class young men who faced deportation as forced labourers. As a result, the students at the "Von-Bissing University" were ostracised by much of patriotic society. In response, they adopted a defiant attitude, as the picture clearly shows: well-dressed young men and women insolently marching through a heavily occupied city. Tellingly, the parade was led by a Flemish prisoner of war in full uniform: a reference to army prestige.

Obviously, the image refers to tensions around wartime Flemish nationalism. But, I would argue, there is much more to it: the image illustrates the impossible situation of young men under occupation. It is, therefore, linked to forms of rebellion that did not have a linguistic component, such as the circle around the dadaist poet Clément Pansaers. In all of these cases, the impossible position of young people, especially educated young men, in German-occupied Belgium alienated some from a patriotic culture that offered only hard choices: army volunteering, resistance – or invisibility and shame. And so some, in response, defiantly defined themselves as being above the fray – which, in the circumstances, amounted to an endorsement of the occupation regime's claims to legitimacy.

Having analysed the different conceits and attitudes of the occupied population, it is now time to turn to the occupiers. How did they seek to make sense of their experience? What images might illustrate *their* quest for sense?

A major dimension of the occupation experience, for both the occupied and the occupiers, was the memory of the explosion of violence in the summer of 1914, when 5,500 unarmed civilians had been massacred by the invading army. The occupation regime as an entity, but also individual occupiers, counteracted the memory of these shocking events by presenting their action as essentially benevolent.

Image 8: The occupiers: benevolence

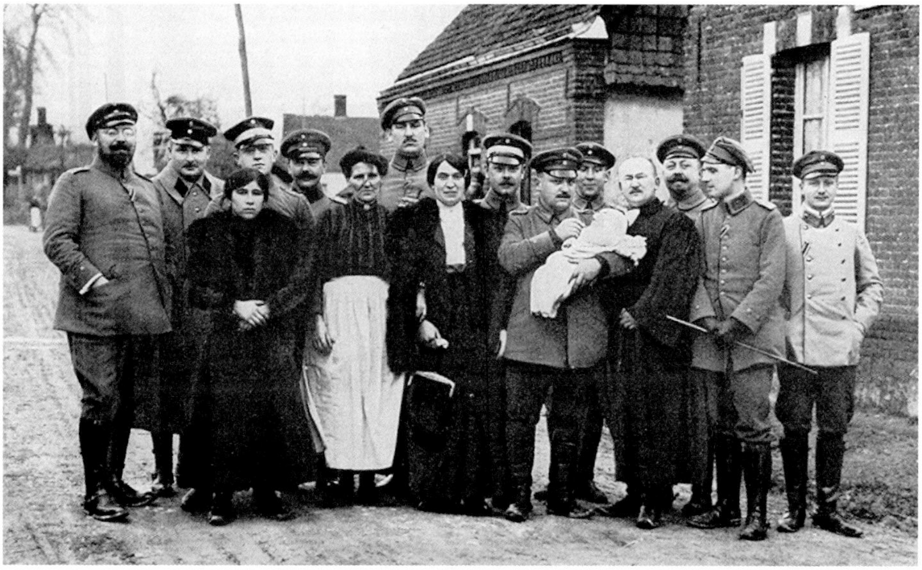

2.8. *Kindtaufe in Feindesland*, 1915. Walther Stein, *Um Vaterland und Freiheit. Wirklichkeitsaufnahmen aus dem grossen Krieg*. Siegen/Leipzig: Hermann Montanus Verlagsbuchhandlung, 1915, vol. 3, ill. 93, 68.

This benevolent image is clearly expressed by pictures like this, which appeared in compendia aimed at a German home front audience. This particular picture shows a group of German soldiers, one holding a baby, together with civilian women on an unidentified *chaussée*. The image, entitled *A Child's Christening in Enemy Land*, bears the caption : "The Army medic, who was the first to dispense care, holds the child; next to him is the Army chaplain who christened it." The complete absence of civilian men is noteworthy: in this image, it is the men in uniform who offer care and protection to the grateful women and the helpless newborn.

Another point to be made is that, like the occupied, the occupiers defined themselves with regard to those who had fallen in battle.

Image 9: Soldiers' sacrifice (II)

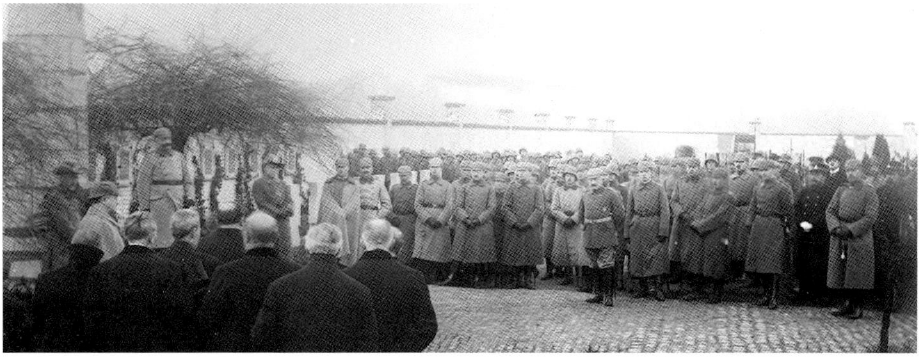

2.9. Aalst (East Flanders): unveiling of the monument to the German fallen, in the presence of occupying troops and the local authorities, 16 December 1916. Verz. Stadsarchief Aalst.

This image shows a type of ceremony that occurred right across the occupied country. As the occupying troops unveiled monuments to their fallen, occupier and occupied came together. Local dignitaries were entrusted with the care of the monuments and the graves. On this occasion, the Burgomaster of Aalst (Alost) in East Flanders made a dignified speech stressing that

> "the bitter sufferings of our ... Fatherland have created a deep and insurmountable gulf between us Belgians and the Germans. But civilized peoples respect death; they know that hostility ... must vanish in front of the grave, to leave nothing but ... a general feeling of profound pity for those youths whose finest years were cut short in that cruel chaos."[21]

This telling speech indicates that such unveiling ceremonies were loci, perhaps not of reconciliation as such, but certainly of encounter.

Another remarkable element is that the German fallen were buried, although cremation had become legal in most German states before the war, and engineers had even developed blueprints for mobile crematoria to be used near battlefields. Yet, in the event, only one crematorium was built during the First World War; very few of the war dead were cremated; and the cremation movement toned down its campaign for the duration of the war.[22] The wider point to be made here is that burial rites found themselves in between the traditional and the novel – as did other forms of culture during the Great War.

Examples of straddling of the traditional and the new abound in the war's memory. This essay's last image indicates as much.

Image 10: Memory

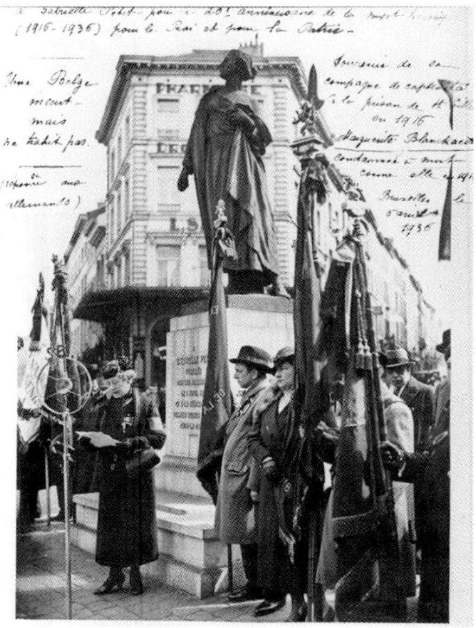

2.10. Statue to Gabrielle Petit [1893-1916], Sint-Jansplein, Brussels. Sculptor Egide Rombaux (1924). Picture taken during a commemoration ceremony in April 1936. Royal Museum of the Armed Forces and Military History, Belgium.

This 1923 statue to a resistance agent of the First World War who had been executed in 1916 is couched entirely in prewar mode. It is the work of Égide Rombaux (1865-1942), who had been one of Belgium's best-known public sculptors for several prewar decades. At the same time, the pedestal was designed by the distinguished architect Adrien Blomme (1878-1940), who was soon to revolutionise the Brussels cityscape with magnificent Art Déco buildings.[23] Likewise, for all its official aura, the monument was in no way commissioned by the state; it was conceived and sponsored by civil society and individual citizens. And while it glorified Belgian patriotism, its message of heroism would prove sufficiently capacious to allow for its image to be invoked by even radical anti-Belgian patriotism.[24]

The monument, like the other images shown in this essay, was an effort to make sense of the baffling and bitter occupation experience. The exit from occupation deepened the confusion. Who had been to blame, who had behaved well? Had it all been for nothing or had it been a glorious test of national and individual mettle? Occupied civilians felt that their sufferings were not always understood by those who had spent the war at the front or in exile. Their need for an overarching symbol of *civilian* valour brought forth the glorification of executed resisters: their images allowed the newly-liberated to think through the past occupation, for amidst increasing corruption and doubt *they*, at least, counted as blameless and purposeful figures. Their lives and fates were invoked retrospectively to give shape to the mind-numbing murk of the occupation.

Concluding remarks

By way of a very brief conclusion, suffice it to say that, just as in art there is no clear First World War caesura, which is the main message of this volume, culture in the widest sense lacks such a caesura too. Traditional groups engaged in new forms of expression (Catholic confraternities, for instance, kept underground papers afloat); avant-garde students claimed the status of *Bildungsbürger*; charity co-existed with more structural forms of solidarity. Rather than an end-point of one culture and the beginning of another, the war in its different theatres – military occupation being one of them – begat what one might call a re-crystallisation of cultures. For all that it was a cataclysm, the First World War, at least in Western Europe, was folded into cultures – it changed them, but it did not shatter them.

Notes

1 Written by Satie (music) and Cocteau (scenario) for Diaghilev's Ballets Russes, *Parade* premiered on 18 May 1917 in Paris, with costumes and sets by Picasso and choreography by Massine (who danced). Ernest Ansermet conducted.

2 See the insightful analysis by Leonard V. Smith in Audoin-Rouzeau, Becker and Smith, *France and the Great War 1914-1918*, (Cambridge University Press, 2003).

3 Sébastien Vogt, « La dévotion des combattants à la « petite Soeur » Thérèse de Lisieux pendant la Première Guerre mondiale » (Master's Thesis, Université de Strasbourg, 2012). For one example of such an image, see the Cover of *Pluie de Roses : interventions de Sr Thérèse de l'Enfant-Jésus pendant la guerre*, Bar-le-Duc, Le Carmélites de Lisieux, 1920.

4 John Horne, "Inventing the 'Front' : Cognition and Reality in the Great War," lecture, (University of Kent, 8 December 2016).

5 As laid out in the foundational text by Ruth Benedict: *Patterns of Culture* (1934).

6 Wolfgang Mommsen, *Max Weber und die Deutsche Politik 1890-1920*, 2nd revised ed. (Tübingen, 1974), 218.

7 Hubert Roland, *La "colonie" littéraire allemande en Belgique 1914-1918* (Brussels : Labor, 2003).

8 "Le régime brumeux et fade de la cellule", Archives et Musée de la Littérature (AML), Bruxelles, Edmond Picard, *La Guerre Européo-allemande*, unpublished manuscript, M.L. 2229/1-2 ; entry of 3 February 1915.

9 The text of the pastoral letter in Fernand Mayence, La correspondance de S.E. le Cardinal Mercier avec le gouvernement-général allemand pendant l'occupation 1914-1918 (Brussels-Paris : Albert Dewit – Gabalda, 1919), 448-467.

10 Sophie De Schaepdrijver and Emmanuel Debruyne, "*Sursum Corda*: The Underground Press in Occupied Belgium, 1914-1918," *First World War Studies* 4:1 (March 2013), 23-38.

11 Sophie De Schaepdrijver, "Occupation, Propaganda, and the Idea of Belgium," in *European Culture in the Great War: the Arts, Entertainment, and Propaganda, 1914-1918,* ed. Aviel Roshwald and Richard Stites, (Cambridge University Press, 1999), 267-294.

12 On this charity see Sophie De Schaepdrijver and Tammy Proctor, *An English Governess in the Great War: The Secret Brussels Diary of Mary Thorp* (New York: Oxford University Press, 2017).

13 Sophie De Schaepdrijver, "Measuring lost time: civilian diaries under military occupation," in *Inside World War One? Ego-documents and the Experience of War,* ed. Richard Bessel and Dorothee Wierling, (Oxford: Oxford University Press 2018), 57-81.

14 Sophie De Schaepdrijver, "Patriotic Distance," 1914-1918-online. International Encyclopedia of the First World War, https://encyclopedia.1914-1918-online.net/article/patriotic_distance?version=1.0.

15 Sophie De Schaepdrijver, "Polichinelles dans la ville: la vision de l'Allemand dans les caricatures," in *L'humour s'en va-t-en guerre. Bruxelles et la caricature en 14-18*, ed. Serge Jaumain and Valérie Piette, Brussels, Archives de la Ville (series *Fontes Bruxellae*, 2, 2005) 101-107.

16 On "Maison Norine," the venture of Honorine Deschryver and her husband Paul-Gustave Van Hecke, see the dissertation in progress by Nele Bernheim (VUB/UA).

17 Sophie De Schaepdrijver, "Antimémoire d'une antimémoire: les occupations d'un écrivain belge," in *Mémoires et antimémoires littéraires: la première guerre mondiale*, ed. Annamaria Laserra, Nicole Leclercq and Marc Quaghebeur (Frankfurt-Brussels: P.I.E.-Peter Lang, 2008) Vol. I, 19-32.

18 On this shift see Sophie De Schaepdrijver, *Gabrielle Petit: The Death and Life of a Female Spy in the First World War* (London: Bloomsbury Academic, 2015) Chapters 4 and 5, passim.

19 AML, Adrien Bayet, *Journal d'un Bruxellois pendant l'occupation allemande*, M.L. 3546 notebooks 1 to 25.

20 See an analysis of this aspect of the occupation in Sophie De Schaepdrijver, "No country for young men: patriotism and its paradoxes in German-occupied Belgium, 1914-1918," in *Breaking Empires, Making Nations: The First World War and the Reforging of Europe,* ed. Richard Butterwick-Pawlikowski, Quincy Cloet and Alex Dowdall (Warsaw: The College of Europe at Natolin, 2018) 124-153.

21 Text of the speech by Burgomaster Jaak Van den Bergh on the back of the photo; City Archives Aalst.

22 Simone Ameskamp, *On Fire: Cremation in Germany, 1870s-1934* (Ph.D. dissertation, Georgetown University, 2006) 338-339; id., "Fanning the Flames: Cremation in late imperial and Weimar Germany," in *Between Mass Death And Individual Loss: The Place of the Dead in Twentieth-Century Germany,* ed. Alon Confino, Paul Betts and Dirk Schuman (Berghahn Books, 2013) 93-112, 97.

23 Blomme designed, a.o., the present rectorate of the Université Libre de Bruxelles (1928) and the striking main tower and brewery-hall of the Wielemans-Ceuppens brewery, a modern art centre since 2007. Françoise Blomme, *À la rencontre d'Adrien Blomme (Brussels : CIVA, 2016).*

24 Sophie De Schaepdrijver, *Gabrielle Petit*, op.cit.

14/18 Rupture or Continuity? Belgian Art Around World War I in the Collections of the Royal Museums of Fine Arts[1]

INGA ROSSI-SCHRIMPF & LAURA KOLLWELTER

World War I, the occupation, the horror of battlefields and the exile of more than a million Belgians have a significant impact on the country's artistic production. Nobody is indifferent to the life-altering events related to this war. For some, the experience consolidates an already present style; for others, it constitutes a revolution leading to new artistic adventures.

The historiographical consensus of the Great War as a catalyst for change, upheaval and revolution in life as well as art is well established. While this narrative is widely accepted, it tends to overlook the continuation of styles and artistic approaches rooted in a linear tradition that is only slightly, if at all, impacted by the war. The exhibition shed a light on this dichotomy and this coexisting of artistic propositions from 1910 to 1925 by focusing on Belgian artists living and working in and outside the Kingdom. It availed itself solely of the particularly rich collection of paintings, sculpture and drawings of the Royal Museums of Fine Arts of Belgium, hence also offering a visualisation of how this rich and important period in Belgian art history is represented in its largest national art museum.

Collecting Belgian art of the early 20th century

In the years 1910 to 1925, the acquisition policy of the then Royal Museums of Painting and Sculpture of Belgium (today Royal Museums of Fine Arts of Belgium) depended largely on the Administration for Fine Arts of the government.[2] The museums were run by a board, and as from 1907 art historian Hippolyte Fierens-Gevaert (1870-1926) became its secretary before joining as a member. Just after the war, in 1919, he became the first chief curator of the museums. The possibilities for acquisitions were very restricted. Even more so for living artists or artists who had been dead less than 10 years of whom the government administration had the sole right to acquire works. The museums' board could only reject or accept the acquired works for its collections. It could also submit to the administration a sort of wish list. These guidelines as well as the composition of the board of mostly conservative members led to a non-existent or weak representation of contemporary artists and progressive talents. This lack of official recognition in their home country of internationally successful Belgian artists was regularly noticed by foreign visitors. However, some artists, such as Fernand Khnopff (1858-1921), entered the collections as from 1900. During the war, acquisitions were not possible. When the administration of Fine Arts as well as the board for the museums took up its acquisition policy after the war, closing the gaps with works by important Belgian artists of the late 19th century to the first decade of the new century was the priority. This contained of course the risk of again delaying the broadening of the collection to the younger generation. In fact, until 1925 only a few contemporaries of the generation born after 1882 entered the collections. Even though private initiatives such as the "L'Art Vivant" association intended to lend support. Priority was given to artists linked to the village of Sint-Martens-Latem. The *Pietà* by Albert Servaes (1883-1966) had already been acquired in 1920, two drawings by George Minne (1866-1941) were donated by "L'Art Vivant" the same year. Several works by James Ensor (1860-1949) had been finally acquired and assigned to the Brussels museum as well. But often, even artists of a certain national tradition could only sell a work to the museum collection rather late in the 1920s. For example Constant Permeke's (1886-1952) work *The stranger* was acquired thanks to a patron in 1927. Consequently, when the Museum of Modern Art reopened in February 1924 after renovation works, press articles criticised the lack of works by William Degouve de Nuncques (1867-1935), Rik Wouters (1882-1916) and by what they estimated progressive artists. Of the latter, there have only been works by Servaes, Gustave van de Woestyne (1881-1947), Ramah (1887-1947) and Valerius De Saedeleer (1867-1941).

We have to wait until the end of the 1920s for the establishment of a larger contemporary Belgian collection. In 1927, the museums, with the help of several donors and patrons, assembled an important number of works by artists of Sint-Martens-Latem, Nervia or individual talents such as Léon Spilliaert (1881-1946) in honour of the late Hippolyte Fierens-Gevaert, who had died the year before (fig. 3.1). Examples are *Béatrice* by Gustave De Smet (1877-1943) and *Sunday* by Frits van den Berghe (1883-1939). In 1929, the press announced the creation of a room entirely dedicated to the sculptor George Minne. The selection of artists not surprisingly followed confirmed collection guidelines and an official image of contemporary Belgian art that emphasised a certain rootedness in national traditions and a moderate modernity as also supported by the former chief curator and organiser of the Belgian contributions to the Venice Biennale between 1907 and 1926. The rediscovery and revalorisation of the Flemish Primitives in which Fierens-Gevaert equally participated as in the image building of contemporary Belgian art to the outside, may explain partly why those contemporary movements building up on such pictorial traditions prevailed in official collections and exhibitions. Another reason is probably to be found in the identity crisis due to the German invasion and the First World War. Accordingly, abstract artists did not enter the collections before the end of the Second World War when new abstraction became significant.

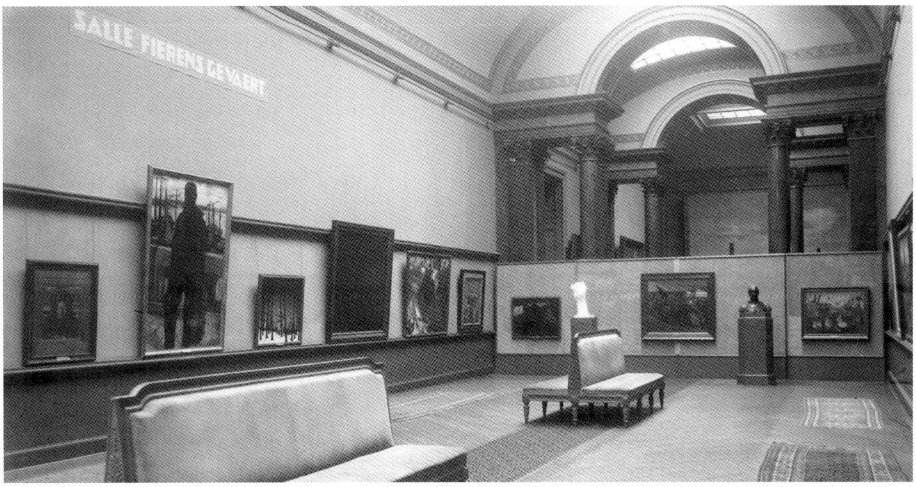

3.1. View of the room dedicated to former head curator Paul Fierens-Gevaert, inaugurated on 17 December 1927, with works by among others Frits van den Berghe, George Minne, Eugène Laermans, Valerius de Saedeleer, Edgard Tytgat. Archives of the Royal Museums of Fine Arts of Belgium.

In a certain manner, the acquisition policy of the museums during most of the 20th century was characterised by a sort of swing to catch up with what was missed out on before. Today, the collections hold a large diversity of artists and works of early 20th-century art and the museums have participated since the 1980s in the rediscovery and research on this fascinating period of Belgian art history. The selection of works on display during the exhibition could only give a glimpse of this collection and could have filled a much larger floor layout.

Art in the lull: Belgian art and artistic scene 1910 to 1914

While Fauvism, Expressionism, Cubism, Orphism or Futurism were radically changing artistic conceptions in France, Germany and Italy, Belgian artists, art critics and collectors stayed obliged to Post-Impressionism, be it the Luminism of Emile Claus (1849-1924) or the Brabant group including Rik Wouters, Willem Paerels (1878-1972) or Auguste Oleffe (1867-1931), and to late Symbolism, although representatives of Belgian Symbolism themselves declared it already outdated.[3] James Ensor was the idol of many of the young artists. They focused on his early dark and 'realistic' works of the 1880s. The modernity of his topics such as the masks, the masses and the grotesques or the nervous, free lines of his etchings did not inspire them as they did German artists. At a moment when ground-breaking exhibitions took place – such as The Armory Show (1913) in New York, the "Sonderbund" Exhibition (1912) and the "Werkbund" Exhibition (1914), both in Cologne and each featuring a significant contribution by a Belgian artist of the fin-de-siècle generation (George Minne and Henry van de Velde), or the touring exhibition of Italian Futurism (1912) which was also on show in Brussels – Belgian art appears quite self-sufficient. "I continue",[4] seemed to be the overall slogan and not only the state of mind of Rik Wouters when leaving the conference held by Boccioni and Marinetti in Brussels in 1912. However, younger artists did not even need to go far to keep track of the latest evolutions in the arts, either at home – Parisian Orphism and Cubism at the Cercle des Indépendants in Brussels in 1911, Italian Futurism at the Galerie Giroux in Brussels in 1912 or German Expressionism with Kandinsky also at the Galerie Giroux in 1913 – or a few hours by train in Paris or Cologne. With the Salon des Indépendants and the Gallery Georges Giroux new actors tried to aerate Belgian artistic life. According to Paul van Ostaijen (1896-1928) in his essay on the birth of Expressionism in Flanders, young Belgian artists were not prepared for these artistic "revolutions" at the time.[5] As other critics in retrospect and some artists of the time, he concluded that Belgian art was stuck in bourgeois, pre-war Impressionism. In 1918, still in occupied Belgium and probably not aware of evolutions outside, he mentioned Rik Wouters, the brothers Oscar (1887-1970) and Floris (1889-1965) Jespers and Paul Joostens (1889-1960) as those who led out of this impasse and James Ensor as its precursor.

The Jesper brothers and Joostens were part of the then youngest generation of artists who only began their training and careers around 1910. At that moment, Belgian artists were indeed still strongly influenced by Impressionism and Symbolism. The exhibitions of *La Libre Esthétique*, founded in 1893, were still on-going and Impressionism and Neo-Impressionism had been consecrated in a retrospective exhibition in 1904. More recent initiatives such as *Kunst van Heden* in Antwerp showed a similar broadband of art works. This association organised comprehensive exhibitions on contemporary Belgian art in Berlin and Cologne in 1908 and 1914. The duality of Belgian art and culture as well as tradition and the figureheads of the late 19th century were emphasised. The modern school and a new generation were represented by the Brabant painters. The secretary of *Kunst van Heden* as of 1908 was Jules Schmalzigaug (1882-1917).[6] His example is quite instructive regarding the struggle of young Belgian artists to emancipate themselves from the heavy heritage of 19th-century fin-de-siècle. Considering that Belgian art life was stagnating, he was convinced that only artistic exile could counteract this. After first training in Germany and a short stay in the city of Bruges, he thus left Belgium in 1910 for Paris before going to Venice. Though Schmalzigaug found his artistic "home" in the formal language of Futurism, he also crossed the art historical past in search of renewal. This duality between modernity and tradition will also be essential in the interwar period. In November 1913, the young artist wrote to a friend, "There is a new world for us and we hesitate?"[7]

Clash of 1914: Geographical dispersal and the need to take a position

In 1914, the exhibition of *La Libre Esthétique* took place as usual, inviting for the first time the "Bleus" (Greenhorns) as the young painters of the Brabant group have been called. The Salon Triennal was held from May on in Brussels. In July, Belgian, English, French and many German summer visitors rushed to the Belgian coast and its famous seaside resorts to spend some relaxing weeks.

> "In Le Coq, the small seaside resort near Ostend ..., the same unconstraint reigned as elsewhere. ... The only disturbance came from a newsboy who, to stimulate business, shouted the threatening captions in the Parisian papers: *L'Autriche provoque la Russie, L'Allemagne prépare la mobilisation.* We could see the faces of those who bought copies grow gloomy, but only for a few minutes. After all, we had been familiar with these diplomatic conflicts for years; they were always happily settled at the last minute, ... But the bad news piled up and constantly became more threatening. ...; one saw Belgian soldiers who had never before been seen on the beach, ... It appeared completely ridiculous to me that while thousands and tens of thousands of Germans were enjoying at their leisure the hospitality of this small, impartial country, an army should stand in readiness at the frontier prepared to march in. ... Then came the critical last days of July ... One sensed the serious situation. At once an icy wind of

> fear blew over the beach and swept it bare. People left the hotels by thousands and stormed the trains, ..."[8]

The First World War started on 28 July 1914. On 4 August, the German army invaded neutral Belgium. On 19 August the Germans entered Brussels. In October the first battle of Ypres started. The trench warfare devastated the Flemish landscape. In the meantime hundreds of thousands of Belgians fled, among them a large number of artists, critics, collectors etc. For the following four years Belgian art life took place for a large part outside Belgium, in exile. Inside Belgium under occupation, censorship and cultural policy forced artists and intellectuals to take positions. This disintegration of the Belgian art scene, on the one hand, and the loss of the positive ties with the Germanic brother in the East impacted on Belgian culture and cultural identity deeply and long-lastingly.[9] The duality between the Latin and the Germanic as it had been emphasised since the late 19th century became a divisive issue.

In 1914 the era of *La Libre Esthétique* ended. The geographic dispersal of artists leaving their homes led to quite different artistic situations according to where the artists went. Artistic exile in order to renew art, as Jules Schmalzigaug professed before the war, now often became a burden. Nevertheless, confrontation with a different culture and art scene for those in exile largely influenced their artistic creation. Those who stayed in Belgium equally got impulses from the occupying forces. Numerous German artists, art historians, art critics, art dealers, writers and other intellectuals arrived as soldiers or employees of the occupying administration. Censorship influenced the information available to artists, increasing the influence of German art journals such as *Die Aktion* or *Der Sturm*. Thus, for four years Belgian artists would follow very different paths: they were either cut-off from modern artistic life in rural exile like Gustave van de Woestyne in Wales or in a sort of inner emigration as chosen by Jakob Smits (1855-1928) in the Flemish countryside; they opened up to international vanguard movements either in exile in the neutral Netherlands like Gustave De Smet or Georges Vantongerloo (1886-1965), on an individual itinerary up to southern France like Marthe Donas (1885-1967) or even in contact with the occupier like Jozef Peeters (1895-1960). Yet others were enrolled, even though the front experience was not the most influential on modern art in Belgium. It was certainly dispersal and occupation that most changed the Belgian art scene during the First World War (p. 81, fig. 1.1). The artistic effects were not always perceptible; pictorial or sculptural language did not change for everyone, but could also be strengthened by the experience from 1914 to 1918. Finding their artistic response to exile, war and occupation was one challenge. Another was reconciliation and the reconstruction of the Belgian art scene afterwards, when the occupier left and the exiled slowly came back.

1910 to 1925: a selection from the collection

The diversity of the works in the collection and of the small selection finally exhibited is remarkable. Be it styles, techniques or subjects, the artistic creation before, after and during World War I was manifold. Through five main sections, the keywords rupture and continuity are illustrated in all their complexities. One realises that even in one same section examining a same artistic movement, notions of changes and constants can appear simultaneously. Some artists' styles might remain the same before and after the war but their personal and social life experiences a breach. For others, the physical rupture as a result of exile results in a break with a more traditional style practised in pre-war Belgium. Yet others remain in Belgium but are influenced by the international urgency of change and revolution.

The following paragraphs analyse the five aforementioned sections of the exhibition and expand on their role in the pre- and post-war context while also trying to put an emphasis on the four years of the war. Trying to answer the question of rupture and continuity as suggested by the exhibition's title, this is not an exhaustive survey but rather a walk through the exhibition and along the selected art works.

Rik Wouters and Ferdinand Schirren: Beyond Ensor

Rik Wouters and Ferdinand Schirren (1872-1944) introduce us to prewar art in Belgium (fig. 3.2).

The years 1914-1918 alter the fates of both artists. Schirren stays in Belgium where he continues to paint and draw and continues exhibiting during and after the war. He develops his style and his career really takes off. After the war, he shows in the most important interbellum galleries Georges Giroux and Le Centaure. His work is also appreciated by the younger generation of the avant-garde such as *7 Arts* and "La Lanterne Sourde".[10] In 1926 he signs a contract with the Belgian poet and gallerist Paul van Ostaijen.[11] Ferdinand Schirren was fortunate not to have been negatively affected by World War I. The second World War will however put an end to his artistic creation. Given his Jewish ancestry and the ensuing danger of persecution, he tries to live a discreet live and retires from the art scene.

Wouters was given a unique opportunity in Belgian art history in 1912 by signing a contract and being exclusively represented by one gallery. Georges Giroux in his eponymous gallery allows Wouters to get a monthly salary of 200 francs in exchange for exclusive rights on the selling and promoting of all of Wouters' paintings, drawings and sculptures.[12] In 1914 he is mobilised in the Belgian army and later interned in a camp in the Netherlands. Being able to join his wife in Amsterdam in 1915, Wouters continues to work in exile. His health is however quickly deteriorating, and in July 1916 he succumbs to his multiple ailments inflicted by a cancer and numerous operations that result in his death at the young age of thirty-three.

The Flautist (fig. 3.3), dated around 1914, is one of the key examples of Wouters' paintings. While the male subject is very rare in Wouters' oeuvre, his use of pure colour, applied in broad yet dynamic brush strokes, and his use of the canvas as a vibrant surface shimmering through the colour applications render his typical play with colour and light form-determining entities.

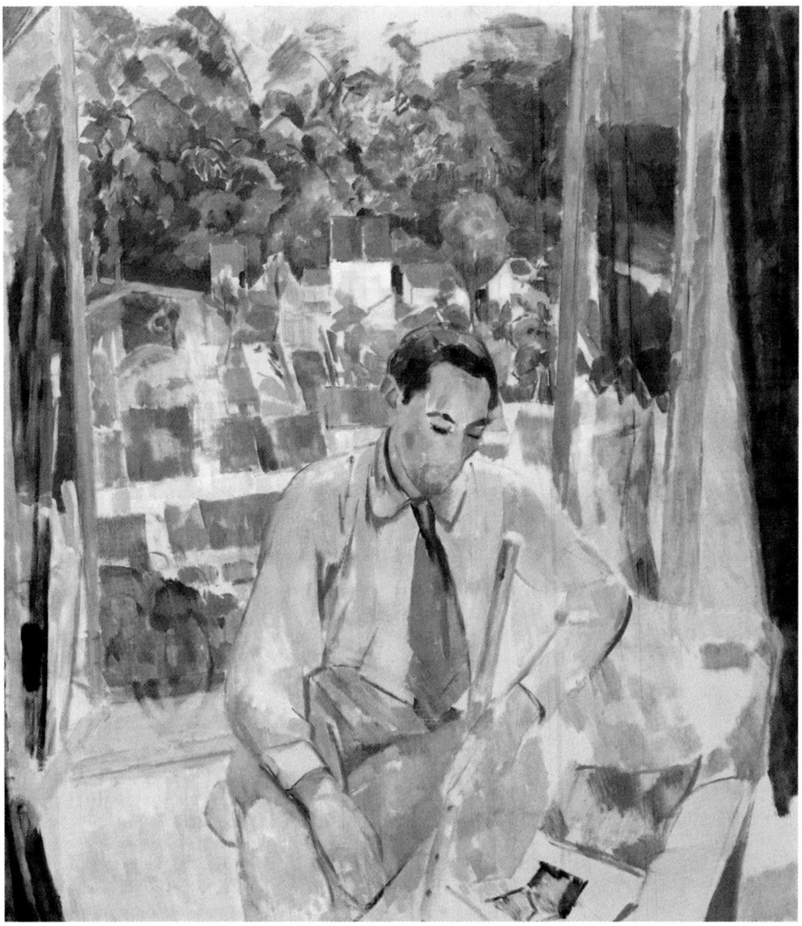

3.3. Rik Wouters, *Flautist*, 1914, oil on canvas, 133,5 x 115 cm. Brussels, Royal Museums of Fine Arts of Belgium, Inv. 4742.

All the same, neither Wouters nor Schirren crosses the line into more radical styles contemporary to their creation, such as Expressionism, Fauvism or Cubism. Their quiet, intimate and serene interiors, staging the feminine figure, in Wouters' case almost exclusively his wife Nel, are rooted in Belgian fin-de-siècle art, rather than in the untamed exploration of colour and (self-)expression as seen in painting in France and Germany at the same period. Without denying the modernity in some conceptions of Rik Wouters in retrospect, instead of initiating a new movement, these two artists should rather be considered as standing at the end of a long impressionistic movement.[13]

Some critics retrospectively lamented this tardiness of Belgian Art on an international level:

> "One has to admit it: at the beginning of the war of 1914, we, in Belgium, were neither strongly 'European' nor strongly 'modern'; while elsewhere illuminated researchers had already started to disrupt the form and renew the spirit of painting and sculpture, we still held on, with a singular obstinacy, almost voluptuously, to impressionism, or rather to our local neo-impressionism"[14].

Modern and avant-garde art do not gain ground in prewar Belgium. Artists and critics interested in these new developments have to turn their gaze across the Belgian borders.

Jules Schmalzigaug: a new world

This is exactly what the painter Jules Schmalzigaug is doing. Unlike Wouters and Schirren, whose main successes can be observed inside Belgium, Schmalzigaug will, during his lifetime, not be acknowledged in his home country. His career mainly unfolds in France and Italy where he is introduced to the futurist movement. It is during a stay in Paris in 1912 that he sees his first futurist exhibition at the Bernheim-Jeune gallery. In 1913 he is introduced to some of the chief members of Futurism such as Umberto Boccioni and Giacomo Balla with whom he starts to exchange ideas on a regular basis.

The same year, in a letter to his brother, Schmalzigaug asks:

> "What would you say if one day I were to orient myself to, what is called stupidly 'Futurism', a word that signifies nothing at all and smells like the large crate at the salvation army."[15]

This resentment towards the term Futurism is related to the fact that Schmalzigaug, while adhering to the futurist style, is interested in neither their social nor their political program. He does not subscribe to the futurist view of the glorification of war and violence and the exaltation of the machine. Moreover, coming from a bourgeois environment himself, he does not identify with the futurist claim to eradicate the upper middle class. He seeks a purely formal Futurism that is "seeking to translate the sense of the movement by decomposing the form".[16]

It is thus on a formal level, not on an ideological one, that Schmalzigaug can today be considered the only Belgian futurist. Undeniably he understands his outstanding position in a Belgian context as early as 1913: "I can say that today, I am exceeding in my intentions – everything that comprises the Belgian School today".[17]

In a work such as *Madame Nelly Hurrelbrinck* (fig. 3.4), these futurist techniques become obvious. The light cone under which the female figure sits breaks up into geometrical fragments. Meanwhile the background is animated by the flickering brush-strokes. Aesthetically, this work is reminiscent of the hectic rendering of movement and the breaking up of light in the works of Gino Severini as well as Umberto Boccioni.

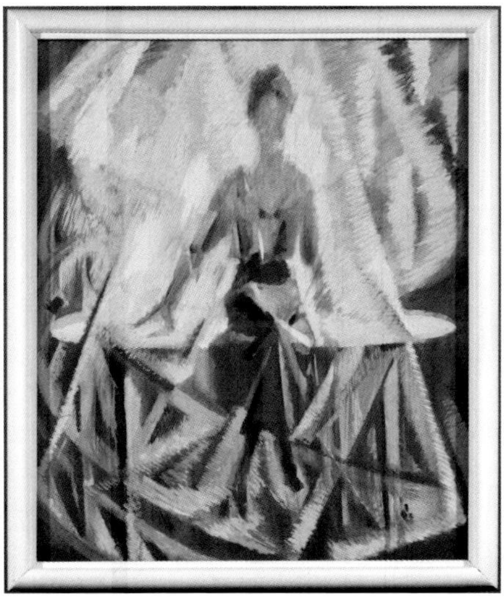

3.4. Jules Schmalzigaug, *Madame Nelly Hurrelbrinck*, ca. 1917, distemper on triplex, 120 x 101 cm (unfinished). Brussels, Royal Museums of Fine Arts of Belgium, Inv. 7557.

The beginning of the war turns Schmalzigaug's world completely upside down. He seeks refuge in the Netherlands and has to leave a tightly knit network of colleagues behind in Italy. At the Dutch seaside resort of Scheveningen he meets many Belgian artists such as Edith Van Leckwyck (1899-1987) and Georges Vantongerloo (1886-1965) with whom he takes on the role of mentor and teacher. At the same time his own artistic development is suffering from the isolation of exile.

After immigrating to Scheveningen, his view on the creative and international process of creation is shattered:

> "[t]he war represents a general paralysis of the creative possibilities. The imagination of the artist is stricken by a kind of mental neurasthenia and the cosmopolitan bonds that linked the experimental [artists] of different countries are brutally broken."[18]

Schmalzigaug cannot cope with these changes and takes his life in 1917. Just like Rik Wouters', Schmalzigaug's career is disrupted at its height and ends tragically during war.

The formal language of Futurism emerges inside Belgium only with the end of the war. While the Galerie Georges Giroux held a futuristic show in 1912 that attracted the attention of some individual critics but did not profoundly change the cultural scene,[19] post-war interest in Futurism is growing. Artists such as Paul Joostens and Prosper De Troyer (1888-1961) are intrigued by the futuristic style. De Troyer's painting *The Seamstress* (fig. 3.5) from 1920 merges the fragmentation of movement and space gravitating towards cubo-futuristic aesthetics. The manual labour of the female figure is transformed into a mechanical sequence of movements, transforming the seamstress into a machine-like producer. This subject matter could just as easily have been found in the body of work of Rik Wouters or Ferdinand Schirren. However, where they portray a handywoman in a private environment, Prosper de Troyer turns his figure into a statement of mass production in a modern age.[20]

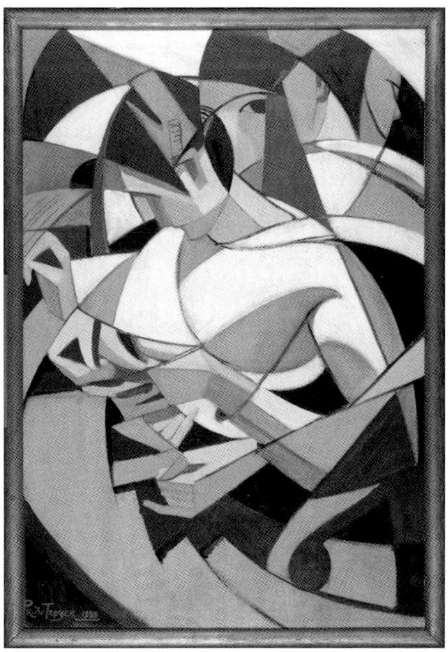

3.5. Prosper de Troyer, *The seamstress*, 1920, oil on wood, 150 x 99 cm. Brussels, Royal Museums of Fine Arts of Belgium, Inv. 7939.

Abstraction, avant-garde and the community

This new formal experimentation of Prosper de Troyer is a result of a new wind that is already being felt in Antwerp during the war, when Floris (1889-1965) and Oscar (1887-1970) Jespers, Paul Joostens and Paul van Ostaijen form the Bond Zonder Gezegeld Papier in 1917. They are distancing themselves from the dominant impressionist tendencies and turning the Belgian art scene on its ear by opening up their doors to the European modernist movements. They are now studying German Expressionism, Italian Futurism or French Cubism. However their access to these artworks and ideas is restricted as the magazines and reproductions that are circulating inside Belgium are being censored by the occupier.[21]

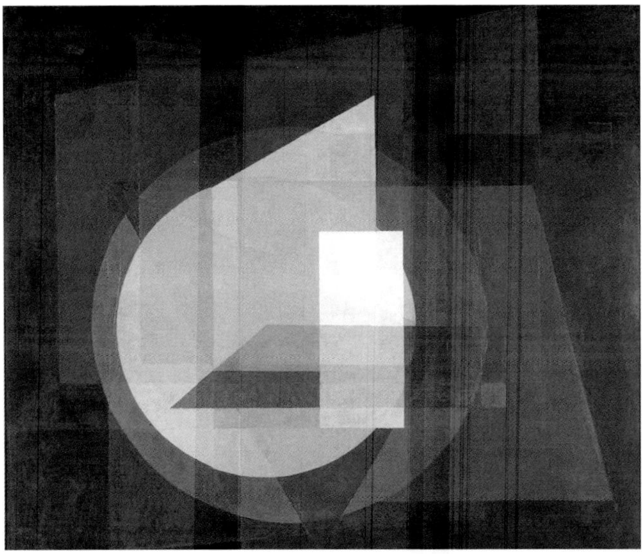

3.7. Jozef Peeters, *Huile n°21*, 1924, oil on canvas,144 x 166,5 cm. 99 cm. Brussels, Royal Museums of Fine Arts of Belgium, inv. 6892.

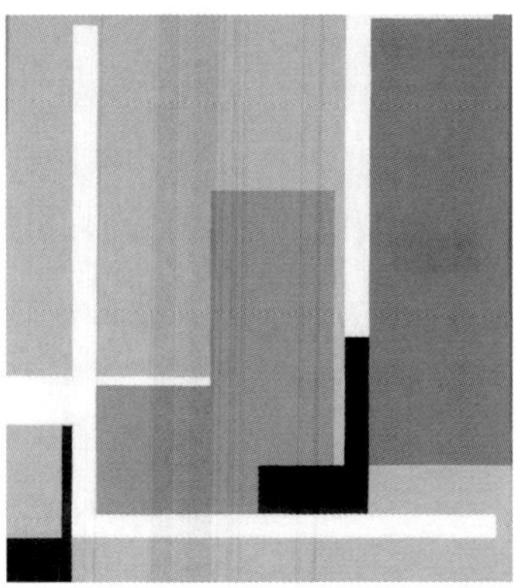

3.8. Marthe Donas, *Construction*, (1920), oil on wood, 48 x 42 cm. 99 cm. Brussels, Royal Museums of Fine Arts of Belgium, inv. 12035.

After the war and with the free circulation of information, a young generation of artists is constituting an avant-garde that seeks involvement with international movements. The newly formed Kring Moderne Kunst, for example, is in contact with De Stijl and the futurist movement.[22] Theo van Doesburg (1883-1931) accordingly visits Brussels and Antwerp in 1920 and 1921 and influences an admittedly small but excited and driven group of artists wanting to explore new forms of artistic expression. They adhere to an international network by theorising and publishing their texts and works in magazines that then can be distributed throughout Europe.

Jozef Peeters plays one of the leading roles in the establishment of this new art in Belgium. He organises three Congresses of Modern Art where international and Belgian modern art is at the forefront. With the writer Fernand Berckelaers alias Michel Seuphor (1901-1999) he also publishes the magazine *Het Overzicht*. Founded in 1921 it promotes, together with the Brussels *7 Arts* magazine founded in 1922, a new, communitarian art, that finds its perfect incarnation in the geometric form. Constructivist notions are thus introduced and a pure geometrical abstraction is developed. The aforementioned magazine, *7 Arts*, based in Brussels and founded by the brothers Pierre (1898-1976) and Victor (1897-1962) Bourgeois, Pierre-Louis Flouquet (1900-1967), Karel Maes (1900-1974) and Georges Monier (1892 – 1973), promotes this abstraction while at the same time exploring other forms of art, as its title suggests. Be it architecture, literature or cinema, they are valuing the interconnectivity of all arts with a modern society.

Adhering to the movement, but coming from a more individual path is the female artist Marthe Donas (1885-1967), who was introduced to modernist movements outside Belgium during the War. Donas explored multiple art forms, from Cubism to Cubo-Futurism and abstraction through a tumultuous path laid out for her by the incidence of war and the exile resulting from it. While the exiled artist Georges Vantongerloo got acquainted with abstract art in the Netherlands, Donas meets the avant-garde in Paris. Her career is quite unusual, not only because of her gender but also because for a while she was the most successful Belgian modernist artist, without being recognised as such in her home country. This is mostly due to the fact that her career started in exile, and after the war she did not immediately adhere to the Antwerp avant-garde around Jozef Peeters but rather stayed in Paris where she was a member of the exhibition group La Section d'or. In a work such as *Construction* (Inv. 12035) her most radical research into formal abstraction is visible: a purely constructed amalgamation of strictly geometrical and non-referential forms as can be observed throughout European art at the time. Artists such as Pierre-Louis Flouquet do not go quite as far in the reduction of form. Allusions to the figurative can still be seen with his anthropomorphic forms and his use of lettering. The same can be said for Victor Servranckx (1897-1965). In his *Opus 47* (fig. 3.9), the composition of large geometrical surfaces is creating an engine-like structure, alluding to the mechanical world.

While these different explorations are at their height in the beginning of the 1920s, a return to a less "revolutionary" art form can however be observed within the Belgian avant-garde in the second half of the 1920s. The limits of exploring the geometrical form had quickly been reached. Either figuration is reintroduced, the rigid form makes way for a lyrical abstraction, allowing a more poetical interpretation of the work or painting to be abandoned for the applied arts and design. Furthermore, the lack of critical and/or financial acclaim of this geometrical abstraction on a national but also international level leads these artists to different forms of expression.

The belief in their art and ideological programme did not however leave all of the artists: "[w]e continue the effort. And if our generation cannot impose it, may the next one take off where we left it."[23]

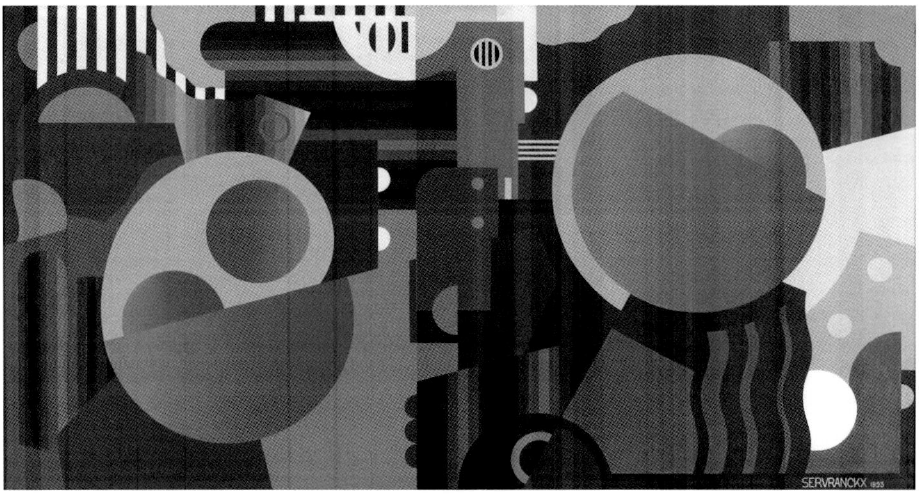

3.9. Victor Servranckx, *Opus 47*, 1923, oil on canvas, 113 x 210,5 cm. Brussels, Royal Museums of Fine Arts of Belgium, Inv. 6859.

Flemish Expressionism at large

While the abstract and constructivist movement has difficulties arousing a strong interest in Belgium, another movement is met with enormous enthusiasm in the Belgian art world. Flemish Expressionism (fig. 3.11–12) is received very positively and sells extremely well after 1918. Its three main representatives, Constant Permeke, Frits Van den Berghe and Gustave De Smet, return to Belgium after having sought exile during the war years where the path to this new art was laid.

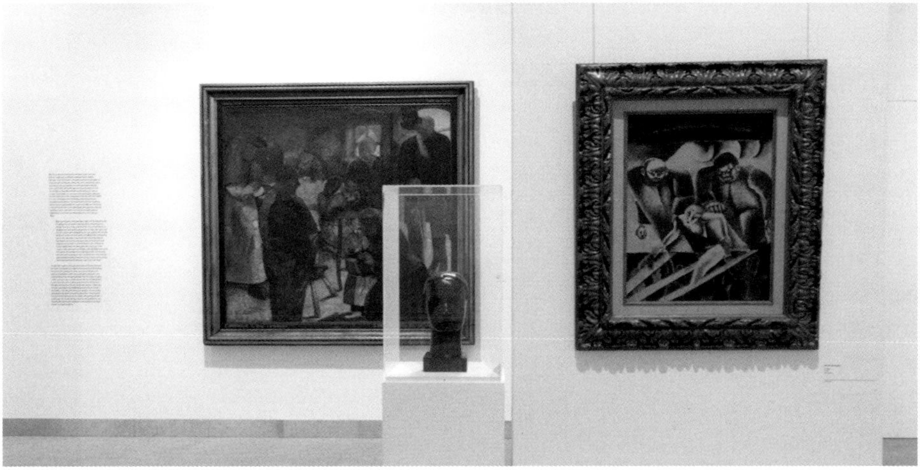

3.11 View of the exhibition "14/18. Rupture or Continuity," 2018, with works by Constant Permeke, Jozef Cantré and Frits van den Berghe.

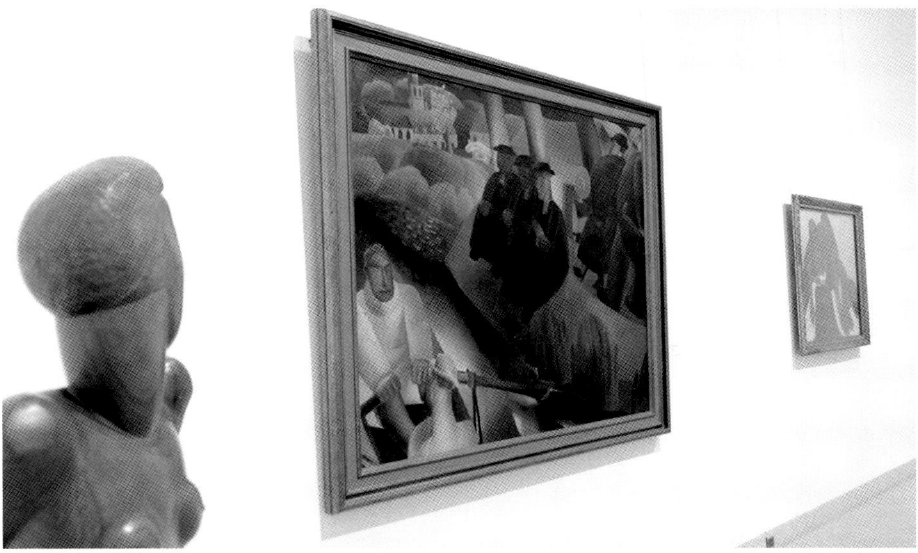

3.12 View of the exhibition "14/18. Rupture or Continuity," 2018, with works by Oscar Jespers, Frits van den Berghe and Albert Servaes.

The years in exile are thus crucial in their artistic development and in the formation of what we call Flemish Expressionism. Gust de Smet and Frits Van den Berghe live in the neutral Netherlands during the war. Here, they are introduced to all the modernist European movements, and especially to Cubism, by the French artist Henri le Fauconnier (1881-1946). They possibly discover German Expressionism in a 1916 exhibition in The Hague organised by the Berlin gallery Der Sturm[24] which also publishes a monthly magazine distributed in the Netherlands. Gust De Smet was later on also to subscribe to Paul Westheim's *Kunstblatt*, another important mouthpiece of Expressionism. Van den Berghe and De Smet, as well as the critic André De Ridder, correspond with their friend and colleague Constant Permeke and inform him of the newest developments in modern art.[25] Permeke moved to England during the war. While the information given by his friends certainly resonates with him, he lives and works in a quiet isolated region in Devon and his stylistic development was thus a more personal one.

The large oil canvas *The Foreigner* (p. 82, fig. 1.2) from 1916 can be considered as a turning point in Permeke's work. Knowing its historical context and title, the work immediately evokes a sense of displacement, reflecting the possible psychological troubles of the exiled. The ambiguity of the work however lies in the fact that the spectator does not know if the foreigner is a stranger seeking refuge and safety from these villagers or if, on the contrary, the figure is a foreign oppressor, disrupting the peace. Stylistically, *The Foreigner* showcases what will later be considered characteristic of Permeke's work: large and boxy figures in a tight space whose features are lost in the thick paste of the earthy oil paint.

At the return of the three artists shortly after the armistice, a newly formed gallery network welcomes them. Paul-Gustave van Hecke and André de Ridder with the painter Gust De Smet found the gallery Sélection in 1920. Its purpose, along with that of an eponymous art review, is to encourage and promote modern art, and Flemish Expressionism in particular. In the figure of Walter Schwarzenberg and his important gallery Le Centaure in Brussels, the painters are also finding a fierce defender of their art.

While their technique is vastly different from what they did in Sint-Martens-Latem before the war, the subjects of Permeke, De Smet and Van den Berghe mostly stay the same. They still show a proclivity for rural landscapes and the exaltation of the countryside. They also represent the human figure, and more precisely the simple people, peasants, fishermen or villagers.

The experience of being forced to leave their home country and being exposed to new art movements accordingly has an important impact on artists such as Gust

De Smet and Constant Permeke. It would however be wrong to suggest that the experience of exile invariably leads to a radical change in style.

Artists of the first generation of Sint-Martens-Latem's such as Albert Servaes, staying in the Flemish countryside during occupation, or George Minne and Gustave van de Woestyne, both exiled in Great Britain, remain true to their pre-war style. Minne, while still exploring the religious figure and themes such as grief, isolation and solace, changes his medium.[26] Unable to afford materials for sculpting, he has to resort to drawing during the war years. During, and in the immediate after-war period Minnes' depictions of the broken, shelter-seeking, saintly figures such as his *Pietà* (fig. 3.13) of 1921 can be read as perfect metaphors for the experienced war traumas of individuals as well as of the entire Belgian nation. In the 1920s Minne turns to more classical forms. Next to him artists from Sint-Martens-Latem such as Albert Servaes but also the Nervia group under Anto Carte (1886-1954) and Louis Buisseret (1888-1956) will emphasise medieval traditions. The subject matter often has religious conotations while formally relating to other "objective" tendencies and the question of a return to order.

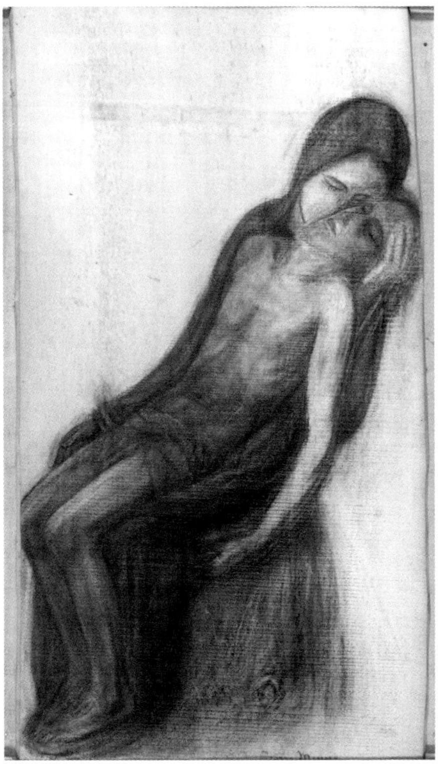

3.13. George Minne, *Pietà*, 1921, charcoal on wood, 107 x 54 cm. Brussels, Royal Museums of Fine Arts of Belgium, Inv.4330.

Artists at war

World War I saw the appearance of new fighting techniques, including the creation of trenches and the use of toxic gas as a deathly weapon. The battles were long and exhausting, and often conducted at a distance – the war of attrition – which posed new problems for artistic representation. With the artists aghast and often paralysed by this new, atrocious, inhumane and often even invisible face of the war, the actual battlefields were only rarely depicted.[27]

At the front itself the official forces understand the need for representation of this war beyond documental photography and create a specialised unit:

> "The current war is not a succession of battles but a latent state of which it was important to fix its aspects and characteristics. To the litteral documents furnished by photography and cinema, it befitted to add others, born from human sensitivities, and the documentary service of the army had the idea of calling upon a certain number of well known artists ...."[28]

The *Section Artistique de l'Armée belge en Campagne* was created in 1916. Its primary purpose was to document the war at the front. However, these artists employed by the Belgian state tended not to represent the battles, limiting themselves to the ruins and debris caused by warfare and to portraits of the soldiers.

Twenty-six artists make up this official *Section* between May 1916 and July 1918. Most of them work in a luminist Realism, but not all of their styles are homogenous. However subject and form always stay detached from personal opinion. Their methods are not expressive in that they do not reflect any inner turmoil caused by the war. One exception might be Achille Van Sassenbrouck (1886-1979) who introduces an expressive use of colour and brushwork that is explained by war-induced psychological trauma reflected in his art.[29] His *Ruins of the church of Nieuwpoort* (fig. 3.14) uses these new brushstrokes. In vivid colours and thickly applied pure paint, the ruin is a symbol of the disrespect of the enemies, destroying Belgian cultural and religious heritage.

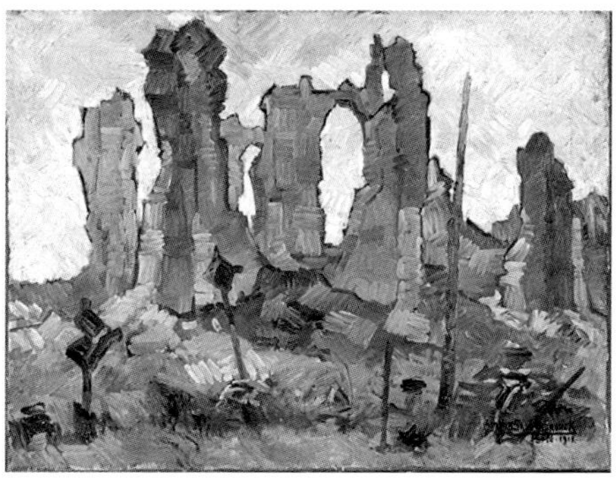

3.14. Achille Van Sassenbrouck, *Ruins of the church of Nieuwpoort*, 1918, oil on canvas, 54,2 x 69,6 cm. Brussels, Royal Museums of Fine Arts of Belgium, Inv. 10076.

Curiously, it is predominantly those artists who remain civilians in occupied Belgium or are refugees in exile and thus have not experienced the trauma of the front that painted battle scenes, death and affliction, probably drawing on verbal accounts and photographs but also adding elements of the fantastical. Jules de Bruycker's (1870-1945) *The cathedral of Reims* (fig. 3.15) leaves the realm of reality and depicts war in all its cruelties as a real Armageddon of abominable horrors and nightmares. Like Van Sassenbrouck, he also uses the ruin as a sign of destruction, but rather than pretending to show a neutral landscape that is subtly used for propaganda purposes, De Bruycker populates the sombre drawing with masses of people fleeing and dying. After the war, Paul Joostens staged the devastating effects of the bombing of the cathedral of Reims in a very different manner (fig. 3.16).

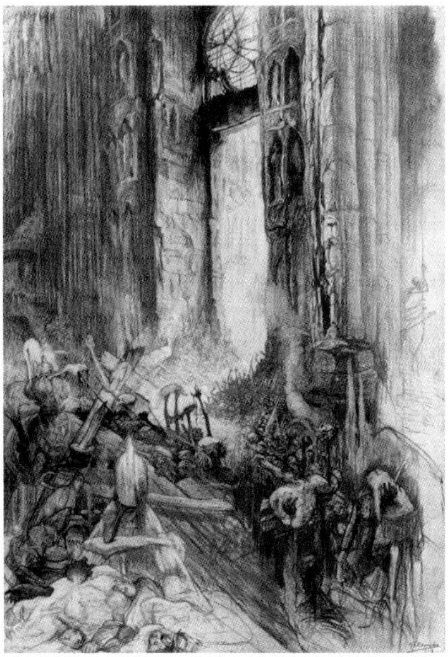

3.15. Jules de Bruycker, *The cathedral of Reims*, 1918, black pencil on paper, 99,5 x 67 cm. Brussels, Royal Museums of Fine Arts of Belgium, Inv. 4488.

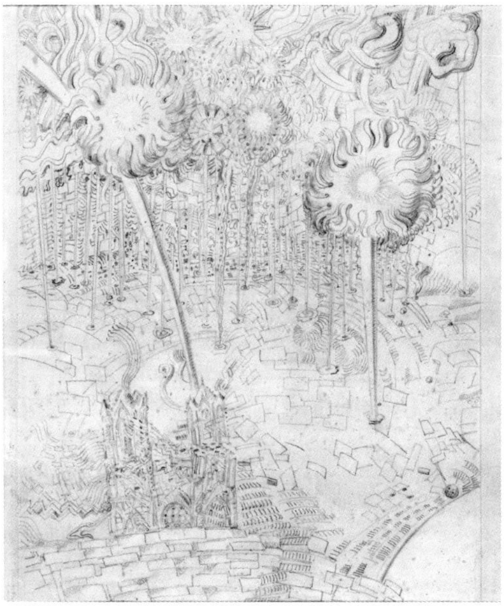

3.16. Paul Joostens, *Composition (The war) [Reims]*, s.d., pencil on paper, 59,2 x 48 cm. Brussels, Royal Museums of Fine Arts of Belgium, Inv.7933.

Conclusion

The diversity of interbellum art in Belgium is extremely vibrant. Alongside the important legacy of fin-de-siècle aesthetics still very popular in the post war years, new developments such as Constructivism and Expressionism are emerging. Dadaism is a more marginalised movement but leads with an artist like E.L.T. Mesens (1903-1971) to the very central movement of Belgian Surrealism that dominates the Belgian art historical narrative in the second half of the 1920s. The hanging of the collection for the exhibition *14-18 Rupture or Continuity* can hence be understood as an interlude between the Museum's Fin-de-Siècle collection and its Magritte Museum.

While the Royal Museum of Fine Arts' collection holds masterpieces from every large movement in Belgium at the beginning of the 20th century, two key Belgian figures in the national and international account of art history are missing. On the one hand, Frans Masereel (1889-1972) with his groundbreaking oeuvre of woodcuts and graphic work and his important role in the international pacifist movement is noticeably lacking as print is not the scope of the museum collection. Furthermore, the determining early work of Georges Vantongerloo as co-signer of the Dutch De Stijl manifesto is absent from the Museum's collection. While these two artists would have completed the show, their absence in the largest national museum of fine arts is in and of itself an important fact in the history of acquisition of the Museum and in the appreciation in Belgium of these artists in the second half of the 20th century.

In its entirety the exhibition demonstrates the complexity of the question "Continuity or Rupture?" asked in the title. The two words have to be read on different levels, from stylistic, to political, to geographical and societal and even personal points of views. They are not mutually exclusive but rather to be understood in a complex web where clinging to traditions or being open to new influences coming from abroad are two sides of one artistic society in its whole, juxtaposing different personalities in these unsettling years at the dawn of the 20th century.

Notes

1 This article refers to the focus exhibition held at the Royal Museums of Fine Arts in the Patio exhibition space from 29 September 2016 to 22 January 2017.

2 For the collection history of the RMFAB in this period please refer to Michèle Van Kalck, "Les collections", in Michèle Van Kalck (ed.), *Les Musés royaux des Beaux-Arts de Belgique. Deux siècles d'histoire, vol. 1*, (Brussels: Dexia Banque/ Racine, 2003), 227-275, and especially 248-252 in the section "L'art modern"; Virginie Devillez, "Les collections", in *ibid.*, 338-412, and especially "L'art moderne. Les collections, entre modernité et tradition (1919-1927)", 397-400.

3 On Belgian art at the dawn of the 20th century in a continued perspective, we refer among literature

on more specific aspects to Robert Hoozee et. Al., *L'art moderne en Belgique. 1900-1945* (Antwerp, Mercator Fonds,1992); Piet Boyens, *L'art flamand. Du symbolisme à l'expressionisme à Laethem-Saint-Martin*, (Tielt: Lannoo, 1992); Philippe Roberts-Jones, *Du Réalisme au Surréalisme, Belgique art du temps*, (Brussels, Laconti,1969).

4 Olivier Bertrand, *Rik Wouters. Visies op een levensloop. Nel Wouters onuitgegeven herinneringen* (Brussels: Belgian Art Research Institute, 2000), 234.

5 Paul Van Ostaijen, "Ekspressionisme in Vlaanderen", in *Paul Van Ostaijen, Verzameld werk. IV. Proza: Besprekingen en beschouwingen*, (Amsterdam: Bakker, 1979), (originally in De Stroom, 1918).

6 See on this artist *Jules Schmalzigaug: Un futuriste belge*, Cahiers des Musées royaux des Beaux-Arts de Belgique, vol. 8 (2010); *Jules Schmalzigaug: Futurist* (Oostende, Mu.ZEE, 29.10 2016 – 05.03 2017).

7 Jules Schmalzigaug to Richard Baseleer, 3.11.1913, AACB, inv. 15.108. "Er is een nieuwe wereld voor ons en wij zouden twijfelen? En wat dan nog als ik me vergis!" (translated by the author).

8 Stefan Zweig, *The World of Yesterday. An Autobiography* (London/ Toronto/ Melbourne/ Sidney: Cassell and Company Ltd. 1947), 170-172.

9 Cf. among others, Sophie De Schaepdrijver, "*Ô faiseuse de crépuscule.* Deutschlandbilder in Belgien im Großen Krieg," in Hubert Roland, Marnix Beyen, Greet Draye, ed., *Deutschlandbilder in Belgien 1830-1940* (Münster: Waxmann, 2011), 292-310.

10 For Schirren and his links to he Belgian avant-garde see Virginie Devillez, "1920-1940 Entre animisme et modernité, l'énigme Schirren," in *Ferdinand Schirren*, Cahiers des Musées royaux des beaux-Arts de Belgique, vol. 11 (2011), 95-107.

11 Adrien Grimmeau, "Biographie", in *ibid.*, 95-107.

12 For more information on Rik Wouters and his carreer as a painter, sculptor and draftsman see *Rétrospective Rik Wouters*, Bruxelles, Musées royaux des Beaux-Arts de Belgique, 10.03 2017 – 02.07 2017.

13 *Lust for Life*, Mechelen, Hof van Busleyden, 26.08 2016 – 11.12 2016; Antwerpen, MoMu – ModeMuseum Provincie Antwerpen, 17.09 2016 – 26.02 2017, 81.

14 André De Ridder, "L'école belge contemporaine," in *Cahiers de Belgique*, 4, 4-5 (avril - mai 1930), 177. "Il faut bien l'avouer : au moment où éclatait la guerre de 1914, nous n'étions, en Belgique, ni fort « européen », ni fort « modernes » ; alors qu'ailleurs des chercheurs illuminés avaient déjà commencé à bouleverser la forme et à rénover l'esprit de la peinture et de la sculpture, nous nous accrochions encore, avec une singulière obstination, presque voluptueusement, à l'impressionnisme ou, pour mieux dire à notre néo-impressionnisme local" (translated by the author).

15 Jules Schmalzigaug to Walter Schmalzigaug, 27 March 1913, AACB, inv. 15.085. "Que dirais-tu si je m'orientais un jour vers ce qu'on désigne sous le titre si idiot de 'futurisme', mot qui ne signifie rien du tout et qui sent la grosse caisse comme l'armée du salut." (translated by the author).

16 Jules Schmalzigaug to his parents, 15 November 1913, AACB, inv. 15.110.

17 Jules Schmalzigaug to his parents, 15 November 1913, AACB, inv. 15.110. "Je peux dire que je dépasse aujourd'hui dans mes intentions – tout ce que comprend l'école belge d'aujourd'hui." (translated by the author).

18 An Paenhuysen *De nieuwe wereld: De wonderjaren van de Belgische avant-garde (1918-1939)*, (Antwerpen: Meulenhoff/Manteau, 2010), 56. "De oorlog betekende een algemene verlamming van de creatieve mogelijkheden. De verbeelding van de kunstenaar werd getroffen door een soort mentale neurasthenie en de kosmopolitische banden die de experimentelen van verschillende landen verenigen, werden brutaal verbroken." (translated by the author).

19 Cf. Bart Van den Bossche, "Futurism in Belgium 1909-1940", in *Jules Schmalzigaug: Futurist, Oostende*, *op. cit.*, 265-271.

[20] Kurt De Boodt, *Prosper De Troyer. Schilder in Beweging*, (Antwerpen: Pandora Publishers, 2013), 35.

[21] Inge Henneman, "Paul van Ostaijen en de Antwerpse avant-garde – 1917-1925", in *1900-1930. Vlaams Expressionisme in Europese context*, Gent, Museum voor Schone Kunsten Gent, 10.03 1990 – 10.06 1990, 189.

[22] Frederik Leen, "In cirkels en Kringen. Kunstenaarsgroepen en -bonden van de voorhoede in België 1917-1929", in *Avant-Garde in België*, Brussel, Museum voor Moderne Kunst, 18.09 1992 – 13.12 1992: Antwerpen, Koninklijk Museum voor Schone Kunsten, 20.09 1992 – 06.12 1992, 28.

[23] Cited in Serge Goyens de Heusch, *7 Arts. Bruxelles 1922-1929. Un front de jeunesse pour la révolution artistique* (Brussels: Ministère de la Culture Française de Belgique, 1976), 49. "Nous continuons un effort. Et si notre génération ne parvient pas à l'imposer, que la suivante la reprenne là où nous l'aurions laissé" (translated by the author).

[24] The German presence of Der Sturm in the Netherlands is linked to a lucrative propaganda programme initiated by Herwarth Walden for the German State. Cf. Kate Winskell:. "The Art of Propaganda: Herwarth Walden and 'Der Sturm' 1914–1919". in *Art History* 18, 3 (1995), 329.

[25] Willy Van den Bussche, "Permeke in Engeland", in *1900-1930 Vlaams Expressionisme in Europese Context, op. cit.*, 73-75.

[26] The rupture or crisis of Minne's works has already taken place between 1910 and 1912 when he executes more 'muscled', realistic sculptures depicting always the same worker and reinforces his activities as a draftsman of religious scenes. In 1914 his obsession with the 'Mother and child' motive develops.

[27] For further information see Philippe Dagen, *Le silence des peintres: Les artistes face à la Grande Guerre* (Paris: Fayard, 1996). Mark Connelly, "Visualization of Violence", in 1914-1918 online. International Encyclopedia of the First World War, https://encyclopedia.1914-1918-online.net/article/visualization_of_violence?version=1.0 (accessed 6 March 2018). Sue Malvern, "Art", in 1914-1918 online. International Encyclopedia of the First World War, https://encyclopedia.1914-1918-online.net/article/art?version=1.0 (accessed 6 March 2018). Claire Maingon, *L'art face à la guerre* (Vincennes: éd. PUV, 2015).

[28] *Section artistique de l'armée. 2e exposition. Catalogue*, La Panne, 13.03 – 31.03.1917, 2. "La guerre actuelle n'est pas une succession de batailles, mais un état latent dont il importait de fixer les aspects et les caractéristiques. Aux documents littéraux que fournissent la photographie et le cinéma, il convenait d'en ajouter d'autres, nés de la sensibilité humaine, et le service documentaire de l'armée a eu l'idée de faire appel à un certain nombre d'artistes connus (...)" (translated by the author).

[29] Sandrine Smets, "Achille Van Sassenbrouck. Verminkt lichaam, helend werk", in *Oorlog & trauma: soldaten en ambulances 1914-1918*, Ieper, In Flanders Fields Museum, 1.11.2013 – 30.6.2014: *soldaten en psychiaters 1914-2014*, Gent, Museum Dr. Guislain, 1.11.2013 – 30.6.2014, 117.

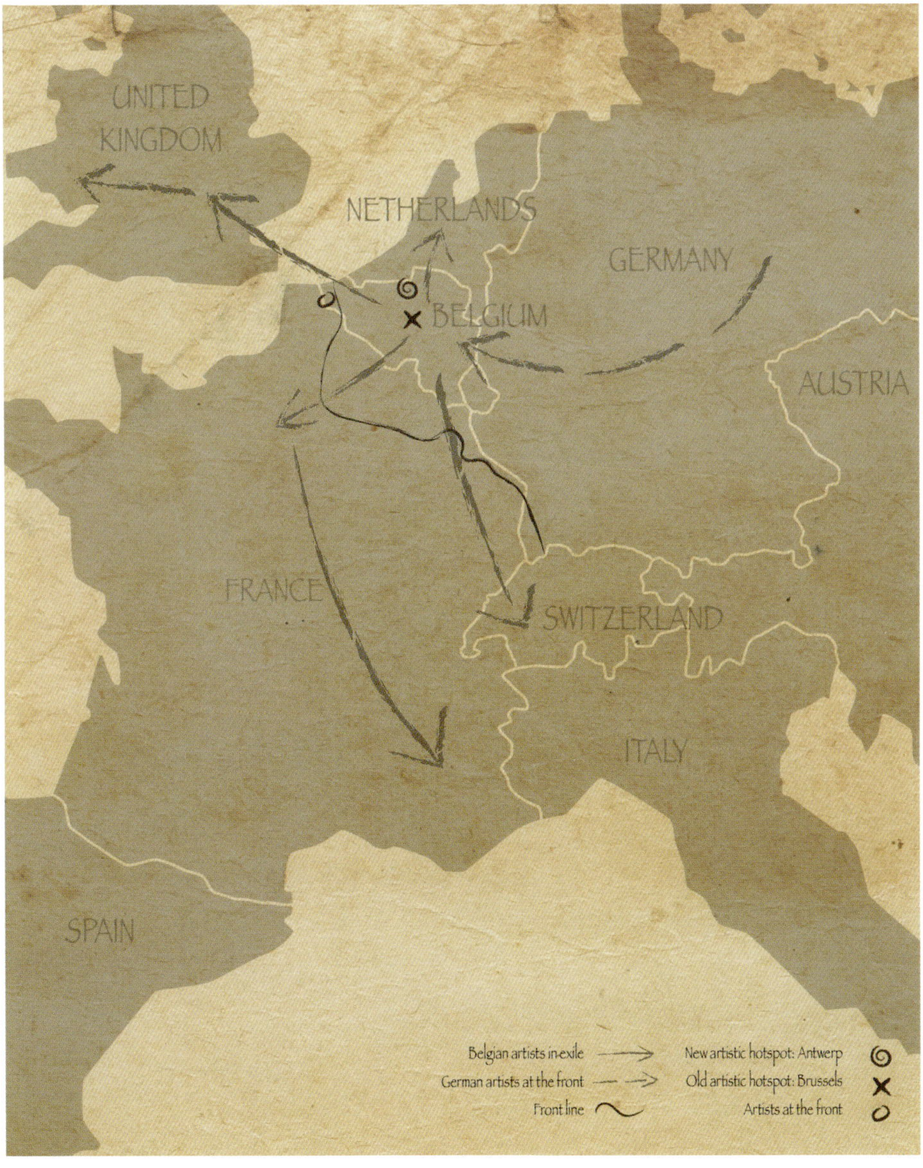

1.1. Map of migrations of Belgian artists.

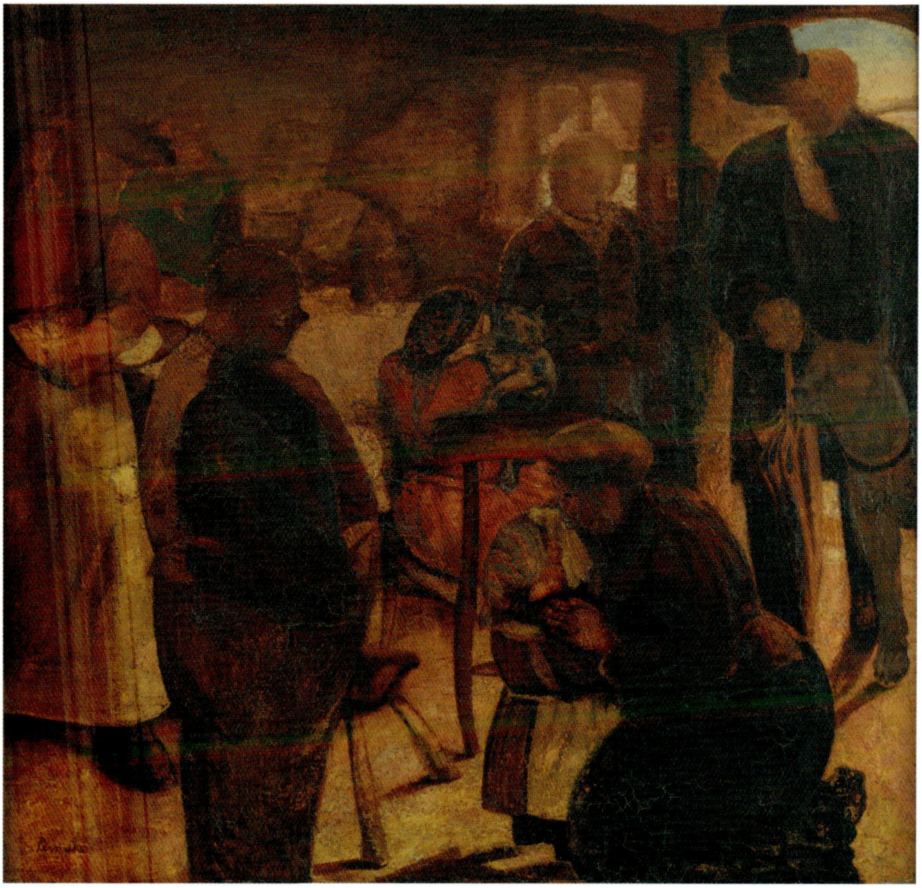

1.2. Constant Permeke, *The Stranger*, 1916. Oil on canvas, 173 x 180 cm. Brussels, Royal Museums of Fine Arts of Belgium, Inv. 4655.

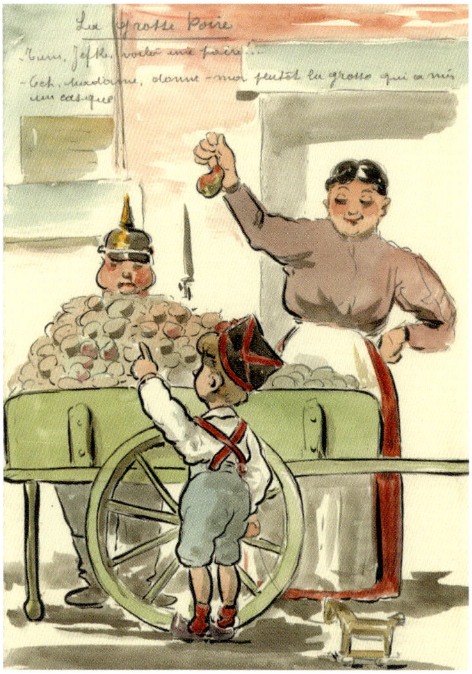

2.5. Satirical image "La Grosse Poire," signed René [possibly René De Pauw, 1887-1946], n.d. [1915?]. Brussels City Archives, Fonds Keym 59/64.

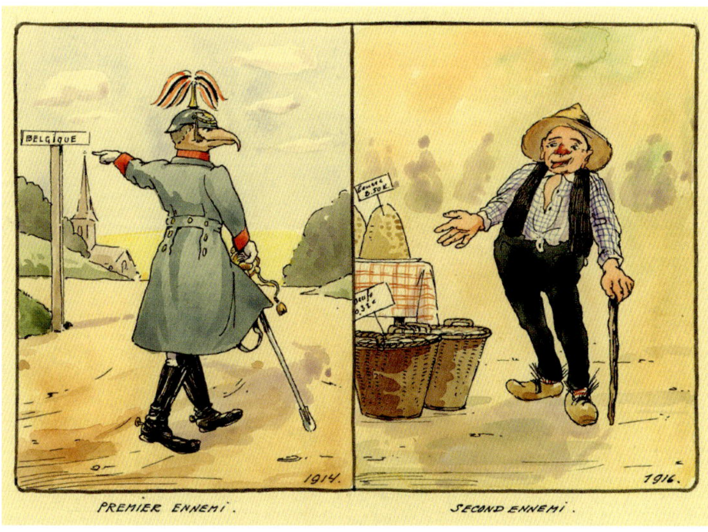

2.6. Brussels caricature "L'ennemi de 1914 – l'ennemi de 1916." Brussels City Archives, Fonds Keym.

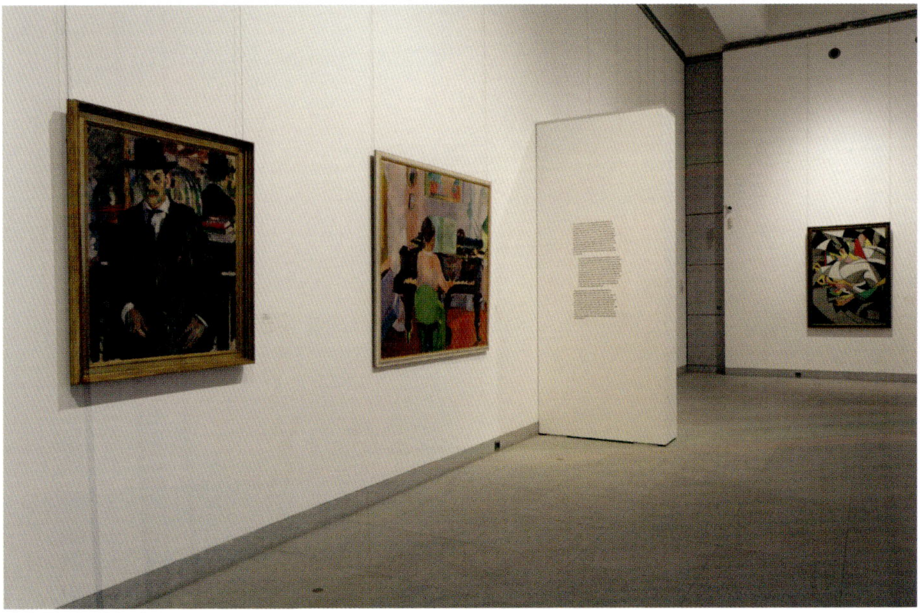

3.2. View of the exhibition "14/18. Rupture or Continuity," 2018, with works by Rik Wouters, Ferdinand Schirren and Prosper de Troyer.

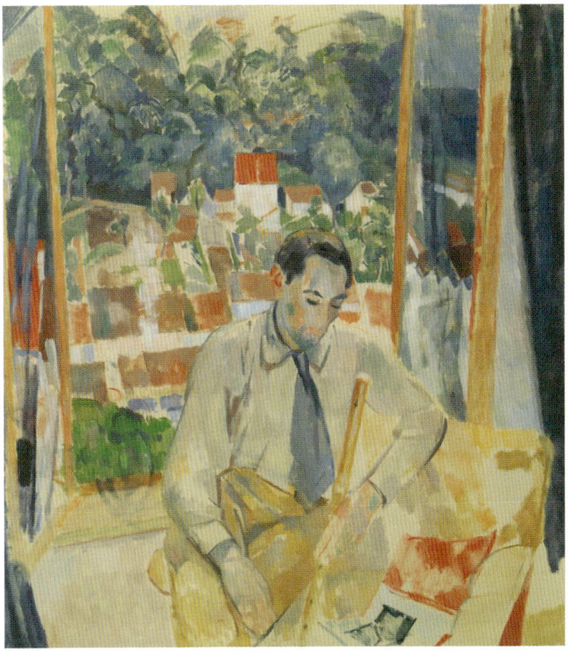

3.3. Rik Wouters, *Flautist*, 1914, oil on canvas, 133,5 x 115 cm. Brussels, Royal Museums of Fine Arts of Belgium, Inv. 4742.

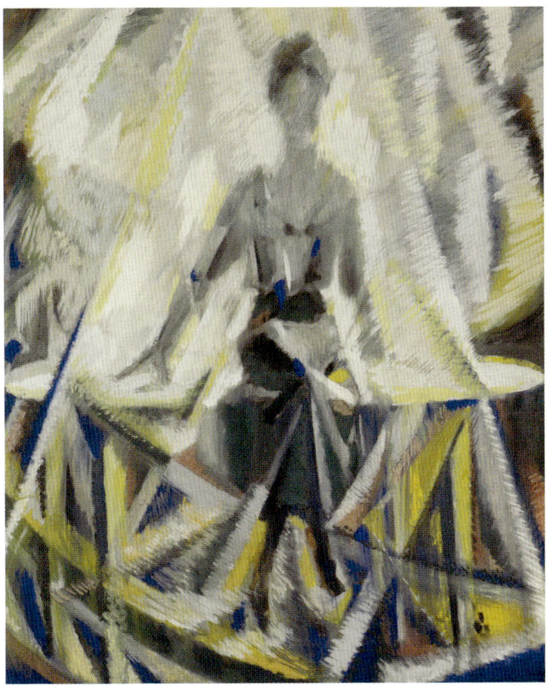

3.4. Jules Schmalzigaug, *Madame Nelly Hurrelbrinck*, ca. 1917, distemper on triplex, 120 x 101 cm (unfinished). Brussels, Royal Museums of Fine Arts of Belgium, Inv. 7557.

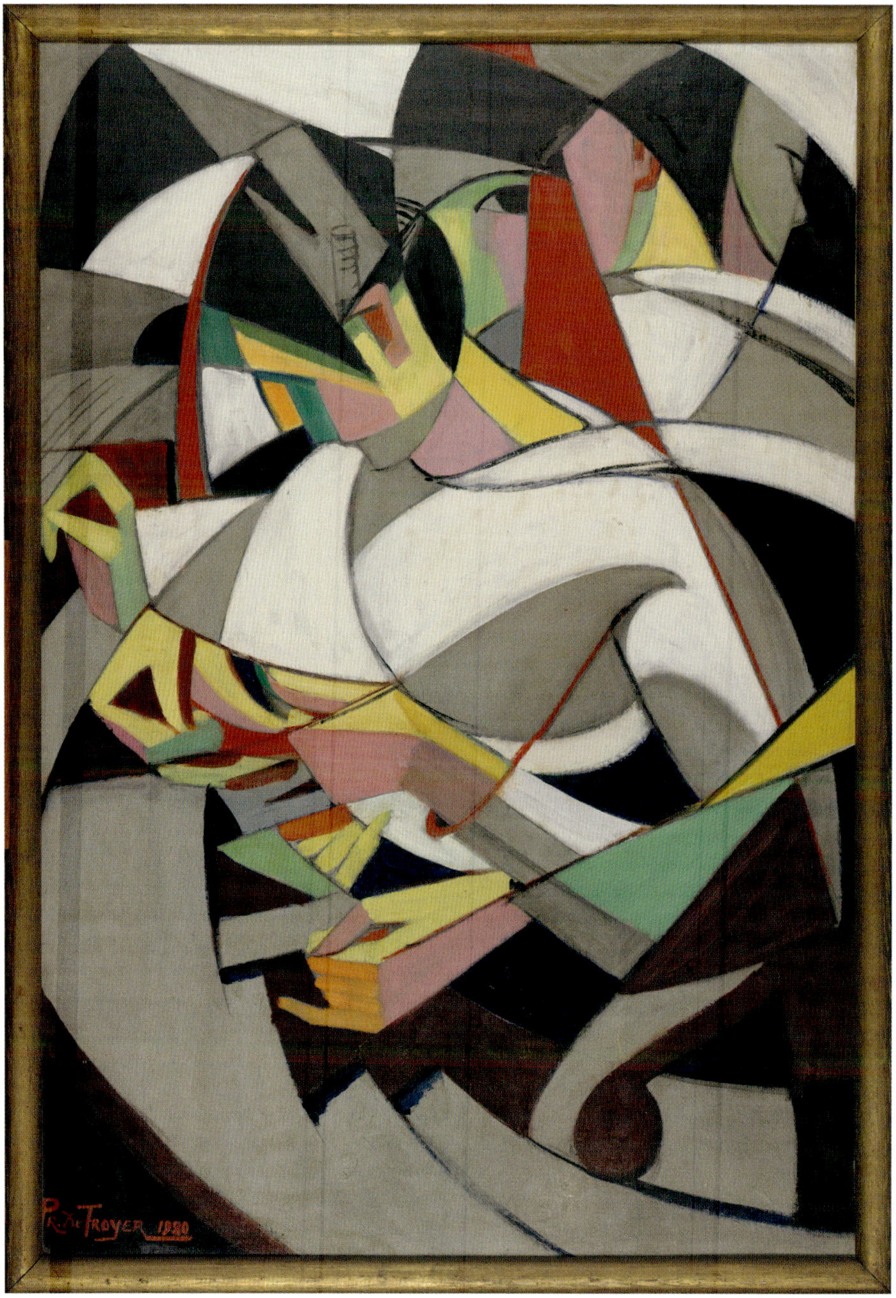

3.5. Prosper de Troyer, *The seamstress*, 1920, oil on wood, 150 x 99 cm. Brussels, Royal Museums of Fine Arts of Belgium, Inv. 7939.

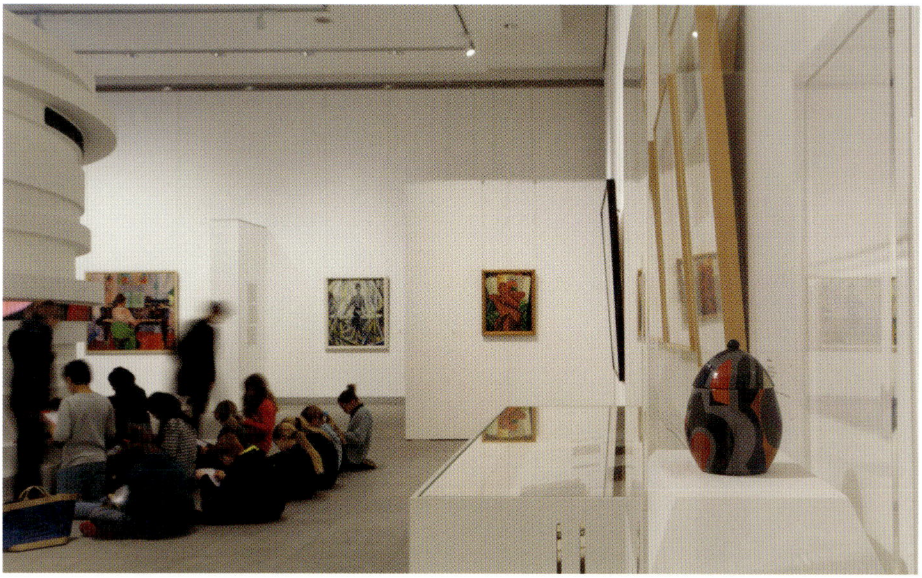

3.6. View of the exhibition "14/18. Rupture or Continuity," 2018, with works by Ferdinand Schirren, Jules Schmalzigaug, Pierre-Louis Flouquet and Jan Cockx.

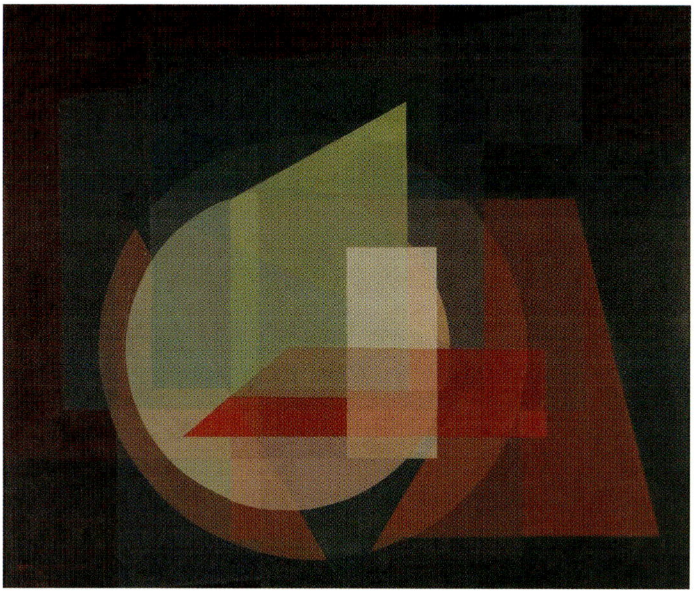

3.7. Jozef Peeters, *Huile n°21*, 1924, oil on canvas,144 x 166,5 cm. Brussels, Royal Museums of Fine Arts of Belgium, inv. 6892.

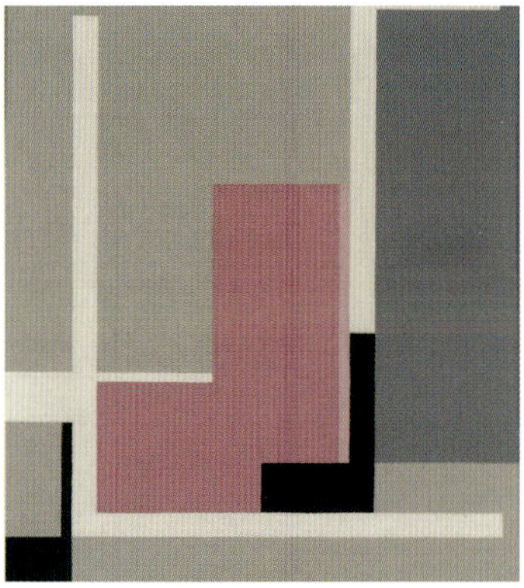

3.8. Marthe Donas, *Construction*, (1920), oil on wood, 48 x 42 cm. Brussels, Royal Museums of Fine Arts of Belgium, inv. 12035.

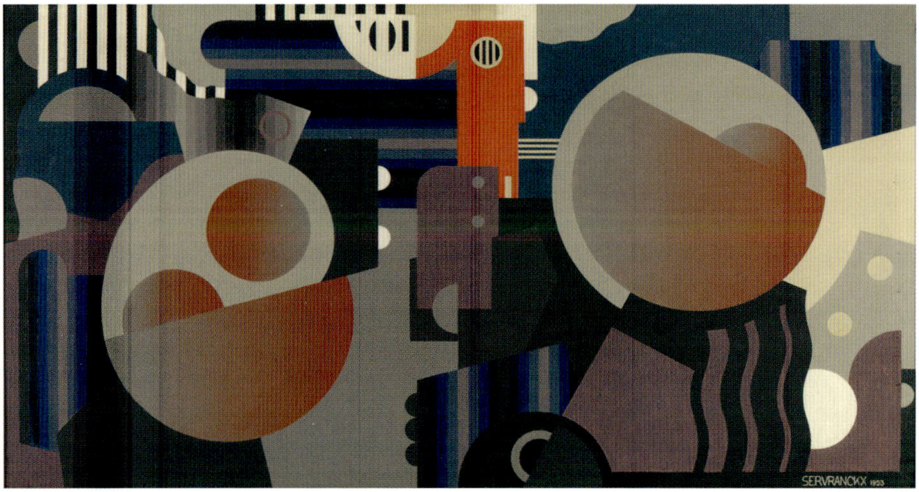

3.9. Victor Servranckx, *Opus 47*, 1923, oil on canvas, 113 x 210,5 cm. Brussels, Royal Museums of Fine Arts of Belgium, Inv. 6859.

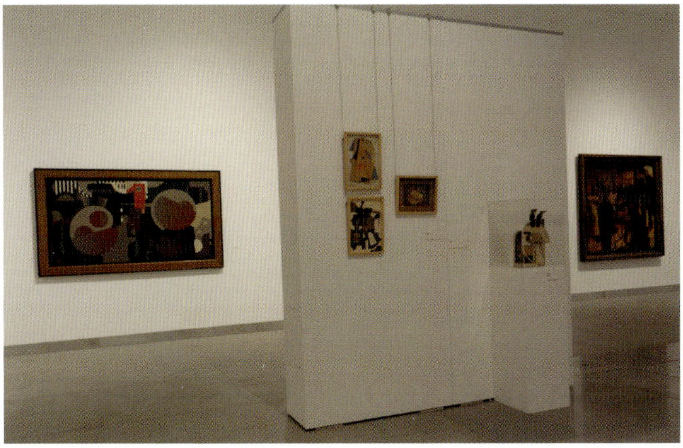

3.10. View of the exhibition "14/18. Rupture or Continuity," 2018, with works by Victor Servranckx, Paul Joostens and Constant Permeke.

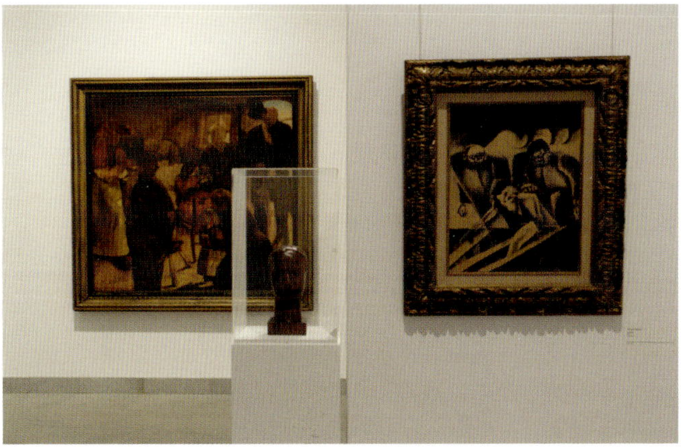

3.11. View of the exhibition "14/18. Rupture or Continuity," 2018, with works by Constant Permeke, Jozef Cantré and Frits van den Berghe.

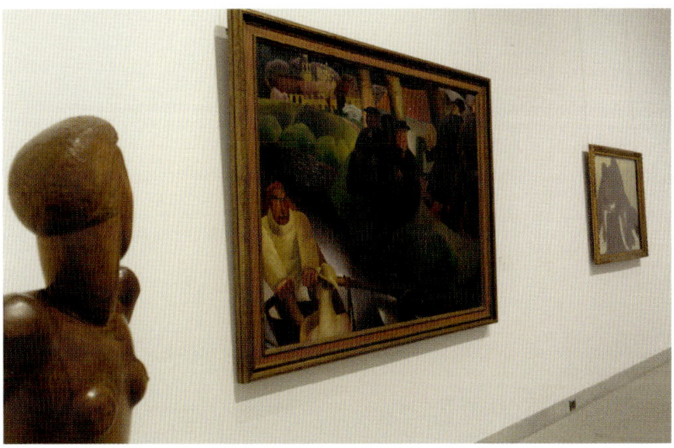

3.12. View of the exhibition "14/18. Rupture or Continuity," 2018, with works by Oscar Jespers, Frits van den Berghe and Albert Servaes.

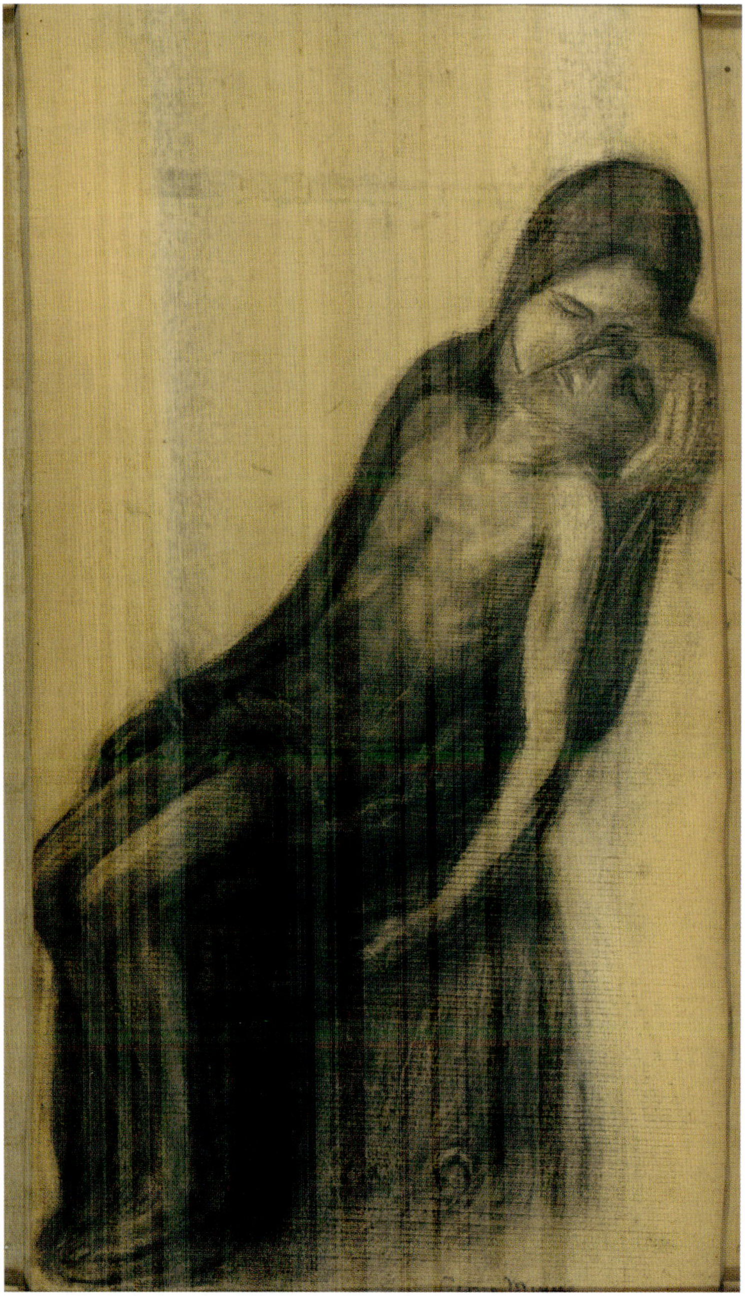

3.13. George Minne, *Piëta*, 1921, charcoal on wood, 107 x 54 cm. Brussels, Royal Museums of Fine Arts of Belgium, Inv.4330.

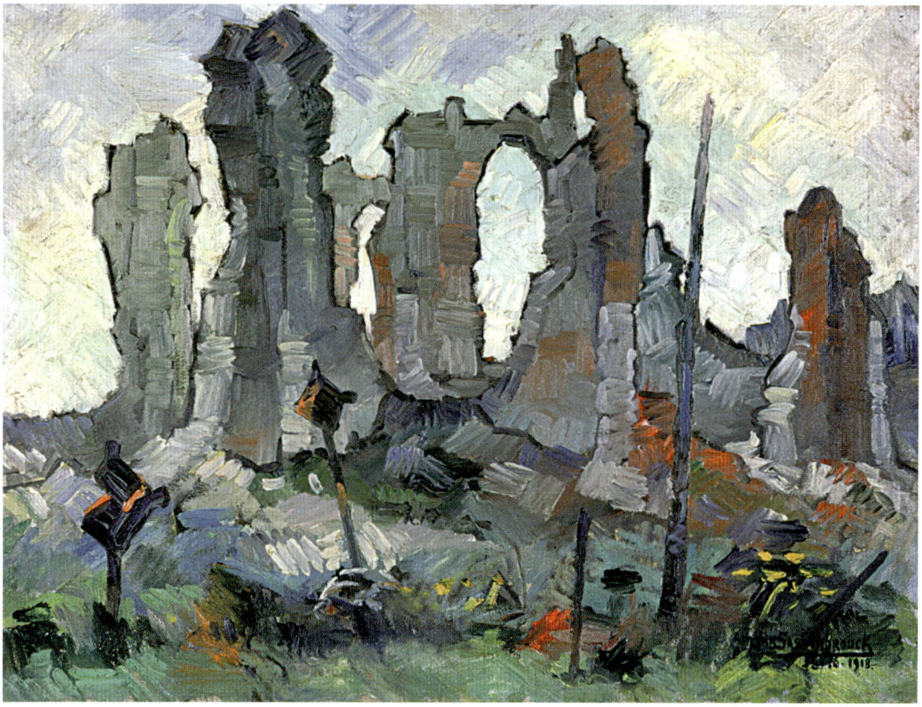

3.14. Achille Van Sassenbrouck, *Ruins of the church of Nieuwpoort*, 1918, oil on canvas, 54,2 x 69,6 cm. Brussels, Royal Museums of Fine Arts of Belgium, Inv. 10076.

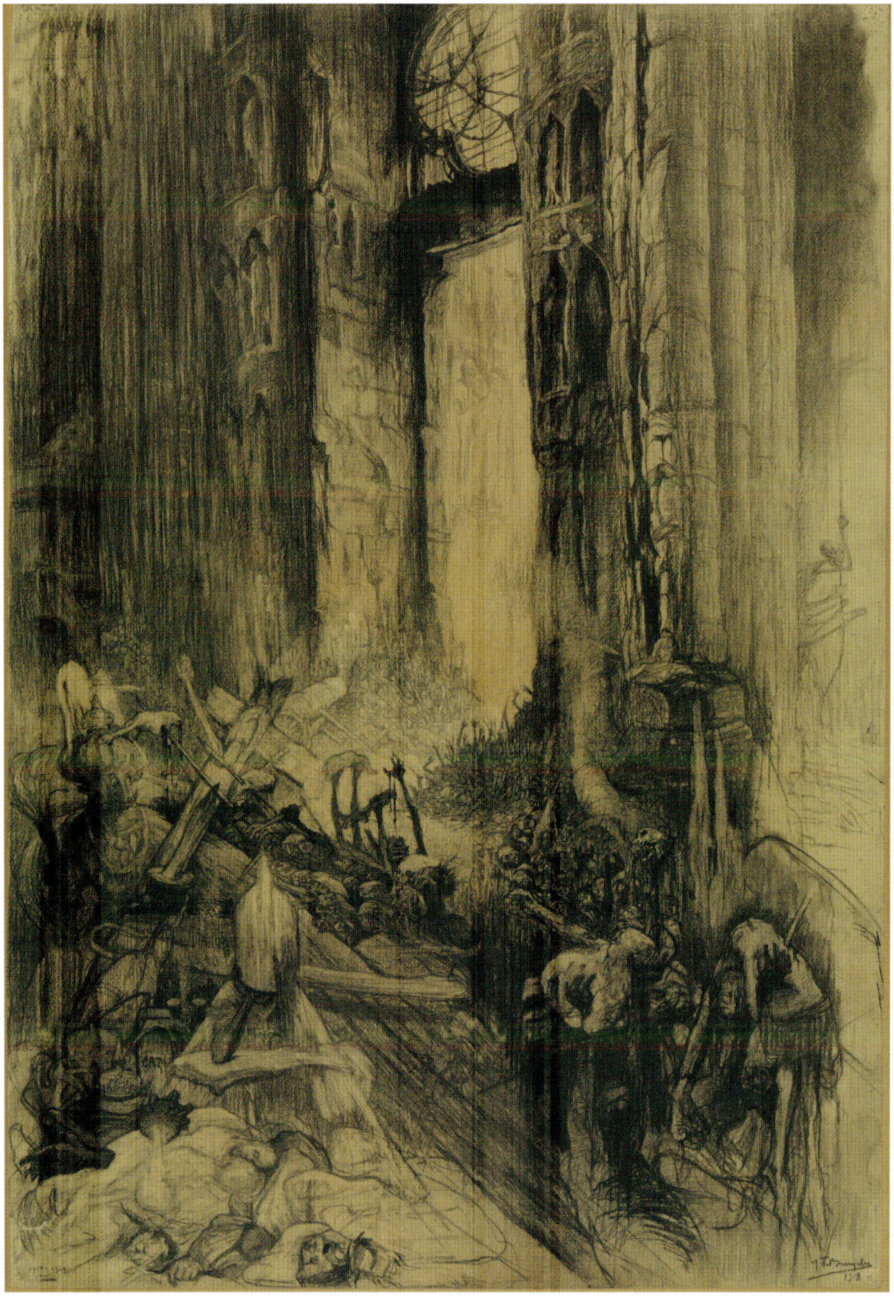

3.15. Jules de Bruycker, *The cathedral of Reims*, 1918, black pencil on paper, 99,5 x 67 cm. Brussels, Royal Museums of Fine Arts of Belgium, Inv. 4488.

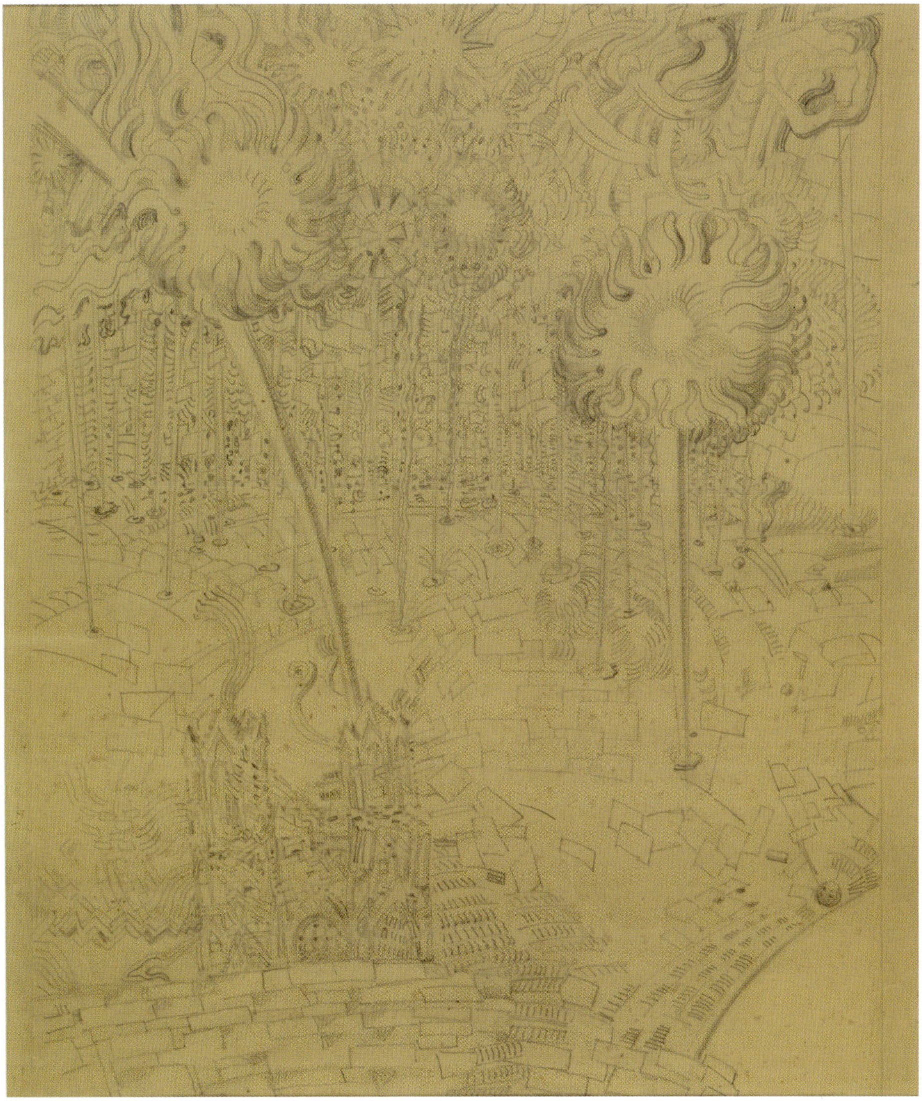

3.16. Paul Joostens, *Composition (The war) [Reims]*, s.d., pencil on paper, 59,2 x 48 cm. Brussels, Royal Museums of Fine Arts of Belgium, Inv.7933.

Artists at war and abroad – On the front and in exile

L'art en guerre !
L'État belge, mécène des artistes combattants : politique bienveillante ou nécessité impérieuse ?

Sandrine Smets

Avec l'invasion d'août 1914, les artistes belges connaissent des destinées variées : imposées à certains ou résultant d'un choix personnel pour les autres. Les plus jeunes, nés à partir de 1880, sont mobilisés. Parmi les autres, plus âgés ou réformés, quelques-uns se portent volontaires pour la durée de la guerre, d'autres choisissent de rester en Belgique ; bon nombre d'entre eux décident de fuir le pays et de vivre en exil. Pendant la guerre de mouvement, entre août et octobre 1914, quelques combattants artistes sont faits prisonniers ; ceux-ci passent les quatre années en captivité. Quelques-uns encore, qui participent au siège d'Anvers, se retirent aux Pays-Bas après la reddition de la ville le 10 octobre 1914, et sont incarcérés pour la durée de la guerre dans des camps d'internement. En trois mois, la communauté artistique belge se trouve dispersée et placée dans une situation de haute vulnérabilité, car brutalement dépourvue de sources de revenus et, souvent, privée de moyens de travailler.

S'appuyant sur des archives encore inexplorées et revisitant la littérature existante, la présente contribution vise à cerner la politique de l'État belge vis-à-vis des artistes, en particulier les artistes combattants. Dans un premier temps, nous étudierons les actions de l'État en faveur des artistes, au travers des politiques menées par le ministère des Sciences et des Arts, d'une part, par le ministère de la Guerre, d'autre part. Nous évoquerons ensuite la question de l'instrumentalisation de l'art en temps de guerre. Nous envisagerons enfin le pouvoir des images en dressant un panorama de la production artistique des peintres officiels et en montrant comment elles ont été exploitées par l'État. Nous conclurons en repositionnant notre propos à travers le prisme de la problématique : rupture ou continuité ?[1]

Protéger les artistes

Dès l'automne 1914, l'État belge réagit pour pallier la précarité des artistes. Les acteurs officiels principaux sont le ministre des Sciences et des Arts, Prosper Poullet, établi tantôt à La Haye tantôt au Havre, et le directeur de l'administration des Beaux-Arts, Paul Lambotte, installé à Londres. L'abondante correspondance entre les deux hommes permet de cerner la politique de secours mise en place.[2]

L'État s'occupe d'abord d'assurer les besoins premiers des artistes exilés (logement, nourriture, vêtements) et d'offrir une aide pratique pour les accompagner dans les démarches quotidiennes dans le pays d'accueil (traduction de documents, encaissement de chèques, etc.).[3] Le sort des artistes restés en Belgique, qui ont vécu l'invasion et ses tourments et subissent à présent le régime d'occupation, inquiète davantage. En 1915, la reine Élisabeth accorde un subside de 50 000 francs pour aider les artistes, 80 % de la somme étant, selon ses vœux, réservés aux artistes de la Belgique occupée.[4] Se constitue à Londres un comité chargé de la distribution du fonds ; celui-ci comprend des artistes, le peintre Alfred Bastien et le sculpteur Victor Rousseau, un représentant politique, Jules Destrée, et un représentant de l'administration des Beaux-Arts, Paul Lambotte.[5] Pour collecter des fonds supplémentaires, Paul Lambotte organise en Grande-Bretagne[6] une multitude d'expositions d'art belge avec les œuvres présentées à la Biennale de Venise de 1914[7] et à l' « Esposizione Internazionale di Bianco e Nero » à Florence,[8] rapatriées à Londres du fait de la guerre. Ces expositions sont l'occasion pour les artistes de vendre et, pour l'État, de faire quelques bénéfices sur les droits d'entrée, mais surtout de faire circuler les œuvres dans des locaux généralement mis gratuitement à la disposition de l'État belge, évitant ainsi de dépenser des sommes importantes pour leur magasinage. En outre, Paul Lambotte organise des conférences sur l'art belge, des rencontres littéraires, notamment avec Maurice Maeterlinck, prix Nobel de Littérature en 1911, des concerts et participe à la publication de livres tels le *Book of « Belgium's Gratitude »* et le catalogue « *Belgian Art in Exile* ». L'argent ainsi réuni est redistribué aux artistes nécessiteux, selon les besoins et les situations,[9] avec discernement, car certains artistes sont d' « effrontés quémandeurs »,[10] et toujours peu à la fois.[11] Paul Lambotte se charge personnellement d'octroyer des aides financières aux artistes en Grande-Bretagne, il envoie régulièrement des subsides aux Pays-Bas distribués par la princesse de Ligne, tandis que ceux envoyés à Bruxelles sont attribués par le Directeur général de l'Administration des Beaux-Arts resté à Bruxelles, Ernest Verlant.

Qu'en est-il des artistes combattants ? Paul Lambotte mentionne uniquement l'aide apportée à l'un d'entre eux arrivé en Grande-Bretagne en mars 1915 :

> « Marc-Henry Meunier, brancardier, vient de rentrer épuisé moralement et physiquement. Il est sans ressources. Il a obtenu l'hospitalité et des soins gratuits à la campagne, mais il y a les trajets en chemin de fer, les vêtements à remplacer, le blanchissage... »[12]

Ce n'est qu'en 1917 que Paul Lambotte crée une œuvre philanthropique *Belgian Artists at the Front*. Son but est d'envoyer aux artistes-soldats le matériel nécessaire à la pratique de leur art pour « leur éviter une dépression nerveuse ».[13] Force est donc de constater qu'ils sont négligés, en tout cas dans un premier temps, par leur ministère de tutelle. Est-ce parce que les artistes engagés sous le drapeau sont pris en charge par le ministère de la Guerre, entendons par là qu'ils sont « logés, nourris, blanchis » et qu'ils perçoivent la solde réglementaire ? Quelle est la position des autorités militaires ?

Mobilisés ou volontaires, les artistes combattants sont incorporés dans les différentes unités combattantes, sans distinction aucune. Malgré la pénibilité des conditions de vie sur le front, nombre d'entre eux reprennent le crayon ou le pinceau pour témoigner de l'histoire et exprimer leur vécu. La pratique artistique interroge les autorités militaires. Elle est cependant rapidement jugée utile à la tactique militaire : soit pour effectuer des relevés dessinés des positions ennemies afin d'orienter les tirs de l'artillerie, soit pour mettre en œuvre diverses techniques de camouflage destinées à tromper l'ennemi. Elle est en même temps identifiée comme moyen de distraction profitable au moral des troupes, tout en suscitant la méfiance par crainte de voir diffuser des images porteuses de renseignements classés top secret. Aussi l'armée belge décide-t-elle en 1915 d'admettre sa pratique et de la contrôler par l'octroi d'autorisations de dessiner et peindre sur le front. Parallèlement, les initiatives culturelles, telles que concours de dessin ou expositions d'œuvres et d'artisanat de guerre, se multiplient. Celles-ci stimulent la production artistique, mais elles contribuent surtout à une réflexion sur l'utilité de l'art de guerre.

Ainsi, l'État[14] décide la création de la section artistique de l'armée belge en campagne en mai ou juin 1916. Elle est rattachée à la 2e section de l'état-major général en charge du renseignement. S'ils conservent un statut militaire, les artistes membres sont libérés de toute obligation militaire pour qu'ils puissent entièrement se consacrer à leur art. La seule rétribution perçue est la solde réglementaire avec laquelle ils doivent assurer leur propre subsistance. Les artistes sont libres de choisir les lieux et les sujets à représenter, pour autant qu'ils soient exécutés sur le secteur belge du front ou dans les zones d'étapes belges en France. Les œuvres demeurent propriété de leur auteur, mais ne peuvent être publiées ou vendues sans l'assentiment de la censure. Le gouvernement s'accorde un droit de préemption et un droit de reproduction sur toutes les œuvres produites par les artistes membres, quel qu'en soit leur propriétaire. La section artistique compte vingt-six membres, la plupart volontaires de guerre, à la moyenne d'âge élevée, qui se regroupent principalement dans deux localités proches du front : Nieuport et Loo. Leur mission : documenter la guerre.

Instrumentaliser l'art

Comment expliquer le revirement d'attitude significatif vis-à-vis des artistes combattants qui s'opère en 1916 ? Après les tragiques désillusions de 1914 et l'enlisement désastreux de 1915, avec ses offensives répétées, aussi meurtrières qu'inutiles, la lassitude s'installe.[15] Les troupes commencent à exprimer leur lassitude et les opinions publiques gorgées de sentiments patriotiques s'essoufflent progressivement. Les états belligérants, parfois partagés entre une paix négociée et une volonté jusqu'au-boutiste d'en finir par les armes, doivent financer coûte que coûte la guerre, tout en cherchant sur le plan diplomatique les alliances qui mèneront à la victoire. En 1916, les gouvernements doivent tirer les leçons de la guerre de tranchées et envisager de nouvelles stratégies. Simultanément, ils doivent à tout prix remobiliser les esprits, ce qui n'est possible que par un strict contrôle de l'information, basé sur la censure et la propagande. Les systèmes d'information et de propagande spontanée, qui se sont mis en place de façon empirique dans les premiers mois de la guerre, se structurent en 1915 en services officiels. 1916 contraint l'ensemble des états belligérants à renforcer par une réorganisation en profondeur les organes de censure et de propagande.

Le défi majeur de la propagande belge est de rappeler au monde entier l'implication de l'armée belge dans le conflit.[16] La Belgique est en effet prisonnière de son image de « Poor Little Belgium ». Dès 1914, l'invasion allemande du territoire national, la violation de la neutralité du pays, les récits d'atrocités commises par l'envahisseur et l'occupation autoritaire, qui affame un peuple, offrent à la propagande alliée l'occasion de planter leur décor, leur lecture des événements : les Allemands sont responsables d'une guerre abjecte ; les Franco-Britanniques sont intervenus pour défendre le Droit. Cette simplification outrancière des enjeux est propre à la propagande qui doit clarifier pour convaincre. Mais cette image de la Belgique victime devient progressivement caricaturale. Si l'État belge veut obtenir le soutien d'états neutres et recevoir de nouveaux crédits, il doit minimiser cette image n'incitant que commisération pour imposer celle d'une nation belligérante à part entière. Au printemps 1916, les autorités belges procèdent à une profonde réorganisation de la propagande. Celle-ci a besoin de nouvelles images. La création de la section artistique à l'été 1916 s'inscrit dans ce programme global, dans la foulée des services photographique et cinématographique de l'armée belge.

Soulignons la symétrie dans l'organisation de missions artistiques sur le front chez les Alliés. En France, le sous-secrétariat d'État aux Beaux-Arts reprend en 1916 l'organisation des missions artistiques, succédant ainsi au musée de l'Armée très critiqué tant pour le choix des artistes que pour la qualité jugée médiocre de leurs œuvres. Au Royaume-Uni, la « Wellington House », département secret chargé de la propagande britannique, engage en mai 1916 le premier artiste de guerre officiel[17] et crée en juillet une section de propagande picturale. Les programmes belge, français et britannique poursuivent les mêmes objectifs : documenter le conflit par des œuvres, qui peuvent servir à la propagande.

Pour les Belges, créer un statut d'artiste officiel permet de certifier l'authenticité des images peintes. L'introduction au catalogue de la deuxième exposition de la section artistique insiste sur leur valeur testimoniale, niant de cette façon leur valeur propagandiste :

> « Le public ne s'attend guère à trouver ici des “tableaux de bataille”. Des tableaux de bataille, des peintres en pantoufles en fabriquent dans des ateliers bien chauffés de Montmartre et de Kensington pour l'édification de journaux illustrés. »[18]

L'auteur dénonce ici les artistes planqués, ceux qui peignent la guerre à l'arrière d'après des photographies, sans avoir fait l'expérience du front, pour la presse. Quelques paragraphes plus loin, il souligne la véracité du témoignage des artistes officiels belges : « tous soldats et ayant longtemps partagé, comme tels, les peines et les émotions des combattants ».[19] Le statut de l'artiste intervient donc aussi dans les mécanismes de la propagande de guerre.

Persuader par l'image

L'image est essentielle pour la propagande, car elle est un medium particulièrement efficace pour fabriquer des messages persuasifs.[20] Parce qu'elle suscite des émotions, parce qu'elle est presque spontanément mémorisée et parce qu'elle garantit l'authenticité de l'événement représenté. Mais pourquoi utiliser des œuvres d'art comme matériel visuel alors que la photographie envahit la presse illustrée ?

Rappelons d'abord que les missions artistiques officielles belges et alliées interviennent alors que le matériel visuel pouvant servir à la propagande se fait rare, souvent par manque de moyens ou par désorganisation, mais aussi à cause des difficultés ou interdictions de photographier sur le front. Elles viennent donc pallier le manque de matériel photographique. Mais, les responsables de la propagande ont certainement vu en l'œuvre d'art d'autres atouts.

La photographie est en effet souvent perçue comme une image littérale de la réalité, à laquelle le spectateur est confronté de façon brutale, sa véracité ne peut être mise en cause. Tandis que le témoignage artistique est une image fabriquée par l'homme, il place le spectateur à une distance un peu plus lointaine de la réalité crue. Il n'en atteste pourtant pas moins l'authenticité des faits. Mais, sa forme et son langage sont plus à même d'entraîner le spectateur dans une voie émotive. Image photographique et image peinte, « chaque type de support a ses contraintes et son langage propre, ses limites et ses effets spécifiques ».[21] Les deux médias doivent donc être envisagés comme des vecteurs complémentaires de propagande. Si tous deux en appellent aux émotions du récepteur, c'est l'intensité de la charge émotive qui est décisive dans le processus de persuasion. Voilà l'objectif poursuivi par la propagande : faire prendre conscience et susciter l'adhésion à une cause.

La première condition du pouvoir de persuasion d'une image réside dans sa lisibilité. Le contenu de l'image doit être instantanément identifié du public et aussitôt mis en corrélation avec le conflit. Il n'est dès lors pas étonnant que l'État ait choisi comme membres de la section artistique des artistes inscrits dans la tradition figurative, sans pour autant se limiter à un style.

Les artistes officiels belges sont en effet issus de différentes générations et écoles. Certains perpétuent le réalisme académique ou des styles de la fin du XIXe siècle, tels que le symbolisme et le postimpressionnisme. D'autres optent pour des courants d'avant-garde, basés sur une réflexion quant au rendu de la lumière, à l'utilisation de la couleur et à la déformation des volumes, tels que le fauvisme et, dans une moindre mesure, l'expressionnisme. Les mouvements plus novateurs tels le cubisme en France, le futurisme en Italie et le vorticisme en Grande-Bretagne, sont absents de la production belge.

Parmi les peintres révolutionnaires, citons le cas exemplaire de l'artiste de guerre britannique C.R.W. Nevinson[22] qui, influencé par le futurisme italien, réalise au début de la guerre des œuvres vorticistes puissantes, puis revient à un style figuratif académique pour s'assurer que ses œuvres véhiculent un message intelligible du plus large public. Ainsi, « *Returning to the trenches* » (1914),[23] qui transforme une colonne de soldats marchant telle une mécanique guerrière inébranlable, cède la place à « *The Paths of Glory* » (1917),[24] qui montre deux soldats en uniforme britannique aux corps sans vie allongés dans la boue, face contre terre, entremêlés dans un réseau de fils barbelés. Le réalisme des soldats morts et le fait qu'ils ne donnent pas l'image de héros conduisent les autorités britanniques à censurer la peinture. Nevinson décide malgré tout de l'exposer en mars 1918 à Londres, mais y fixe un bandeau de papier couvrant la toile sur lequel on peut lire « Censuré ». La représentation figurative combinée à un style académique revêt ainsi un caractère fondamental dans l'efficacité de l'image.

La totalité de la production artistique belge de la Grande Guerre ne peut pas pour autant être qualifiée de fade. Quelques artistes cherchent à faire sentir la violence vécue. Transcrire un ressenti, exprimer des émotions, traduire des sensations deviennent le nouveau défi et trouvent des formes nouvelles. Chez certains, le traumatisme d'une blessure engendre un tel bouleversement, qu'il enfante un nouveau langage artistique. Citons le peintre Achille Van Sassenbrouck, blessé le 10 décembre 1915, qui exprime la violence dévastatrice, dont il a été victime, par l'utilisation de couleurs vives très contrastées et qui cerne les formes d'un trait noir, comme pour reconstruire son schéma corporel, offensé par la brutalité des explosions de l'artillerie.[25] On note les mêmes caractéristiques dans l'œuvre de guerre de Marcel Canneel : couleurs vives, presque violentes, fragmentation des formes et utilisation des aplats. Un artiste chez qui, dès la fin du conflit, les couleurs redeviennent réalistes et la touche se fait moins énergique, plus sereine. Ici, c'est l'intensité du langage des peintres qui frappe les esprits, provoque une réaction émotionnelle forte et confère à l'image toute sa puissance persuasive.

Au-delà de la forme, le contenu constitue la seconde condition de l'efficacité de l'image. Celui-ci est d'abord déterminé par le regard de l'artiste. Qu'ont-ils montré de la guerre ? La Première Guerre mondiale sonne le glas des scènes héroïques de batailles enracinées dans la tradition de la peinture d'histoire. Le décorum des champs de bataille disparaît, les armées s'enterrent, tandis que le feu de la guerre mécanisée se fait de plus en plus violent et les armes chimiques opèrent de façon sournoise. Finis les affrontements rangés, place aux explosions, aux sombres nébuleuses et aux gerbes de terre. Les combats sont essentiellement visibles dans leurs effets sur le paysage et sur le patrimoine. D'autres motifs se développent : la vie quotidienne dans les tranchées et à l'arrière, ou encore le portrait des camarades et l'autoportrait qui fait son apparition. Par autocensure, la mort, pourtant inhérente à la guerre, est presque passée sous silence. Rappelons que les artistes officiels jouissent d'une liberté totale dans le choix des sujets à peindre. Si leurs œuvres sont conçues à l'origine par leurs auteurs comme des documents artistiques, elles ont largement été utilisées par les autorités belges à des fins de propagande. C'est dans ce corpus d'images que les responsables de la propagande choisissent les images les plus à même de véhiculer les messages souhaités.

Quels sont ces messages ? Et quelles images peuvent les véhiculer ? Pour l'historienne Laurence van Ypersele, « la propagande de guerre cherche toujours, d'une part, à désigner l'ennemi, en le diabolisant tout en le minimisant, et d'autre part, à unifier son propre camp, en légitimant son combat et en exaltant son identité ».[26] Partant de cette définition du message propagandiste en temps de guerre, nous proposons ici d'étudier quatre œuvres de la production artistique officielle belge, qui présentent les caractéristiques de celles sélectionnées pour les expositions de propagande, en cherchant à cerner le choix des motifs par l'émetteur, à déterminer le degré de réalité du motif choisi, à décrypter le message véhiculé par le motif, et à comprendre comment le récepteur est susceptible de le décoder.

Fernand Allard l'Olivier peint une scène militaire représentant un soldat dans la tranchée, occupé à l'entretien de son arme (ill. 4.1).[27] Assis devant la porte d'un abri, il est vêtu de façon décontractée, col de la veste ouvert et bottines délacées. Il porte un petit bonnet tricoté, coiffe non réglementaire typique des envois faits par les femmes

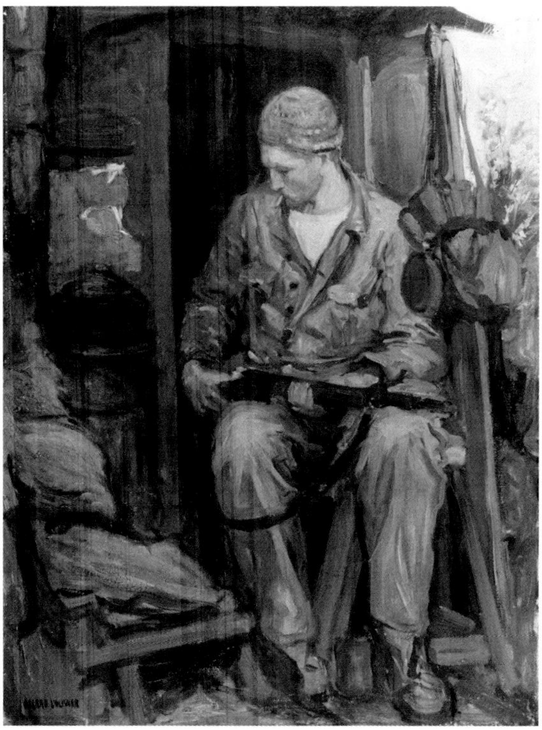

4.1. Fernand Allard l'Olivier, « Fantassin au repos dans la tranchée », s.d., huile sur toile, 73 x 54 cm. Bruxelles, Musée royal de l'Armée et d'Histoire militaire. Inv. n° 201000112.

de l'arrière qui tricotaient calots, écharpes, moufles et chaussettes aux hommes du front pour leur offrir un peu de chaleur. Son attitude décontractée, dans une posture vigilante, mais non belliqueuse, témoigne-t-elle avec exactitude de la conjoncture de l'armée belge ? La zone du front tenue par l'armée belge est en effet réputée calme. Contrairement aux stratégies meurtrières des Alliés français et britanniques, la volonté du roi Albert était d'épargner autant que possible les hommes de son armée.[28] En outre, les conditions du terrain, avec la mise sous eau d'une grande partie du secteur belge, expliquent également l'absence d'assauts suicidaires, tels que pratiqués à Verdun, dans la Somme et au Chemin des Dames. Les conditions de vie en première ligne n'y sont pas pour autant moins pénibles. L'humidité de la zone inondée, le climat passant du froid piquant en hiver aux chaleurs suffocantes l'été, le manque d'hygiène qui s'accompagne de la présence lassante de nuisibles, les sempiternels déchaînements de l'artillerie qui viennent interrompre les périodes de calme, sans compter l'odeur nauséabonde des cadavres en décomposition, provoquent de nombreuses maladies et minent le moral des troupes. Cependant, si l'armée belge ne participe pas directement aux grandes offensives des Alliés, elle y contribue tantôt en reprenant une partie des secteurs gardés par les Français ou les Britanniques afin de libérer des hommes et de renforcer d'autres secteurs, tantôt en augmentant son degré d'activité pour éviter que les troupes allemandes ne soient retirées du front belge et placées ailleurs.[29] Aussi la peinture d'Allard l'Olivier est-elle en parfaite adéquation avec la réalité du terrain.

Comment cette image est-elle susceptible de gagner le consentement des populations ? L'absence d'agressivité dans l'attitude du soldat belge, associée à l'action d'entretenir son arme, vise d'abord à pointer la responsabilité de l'ennemi dans le déclenchement du conflit. Autrement dit, si cet homme a dû prendre les armes, c'est parce que l'ennemi a envahi le territoire belge, il ne fait que de le défendre. La présence du bonnet tricoté n'est pas anodine. D'une part, il montre aux femmes que les envois parviennent au front et que les accessoires viennent à point ; d'autre part, il les mobilise en suggérant la nécessité de maintenir l'effort de guerre. Mais, pour le public belge, l'image se veut également rassurante. L'homme est convenablement équipé pour combattre, outre son arme posée sur les genoux, son équipement (cartouchière, sac à pain et gourde) pend à sa gauche ; il semble aussi correctement nourri, une marmite repose sur un réchaud de campagne à sa droite ; enfin, l'homme, cigarette sur le bout des lèvres, paraît calme, concentré et imperturbable. Pour le public international, l'image met surtout en exergue la participation de l'armée belge au conflit et sa détermination, tout en légitimant son action.

Lorsqu'Alfred Bastien illustre une colonne de soldats britanniques aveuglés par l'ypérite,[30] il dénonce l'utilisation illicite d'armes par l'ennemi et montre la nature perverse de l'ennemi. L'emploi d'une arme chimique avait en effet été interdit par les Conventions de La Haye de 1899. Or, les Allemands ont été les premiers à utiliser les gaz en avril 1915 sur le front belge, et n'ont pas cessé d'améliorer leur efficacité : l'ypérite ou gaz moutarde, utilisé pour la première fois près d'Ypres en septembre 1917, attaque la peau, les yeux, toutes les muqueuses, et les poumons. Notez que le camp adversaire ne tarde pas à faire usage de gaz, mais évidemment, sous le couvert de la riposte !

Ici, c'est la touche colorée et dynamique de Marc-Henry Meunier qui sert à sublimer la désolation qui accompagne les désastres de la guerre (ill. 4.2).[31] Le paysage de ruines, en perpétuel changement, fascine les artistes qui en multiplient les vues. La propagande belge fait un large usage de ce motif pour dénoncer les méfaits commis par l'ennemi.[32] La vision du patrimoine détruit provoque la colère du spectateur, et devient par conséquent le ferment d'un sentiment patriotique fort. Montrer la violation du patrimoine, ce n'est pas seulement montrer le non-respect des lois internationales par l'armée allemande, c'est aussi rappeler la nation violée et, par là, légitimer la cause défendue.

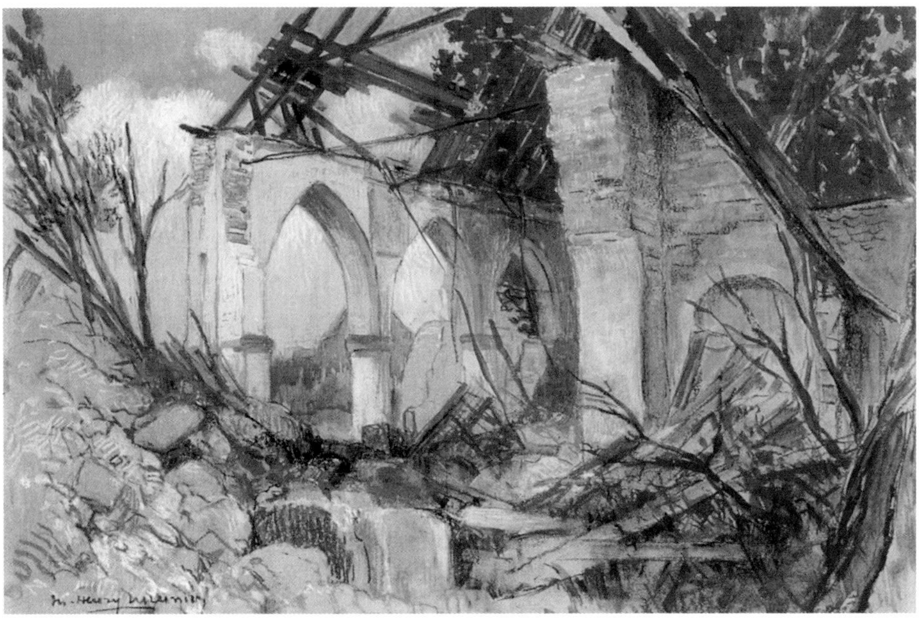

4.2. Marc-Henry Meunier, « Ruines de l'église de Saint-Jacques-Capelle », 1917, fusain, gouache et pastel sur papier, 51,6 x 74,4 cm. Bruxelles, Musée royal de l'Armée et d'Histoire militaire. Inv. n° 88100021.

L'interprétation de certaines images est parfois équivoque. Dans *Le chemin de la victoire à Westrozebeke* (ill. 4.3),[33] Allard l'Olivier donne une image brute des combats : les hommes blessés quittant le front, la relève avançant d'un pas décidé, les cadavres des chevaux, victimes collatérales du conflit, dont on ôte la viande, et en marge, dans l'angle inférieur droit, des cadavres humains, anonymes – leur visage est hors cadre – alignés sur le sol. Cette vision de la guerre provoque davantage la répulsion, le recul, le rejet. Le titre « *Le chemin de la victoire* » suggère toutefois une victoire proche. En effet, le peintre illustre les tout premiers jours de l'offensive finale, élaborée par les Alliés et à laquelle la Belgique prend part, sous peine de voir la victoire lui échapper. Le 28 septembre 1918, premier jour de l'offensive, les Belges lancent une attaque d'infanterie entre Ypres et Dixmude, en marge d'un feu virulent de l'artillerie, et permettent aux Alliés de progresser rapidement jusqu'à la colline de Westrozebeke et de libérer Zonnebeke, Poelkapelle, Langemark, Passendale et Houthulst. Deux jours de combats très meurtriers sont encore nécessaires pour reprendre le village de Westrozebeke aux Allemands.

L'œuvre exhorte donc la population à consentir un dernier sacrifice afin de triompher sur le mal ! Mais, les images, utilisées pour persuader, pour susciter l'adhésion à une cause, peuvent *a contrario* avoir un effet dissuasif, notamment lorsque l'image déclenche la peur ou le dégoût. Ce constat explique peut-être les réticences de la

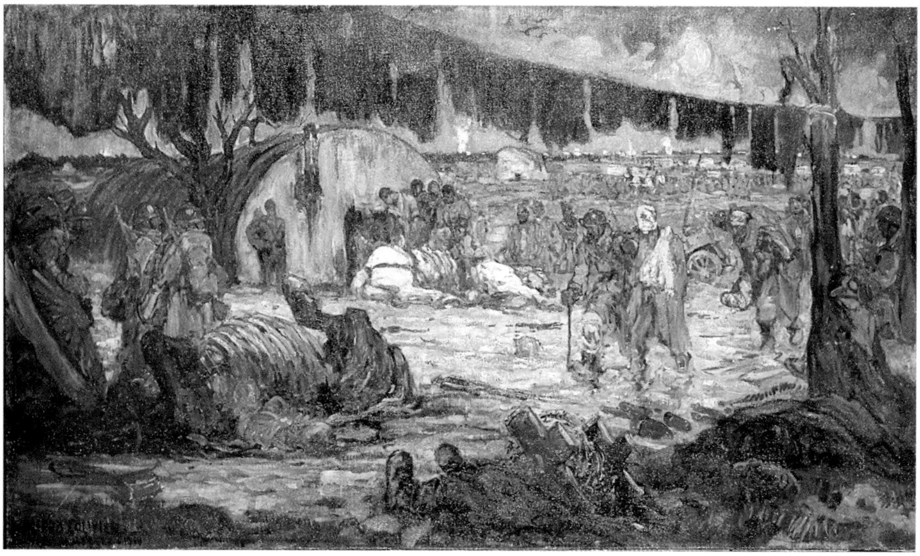

4.3. Fernand Allard l'Olivier, « Le chemin de la victoire à Westrozebeke », 1918, huile sur toile, 98 x 162 cm. Bruxelles, Musées royaux des Beaux-Arts de Belgique (en dépôt au MRA). Inv. n°10076/54.

propagande à utiliser les images de la mort qui pourraient être contre-productives du fait de leur décryptage potentiellement antinomique. Sans doute, l'image peinte par Allard l'Olivier était-elle surtout destinée à clamer au plan international la participation belge à la victoire, en vue des négociations à mener dans le cadre de l'élaboration des traités de paix.

Conclusion

Si la section artistique trouve ses origines dans le besoin pressant d'images destinées à la propagande, les artistes membres n'ont pas à proprement parler produit des œuvres « engagées ». Ils ont représenté la réalité de la guerre ou, plus précisément, ils ont proposé, au travers de celles-ci, une interprétation du réel. C'est au sein de ce corpus que la sélection s'opère, transformant ces œuvres en supports de propagande. Bien que polysémiques et donc sujettes à différentes interprétations, les œuvres d'art véhiculent des messages qui, adressés à un public déterminé, se prêtent en réalité peu à l'ambiguïté, car elles font écho à des représentations déjà existantes. Ainsi, comme le souligne Laurence van Ypersele, « tout système de propagande, pour être percutant, doit intégrer le vécu du public ciblé, ses croyances, ses espoirs et ses craintes. »[34]

Rupture ou continuité ? Que ce soit le mécénat d'État qui s'adapte au temps de guerre, l'instrumentalisation massive des arts dans la propagande de guerre ou l'art issu du conflit, la tendance générale est à la continuité. Les ruptures sont ponctuelles et montrent davantage la nécessité de s'adapter aux circonstances guerrières, qu'une cassure irrévocable. Après la guerre, c'est en effet le retour à l'ordre. Les artistes se remettent à l'ouvrage, abandonnant le motif militaire pour traiter de plus paisibles sujets. L'État reprend vis-à-vis des artistes ses prérogatives d'antan. Alors que les achats d'œuvre avaient quasiment cessé pendant quatre ans, ils se rétablissent lentement. Dans un souci mémoriel, l'État achète aux artistes officiels de l'armée belge. Jusqu'en 1925, leurs œuvres sont régulièrement présentées dans le cadre d'expositions de souvenirs de guerre. Elles tombent ensuite dans une longue léthargie...

Explorer le lien entre l'art et l'État, entre les artistes et le mécénat étatique, entre l'esthétique et la politique est un vaste champ d'investigation qui doit faire appel à plusieurs concepts interdisciplinaires et mérite dans le futur encore de nombreuses recherches. Pour l'heure, nous espérons avoir accompagné le lecteur à poser un regard différent sur la production artistique de guerre et à appréhender son pouvoir persuasif, que nous résumerons en citant Buffon qui, discourant sur l'éloquence, affirmait : « il ne suffit pas de frapper l'oreille et d'occuper les yeux, il faut agir sur l'âme et toucher le cœur en parlant à l'esprit ».[35]

Notes

1 L'auteure tient à remercier vivement la professeure Sophie De Schaepdrijver et la professeure Laurence van Ypersele pour leurs précieux conseils, ainsi qu'Émilie Gaillard et Aude Piernas pour leur relecture attentive.

2 Archives générales du Royaume (ci-après AGR), Bruxelles. Fonds Prosper Poullet.

3 AGR. Fonds Prosper Poullet, Dossier 136. Lettre de Paul Lambotte à Prosper Poullet, dd. 5 mars 1915 : « je les case, j'encaisse leur chèque, je fais leurs traductions, ... ».

4 *Ibid.*, Lettre de Paul Lambotte à Prosper Poullet, dd. 10 novembre 1915. La répartition du subside est mentionnée lors de l'annonce de son renouvellement pour l'année 1916.

5 *Ibid.*, Lettre de Paul Lambotte à Prosper Poullet, dd. 7 mai 1915.

6 Plus tard, d'autres expositions verront également le jour en Europe et en outre-Atlantique.

7 Archives historiques des Arts contemporains, la Biennale de Venise, 1914. Voir : http://asac.labiennale.org/it/passpres/artivisive/annali.php?m=222&c=a.

8 *Catalogo della Esposizione internazionale di bianco e nero (Firenze, 10 maggio-20 giugno 1914), Società delle belle arti in Firenze* (Firenze, 1914). Voir : http://catalogue.bnf.fr/ark:/12148/cb44416888t.

9 AGR. Fonds Prosper Poullet, Dossier 136. Lettre de Paul Lambotte à Prosper Poullet, dd. 31 mars 1915.

10 *Ibid.*, Lettre de Paul Lambotte à Prosper Poullet, dd. 6 avril 1915.

11 Id.

12 AGR. Fonds Prosper Poullet, Dossier 136. Lettre de Paul Lambotte à Prosper Poullet, dd. 31 mars 1915.

13 « Monsieur Paul Lambotte, Directeur des Beaux-Arts de Belgique representing officially, in Great Britain, the Ministry of Fine Arts and Sciences, has undertaken to send to all soldier-artists now with the Belgian Army, instruments for orchestras bands, etc., and for the painters and draughtsmen, all the different requisities they need to enable them to practice and keep themselves trained and avoid moral depression. This fund – supported by voluntary contributions only – desires very much to be able to send regularly, every month, a supply of these necessaries, and about 200 dollars are needed. » Soulignons que la citation est extraite d'un document destiné à lever des fonds. In : Archives du Musée royal de l'Armée et d'Histoire militaire, Bruxelles (ci-après AMRA). Fonds Moscou, Dossier 4337.

14 La section artistique est créée par le ministère de la Guerre, ce qui n'exclut pas que le ministère des Sciences et des Arts, voire également le ministère des Affaires étrangères, aient eu un rôle à jouer. Le dossier personnel d'Armand Massonet mentionne d'ailleurs qu'il est « passé par ordre du G.Q.G. à la mission du ministre des Sciences et des Arts à La Panne ». AMRA. Dossier personnel, Armand Massonet. Sur la section artistique voir : Sandrine Smets, « Créer sous le feu. Origines et organisation de la section artistique de l'armée belge », *Bulletin du Musée royal de l'Armée et d'Histoire militaire. Contributions à l'étude du patrimoine militaire* 3 (2014) 124-43.

15 Jean-Yves Le Naour, *1916. L'enfer* (Paris : Perrin, 2014).

16 Michaël Amara, « Une icône... des propagandes au cœur du conflit. Les grands défis de la propagande belge durant la Première Guerre mondiale », in *La petite Belgique dans la Grande Guerre. Une icône, des images. Actes du colloque de Namur 24-27/11/2010*, éd. Bénédicte Rochet et Axel Tixhon (Namur, Presses universitaires de Namur, 2012), 21-35.

17 Le graveur écossais Muirhead Bone (1876-1953).

18 *Section artistique de l'Armée. 2e Exposition (La Panne, 15-31 mars 1917)* (Dunkerque, 1917), 1. L'introduction est signée du monogramme « J.D.M. ».

19 *Section artistique de l'Armée. 2e Exposition... op. cit.*, 2.

20 Helene Joffe, « Le pouvoir de l'image : persuasion, émotion et identification », *Diogène* 217 (2007/1) 102-115.

21 Laurence van Ypersele, « Propagandes de guerre et consentements des populations », in *Questions d'histoire contemporaine. Conflits, mémoires et identités*, éd. Laurence van Ypersele (Paris, Presses Universitaires de France, 2006), 186.

22 Charles E. Doherty, « Nevinson's Elegy: Paths of Glory », *Art Journal* 51/1 (1992): 64-71.

23 Christopher Richard Wynne, Nevinson, (1889-1946), *Returning to the trenches*, 1914, huile sur toile, 51,2 x 76,8 cm. Ottawa, National Gallery of Canada. Inv. n° 4800.

24 Christopher Richard Wynne, Nevinson, (1889-1946), *Paths of glory*, 1917, huile sur toile, 45,7 x 60,9 cm. Londres, Imperial War Museum. Inv. n° IWM ART 518.

25 Sandrine Smets, « Achille Van Sassenbrouck. A Wounded Body, a HealingŒuvre », in *War & Trauma* (Ieper/Gent/Furnes, In Flanders Fields Museum/Museum Dr. Guislain/Hannibal, 2013), 114-119.

26 Laurence van Ypersele, « Propagandes de guerre... », *op. cit.*, 186.

27 Fernand Allard l'Olivier, (1883-1933), *Fantassin au repos dans la tranchée*, s.d., huile sur toile, 73 x 54 cm. Bruxelles, Musée royal de l'Armée et d'Histoire militaire. Inv. n° 201000112.

28 Luc Vandeweyer, *De eerste wereldoorlog. Koning Albert en zijn soldaten* (Anvers : Standaard Uitgeverij, 2005).

29 Tom Simoens, « De operaties van het Belgische leger tijdens de stellingsoorlog (1914-1917) », in*14-18 Oorlog in België*, éd. Luc Devos et al. (Leuven : Davidsfonds, 2014), 245-264.

30 Alfred, Bastien, (1873-1955), *Écossais aveuglés par l'ypérite*, 1917, huile sur toile, 64 x 88,5 cm. Bruxelles, Musée royal de l'Armée et d'Histoire militaire. Inv. n° 9900718.

31 Marc-Henry, Meunier, (1873-1922), *Ruines de l'église de Saint-Jacques-Capelle*, 1917, fusain, gouache et pastel sur papier, 51,6 x 74,4 cm. Bruxelles, Musée royal de l'Armée et d'Histoire militaire. Inv. n° 88100021.

32 Sandrine Smets, « Paysage de ruines ou ruine du patrimoine. *Topos* de la vision apocalyptique des artistes belges et français de la Grande Guerre », in *Actes de la Journée d'étude France-Belgique « La France et la Belgique occupées (1914-1918) : regards croisés » 25 avril 2008 – Cahier de l'IRHiS n° 7* (Lille, Université Charles-de-Gaulle – Lille 3, 2009), 46-57.

33 Fernand Allard l'Olivier, (1883-1933), *Le chemin de la victoire à Westrozebeke*, 1918, huile sur toile, 98 x 162 cm. Bruxelles, Musées royaux des Beaux-Arts de Belgique (en dépôt au MRA). Inv. n°10076/54.

34 Laurence van Ypersele, « Propagandes de guerre... », *op. cit.*, 186.

35 Georges-Louis Leclerc, comte de Buffon, *Discours sur le style*, discours prononcé à l'Académie française le jour de sa réception, le 25 août 1753.

'My heart is sore about brave Belgium' – Artistic Exodus: Belgian Refugee Artists in Great Britain during the Great War

Caterina Verdickt

Introduction

The German invasion of Belgium in August 1914 caused the flight of a vast contingent of Belgian civilians, who found refuge in neighbouring countries.[1] The artistic interaction and the cultural importance of Belgian artists in exile in Great Britain has been scarcely researched.[2] Of the many Belgians who fled German occupation, 250,000 lived in Great Britain during the war, where they were warmly welcomed and hosted, since Britain felt partly responsible for the agony of the Belgians. These refugees were housed, cared for and temporary employment was sought for them. British cultural society offered various opportunities for the exiles and, apart from the people themselves, Belgium's heritage was cared for, and the reconstruction of the nation prepared and researched by British architects.[3] Among the thousands of Belgian refugees, there was a substantial group of artists and architects. According to the data of T.T.S. De Jastrzebski, an official in charge of registration, 536 civil engineers and architects lived in Great Britain during the Great War along with 1,289 male artists and 387 female artists.[4]

So far, my archival research has shown that a significant number of artists who were among these Belgian refugees can be identified. However, due to the scattered events of the war, one cannot speak of a logical and well-conducted cultural policy. These artist-refugees landed in Great Britain and were then dispatched all over the country: they settled in London, Glasgow, Devonshire, Wales and Cornwall.

The experiences of the Belgian artists were partly described by art critics such as Paul Buschmann (1877-1924), who equally sought refuge in Britain during the war.[5] In December 1914 the first article in a series of three was published under the title "Belgian Artists in England" in *The Studio*.[6] Buschmann wrote:

> "Whilst the German army has been busy destroying or spoiling the art treasures of Belgium, the English people have been quick to offer asylum to the distressed Belgian artists, who have come amongst them under such tragic circumstances, and to cheer them up in the adversity which has befallen them."[7]

At the beginning of the war the tendency of such articles was positive and inspired. Kinship between British and Belgian culture was emphasised. Similarities between the two cultures were stressed and no mention was made of the refugees' possible suffering in the guest country. On the contrary, Buschmann wrote that "the Belgian artists who have now sought refuge in England will not feel quite out of their element; all those I have met here, partners in the misfortune which has befallen the country, have expressed themselves delighted with the reception everywhere accorded to them".[8] In his second article, published in February 1915, Buschmann wrote that Belgian artists often found their own country too small and its boundaries too limited. Travelling to other countries in search of expertise and inspiration was a longstanding tradition in their métier, as shown by their predecessors Jan van Eyck and Peter-Paul Rubens long before.[9] Buschmann did not mention the less magical parts of Great Britain, such as the industrial cities with challenges such as poverty and hardship, nor did he mention the difficulties the refugees encountered during their exile. He did however acknowledge that "Times are not propitious to artistic creation and it may be some time yet before fresh impressions will be reflected by the Belgian artists in works of durable value"; but he continued "artists will at least have acquired something by their forced stay in England; it will have enlarged their views, enriched their minds, and awakened a wholesome enthusiasm for newly discovered beauty."[10]

Belgian arts and artists dominating the British exhibition scene

The cause of the Belgians, their national heritage, their culture and their arts soon became a matter of national British interest. From October 1914 on, many exhibitions with Belgian art were held throughout the country. These exhibitions were organised in order to raise awareness of the Belgian cultural heritage and at the same time to show how its century-old artistic tradition, rooted in history, was being destroyed by the Germans on the continent. Belgian art was shown in a variety of forms and matters. These were exhibitions of paintings, of sculpture but equally of furniture, or of lacemaking or puppetry. Every aspect of Belgian art, all kinds of arts and all sorts of exhibitions were organised.[11] For example in November 1914 a first collective exhibition of Belgian masterpieces was held in London. This show was set up specifically to help Belgian artists in need. More than 100 works of art made by well-known artists were on show in the McLean Galleries, a typical late Victorian commercial art gallery. Mc Leans was a print seller and art dealer located at 7 Haymarket in London.[12] The works of arts exhibited here were smuggled into Britain, having passed through the German lines, according to the *Daily Telegraph* of 24 November 1914.[13]

It can be seen as almost an exception in wartime London, where the art scene was in low spirits, that an exhibition was organised not for the sake of benefit or charity, but merely for art's sake. The 1914 Autumn exhibition at the Goupil Gallery was one of those few events not organised for charity. This gallery, again a characteristic 19th century print seller, print publisher and commercial art gallery, was the London branch of the French Maison Goupil.[14] Mainly British art was on show here, although the work of one Belgian artist, Alexander Marcette (1853-1929), was represented by some drawings.[15] Yet, the Goupil Gallery did not escape the Belgian Art frenzy either. The exhibition of works by Belgian artists was organised at the Goupil Gallery in the winter of 1914. For this particular Belgian Art exhibition, the Duchess of Vendôme, Henriette, sister of King Albert I, acted as the president, and the diplomat Jacques de Lalaing (°1889) as vice-president. This exhibition, which was relatively successful, was prepared for the benefit of the Funds for the Immediate Relief in Belgium. A large number of Belgian artworks was brought together and was to be sold in order to collect funds. Paul Buschmann reviewed the exhibition in *The Studio* and wrote that it "had a quite distinctive appearance and proved a gratifying success", and according to him some of Belgium's best-known artists were represented.[16]

As for interior design arts and crafts, they too found their way to the British public. In December 1914, around the same period as the aforementioned exhibitions, the "Handicrafts Exhibition by Belgian Refugees" was held at Hampshire House Social Club in Hoglane, Hammersmith in West London. Wood carving of the highest quality, according to the *Daily Telegraph*, and embroidery made by Belgian refugees was on show.[17] The Hampshire House, founded in 1912, was an organisation where educative projects and recreational activities were held. The Hampshire House Trust had its own properties where, during the first months of the war, Belgian refugees were accommodated and cared for by followers of William Morris. Morris was once a resident of Hammersmith Mall and his home came to be a centre for the Arts and Crafts movement.[18] The work of the Belgians was exhibited at the same location in which, before the war, the work of William Morris, May Morris and Frank Brangwyn had been on show. [19] The aforementioned show was followed by another exhibition of the work of Belgian craftsmen. It too was held at Hampshire House Social Club in June 1915.[20]

One type of Belgian craft that in particular interested the British public was lacemaking. According to the critic in the *Journal of the Royal Society of Arts* lacemaking was a craft that became quite popular again:

> "For some years past English women have been taking an interest in it, and in many English counties a quite remarkable revival of the art has taken place. On the other hand, the devastation of Belgium, and the quantities of Belgian lace which have come over to England, have reminded us very forcibly that our own hand-made lace industry is not only younger but smaller and more exotic than that of the gallant little country on the other side of the Channel." [21]

The Women's International Art Club organised an exhibition at the Grafton Galleries and included amongst their exhibits a collection of lace. On show was old Flemish lace and modern Belgian work, and some of it was for sale. The lace originated mainly from private collections and was lent by its owners. [22] It is interesting to note that these Grafton Galleries, founded in 1891 as art gallery and rooms for public venues, were used as the scene for reviving lacemaking. Earlier on the Grafton Galleries, situated "in the heart of London's elite gallery district" had been the place where the frontman of the British modern movement, Roger Fry, had organised his iconic two major exhibitions on Post Impressionism in 1910 and 1912: two exhibitions that had a dramatic impact, that evoked "art-quakes".[23] The Grafton also hosted the Allied Artists Association avant-garde and modern art exhibitions from 1916 until 1920.[24]

Apart from these "Belgian Art exhibitions", many other initiatives such as books on Belgian art, Belgian towns and Belgian architecture were published and lectures were held on the same subjects. Books on the Belgians and their culture included *King Albert's Book* in 1915 and *Allies in Art* in 1917,[25] *Belgium* by Frank Brangwyn 1916 and *Little towns of Flanders* woodcuts by Albert Delstanche 1915, which was accompanied by a preface by Emile Verhaeren. All these books portrayed Belgium as picturesque, small, cute and endearing, a little country rooted in history.

Besides these publications, many an artist, writer, poet or sculptor acted as cultural ambassador and gave lectures throughout the country. Sir Henry Trueman Wood (1845-1929) from the Royal Society of Arts lectured on Belgian art and culture, as did M.G. Rosier, the director of the Academy of Fine Arts of Malines.[26] Emile Verhaeren toured the country with Emile Vandervelde and Emile Claus, lobbying and lecturing on Belgium's behalf. Verhaeren also wrote several poems such as "La

Belgique sanglante", published in 1915. His work was picked up by British peers such as Ezra Pound, who commented on his poetry in a 1917 publication.[27]

Conservative image to the front and a progressive heart to the back

The greater part of the abovementioned initiatives should be seen in the context of charity and propaganda. Until the end of 1915 "everyone was Belgian mad for a time."[28] Countless initiatives were taken: Belgian Days and Flag Days were organised, committees formed, concerts held, and so on. Every suggestion was more or less accepted in order to create awareness and collect funding. In the first months of the war and up to the end of 1915, Belgian art as a theme and caring for Belgian refugees was "high in demand" in British society. When one takes a closer look at what was exhibited, one sees the same conservative approach coming through every time. Modern painters, sculptors and designers were absent at these venues. What was shown was conventional, conformist and traditional art. The work of artists such as Constant Permeke, Gustave Van de Woestijne, Henry van de Velde and George Minne was missing or was marginalised. Why was that the case? Was a deliberate motive at play here? Belgian art was presented as rural, traditional, conformist and conventional. Belgium itself was presented as a little country, small and brave. Its citizens poor, martyrs, without will even, to be pitied as passive heroes, almost unreal in their pathos (fig. 5.1). This strong propagandistic current took over and dominated the British exhibition arena. The image constructed of the Belgians and their identity was biased towards the interests of the greater politics and their propaganda mechanisms. Historian Pierre Purseigle stated that

> "the exiles' experience bred a hatred of the enemy that lay at the heart of war cultures and increasingly focused on the person of the enemy. The systematic moral condemnation of the foe moreover strengthened by a recourse to sacred images and words to invoke the martyrdom of the invaded and devastated areas".[29]

Expert in migration studies Robin Cohen formulated that in case of a diaspora, such as was the case with the Belgians, the "old country" always had some claim on their loyalty and emotions.[30]

"Upon arrival the exiles were ascribed their identity"[31] wrote Purseigle, and in the case of the Belgian refugee artists it was one of obligatory conservatism. The movement towards modernism that had set in before the Great War seemingly ceased to exist, or was at least pushed to the background. During the war and in the early days after the war, the historicising countermovement in the discourse on arts, architecture and interior design was rekindled. A tendency to hold on to old values took hold. As if clinging on to architectural, cultural and artistic roots could prevent further losses. "Having to leave their home country and becoming uprooted triggered a need to reconstitute their identities".[32] People who have suddenly lost everything are first to claim their history and culture, in order to secure at least their identity. Innovations and new forms of art are then not the first priorities that come to mind. And thus the pace of modernism slowed down. Regaining strength after the traumatic events and destruction meant going back to old values and artistic traditions and meant re-anchoring in history, such as seen in the lacemaking exhibition.

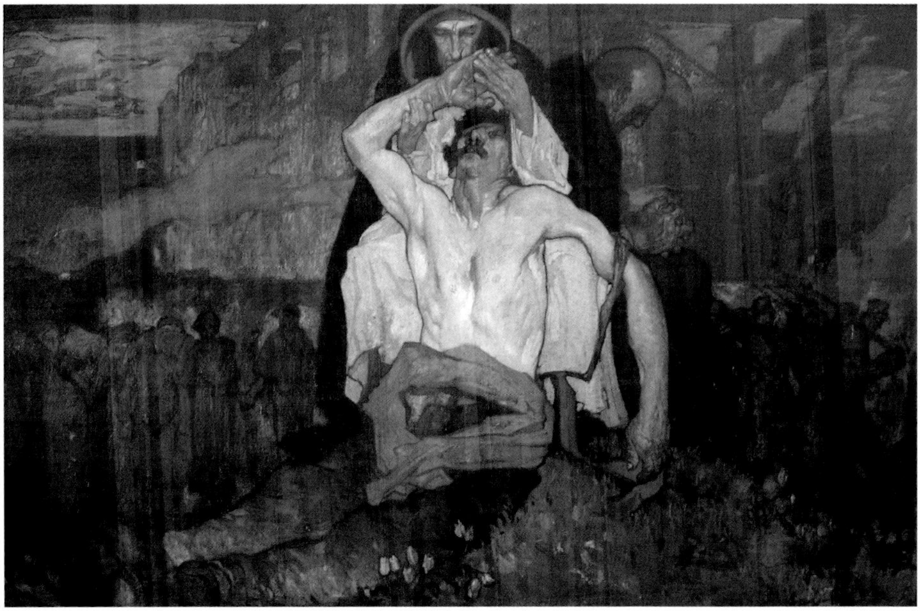

5.1. Frank Brangwyn, *Mater Dolorosa Belgica*, 1915, oil on canvas, 159 x 234 cm. William Morris Gallery, London Borough of Waltham Forest, BrO3.

In 1915 the Belgian refugee artists in Britain united themselves, with the founding of a committee, located at the Victoria Hotel near Trafalgar Square. This committee was a part of British Gifts for Belgian Soldiers, a union of different committees, under the presidency of Emile Vandervelde (1866-1938), Minister of State. The committee collected works of art from the members, which would then be auctioned for charity.[33] The artists accepted Paul Lambotte as their chairman. Another group was the Belgian Artists Committee, who chiefly gave concerts and travelled the country with their music. Their offices were located in Hotel Cecil in London, in the same building as the RAF, and again Emile Vandervelde functioned as president, and here too Paul Lambotte secured his patronage, next to the English composer J.H. Maunder (1858-1920), conductor Paul Kochs, A. Coryn, R. Boin and Armand Varlez as members.[34] A third union of Belgian artists, The League of Belgian Artists composed an edition named *Belgian art in Exile*, for which they were assisted by Frank Rutter, again by Paul Lambotte and Frank Brangwyn.[35] Brangwyn and Lambotte, who were acquainted long before the war,[36] worked together on several projects during those years.[37] Brangwyn also provided help for various Belgian artists in Britain. He assisted the painter Edgar Gevaert during his period of convalescence after he was hurt in battle and he lent the graphic artist Jules de Bruycker material, etches and acid so that he could continue his work.[38] Brangwyn was seen as one of the greatest artists of his time, a fact underlined by Octave Maus of *La Libre Esthétique* who wrote to Paul Lambotte from his exile base in Switzerland.[39]

The driving force behind Belgian conformist art: Paul Lambotte

In all these circles, the enigmatic Paul Lambotte (1862-1939), director of the Belgian Ministry of Arts and Sciences in 1914, plays a central role (fig. 5.2). Understanding his role is essential to grasping the underlying mechanisms behind these events, exhibitions, lectures and editions and the deliberately conservative profile of Belgian artists and Belgian art. So far, no monography or other thorough study has been done on Paul Lambotte. Aside from Virginie Devillez's paragraphs on Paul Lambotte,[40] all one can know of his work is to be derived from primary sources and archive material. It is clear that he was originally a solicitor and before the war had been engaged in large cultural events, such as the "Exposition Universelle" held in Paris in 1900, as the secretary of the Belgian section.[41] It is around that time that his relationship with several artists such as Georgiana Burne Jones, the wife of the painter Edward Burne Jones and a close friend of William Morris originated.[42] When Lambotte fled to Great Britain with a delegation of the Belgian government, he maintained and expanded his large network with several prominent members of British high society and its cultural circles. Devillez described Lambotte as a patriotic hero, with a calm and abstemious bourgeois taste, and did mention the many exhibitions Lambotte organised, but she did not elaborate on the matter.[43]

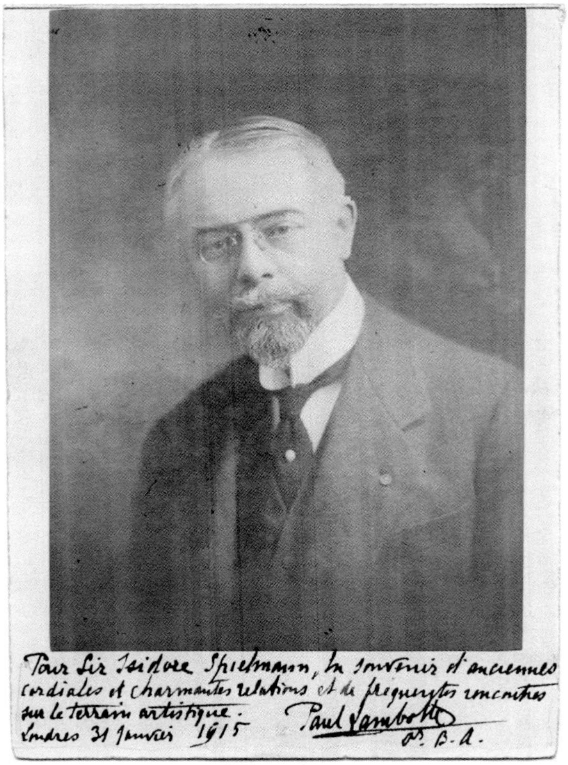

5.2. Paul Lambotte by unknown photographer, vintage print, (1915?), 16,9 x 12,3 cm.

It is significant that the members of Lambotte's network came primarily from traditional institutions like Cecil Smith from the Victoria & Albert Museum and Henri T. Wood from the Royal Society of Arts. Another example is the assistance he sought from the artist and duchess Violet Rutland for the Belgian Funds for Soldiers.[44] Such connections often resulted in artistic materialisations, as was the case with Rutland's daughter Lady Diana Manners who was immortalised by Belgian refugee artist Victor Rousseau with a marble bust, exhibited in London and published in *The Connoisseur*.[45] Other connections dating from the war years were with the painter H. Hughes Stanton (1870-1937), Scottish painter James Guthrie (1859-1930), Welsh sculptor William Goscombe John (1860-1952) and the art historian, editor of the *Burlington Magazine* and former director of the National Portrait Gallery, Lionel Cust (1859-1929).[46] The last invited Lambotte to become a member of the Burlington Fine Arts Club, located at 17 Saville Row.[47]

Lambotte's abovementioned connections concerned mainly high class, traditional figures with Victorian and 19th century aesthetics. The discourse in Lambotte's letters was chiefly one of conservatism and patriotism. He used these connections either to get articles on Belgian art published[48] or when he sought help to get an exhibition organised such as the 1915 Belgian Art exhibition at the National Museum and Galleries in Cardiff in which he was assisted by William Goscombe John. In other letters a strident rhetoric of heroism, pathos and radical unforgivingness towards Germany, the enemy, was maintained.

> "This war is very dreadful. My heart is sore about brave Belgium, and all her people. Your beautiful old historic towns which I am glad to have seen. Some of them we shall never see again. May the murderous devastators be severely punished!"[49]

wrote painter Thomas Austen Brown (1859-1924) to Paul Lambotte on 13 September 1915.

Lambotte's friendship with the iconic British writer Rudyard Kipling (1865-1936) during those years was symbolic of the conservative ideas and narratives that he and Lambotte, as the bearers of culture, followed. Kipling had been a proponent of the war and had anticipated it long before it was even declared.[50] Kipling wrote that "Germany is running this war, of set purpose without the faintest regard for any law human or divine".[51] He was motivated and appalled by the German atrocities and wrote to his large and extensive network for assistance and aid for the Belgian cause; for instance to Theodore Roosevelt he wrote,

> "I wish you could spend half a day with the Belgian refugees as they come into Folkestone. The look on their faces is enough without having to hear their stories which are like tales from hell".[52]

The author of the Jungle Book and the Belgian official became good friends. They visited each other's houses and met the families.[53] At the end of the war, Kipling's admiration and disposition did not alter; when Lambotte and his family were returning home to Belgium, Kipling asked them, "How does it feel to return to one of the greatest of the peoples?"[54]

Lambotte's taste or modus operandi did not change in the four years of his exile in London either. He would ceaselessly push and promote Belgian artists and Belgian art. However, he focussed mainly on those who created conservative and conformist art. He followed a policy of "safe" art and avoided any kind of confrontational art or art that might create controversy. Lambotte used his network to help and introduce artists to British colleagues or peers. Often he succeeded in individual actions; he for instance took the painter Albert Baertsoen (1866-1922) to visit the studio of society painter John Singer Sargent (1856-1925), whom Lambotte had known since 1899.[55] After this visit Baertsoen was invited to use Sargent's studio, and he did some of his refugee work there.[56] As for larger-scale events such as exhibitions Lambotte put pragmatism before vision. He assisted with and organised, as mentioned above, many of these events, such as the War Relief Exhibition in 1915 at the Royal Academy. In the autumn of 1914 the board of the Royal Academy decided to organise a War Relief Exhibition on behalf of the Red Cross and the Artists' General Benevolent Institution. A few weeks later, in December 1914 a Belgian section was added to the show, and for this section Lambotte's cooperation was sought. The British royals took on patronage and the board collaborated with the Royal Scottish Academy and the Royal Hibernian Academy to curate the exposition. Lambotte delivered a list with the names of 53 Belgian artists residing in Britain as refugees. The profits of the Belgian section were to go to these Belgian artists. Sir Edward Poynter (1836-1919), the president of the Royal Academy, saw an opportunity in presenting these Belgian artists to the British public.[57] Curating this exhibition was by no means an easy task. At first the idea was to transport two collections of Belgian art from Venice and Lyon to London. However due to the war transport became an insurmountable difficulty. As a solution two Belgian collections of sculpture, which were kept in Aberdeen and Glasgow, were thus exhibited in lieu of the aforementioned collections.[58]

As a whole, the exhibition was loosely structured, with no elaborate vision. No theme was chosen for the exhibition, nor did it focus on a style, a group, or an "ism". The exhibition was simply a collage of what was at hand and its merits did not lie in presenting quality, avant-garde or modern art or any contemporary art. Lambotte, the profiler of the Belgian artistic community, did his utmost to preserve the goodwill towards the poor little Belgians and put his energies in that direction. Buschmann commented that Lambotte "succeeded in collecting a hundred works, all of which have been sold for the immediate relief of the artists who remained in Belgium". In his review of the exposition Buschmann wrote that "[t]he English public has displayed a peculiar interest in Belgian art; besides the important exhibition now on at Burlington house some smaller selection of Belgian works have been on view in London galleries."[59] Buschmann commented on each participating artist and included a series of photographs.[60] He acknowledged that the exhibited works were traditional and that some of them were "works of more or less minor importance: sketches, water-colours, etchings".[61] The British section of the exhibition was reviewed in *The Connoisseur*, but the Belgian section was not. Was this brought about by the belated opening of the Belgian section or was it due to a lack of interest in Belgian art? That is unclear. *The Burlington Magazine* however did review the exhibition. The critic W.T. Whitley wrote that

> "it was not to be expected that the Belgian section of the War Relief Exhibition at The Royal Academy should represent adequately the art of the country whose brave sons have lately gained the admiration of the world".

Whitley thought it to be miraculous that an exposition of this kind had taken place in the first place and thus he congratulated Paul Lambotte on his realisation.[62]

Lectures were another medium Lambotte used to reach out to the British public. In April 1915 he lectured at the Royal Society of Arts. The content of that lecture was published a year later in the spring of 1916. Lambotte felt that the British public was unaware of Belgian art, and specifically of Belgian modern art. However his own focus in his talk stopped in 1900. Was he himself unaware of modern art of the last 14 years before the war? He did not mention sculpture and vaguely stated that Belgian architecture did have an original outlook.[63] In another lecture at the Royal Society he gave his impressions of London, proclaimed he was a fervent devotee of the city and was full of praise for her parks and other seductions: the unexpected contrasts, the richness of her art treasures and the artistic effects of extreme individual liberty.[64] But Lambotte himself did not apply that kind of liberty to his [own selection of] artists. Any kind of art remotely connected with German art he banished from the scene of these exhibitions. For example, George Minne's art was excluded for he had been renowned in pre-war Germany and at the Wiener Secession, which made Minne and his art less desirable. Another disadvantage in Minne's case was the fact that in 1914 Minne tried to have his sons excluded from immediate combat, as they were in Military Service, and with this in mind he lobbied certain officials on their behalf. Minne did not succeed, but nonetheless the very attempt [to protect his sons from combat] made him persona non grata with Lambotte for the rest of the war. The constant anguish over the wellbeing of his children held Minne hostage for the entire period of the war. Over and over he drew mothers holding their children in a protective embrace. Like a mantra, or in his own words like a prayer, pleading to whatever power to keep them safe.[65]

Conclusion

The work of the many Belgian refugee artists who were exiled in Great Britain during the Great War achieved a great deal of attention in the first two years of the war. Every form of art: sculpture, paintings and crafts, found its way on to the exhibition scene in the London area and the rest of the country. Belgian culture and Belgian heritage were promoted by cultural ambassadors of all kinds by means of lectures and publications, executed by important Belgian artists or culture bearers, and by their British peers alike. The conditions of the war however proffered restrictions and a conservative programme. Foreign influences, and especially German, and thus hostile, influences in art were altogether to be excluded from the exhibition scene, as seen in the case of George Minne. Modern and avant-garde painters, sculptors and designers were absent at the pragmatically arranged exhibitions, which were often completed in haste, and seldom accompanied by a conceptualised or artistic vision. These venues were in general organised by members of the Belgian government, such as Paul Lambotte, and or the British government, or were at least controlled or supervised by governmental bodies. The works of art shown were conventional, conformist and traditional. A politics of safe art was followed and any kind of confrontational art, or art that might create controversy, was to be avoided, thus securing the ongoing benevolence offered by British society towards the larger contingent of Belgian refugees.

Notes

1 Peter Cahalan, *Belgian Refugee Relief in England during the Great Wa,* (London – New York, 1982) and Michael Amara, *Des Belges à l'épreuve de l'exil,* (Brussel, 2008).

2 Little more has been published on the topic than my previous publications: Caterina Verdickt, *Belgische kunstenaars in Groot-Brittannië tijdens de Eerste Wereldoorlog 1914-1918* (Lic. Verh., KUL, 1999) and Robert Hoozee, Caterina Verdickt, e.a., *Kunst in Ballingschap. Vlaanderen, Wales en de Eerste Wereldoorlog.* Exhibition catalogue (Ghent, 2002).

3 Pieter Uyttenhove, "Internationale inspanningen voor een modern België," in *RESURGAM De Belgische wederopbouw na 1914,* ed. Marcel Smets (Brussels, 1985), 33-68.

4 Katherine Storr, *Excluded from the Record. Women, Refugees and Relief. 1914-1929* (Oxford, 2009) 65 and T.T.S. De Jastrzebski, "The Register of Belgian Refugees," in *Journal of the Royal Statistical Society*, vol. LXXIX, II (March 1916), 149-150.

5 Sylvia Van Peteghem, "Hoe staat het nu toch met Onze Kunst? Een briefwisseling tussen L.J Veen en Paul Buschmann sr. en jr. (1900-1919)," in *Jaarboek Letterkundig Museum 3*. Nederlands Letterkundig Museum en Documentatiecentrum, (Den Haag 1994), 16-18.

6 Paul Buschmann, "Belgian artists in England," in *The Studio*, Vol. LXV, No. 261 (December 1914), 183–210.

7 Paul Buschmann, 1914, 183.

8 Paul Buschmann, 1914, 184.

9 Paul Buschmann, "Belgian artists in England," in *The Studio*, vol. 64 (February 1915), 43-44.

10 Paul Buschmann, February 1915, 44.

11 *Standard*, 28 October 1914

12 Pamela Fletcher, "Shopping for art: the rise of the commercial art gallery, 1850s-90s," in *The Rise of the Modern Art Market in London 1850-1939, ed.* Pamela Fletcher and Anne Helmreich (Manchester, 2011), 52-60.

13 *Daily Telegraph*, 24 November 1914 and Paul Buschmann, 'Belgian Artists in England', in *The Studio*, vol. 64 (February 1915), 46 quoted in Caterina Verdickt, 1999, 14.

14 Anne Helmreich, 'The Goupil Gallery at the intersection between London, Continent and Empire', in *The rise of the modern art market in London, 1850-1939,* ed. Pamela Fletcher and Anne Helmreich, (Manchester: Manchester University Press, 2011), 65-84.

15 'Autumn Exhibition at the Goupil Gallery', in *The Connoisseur*, vol. 41, no. 161 (January 1915), 54.

16 *Exhibition of Works given by Belgian Artists*, exhibition catalogue, London, Goupil Gallery, s.d and Paul Buschmann, (February 1915), 44-46.

17 *Daily Telegraph*, 5 December 1914.

18 Judith Collins, *The Omega Workshops* (London, 1984), 108.

19 Ruth Levitas, "After Morris: Warwick Herbert Draper and the pursuit of Utopia," in *William Morris in the Twenty-first Century*, ed. Phillippa Bennet and Rosie Miles (Bern, 2010), 32-33.

20 Martin Hopkinson, 'Belgian Prints in Britain during World War I', in *Print Quarterly*, XXXIII, 4 (2016), 421.

21 'Arts and Crafts', in *Journal of the Royal Society of Arts*, Vol. 63, No. 3251 (March 1915), 379-381, quote 380.

22 "Arts and Crafts," in *Journal of the Royal Society of Arts*, Vol. 63, No. 3251 (March 1915), 380.

23 Anna Gruetzner Robins, "Marketing Post-Impressionism: Roger Fry's commercial exhibitions," in *The rise of the modern art market in London, 1850-1939*, ed. Pamela Fletcher and Anne Helmreich, (Manchester: Manchester University Press, 2011), 85.

24 Pamela Fletcher and Anne Helmreich, ed., 2011, 305.

25 Caterina Verdickt (2002), 56-59.

26 Caterina Verdickt (1999), 23.

27 Quoted by Ezra Pound in "Emile Verhaeren," in *Poetry,* vol. 9, no. 5 (February 1917), 257.

28 Pierre Purseigle, "A wave on to Our Shores; The Exile and Resettlement of Refugees from the Western Front, 1914 – 1918," in *Contemporary European History,* 16, 4 (2007), 441.

29 Pierre Purseigle (2007), 434.

30 Robin Cohen, quoted by Jutta Vinzent, *Identity and Image. Refugee artists from Nazi Germany in Britain (1933-1945),* (Weimar, 2006), 169.

31 Pierre Purseigle (2007), 439.

32 Jutta Vinzent, *Identity and Image. Refugee artists from Nazi Germany in Britain (1933-1945)* (Weimar, 2006), 63.

33 ANTWERPEN, Letterenhuis, L 1606, *Brief van Paul Lambotte aan Jozef Muls*, 15 april1915, inv. nr.: 43799/231.

34 Armand Varlez, *Les Belges en Exil* (London, 1917), 124-133.

35 Brussels, Royal Library of Belgium, Manuscripts, Paul Lambotte inv. no.KBR, hs, II 7133/302 23/12/1918 and 26/2/1918.

36 Brussels, Royal Library of Belgium, Manuscripts, Paul Lambotte inv. no.KBR, hs, II 7133/124 7/2/1894.

37 Brussels, Royal Library of Belgium, Manuscripts, Paul Lambotte inv. no.KBR, hs, II 7133/126 16/07/1916.

38 Brussels, Royal Library of Belgium, Manuscripts, Paul Lambotte inv. no. KBR, hs, II 7133/128a 6/8/1916,

39 Brussels, Royal Library of Belgium, Manuscripts, Paul Lambotte inv. no. KBR, hs, II 7133/609a 20/7/1919.

40 Virginie Delvillez, *Kunst aan de orde* (Brussels, 2003), 34-35.

41 Brussels, Royal Library of Belgium, Manuscripts, Paul Lambotte inv. no. II 7133/514.

42 Brussels, Royal Library of Belgium, Manuscripts, Paul Lambotte inv. no., II 7133/150 19/7/1898 and 13/3/1894.

43 Virginie Delvillez, 2003, 35.

44 Brussels, Royal Library of Belgium, Manuscripts, Paul Lambotte inv. no. II 7133/ 340 a 10/03/1917.

45 Paul Lambotte, "Belgian Artists in England", in *The Connoisseur*, vol. 50, nr. 200 (April 1918), 189a.

46 Brussels, Royal Library of Belgium, Manuscripts, Paul Lambotte inv. no., II 7133/363, 370, 371, 378, 204:a and 220.

47 Brussels, Royal Library of Belgium, Manuscripts, Paul Lambotte inv. no., II 7133/220 a, 5/1/1915.

48 Paul Lambotte, "L'Evolution de l'Ecole Belge de Peinture (1830-1900)," in *Journal of The Royal Society of Arts*, vol. 63, no. 3255 (9 April 1915), 469-479.

49 Brussels, Royal Library of Belgium, Manuscripts, Paul Lambotte inv. no., II 7133/143a 13/9/1915.

50 Adam Hochschild, *To End all Wars, A story of loyalty and rebellion, 1914 – 1918* (New York, 2011), 96.

51 Letter to Frank N. Doubleday, 11 September 1914, published in *The Letters of Rudyard Kipling. Volume 4: 1911 – 1919,* ed. Thomas Pinney (Iowa, 1999), 254.

52 Letter to Theodore Roosevelt, 15 September 1914, published in The Letters of Rudyard Kipling. Volume 4: 1911 – 1919, ed. Thomas Pinney (Iowa, 1999), 255.

53 Brussels, Royal Library of Belgium, Manuscripts, Paul Lambotte inv. no. II 7133/445a 26/06/1915, II 7133/444b 7/09/1917, II 7133/443b 11/09/1917 and II 7133/446a 22/12/1919.

54 Brussels, Royal Library of Belgium, Manuscripts, Paul Lambotte inv. no. II 7133/440a 5/12/1918.

55 Brussels, Royal Library of Belgium, Manuscripts, Paul Lambotte inv. no. II 7133.

56 Brussels, Royal Library of Belgium, Manuscripts, Paul Lambotte inv. no., II 7133/24n 24/12/1918.

57 London, Royal Academy of Arts, *Minutes of meetings,* 17 November 1914, inv.nr.: CXXIII, 1913-1918 and *A Book of Belgium's Gratitude*, London, 1916, 206 quoted in Caterina Verdickt, 1999, 17.

58 London, Royal Academy of Arts, *Minutes of meetings*, 23 November 1914, inv.nr.: CXXIII, 1913-1918, 241 and Paul Buschmann, 'Belgian Artists in England', in *The Studio*, vol LXIV (April, 1915), 260 quoted in Caterina Verdickt (1999), 18.

59 Paul Buschmann (February 1915), 44.

60 "The War Relief Exhibition at the Royal academy," in *The Connoisseur,* vol. 41, nr. 162, (February 1915),110-112 and Paul Buschmann (April 1915), 260-266.

61 Paul Buschmann (February 1915), 44.

62 W.T. Whitley, "Notes. Belgian Art," in *The Burlington Magazine for Connoisseurs*, vol. 26, no. 144 (March 1915), 256.

63 Paul Lambotte, "L'Evolution de l'Ecole Belge de Peinture (1830-1900)," in *Journal of The Royal Society of Arts*, vol. 63, no 3255 (April 1915).

64 "The London Society. Summary of Lecture to be given by Monsieur Paul Lambotte," 21 June 1917 at 5 pm in the Hall of the Royal Society of Arts, "Impressions of London".

65 Brussels, RMFAB, AHK, *Letter Paul Lambotte to George Minne*, 21 May 1915, inv. no. 16 511, *Letter George Minne to René Van Herreweghe*, 2 April 1919, inv. no. 8231 and Robert Hoozee, *George Minne en de kunst rond 1900*, tent.cat. Gent, MSK, 1982, 207.

Jacob and Louise De Graaff – Patrons of Modern Belgian Artists in Exile

LAURA KOLLWELTER

Introduction

At the time of the Great War a handful of Belgian artists, seeking refuge in Great Britain, find not only advocates for their art but also financial facilitators and even friends in the couple of Jacob and Louise De Graaff.

Jacob De Graaff was born in 1873 in Rotterdam, son of the successful merchant Jan De Graaff and brother to Marie De Graaff a batik artist working mainly in the Hague.[1] It is through Marie that Jacob De Graaff met Louise Bachiene, illustrator and designer, whom he would marry in August 1899.[2] One year later, the couple moved to London where Jacob De Graaff founded an import-export business with one seat in London, one in Sydney. Louise De Graaff's artistic education and Jacob De Graaff's wealthy upbringing led the couple to cultivate an art collection. Before 1914 the collecting was mainly focused on Dutch artists of the school of the Hague such as Johannes Hendrick Weissenbruch or of the Amsterdam impressionists such as Georg Hendrik Breitner .

A chance encounter during the war years[3] changed De Graaff's outlook on art, collecting and patronage for good. According to his own account, De Graaff overheard three Flemish men talking about the outdated character of an Alfred Stevens painting in the National Gallery.[4] Curious, De Graaff approaches them and learns that their names are Hippolyte Daeye, Léon De Smet and Gustave Van de Woestyne. Painters themselves, they are exiled in Britain due to the German occupation of Belgium. Through these three artists, Jacob and Louise De Graaff will be introduced to the exiled artists of Sint-Martens-Latem, a small village near the Flemish city of Gent, where from the end of the 19th century on, a small artistic colony has settled. A rich correspondence of almost 400 letters with ten Belgian artists and one artist's widow allows us to trace these encounters and give an insight into the relationship of the Dutch couple to the artists, their business arrangements as well as their personal lives from 1917 to well after De Graaff's death in 1947 when Louise De Graaff would take over the correspondence.[5]

World War I – Exiled artists and relief structures

The Dutch businessman cannot be included in the numerous wartime charity and relief funds for Belgian refugee artists in Great Britain.

These refugee aids were often a very politicised spectacle. For example, the work of the official Belgian Relief Fund or the Belgian Refugee Aid presided over by Paul Lambotte, Director of the Fine Arts at the Ministry of Science and Arts in Belgium, were organising charity exhibitions of Belgian artists throughout the country. Their main goal is not necessarily to show the newest explorations of modern ideas, but rather a demure look at nationally recognised artists which could please a large crowd and thus encourage sales. Given Paul Lambotte's known anti-modernist views, it is no surprise that artists such as Jean Delville or Emile Claus will be favoured over, for example, Gustave Van de Woestyne, Edgard Tytgat or Valerius De Saedeleer, who consider themselves modern painters.

Meanwhile in Wales, the Davies sisters had a philanthropic goal in promoting Belgian art.[6] Margaret and Gwendoline Davies, rich heirs to their grandfather's industrial successes, invited a number of Belgian painters, sculptors and musicians to find exile in Wales where they helped them obtain housing and work. With the help of the Belgian Fabrice Polderman, professor working in Cardiff and Rafaël Petrucci, son-in-law of the painter Alfred Verwée who in turn worked for the British minister George Lloyd, they arranged for the artists George Minne, Valerius De Saedeleer and Gustave Van de Woestyne[7] to settle in Wales (fig. 6.1). While the altruistic and philanthropic intentions of the Davies' are undeniable, by recruiting mainly actors of the creative world, they also hoped to further cultural renewal in their region. Their intentions were made public on several occasions:

> "The study of painting and sculpture is in a deplorably backward condition in Wales. Shall we take immediate advantage of the unexpected presence in our midst of this brilliant group: take counsel with them and give them facilities to exercise their genius and give our young arts students the chance of seeing them at work?"[8]

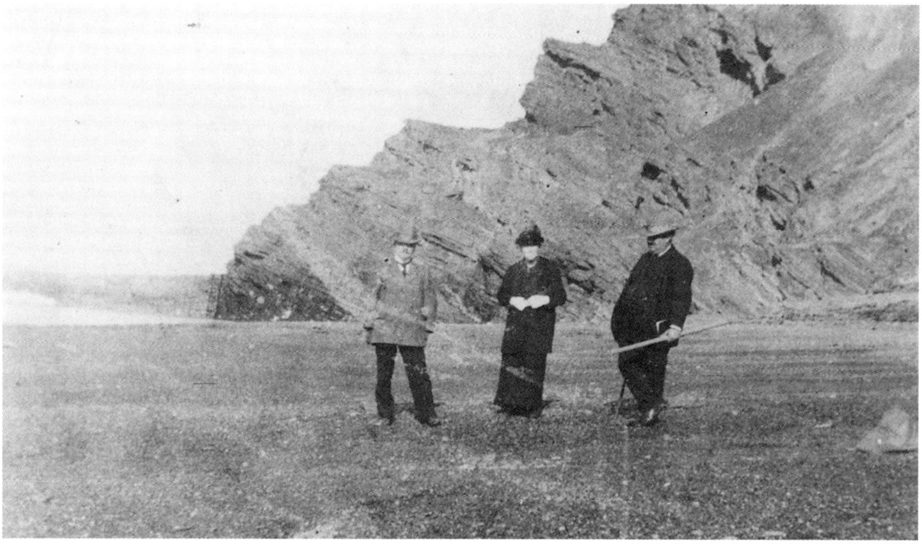

6.1. George Minne, Josephine Minne et Albijn van Abeele en exile au Pays de Galles, Brussels, Royal Museums of Fine Arts of Belgium / Archives of Contemporary Art of Belgium, Inv. 001171.

Encouraging the population to welcome the Belgian refugees and understanding the unique cultural possibilities that they represent, one can read:

> "One of the chief blessings to Wales of the war should be the intellectual and artistic stimulus which we may derive from the presence in our midst of foreign poets, artists, and musicians."[9]

Here, modern art, and foreign art at that, was instrumental in provoking an awakening of Welsh culture.

From collecting to promoting – The far reaching support of the De Graaff couple

The two examples given above, while helpful for a number of Belgian artists in exile, are also political in nature. Their main actors are seeking to promote a certain agenda, whether that be charity and political propaganda or the promotion of a region by displaying a welcoming culture, while at the same time taking advantage of the situation in order to improve one's own. Jacob and Louise De Graaff are to be considered as individual art collectors with a philanthropic streak for some of the artists who did not get support from the official authorities. Their relationship to the Belgian artists is unbiased given that they behave as personal rather than political actors. The couple are private patrons with no ties to any sort of relief fund or governmental institution. Their collecting is a personal choice without a means to an end paired with a genuine generosity and in some cases real friendship towards the artists.

Gratitude is thus the main sentiment that Belgian artists express towards the De Graffs. Léon De Smet writes to Jacob De Graaff in December 1918: "I thank you, you have come to help me at one of the most critical moments of my life."[10]

In retrospect, Tytgat calls De Graaff the "man who, at the most painful period, was a precious balm for the Belgian artists".[11] De Saedeleer writes,

> "I will never find the right words to tell you what you did for me, before my visit to you I was like a man whose hands and feet where tied up, completely powerless. Despite my will and confidence, it was impossible for me to continue ... my work. Now, with the help that you gave me I can start again and give it my all and I am sure that I can ask you in a couple of months to come and see what [I] can produce; my visit to you in London has given me confidence in my work."[12]

In another letter he says, "You brought me joy and laid the first stone on which I can now continue to build".[13] The ultimate and official token of this gratitude will be presented to De Graaff in 1926 when he receives the Belgian Knighthood of the Crown for his support for Belgian refugees during the war.[14]

But what are these artists grateful for? How have Jacob and Louise De Graaff helped and encouraged them? Their support of this handful of Belgian artists exiled in Great Britain is first and foremost evident in their buying of artworks. During the war years Jacob De Graaff will buy *Welsh Landscape* by Valerius De Saedeleer, *The Sleepers* and a study of *My Daughter as a Refugee in Wales* by Gustave Van de Woestyne, *Nude Girl with Cat* by Hippolyte Daeye and furthermore *True Stories* by Constant Permeke. He also let Edgard Tytgat make a painting of his mansion in Highgate called *Insulinde*, which he later bought, and further commissioned a portrait of his wife by the painter Gustave Van de Woestyne.

However, the couple's generosity is not solely showcased in their buying of artworks. Both of them are considered to have been very sociable. They organised large parties at their home and were also generously inviting their new Belgian acquaintances to the theatre and ballet. We know that Daeye, Van de Woestyne and Tytgat saw Dihagilev's ballets because of De Graaff. The couple also gives away money without asking anything in return and makes Christmas presents to the kids of Van de Woestyne.[15] They make presents to Victor Lorein's two boys[16] and help Hippolyte Daeye's boy Maurice out when he needs study advice from a businessman. They will also host Marie and Elisabeth De Saedeleer, Valerius De Saedeleer's daughters, in London and buy supplies for their tapestry works that they do on the basis of other artists' paintings, of which De Graaff himself buys one. In 1818 he will help Léon De Smet's parents who arrive in the Netherlands with no allowances.[17] And Karel Van de Woestijne (Gustave's poet brother) will stay with the De Graaffs when visiting London for a lecture in 1919. The list goes on and the occasions on which the De Graaffs give loans, make advance payments for works not yet started or help the artists by developing photographs for them, acting as middlemen to translate or just talk to their British and Dutch friends about the Belgian artists are numerous.

The help of the couple is of large importance to some of these artists, especially as most of them will not be highly successful in Great Britain during the war. One major exception certainly is Léon De Smet who during his stay will integrate into London high society. He already knew the German painter Georg Sauter who had lived in Britain since 1889 and was married to John Galsworthy's sister. He counts the writers John Galsworthy and Bernard Shaw among his friends and will paint portraits of them as well as of Thomas Hardy and Joseph Conrad. Galsworthy will also buy works by De Smet[18] and will furthermore help out by accommodating him and his wife as well as Jules de Bruycker in his farmhouse Wingstone, located in Devon.[19] Léon De Smet shows on multiple occasions in the renowned Burlington and Leicester galleries and will paint multiple members of high society. Having said that, he complains about the situation in Great Britain where it seems useless to him to even try and show his works; he longs for the time where he can send his work back to Belgium to show it in the Salons.[20] De Smet's complaining despite his achievements can be seen as a form of homesickness of an exiled artist. It also functions as a way to understanding how much struggle the more unsuccessful artists must have had to endure professionally as well as psychologically, when even the more successful ones are unsatisfied with the situation.

Léon De Smet is thus building his own network in London. Meanwhile other Belgian artists will ask Jacob De Graaff for help in order to meet some important players on the London art scene. In a letter from the Leicester Galleries to George Minne, they let him know that Jacob De Graaff already introduced them to Minne's work.[21] While the exhibition in the end did not take place for logistical reasons, De Graaff did play his role in presenting the exiled artists to London galleries helping them to enlarge their potential buyer base.

De Saedeleer asks for active advice from De Graaff in 1920, when he is still living in Wales and sees an opportunity to exhibit in the British capital. Should he show at the Leicester Gallery, or rather at the Twenty One Gallery?[22] Some days later it seems that De Graaff suggested a third option, the Burlington Galleries. De Saedeleer writes:

> "I would be happy to show at the Burlington Galleries ... May I ask you to be so nice as to give me the necessary information concerning the Burlington Galleries, what are the conditions [to show there]?"[23]

He also wants to know De Graaff's honest opinion on the Burlington Galleries. After getting all the information needed, he will show thirty of his works at the Burlington Galleries in April 1921 as a direct result of De Graaff's counselling. He even asks the couple to go and check on the hanging of his works before the opening as he is scared he will not be able to come. Since De Graaff introduced De Saedeleer to the gallery, he also trusts him to evaluate their work and undertake possible changes in the showing of his art.[24]

While the circumstances are not quite certain, the most significant introduction that De Graaff made was introducing Gustave Van de Woestyne to David Van Buuren, who would later become his most important buyer and patron. Van Buuren and De Graaff might have known each other from business before the war. It is also possible that both met during sales at the Gallery Georges Giroux in Brussels during the interbellum years.[25] Either way, there was a triangular link between these men. *Children's table*, a large painting of Gustave Van de Woestyne's daughters was bought by the De Graaffs in 1920 and donated by Louise De Graaff to David and Alice Van Buuren. Wether this donation was made out of an act of friendship between the De Graaffs and the Van Buurens or on the request of the artist is uncertain.

Inner circles – Belgian artist solidarity

De Graaff furthers the artists' careers by buying their works and introducing them to the cultural circles of London. In order to understand the collection of Belgian art in De Graaff's possession, the promotional role of the Belgian artists for one another is crucial. They are heavily advocating their own art but even more so the works of their colleagues and friends. They have quite an established network which is no coincidence given that most of them already knew each other in Belgium, including a number of them in Sint-Martens-Latem. They thus have a profound knowledge of one another's art facilitating their discourses towards De Graaff. In a way, they become each other's perfect lobbyists.

It is like this that De Graaff will turn to Daeye to be introduced to Constant Permeke's work. Permeke himself lives secluded in Devon and later in Sidmouth and Sidford.[26] He will nevertheless sporadically exhibit in and around London. Two of his gouaches, *Woman and Child* and *Grandmothers,* were shown in the Belgian Exhibition of Modern Art in Kingston-upon-Thames and Oxford in 1915.[27] At the latest in 1918 some of his work can be found at the London Dicksee's Gallery.[28] De Graaff will come to see Permeke's work at Daeye's studio which he is renting from the British painter Ethel Walker whom Daeye will also introduce to De Graaff.[29]

Jules de Bruycker will give De Graaff Lorein's contact. Gustave Van de Woestyne tells De Graaff about the work of Valerius De Saedeleer. This is a prime example of friends helping friends. Van de Woestyne is the godfather of Elisabeth De Saedeleer[30] and thus a very close friend of the family.

Meanwhile in 1920 Léon De Smet is introducing De Graaff to his brother Gust De Smet when Gust is still living in the municipality of Blaricum in the north of the Netherlands where he sought refuge during the war years. Gust De Smet implores De Graaff to buy his art as nobody else is buying his work anymore and he is in desperate need of tools.[31] And indeed, in the course of four months, De Graaff will buy four works by Gust De Smet.[32]

Finally, in 1918, De Graaff is contacted by Nell Wouters who heard from Edgard Tytgat that the businessman would be interested in buying works by her deceased husband Rik Wouters.[33] Nell refuses to sell anything before she moves back to Belgium (she is still living in Amsterdam at the time) and has exhibited her husband's work inside and outside the country.[34] Indeed, it seems that De Graaff will not buy a Wouters before 1923, when Tytgat contacts Nell again in order to fix an appointment.[35] Léon De Smet as well as Tytgat warn De Graaff that Wouters' work is not appreciated by them.[36] Tytgat calls it outdated and assures De Graaff that Van de Woestyne shares this opinion.[37] The Dutchman does not seem to listen to this advice. On the contrary, he bought eight paintings as well as at least two sculptures, one of them a bronze bust of his friend Edgard Tytgat from 1910. Furthermore, De Graaff bought one of the fifty-two Stols Albums. This series of etchings was reedited by Nell Wouters in 1927.[38]

Interbellum – A shift in the artist-collector relationship

After the armistice the artists slowly move back to Belgium. Some, such as Permeke, cannot wait to finally return home. Often however these moves are made reluctantly. A lot of doubt as to staying or moving back is palpable. De Saedeleer writes to De Graaff, "We don't know yet what we are going to do, the news of Belgium are so discouraging. Here we are happy and the future is so uncertain."[39]

Later on, De Saedeleer's discourse will become a more nuanced one. He admits that his art, has never really rooted in Wales[40] which at the end will outweigh his daughters' success in tapestry weavings in Wales and make them return to Belgium. Daeye's family is moving back to Belgium in autumn of 1919, Daeye himself will however keep his studio in London before moving back for good in March 1920. When Tytgat moves back to Brussels in the summer of 1919, he deplores its size and talks about the 'Spleen' of London, a malady which haunts him since his return to Belgium[41]. Tytgat is not the only one having trouble returning to the seemingly provincial Belgian cities. Van de Woestyne also would have preferred staying in England. The move back is harder than expected, the cosmopolitan feel of London being missed by many of the artists. By 1925 however, everyone except for Léon De Smet has returned to Belgium. Sint-Martens-Latem being revived and the Flemish Expressionism thriving, the artists find in Belgium a degree of esteem and popularity that they did not manage to achieve in exile.

The return to Belgium will not disrupt the correspondences with De Graaff. The artists continue to promote their art to him by sending works and photographs of works to look at. Minne sends photographs and smaller sculptures to De Graaff in the hopes of him buying them or showing them to potential buyers in his circle. The Belgian artists inform De Graaff regularly on their exhibitions held in Belgium and send him clippings talking about their work. They will also constantly ask the patron to loan their paintings kept in De Graaff's collection in order to be shown in different exhibitions. De Graaff always complies. Tytgat talks to De Graaff about the periodical *Sélection* and urges him to get it in order to read about his production but also the ones of his colleagues; he even gives him an address in London where he might find it.[42] *Sélection* is indeed a periodical, but also the name of an art space founded by André De Ridder and Paul-Gustave van Hecke, introducing the Flemish Expressionism of Sint-Martens-Latem into Brussels and throughout Belgium. While visiting his friends in Flanders and Brussels, Jacob and Louise De Graaff will be introduced to this emblematic art space as well as to the important Brussels art galleries such as Walther Schwarzenberg's "Le Centaure" and the Georges Giroux gallery.

It is on this new local market that Jacob De Graaff continues to support his Belgian artist friends. He will for example buy one of multiple Gust De Smets from 'Sélection' in 1921, one painting and three watercolours by Rik Wouters at "Galerie Georges Giroux" in 1923 and two drawings by George Minne as well as Permeke's *Mother and Child* at "Le Centaure" in 1927. Hippolyte Daeye will tell him about the "Groupe des 9", a union of nine artists showing at "Le Centaure" comprising Permeke, Van de Woestyne, Gust De Smet, Frits van den Berghe, Edgard Tytgat, Hippolyte Daeye, Willem Paerels, Ramah, Oscar Jespers. The three last, whom De Graaff probably never met, will be of no interest to him in the interbellum. Incidentally, it is to be noted that except for the artists he met during the war years, De Graaff will not show any interest in living Belgian artists. This might be due to the fact that the Brussels' galleries, next to national artists, showed and promoted many artists from France who were a lot more prestigious and well established than their Belgian counterparts. At "Le Centaure", he will have the opportunity to see, amongst many others, works by Charles Dufy and also bought a Marc Chagall and a Maurice de Vlaminck in 1927.

Furthermore, he will ask some of his Belgian acquaintances to buy art for him, in Brussels as well as Paris. Van de Woestyne will buy works by Charles Dufresne at "Le Centaure" gallery. When he travels to Paris in 1923 he buys eight works for De Graaff including, one Hermine David, two Modiglianis and two Sacharoffs as well as two Foujitas and one Utrillo (fig. 6.2). He is also on the lookout for a Gaugin and a Douanier Rousseau in Paris and advises De Graaff on the quality of Marie Laurencin's paintings: "Marie Laurencin is not what she used to be. If you've seen one of her works, you've seen them all."[43] De Graaff will in a way take this to heart since one can only find one Laurencin in his collection, which, in Van de Woestyne's opinion, seems to suffice.

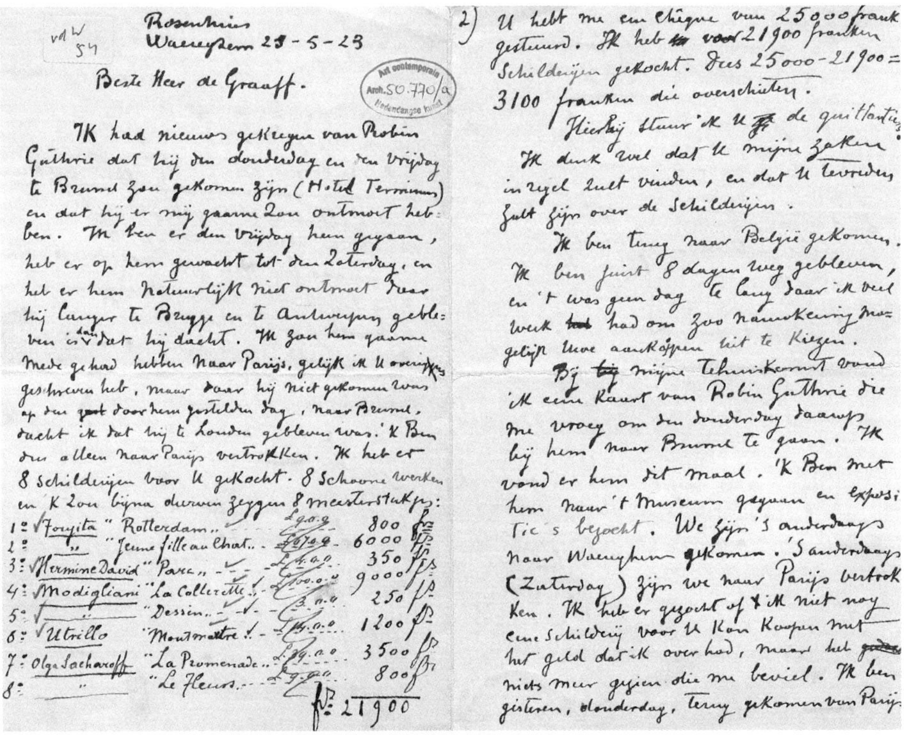

vdW 54

Art contemporain Arch. 50.770/a

Rosenhuis
Waereghem 29-5-23

Beste Heer de Graaff.

Ik had nieuws gekregen van Robin Guthrie dat hij den donderdag en den Vrijdag te Brussel zou gekomen zijn (Hotel Terminus) en dat hij er mij gaarne zou ontmoet hebben. Ik ben er den Vrijdag heen gegaan, heb er op hem gewacht tot den Zaterdag, en heb er hem natuurlijk niet ontmoet daar hij langer te Brugge en te Antwerpen gebleven is dan dat hij dacht. Ik zou hem gaarne mede gehad hebben naar Parijs, gelijk ik U overigens geschreven heb, maar daar hij niet gekomen was op den door hem gestelden dag, naar Brussel, dacht ik dat hij te Londen gebleven was. 'K Ben dus alleen naar Parijs vertrokken. Ik heb er 8 schilderijen voor U gekocht. 8 Schoone werken en 'K zou bijna durven zeggen 8 meesterstukken:

1: √Foujita "Rotterdam" £9.0.0 800 fr
2: " "Jeune fille au Chat" £70.0.0 6000 fr
3: √Hermine David "Parc" £4.0.0 350 fr
4: √Modigliani "La Collerette" £100.0.0 9000 fr
5: √ " "Dessin" £3.0.0 250 fr
6: √Utrillo "Montmartre" £14.0.0 1200 fr
7: Olga Sacharoff "La Promenade" £39.0.0 3500 fr
8: " "Le Fleurs" £9.0.0 800 fr

fr 21900

2) U hebt me een chèque van 25000 frank gestuurd. Ik heb voor 21900 franken schilderijen gekocht. Dus 25000-21900 = 3100 franken die overschieten.

Hierbij stuur ik U de quittanties. Ik denk wel dat U mijne zaken in regel zult vinden, en dat U tevreden zult zijn over de schilderijen.

Ik ben terug naar België gekomen. Ik ben juist 8 dagen weg gebleven, en 't was geen dag te lang daar ik veel werk had om zoo nauwkeurig mogelijk uwe aankoopen uit te kiezen.

Bij mijne tehuiskomst vond ik eene kaart van Robin Guthrie die me vroeg om den donderdag daarop bij hem naar Brussel te gaan. Ik vond er hem dit maal. 'K Ben met hem naar 't Museum gegaan en exposities bezocht. We zijn 's anderdaags naar Waereghem gekomen. 'S anderdaags (Zaterdag) zijn we naar Parijs vertrokken. Ik heb er gezocht of ik niet nog eene schilderij voor U kon koopen met het geld dat ik over had, maar heb niets meer gezien die me beviel. Ik ben gisteren, donderdag, terug gekomen van Parijs.

6.2. Letter of Gustave van de Woestyne to Jacob De Graaff, 29.05.1923, Brussels, Royal Museums of Fine Arts of Belgium / Archives of Contemporary Art of Belgium, Inv. 50.770.

Meanwhile, Tytgat is buying four works at the Giroux gallery for De Graaff including one Evenepoel and one Ensor. The Ensor purchase should come as no surprise as Tytgat is highly praising his art to De Graaff: "I don't think it is necessary to talk about his exhibition, it is more than a miracle, it is magic and surely he is the master of our era."[44] The two other works are by Utrillo and Jongkind.

Léon De Smet is also perusing the Paris art market for De Graaff. In 1920, while visiting Paris, he is chasing a Modigliani for his Dutch friend. He also seems to play the middleman between De Graaff and Kees Van Dongen, asking permission to exhibit one of the works by Van Dongen that De Graaff owns. And De Smet is also buying art for the Dutchman. Amongst the paintings that he finds for his patron in Paris in 1921 is one Favory and one Bissière and in 1926 a Zadkine[45] which receives high praises from two of Brussels' most important art dealers: "[y]esterday, I received a visit from Van Hecke and Schwartzenberg ... They both find it the best that [Zadkine] has ever done."[46]

With the help from Léon De Smet and Gustave Van de Woestyne, De Graaff gets a certain reputation in Paris. In a letter from 1926 Léon De Smet explains," You have to understand, here in Paris, you are known as the big art lover from England, which is why I am getting loads of invitations ...."[47]

We do not know the exact arrangements of these purchases. Van de Woestyne does write: " ... remember, you told me that, if I see something that is really good, I should buy it for you".[48]

This vague guideline does not however answer questions such as: Does De Graaff pay them some sort of commission? Does he reimburse their trips to Paris, maybe promise to support their art in return? Or do the Belgian artists only buy when they are in Paris anyway and do not ask anything in return of De Graaff as a gesture of friendship and gratitude?

Furthermore, Daeye but more so Van de Woestyne will start to mentor Robin Guthrie, a young artist whom De Graaff seems to have taken under his wing. De Graaff asks both of them to welcome him in Belgium, show him around and take him to Paris. Léon De Smet will send the young artist an entire list of museums and galleries to visit while in Paris in 1920.[49] Van de Woestyne, through De Graaff gives artistic advise to the young artists: 'I am convinced that a young painter has to have pursued academic studies. He also has to know the masterpieces, not only the old Italians but also the Egyptians, the Japanese, the Persians, the Chinese etc. etc.'[50] He then continues to also send Guthrie addresses of merchants and urges him to visit Paris to get acquainted with contemporary art.

After the war, the relationship between De Graaff and his protégés does change. While he is still buying works by the artists he met in Great Britain, some of them will become his art advisers and even his art buyers. De Graaff now depends to a certain extent on the goodwill of the artists he supported during the war. They are perusing the galleries for him and keep him updated on the comings and goings in Paris and Brussels. Conversely to the war years, where the artists promoted themselves to De Graaff, they are now becoming *his* lobbyists, promoting him as a trustworthy and well established buyer and art lover in Belgium as well as in the French capital. A certain emancipation is also palpable when the three above mentioned artists advise Guthrie. In England, De Graaff had his network and his knowledge was precious. During the interbellum, it is the Dutchman who actively asks for advice in order to steer a new generation of artists in the right direction, trusting that his Belgian friends know the way.

The De Graaffs and the Belgian artists – A relationship built on reciprocity

In June 1930 Jacob and Louise De Graaff and Louise Bachiene move to the South of France. They still keep in touch with a couple of artists such as Van de Woestyne and Tytgat but stop buying Belgian art and focus more on contemporary artists of the Parisian market. After Jacob De Graaff's death in 1947, his wife Louise De Graaff starts donating a large part of their collection to different Museums in Belgium, most notably, her own portrait by Gustave Van de Woestyne, which today is at the Royal Museums of Fine Arts of Belgium (fig. 6.3), but also to the Boymans van Beuningen Museum in Rotterdam. Her most important donation will be to the Hannema-De Stuers Foundation[51] in the Netherlands. After her passing, seventy paintings, drawings and sculptures by Belgian artists were given to the foundation, making it one of the most important collections of Belgian art outside the country's borders.

The patronage of a handful of Belgian artists by the De Graaff couple has shaped the refugee experience of these artists during World War I. A personal bond has been established, granted, stronger with some artists (Tytgat, Daeye, Van de Woestyne, Léon De Smet, Minne) than with others (De Bruycker, Lorein, Permeke etc). With his financial support Jacob De Graaff allows these artists to continue with their work even though they found little to no support within the official institutions. Except from some local artists such as Ethel Walker, Frank Brangwyn or Marcel Jeffreys, the last two with roots in Belgium, they also do not have extensive contacts to the local artistic circles. In addition, only a few of them, such as Van de Woestyne who mainly

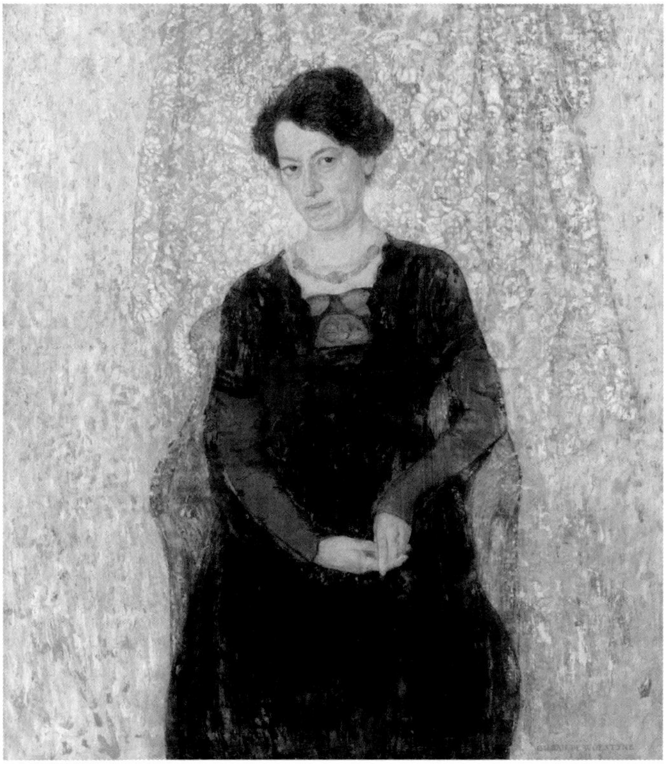

6.3. Gustave van de Woestyne, *Portrait de madame Louise de Graaff*, 1919, oil on canvas, 122 x 107 cm. Brussels, Royal Museums of Fine Arts of Belgium, Inv. 6520.

lived off portrait commissions, or Edgard Tytgat with his book illustrations, had regular income. Their need for a patron was thus crucial for their artistic production.

De Graaff was an important patron for these artists; nonetheless it seems that he had no direct influence on their views on art and culture. On the contrary, it is they who shaped his taste for modern art. This new found interest can be directly traced back to the encounter with Van de Woestyne, Daeye and Léon De Smet. It could be argued that without the refugee immigration during the war, De Graaff's understanding and access to modern art would not have taken place or at least would have only been awoken after the war and probably focused less on the Belgian market but instead limited to the French one. It can also be argued that without the meeting of the Belgian artists in exile, De Graaff would not have been introduced to the thriving art scene that was developing in Brussels during the interbellum.

The relationship between Jacob and Louise De Graaff and the Belgian artists is an exemplary illustration of mutual understanding and support. It underlines the strong network of Belgian artists before, during and after the war and the trust the De Graaff couple had laying in their judgment.

At the end of their lives, their important collection of almost four hundred artworks, from sculptures, to paintings, drawings and etchings, was made up by one fourth of Belgian art.

Notes

1 Marjan Groot, *Vrouwen in de vormgeving in Nederland 1880-1940* (Rotterdam: uitg. 010, 2007), 483.

2 *Ibid.*, 455.

3 The date of the encounter is 1915. This date is given by Jacob De Graaff himself in an exhibition catalogue of 1947: *Les Peintres et Graveurs Belges Contemporains* (Bordeaux 1947). However, given that the earliest correspondences that we know of start with Hippolyte Daeye on 28 May 1917 and the fact that De Graaff makes some attestable mistakes remembering the war period some thirty years later, it is possible that the meeting of the Belgian artists took place at a later date.

4 Probably the work *The Present* about 1866-1871, acquired in 1917 by the National Gallery, which would corroborate the theory of the encounter not before 1917.

5 The ten artists are: Hippolyte Daeye, Léon De Smet, Gustave Van de Woestyne, Edgard Tytgat, Valerius De Saedeleer, George Minne, Jules de Bruycker, Victor Lorein, Constant Permeke, Gust De Smet. As for the widow, it is Nell Wouters, wife of the late Rik Wouters.

6 For detailed information on the patronage of the Davies family during the war see Vincentelli Moïra, "The Davies family and Belgian Refugee artists and musicians in Wales," https://www.aber.ac.uk/en/media/departmental/informationservices/pdf/specialcollections/the-davies-family-and-belgian-refugee-artists-and-musicians-in-wales.pdf
and *Kunst in ballingschap: Vlaanderen, Wales, en de Eerste Wereldoorlog* (Antwerp: Pandora, 2002), exhibition catalogue, Museum voor Schoone Kunsten, Gent, 12.01.-17.03.2002, Hannema-de Stuers Fundatie, Heino/Wijhe, 30.03.-02.06.2002, National Galleries of Wales, Cardiff, 22.06.-15.09.2002. and Caterina Verdickt, "The case of Elisabeth De Saedeleer (1902-1972): The influence of Welsh hospitality in the Great War on Belgian Modernist interior design," *The British Art Journal*, Volume XV, No.3.

7 Gustave Van de Woestyne, with wife and children, moves to London in 1917.

8 "Notes of the Month," *The Welsh Outlook* (November 1914), 457.

9 "Notes of the Month," *The Welsh Outlook* (December 1914), 497.

10 Valerius De Saedeleer to Jacob De Graaff, 13.12.1918, Inv. 50597, RMFAB/ACAB. 'Je vous remercie, vous m'êtes venu en aide dans un moment le plus ctirique de ma vie'.

11 Edgard Tytgat to Jacob De Graaff, 23.12.1931, Inv. 44869, RMFAB/ACAB. '(...) homme qui a été à l'époque la plus douloureuse un baume précieux pour les artistes belges'.

12 Valerius De Saedeleer to Jacob De Graaff, 29 March 1919, Inv. 50602, RMFAB/ACAB. "Pour vous dire ce que vous avez fait pour moi je ne trouverai jamais de mots assez juste pour l'exprimer, avant ma visite chez vous j'étais comme un homme lié aux bras et pieds totalement impuissant, malgré la grande volonté et confiance j'étais dans l'impossibilité de continuer le travail[...]maintenat avec

l'aide que vous m'avez donné je peux de nouveau reprendre ce travail et y mettre toute ma volonté et ma force et je suis sure [sic] de pouvoir vous prier dans quelques mois de venir voir ce que nous pouvons produire ; ma visite chez vous et à Londres m'a donné la confiance dans mon travail. "

13 Valerius De Saedeleer to Jacob De Graaff, 1 May 1919, Inv. 50606, RMFAB/ACAB. "vous m'avez apporté du Bonheur et mis la première pierre sur laquelle je peux continuer à bâtir."

14 Being considered the most notorious collector of Belgian artists in exile, the Minister for Sciences and Arts introduces the request for De Graaff's decoration in 1926.

15 Mrs. Van de Woestyne to Jacob De Graaff, 5 January 1919, Inv. 50720, RMFAB/ACAB.

16 Victor Lorein to Jacob De Graaff, undated, Inv. 40189, RMFAB/ACAB.

17 Léon De Smet to Jacob De Graaff, 2 April 1918, Inv. 50522, RMFAB/ACAB.
For details on the refugee status in the Netherlands see Michäel Amara, *Des Belges à l'épreuve de l'exil: Les réfugiés de la Première guerre mondiale / France, Grande-Bretagne, Pays-Bas, 1914-1918*, 2e tirage, Histoire 1 (Bruxelles, Paris, Le Plessis-Pâté: Éditions de l'Université de Bruxelles; diff. Sodis; diff. ToThèmes, 2014).

18 Léon De Smet to Jacob De Graaff, 13.08.1919, Inv. 50538, RMFAB/ACAB.

19 James Jack Gindin, *John Galsworthy's life and art: An alien's fortress* 1 (London: MacMillan, 1987), 348.

20 Léon De Smet to Jacob De Graaff, 5 July 1919, Inv. 50537, RMFAB/ACAB.

21 The Leicester Galleries to Geoge Minne, 16. December 1918, Inv. 16.552, RMFAB/ACAB.

22 Valerius De Saedeleer to Jacob De Graaff, 20 October 1920, Inv. 50621, RMFAB/ACAB.

23 Valerius De Saedeleer to Jacob De Graaff, 30 October1920, Inv. 50622, RMFAB/ACAB. 'je serais content d'avoir les Burlington Galleries [...]. Je vous demande d'avoir la bonté de prendre les renseignements nécessaires aux Burlington Galleries, quelles sont leurs conditions?'

24 Valerius De Saedeleer to Jacob De Graaff, 28 March 1921, Inv. 50628, RMFAB/ACAB.

25 Françoise Lechien-Durant und Paul Eeckhout, *Musée David et Alice Van Buuren: Maison de mémoire* (Brussels: Racine, 1995), 100.

26 Willy van den Bussche, "Permeke in England," in *Vlaams expressionisme in Europese context*, (Snoeck-Ducaju & Zoon Ludion: Gent, 1990), exhibition catalogue: Museum voor Schone Kunsten, Gent, 10.03-10.06.1990, 73-75.

27 Exhibition of Belgian Art, Oxford, May-June 1915 and Belgian Exhibition of Modern Art, Municipal Art Gallery, Kingston-upon-Thames, London, 15.03 – 27.03.1915.

28 We do not know how the contact between artist and gallery was established. However, the gallery held an exhibition of the Artist's War Fund in October 1914.
See Hippolyte Daeye to Jacob De Graaff, 16 (?). 09 (?) 1918, Inv. 39085, RMFAB/ACAB.

29 After this encounter, Jacob de Graaff will buy multiple of Ethel Walker's works and begins a correspondence, kept today at the Tate in London.

30 Gustave Van de Woestyne is also godfather to Permeke's girl born in England in 1918. It goes to show that many of these artists had a very important bond to one another.

31 Gust De Smet to Jacob De Graaff, 15 January 1921, Inv. 39255, RMFAB/ACAB.

32 *'Vissersdorp', 'Stadzicht', 'Meijeskop'* and *'Bloemen'.*

33 Nell Wouters to Jacob De Graaff, 20 December 1918, Inv. 40173, RMFAB/ACAB.

34 Nell Wouters to Jacob De Graaff, 20 December 1918, Inv. 40173, RMFAB/ACAB.

35 Edgard Tytgat to Jacob De Graaff, 2 January 1923, Inv. 50663, RMFAB/ACAB.

36 Léon De Smet to Jacob De Graaff, 16 May 1926, Inv. 5066, RMFAB/ACAB.

37 Edgard Tytgat to Jacob De Graaff, 11 December 1924, Inv. 50672, RMFAB/ACAB.

38 Vanruysseveldt, Peter, *De onbekende werken van Rik Wouters – Catalogus van het grafische werk / catalogue de l'oeuvre gravé [sic] /* (Antwerp: Pandora, 2007), 20.

Comprised of 35 etchings, the Stols Album of the De Graaff collection only has 34, "Les rendez-vous, soir de pluie" is missing. The album today belongs to the Hannema-De Stuers Foundation, the whereabouts of the 35th etching of the album is unknown.

39 Valerius De Saedeleer to Jacob De Graaff, Inv. 50600, RMFAB/ACAB.'Nous ne savons pas encore ce que nous alons [sic] faire, les nouvelles de la Belgique sont si décourageant, ici nous sommes si heureux et l'avenir est si douteux.'

40 As cited in Piet Boyens, *L'Art flamand: Du symbolisme à l'expressionnisme à Laethem-Saint-Martin* (Tielt, Sint-Martens-Latem: Lannoo; Art Book Company, 1992), 104: "I have tried, with daily walks, to familiarise myself with the land and the sky, but despite my sustained efforts, they remained mute for me and I understood that reproducing this foreign atmosphere will never be within my reach. It is this that can be attributed to the fact that most of my works of this period are devoid of the emotions which in my country were coming naturally to me."

41 Edgard Tytgat to Jacob De Graaff, 5 August 1920, AACB Inv. 50653, RMFAB/ACAB.

42 Edgard Tytgat to Jacob De Graaff, 2 May 1926, Inv. 50677, RMFAB/ACAB.

43 Gustave Van de Woestyne to Jacob De Graaff, 25 May 1923, Inv. 50770, RMFAB/ACAB. 'Marie Laurencin, is niet meer wat ze vroeger was. Las U eeb werk van haar ziet, hebt U ze allemaal gezien.'

44 Edgard Tytgat to Jacob De Graaff, 15 January 1920, Inv. 50652, RMFAB/ACAB. 'je crois qu'il n'est pas necessaire de vous parler de son exposition, c'est plus qu'une merveille, c'est magique et, surement [sic] c'est le maître de notre époque.'

45 Jacob De Graaff will also be starting a correspondence with Ossip Zadkine today in the 'Bibliothèque Nationale de France' in Paris.

46 Léon De Smet to Jacob De Graaff, undated, Inv. 50570, RMFAB/ACAB. 'Ik ontving gisteren het bezoek van Van Hecke en Schwartzenberg[...]. Zij vinden het, het mooiste [Zadkine] dat hij ooit deed.'

47 *Ibid.* 'U moet weten dat Uw naam hier te Parijs is gekend, als den groote [sic] kunstliefhebber van England, waardoor ik heel wat uitnodigingen [...] krijg.

48 Gustave Van de Woestyne to Jacob De Graaff, 28 October 1922, Inv. 50762, RMFAB/ACAB.

49 Léon De Smet to Jacob De Graaff, undated, Inv. 50555, RMFAB/ACAB.

50 Gustave Van de Woestyne to Jacob De Graaff, 15 December 1920, Inv. 50753, RMFAB/ACAB. 'Ik ben overtuigd dat een jonge schilder moet Akademische [sic] studiën gedaan hebben. Hij moet ook de Meesterwerken kennen, niet alleen de oude Italianen maar ook de Egyptenaren, de Japaners [sic], de Persen, de Chinezen enz. enz.'

51 Dirk Hannema is an acquaintance of the De Graaffs already in the 1920's. He will become a good friend of the couple in 1930. In 1957, Dirk Hannema creates the Hanemma – De Stuers Foundation in Kasteel het Nijenhuis in the Netherlands. See: *De collectie De Graaff-Bachiene: Schilderijen, Beeldhouwwerken, Tekeningen en Grafiek* (Heino/Wijhe, Gent, 1992), exhibition catalogue, Hannema-De Stuers Fundatie, Heino/Wijhe, 11.04.-31.05.1992, Museum voor Schone Kunsten, Gent, 13.06-30.08.1992.

Occupation – Influences on the Art Market and the Intercultural Exchanges

Belgian Art During the First World War: Exhibitions and Salons in Brussels

Werner Adriaenssens

> "In spite of oppression, the high cost of living, the price of butter, etc, art has stood its ground and has not come to a standstill. We have as many exhibitions as in peacetime, if not more."[1]

There was no let-up in artistic life in Belgium during the First World War. Indeed, an active cultural policy was pursued by the Germans.[2] The art market flourished in Brussels, with public buildings and private galleries hosting exhibitions of the work of contemporary Belgian artists, albeit that there was no link with the cultural policy of the Germans. The focus of those exhibitions was on painting, and the works shown were ultra "salonfähig" (respectable) in terms of both theme and style. War themes and "avant-garde" works were nowhere to be seen.

There are few sources available for reconstructing the forgotten history of those art exhibitions. Archives either have not survived or are inaccessible. Upon the outbreak of war, many periodicals and magazines closed down and new publications were a rarity. In consequence, the major source is the daily and weekly newspapers that reappeared on the streets from the end of 1914 on. Although they are a mine of information, they have to be treated with caution, since the press was censored by the German occupier. Additional information is provided by exhibition catalogues and a few scarce occasional publications.

The intention here is not to provide an exhaustive narrative of all the facts and to list and discuss all the exhibitions in the galleries then active, but rather to examine how that specific aspect of cultural life in occupied Brussels flourished again and what the reason for its success was.[3]

The 1914 exhibition season

1914 was a busy season for exhibitions, notable fixed events during the spring being the *La Libre Esthétique* and *Pour l'Art* Salons at the Museum of Modern Art. There was a whirl of gallery life, too, including the seven exhibitions organised at the Galerie Georges Giroux from January to June, the most memorable of which was that of the works of Rik Wouters. The Salle Studio, headed by Isy Brachot, also had a busy programme, and other players included the Galerie d'Art and the Salle Aeolian. From 9 May to 2 November, the Cinquantenaire hosted the chief event of the season, the Exposition Générale des Beaux-Arts, better known as the Salon Triennal.[4]

The Brussels museums

The Brussels museums closed with effect from 1 August 1914, as mobilisation made it impossible to guarantee their proper operation and security. In mid-December of that same year, the head of the Imperial German Government-General of Belgium, Governor-General Moritz von Bissing, ordered that they be reopened, "… so that the people of Brussels and German soldiers should not be deprived of the opportunity to admire their collections".[5] The various sections of the Cinquantenaire, as well as the Porte de Hal and the Wiertz Museum, reopened on 2 January 1915, and the Museums of Modern Art and of Old Masters on 23 and 24 January respectively.

On 20 February, less than a month after its reopening, the Museum of Modern Art saw the inauguration of the "Salon des Beaux-Arts". For that purpose, the museum rooms of the Old Palace were placed at the disposal of a committee whose aim was to help needy artists.[6]

The Fédération Professionnelle des Beaux-Arts

The "Salon des Beaux-Arts" was the first big art exhibition to be organised in Brussels during the war. A proportion of the proceeds was earmarked for the "Fédération Professionnelle des Beaux-Arts" (Professional Federation of the Fine Arts), which played a stimulating role in the organisation of exhibitions during the early part of the war.

The "Fédération" was set up in September 1914, with the goal of providing support for artists who found themselves without an income; it paid them a monthly sum to help them survive, and also provided paint and plaster to enable them to work.[7] An important part in all that was played by the painter-architect William Jelley;[8] it was he who, in November 1914, in order to encourage creativity, opened the Labor atelier, where models were hired and materials collected.[9]

From the outset, the "Fédération" was supported by funding from the artists' associations; indeed, the "Cercle Artistique et Littéraire", the "Société royale des Aquarellistes" and *Pour l'Art* transferred to it the entirety of their cash balances. With Ernest Blanc-Garin, Henri Cassiers, Camille Gaspar and Philippe Wolfers, those associations were also well represented on the board of the "Fédération".[10]

In addition, the "Fédération" was also subsidised by the "Comité National de Secours et d'Alimentation" (National Committee for Relief), which itself was financed by leading Belgian businessmen.[11] The committee took on the distribution of the goods of the Commission for Relief in Belgium, the aid organisation that purchased food and other necessities of life for dispatch from the United States to Belgium.

It quickly became apparent that the funds available were insufficient to meet the cost of rising need, and it therefore proved necessary for the "Fédération" to generate additional funding.

Paul Lambotte's initiative

Paul Lambotte, Director of Fine Arts and member of the organising committee of the Salon Triennal of 1914, was concerned about the fate of artists remaining behind in Brussels. He himself had left for London in November 1914, but not without proper preparation for his flight, succeeding in smuggling with him a hundred or so works by Brussels artists[12] for inclusion in a charity exhibition organised in the British capital.[13] The exhibition opened on 16 November at Goupil & C°,[14] a Paris art house with branches in London and Brussels, among other places. However, the works were not offered for sale there, since Lambotte had requested the artists, or the artists had stipulated, that they be put into a charity raffle,[15] for which a publicity campaign was mounted.[16]

Although this was a well-intentioned initiative, there was a negative reaction from the Brussels artists. In an open letter, remarks were made by an unspecified group of artists:

> "It is all to the good that an attempt is being made to have Belgian art benefit from the sympathy recently aroused towards us in friendly countries. Our artists are better off being known, appreciated and liked, and also value the fact that people buy their works. However, because all the compatriots of M. the Director of Fine Arts deserve that sympathy without discrimination, it is surprising that M. Lambotte has omitted to invite a very large number of

> painters to participate in this Belgian exhibition in London. Is that foreign sympathy to be channelled for the benefit of a few friends of the Directorate, or does the Directorate count on spreading the profits of its initiative among all those – friends or personal enemies – who have contributed towards the artistic fame of our country? Or could it be that this benevolent preoccupation has the sole goal of providing a fig leaf for the flight of officials who have no other reason for following the Government? But that is an unworthy thought and it is known that the artists ... are good fellows. They still hope that M. Lambotte will concern himself actively with the precarious future of all painters and be successful in the undertaking".[17]

The message clearly touched a nerve. Lambotte's alleged jumping of ship was greeted with indignation. The politician Paul Wauwermans came to his defence, arguing that, at the outset, it had never been Lambotte's intention to organise a Belgian exhibition in London; rather, he had looked to arrange a sales exhibition in Belgium, but that had proved unworkable. The exhibition at Goupil & C° appeared to be the only viable alternative.[18] It seemed likely that the event had been effectively organised from Brussels via the gallery's branch there.

That defence did not entirely quell the discontent, and a harsh retort followed, concluding with the following words:

> "For the Directorate of Fine Arts, not only are few chosen, but few are indeed called. It is that we are protesting about. And in our opinion the Directorate has either overstated its initiative or poorly executed its mandate" [19].

The reactions to Lambotte's initiative indicate two frustrations. On the one hand, the Brussels artists felt themselves abandoned by the Belgian Government, the representatives of which had fled and which was suspected of partisanship and favouritism. On the other, the incident brought a great discontent into the open, as there was no opportunity whatsoever in Brussels to sell work.

The discussion flared up again briefly at the end of January 1915 on the occasion of Belgian participation at the Panama-Pacific International Exhibition in San Francisco: "Is foreign sympathy to be channelled for the benefit of a few friends of the Directorate?".[20] However, nothing further occurred, as preparations were taking place concurrently for the Salon des Beaux-Arts, an initiative that did indeed meet the complaints of the Brussels artists.

The "Salon des Beaux-Arts" and the "Salon d'Automne" in the Museum of Modern Art

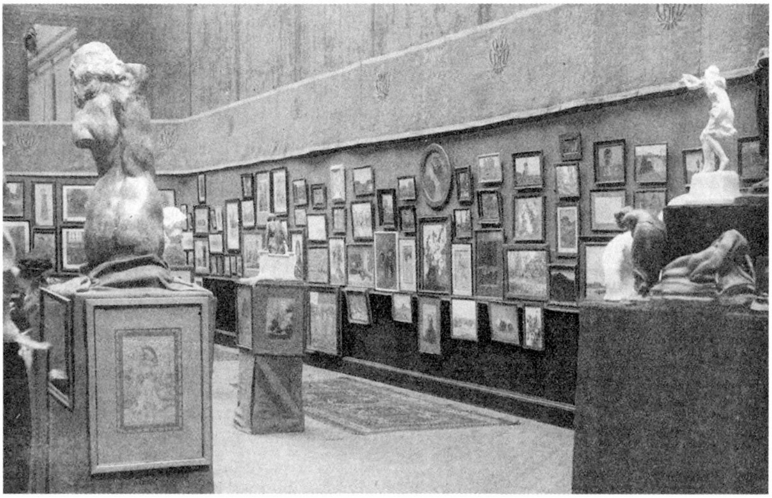

7.1. Museum of Modern Arts, Salon d'Automne, the room with the raffle prizes, 2 October – 14 November 1915. *Salon d'Automne, 1914 Illustré*, n° 58 (1915): s.p.

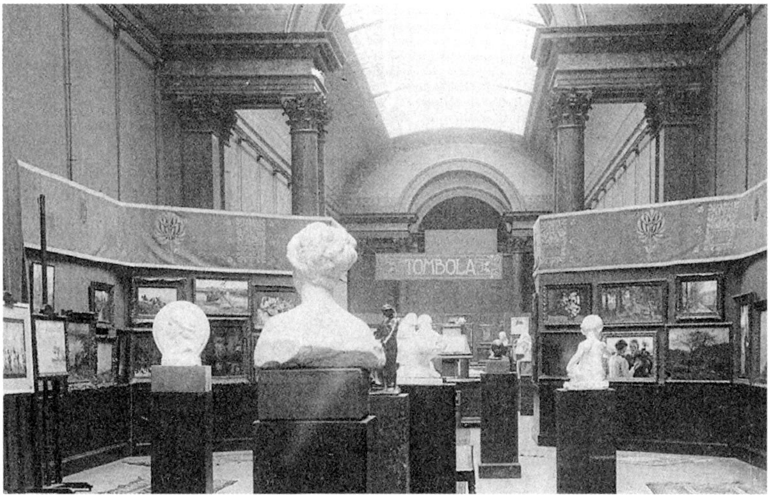

7.2. Museum of Modern Arts, Salon d'Automne, 2 October – 14 Novembre 1915. *Salon d'Automne, 1914 Illustré*, n° 58 (1915): s.p.

Just a few days after the Museums of Old Masters and of Modern Art had been reopened, the secretary-general of the Directorate of Fine Arts sent a letter to the management committee, notifying it that the rooms of the Old Palace were available for use by "a group of artists, with a view to organising an exhibition there with the aim of aiding artists without means of support".[21] Just a few days later, on 29 January 1915, Jacques de Lalaing, chairman of the museum committee, was officially notified by the painters Adolphe Crespin and Victor Creten, the secretaries of the group. That occurred on the advice of Ernest Verlant, General Director of Fine Arts and Lambotte's superior.[22] The idea for such an exhibition had already been launched at the end of the previous November by *Le Quotidien*,[23] when the discussion over Lambotte's action was exercising the feelings of artists in Brussels, and it is likely that a start was made then with the organisation of the exhibition.

The Salon des Beaux-Arts was a large-scale exhibition and was accompanied by the publication of a catalogue. The organising committee consisted solely of artists, but acquired official character through the honorary chairmanship of Ernest Verlant and Émile Jacqmain, Aldermen of Public Education and of Fine Arts respectively of the town of Brussels.[24]

The Salon met two important points of discontent. On the one hand, it was a sales exhibition for Brussels artists who had remained in the occupied capital.[25] On the other, it had a charitable side in that it was linked to a raffle to which each participating artist had contributed at least one work.[26] The tickets cost twenty francs each and guaranteed a prize.[27] The entire proceeds of the entry tickets and ten per cent of the sale price of the works on display went in full to the "Fédération Professionnelle des Beaux-Arts" and to the "Comité d'Aide et Protection aux Artistes".[28] The latter was an initiative of Baron Lambert and also operated under the auspices of the "Comité National de Secours et d'Alimentation". Initially set up for all artists, this last came in time to direct its efforts chiefly to wordsmiths and people from the world of theatre and opera.[29]

The Salon was trumpeted as a success that had exceeded all expectations. Although all the raffle tickets had been sold, however, the number of registered entry tickets – 5485 – pointed rather to a relatively modest attendance. Sales were disappointing, too: only fifteen of the 175 works were purchased.[30] The artists were left to nurse their hunger.

Substantial responsibility for this undoubtedly lay with the organisation. Quality was not a concern, the only selection criterion being format: in order to display as many works as possible, only those less than a metre and a half square were accepted.[31] The committee made no judgement, aiming only at quantity.[32] Mindful of the reproach that Lambotte must have been aware of, however, there was certainly no wish to exclude anyone. The result matched this:

> "It is not, ..., unimportant that, in such an exhibition, no community of taste, ideas or trends can be discerned among the exhibitors. On display are works by 300 painters, engravers, sculptors, watercolourists and etchers, all of merit in their various ways; the catalogue runs to no less than 420 items, but it would be, ..., puerile to suggest that these were 420 masterpieces".[33]

Neither is it clear whether the works were produced especially for the exhibition. It is, in any case, a fact that the raffle prizes often dated from before the war.[34]

The Salon d'Automne (7.1 and 7.2) opened on 2 October 1915 in the rooms of the Old Palace, preparations having begun in the summer.[35] Its organisation and principle were the same as for the Salon des Beaux-Arts, except for the organising committee, which was enlarged; and the only interested party was the "Fédération Professionnelle des Beaux-Arts".[36] Boasting 613 catalogued items, this exhibition was even more comprehensive than the preceding one. However, whereas – in view of its charitable nature – that earlier exhibition had enjoyed a degree of restraint in the criticism of the quality of the works on show, no such restraint was accorded the later one. It was particularly the careless appearance of the exhibition that attracted negative comment. Not only was there an impression of its having been set up too hastily, but the over-abundance was also disapproved of: "[s]ome works have really been sacrificed; placement has continued down to floor-level, and into show-cases blocking the way".[37] The qualitative difference was also denounced: "... 'there are infinitely more pieces of canvas than masterpieces'.... Why is it tolerated?"[38]. The jury was accused of voluntarism,[39] each work having indeed been accepted unreservedly. Clearly, the committee did not want to offend anyone.

Contrary to what happened with the Salon des Beaux-Arts, there was virtually no reporting regarding the success of this exhibition; there was also no statement of income and expenditure. The fact that the closing date was postponed a couple of times (from 6 to eventually 14 November[40]) may indicate that the exhibition was not a hit. It was clear that the formula of combining charity and art within a museum context did not work, and consequently it was not repeated.

The reopening of the Salon Triennal

The official character of the Salon d'Automne prompted one journalist to see it as a smaller version of the Salon Triennal.[41] On the outbreak of the war, that event had been shelved, a situation that appeared to be unchanged in January 1915, when Paul

Lambotte replied to concerned artists that everything was still in place, undamaged and intact.[42] The Salon reopened in April [43] and it quickly became apparent that it was attracting an interested public that was effectively purchasing works of art. The resulting freed space had consequently to be filled with new works, a situation that acted as a spur to artists:

> "'A smart curator who never tires of selling and a galaxy of artists who never tire of painting!' Here we have an explanation for the turnaround on the picture rails; here we have the old Triennal 1914 guard, despite the years, the ever-so-piquant attraction of eternal youth and the novelty. And no complaint is being heard from the artists!".[44]

In accordance with the tradition of this Salon, the new works were judged by a committee.[45] This was necessary, since the event was traditionally aimed at a wealthy public.[46] The reopening of the Salon represented a partial move on the part of officialdom to meet the urgings of artists looking to exhibit their works with a view to selling them.

The private galleries

A conclusion drawn in May 1915 was that "artists are decidedly not among the idle at present".[47] Correctly so, as, besides the charitable art exhibitions being held in official buildings, the year also saw most private galleries reopening their doors.[48]

The Salle Studio

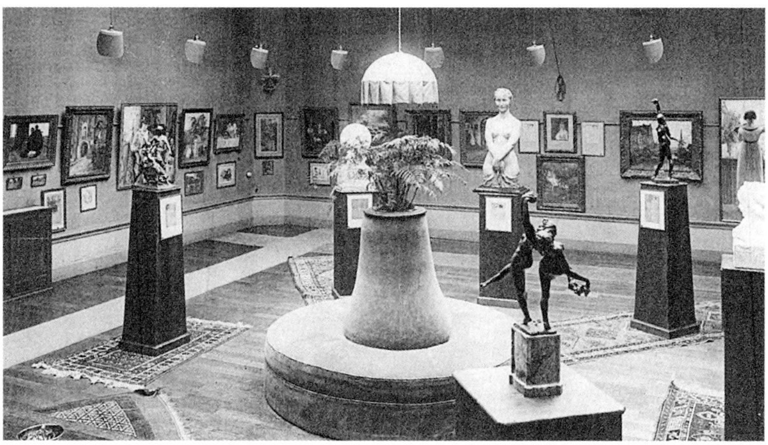

7.3. Salle Studio, Salon d'Été, 31 July — 31 August 1915. *Le Salon d'Été, L'Événement illustré*, 26 (1915): 51.

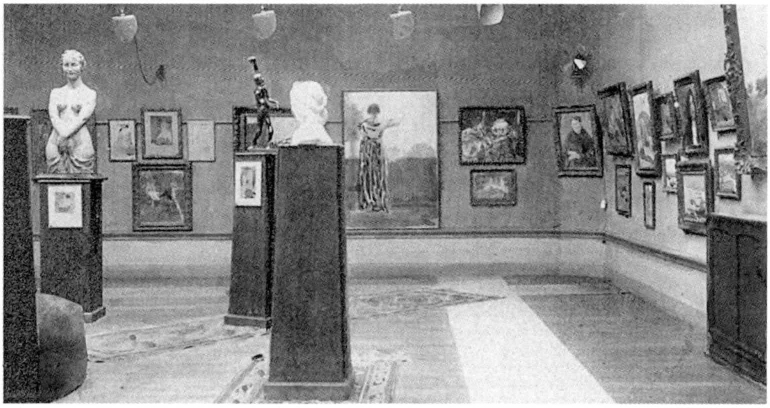

7.4. Salle Studio, Salon d'Été, 31 July — 31 August 1915. *Au Cercle "Studio". – L'Exposition de nos Peintres*, *1914 illustré*, n° 51 (1915): s.p.

The first art exhibition in occupied Brussels took place from 12 to 31 December 1914 in the Salle Studio. The plan was clear: "... to permit artists, ..., to remain in contact not only with critics or admirers of their work, but also with its buyers".[49] In this way, the gallery's director, Isy Brachot, was the first to respond to the complaint levelled by Brussels artists at Paul Lambotte's initiative. By concentrating on sales, Salle Studio automatically brought its focus to bear on art lovers, and more particularly on the gallery's regular clientele, so as to re-establish contact. That basis implied an essential difference from the purely charitable art exhibitions that were to take place in 1915 in the Museum of Modern Art and at which quantity was paramount. Brachot placed the emphasis on quality, so that much more emphasis was placed on the selection of works, which were displayed in optimal circumstances: "... dabblers of no use in this respect, are carefully weeded out".[50] This was contrary to the general expectation of an exhibition organised in wartime: "That one doesn't conceive of this small wartime gallery – ... – containing hastily thrown together 'junk', over-stylish canvasses...".[51] The exhibition nevertheless had a philanthropic character in that it was combined with a raffle whose tickets went for the considerable sum of fifty francs. The proceeds of the tickets, together with part of the profit from the sale of entry tickets and catalogues, and a percentage on the sale of works were used by the gallery itself to purchase exhibited art works for the raffle. The profit was paid out to the "Fédération Professionnelle des Beaux-Arts".[52] It was a businesslike and intelligent way to maintain control of standards and to guarantee quality to potential clients.

With the first exhibition proving a successful testing of the waters, it took only until 2 January 1915 for a new exhibition to open in the gallery,[53] but the real start came with an exhibition of paintings, sculptures and decorative art which ran from 6 March to 6 April 1915.[54] From then on, the gallery worked at full throttle, until the end of 1916 hosting more than twenty exhibitions (7.3-7.4) with highly divergent and original themes: solo and group exhibitions; winter, spring and summer exhibitions; thematic events devoted to watercolourists, pastellists and graphic art, for example, or the very successful Salon d'Art féminin devoted exclusively to work by female artists.[55] These sales exhibitions were interspersed with the occasional charitable event, one instance of which was the "Exposition Nationale de Peinture et de Sculpture" organised in September 1916 under the patronage of Verlant and Jacqmain, and in aid of the wives and children of front-line soldiers.[56] The ambition for 1917 and beyond was to organise twenty exhibitions a year. It is clear that Brachot was attempting to bind the public to the gallery, a goal reinforced by his founding of the "Cercle d'Art du Studio" in 1917. Subscription to this was hefty, but it entitled the subscriber to free entry to all exhibitions, the luxury album "Studio Noël" and a multiple of an established artist.[57]

The Salle Studio exhibitions did not all enjoy unanimous acclaim, but in general can be said to have received positive ratings. The fact is, too, that their quality and regularity, together with the creation of the "Cercle d'Art du Studio", meant that they could count on a steady clientele.[58]

The Galerie Georges Giroux

During the First World War, the Galerie Georges Giroux was overtaken by the Salle Studio as the most active art gallery in Brussels. Indeed, it resumed activities only in May 1915 (7.5), after its management, during the first part of that year, had offered it as a venue for charitable events, such as a concert.[59]

The first wartime exhibition was of paintings and sculptures, though there was no clear theme or link between the artists.[60] What occasioned the re-opening was sketched decades later by Jules Elslander – with Giroux, a co-director of the gallery:

> "La Galerie Giroux had closed its doors. What did we still have to offer artists? We were going to war ...! But a little while later I convinced Giroux to reopen; I had met the painter [Philippe] Swyncop who told me he had sold a canvas! And why not, after all? Apprehensively, we tempted our luck and a few artists brought us some pictures".[61]

Although there is now no way of verifying its veracity, this account is certainly plausible, particularly as artistic life in Brussels was beginning to burgeon again around the time Giroux restarted, albeit that the paintings shown at the opening exhibition were apparently likewise not new works and were, it was said, at best works retouched by their painters.[62] For subsequent exhibitions, however, new works were indeed created.[63] Activity at Giroux also breezed along with thematic and group exhibitions,[64] as well as the occasional charitable event, such as the exhibition of painted meal sacks, which last the "Comité National de Secours et d'Alimentation" made available to the artists of the "Fédération Professionnelle des Beaux-Arts".[65]

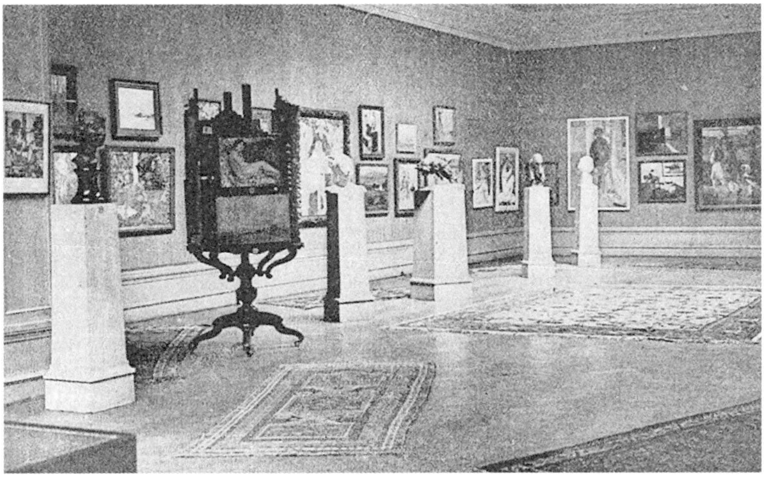

7.5. Galerie Georges Giroux, Exposition 12 May – 15 June 1915. Marcel Dekoster, "La Vie Artistique et Littéraire," *Le Temps Présent*, 33 (1915): 477.

With exhibitions devoted to young talent, Giroux appeared the most progressive in the gallery world. Nevertheless, the frequency with which exhibitions were mounted at the Salle Studio during the First World War indicates greater attendance on the part of the public, which undoubtedly had an impact on sales. Not unimportant in this respect was the fact that artists were often required to pay a considerable fee to exhibit at the Salle Studio. A consequence of this was that only those with means – often an older generation of artists – were able to show their work;[66] in most cases, these artists enjoyed an established reputation and their work could count on the approval of a faithful public.[67] For the less well-off, still seeking to make their names, that fee represented an obstacle. The Galerie Giroux attempted to be forthcoming in that respect, but the scope of its response was necessarily limited. Economic reality was, after all, a determining factor for a private gallery, and even more so – certainly – in wartime.

Reasons for the burgeoning of the Brussels art market

The fact that sales exhibitions were organised at an unrelenting tempo in private galleries in Brussels during the First World War indicates that there was a monied public in the capital. That picture is emphasised by the reopening of the Salon Triennal which, for the further course of the war, continued to function as an official sales point. The success of the Brussels art auctions was a further sign. Among these, the public auctions organised by Giroux attracted a select public,[68] with hammer prices exceeding expectations:

> "Decidedly, seeing the press of people at these gatherings, one would say that buying paintings, antiques, art objects, curios and the like represents a good investment at the moment".[69]

As regards Belgian painting, indeed, record prices were sometimes achieved.[70] Jules Elslander offered the following reason for the flourishing of the art market during the war: "Then came the epoch of the nouveaux riches, those called the 'Soap Barons', ...".[71] Those war-profiteers would certainly have been among the interested public, but it is not possible that the success of the art market was down to them alone. It appears plausible that, in the uncertain years of war, art was seen as a sound investment. With the value of money depreciating fast, art was regarded as holding a fixed value; to limit risk, works were consequently bought chiefly from artists with an established reputation, the same mechanism probably determining the selection of contemporary artists. The situation of the war left little scope for experiment, in the sense that the risk of loss had to be kept as limited as possible. It appears obvious, therefore, that preference was given to society painters of recognised quality whose style was to the taste of a loyal clientele among the *bourgeoisie*. Telling within that context is the following passage from the critique of the spring exhibition organised in the Salle Studio in 1915:

> "'The Japanese Prints' by Fernand Toussaint is a product of the painter's habitual palette; it is sentimental and to many people's taste; [Herman] Richir and F.[irmin]. Baes are exhibiting coloured photography. .... These and other names draw the public to the Salle Studio and sell canvases there; but what encouragement does it give to young people with talent?" [72]

The public attending gallery-organised exhibitions explained the limited success of charitable art exhibitions in general and those held sporadically in actual galleries. With the accent on charity, the qualitative benchmark was automatically set lower; indeed, the public attracted by philanthropic work had other things in mind than the purely artistic or investment.

The dominance of painting

"Exploitation of the vogue for exhibitions of paintings is in full swing"[73] was the story of the summer of 1915; painting, indeed, dominated virtually all exhibitions. The galleries had nevertheless also paid attention to sculpture and the applied arts in the beginning, albeit that these last could never attract much notice.[74] A telling example concerns the architect Léon Sneyers, who had run the small decoration business 'L'Intérieur' since 1911. At the end of 1917, with a view to organising exhibitions of paintings and graphic art, he expanded his exhibition space in the rue de Namur, naming it La Galerie Sneyers.[75] In spite of the scant attention given to the applied arts, he continued his attempts to excite durable interest in them, one event in his gallery being "L'Art dans Tout", which he organised in 1918. That, too, hardly stirred the public.[76] Sculpture suffered the same fate. On the occasion of the Salon d'Automne in 1915, it had already been remarked that sculpture was under-represented.[77] Already it was clear that the preference was for painting, a situation that was to persist throughout the war.: "...; they [the painters] are the pets of the great majority of the public!".[78]

In the specific circumstances of war, there was nothing illogical in the public's preference for painting rather than sculpture. An investment in painting was not only safer, but much more practical. However, that was certainly not the only consideration; the very short supply of resources also played a part: not only were raw materials such as marble very scarce, but the Germans began in December 1915 to requisition bronze, thereby excluding the possibility of casting any further sculptures, never mind of exhibiting them. All that the sculptors were left to exhibit were terracotta and plaster items, but these failed to capture the interest of the target public. Set against this was painting, which could achieve maximum effect with relatively few and inexpensive materials.

"There is no lack of exhibitions in Brussels. Along the Rue Royale, from the Schaerbeek to the Porte de Namur, they are everywhere to be seen".[79] That was the reality during the First World War. The gallery world capitalised successfully on the public's interest for paintings, and the painters themselves enjoyed a certain fame in society circles. It is noticeable, too, that the works bear no reference to the events of the war or their consequences. In occupied Brussels, not only would any such paintings or exhibitions of them have been censored, but the gallery-frequenting public would not have bought them; rather, then, they are generally peaceful, charming and even idyllic. Because of their fashionable character, moreover, the exhibitions posed no problems for the Germans, making it possible to report on them fairly freely under the censor.

After the war, most galleries continued their activities. One of the first exhibitions after the Armistice was the Salon Anti-Boche in the Salle Aeolian, at which satirical and humorous works were shown that had been produced by those same gallery artists during the hostilities...[80]

Notes

1 "*Les expositions*," *L'indépendance Belge* (26 September 1918) : "En dépit de l'oppression, de la vie chère, du prix du beurre, etc. l'art se raidit et ne chôme pas. Nous avons autant d'expositions qu'en temps de paix sinon plus".

2 Ulrich Tiedau, "De Duitse cultuurpolitiek in België tijdens de Eerste Wereldoorlog", *Bijdragen tot de eigentijdse geschiedenis 11* (2003): 21-45.

3 This article is the first and summarised account of an extensive study conducted on this subject.

4 *Exposition Générale des Beaux-Arts (Salon Triennal)*. Brussels: Cinquantenaire, 1914, 9.

5 "Dernières dépêches," *Le Messager de Bruxelles*, 3 January 1915 : "(...) afin que la population bruxelloise et les soldats allemands ne soient pas privés de l'occasion d'admirer ces collections".

6 Archives of the Royal Museums of Fine Art of Belgium, File "Musea", Register "Notulen Commissie", D. 49/B 1901-1923, letters 26 January 1915, 29 January 1915 and 17 March 1915.

7 "À la *Fédération Professionnelle des Beaux-Arts*," *Le Bruxellois*, 17 October 1915.

8 "Pour les artistes," *Le Quotidien*, 7 February, 1915.

9 "Le 'Labor'," *Le Quotidien*, 12 November 1914.

10 "À la *Fédération Professionnelle des Beaux-Arts*," *Le Bruxellois*, 17 October 1915.

11 "Pour les artistes," *Le Quotidien*, 15 August 1915.

12 "Pour les artistes," *Le Bien Public*, 27 November 1915 indicates that the works concerned were canvasses, watercolours and etchings by such artists as Firmin Baes, Geo Bernier, Henri Thomas, Jean Gouweloos, Franz Gaillard, Maurice Hagemans, Theo Hannon, Maurice Langaskens, Georges Lemmen, Amedée Lynen, Jules Merckaert, Marc-Henri. Meunier, Henriette Meunier, H. Smits, Jean François Taelemans, Louis Titz and Carl Werlemann.

13 "Pour nos artistes," *L'Indépendance belge (published in England)*, 11 November 1914.

14 "Une exposition d'œuvres belges," *L'Indépendance belge (published in England)*, 18 November 1914.

15 "Mise au point," *La Belgique*, 22 November 1914.

16 "La détresse des artistes" *Le Quotidien*, 18 November 1914.

17 "Nos artistes peintres," *La Belgique*, 20 November 1914: "Que l'on essaye de faire profiter l'art belge des sympathies récemment éveillées en notre faveur dans les pays amis, rien de mieux. Nos artistes valent qu'on les connaisse, qu'on les apprécie, qu'on les aime. Ils valent même qu'on achète leurs œuvres. Mais comme ces sympathies sont indistinctement méritées par tous les compatriotes de M. le Directeur des Beaux-Arts, il est étonnant que M. Lambotte ait oublié d'inviter un très grand nombre de peintres à participer à ce Salon belge de Londres. La sympathie étrangère sera-t-elle donc canalisée au profit de quelques amis de la direction, ou la direction compte-t-elle étendre le bénéfice de son initiative à tous ceux, amis ou ennemis personnels, qui ont contribué à la renommée artistique de notre pays? Autre hypothèse: cette bienveillante préoccupation aurait-elle pour seul but d'excuser la fuite de fonctionnaires qui n'avaient pas d'autres raisons de suivre le Gouvernement? Mais cette hypothèse est méchante et l'on sait que les artistes (...) sont de bons enfants. Ils espèrent encore que M. Lambotte se préoccupera activement et avec succès du sort précaire de « tous » les artistes-peintres".

18 "Mise au point," *La Belgique*, 22 November 1914.

19 "Les artistes," *La Belgique*, 26 November 1914: "Pour la direction des Beaux-Arts, non seulement il y a peu d'élus, mais il y a même peu d'appelés. C'est contre quoi nous protestons. Et nous estimons que la Direction ou bien a exagéré son initiative ou mal exécuté son mandat".

20 Le Vieil Hibou, "Un comble," *Le Messager de Bruxelles* (28 January 1915): "La sympathie étrangère serait-elle donc canalisée au profit de quelques amis de la direction?".

21 Archives of the Royal Museums of Fine Art of Belgium, File "Musea", Register "Notulen Commissie", D. 49/B 1901-1923, letter 26 January 1915: "Un groupe d'artistes en vue d'y organiser une exposition dans le but de venir à l'aide des artistes sans ressources".

22 Archives of the Royal Museums of Fine Art of Belgium, File "Musea", Register "Notulen Commissie", D. 49/B 1901-1923, letter 29 January 1915.

23 R. De Man, "Pour les Artistes. Une idée du 'Quotidien'," *Le Quotidien*, 22 November 1914.

24 *Salon des Beaux-Arts 1915. Catalogue*. Brussels: Museum of Modern Art, 1915: 5. Also among the group of artists, besides the above-mentioned secretaries Creten and Crespin, were the painters Henri Cassiers, Fernand Khnopff, Alfred Verhaeren and Rodolphe Wytsman, and the sculptors Pieter Braecke, Godefroid Devreese and Egide Rombaux.

25 Scaldis "L'Actualité. L'Art à Bruxelles. L'Exposition au Musée Moderne," *Le Bruxellois*, 26 February 1915.

26 "La tombola du Salon," *Le Quotidien* (4 April 1915). During the exhibition, more than 100 additional works were donated by the artists.

27 Scaldis "L'Actualité. L'Art à Bruxelles. L'Exposition au Musée Moderne," *Le Bruxellois*, 26 February 1915.

28 *Salon des Beaux-Arts 1915. Catalogue*. Brussels: Museum of Modern Art, 1915, 6.

29 "Rapport critiques sur l'action du comité Aide et Protection aux Artistes," *Le Bruxellois*, 12 June 1916.

30 Le Vieil Hibou, "Le Salon des Beaux-Arts," *Le Messager de Bruxelles*, 28 April 1915.

31 Scaldis "L'Actualité. L'Art à Bruxelles. L'Exposition au Musée Moderne," *Le Bruxellois*, 26 February 1915.

32 R. De Man, "Pour les Artistes. Une idée du 'Quotidien'," *Le Quotidien*, 22 November 1914.

33 C. D., "L'Exposition des Beaux-Arts," *Le Messager de Bruxelles*, 3 March 1915: "Ce n'est pas, (...), une mince affaire que de se rendre compte d'un pareil salon où l'on ne peut chercher entre les exposants, aucune communauté de goûts, d'idées ou de tendances. Il y a là des œuvres de trois cents peintres, graveurs, sculpteurs, aquarellistes et aquafortistes, tous méritants à des titres divers; le catalogue ne porte pas moins de 420 numéros, il serait, (...), puéril d'affirmer que ce sont 420 chefs-d'œuvre".

34 *Salon des Beaux-Arts 1915. Catalogue*. Brussels: Museum of Modern Art, 1915. For example: Khnopff offered etchings all of which dated from around the turn of the century (30, nos. 234-238); the etching *L'Escalier Rouge* by Henri Thomas dated from 1912 (41, no. 358) and the drawing offered by Georges Creten bore the date 1914, under which the raffle was mentioned with the date 1915 (17, no. 86, private collection). In general, the works earmarked for the raffle were mostly graphic studies, plaster casts or medallions: in other words, often studio works or multiples.

35 Archives of the Royal Museums of Fine Art of Belgium, File "Musea", Register "Notulen Commissie", D. 49/B 1901-1923, letter 7 August 1915.

36 *Salon d'Automne 1915. Catalogue*. Brussels: Museum of Modern Art, 1915, 5. The committee was enlarged to include the member-artists Louis-Henri Devillez, Alexandre Marcette and Auguste Oleffe.

37 "L'Ouverture du Salon d'Automne," *Le Progrès*, 5 October 1915.

38 "Chronique artistique. Le Salon d'Automne de 1915," *Le Messager de Bruxelles*, 21 October 1915 : "Il y a vraiment bien des œuvres sacrifiées; on a accroché jusqu'à ras de terre, aux vitrines encombrant le passage". The qualitative difference was also denounced: "(...) il y a là 'infiniment plus de mètres de toiles que de toiles de maîtres'.(...) Pourquoi les a-t-on tolérées?".

39 "L'Ouverture du Salon d'Automne," *Le Progrès*, 5 October 1915.

40 Cf. "Le Salon d'Automne," *Le Quotidien*, 7 November 1915; "Le Salon d'automne," *Le Quotidien*, 13 November 1915.

41 "Le Salon d'Automne," *Le Quotidien*, 24 October 1915.

42 "Le dernier Salon," *Le Vingtième Siècle*, 21 January 1915.

43 This can be inferred from "À Anvers," *Le Progrès*, 12 April 1915, in which it is stated that artists requesting it could recover their works. In May, a number of paintings were stolen during opening hours: "Important vol au Salon Triennal," *Le Quotidien*, 15 May 1915. The *Salon* remained open until after the Armistice.

44 "À Bruxelles. L'exposition de 1914," *L'Indépendance belge*, 20 June 1918 : "Un conservateur habile qui ne se lasse pas de vendre et une pléiade d'artistes qui ne se lassent pas de peindre! Ainsi 'explique le renouvellement des cimaises; ainsi le vieux Triennal 1914 garde, malgré les années, les attraits si piquants de l'éternelle jeunesse et de la nouveauté. Et ce ne sont pas les artistes qui s'en plaindront!".

45 Octave Maus, "Lettre de Lausanne. La Peinture en Belgique," *L'Indépendance belge*, 13 June 1918. The committee consisted of Ernest Verlant, Fernand Khnopff, Constant Montald and Alfred Verhaeren.

46 "À Bruxelles. L'exposition de 1914," *L'Indépendance belge*, 20 June 1918.

47 B.-O.-N., "À la Salle Giroux," *Le Messager de Bruxelles,* 16 May 1915 : "*Les artistes ne sont décidément pas du côté des chômeurs de l'heure présente*".

48 In 1915, there were many more art exhibitions of a charitable nature than those discussed here. Another initiative for the benefit of the Fédération Professionnelle des Beaux-Arts was the exhibition held from March to September in the Palais de Glace.

49 "Une exposition d'art à Bruxelles," *L'information de Bruxelles*, 13 December 1914: "(...) permettre aux artistes, (...), de rester en contact non seulement avec ceux qui critiquent ou admirent leurs œuvres, mais encore avec ceux qui les achètent".

50 "À la Salle Studio," *Le Quotidien*, 18 December 1914: "(...) les amateurs inutiles en l'occurrence, ont été éloignés avec soin".

51 "À la Salle Studio," *L'Écho de la presse internationale*, 17 December 1914: "Qu'on s'imagine pas que ce salonnet de guerre – (...) – contienne des 'rossignols' hâtivement rassemblés, des toiles mal léchées..."

52 "Salle Studio," *Le Quotidien*, 9 December 1914; "À la Salle Studio," *La Belgique*, 27 December 1914. With the proceeds, the gallery was able to purchase 27 works, which were raffled on 24 December.

53 "À la Salle Studio," *Le Quotidien*, 1 January 1915.

54 Mario, "Le Salon du Studio," *Le Bruxellois*, 21 March 1915.

55 G. Germain, "Les Salons du 'Studio'," in *Studio-Noël-Salon* (Brussels: I. Brachot, 1916) : s.p.

56 "L'Exposition Nationale," *Le Messager de Bruxelles*, 2 September 1916.

57 Isy Brachot, "Cercle artistique du Studio," *Studio Noël 1917* (Brussels: I. Brachot, 1917): s.p. For 1917, it was a Marcel Hess lithograph; for 1918, a Franz Charlet etching.

58 The list of subscribers was published in the catalogues issued for the exhibitions. For the complete list for 1916 and 1917, cf. "Membres abonnés aux expositions de la Salle 'Studio'," *Studio-Noël-Salon* (Brussels: I. Brachot, 1916) : s.p.; "Membres du Cercle Artistique du Studio," *Studio Noël 1917* (Brussels: I. Brachot, 1917), s.p.

59 "Pour les 'Éprouvés des temps présents'," *La Belgique*, 18 February 1915.

60 "Exposition de la Galerie Giroux," *La Belgique*, 13 May 1915. The exhibition ran from 12 May to 15 June 1915.

61 Jean-François Elslander, *Figures et Souvenirs d'une Belle époque* (Brussels: La Renaissance du Livre, 1944), 53 : "La Galerie Giroux avait fermé ses portes. Qu'y avait-il encore à faire pour les artistes? Nous partions en guerre (...)! Mais quelque temps après je décidai Giroux à rouvrir: j'avais rencontré le peintre [Philippe] Swyncop qui me dit avoir vendu une toile! Pourquoi pas après tout? Timidement on tenta l'aventure. Quelques artistes nous apportèrent des tableaux".

62 "À la Salle Giroux," *Le Messager de Bruxelles*, 16 May 1915.

63 It is noticeable that a particularly large number of paintings produced during the First World War bore a year on them. It is not beyond the bounds of probability that this represented a statement: "painted during the war!".

64 A few examples: Les Indépendants; Le Portrait; Exposition Philibert Cockx, Jos Albert and Jehan Frison; Salon d'Hiver (1916); Alfred Delaunois; Les artistes disparus (1917); Exposition Fernand Khnopff, Victor Creten, Alfred Verhaeren, Londot, Xavier Mellery (1918).

65 "Pour les artistes," *Le Quotidien*, 15 August 1915.

66 "Nos Peintres," *Le Temps Présent*, 34 (1915), 503.

67 Marcel Dekoster, "Salle Studio," *Le Temps Présent*, 33 (1915), 477.

68 "À travers les ventes publiques," *Le Messager de Bruxelles*, 20 December 1916.

69 C. H., "À Travers les Ventes publiques. À la Galerie Giroux – La vente des tableaux Marlier. – À la salle Aeolian – La vente de la collection dépendant de la succession Théo Hannon," *Le Messager de Bruxelles*, 12 January 1917: "Décidément, à voir l'empressement des amateurs qui assistent à ces réunions on dirait que l'achat de tableaux, d'antiquités, d'objets d'art, de bibelots, etc. constitue un bon placement en ce moment".

70 Octave Maus, "Lettre de Lausanne. La peinture en Belgique," *L'Indépendance Belge*, 13 June 1918. Referred to here is the collection of seventeen works of Ensor, which were auctioned on 30 March 1918 by the Galerie Royale in Brussels.

71 Jean-François Elslander, *Figures et Souvenirs d'une Belle époque* (Brussels: La Renaissance du Livre, 1944), 53 : "Puis vint l'époque des nouveaux riches, ceux qu'on appelait alors les 'Barons Zeep', (...)".

72 Marcel Dekoster, "Salle Studio," *Le Temps Présent* 33 (1915), 477 : " 'Les Estampes Japonaises' de Fernand Toussaint font partie de la gamme habituelle du peintre; c'est de la guimauve et c'est bien goûté; [Herman] Richir et F.[irmin]. Baes exposent de la photographie en couleurs. (...). Ces noms et d'autres amèneront le public Salle Studio et y feront vendre des toiles; mais quel encouragement en résultera-t-il pour les jeunes et qui ont du talent?".

73 "Au Studio," *Le Bruxellois*, 15 August 1915: "L'exploitation de la vogue des expositions de peintures bat son plein".

74 Marcel Dekoster, "Salle Studio," *Le Temps Présent* 33 (1915), 477.

75 "Constant Montald inaugure la Galerie Sneyers," *L'Événement illustré* 145 (1917), 840.

76 Charles Debonnets, "Galerie Sneyer: L'Art Décoratif," *Le Messager de Bruxelles*, 26 May 1918.

77 "Le Salon d'automne. Statuaires," *L'Écho de la Presse Internationale*, 13 October 1915.

78 Le Diable Boiteux, "Un plaidoyer," *Le Quotidien*, 9 April 1916: "(...); ils [les peintres] sont les enfants préférés de l'immense majorité du public".

79 Lukas, "*Kunstkroniek*," *Gazet van Brussel*, 19 March 1918: "Tentoonstellingen ontbreken te Brussel niet. Van de Schaarbeeksche tot aan de Naamsche poort, langs de Koninklijke straat is er geen mangel aan dusdanige instellingen".

80 "L'Art et les Boches," *L'Étoile Belge*, 1 December 1918. This exhibition opened on 3 December and showed works by, among others, Amedée Lynen, Gustave Flasschoen, Victor Mignot, Philippe Swyncop, Ramah, Anto Carte, Roméo Dumoulin and Firmin Baes.

« Rencontres interculturelles » et occupation : un nouvel élan pour les transferts culturels belgo-allemands après 1918

CHRISTINA KOTT ET HUBERT ROLAND

La présence de nombreux écrivains, artistes et intellectuels allemands conscrits en Belgique occupée en 1914-1918 a généré une intensité de « rencontres interculturelles », dont la dynamique contradictoire et les modalités ambivalentes et complexes ont été étudiées, notamment dans nos recherches doctorales respectives[1]. À l'initiative de ces rencontres, on trouvait une série d'intellectuels allemands « belgophiles » (écrivains, éditeurs, publicistes, historiens d'art s'intéressant au patrimoine artistique belge, etc.) qui, soit avaient déjà circonscrit la Belgique dans le périmètre de leurs activités depuis le début du XXe siècle, soit profitèrent du regain d'intérêt pour tous les aspects de la « question belge » et des nouvelles opportunités offertes par la politique culturelle allemande sous l'occupation pour développer des projets en germe ou susciter de nouveaux projets.

Au moment de l'accomplissement de nos recherches doctorales entamées dans les années 1990, nous étions en premier lieu soucieux d'une recherche empirique dans des fonds d'archives inexplorés, qui n'avait pas été menée jusque-là. Depuis lors, le domaine des transferts culturels s'est considérablement développé et nous permet à présent une meilleure mise en perspective critique et théorique. C'est ainsi que la situation des écrivains et artistes en Belgique occupée illustre parfaitement une des thèses récemment énoncée par Hans-Jürgen Lüsebrink, selon laquelle les situations de guerre peuvent aussi contribuer à « intensifier les échanges interculturels et produire [...] des effets à la fois inattendus et paradoxalement créateurs de contacts » ; elles sont ainsi à même de susciter « des formes de curiosité et d'intérêt, voire de fascination et d'identification pour le pays voisin »[2] et redéfinissent, par le biais du contact direct et intensif, les paradigmes de perception et de représentation des uns et des autres. Par ailleurs, les historiens Martin Aust et Daniel Schönpflug ont également énoncé le paradoxe apparent selon lequel « c'est justement dans des constellations de rejet fondamental que l'échange entre individus, groupes ou sociétés peut être particulièrement intense et nécessaire »[3].

Sur le plan des continuités, l'objectif de la présente contribution sera d'étudier l'impact de moyen et de long terme de la médiation et des transferts culturels en temps de guerre, de même que leurs répercussions sur la modification des schèmes des identités collectives, et ce dans le sillage de la très active propagande culturelle menée au service de la « Flamenpolitik » en 1914-1918. C'est en effet bien cette dernière qui a stimulé ou relancé l'intérêt pour un « patrimoine » artistique belge ou flamand, sous sa forme matérielle ou immatérielle.

La première partie de cet article prendra pour objet la pérennisation du projet de constitution d'un patrimoine littéraire flamand en 1915-1918 à travers le programme éditorial spécifique de la « *flämische Serie* », conçu à la base par le directeur de la maison d'édition de l'« Insel-Verlag », Anton Kippenberg. La seconde partie portera sur le projet allemand d'inventorisation photographique du patrimoine artistique belge lancé en 1917-1918 et dont la postérité s'avérera encore plus exemplaire, en ceci qu'elle débouchera *in fine* sur une véritable collaboration transnationale entre chercheurs belges et allemands.

La raison patrimoniale affichait pendant la première occupation sa souveraine indépendance par rapport aux contingences politiques immédiates. On sait toutefois qu'elle fut aussi directement soumise aux impératifs de la propagande culturelle, qui mit à sa disposition des moyens dont elle n'eût pas bénéficié autrement. Si une même ambivalence fondamentale continua de caractériser le rapport à la culture de l'autre (notamment lorsque certains médiateurs allemands déjà actifs en 1914-1918 poursuivirent leur travail dans le cadre des structures idéologiques imposées par le pouvoir national-socialiste après 1933), la question des marges d'indépendance des médiateurs allemands dans les modalités du partenariat avec les acteurs culturels belges mérite en tout cas d'être posée.

Le patrimoine littéraire flamand (et belge) comme objet de transfert culturel « à succès » en Allemagne

La « série flamande » de l'« Insel-Verlag » fut portée par un réseau de traducteurs et médiateurs de cet éditeur autour de son directeur Anton Kippenberg, conscrit en Belgique occupée. Même si l'éditeur s'efforça de relativiser la portée politique du projet, on sait que la mutation de Kippenberg en Belgique occupée (comme responsable d'un journal de guerre) et de l'auxiliaire du projet Rudolf Alexander Schröder, poète patriote et amateur de littérature flamande, fut en effet organisée dès le début de l'année 1915 avec le soutien d'une personnalité de l'industrie allemande, Eberhard von Bodenhausen, directeur des ateliers Krupp à Essen[4].

Nonobstant la solution politico-militaire qui prévaudrait immédiatement à l'issue du conflit, les différents protagonistes entendaient œuvrer dès le départ à un rapprochement entre élites culturelles grâce à ce projet qui ambitionnait de tisser des relations intellectuelles entre l'Allemagne et la Flandre. La politique culturelle allemande, « autre canal d'influence indirecte »[5] à côté de la pénétration économique, est en effet mise en œuvre par la « Politische Abteilung » de l'Administration civile allemande sous la direction d'Oscar von der Lancken-Wakenitz et menée en direction des milieux flamands. Le secteur de l'édition du livre, alliant les intérêts économiques et le dialogue culturel, s'avérait pour ce faire tout indiqué. Et le concept d'une collection de poche accessible comme l'« Insel-Bücherei » montrait le souci de popularisation, de même que l'intention de diffuser l'idée d'une entité culturelle flamande, plutôt que belge, auprès d'un large public. La « flämische Reihe » obéit ainsi à une double logique entre 1915 et 1918 : dresser un patrimoine d'œuvres flamandes, essentiellement de langue néerlandaise, depuis la mystique médiévale de Jan van Ruysbroeck et Hadewijch jusqu'au grand classique du XIXe siècle, *De leeuw van Vlaanderen/Der Löwe von Flandern* d'Henri Conscience ; mais aussi permettre à des auteurs contemporains comme Stijn Streuvels et Felix Timmermans de réaliser une percée internationale.

Sur le long terme et depuis une perspective contemporaine, on constate que la Flandre et les Pays-Bas se sont établis comme un partenaire politico-culturel de poids en Allemagne, comme en témoigne le fait qu'au jour d'aujourd'hui cet espace culturel est le seul, avec l'Inde et le Brésil, à avoir pu s'exposer à deux reprises dans le cadre de la Foire du Livre de Francfort (Frankfurter Buchmesse)[6]. Le seul mérite de cette situation ne revient certes ni à la « Flamenpolitik » de la Première Guerre mondiale ni à Anton Kippenberg seul. Car l'intérêt particulier pour la littérature flamande s'inscrit en Allemagne dans une longue durée qui remonte au lendemain de la Révolution belge et il n'a jamais discontinué depuis[7]. Dès le départ, cet intérêt se caractérisa au XIXe siècle par une forte dimension philologique et un intérêt pour le patrimoine populaire, mais aussi linguistique et littéraire, incarné par les figures exemplaires de Jacob Grimm et de Hoffmann von Fallersleben, dont la démarche du récolement de sources à la fois orales et écrites se situait dans une tradition typiquement romantique[8]. Dès le départ également, une motivation d'ordre idéologique fut clairement perceptible chez les savants et autres voyageurs allemands qui entendaient aider le « petit frère germanique » à se constituer ses propres bases culturelles à l'aide du modèle allemand, dans la perspective de l'émanciper des influences françaises qui déterminaient, comme on le sait, les structures de la société belge au XIXe siècle. Dans le contexte du nouvel ordre européen d'après 1815, la figure nationaliste emblématique d'Ernst Moritz Arndt agita en effet le spectre de l'impérialisme français, lorsqu'il publia en 1834 une brochure sur la Belgique[9], qui fit d'ailleurs l'objet d'une réédition en 1918[10]. Sans être une adepte d'un tel militantisme, l'intellectuelle Luise von Ploennies (1803-1872), qui voyagea en Belgique et publia ses souvenirs en 1845, se considérait comme une émissaire de la *Germania*, envoyée pour chérir et libérer un membre de la famille, à savoir le peuple flamand, étouffé par la « belle-mère française »[11]. Son intérêt pour la Belgique et le mouvement flamand devint une histoire de famille : sa fille Maria rassembla plus tard une anthologie de légendes belges, *Die Sagen Belgiens* (Verlag von F.S. Eisen) ; elle avait épousé le germaniste Johann Wilhelm Wolf (1817-1855), auteur pour sa part d'une anthologie de *Niederländische Sagen* (Leipzig, Brockhaus, 1843) dédiée à l'historien national Leopold von Ranke[12].

Que la littérature flamande et néerlandaise soit donc devenue l'objet d'un transfert culturel « à succès » est aujourd'hui indéniable. Au mois d'octobre 2016, les bulletins d'information mensuels de la Frankfurter Buchmesse évoquaient le chiffre de 360 nouvelles traductions (en ce compris) les rééditions, dont 309 de nature proprement littéraire[13]. La question du patrimoine historico-littéraire figure toujours au centre de cet intérêt. Certains éditeurs, comme Severus, se concentrent actuellement sur la réédition d'œuvres canoniques d'histoire de la littérature flamande et néerlandaise. Ils rééditent ou adaptent des traductions parues après 1900, voire pendant la Première Guerre mondiale, comme la très populaire épopée flamande d'Henri Conscience *De leeuw van Vlaanderen/Le lion des Flandres* (1838), traduite en 1916 par Severin Rüttgers pour l' « Insel-Verlag ». Si cette dernière ne fut à l'époque éditée qu'à 10 000 exemplaires, elle dut aussi souffrir de la concurrence d'une autre traduction, réalisée par Walter van der Bleek – le même qui avait réédité l'ouvrage d'Arndt en 1918[14] – et parue la même année chez l'éditeur berlinois Borngräber. L'orientation politique de ce dernier ouvrage, dédié au gouverneur général de Belgique occupée Moritz Freiherr von Bissing, mena à quelques retouches qui favorisèrent une lecture idéologique du texte[15].

On le constate ainsi à la lecture des travaux spécialisés qui continuent de se pencher sur l'histoire des traductions de langue flamande et néerlandaise en Allemagne, la matière abonde et un regard d'ensemble sur ces continuités intellectuelles fait encore défaut. Il serait seul à même de pouvoir évaluer la dimension clairement idéologique de certains projets (mais pas nécessairement des autres), de comparer et contraster les éditeurs, traducteurs et autres agents de médiation, notamment pendant les périodes de guerre et de conflit, qui ont manifestement donné des impulsions décisives au dialogue culturel germano-flamand et germano-belge. Ces moments particuliers – et tout particulièrement la première occupation allemande en Belgique – ont effectivement généré l'opportunité d'une concentration des instances médiatrices de diffusion : acteurs privés et indépendants (traducteurs, journalistes, éditeurs), acteurs institutionnels (« Kulturpropaganda »), instances de médiation (presse et revue). Toute une série d'acteurs privés, notamment des traducteurs indépendants, ont ainsi pu valoriser leur travail de médiation à l'intérieur d'une fonction officielle et multiplier les projets en fonction de moyens financiers conjoncturels plus conséquents. De par la qualité des relations tissées avec les auteurs, des perspectives de collaboration à moyen terme sont nées et ont continué de porter leurs fruits jusqu'à la Seconde Guerre mondiale, et même, comme on l'a vu, jusqu'à aujourd'hui.

La question de l'instrumentalisation politique et idéologique s'est posée de manière plus acerbe sous le national-socialisme, lorsque Kippenberg poursuivit et élargit son programme de littérature flamande dans les années 1930 et 1940. Le fait qu'Insel poursuivit ses activités sous le système nazi suscita la colère des milieux de l'exil antifasciste, représentés en Belgique par le journaliste néerlandais Nico Rost. Commentant le fait que Kippenberg et Schröder représentaient l'Allemagne officielle lors d'un festival des Lettres flamandes en Belgique en 1937, celui-ci écrivit dans la revue belge *Combat* :

> « Schröder et Kippenberg ont séjourné longtemps en Belgique pendant la guerre et ont tâché de faire connaître en Allemagne la littérature flamande moderne. Dans quel dessein ? Voulaient-ils par ces traductions effacer toutes les cruautés des Allemands pendant la guerre en Belgique et créer l'illusion d'une Allemagne qui était toujours le pays « der Dichter und Denker » ? Maintenant, sous Hitler, le même phénomène se présente. N'avez-vous pas remarqué, combien de romans flamands modernes, soit de Streuvels, de Teirlinck, de Roelants, de Pillecyn et de Walschap, ont été traduits en allemand au cours des dernières années ? [...] Toutes ces œuvres peuvent paraître en Allemagne parce que leur caractère n'est pas en contradiction avec l'idéologie du fascisme et beaucoup d'entre elles correspondent aux postulats de la Blubo de Hitler »[16].

À y regarder toutefois de plus près, la position de Kippenberg sous le Troisième Reich fut aussi ambivalente qu'elle l'était déjà pendant la première occupation allemande. Certes, l'éditeur avait intériorisé la contrainte de la « mise au pas » (« Gleichschaltung ») et il ne publia pas d'auteurs fondamentalement indésirables aux yeux du régime[17]. Il continua avec constance d'éditer ses auteurs flamands de prédilection, véhiculant avec efficacité cette vision traditionnelle de la Flandre qui avait trouvé son public : Stijn Streuvels et Felix Timmermans, dont l'édition de *Pallieter* atteignit 217 000 exemplaires en 1944 ; le nouveau venu Ernest Claes, dont le succès commercial fut également non négligeable. Mais il est aussi intéressant de constater que la promotion des auteurs belges et « flamands de langue française » continua de bénéficier du transfert mis en place durant la « Flamenpolitik », ce qui fait que l'autonomie culturelle du transfert dépassa en réalité la logique directe de son instrumentalisation politique. Insel n'a ainsi jamais cessé de faire la promotion de son auteur belge fétiche d'avant 1914, Émile Verhaeren, là où ce dernier avait été mis à l'index de par son comportement virulemment anti-allemand dès les premiers jours du conflit et jusqu'à sa mort accidentelle à l'automne 1916. Kippenberg s'était permis de faire paraître par la suite en 1917 (et en marge de la « série flamande ») la traduction des *Blés Mouvants* du poète belge, que le jeune écrivain expressionniste allemand Paul Zech avait réalisée à la veille de la guerre[18]. Dès les lendemains de la guerre, il reprenait encore des récits de Verhaeren (*Fünf Erzählungen*) dans une traduction de Friderike Maria Zweig, puis publiait en 1923 la monographie que Verhaeren avait consacrée à Rembrandt et qui fut tirée à 45 000 exemplaires. (ill. 8.1)

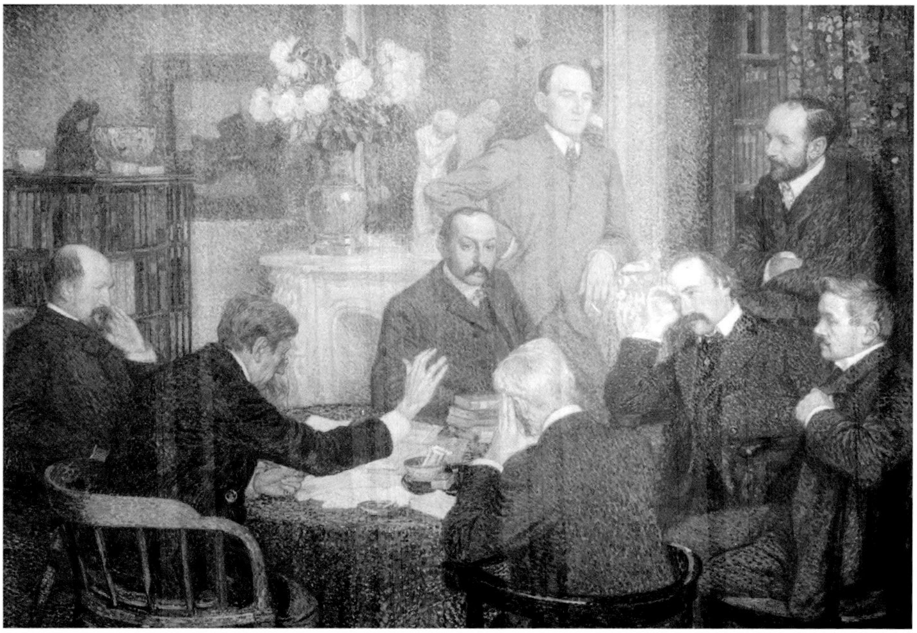

8.1. *La lecture d'Emile Verhaeren*. Reproduction photographique en n/b du célèbre tableau de Théo van Rhysselberghe (1903, Musée des Beaux-Arts de Gand) dans le cadre de l'inventaire photographique allemand, 1917-1918, KIK-IRPA, Bruxelles (Belgique), cliché B018257.

Jusque et y compris sous le Troisième Reich, des auteurs flamands francophones continuèrent donc de bénéficier de la promotion de la littérature flamande en Allemagne, ceci en totale contradiction avec les principes idéologiques de la « Flamenpolitik », dont l'objectif consistait pourtant à émanciper la Flandre des schèmes du modèle culturel français. Certes la fortune du *Till Eulenspiegel* de Charles De Coster dans son habit allemand se poursuivit en toute autonomie sous le couvert du roman historique. Mais il y eut aussi l'émergence de la romancière anversoise contemporaine Marie Gevers, dont on compte sept traductions chez plusieurs éditeurs entre 1935 et 1943. Son ouvrage *Heideglöcklein oder Das Glück von Sankt Anton*, publié en 1938 à Regensburg, le fut même avec des illustrations de Felix Timmermans[19].

La collaboration entre Gevers et Timmermans scellait par ailleurs une dimension visuelle et picturale essentielle quand il est question de la transmission d'un patrimoine culturel belge et flamand. Aujourd'hui encore, la « Belgique picturale » fait toujours partie intégrante de la reconnaissance et du succès de son transfert ; on peut même aller jusqu'à dire que, vu d'Allemagne, il s'est agi d'une des conditions nécessaires de sa réalisation depuis au moins la monographie que Wilhelm Hausenstein, éditeur de la revue *Der Belfried* en Belgique occupée, avait consacrée à « Bruegel le Belge »[20].

De l'inventorisation photographique belge de 14-18 aux clichés allemands de l'IRPA, un transfert culturel du temps de guerre ?

À sa création en 1957, l'Institut royal du patrimoine artistique à Bruxelles héritait d'une collection de plus de 10 000 plaques de négatifs sur verre, issue d'un inventaire photographique du patrimoine artistique belge entrepris pendant l'occupation de la Première Guerre mondiale par une trentaine d'historiens de l'art, d'architectes et de photographes allemands. Intégrée et dispersée dans la photothèque de l'Institut, cette collection n'avait pas suscité l'intérêt des chercheurs jusqu'à tout récemment, lorsqu'elle a bénéficié d'un projet de recherche financé dans le cadre des commémorations de 14-18[21]. La question qui nous occupera dans cette seconde partie sera la suivante : peut-on considérer cet inventaire photographique du patrimoine artistique belge par des historiens de l'art allemands, ainsi que ses résultats, « les clichés allemands » de l'IRPA, comme les produits d'un transfert culturel transnational au sein de l'histoire de la conservation du patrimoine, entre le XIXe et le XXIe siècle ?

De prime abord, et vu sur le court terme, l'inventaire photographique allemand, à mi-chemin entre mesure de politique culturelle officielle et projet scientifique, ressemble à une entreprise expansionniste s'inscrivant dans la politique d'annexion du Gouvernement général impérial allemand (« Kaiserliches Deutsches Generalgouvernement Belgien »). Les liens de l'inventaire photographique avec la « Flamenpolitik » sont alors étroits : Erwin Hensler (1882-1935), le responsable du projet (« Geschäftsführer ») au sein de l'administration d'occupation, est membre de la section II B du Gouvernement général, chargée non seulement de la surveillance de la presse et de la publication de textes de propagande, mais aussi de la coordination avec la « Politische Abteilung » qui, quant à elle, fait partie de la « Zivilverwaltung ». Les principaux acteurs du volet culturel de la « Flamenpolitik » au sein de la « Politische Abteilung », l'archiviste Pius Dirr (1875–1943) et le sculpteur Hans Albrecht von Harrach (1873-1963), sont également les interlocuteurs de l'historien de l'art Julius Baum (1882-1959), pendant qu'il occupe un poste à la section II B entre fin 1914 et juin 1915, date à laquelle il est renvoyé en Allemagne pour avoir divulgué des informations considérées comme confidentielles[22]. Dans le cadre de ses activités de propagande, Baum donne des conférences au sujet du patrimoine artistique belge et surtout bruxellois, publie des brochures et guide des personnalités allemandes de haut rang à travers la ville[23]. Ce même Baum deviendra, fin décembre 1916, l'initiateur de l'inventaire photographique, qu'il justifie entre autres en invoquant l'appartenance de la Belgique actuelle « aux anciens territoires allemands »[24]. En mai 1918, au début de la seconde campagne photographique, Paul Clemen, conservateur du patrimoine de Rhénanie et l'organisateur du projet, affirme que « le mouvement flamand sur lequel nous nous appuyons a bien sûr une incidence très forte sur notre travail. Ce sont surtout les monuments flamands que nous voulons mettre en évidence »[25].

En termes de quantité, le fonds dispose en effet d'un nombre supérieur de clichés pris dans les régions flamandes. Or, malgré l'inscription évidente du projet dans la « Flamenpolitik », un examen plus approfondi confirme l'idée que l'inventaire photographique est loin d'être une simple arme politique pour attirer la sympathie des milieux flamands, voire flamingants. Premièrement, il s'agit en effet d'un projet scientifique qui s'appuie sur le concept d'une présupposée existence de liens ancestraux germano-belges, qui se seraient traduits également dans les styles et les productions artistiques ainsi que dans leur diffusion. Ce concept se basait d'un côté sur des critères linguistiques et raciaux (parenté entre la langue flamande et le bas allemand, etc.) et de l'autre sur des liens historiques fondés sur l'existence d'entités politiques ou religieuses placées sous l'égide « germanique ». Celles-ci, à l'instar de la principauté épiscopale de Liège, faisant partie du Saint-Empire romain germanique, dépassaient les frontières étatiques existantes en 1914. À ce titre, il est intéressant de constater que l'inventaire devait initialement se limiter notamment à ces régions limitrophes, en l'occurrence wallonnes. Deuxièmement, il s'agit d'un projet de « pénétration scientifique à long terme », basé sur une expertise scientifique justifiée par une suprématie allemande dans les domaines nécessaires à la réalisation d'un inventaire photographique : l'histoire de l'art et de l'architecture, l'inventorisation patrimoniale et la photographie documentaire d'œuvres d'art et de monuments. Par ces deux ancrages, le projet d'inventaire s'inscrit dans une volonté de conquérir la sympathie des milieux cultivés du pays occupé, donc plutôt francophones, mais pas exclusivement, et les milieux scientifiques non seulement belges, mais internationaux, afin de se procurer, au final, une longueur d'avance dans la compétition scientifique internationale. Il convient de rappeler qu'avant la guerre, la discipline de l'histoire de l'art s'était organisée à l'échelle internationale – essentiellement européenne – et qu'elle était dominée par les représentants de langue allemande (autrichiens et allemands). Les accusations de barbarie et de vandalisme, prononcées à l'encontre de toute la nation allemande suite aux destructions patrimoniales de Louvain et de Reims perpétrées par ses armées, avaient mis en cause cette suprématie, qu'il s'agit en quelque sorte de reconquérir par le biais de ces projets scientifiques.

Mais à y regarder de plus près, et sur le long terme, l'inventaire photographique s'avère être le produit d'un nœud de communications transnationales et transculturelles, à plusieurs échelles : intellectuelle, artistique, personnelle, économique, politique, etc.

Premièrement, comme tout projet mettant en jeu les représentants de plusieurs nations ou ethnies, il se nourrit de perceptions de l'autre et de soi-même, qu'elles soient antérieures ou contemporaines au conflit : les Allemands sont vus comme 'barbares', 'vandales', ou comme des individus arrogants, pédants, militaristes tandis que les Belges sont perçus comme indisciplinés, incompétents, mal-organisés, et faibles politiquement. Deuxièmement, le projet d'inventaire photographique bénéficie de la présence de médiateurs transnationaux, à l'instar de l'archéologue Gerhard Bersu (1889-1964), ancien responsable d'un « Kunstreferat » au sein de la « Zivilverwaltung » à Bruxelles entre 1916 et 1918, et personnage clé des négociations germano-belges après 1918 en tant que délégué allemand pour les questions de restitution culturelle. Bersu coopère avec Eugène van Overloop (1847-1926), directeur du musée du Cinquantenaire et son successeur Jean Capart (1877-1947), le premier étant convaincu en 1914 qu'une coopération officieuse entre « Fachleute » (experts) des deux camps n'était pas inconciliable avec une attitude patriotique pendant l'occupation. Troisièmement, les sources documentaires sur lesquelles s'appuient les experts allemands, qui possèdent une bonne connaissance du paysage artistique belge ou d'une partie de celui-ci, lors de la préparation du projet et de son programme, sont d'origine essentiellement belge. L'étude de ces sources, leur translation vers le contexte culturel allemand et leur intégration dans le corpus de recherche des historiens de l'art germanophones constituent également des processus de transferts et de circulations du savoir.

Une fois sur place, dans le pays occupé, le contact direct avec d'un côté les objets patrimoniaux, et de l'autre, les responsables belges, pouvait soit infirmer soit confirmer ces connaissances ainsi que les images de l'autre et de soi-même chez les occupants. Du côté des occupés, cette confrontation pouvait provoquer différents processus de transfert ou d'apprentissage, pour reprendre les termes forgés par Aust et Schönpflug : de l'acculturation en passant par « l'apprentissage sectoriel » aux « transferts négatifs » (ou transfert par inversion)[26]. Dans les milieux de l'histoire de l'art et de la conservation du patrimoine, c'est surtout le concept « d'apprentissage sectoriel » qui semble adapté, à savoir « lorsque des acteurs historiques tout en rejetant l'idéologie sous-tendant une action de l'autre camp pouvaient témoigner de l'admiration pour des réalisations techniques, économiques ou artistiques de ce même camp ennemi »[27]. C'est le cas du côté belge : d'une part on rejette l'occupation et l'idée d'hégémonie culturelle allemande, de l'autre on admire les réalisations techniques de l'ennemi, et notamment le résultat de l'inventaire photographique allemand (ill. 8.2 et 8.3).

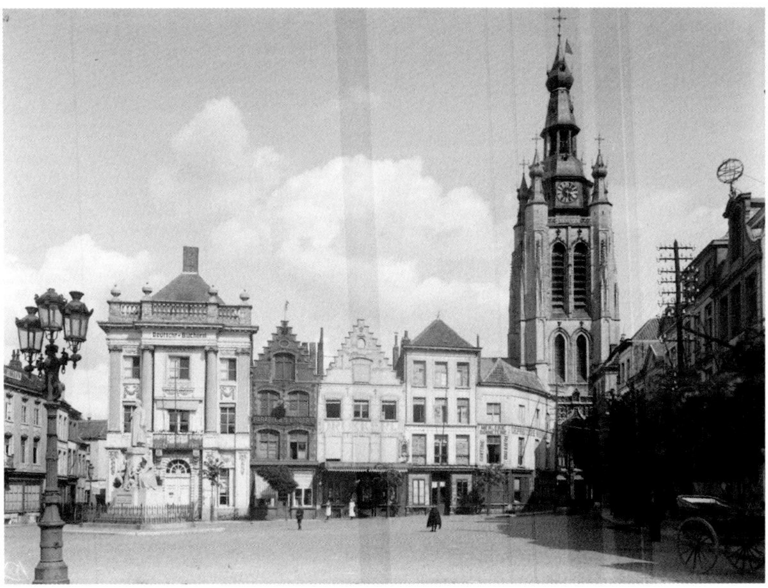

8.2. La Grand Place de Courtrai avec la porte Saint-Martin. A gauche, la « Deutsche Bücherei », une bibliothèque destinée aux militaires allemands. Cliché pris dans le cadre de l'inventaire photographique allemand, 1917-1918, KIK-IRPA, Bruxelles (Belgique), cliché B017649.

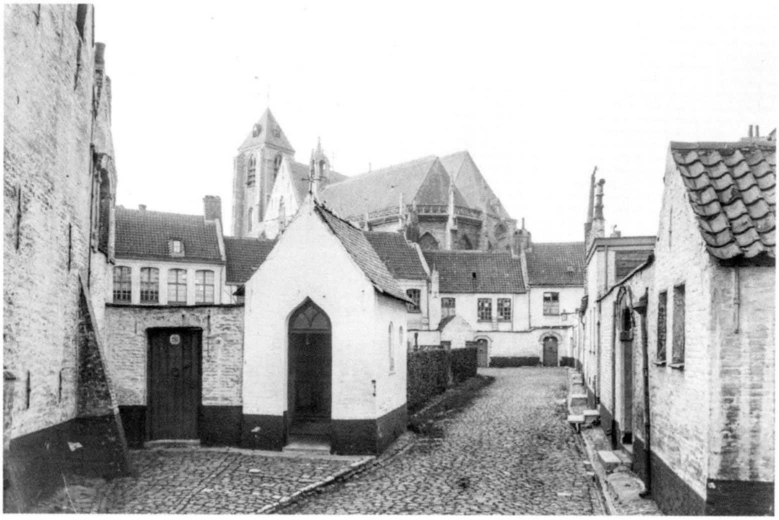

8.3. La Chapelle Notre-Dame-aux-Neiges (Onze-Lieve-Vrouw-ter-Sneeuw) au béguinage Sainte-Élisabeth de Courtrai (Begijnhof Sint-Elisabeth). Cliché pris dans le cadre de l'inventaire photographique allemand, 1917-1918, KIK-IRPA, Bruxelles (Belgique), cliché B017649.

Ces deux attitudes furent cependant dissociées dans le temps : pendant l'occupation, les autorités belges manifestent, pour la plupart, des réticences, voire des résistances vis-à-vis de l'inventaire photographique et de ses acteurs, comme le confirme cette remarque de Paul Clemen : « ... il faut prendre contact avec les autorités belges qui sont bien sûr assez réticentes et tout le monde doit toujours être caressé dans le sens du poil car il y en a toujours un qui est grippé[28]. » Après l'Armistice et le retrait des troupes d'occupation, le rapatriement de l'inventaire photographique en Allemagne est avant tout ressenti comme un vol et une perte pour la Belgique. Puis, l'admiration pour les résultats, mais aussi la volonté de « récupérer » ce qui est considéré comme bien national belge, vont constituer les motivations principales, côté belge, d'entamer des négociations avec les Allemands. En effet, dès 1921-1922, Eugène van Overloop entreprend des démarches en vue du rachat de l'inventaire photographique allemand. En 1924, l'affaire piétine, ce qui amène van Overloop à vanter auprès du ministre des Sciences et de Arts les mérites du « service photographique » allemand sous la direction du professeur Paul Clemen, en faisant référence à la « superbe publication » de ce dernier, « Die Kunstdenkmäler der Rheinprovinz », selon van Overloop le « type le plus parfait des inventaires régionaux que suivent présentement les Hollandais et que notre Commission Royale des Monuments de Belgique se propose d'imiter, à son tour[29]. » Il en vient ensuite aux prouesses techniques :

> « Disposant des appareils les plus perfectionnés, en même temps que d'opérateurs de premier ordre, l'entreprise produisit, en grande quantité, les superbes clichés [...] », donc en somme des « documents précieux, judicieusement choisis et parfaitement exécutés [...] »[30]

dont il a eu l'honneur de soumettre un échantillon au ministre. Cependant, la reprise des clichés allemands ne se justifie pas uniquement par leur qualité extraordinaire, mais aussi par leur signification nationale : « Il s'agissait des résultats d'une opération d'ordre national, que les Allemands avaient réalisés en nos lieu et place [...] » et « il y avait donc quelque chose de honteux pour notre sentiment national à ne pas épuiser tous les moyens de faire nôtre ce travail de l'envahisseur et de lui reprendre ce portrait emporté de notre patrie »[31].

Cependant, dans l'idée de pouvoir un jour renouer les contacts avec les experts allemands, donc de reconstituer les liens interrompus par la guerre, les Belges renoncent à reprendre les plaques photographiques par la force en Rhénanie occupée – action entre autres rendue impossible du fait de leur dispersion au début des années vingt – ou d'exiger la « restitution » de la collection en vertu de l'article 238 du traité de Versailles. Cette attitude loyale respectant l'esprit scientifique rencontre la plus haute estime du côté allemand, comme l'exprimera Paul Clemen dans une lettre de septembre 1940, au moment où il est question de reprendre à nouveau l'inventaire photographique en Belgique envahie, dans le double sens du terme[32]. Selon Clemen, la saisie de la collection se justifiait d'autant moins en 1940 que le transfert des plaques photographiques en tant qu'objets vers la Belgique s'était fait sur la base du volontariat et de rapports de loyauté entre experts de part et d'autre, car « du point de vue scientifique, il ne fait aucun doute que le dépôt et la gestion des plaques à Bruxelles semblent être la bonne solution et que c'est l'endroit où il y a la possibilité pour la communauté scientifique internationale d'exploiter ces fonds de plaques dans le sens où nous l'avions envisagé lors de la fondation de notre organisation. »[33] Le rachat de l'inventaire photographique par les Musées royaux d'art et d'histoire se déroule en deux étapes dans le cadre du paiement des réparations et sous l'égide de la Commission des réparations. Le premier lot constitué des 540 plaques photogrammétriques est cédé en 1925, le deuxième fort de 10 011 plaques photographiques d'autres formats suivra en 1927. Dès lors, la « Belgische Inventarisation » ou « Inventarisation der belgischen Kunstdenkmäler » devient « la Collection allemande » et plus tard « les clichés allemands ».

Mais le transfert ne s'achève pas au passage matériel des plaques photographiques d'un pays, d'une institution à l'autre. Tout au contraire, car il ne fait que commencer, avec la diffusion, la réception et la fortune critique des « clichés allemands » en

Belgique et dans le monde. Tout d'abord en Allemagne même, car en 1923, Paul Clemen et ses anciens collaborateurs publient comme résultats de leurs travaux en Belgique occupée les deux volumes *Belgische Kunstdenkmäler*.[34] Cette publication, prévue en réalité dès la conception de l'inventaire photographique, témoigne de la reprise de l'autonomie scientifique par rapport au politique, dont l'influence subsiste néanmoins dans la préface par Paul Clemen et dans le soutien financier apporté par le ministère allemand de l'Intérieur. Au niveau scientifique, ces volumes incarnent la volonté de la communauté scientifique allemande de maintenir le pouvoir d'interprétation sur les sources belges, et ce à l'échelle internationale.

En effet, plusieurs instituts et bibliothèques spécialisés en histoire de l'art s'intéressent à la collection et font l'acquisition d'un nombre important de clichés en amont, mais aussi en aval de l'achat des plaques photographiques par la Belgique : le Victoria and Albert Museum à Londres, la Kunstbibliothek à Berlin, la Staatsbibliothek de Bavière à Munich, le professeur Arthur Kingsley Porter ainsi que le Fogg Art Museum à l'université Harvard – mais aussi le musée de Gand qui préfère commander des clichés à Bonn plutôt qu'au musée du Cinquantenaire[35] ! À cela, il faut ajouter les tirages restés à l'université de Bonn, et ceux cédés dans le cadre des réparations de guerre à l'Université de Louvain. Intégrés dans les archives photographiques de quelques-unes des plus grandes institutions de recherche en histoire de l'art, les « clichés allemands » contribuent à diffuser la vision allemande du patrimoine belge à l'échelle internationale. Mais en même temps, la communauté scientifique et les institutions du patrimoine et de l'histoire de l'art en Belgique bénéficient non seulement des réseaux internationaux créés et alimentés par les Allemands – grâce aux relations entre experts existant dans l'avant-guerre – mais aussi de la grande qualité esthétique et technique des prises de vue. En 1940-44, les autorités d'occupation renoncent au final à la saisie des « clichés allemands », tout en obtenant l'autorisation de dupliquer une partie des négatifs de 1917-18 pour le compte des archives photographiques de Marburg (Bildarchiv Foto Marburg) qui possèdent de ce fait également une partie du fonds. L'inventaire photographique national, quant à lui, est repris par le Service photographique au musée du Cinquantenaire sous la direction de Paul Coremans entre 1940 et 1945[36]. Après 1945, les « clichés allemands » sont consultables, mais ils ne sont ni étudiés ni mis en valeur jusque dans les années 2000 lorsque débutent leur digitalisation et leur mise en ligne[37]. Numérisés en haute définition, ils livrent désormais de précieuses informations à la fois sur le patrimoine artistique belge et sur la vie sous l'occupation en 14-18.

Conclusion

Si l'on analyse donc le projet de l'inventaire photographique sur le court terme, et dans le cadre étroit des circonstances politiques de sa création, les « clichés allemands » demeurent le résultat d'une entreprise nationaliste et expansionniste. Si toutefois l'on regarde sur le long terme, et dans un cadre plus vaste, celui de l'institution de la conservation du patrimoine et des relations germano-belges au XXe siècle, on peut très clairement affirmer qu'il s'agit là du produit d'un transfert transnational, et ce avec des ramifications vers d'autres espaces géographiques ainsi que des répercussions jusqu'à nos jours. Un même constat vaut pour la mise en valeur du patrimoine littéraire flamand. L'opération du transfert débouche ici aussi sur un surcroît de reconnaissance internationale, les traductions allemandes de littérature belge et flamande ayant régulièrement servi de pivot vers l'Europe de l'Est.

Le fait qu'une telle « mise en réseau » aux répercussions de long terme fut favorisée au départ dans le cadre d'une occupation militaire pose des questions d'ordre éthique, qui débordent du cadre de cette contribution, mais l'analyse des retombées positives du transfert né en temps de guerre ne doit pas être comprise comme une forme de « normalisation » d'une situation d'occupation par la force, illégitime au regard du droit international.

Notes

1 Christina Kott, *Préserver l'art de l'ennemi ? Le patrimoine artistique en Belgique et en France occupées, 1914-1918* (Bruxelles : Peter Lang P.I.E., 2006) ; Hubert Roland, *Die deutsche literarische « Kriegskolonie » in Belgien 1914-1918. Beitrag zur Geschichte der deutsch-belgischen Literaturbeziehungen 1900-1920* (Bern : Peter Lang, 1999); traduction française revue et augmentée par l'auteur: *La 'colonie' littéraire belgo-allemande 1914-1918* (Bruxelles : Archives et Musée de la Littérature, 2003).

2 Hans-Jürgen Lüsebrink dans l'introduction au dossier *Europa zwischen Text und Ort – L'Europe entre Texte et Lieu/ Interkulturalität in Kriegszeiten (1914-1954) – Interculturalités en temps de guerre (1914-1954)*, éd. Valérie Deshoulières, H.-J. Lüsebrink & Christoph Vatter = *Jahrbuch des Frankreichzentrums der Universität des Saarlandes* (2013), Bd. 12. (Bielefeld: transcript Verlag, 2013), 100-101 et 103.

3 Martin Aust et Daniel Schönpflug, « Einführende Überlegungen zu einer Interpretationsfigur der Geschichte Europas im 19. und 20. Jahrhundert » : in *Vom Gegner lernen. Feindschaften und Kulturtransfers im Europa des 19. und 20. Jahrhunderts,* éd. Martin Aust et Daniel Schönpflug (Francfort/ New York: Campus, 2007), 7.

4 Concernant tous les détails de « l'entreprise flamande » de l' Insel-*Verlag*, cf. Roland : *La 'Colonie' littéraire*
allemande en Belgique 1914-1918, 130ff.

5 Cf. l'introduction de Michael Amara et Hubert Roland à l'édition critique de *Gouverner en Belgique occupée. Oscar von der Lancken-Wakenitz – Rapports d'activité 1915-1918* (Bruxelles : P.I.E.-Peter Lang, 2004), 20.

6 La tradition des « pays hôtes » de la « Buchmesse » s'est ouverte avec l'Inde en 1986. La littérature de Flandre et des Pays-Bas a été accueillie en 1993 et en 2016. À noter encore qu'à l'exception des « Pays catalans » en 2007, la Flandre est la seule entité sous-étatique qui a pu s'exposer à Francfort.

7 Cf. Herbert Van Uffelen, *Moderne niederländische Literatur im deutschen Sprachraum 1830-1990* (Münster: Zentrum für Niederlande-Studien, 1993).

8 Cf. Marcel De Smedt, « Philologische Kontakte zwischen Deutschland und Flandern in der ersten Hälfte des 19. Jahrhunderts », in *Deutschlandbilder in Belgien 1830-1940,* éd. Hubert Roland, Marnix Beyen, Greet Draye (Münster: Waxmann, 2011), 71-91.

9 Ernst Moritz Arndt, *Belgien und was daran hängt* (Leipzig, Weidmann'sche Buchhandlung, 1834).

10 Ernst Moritz Arndt, *Um Flandern und Brabant. Die Frage über die Niederlande und die Rheinlande, Belgien und was daran hängt*. Im Auftrage d. Freiwilligen Aufklärungskorps zur See u. zur Luft, Reichsverband E.V. von 1913, herausgegeben von K.H.L. Walter van der Bleek, mit einer Erklärung d. Bevollmächtigten d. Rates von Flandern Achilles Brijs-Schouppe (Berlin: Boll und Pickardt, 1918). Cité d'après Jan Ceuppens, « De Germaanse leeuw. Consciences *Leeuw van Vlaenderen* als inzet van Duits-Vlaamse betrekkingen 1840-1918 », in *Verslagen & Mededelingen van de Koninklijke Akademie voor Nederlandse Taal- en Letterkunde*, vol. 123, n° 2-3 (2013), 233-247.

11 « [I]ch wurde als die Gesandtin betrachtet, welche die Germania ihrer lange unter dem Druck der französischen Stiefmutter seufzenden Schwester hinüberschickte, um ihr die Versicherung ihrer nicht erloschenen Liebe zu bringen »: Luise von Ploennies, *Reise-Erinnerungen aus Belgien* (Berlin: Verlag von Duncker & Humblot, 1845), VII-VIII.

12 Cf. également Hubert Roland, « Construction identitaire et regard de l'autre. Récits de voyage allemands et français en Belgique 1830-1850 », dans Stéphanie Vanasten & Matthieu Sergier (eds.), *Literaire* belgitude *littéraire.* Bruggen en beelden. *Vues du Nord. Hommage aan Sonja Vanderlinden* (Presses Universitaires de Louvain, 2011), 133-152.

13 Heinz Eickmans, « Ehrengast der Frankfurter Buchmesse 2016. Flandern und die Niederlande: Was sie teilen und was sie teilt », in *literaturkritik.de*, Nr. 10, Oktober 2016: http://literaturkritik.de/id/22567 (consulté le 29.10.2017).

14 Cf. note 10.

15 Ceuppens, *op. cit.*, 244-246.

16 Nico Rost, « À propos du festival des Lettres flamandes », in *Combat*, 4 décembre 1937. L'expression *Blubo* se réfère à l'esthétique nazie du *Blut und Boden*.

17 Heinz Sarkowski, *Der Insel-Verlag 1899-1999. Eingeleitet von Siegfried Unseld* (Frankfurt/M.-Leipzig: Insel, 1999), 297ff. On lit par exemple que « Kippenberg se comporta vis-à-vis des autorités du nouveau gouvernement de manière extrêmement prudente et, vue de l'extérieur, loyale. Il évita tout ce qui aurait pu jeter de l'ombre sur la maison d'édition », 298.

18 Cf. Hubert Roland, « Un Verhaeren expressionniste. La traduction allemande des *Blés mouvants* (*Die wogende Saat*, 1914/1917) par Paul Zech », dans *Verhaeren en son temps*. Dossier dirigé par Paul Aron et Jean-Pierre Bertrand = n°50-51/2016 de *Textyles. Revue des lettres belges de langue française*, 89-102.

19 Julie Crombois a consacré un article à la réception allemande de Marie Gevers, qui paraîtra à l'automne 1918 dans le *Journal of Dutch Literature*.

20 Wilhelm Hausenstein, *Der Bauern-Bruegel. Mit einem Vorwort zur neuen Ausgabe über Bruegel den Belgier. Mit sechsundsechzig Abbildungen nach Gemälden, Kupferstichen und Zeichnungen* (München: Piper Verlag, 1916).

21 Ce projet de recherche scientifique est mené par l'Institut royal du Patrimoine artistique (IRPA) à l'initiative de la Chancellerie du Premier ministre, dans le cadre de la commémoration de la Première Guerre mondiale en Belgique avec le soutien de la Loterie Nationale et de BELSPO (Politique

scientifique fédérale). Il regroupe expositions, campagnes de digitalisation et de rephotographie ainsi que des publications grand public et scientifiques, voir https://picturingbelgium14-18.com/. Les clichés peuvent être consultés sur le portail balat : balat.kikirpa.be/tools/14-18/.

22 Archives privées Julius Baum (Eva Baum, Stuttgart Degerloch), manuscrit « Adieu Bruxelles », mai-juin 1915. Au sujet de Julius Baum, cf. Myrah Adams, *Julius Baum. Museumsdirektor zwischen Tradition und Moderne* (Ulmer Museum: Ulm, 2005) ; Ulrike Wendland, *Biographisches Handbuch deutschsprachiger Kunsthistoriker im Exil. Leben und Werk der unter dem Nationalsozialismus verfolgten und vertriebenen Wissenschaftler* (München: Saur, 1999), Vol. 1, 27–31.

23 Toute une littérature de popularisation de l'art en Belgique en direction du public germanophone voit ainsi le jour ; rien que pour l'année 1915 : Eugen Lüthgen, *Belgische Baudenkmäler* (Leipzig: Insel-Verlag, 1915); Julius Baum, *Brüssel als Kunststätte* (Strasbourg : Heitz, 1915) ; Richard Graul, *Alt-Flandern. Brabant, Artois, Hennegau, Lüttich, Namur*, (Dachau/Munich : Roland-Verlag, 1915).

24 Julius Baum à Louis Laiblin, le 11 mars 1917 (*Stadtarchiv Pfullingen*, Archives privées Laiblin, n° 70). Ce fut grâce au don de Laiblin, un mécène privé, que le projet a pu démarrer.

25 Lettre circulaire de Paul Clemen à sa famille, le 5 mai 1918 (Archives privées de Paul Clemen, *Amt für Denkmalpflege* à Brauweiler, dossier « Briefe Kriegszeit 1914-1918 »).

26 Aust/Schönpflug 2007, *op.cit.*

27 *Ibid.*, 20.

28 Paul Clemen, lettre circulaire du 30 septembre 1917 (Archives privées de Paul Clemen, *Amt für Denkmalpflege* à Brauweiler, dossier « Briefe Kriegszeit 1914-1918 »).

29 Van Overloop à Daxhelet, directeur général au ministère des Sciences et des Arts, le 3 décembre 1924 (Archives des Musées Royaux d'Art et d'Histoire, Bruxelles, dossier 146/8 (Acquisitions)).

30 *Ibid.*

31 *Ibid.*

32 Paul Clemen à Franz Wolff Metternich, le 3 septembre 1940 (Archives privées de Franz Graf Wolff Metternich, à Brauweiler, *Archivberatungs- und Fortbildungsstelle, Landschaftsverband Rheinland*, et *Vereinigte Adelsarchive*, n° 167).

33 Extrait d'un rapport du 4 mai 1927 adressé par Clemen aux membres de l'ancienne commission pour l'inventaire des monuments belges (Archives privées de Franz Graf Wolff Metternich, à Brauweiler, *Archivberatungs- und Fortbildungsstelle, Landschaftsverband Rheinland*, et *Vereinigte Adelsarchive*, n° 167).

34 Un 3e volume sous forme d'inventaire était d'ailleurs prévu, mais n'a jamais vu le jour.

35 Voir les correspondances au sujet de ces acquisitions aux Archives du Kunsthistorisches Institut de l'université de Bonn, dossier « Belgische Inventarisation – Fotos, 1925-29, 1933 ».

36 Christophe Piron, « Le rôle des Services photographiques et du Laboratoire des Musées royaux d'Art et d'Histoire dans la sauvegarde du patrimoine artistique belge durant la Seconde Guerre mondiale », in Bulletin *de l'IRPA* (Institut Royal du patrimoine artistique/Koninklijk Instituut voor het kunstpatrimonium) 33, (2009-2012), 2013, 257-287.

37 Marie-Christine Claes, « Un héritage bénéfique des deux guerres mondiales. Le concept et les collections de l'IRPA », *Bruxelles Patrimoines* 011-012 (numéro spécial – septembre 2014), Journées du Patrimoine Région de Bruxelles-Capitale, 061-073, ici 064.

Precursors or Followers? The German Art Scene and the Role and Image of Belgian Art Around World War I

INGA ROSSI-SCHRIMPF

German-Belgian as well as Austrian-Belgian cultural and literary relations have been the focus of research for several decades now.[1] The interest in this topic arose with the rediscovery and revalorisation of Symbolism and Art Nouveau. It is by now no longer a secret that Belgian writers such as Maurice Maeterlinck (1862-1949) or Emile Verhaeren (1855-1916) and artists such as Fernand Khnopff (1858-1921), Constantin Meunier (1831-1905), George Minne (1866-1941) or James Ensor (1860-1949) have been very well received in the German speaking world from the end of the 1890s. Lately, a few studies have also looked into the contacts between the young Belgian and German Avant-garde just after World War I, emphasising the links between the gallery and art magazine *Der Sturm* and the circles around *Het Overzicht* and *7 Arts*.[2] Less well-known is the collaboration between the Belgian art dealer, critic and exhibition organiser Paul-Gustave van Hecke (1887-1967) and the German art dealer Alfred Flechtheim (1878-1937).[3]

There are many facets of this exchange and an extensive history and general overview of these interactions is still outstanding. The purpose of this contribution is to tackle the assertion of a reverse movement of the influence in Belgian-German art relations after World War I[4] by analysing the relationship between image and self-image of Belgian art in the German speaking perception and of the position that Belgian art held to the east from the country's borders. It will highlight the continuities, transformations and discontinuities from the turn of the century period to the interwar years and answer the question of a transformation of Belgian art from precursor to follower of German art. One key factor is the notion of the "terre-entre-deux", which on the one hand relates to the construction of a Belgian identity at the end of the 19th century as well as the special cultural interest that foremost German cultural and political actors showed towards Belgium.

"Junge Kunst in Belgien", 1925: Snapshot by Hannes Meyer

My point of departure for this contribution is some central arguments from an article written by Swiss architect and later director of the Bauhaus, Hannes Meyer (1889-1959), published in 1925 in the Swiss magazine *Das Werk*. Hannes Meyer, who trained as an architect in Germany, caught up with the international avant-garde after having built the co-operative settlement *Freidorf* near Basel from 1919 to 1923. He was then largely involved with collective architecture and works for co-operatives. In 1924, Meyer designed the Swiss pavilion for the International Exhibition of Co-operatives in Ghent and stayed for six months in Belgium to follow up this project and the performances in the so-called "Co-op Theatre".[5] During this period, on the recommendation of Belgian, former Basel-based artist Jules de Praetere (1879-1947),[6] he came into contact with Belgian artists and art critics involved with or close to the Belgian art magazine *Sélection*[7] founded in 1920 by Paul-Gustave van Hecke and André De Ridder (1888-1961). He also met architect and co-editor of the modernist art magazine *7 Arts,* Victor Bourgeois[8] (1897-1962) in Brussels and artist and co-editor of *Het Overzicht,* Jozef Peeters (1895-1960) in Antwerp. A regular exchange of letters followed these encounters. From that moment on *7 Arts* reported regularly on Meyer's work and the Swiss also became involved as co-editor of the architecture section in *De Driehoek*, the magazine which followed *Het Overzicht* after its dissolution in 1925.

This interaction has to be placed in the context of the international avant-garde movement and of the belief in community art. Nevertheless, as the involvement of the figure of the Flemish applied artist Jules de Praetere as mediator suggests, it is not disconnected from pre-war positions. This accords with the importance of Henry van de Velde for the same actors and circles as Eva Francioli explains equally in her article in this volume. German architect and critic Adolf Behne (1885-1948), co-founder of the *Arbeitsrat für Kunst* in Berlin, was another figure who in this context became largely involved as correspondent of *7 Arts*. Both Meyer and Behne promoted Belgian art and architecture in their home country, mainly through articles. The article "Junge Kunst in Belgien" by Meyer reflects quite closely the overall convictions and interests, but also relations of the Swiss himself. It restates common ideas on Belgian art as we found them in the forewords to the catalogues of several official Belgian exhibitions and in art criticism in German, but also Austrian, newspapers, art magazines or books as from the 1890s. It spread over two issues of *Das Werk* in September and October 1925 and was richly illustrated by images of architecture, fine arts, applied arts as well as a Minerva car and a motorcycle by the Fabrique Nationale. Meyer's intention was, as he wrote, to give a neutral "cross section of young Belgian artistic expression.".[9] Indeed with photographs of buildings and settlements by architects such as Victor Bourgeois or Louis van der Swaelmen (1883-1929), art works by Gustave De Smet (1877-1943), Oscar Jespers (1887-1970), Jozef Cantré (1890-1957), all of them linked to *Séléction*, as well as by abstract artists like Pierre-Louis Flouquet (1900-1967), Victor Servranckx (1897-1965), Paul Joostens (1889-1960), Karel Maes (1900-1974) or Jos Léonard (1892-1957), this article can be said to be, regarding the aesthetic spectrum, one of the most comprehensive overviews of contemporary Belgian artistic expression that exist in the German language in the interwar period. Nevertheless, the accent was laid on architecture and modernist visions (fig. 9.1-3), quite unlike the 1925 Spring exhibition of Belgian art in Basel in which Meyer was involved and which was clearly in line with the portfolio of *Séléction*, to Meyer's disappointment excluding abstract art but including the precursors Constantin Meunier, George Minne and James Ensor.[10]

Meyer tries to create a special, cultural tie between Switzerland and Belgium when he emphasises right at the beginning of his article the convergence between the two countries as multilingual and multicultural nations. But then he pursues directly with a widespread common place on Belgium as a buffer state ("Puffer- oder Zwischenstaat") and a land of contradictions. Right here we are in the heart of the question of Belgium's quest for identity since the late 19th century and by that also its crises due to German invasion and occupation. The question is, what value does this pre-war (self-) image of Belgian identity still have in the post-war era, and certainly how did it slip into the article of a radical leftist and modernist architect? According to Hannes Meyer, and he must be largely inspired in this by former German art critics as well as by Jules de Praetere, this Belgian specificity warrants the top performances ensured by Belgium in the arts and elsewhere.[11] Belgium is rich because of its contrasts. This is pretty much the same as stated in the preface to the exhibition of Belgian art organised in Cologne in 1914 by the Antwerp art association *L'Art Contemporain.*[12] Meyer recalls on the same occasion and to introduce his subject the pre-war achievements of Belgian art and the trios of names that according to him dominated those achievements in literature (Rodenbach – Maeterlinck – Verhaeren), painting (Meunier – Laermans – Ensor) and architecture (Hankar – Horta – Van de Velde).[13]

Meyer's presentation of Belgian art dates back in several ways to a pre-existing discourse and tradition of Belgian-German artistic relations. We could say rupture and continuity, or perhaps rather transformation.

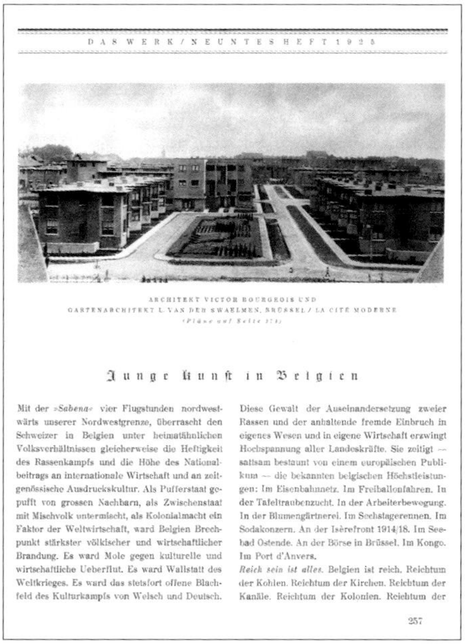

DAS WERK / NEUNTES HEFT 1925

ARCHITEKT VICTOR BOURGEOIS UND
GARTENARCHITEKT L. VAN DER SWAELMEN, BRÜSSEL / LA CITÉ MODERNE
(Pläne auf Seite 274)

Junge Kunst in Belgien

Mit der »*Sabena*« vier Flugstunden nordwestwärts unserer Nordwestgrenze, überrascht den Schweizer in Belgien unter heimatähnlichen Volksverhältnissen gleicherweise die Heftigkeit des Rassenkampfs und die Höhe des Nationalbeitrags an internationale Wirtschaft und an zeitgenössische Ausdruckskultur. Als Pufferstaat gepufft von grossen Nachbarn, als Zwischenstaat mit Mischvolk untermischt, als Kolonialmacht ein Faktor der Weltwirtschaft, ward Belgien Brechpunkt stärkster völkischer und wirtschaftlicher Brandung. Es ward Mole gegen kulturelle und wirtschaftliche Ueberflut. Es ward Wallstatt des Weltkrieges. Es ward das stetsfort offene Blachfeld des Kulturkampfs von Welsch und Deutsch. Diese Gewalt der Auseinandersetzung zweier Rassen und der anhaltende fremde Einbruch in eigenes Wesen und in eigene Wirtschaft erzwingt Hochspannung aller Landeskräfte. Sie zeitigt — sattsam bestaunt von einem europäischen Publikum — die bekannten belgischen Höchstleistungen: Im Eisenbahnnetz. Im Freiballonfahren. In der Tafeltraubenzucht. In der Arbeiterbewegung. In der Blumengärtnerei. Im Sechstagerennen. Im Sodakonzern. An der Isèrefront 1914/18. Im Seebad Ostende. An der Börse in Brüssel. Im Kongo. Im Port d'Anvers.

Reich sein ist alles. Belgien ist reich. Reichtum der Kohlen. Reichtum der Kirchen. Reichtum der Kanäle. Reichtum der Kolonien. Reichtum der

257

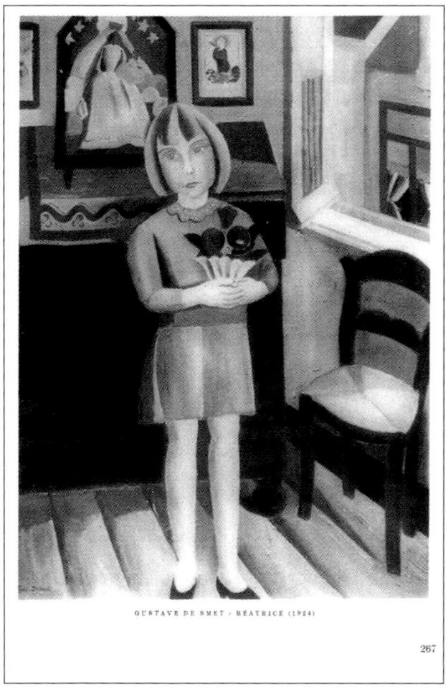

GUSTAVE DE SMET / BEATRICE (1924)

267

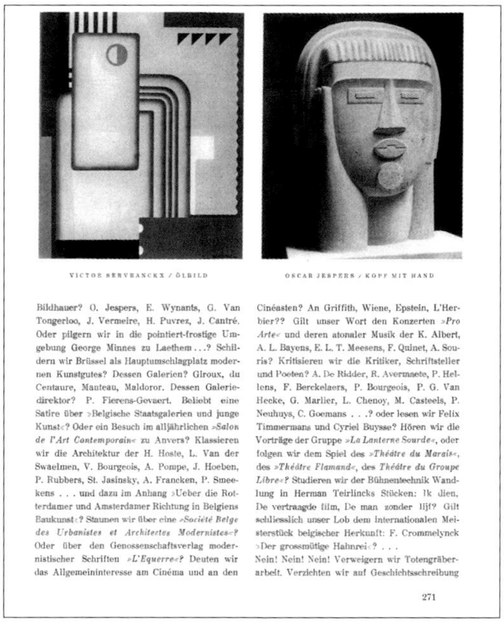

VICTOR SERVRANCKX / ÖLBILD

OSCAR JESPERS / KOPF MIT HAND

Bildhauer? O. Jespers, E. Wynants, G. Van Tongerloo, J. Vermeire, H. Puvrez, J. Cantré. Oder pilgern wir in die pointiert-frostige Umgebung George Minnes zu Laethem ...? Schildern wir Brüssel als Hauptumschlagplatz modernen Kunstgutes? Dessen Galerien? Giroux, du Centaure, Manteau, Maldoror. Dessen Galeriedirektor? P. Fierens-Gevaert. Beliebt eine Satire über »Belgische Staatsgalerien und junge Kunst«? Oder ein Besuch im alljährlichen »*Salon de l'Art Contemporain*« zu Anvers? Klassieren wir die Architektur der H. Hoste, L. Van der Swaelmen, V. Bourgeois, A. Pompe, J. Hoeben, P. Rubbers, St. Jasinsky, A. Francken, P. Smeekens ... und dazu im Anhang »Ueber die Rotterdamer und Amsterdamer Richtung in Belgiens Baukunst«? Staunen wir über eine »*Société Belge des Urbanistes et Architectes Modernistes*«? Oder über den Genossenschaftsverlag modernistischer Schriften »*L'Equerre*«? Deuten wir das Allgemeininteresse am Cinéma und an den Cinéasten? An Griffith, Wiene, Epstein, L'Herbier?? Gilt unser Wort den Konzerten »*Pro Arte*« und deren atonaler Musik der K. Albert, A. L. Bayens, E. L. T. Meesens, F. Quinet, A. Souris? Kritisieren wir die Kritiker, Schriftsteller und Poeten? A. De Ridder, R. Avermaete, P. Hellens, F. Berckelaers, P. Bourgeois, P. G. Van Hecke, G. Marlier, L. Chenoy, M. Casteels, P. Neuhuys, C. Goemans ...? oder lesen wir Felix Timmermans und Cyriel Buysse? Hören wir die Vorträge der Gruppe »*La Lanterne Sourde*«, oder folgen wir dem Spiel des »*Théâtre du Marais*«, des »*Théâtre Flamand*«, des *Théâtre du Groupe Libre*«? Studieren wir der Bühnentechnik Wandlung in Herman Teirlincks Stücken: Ik dien, De vertraagde film, De man zonder lijf? Gilt schliesslich unser Lob dem internationalen Meisterstück belgischer Herkunft: F. Crommelynck »Der grossmütige Hahnrei«? ...

Nein! Nein! Nein! Verweigern wir Totengräberarbeit. Verzichten wir auf Geschichtsschreibung

271

9.1 -9.3 Three pages from the article by Hannes Meyer in *Das Werk*, 1925.

The image and self-image of Belgian (contemporary) art

Meyer serves several common places of German art criticism and perception of Belgian contemporary art. The image of Belgium as a nation of contrasts and mediating land between the Romance and Germanic cultures – with the contrast of Walloon and Flemish mentality and tradition – is a recurring motive of Belgian self-image and of the ruling image in the German perception of Belgian culture in the period from the end of the 19th century until the First World War. Research on this topic has been carried out in the field of literature for many years and evidence does not need to be added.[14]

The dualism between the cities of Seraing (elsewhere it is Mons), thus industrial Wallonia, and Bruges, thus medieval rootedness and mystic silence, echoes two main streams of German interest in Belgium since the 19th century: Belgium as an economic force and a forerunner in industrialisation with social issues and social revolution as consequences; Belgium as an artistic hotspot with a strong (Flemish) tradition. Meyer pays tribute to this pre-war discourse on Belgian art by putting in the foreground next to industrial products, social housing projects and collective art Belgian dualism and judging the Flemish contribution as unequally higher than the Walloon, although he says himself that such a "vivisection", as he calls it, is not constructive. Where the pre-war discourse emphasised the contrast between Mons or Seraing and Bruges, which, according to German-speaking art critics, was exemplified in art by the mystical works of Fernand Khnopff in opposition to the social art of Constantin Meunier, Meyer now tries to reconcile Brussels and Antwerp, and actually *7 Arts* and *Het Overzicht/ De Driehoek* in the new spirit of internationalism (and abstract art).[15] The selection of images in the article supports this intention. It is also quite striking that we find reference to key words such as mysticism, Flemish tradition or mentality and the "Nordic myth" which were commonly used around 1900. For Meyer contemporary Belgian art wants to exaggerate the visible in favour of the emotional, to prefer visionary content and the inner vision instead of the physical eye. That again puts Flanders in the centre of artistic Belgium, as "the land where you find next to roman passion the fire of Nordic mysticism."[16]

Even if Meyer tries to overcome this dualistic view on Belgian art, strong images of the pre-war concept of Belgian art are still or again alive. This is equally expressed through the promotion of Flemish Expressionism by the editors of the art magazine *Sélection* or by governmental art administration.[17] Roland Baumann stated several years ago that the dualistic image of Belgium converged during the war and occupation in the minds of Germans like Wilhelm Hausenstein (1882-1957) in a unified discourse of pan-Germanic socialism.[18] This shift continued after the war but then as socialism under the sign of inter- and intra-national reconciliation. In this sense, the intense contacts and exchange between the modernist and socialist avant-gardes in the aftermath of the war are just another phase of a continuous evolution.

Continuity or discontinuity of the influence of the fin-de-siècle and pre-war generations

If pre-war discourse on Belgian art is still prevalent in 1925, how is it with the renowned influence and reception of Belgian artists and art works from before 1914? Meyer's own answer is the following:

> "The manometer of those artistic efforts are today corrupt. But how close to us present-day artists are the precursors in the past: Verhaeren in the Dynamic, Ensor in Nihilism, Van de Velde in the Aesthetics."[19]

And further he writes, "If we resume under the collective name 'young art' all isms from after impressionism, then James Ensor is the beginning of 'Young Belgian Painting'".[20] This recalls the title of the sixth exhibition at Herwarth Waldens gallery Der Sturm in 1912, entitled "Jungbelgische Kunst". Only two artists exhibited under this grand title, the aforementioned James Ensor and young Rik Wouters. Meyer puts two other artists of this generation as predominant next to Ensor: Meunier and Eugène Laermans (1864-1940). This might be astonishing, given the fact that Meunier's success was very time-limited and faded after his death in 1905, and that the success and influence of Laermans was limited. But it fits absolutely with Meyer's socialist convictions. To him Meunier and Laermans, but also Léon Frédéric (1856-1940), were much more progressive and noteworthy than George Minne and the whole "mystic school" of Sint-Martens-Latem.

As from the 1890s, Belgian artists whose work was shown at the exhibitions of *Les XX* and *La Libre Esthétique* in Brussels were present in German Secessions and in the circles supporting cultural reform. In the first decade of the 20th century, it was a symbol of progressive spirit to live in a Henry van de Velde interior with a *Kneeling boy* by Minne in a prominent place and a Théo Van Rysselberghe (1862-1926) above the sofa. In Vienna, it was a Josef Hoffmann interior and the Belgian sculptor was installed next to a painting by Gustav Klimt (1862-1918). Meunier with his industrial workers was for a few years the eminent artist. Meunier was somehow outdated by George Minne the beginning of whose German success lies in the integration in Jugendstil aesthetics and the mediation by Henry van de Velde (1863-1957). In general, it is striking that Belgian sculpture was very much present and seen as the greatest Belgian force in contemporary art around 1900.[21] Besides the artistic interest in Belgian art works, the economic aspect of this exchange should not be denied. With Germany and the Austro-Hungarian Empire, a huge art and exhibition market opened up for Belgians just before 1900 and was exploited as much as possible. Exchange and interaction in this aspect can be clearly described and quantified. Even today German museums hold a large number of works by Belgian artists of the period 1880 to 1930. The answer to the question of aesthetic transfer is less obvious. Superficial adoption of iconography or motifs is actually not interesting and long-lasting. The adoption and understanding of the actual meaning and essence of the art of the other, the precursor, is of importance, but often very subtle. Nevertheless, artists as diverse as those of *Die Brücke*, Paul Klee (1879-1940), Ernst Barlach (1870-1938), Käthe Kollwitz (1867-1945), Wilhelm Lehmbruck (1881-1919) or George Grosz (1893-1959) were clearly inspired by the Belgians.

In the years just before the war, the importance that was given by certain actors and circles to key figures of Belgian art was consolidated. Not Meunier and Laermans, however. And despite his etchings being already present in German public collections since the mid-1890s, James Ensor remained an insider tip in artists' circles. The exhibition of his works next to those by Rik Wouters at the famous Berlin gallery Der Sturm in 1912 and his promotion by official Belgian exhibitions as in Berlin (1908) and Cologne (1914) had no decisive echo in newspapers or art magazines. More influential was the diffusion of his graphic works.[22] The first work catalogue of his etchings was published in 1913 by Herbert von Garvens-Garvensburg.[23] Alfred Kubin (1877-1959), Paul Klee and George Grosz all got to know Ensor's art through his etchings. Emil Nolde (1867-1956) was one of the first German artists to visit the master of Ostend in 1911.[24] During German occupation a sort of small pilgrimage to Ostend of German artists, art historians and critics to his studio happened. Ensor is certainly the artist who had the most long-lasting and widespread influence on German art, long after World War II. We can just give the etchings of Horst Janssen (1929-1995) as one example. The fact that young artists of the CoBrA movement, like Asger Jorn (1914-1973), were regular hosts at von Garvens-Garvensburg's place in his Danish exile and would have been able to see works by Ensor there may underpin equally the long-term influence of the reception of Belgian art in Germany at the beginning of the 20th century. Ensor can definitively be said to be the precursor of various expressionist to surrealist tendencies. His depiction of masses, of the threatened and exposed individual, of masks, his sarcasm and irony towards his contemporaries and artistic features as light and the liberty of graphic lines inspired many German artists between 1910 and 1940. Not least because it was in line with their own experience in a changing and destabilised world. (fig. 9.4 and 9.5) However, it is noteworthy that Ensor was almost completely absent in Vienna and that his public presence in Germany would only really become important at the end of the 1920s with major exhibitions and acquisitions by museums. Not surprisingly, around 1930, his masks would again become a great inspiration for young German artists facing the impending fascist terror.[25]

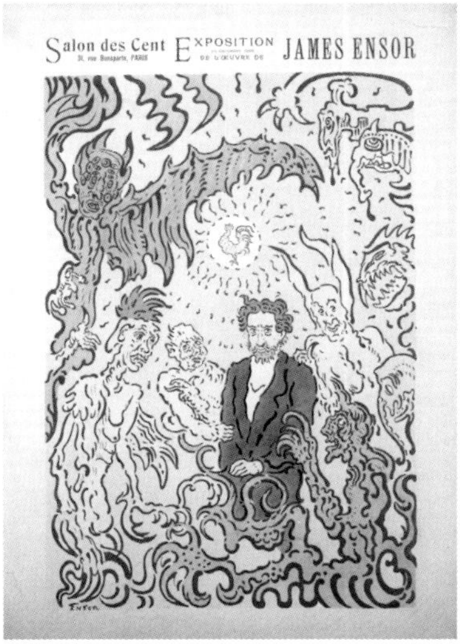

9.4. James Ensor, *Salon des Cent. 31, rue Bonaparte, Paris. Exposition en décembre 1898 de l'oeuvre de James Ensor/* Démons me turlupinant,1898, colour lithograph, 649 x 468 mm, Brussels, Royal Museums of Fine Arts of Belgium, inv. 7526.

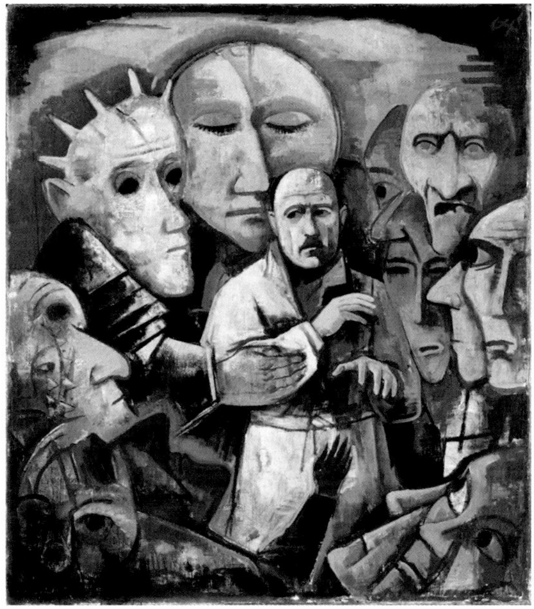

9.5. Karl Hofer, *Selbstbildnis mit Dämonen* (ca. 1928), oil on canvas, 147 × 124 cm, Ettlingen, Schloßmuseum (Dauerleihgabe Nachlaß Hofer Nr. 381).

George Minne was canonised in the years 1912 to 1914 in three very important exhibitions in Germany: the "Sonderbund" exhibition in Cologne in 1912, and two exhibitions in Mannheim that were exclusively dedicated to sculpture in 1912 and 1914. In the "Ausdrucksplastik" exhibition he was next to Aristide Maillol (1861-1944) the sole foreign sculptor, and at the "Sonderbund", he was set as one of the precursors next to Vincent Van Gogh (1853-1890), Paul Gauguin (1848-1903) and Paul Cézanne (1839-1906). The artists of the *Brücke* had already in 1906 intended to ask him to become member of their association, next to Edvard Munch (1863-

1944). The expression, introspection and simplified forms of his sculpture as well as the use of wood and his graphic work emphasising the aesthetics of medieval woodcuts inspired more than one German and Austrian artist.[26] Gustav Friedrich Hartlaub, director of the Kunsthalle in Mannheim, said of Minne in his foreword to the Ensor exhibition catalogue in 1928 that he was until then the only Belgian artist who undisputedly entered in European memory. Today, he certainly is, after Ensor and van de Velde, the Belgian artist of his generation who is still present in German art memory as confirmed by a monographic exhibition in 2013.[27] Henry van de Velde was honoured in that same year in Germany by a thematic year with several exhibitions.[28] He can be qualified as the most important mediator between the German and Belgian art scenes around 1900. In 1914, at the other famous exhibition in Cologne, the *Werkbund* exhibition, showed the "Werkbund Theatre" by van de Velde, which Meyer equally mentioned. Ole W. Fischer points out later in this volume the influence that this project had on post-war architecture (p. 287-288).

In 1912-14, the generation of *Les XX* and *La Libre Esthétique* artists was recognised as the precursors of a new art which had blossomed in Germany since 1905.[29] The presence of Rik Wouters (1882-1916) in Berlin could have been the beginning of a new generation entering Germany. Several voices in the late 1920s relate very positively to Wouters and Leo van Puyvelde (1882-1965), the chief curator of the Brussels museum, cited him in the 1929 exhibition catalogue on Belgian art (Frankfurt, Kunstverein) as precursor next to Minne and Ensor. But would his work have brought a new impulse to German art? Although he was inspired by artists that influenced equally young German artists, for example Cézanne, the new artistic generation in Belgium was only about to liberate itself from a sort of stagnation that had overcome Belgian art in the first decade of the 20th century. Two exhibitions shown in Berlin and in Brussels the same year, Italian Futurism (1912) and Kandinsky (1913), had for example not the same direct artistic impact on both sides of the border. This was the concern of one of the few young artists who was already opening up his horizon: Jules Schmalzigaug (1882-1917). Interesting for our topic of German-Belgian affinity in the art based on the emphasised duality is his assertion that activist Flemish were blind to all new international tendencies and the rapid cultural renewal abroad.[30] The dualist identity seemed to be affected by the Flemish movement with a backlash to tradition and rootedness and a crisis of Belgian identity arose already before the war at the very moment when international avant-garde movements were present in Belgium.[31]

The new generation and its interconnections

With the outbreak of the war, the artistic scene in Belgium burst, between exile, inner emigration and collaboration. There was now a forced intercultural exchange between Belgium and Germany, and the old ties changed. Those artists who were present just before 1914 in the circles of German artistic renewal, George Minne, James Ensor, Henry van de Velde and Rik Wouters, followed different paths: the first fled the Germans into Welsh isolation and the fourth died in Dutch exile; Ensor stayed; van de Velde became an "enemy alien" and lost his position in Weimar. Germans in occupied Belgium concentrated on cultural and artistic respect mainly on ancient art and architecture treasures and on the so-called "Flamenpolitik".[32] When the war was over, it was then the opposite: Germans had major problems in coming to Belgium as there were many restrictions, but often as a former occupier they did not feel well that it was right either to return to this country. The relations between the figures of the turn-of-the-century exchange were at least disturbed for a while. But the artistic Belgian and German landscape had also changed. Utilitarian and abstract art as well as a larger solidarity between artists was one reaction to the war and the misery that followed. Hannes Meyer alludes to the now stronger international component and the new awareness or presence of progressive movements like Dadaism, Surrealism or constructivism and abstract art:

> "With the retreat of the enemy, the post-war period began. Reparation and reconstruction. Standardization and air service and propaganda movie and abstract art. Henry Ford and Handley-Page and Charlie Chaplin and Fernand Leger. Bolshevism and Dadaism and Surrealism and Zenitism and Super idealism. The new Internationale moves to young Belgium. The geography of this virgin soil is impressive like a moonscape. The old forces expired. New circles were founded. Most of the time concentrating around a magazine."[33]

Alfred Behne also recognised "much that was enjoyable" in Belgian art and architecture but also criticised the antiquarianism that characterised the reconstruction of the devastated territories.[34] It must be said that directly after the war Belgian-German cultural transfer concentrated on pacifist and on modernist circles, though this was not exclusive. It was part of a larger internationalist network and related partly to the will for reconciliation of a few Belgians. Socialist and even communist positions were part of this movement for a new world. From a German point of view, this fits with the already existing image of Belgian as a forerunner in industrialisation and thus in social revolution.[35] If there is something relatively new in this exchange at the outcome of the war, it is to be found in Belgian reception of German art in the avant-garde circles around the expressionist-pacifist art magazine *L'Art Libre*, the *Lumière* group with its accent on graphic arts, especially woodcuts, and the modernist circles in Brussels with *7 Arts* and in Antwerp with *Het Overzicht* and the *Kring Moderne Kunst*. We now observe parallel movements as well as an emancipation of the relations with a more reciprocal flow of interest and influence. Information on German artists and movements was intensified in respect of what can be found in Belgian art magazines as *L'art moderne* before the war. Nevertheless and although promoted by Herwarth Walden as such, artists such as Jozef Peeters, Victor Servranckx or Karel Maes cannot be labelled clearly either as precursors or followers.

L'Art Libre and Paul Colin were focussing on expressionism, and their network is that of the *Clarté* movement. They try to reconcile the nations including Germany, and even more they give the Germans space to rectify the image of the role of German writers, intellectuals and artists during the war. They also seem to see their role as a bridge between German pacifist circles around René Schickele and Kasimir Edschmid and France. For example, they emphasise that they are the first French-speaking magazine to publish in its entirety a manifesto by German intellectuals entitled "Appel à la jeunesse intellectuelle française".[36] Regular texts on German expressionism are equally published and Paul Colin in general distinguished himself as mediator between Germany, Belgium and France, but all of this had very little or no effect on artistic practice in fine arts.

In fact, the relation to expressionism as a German art movement – even if Belgian art critic André De Ridder tried to label it genuinely French[37] – was at least ambiguous in Belgium at that time and the movement was already in decline in Germany. It was also too clearly linked with German occupation; one example is the magazine *Résurrection* by Clément Pansaers (1885-1922) and financed by the occupying authorities. Belgian or Flemish expressionism had therefore to differentiate itself from the homonymous movement in Germany. His own roots in Belgian pre-war art were thus emphasised. Flemish (Belgian) expressionism established itself more clearly during exile in Great Britain (Constant Permeke, 1886-1952) and the Netherlands (Gustave De Smet, Frits van den Berghe). Nevertheless, several facts link it to the influence of German expressionism: the magazines *Die weissen Blätter, Der Sturm, Die Aktion* or *Das Kunstblatt* as sources during war and exile; an exhibition on German expressionists organised by *Der Sturm* was held in The Hague in 1916; after the war woodcuts by German expressionists were regularly shown at the *Lumière* exhibitions in Antwerp. At least in the graphic work of Gustave De Smet, we recognise its influence.

The case is different for Modernism. Modernism had no real nationality, and if it had, it was situated at the cultural periphery which now moved in rapidly to the centre. Germany was of course important here, but not as the motherland of a style promoted as "northern" or "Germanic", but as a transit land and an agitated society where – and that despite all the still existing conservatism, militarism and even wilhelminic attitudes – for a couple of years "everything seemed possible and the artist seemed to have his role to play" (as Will Grohmann stated).[38] It is impossible to detail in this contribution exchanges between Germany, the Netherlands, Hungarian, even Russian artists and Belgium in the first half of the 1920s.[39] The point that is important here and that is also the point with Hannes Meyer's role, is that for the first time in Belgian artistic relations with the German-speaking art world, we can speak of a balanced mutual interest and a collaboration, that means an exchange of ideas on an equal basis.[40] The network of art magazines was in this respect primordial, as were initiatives as the international congresses (all in 1922) in Antwerp, Düsseldorf and Weimar. German written magazines and books were largely consulted in Belgium and one important source on international art.

The presence of young Belgian artists was for a short period concentrated around the gallery Der Sturm with an attempt to integrate the *Novembergruppe*. Frans Masereel was an exception. Those magazines which reported very regularly on Belgian art and artists before 1914 published almost nothing during the years of occupation and rarely in the first years of the 1920s. The special issue on Belgium of *Die Aktion* in 1916 was an exception, as were the contributions in the occupation magazine *Der Belfried*, both political statements. The Flanders issue of *Der Sturm* was the high point of the interaction of the modernist circles in the aftermath of the war who tried to overcome isolation and nationalism.[41] Peeters emphasised the Flemish and the international or supranational of Constructivism in his texts.[42] To him, his own achievements to overcome Impressionism and the contact with Expressionism during Occupation were the beginning of the modern movement in Flanders. Of course, according to him, this is limited to the modernist artists excluding his contemporaries commonly labelled as Flemish Expressionists.

In 1925, another article on "young art" in Belgium was published in German, this time in the German magazine *Der Cicerone* and written by the Belgian Paul Fierens (1895-1956), son of Hyppolite Fierens-Gevaert, then chief curator of the Royal Museums in Brussels.[43] If he and Peeters agreed that Belgian art was for a long time a follower of Parisian movements, he ignores completely all abstract art. From James Ensor and George Minne as precursors of Belgian modern art, he distinguishes two contemporary art schools – Sint-Martens-Latem (Flanders) and Brabant (Brussels). Dualism between Flemish and Walloon artists equally is the topic of his description as the rootedness in tradition up to van Eyck and Brueghel. Through official exhibitions, taking on the pre-war tradition of Belgian or Flemish art exhibitions in Germany, this image of Belgian contemporary art will equally be promoted. This other facet of Belgian art and its German speaking reception will be the main aspect of cultural exchange at the end of the 1920s. The image of Belgian figurative art spread at the end of the 1920s and became prevalent also in retrospect. Belgian art history emphasised for a long time Belgian expressionism and surrealism. The German side almost forgot the intense and utopian transfer with Belgian modernist circles in the direct aftermath of war.

Before/ during/ after – Shifts in the artistic transfer to the East

Thirty years ago, in one of the first studies on Belgian-German artistic relations until the 1920s, Paul Haderman stated that one could present these relations schematically as "an alternate motion of transmitting and receiving following two main currents: first from West to East, then the other way round."[44] This has to be nuanced. We cannot identify a simple reversion of direction of influence or interest. There are rather parallel currents and developments: on the one hand, we can describe a continuous interest of German artists, art critics, dealers and museums in Belgian artists, foremost of the fin-de-siècle generation; on the other hand, there can be found reciprocal interest in the framework of the internationalisation of the avant-garde and the utopia of "community art". This last movement which is more recent can however not be completely disconnected from the interconnections of the years before 1914 – and we think especially of Henry van de Velde and the applied arts movement[45] – nor from the years of the German occupation in Belgium with a sort of forced interculturality and the correlation between Flemish activism and German "Flamenpolitik". The conclusion of our research would be quite different also according to the time frame we choose. If we closed our study with the year 1924 and the Flemish edition of the magazine *Der Sturm,* we would have observed, if not a rupture, a quite important shift. But this has to be contextualised, on the one hand, within the reconstruction of a devised Belgian art scene after war, exile and occupation and the utopian belief in the construction of new world and, on the other hand, within the the political and economic context of inflation and destabilization which affected largely the German art market. If however we take as the final date of our study the beginning of the 1930s, we assert that there is a strong continuity.

Before World War I, Germany and Austria were an important art market and exhibition hub for Belgian artists. Recognition outside Belgium was a warrant for recognition in their home country. Belgian artists and writers had major influence on German expressionism. Nevertheless, although abstract artists saw even more potential in Germany than in their home country. The mercantile aspect became interesting again in the second half of the 1920s but with much less virulence and for a very short period. Here old connections such as those by Alfred Flechtheim or Herbert von Garvens-Garvensburg were taken up again while that of Herwarth Walden for the younger generations came to its end. After World War I, the fascination for Berlin and for tendencies in collective art on the one hand, pacifist ideas according to the *Clarté* movement on the other, became the first motors for Belgian-German cultural transfer. For a while and in vanguard circles the important aspect of the "nordic myth" was of no importance, either in self-image or image.[46] "Collective art" as an international movement makes a big difference between the situation before and after the war. Furthermore, abstract art could not be linked to Flemish Tradition; quite in the contrary to Flemish expressionism and similar courants as the group *Nervia*. The diffusion of Belgian "Pure Plasticity" linked solely to artists' initiatives as well as the network around *Der Sturm* with its last high point being the solo exhibition of Victor Servranckx in 1928 collapsed in a general "return to order".

Big names of the pre-war years then had a major comeback as from 1927 with among others an Ensor solo exhibition in Hannover at the Kestner-Gesellschaft and in 1929 Minne at the galleries of the art dealer Alfred Flechtheim who also promoted Frans Masereel all through the 1920s and had organised in 1914 a touring exhibition of the symbolist William Degouve de Nuncques.[47] As from 1928 with the normalisation of official relations, the Belgian government started to include German venues in its exhibitions programme to promote Belgian (contemporary) art, largely concentrating its selection on Flemish Expressionism and artists linked to *Nervia* or the art magazine *Sélection*. Several articles on these exhibitions as well as individual artist such as James Ensor, George Minne or Anto Carte in German art magazines like *Deutsche Kunst und Dekoration* or *Der Querschnitt* underpin this reconnection with pre-war tradition – in creation as in reception.[48]

Belgian pre-war artists as precursors were confirmed in these years of the late 1920s and again influenced a younger generation, today called the "lost generation". The mutual inspiration of modernist circles in the upheaval for a new world in the early 1920s appears thus as an interlude in an almost clear continuity of the role of several Belgian artists as precursors and of the dualistic identity of Belgian art as an ally against French artistic dominance.

Notes

1 For example Paul Hadermann, "Belgo-German Relations in the Arts, 1890-1918," in *The Ideological crisis of expressionism: The literary and artistic German War colony in Belgium 1914-1918*, ed. Rainer Rumold and Otto K. Werckmeister, Studies in German literature, linguistics, and culture 51 (Columbia, SC: Camden House, 1990), 19-39; Ernst Leonardy and Hubert Roland, eds., *Deutsch-belgische Beziehungen im kulturellen und literarischen Bereich 1890-1940: Les relations culturelles et littéraires belgo-allemandes 1890-1940,* Studien und Dokumente zur Geschichte der romanischen Literaturen 36 (Frankfurt am Main, Berlin, Bern, New York, Paris, ·Wien: Peter Lang; Lang, 1999); for Austrian-German relations see Fabrice van de Kerckhove, ed., *Bruxelles, Vienne 1890-1938* (Brussels: CFC, 1987). We refer equally to a future volume: Piet Defraeye, Helga Mitterbauer, Chris Reyns, eds., *Vienna : 1900 : Brussels*, Workshop Wirth Institute/ University of Alberta, Edmonton, Canada, 10.-12.09. 2015 (Amsterdam: Rodopi, to be published in 2018/2019) to which the author also contributed.

2 An Paenhuysen, "Berlin am Sonntag: Die belgische Avantgarde über das Chicago an der Spree," in Roland; Beyen; Draye, *Deutschlandbilder in Belgien 1830-1940*, 311-331; Nathalie Toussaint, "Contacts des peintres et graphistes belges avec la revue *Der Sturm*," in Leonardy; Roland, *Deutsch-belgische Beziehungen im kulturellen und literarischen Bereich 1890-1940*, 221-245.

3 Some details have been included in Virginie Devillez, "Paul-Gustave Van Hecke, Max Ernst & Co.: die Wahlverwandschaften der deutsch-belgischen Avantgarde 1918-1940," in Roland; Beyen; Draye, *Deutschlandbilder in Belgien 1830-1940*, 424-455.

4 Paul Hadermann, "Echanges belgo-berlinois de l'Art Nouveau aux années vingt," in *Expressionisme à Berlin, 1910-1920: Palais des beaux-arts*, Bruxelles, 22 septembre-4 novembre 1984 (Brussels: Société des expositions du Palais des beaux-arts de Bruxelles, 1984), 33.

5 See on the "Co-op Theatre" the text by Hannes Meyer himself in *Bauhaus* 2, no. 3 (1927), 5.

6 A Belgian-Flemish artist-designer, who got recognition and first appointments as a teacher in Germany, Krefeld and then Düsseldorf. He lived and worked in Switzerland from 1906 to 1921 and was first director of the school and of the museum of decorative arts in Zurich, then in Basel.

7 At least this is what is suggested by the foreword to the 1925 catalogue of the Belgian art exhibition in Basel, *Ausstellung belgischer Kunst 15. März bis 5. April 1925* ([Basel]: [Kunsthalle Basel], 1925).

8 Jacques G. Watelet and Annick de Ville, "La première rencontre de Hannes Meyer et de Victor Bourgeois," *ICSAC* 6/7, Februrar (1987), 297-315.

9 "Querschnitt durch jungbelgische Ausdruckskultur", Hannes Meyer, "Junge Kunst in Belgien," *Das Werk: Architektur und Kunst / L'oeuvre: architecture et art* 12, no. 9 (1925), 275. (translation by the author).

10 *Ausstellung belgischer Kunst 15. März bis 5. April 1925*, organised on the proposal of a group of young Belgian artists and with help from Hannes Meyer. It showed Constant Permeke, Gustave De Smet, Frits van den Berghe, Jules de Praetere, Jozef Cantré, Frans Masereel and Floris Jespers.

11 Meyer, "Junge Kunst in Belgien", 257.

12 *Sonderausstellung der belgischen Kunstvereinigung L'Art Contemporain*, Gemäldegalerie des Kölnischen Kunstvereins (March 1914), 2–3.

13 Meyer, "Junge Kunst in Belgien," 259.

14 See among others Roland Baumann, "Visions allemandes de l'art belge (1891-1944)", in Leonardy; Roland, *Deutsch-belgische Beziehungen im kulturellen und literarischen Bereich 1890-1940*, 191-207; Joachim Schultz, "Mysterium, soziale Revolution, Menschenseele: Das Bild Belgiens in deutschen Literatur- und Kulturzeitschriften zwischen 1900 und 1930. Anmerkungen zu ausgewählten Bei-

spielen," in Leonardy; Roland, *Deutsch-belgische Beziehungen im kulturellen und literarischen Bereich 1890-1940*, 108-122.

15 Meyer, "Junge Kunst in Belgien," 258–59

16 "Ein Streifblick in den belgischen Kreis bildender Künstler zeichnet heute unverkennbar stark diese starke Gesinnung: Das Sichtbare zugunsten des Seelischen zu übersteigern, visionären Gehalt vorzuziehen visueller Gestaltung, und das äussere Auge hintanzusetzen zugunsten des innern Gesichts. Wenig verwundert Flandern als Herz dieses Weltbildes, das Land, allwo neben westlicher Leidenschaftlichkeit je und je nordische Mystik glühte." Hannes Meyer, "Junge Kunst in Belgien," *Das Werk: Architektur und Kunst / L'oeuvre: architecture et art* 12, no. 10 (1925), 304. (translation by the author).

17 Virginie Devillez, *Le retour à l'ordre: Art et politique en Belgique 1918-1945* (Brussels: Dexia, 2003).

18 Roland Baumann, "Visions allemandes de l'art belge (1891-1944)," in Leonardy; Roland, *Deutsch-belgische Beziehungen im kulturellen und literarischen Bereich 1890-1940*, 203.

19 Meyer, "Junge Kunst in Belgien", 260.

20 "Fasst man mit dem Sammelnamen ‚Junge Kunst' alle die ismen einer nachimpressionistischen Zeit, so steht James Ensor (geb. 1860) am Anfang der ‚Jungen belgischen Malerei'." *ibid.*, 262.

21 Cf. among others, Susanne Kähler, "Belgische Bildhauer im Berlin der Jahrhundertwende," *Museums-Journal. Berichte aus den Museen, Schlössern und Sammlungen in Berlin und Potsdam* 8, 4 (Oktober) (1994), 12-14.

22 Félicien Rops and his graphic work should also be mentioned in this respect.

23 Herbert von Garvens, *James Ensor: Maler, Radierer, Komponist; Ein Hinweis mit dem vollständigen Katalog seines radierten Werkes als Anhang* (Hannover: Ey, 1913).

24 See on Ensor and Germany the different studies by Joachim Heusinger von Waldegg, as for example, "Ensor und Deutschland: Die Wirkung des Flamen auf die Künstler des Nachbarlandes," *Kunst & Antiquitäten*, no. 4 (1988), 84-96.

25 *Ibid.*, 88.

26 Cf. on Minne and his reception and artistic influence in Germany and Austria the different publication of the author of this article.

27 Bettina Berg and Ernst van Raaij, eds., *George Minne: Ein Anfang der Moderne = George Minne: voorbode van de moderne kunst* (Köln: Wienand, 2013).

28 Thomas Föhl and Sabine Walter, eds., *Henry van de Velde: Leidenschaft, Funktion und Schönheit und sein Beitrag zur europäischen Moderne* (Weimar: Weimarer Verl.-Ges, 2013).

29 On the same question regarding Vienna and the Austrian part of the Austro-Hungarian Empire, I refer to my article "Terribly modern. Belgian artists and the Secessionist battle for Modern Art," in Piet Defraeye, Helga Mitterbauer, Chris Reyns (Hrsg.), *Vienna : 1900 : Brussels*, Workshop Wirth Institute/ University of Alberta, Edmonton, Canada, 10.-12.09. 2015, Amsterdam: Rodopi (to be published in 2018/19).

30 Cf. Jules Schmalzigaug to his parents, letter, 17.03.1911, MRBAB – AACB, inv. 50.176.

31 Cf. Francis Muls, Hubert Roland, and Dennis van Mol, "Discours internationaliste et conscience identitaire des échanges culturels: l'exemple belgo-allemand," in *Europa! Europa? The avant-garde, modernism, and the fate of a continent*, ed. Sascha Bru and Jan Baetens, European avant-garde and modernism studies 1 (New York: Walter de Gruyter, 2009), 273–74.

32 See the contribution of Hubert Roland and Christina Kott on important aspects of cultural politics during occupation.

33 "Mit abziehendem Feinde bricht die Nachkriegszeit herein. Mit Wiedergutmachung und Wiederaufbau. Mit Standardisierung und Flugdienst und Propagandafilm und abstrakter Kunst. Mit Henry Ford

und Handley-Page und Charlie Chaplin und Fernand Leger. Mit Bolschewismus und Dadaismus und Surrealismus und Zenitismus und Superidealismus. Die neue Internationale zieht ins junge Belgien. Die Geographie dieses Neulandes ist eindrücklich wie eine Mondlandschaft. Die alten Krater sind erloschen. Neue Ringe sind da. In deren Mitte meist eine Zeitschrift. " in Meyer, "Junge Kunst in Belgien", 269. (translation by the author).

34 Adolph Behne, "Pierre Flouquet," *Welt am Abend*, 19.05.1925.

35 Joachim Schultz, "Mysterium, soziale Revolution, Menschenseele: Das Bild Belgiens in deutschen Literatur- und Kulturzeitschriften zwischen 1900 und 1930. Anmerkungen zu ausgewahlten Beispielen," in Leonardy, Roland, *Deutsch-belgische Beziehungen im kulturellen und literarischen Bereich 1890-1940*, 108-122.

36 Edschmid and Kasimir (Aucune), "Appel à la jeunesse intellectuelles française. Manifeste des intellectuels allemands," *L'Art Libre,* Bruxelles, 1, no. 15 (1.11.1919), 173-175.

37 An Paenhuysen, "Berlin am Sonntag: Die belgische Avantgarde über das Chicago an der Spree," in Roland; Beyen; Draye, *Deutschlandbilder in Belgien 1830-1940*, 315.

38 Uwe M. Schneede, "Vorwort", in *Die zwanziger Jahre. Manifeste und Dokumente deutscher Künstler*, ed. Uwe M. Schneede (Köln: DuMont, 1979), 9.

39 See for example: Eva Bajkay, "L'avant-garde hongroise et ses relations avec la Belgique et les Pays-Bas de 1915 à 1925 / De Hongaarse Avant-garde en de relaties met België en Nederland van 1915 tot 1925," in *Avant-garde hongroise / Hongaarse Avant-garde: 1915-1925*, ed. Eva Bajkay et al., Europalia 99 Hungaria (Brussels: BBL; Brepols, 1999-2000), 17-67 ; Nathalie Toussaint, "Interconnexions des avant-gardes picturales entre la Belgique, l'Allemagne et les Pays-Bas de 1914 à 1924: Une exemplification" (Thèse présentée en vue de l'obtention du grade de docteur en Philologie et Lettres (Archéologie et Histoire de l'Art), Philosophie et Lettres (Archéologie et Histoire de l'Art), Université Catholique de Louvain, 2000). These exchanges are also in the focus in the exhibition catalogue *The New Berlin. 1912-1932*, Inga Rossi-Schrimpf, ed. (Tielt: Lannoo; Brussels: Royal Museums of Fine Arts of Belgium (to be published in October 2018).

40 This corresponds to the basic ideas and intentions of modernist circles as formulated for example by one of the Bourgeois brothers: "Telle est la mission de tout art digne de l'époque: l'égalite créatrice des peuples, l'interrogation mutuelle, la collaboration. Périmés sont les régionalismes, mais haïssables les servitudes aux modes étrangères." Pierre Bourgeois, "L'Effort belge et l'Etranger: La Revue allemande 'Bauwelt' consacre un article aux modernistes belges," *7 Arts* 3, 5 (4.12.1924) (1924/25).

41 On these two issues respectively of *Die Aktion* and *Der Sturm* see Laura Kollwelter, "Ein Spiel in drei Akten. Entwicklungsstufen der Zeitschriften *Der Sturm* und *Die Aktion* am Beispiel belgischer Kunstbeiträge," *Expressionismus. Der Sturm und Die Aktion* 5, (2017), 77-86.

42 Jozef Peeters, "Die flämische Kunst der Avantgarde," *Der Sturm: Monatsschrift für Kultur und die Künste* 15, 1 (März) (1924), 4-6.

43 Paul Fierens, "Die junge Kunst in Belgien," *Der Cicerone: Halbmonatsschrift für die Interessen des Kunstforschers & Sammlers* 17, 7 (April) (1925), 363-372.

44 "(...), on peut représenter de façon schématique les relations entre l'Allemagne et la Belgique comme un va-et-vient d'émissions et de réceptions s'effectuant selon deux grand courants : d'abord d'ouest en est et puis inversement." Hadermann, "Echanges belgo-berlinois de l'Art Nouveau aux années vingt", 33. (translation by the author).

45 I join in this the argument of Eva Francioli in this volume, but then transferred to international artistic relations.

46 The deconstruction of the "nordic myth" as warrant for profiling Belgian art in international avant-garde began already before 1914. Muls, Roland and van Mol, "Discours internationaliste et

conscience identitaire des échanges culturels: l'exemple belgo-allemand", 276.

[47] Alfred Flechtheim started his first gallery just before the war and prospected Belgian artists for several years before that. During the war, he was serving in the German army in Flanders. He was then connected with Paul-Gustave van Hecke and co-organised the German section of the Brussels exhibition *L'Art vivant en Europe* in 1931. On Flechtheim cf. Ottfried Dascher, *Alfred Flechtheim: Sammler, Kunsthändler, Verleger*, with the assistance of Rudolf Schmitt-Föller, and Rico Quaschny, 2. Aufl., Quellenstudien zur Kunst Bd. 6 (Wädenswil: Nimbus, 2013). Ensor and Minne had been included in other exhibitions as of the beginning of the 1920s again, but 1927-1930 could be considered as a new highpoint.

[48] For example: Barchan, "Anto-Carte: Brüssel," *Deutsche Kunst und Dekoration* (1928/29), 177; André de Ridder, "James Ensor," *Der Querschnitt* 7 (1927), 918-922.

Politicized Art Around WWI

When Flemish Nationalism, Progressivism, and Avant-Gardism Came Together: 1917-1922

SERGIO SERVELLÓN

Introduction

Belgium witnessed the emergence of abstract art in the first two decades of last century in the wake of developments in other European countries. This artistic trend made an impact first of all on painting, and went on to influence a wide range of disciplines with its distinct social commitment. The combination of a revolution in imagery and the pursuit of a new society are what we now call constructivism. Adherents to and defenders of this brief period are designated as historical avant-gardists, a title which distinguishes them from the group which, as it were, rediscovered abstract art after the Second World War.[1] A yawning silence separates the two periods. The first generation arose in a sweltering and experimental atmosphere where revolutionary, social and political developments led to overtures between politics and art.[2] The title of this article refers to the short period in which the Flemish Movement not only had a distinct social democratic programme, but also called upon avant-garde artists to form a community. In *Ruimte* (Space), the magazine of the old activist Eugeen De Bock, Herman Vos published the journal's manifesto from his cell.[3] Furthermore, we want to link this publication, which appeared for only two years (1919-20), to the entanglement of Flemish nationalism and a budding avant-gardism, with the main examples being the congresses for modern art which Jozef Peeters organised in Antwerp and Bruges.

Even before the 1914-18 war, Europe was hearing calls for change. New artistic trends and organisations were appearing in rapid succession. From Italian Futurism and Parisian Dadaism to German Expressionism, youthful agitation and organisation assailed outmoded art and society. This anti-establishment activity gained momentum after the war because the older generation proved incapable of breaking with the social and moral deficit of the "old order" during peace talks. This prompted idealistic young people to act, think and express themselves differently. Non-conformism went hand in hand with a strong youth movement and a flowering of clubs and societies committed to pacifism, co-operative experiments and a return to "authenticity".[4]

Young people saw the Russian Revolution of 1917 as evidence that the world could be actively "built". In Flanders an "activating" intellectualism also took Flemish nationalist social commitment to a new level. Leo Picard notes that, at the start of the summer holiday of 1914 just before the outbreak of the war, Ghent professor Julius MacLeod warned his students about the difference between progressive Flemish nationalism and what he called "Peasant Flemish nationalism".[5] MacLeod wanted to warn his students against the strong conservative forces within the Flemish Movement which had to be resisted at all times. Lodewijk de Raet and August Vermeylen were figures who personified a "modern face" of the Flemish problem as opposed to a "romantic" intent.

The post-war atmosphere, especially in Antwerp, brought together radical socialists and radical Flemish militants in a melting pot of pacifist, anarchistic and communist inclinations. Young artists felt called to lead the community towards a new society. For a while it looked as though art could play a major part in creating a new and just society. Via a prologue I would like to highlight the continuity between what happened in Brussels during the war and the later situation in the port city of Antwerp.

Prologue: the summer exhibitions of "Doe Stil Voort" and the "Groeningerwacht"

The initial links between the younger generation of artists and the Flemish Movement arose through the activity of all sorts of art organisations and clubs and societies, which became active (again) under the German occupation. The "Doe Stil Voort" art circle, which had been founded originally in Brussels in 1899, conducted its fight for its own language and linguistic rights via cultural activities. In 1917, this initiative gained a new impetus with contributions from artists such as Albert Daenens, Prosper De Troyer and Gust Van Gompel, as well as the president Jef van Hoecke. This line-up shows that there was a strong emphasis on visual art.[6] Initiatives became specific after the opening meeting of 4 April 1917. Firstly, they set up a communal workshop in the Flemish House in Brussels where all users could share models and materials. The Flemish House, situated on the Market Square at no. 16, had already been a sort of headquarters for the Flemish Movement in Brussels for a few decades. All this new momentum must be linked to the collaboration of the Council of Flanders, which had been set up by activist professors and acted as an unofficial parliament within German-Flemish politics. In the short period of the Council's existence (1917-18), it helped to organise lots of cultural activities.

The first group exhibition was organised from 26 May to 11 June 1917. One of the early participants in this first summer exhibition was Felix De Boeck. He was a farmer's son and an aspiring artist who exhibited work from his post-impressionist period from 1917.[7] During that short period, De Boeck painted "in the open air", led by Prosper De Troyer, who introduced him to modernism. It would appear that this way of working was not so easy during the war years, as is evidenced from an archive in which De Boeck was explicitly given permission to travel around as a painter (fig. 10.1). On the back of this "Erlaubnisschein" or permit is a description of the subjects that were actually prohibited from being displayed: scaffolding, ruins and "anything that could provide information for the enemy."[8] In the communal workshop of "Doe Stil Voort" knowledge of the latest artistic trends seeped through mainly via German publications, thanks to De Troyer's contacts. For example, De Boeck was in possession of a German publication about the Italian futurists.[9]

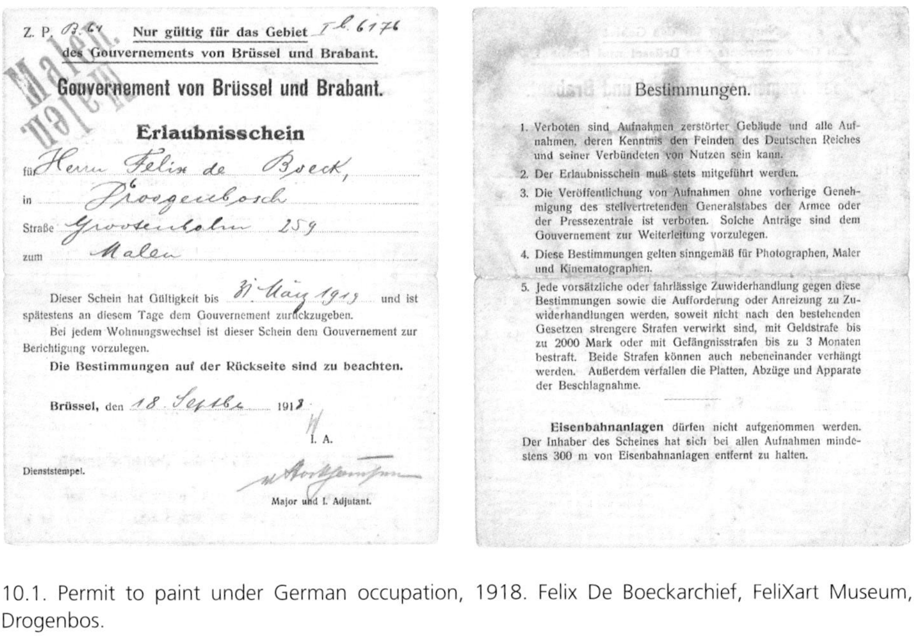
Z. P. Nur gültig für das Gebiet des Gouvernements von Brüssel und Brabant.

Gouvernement von Brüssel und Brabant.

Erlaubnisschein

für Herrn Felix de Boeck,

in

Straße

zum Malen

Dieser Schein hat Gültigkeit bis ... und ist spätestens an diesem Tage dem Gouvernement zurückzugeben.

Bei jedem Wohnungswechsel ist dieser Schein dem Gouvernement zur Berichtigung vorzulegen.

Die Bestimmungen auf der Rückseite sind zu beachten.

Brüssel, den 18 ... 1918

I. A.

Dienststempel.

Major und I. Adjutant.

Bestimmungen.

1. Verboten sind Aufnahmen zerstörter Gebäude und alle Aufnahmen, deren Kenntnis den Feinden des Deutschen Reiches und seiner Verbündeten von Nutzen sein kann.
2. Der Erlaubnisschein muß stets mitgeführt werden.
3. Die Veröffentlichung von Aufnahmen ohne vorherige Genehmigung des stellvertretenden Generalstabes der Armee oder der Pressezentrale ist verboten. Solche Anträge sind dem Gouvernement zur Weiterleitung vorzulegen.
4. Diese Bestimmungen gelten sinngemäß für Photographen, Maler und Kinematographen.
5. Jede vorsätzliche oder fahrlässige Zuwiderhandlung gegen diese Bestimmungen sowie die Aufforderung oder Anreizung zu Zuwiderhandlungen werden, soweit nicht nach den bestehenden Gesetzen strengere Strafen verwirkt sind, mit Geldstrafe bis zu 2000 Mark oder mit Gefängnisstrafen bis zu 3 Monaten bestraft. Beide Strafen können auch nebeneinander verhängt werden. Außerdem verfallen die Platten, Abzüge und Apparate der Beschlagnahme.

Eisenbahnanlagen dürfen nicht aufgenommen werden. Der Inhaber des Scheines hat sich bei allen Aufnahmen mindestens 300 m von Eisenbahnanlagen entfernt zu halten.

10.1. Permit to paint under German occupation, 1918. Felix De Boeckarchief, FeliXart Museum, Drogenbos.

The "Doe Stil Voort" art club organised a double summer exhibition in 1918 in the Brussels Museum of Contemporary Painting. It was here that a large group of pioneers, including Jozef Peeters, Felix De Boeck, Edmond Van Dooren and Prosper De Troyer, met each other and were already expressing the desire to make a clean break from existing artistic norms. The fact that the debate started under the German occupation and emerged later in the wake of the progressive wing of the Flemish Movement, including, for instance, the Congresses for Modern Art organised by Peeters, means that this Doe Stil Voort period is an example of complexity in the combination of politics and art. It seems obvious that the recruitment of these young artists was less innocent than it might appear from the above. Their youthful enthusiasm was harnessed on the basis of their commitment to Flemish nationalism.

The example of Felix De Boeck[10] and the formation of the Groeningerwacht[11] in Drogenbos are good examples here. On 16 November 1917, statutes[12] were drawn up in the dining hall of "Au Cher Ami", which was owned by De Boeck's grandfather. Felix De Boeck was the "scribe" or secretary of the association and Jef Borremans was chairman. An extensive report on an unsuccessful meeting, presumably written by De Boeck, had already been sent to the Groeningerwacht in Brussels. In turn, Willem Gijsels, chairman of that division and also the originator of "Doe Stil Voort", asked the Council of Flanders to mediate in the dispute regarding permission for the event in Drogenbos. He referred to the permission which they had obtained from the occupying German commander (Ortskommandant) of Ruisbroek.[13] This makes it clear that all these associations collaborated with the German occupying forces to promote their activities. Gijsels also asked for the support of the Council of Flanders for both the "Doe Stil Voort" summer exhibitions. He went to great lengths here: "[w]e can certainly consult with the Occupying Forces to make the visit of our artists as profitable as possible."[14]

And so the activity of this young guard went beyond the mere development of artistic expressions; it was part of the programme for Flemish independence. New information now available to us in the archives of the Council of Flanders shows that several artists from the "Doe Stil Voort" group were looking for links with the new collaborating administration. Apart from De Boeck, we also find names of figures such as Paul van Ostaijen, Jos Leonard and Victor Servranckx.

One example of how this Flemish nationalist commitment affected the art production of the abovementioned generation of young artists, can be seen in the work of Felix De Boeck. Like Alfons Marchant during the "Doe Stil Voort" exhibitions, De Boeck made a *Portrait of Borms.*[15] (fig. 10.2) This portrait has the dynamics of futurism with a range of colours leaning towards his earlier expressive fauvist works. At the same time, it is also a forerunner of the distinctiveness of the first abstract works in Flanders, which were powerful, colourful, and dynamic compositions.

This stands in stark contrast to the expressions of Dutchmen Piet Mondriaan and Theo van Doesburg of "De Stijl". De Boeck's portrait of Borms shows nicely how expressive development combines with social commitment. For De Boeck and co, this channelled itself within the Flemish struggle for cultural emancipation and the actions of a progressive section of the Flemish Movement.

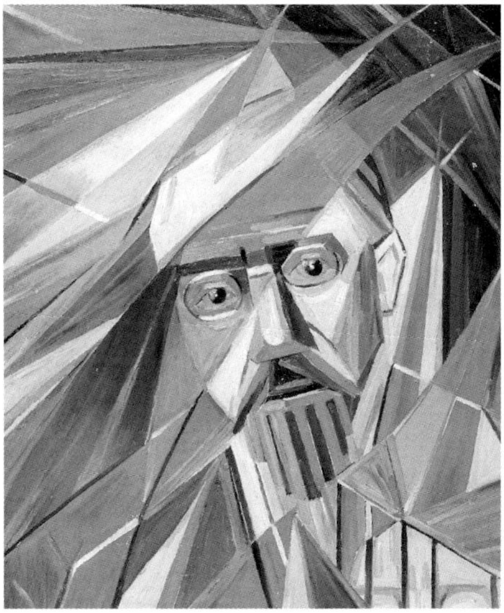

10.2. Felix De Boeck, *Portrait of Borms*, 1919, oil on cardboard, 88 x 71 cm. Collectie Vlaamse Gemeenschap, BK6271a.

Herman Vos: from Dickens to Community Art

Parallel with general voting rights in 1893, a social democratic tendency arose which also developed strongly within the Flemish Movement. This development was to culminate after the First World War in general voting rights for men with a strong growth of the Belgian Workers' Party and attention for the masses. The Front Party, too, committed itself to this with the "socialisation" of the Flemish Movement as a result. This takes us to the significance of the cell letters of Herman Vos.[16] Vos, sociologist and journalist, was a man who was working in the background on the cultural revival in Flanders. After his secondary school studies at the Koninklijk Atheneum van Antwerpen (Royal Grammar School of Antwerp) where Pol De Mont and August Borms had once taught, Herman Vos found a position at the City Statistical Office in Antwerp, which he combined with studies in sociology under Emile Waxmeiler. During World War I, he ended up working in an office set up by Antwerp

City Council to promote relations with the German government. Together with his fellow city officials Marten Rudelsheim, Anton Jacob and Paul van Ostaijen, Vos was a key figure within Antwerp activism. It is important to note that this socially aware group reinforced the left wing of Flemish nationalism by not only campaigning for the linguistic issue, but also by putting the fight against the bourgeoisie, the Roman Catholic Church and capitalism on the agenda. In 1917, on behalf of the National Flemish Students' Union, Vos took up membership of the Council of Flanders, which he abandoned as early as January 1918 after Flanders' declaration of independence. Despite his balanced unionist views, Vos was sentenced to three years in prison, together with Jacob and Rudelsheim. Van Ostaijen fled to Germany after a previous conviction for scoffing at Cardinal Mercier.

From his cell on 17 June 1919 Vos wrote the following words to Eugeen De Bock, whom he knew from the Koninklijk Atheneum and the editorial board of the liberal magazine of the Flemish Union, *De Goedendag*:

> "I'm re-reading Dickens, his 'Pickwick Papers'. I've been revelling in that funny story for three days now. Sometimes I get a fit of the giggles all on my own in the cell. Anyhow, it has a very hygienic effect on an accused who's been 'locked up' for almost seven months. Such therapeutic laughter is like a nervous 'release', which relaxes your brain somewhat. Are you familiar with Dickens? What an artist! I only had a very superficial knowledge of his work; we simply read it much too early. When I think about Pickwick, I come back to the conclusion that Kloos's well-known definition, you know, (art being) 'the most individual expression of...' is not accurate."[17]

In this passage Vos apparently covers a subject which had already occupied both friends for a considerable length of time. In his work *Jeugd in de Stad* (Young people in the City) published in 1918, De Bock testifies to the idiosyncratic mix of influences, from humanitarian expressionism[18] to futurism, which set the pre-war youth of Antwerp apart from the spirit of the "Tachtigers" from the 1880s. Here, De Bock cites explicitly the frequently quoted statement by Willem Kloos that art should be the most individual expression of the most individual emotion. However, Vos and De Bock did share a strong social and ethical concern. Art, or the aesthetic, is a means of raising standards and achieving a just society. And so, it should come as no surprise that Vos re-read Dickens during his imprisonment. Dickens, an English writer, is well known for his social and moral streak. Although Dickens' first novel *Pickwick Papers*, due to its picaresque Don Quichote plot, does not represent later social complaints such as in *Oliver Twist*, the typical caricature of the setting and the characters attracted Vos' attention:

> "Great Art gives us a typical individuality. If it is about what is typical in us, there is no purely aesthetic principle involved, but beauty always defines itself in the background of a spiritual, social, or ethical value. With Dickens it is mainly the social and national English streak of the work which is essential. As the recent German literary movement well understands, there, too, lies the chief moment, namely the ethical principle of the artistic work. Art was never designed to embellish life, but to enliven living forces, from intuition and the subconscious to the most deeply considered thought, to the utmost tension, or at least contribute towards that. That is what typifies German 'Aktivismus' (Activism) and Futurism, and, from what I've seen, also the whole swarm of the French 'petites revues' (periodicals)."

And so the antidote to individualistic art has to emerge from a new "ethical" art. The monthly journal *Ruimte* (Space) wanted to fill this hiatus, with, in the wake of Vos and De Bock, figures such as Marnix Gijsen, Gaston Burssens, Victor J. Brunclair [19] and Maurits van der Moortel.

'Ruimte': an Antwerp experiment

By this time, De Bock had gone into publishing after being dismissed from municipal service in Antwerp City Library due to his activist sympathies, including his position as editorial secretary of *De Stroom* (The Stream). In 1919, he called upon artists to work on a new magazine. With *Ruimte* he managed to reach some of the Antwerp avant-gardists.[20] Figures such as the Jespers brothers, Leonard and Peeters were to make contributions. It was no coincidence that this group, together with the aforementioned writers, were known as "the Friedmann gang", who gathered around Paul van Ostaijen in the Hulstkamp coffee house in Keyserlei, Antwerp.

Eighteen months after the cell letters, Herman Vos developed his ideas in an article entitled "Voor een decadent Vlaanderen?" ("For a decadent Flanders?") which appeared in 1920 in the December edition of *Ruimte*. Earlier, in March 1920, Vos had already published his manifesto "Ter inleiding" (By way of introduction) and thereby introduced the term "community art" for the first time.[21]

Continuing to build on the ideas formulated in his cell letter, Vos took a look at Flanders in the mirror in his article: "We will have to acquire and process a lot of inner refinement in Flanders if we are ever to arrive at a civilisation which looks socially stylish."[22] He then refers to the "ostentatious, perfumed, and poorly educated great establishment" which idolises "mourir en beauté" (dying beautifully). Here Vos alludes to an article by Paul-Gustave van Hecke, namely "Fashion", which had appeared previously in *Het Roode Zeil* (The red Canvas). And so, benefit should not be expected from a development towards the "Salon and Club", a way which would surely be unfeasible for a people which is "a people of plebeians, warring democrats, and some isolated poets."[23]

According to Vos, there is, however, a remedy. "After the disintegration of all spiritual values, after the intellectual differentiation, there is a felt need for ethical integration."[24] He then shows understanding for the furore which Dostojevski was making amongst young people with his "renovation of the Christian principles of sin and atonement", yet he rejects them as too distant from Flemish souls. Yet Vos did believe that change was on the way: "[t]here is a spirit of rebellious pluck abroad in the world. Maybe all that moves the masses will also prove to be a form of an ideal society." In winsome sentences Vos then calls upon artists to take on their assignment and to think in the stead of the community, for the community:

> "O, think for the thousands! ... O, my Flemish brothers, glorious artists who want to make this land a finer place, not a decadent culture, but rather a new social Mesfianism is the rich, yet undiscovered Treasury, which is well worth coveting!"[25]

The ideas akin to those of John Ruskin and William Morris, which reconciled aesthetic beauty and socialism, were thereby linked to a new approach in the Flemish struggle for liberation.

Ruimte was one of those journals which was influenced by humanitarian expressionism. Apart from criticism of the prevailing culture and society, this movement also had a constructive message with a call to action on the one hand and, on the other, a striving for simplification and renewal in form. Romain Rolland, the French pacifist and Nobel Prize winner, added that the mission of art was to be a human ideal. It is mainly in the interpretation of the latter, encroachment upon society, that the revolutionary reactions from after World War I must be understood.

This literary renewal initially had strong links with the Flemish Movement. The group of students who, apart from a call to activism, also published the first humanitarian expressionist poems in the journals *De Goedendag* and *Aula* were largely the same ones as those who later published works in *De Stroom* and, later, *Ruimte*. Here, Van Ostaijen was always the artistic liberaliser who set the tone with *Music-Hall* and *Sienjaal*. This group, which was social and Flemish in its commitment, was later to oppose the "individualists" from magazines in the tradition of *Van Nu en Straks* (From Now and Then), such as *Het Roode Zeil*. The choice of title, *Ruimte*, already betrayed the fact that this would be about more than just a literary struggle. Vos's major contribution evidenced a more social and political interest. The artistic debates on what should be meant by "community art" contributed to an eclectic aesthetic point of view. The theorising about ethics and aesthetics saw a conflict in the publication in mild expressionist poetry and modernist graphic work. Van Ostaijen's distrust of *Ruimte* came from his need to be as avant-garde as possible. That was why he informed De Bock on 17 March 1921 that with *Sienjaal* he wished to set up a journal for "strict-art only".

Paul van Ostaijen: an artistic and social commitment

One of the first Antwerp artists who wanted to bring together art and politics in practice was Paul van Ostaijen.[26] In the statement of principles which appeared in the prospectus of *Sienjaal,* van Ostaijen declared himself to be openly in favour of an "emancipated cubism". By standing up for an image constructed on the basis of set laws, Ostaijen wanted to exclude adhesion to individual taste. In his line of reasoning non-individualist art could not thrive in a bourgeois society. And so the destruction of society as he knew it was the ultimate objective of committed art.

Van Ostaijen also studied at the Koninklijk Atheneum of Antwerp where he joined the Vlaamsche Bond (Flemish Union). From 1914 to 1918, he worked as a clerk at the Antwerp City Hall. Van Ostaijen admitted that his participation in the Flemish Movement was on the basis of a socialist conviction in which the accent was on the social struggle rather than the language problem. During the war, he published Flemish nationalist articles in which he advocated "level-headed nationalism" always with an international view of Flemish liberation. On 24 April 1920, Van Ostaijen published in *De Toorts* (The Torch) an "Open letter to Mr Camille Huijsmans" drafted in Berlin in which he appointed himself as champion of a rapprochement between the Flemish nationalist and social movements:

> "I'm a socialist and regard the solution of the Flemish problem as being along the lines of socialist interests. ... The Flemish Front party is a young democratic party. Her social inclinations lie instinctively in our direction."[27]

In Berlin Van Ostaijen also persuaded his contacts in the Spartacus League that the Flemish Movement was more than a regional movement, but was also aiming for a social solution for an oppressed class. Isidoor Opsomer, who was already part of the artistic establishment, was to express adverse views regarding this link between avant-gardists and social movements and, in a citation written by Georges Marlier in the newspaper *Ça Ira* (4 July 1920), reacted in a hostile manner to "pictorial Bolshevism" ("le bolchévisme pictural").

Jozef Peeters: organiser within a Flemish nationalist network

In that context we should understand Peeters' yearnings to link the revolution of the form (abstraction) to the theoretical demands of the network which helped him to make progress (progressive Flemish Movement). In this political context the conviction grew that artists could help to bring about changes in urbanisation, architecture and design by means of a well-considered "community art". For his Kring Moderne Kunst (Modern Art Circle), which was formed in 1918, Peeters continued to build up the network of social and Flemish-oriented organisations and worked in particular together with De Bock and Vos.

From the start of his activities, Peeters made use of the facilities of the Flemish Movement. The very first exhibition of the Modern Art Circle worthy of mention opened on 24 December 1919[28] in the Nederlandsche Boekhandel at Sint-Jacobsmarkt 9 in Antwerp. This business, set up in 1893, played an important part in cultural emancipation by spreading literature in Dutch. It issued work by figures such as Pol de Mont and Willem Gijsels.[29] The first lecture in Antwerp by Theo van Doesburg, *Classic, baroque, and modern,* took place on 13 February 1920 in the Lutgardis Hall at Sanderusstraat 53 in Antwerp. Before the war, that address accommodated the Sint-Ludgardis School in rooms made available by Marie-Elisabeth Belpaire. She was called the "Mother of the Flemish Movement" because of the many Flemish-oriented initiatives which she supported. The Belpaire Institute at Bomstraat 11 accommodated the 1st Congress for Modern Art on 10 and 11 October 1920. This congress was clearly sympathetic towards Flemish political demands under the impulse of organisers Jozef Peeters and Huib Hoste. With his 2nd Congress for Modern Art in the dining hall of Koninklijk Atheneum on 21, 22, and 23 January 1922, Peeters

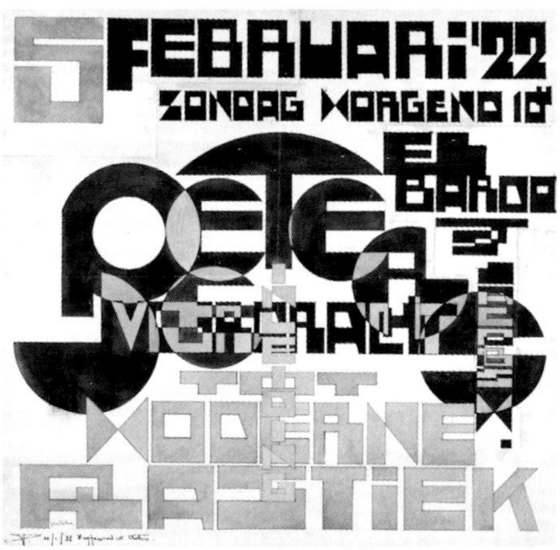

10.3. Poster Jozef Peeters, *Voordracht. Inleiding tot modern plastiek* [Introduction to modern plasticism], 1922. Letterenhuis, Antwerpen.

appointed himself as leader of the Belgian avant-garde at that time. The large-scale exhibition which accompanied the congress, with the cream of the international avant-garde movement, took place in the upper room of the El Bardo public house at Sint-Jacobsmarkt 91. The secretariat of the Flemish Front party was located at that address by the cooperative Malpertuus in May 1920 with the then recently released Herman Vos as secretary.[30] Earlier that year, on 5 February 1922, Peeters had already held a lecture in the El Bardo hall with the title *Inleiding tot moderne plastiek* (*Introduction to modern plasticism*). (fig. 10.3)

At Huib Hoste's suggestion the third congress was linked to the Flemish Scientific congresses and a congress for library staff. A congress took place in Bruges on 5 and 6 August 1922. The exhibition ran from 30 July to 15 August. The main figure in the preparation of the scientific congresses was Jozef Goossenaerts, who was associated with the Front Movement and, as secretary of the Joint Organising Committee, was responsible for the organisation. From 1925, the congresses were organised biannually, one reason why Peeters continued to correspond with Goossenaerts for a long time.[31]

The impact of Vos and De Bock on the young guard of artists was also evident in the intrinsic involvement in the congresses which Jozef Peeters organised in his capacity as secretary of the Kring Moderne Kunst. At the First Congress for Modern Art De Bock gave a speech which was also published in the same number of *Ruimte* in which Vos' article "A decadent Flanders?" had also been included. At the 2nd Congress Vos was to give a lecture entitled "Over de politiek in verband met kunst" ("The relation between politics and art"), which appeared in April 1922 in the literary journal Vlaamsche Arbeid (12th year, no. 4). The fact that Vos was the first speaker after the address of the chairman Hoste shows how much importance the organisers attached to Vos' insights. Moreover, the structure of the lecture was completely in line with what Peeters wanted for those lectures.[32] In line with many culturally critical writings from that period, Vos was to deploy a future projection as the norm, heralding a new world. However, this was done by actively looking to change the present age according to the analogy of the ideas which pre-war German expressionism also cherished. Yet it was the contribution of the anti-individualistic plea which constituted the significance of Vos' speech, the humanitarian expressionist "ethic".

Vos' friend Eugeen De Bock also influenced Jozef Peeters' career development. The lecture by Van Doesburg in 1920 was published in brochure form by "De Sikkel", De Bock's publisher. De Bock was even introduced for a short time as "representative" of "De Stijl" in Flanders, at the expense of Jozef Peeters' ambition. In the tension between a regional position and the desire for participation in an international art event Peeters gradually turned his back on local dogmas. For example, together with Michel Seuphor he transformed the originally broad cultural Flemish nationalist militant publication *Het Overzicht* (The Overview) into an international forum for avant-garde art. The drift of the Flemish Movement towards the right, a development which was to culminate in Vos leaving the Front Party, did not foster further co-operation. The financial bubble which burst into pieces in the autumn of 1929 finally destroyed all avant-gardist cravings of that time. The Return to Order ("Le retour à l'ordre"), in which previously progressive critics such as Georges Marlier conducted a sort of counter-reformation, coincided with a society which found itself confronted with the sober reality.

It was almost another forty years before the pioneers of abstract art in Belgium were rediscovered. The scars of the Second World War, with its sharp left-right polarisation, often coloured research into Flemish history of the "roaring twenties". For instance, it is noticeable that the wider public is hardly aware of van Ostaijen's work as a political and critical art thinker. It is also remarkable that Herman Vos' role in the "Community Art" debate and the organisation of the Antwerp avant-garde movement has hardly been studied at all. The entire *Ruimte* adventure in art history is often defined as a marginal occurrence by "contentious" writers. Robert Melders writes in his study of Peeters: "[Peeters'] sincere Flemish inspiration is almost always ignored, perhaps because the survivors from the right wing of the Flemish Movement have built up a status which could most likely be threatened by the competition."[33]

Ruimte has nevertheless retained its attraction from a cultural-historical point of view, partly due to the tension which it created between social commitment and form renewal. It provided a forum for a generation of creative spirits to crystallise their views and thereby gave an impetus to look deeper and further at the task of art in society.

Notes

1 Relatively little research has been done into Belgian avant-gardism. The most important studies emerged slowly after the 1970s, and mainly from within the museum sector. For a general summary see *Avant-Garde en België 1917-1929,* eds. Eliane de Wilde, Lydia Schoonbaert, Jean-Marie Duvosquel and Joost Geest (Brussels: Gemeentekrediet, 1992). Philippe Roberts-Jones, *Abstracte schilderkunst in België* (Brussels: Gemeentekrediet, 1996). Johan De Smet, ed. *Modernisme: Belgische abstracte kunst en Europa* (Ghent: Museum of Fine Arts in Ghent, 2013).

2 For the general political situation of art between the world wars see Virginie Devillez, *Kunst aan de orde. Kunst en politiek in België 1918-1945* (Ghent: Uitgeverij Snoeck, 2003) and An Paenhuysen, *De Nieuwe wereld. De wonderjaren van de Belgische avant-garde (1918-1939)* (Antwerp: Meulenhoff/Manteau, 2010).

3 This article is an extended and annotated version of an article already published in *Zuurvrij*, the periodical of the Letterenhuis (literature archive), Antwerp. (Servellón 2014).

4 An example of this is the Vlaamsche Bond (Flemish Association), a student group at the Koninklijk Atheneum van Antwerpen / Royal Grammar School in Antwerp and Publisher of *De Goedendag*, which defended both aesthetic and ethical points of view in which ecological, Flemish nationalist and international objectives went hand in hand. Henri-Floris Jespers, *Floris Jespers, and the Gay Twenties*. (Antwerp: Deus Ex Machina The Private Press, 1989), 11.

5 Leo Picard, "The Flemish movement in a new world" in *Het Leven in de jaren 20* Documentation brochure, NDJ Stage for advanced students at Genval, 20-29 August 1963 (Brussels: Ministry of Education, National department for youth, 1963).

6 For an insight into the entwining of literary avant-gardism and the Flemish Movement see Geert Buelens, "Een avant-gardist is (geen) groep. Over de wankele avantgardestatus van de flaminganten tijdens het interbellum" in *Avantgarde! Voorhoede? Vernieuwingsbewegingen in Noord en Zuid opnieuw beschouwd*, eds. Hubert F. van den Berg and Gillis J. Dorleijn (Nijmegen: Vantilt, 2002), 93-102.

7 Dusar, Lutgarde, *Doorheen het leven van Felix De Boeck: zijn vormingsjaren en deelname aan de modernistische kunststrekkingen van de twintiger jaren, geplaatst in het kader van de Europese en Belgische kunstevolutie*, unpublished thesis at the Roman Catholic University of Leuven, Leuven 1973.

8 During the symposium, one of the recurring questions was why there were so few works on the horrors of the war. It is clear that this document at least partly explains why non-mobilised persons had to stay in occupied territory. This document was previously published in Sergio Servellón, "Een ontbolsterende avant-garde. Felix De Boeck tijdens WO I" in *De Groote Oorlog in Vlaams-Brabant*. Themanummer van *Openbaar Kunstbezit Vlaanderen*, ed. M. Vervaeck (Ghent: Openbaar Kunstbezit Vlaanderen, 2014), 18-21.

9 For the importance of the less well-known Prosper De Troyer in the early years of Belgian avant-garde see Kurt De Boodt, *Prosper De Troyer. Schilder in beweging* (Antwerp: Pandora, 2013).

10 At present, David Veltman is conducting doctoral research with a view to publishing a biography of Felix De Boeck for the Biography Institute of the University of Groningen, in co-operation with the FeliXart Museum and the Felix De Boeck Foundation.

11 The Groeningerwacht was an association formed at Antwerp in 1909. The statutes provide the formation of "affiliated association" anywhere in Flanders (Constitution of the Groeningerwacht. File 75 of the Archives Council of Flanders 512782).

12 Groeningerwacht Drogenbosch, in Archives Council of Flanders 512782, file 919.

13 Letter of 9 November 1917 to the Political Department in Archives Council of Flanders 512782, file 1644.

14 Letter from Willem Gijsels to D.K. Heyndrickx on 17 July 1918 in Archives Council of Flanders 512782, file 56, Doe Stil Voort.

15 August Borms became a member of the Council of Flanders in 1917. After the war, the Belgian government started an investigation into the operations of the activists. Borms, too, was on the list of suspects and was arrested. On 6 September 1919, the Brussels Assize Court sentenced Borms to death. Whilst Borms was in prison, he grew into one of the icons of the Flemish Activism and he was admired by many Flemish nationalists.

16 Herman Vos' importance lay historically mainly in the fact that he, as leader of the Front Party, was the final great leader of the social democratic branch of the Flemish Movement. Further to the development which the Flemish Movement was drifting towards, he opted in 1933 to join the Belgian Workers' Party, later the socialist party, for which he occupied two ministerial posts after World War II (Public works and Education). See Bernard Van Causenbroeck, *Herman Vos. Van Vlaams-nationalisme naar socialisme* (Antwerp-Ghent, 1997).

17 Letter from Herman Vos to Eugeen De Bock, 17 June 1919, Fonds Herman Vos, Letterenhuis, Antwerp. I discussed this letter for the first time in my article, Servellón, Sergio, "Gemeenschapskunst

en Zuivere Beelding: twee kanten van dezelfde constructivistische medaille, Victor Servranckx in de jaren 1922-23" in *Victor Servranckx, de jaren twintig* (Ostend: Mu.ZEE-AsaMER, 2012), 36-57.

18 The role of humanitarian expression in the writings of the Flemish avant-gardists is acknowledged in Kris Humbeek, "God geve dat wij Staatsgevaarlijk wezen! Mijn kleine oorlog en de retoriek van het linkse activisme" in *Avantgarde! Voorhoede? Vernieuwingsbewegingen in Noord en Zuid opnieuw beschouwd,* eds. Hubert F. van den Berg Dorleijn, Gillis J. (Nijmegem: Vantilt, 2002), 103-112.

19 See Dieter Vandenbroucke's excellent biography on Victor Brunclair, whose activities can also be regarded as a synecdoche of the combination of art and politics. Vandenbroucke, Dieter, *Dansen op een vulkaan. Victor J. Brunclair, schrijver in een bewogen tijd*, (in Dutch only), Antwerp: De Bezige Bij, 2013.

20 Eugène De Bock, *Een uitgever herinnert zich* (Antwerp: De Sikkel, 1979).

21 Herman Vos, "Ter inleiding," *Ruimte* volume I, no. 1-2 (March 1920), 1-4.

22 This and the following quotations come from Vos, Herman. "Een dekadent Vlaanderen?", *Ruimte* volume I, no. 10-11-12, (December 1920), 118-121.

23 *Ibid.*, 118-121.

24 *Ibid.*, 118-121.

25 *Ibid.*, 118-121.

26 Gert Borgers, *Paul van Ostaijen. Een documentatie* (Amsterdam: Uitgeverij Bert Bakker, 1996).

27 Paul Van Ostaijen, "Open letter to Mr Camille Huijsmans." *De Toorts* (24 April 1920).

28 Flor Bex, *Jozef Peeters 1895-1960* (Antwerp: International Cultural Centre, 1973), 38 and Frederik Leen, "In cirkels en Kringen," in, *Avant-Garde in België 1917-1929* (Brussel: Gemeentekrediet, 1992), 28.

29 Jan Huijbrechts, *Vlaams bewegen in Antwerpen, Een stadsgids met 5 cultuurhistorische wandelingen* (Brussel: Uitgeverij Egmont, 2011), 84.

30 Bernard Van Causenbroeck, *Herman Vos. Van Vlaams-nationalisme naar socialisme* (Antwerp-Ghent: Hadewijch-AMSAB, 1997), 72.

31 List of Jozef Peeters, Letterenhuis, Antwerpen.

32 "We don't want speakers to be historical in their approach, but for educational reasons to expose the pseudo-modern alongside the truth." Letter from Jozef Peeters to J.J.P. Oud, 29 June 1921, Museum of Literature, The Hague, quoted in Sjoerd Van Fassen and August H. den Boef, *Het pseudo moderne nevens het ware. De briefwisseling van de architect J.J.P. Oud met Jozef Peeters en Michel Seuphor, redacteuren van het constructivistische tijdschrift Het Overzicht, 1921 – 1925* (Antwerp: Zacht Lawijd / Garant Uitgevers, 2008), 53.

33 Robert Melders, *Jozef Peeters (1895-1960)* (Antwerp/Amsterdam: Uitgeverij Nederlandsche Boekhandel, 1978).

Albert Daenens (1883-1952): Belgian Artist From Brussels, Flemish Activist and French Publicist, International Anarchist and Antimilitarist Before, During and After World War I

Erik Buelinckx

Two works of art, a drawing and a linocut, the first one made at the end of World War I, the second a couple of years later in the mid 1920s, could show how rupture and continuity at times of great turmoil can have an influence in a political and artistic avant-garde context. The creator of these two works, Albert Daenens, is not well known, but there is no lack of information about him, although mostly hidden in his, until recently unexplored, enormous archive.[1] Albert Daenens cannot be described in a few words. His personal network was extremely vast, but his activities covered multiple fields and, as such, by not really excelling in one domain or another, this could be one of the reasons he remained rather unknown. Before comparing these works of art, we need to know who Albert Daenens was. Wat did he do? What did he stand for? How did he work? And finally, why should we remember him, and give him a rightful place in Belgian and international art history?

Biography and artistic beginnings

Louis Albrecht Daenens, who went by the name Albert, was born in Brussels on 27 February 1883. His mother was Eugenia Daenens (1863-1891), then nineteen years old, his father unknown. Eugenia, who worked as a tailor, mainly for actresses, died when Albert was only 8 years old. From an early age he was raised by his grandparents and his aunt Malvina (1859-1921). The Daenens family came from Ghent and was very active in the Flemish theatre world. Anything connected with theatre would be of lifelong importance for Albert Daenens.

Two little notes in his archive give us an inkling of what the relationship with his mother seems to have been like. He addresses her as "Eugenie" and signs with "your son Albert Daenens". He collects illustrations, stamps and has received a colouring box set. From the letters, we learn that she was always informed how he was doing at school, that he had to work well because that was the only thing they could offer him, referring to a continuous state close to poverty that they lived in. Not much more is known about his childhood, but he was a good student, and at the age of sixteen he went to the art academy of Brussels, where one of his teachers was Adolphe Crespin, and there he won several prizes. In a photograph of Daenens as an adolescent we see him working at an easel. His grandfather, an actor, was an amateur painter too, so he grew up in an artistic environment.

Albert Daenens had a physical disability, one leg was deformed, so a career as leading actor could be forgotten, but since there are more activities in the world of the spectacle, such as directing or designing sets, he kept in touch with that world. People called him "Bère Notje", referring to either "small as a nut", or his handicapped leg.[2] After leaving school he started indeed to work in the theatre world, as an article in *Le Thyrse* shows: "[t]he new sets by Mr. Daenens are really very successful".[3] The play was *Philip II* by Emile Verhaeren, the famous Flemish playwright and poet who wrote in French and was also interested in anarchist ideas.[4]

Daenens' personal records show that he was heavily obsessed with who his father could have been; preferably, in his mind, a well-known and talented individual. By subtracting nine months from his birthday, he tried to figure out which famous people could have been living in or visiting Brussels at that time. Let us not forget that in the obituary of his mother only the following qualifications were mentioned: daughter, sister, sister-in-law and aunt. On a copy of this obituary in his personal archive, he had written in pencil the words "and mother".

Anarchist contacts

An important event in his life was the death of his lover Alice Lebègue at the end of 1912. A police report stated that Daenens, together with some comrades, was under surveillance as a dangerous anarchist:

> "The aforementioned moved from Molenbeek St. Jean with his mistress, one named Lebègue, Alice Jeanne, born in Brussels on March 26, 1886, a single woman, who died, rue Rittweger, 27, November 21, 1912."[5]

It is not clear how Albert Daenens met these other revolutionaries, or how he himself became an active anarchist. One possibility is the Brussels alternative café-scene, especially the cabaret *Le Diable au Corps*. Was it here that Daenens started to build himself a network of multiple, sometimes overlapping tracks? His interests in radical politics, avant-garde art, French literature and Flemish theatre could indeed come together in such places. The cafe-cabaret was a meeting place for Flemish theatre people and French-speaking students from the Université Libre de Bruxelles, mixed with young and old artists and poets of both languages. Some of these young revolutionaries wanted to create in Brussels their own literary-political-artistic magazine that broke radically with the past. Before Daenens himself started the first series of *Haro!*, not knowing what a difficult but interesting path this magazine would take, he collaborated with at least three other journals. These were *La Foi nouvelle* (February 1912 – March 1913) and *En Marge* (July 1912 – September 1913) as radical literary magazines, and the anarchist *Le Révolté* for which he was mentioned in 1913 as acting manager. In a letter from May 1913, answering the question how his involvement would continue regarding *Le Révolté*, he replied that *Haro!* took too much of his resources and that he was not a politician, referring to the pure political line of the journal. Nevertheless, they could always count on him to distribute the journal. In a certain way, Albert Daenens can be seen as part of the bridge between the anarchist movement at the beginning of the century, with some notorious anarchists close to *Le Révolté* and the libertarian colony *L'Expérience* near Brussels, such as Victor Serge, Rirette Maîtrejean, Raymond Callemin and Jean de Boë – all of whom will be later linked in one way or another to the Bonnot Gang – and the Belgian post-war anarchists such as Hem Day and Ernestan. For Albert Daenens this involvement was always part of his artistic activities.

Minor journals

In an interesting study on literary magazines of the period immediately following the First World War, Daphné de Marneffe also pays attention to the pre-war period to describe how all these magazines, individuals and groups are often and historically interconnected.[6] The first issue of *La Foi nouvelle* appeared in February 1912, and presented itself as an artistic, literary and social magazine. Its mission was stated in poetical form:

> "Oh! Small wooden gods and small stone saints, / What crimes for you in this amassed era! / The people no longer believe. Your fine days are past; / Weep in Your Vatican, Successor of St. Peter / The Almighty, alas, is only a chimera /

> That our abused senses went to seek in heaven / In incensed vapours but an artificial rite / Sleepy, mysterious, like an ephemeral dream."[7]

The tone was set, as in other avant-garde manifests. Under the poem another little statement: 'I believe in a more beautiful humanity, daughter of love and reason.'[8] From the first issue on, Albert Daenens was mentioned as a contributor. He designed the cover, which would be printed in different colours over the years. Nevertheless, it was only from the second issue that articles by his hand started to appear. The cover, a blossoming tree with rising sun, was typical of the social-artistic leanings of the magazine and similar imagery was often used at the end of the 19th century for likeminded publications. On the second to last page an overview of the names of collaborators and their areas of expertise was listed. Daenens was responsible for writing about the applied arts. In the Spring issue (1 May 1912), this time with the cover in green, there are four photographic inserts, a study by F. Schirren, the 1912 masterpiece by Rik Wouters, *The Foolish Virgin* aka *The Crazy Violence*, a satirical scene by Ensor, and finally a drawing by Abel Gerbaud.[9] The illustration for the column *La Hotte*, to which Daenens himself contributed texts, was made by him. Here he critiques the slowness or lack of initiative by Belgian officials in honouring artists like Jules De Praetere or Henri van de Velde. On the last page of this issue we see another half-page drawing by Daenens of a person trying to advance against a strong wind. Once again symbolic of the role they saw for themselves as publishing this avant-garde magazine:

> "To the real artists to revolt, we can't expect anything from the current social state, the salvation will come to us from the people, inexhaustible source of new energy. Let us prepare with them the revolution which will chase away this bourgeoisie without ideals, without soul and without brains."[10]

This call by Daenens in his first article on the applied arts may resonate with previous calls by anarchists and artists such as Peter Kropotkin or Henry van de Velde, although both see the artist as an avant-garde person, one who leads, while Daenens clearly wants to walk the road together with the people.[11] Starting from the sixth issue he contributes little illuminations to the different sections of the magazine, but also a page-filling caricature on symbolism. For the double November-December issue in 1912 there is his rather acid critique on religion, and in 1913, the second year of the magazine, one on alcoholism and poverty. He also illustrates a short "tragedy in one scene" by Jules Mellaerts, *La mansarde*, in March 1913. The drawing, depicting a dying young woman suffering from tuberculosis, could well be inspired by the death of his lover Alice Lebègue some months earlier.

Abel Gerbaud, at *La Foi nouvelle* until June 1912, and Paul Ruscart,[12], who will write a last article for the October issue, together with Léon De Roos[13] in July 1912 founded another magazine, *En Marge*, to defend the new ideas in art and literature even more.[14] Daenens, to a lesser extent, would also collaborate, and here he meets War Van Overstraeten, artist and later co-founder of the Belgian Communist Party, who will, under the pseudonym War Campine, write some articles for *Haro!* For this period, we have an interesting additional source about these young revolutionaries in art and politics:

> "Daenens, Louis Albert answers to the following description: / Size 1m55 to 1m57 / Lean and bony figure / Rather yellowish complexion / Blond-red hair, fairly long / Beard blonde-red, square / Limps with the right leg and has therefore an unsteady tread / Always wears a large soft felt hat with wide edges and a 'La Vallière' tie."[15]

Indeed, Daenens and his friends were under observation by the police, and not just by the ordinary local forces, but a special agent from the secret services who had to follow international anarchist activities in Brussels:

> "I've learned that, almost daily, Daenens, Dubois[16] and company, go to rue Paepenkasteel 3, at Gerbaud's place, and hold there, probably, their anarchist press meetings, because it seems that there is a printing machine at that address and that the publication *En Marge* is printed there as well as the new edition of the journal *Le Révolté* under the direction of Daenens, Louis Albert."[17]

Haro! first series (1913-1914)

The successive publication dates of these little magazines show that *En Marge* constituted maybe the transition from *La Foi Nouvelle* to *Haro!*, through its printing press in Uccle (a suburb of Brussels), but what played an additional role was the arrival of the writer Maurice Casteels at *La Foi nouvelle*.[18] His first contribution, *Il faut détruire Carthage*, an anarchist inspired rant, appeared in October 1912, but he had already had an earlier experience with similar magazines, since he was one of the founders of *Le Cynique* in 1910. Some of the people involved in *Le Cynique* will appear later in *La Foi nouvelle* and *Haro!*, such as Marsile Armigny, Louis Fel and René Schmickrath.[19] Together Albert Daenens and Maurice Casteels founded the magazine *Haro!* with following programme in its first issue (fig. 11.1), dated June 1913:[20]

> "HARO! groups only avant-garde writers and artists. / HARO! is in Belgium the first journal of action of modern art in its most intransigent acceptance. / The contributors to HARO! will deal, at the same time as literature and art,

with current events. For if the artist's mission demands silent solitude, he must nevertheless listen to all that may interest other men, and if he interferes with their actions he will show them heroism."[21]

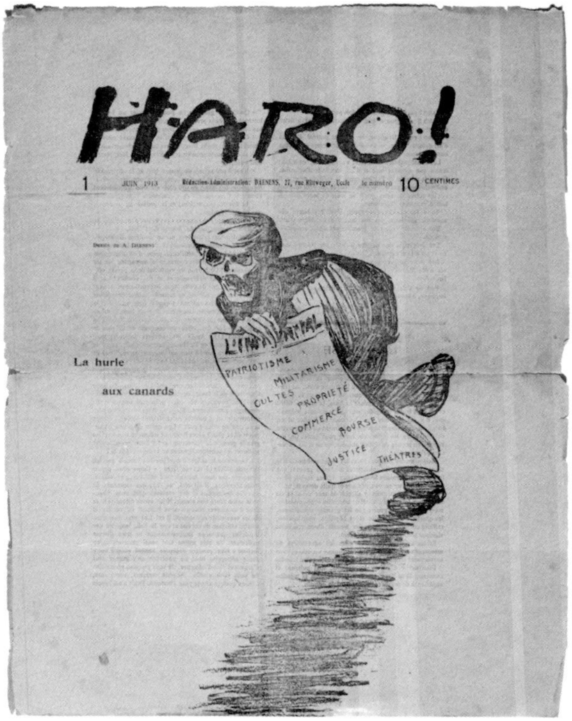

11.1. Albert Daenens, *La hurle aux canards*, 1913, in *Haro!* 1e série, no. 1, p. 1 (July 1913).

The front pages of *Haro!* consisted always of a full-page drawing (for the 2nd and 35th series a full-page linocut) by Albert Daenens. One exception was in October 1913, presenting a half page illustration *Down with the schools*. Within the first two numbers of *Haro!* we rediscover his friends, the French artists Abel Gerbaud and Marcel Bouraine, but also, or better yet, Ferdinand Schirren and then a certain O. Petyt, most likely Oscar Petyt, active in the late 19th and early 20th centuries in Saint-Josse-ten-Noode (Brussels). Issues three and four provide another surprise, with illustrations by Rik Wouters and Léon Spilliaert. Wouters is quite logical because they knew each other from the Brussels-Brabant area, meeting other artists as an informal group later described as *Brabant Fauvism*. In the first issue of *Haro!* Daenens wrote a positive review about him: "Rik Wouters, a sculptor, has this time the heavy task of showing painters the new trends in painting. He managed admirably. ... J. Ensor has made better stuff."[22] In October 1913, a drawing made by Wouters accompanied an article on the right to abortion. Léon Spilliaert may seem more astonishing, but if we look at a lesser known element from Spilliaert's extensive career – from symbolism to dada – we discover that in the first years of the 20th century he made some works with social themes, such as *Man with flag. Crowded mass under a black flag* in 1904. This might very well depict an anarchist rally. Finally, we can mention Charles Counhaye, whose illustrations will also appear in the second series of *Haro!* (1919-1920).[23] Clearly, an interesting group of avant-garde artists was in contact with Albert Daenens and Maurice Casteels.

The first series of *Haro!* ended suddenly, without warning, with the double issue 6-7 in January 1914. The radical pacifist ideology of the magazine was well known, and in a period in which war rhetoric was becoming increasingly important and even some avant-garde art gave way to nationalist regurgitation, magazines like *Haro!* had difficulty surviving.

The war years

During the first years of the war Albert Daenens' activities are not easy to reconstruct. The lack of money, a constant in his life, made him rely heavily on his friends. But some of these friends were considered collaborators with the occupying German regime, and this will have consequences after the war. In the case of Willem Gijssels, we can reasonably assume that he and Daenens probably met each other in the years before World War I at the cafe-cabaret *Le Diable au Corps*. Gijssels was eight years older, now known mainly for some corny Flemish hymns, but what probably impressed Daenens was Gijssels' earlier involvement with the artistic-literary anarchist group *De Kapel* (named after the abandoned chapel in which they held their meetings) in Antwerp around the turn of the century.[24] Gijssels contributed to the journals *Alvoorder* and *Ontwaking*, in which one could find articles by anarchists Kropotkin, Jacques Mesnil and Ferdinand Domela Nieuwenhuis.[25] In 1916 Gijssels became chief editor of *Vlaamsch Leven* (Flemish Life) and in that position, he gave Daenens a press pass, which was of course important because with that pass Daenens could visit museums and galleries without entrance fees. In return, and because he needed the money, Daenens worked as an illustrator for the journal, as can be seen in the serial novel *My bicycle* by the Flemish author Stijn Streuvels.[26] Referring to the theme of rupture/continuity we have already here an example: the style of these illustrations testified to no renovation whatsoever, nor any artistic challenge. These were pure illustrations for a living, perfectly fitting for the journal. Because if we look at his other, more personal, work of that period we will see Daenens experimenting with heavy black and white contrasts, like the illustrations he made for the three stories in the first publication by Maurice Roelants.[27] Proud of his first book Roelants mentioned that "Albert Daenens cut the plates and binding in pear wood, while the writer learned to set this in the noble art of printing."[28] It could well be that these woodcuts were exhibited at the *Doe Stil Voort* exhibition a year later in the Museum of Modern Art of Brussels of some young modern artists, to name a few: the brothers Cantré, Albert Daenens, Felix De Boeck, Prosper De Troyer, Jozef Peeters and Victor Servranckx.[29] Daenens exhibited six paintings and three woodcuts. He was disappointed and angry over some criticisms and wrote letters to the editors of two Flemish newspapers:

> "It is high time that there comes an end to a situation whereby attempts to civilize society threaten to end in shipwreck. / The Flemish people are already retarded enough. Such criticism helps deaden their mind instead of enlightening it. That is a miserable and criminal work."[30]

A politically problematic aspect of Daenens' work is its contribution, from July to November 1918, to the Great-Dutch journal *De Toorts* (*The Torch*), to which many exiled Flemish activists contributed. This contact was facilitated by his friend Gijssels, probably to help him earn a living, because afterwards there was some correspondence about payment problems. However, his illustrations, although similar in style, are nothing like the innocent images as used for *Vlaamsch Leven*, but full-page cover drawings in line with the ideology of the journal. It is not clear that Daenens held the same views, especially considering his radical left-wing political views before and after the war, but nevertheless they can be regarded as ideological statements for the Flemish cause. A few months later, the war was over and Daenens guessed it was better to flee to the Netherlands. A nice anecdote comes from his friend Felix De Boeck: "In the spring of 1918 he [Frits van den Berghe] was at my [Felix De Boeck] place and Albert Daenens made him a false passport, with which Frits was able to go to Holland."[31]

In the Dutch artists' village Blaricum, where Van den Berghe had already lived in 1916, a kind of Flemish exiled artists' colony was formed by the end of the war, with the brothers Jozef and Jan Frans Cantré, the poet René de Clercq and others. Daenens visited them, which proved very fruitful for the second series of *Haro!*.

Haro! second series (1919-1920)

After his stay in The Netherlands, Daenens returned to Belgium. This post-war period is rather complicated in Daenens' life, because of the evolution of some of his acquaintances and friends from collaboration during the World War I, believing that this would further the Flemish cause, towards real ideological World War II collaboration. Due to such evolutions, the political (extreme) left-wing position of this Flemish avant-garde has long been disregarded, as if there was a kind of stain working backwards. Interestingly we can witness something similar through the personal evolution of a few French-speaking writers such as Paul Ruscart, Paul Colin, Michel de Ghelderode and René Baert, just to stay with a few people from Daenens' circle of friends.

So indeed in 1919 Daenens begins with the second series of the magazine, and this is the most fertile, again despite recurrent financial problems. As for the first series, he made the full-page cover and some smaller illustrations inside. Other and now very well-known artists contributed to this magazine which started its first number with the following manifesto:

> "The most abominable crimes that governments have devised against peoples have been committed. The most horrible of wars has just ended. In the name of old and false conventions, ten million men, the youngest, the most entitled to life, have just been mown down, forever defeated. ... Comrades, help us to overthrow the rotten old building! Help us to make the revolution, to drive away the undesirable and the bad. ... Then, with a last and unanimous blow of a pickaxe, we will break open the doors that were obscuring the sun; We shall make the mouldy, decaying, lifeless old world crumble at our feet for ever."[32]

The ideological content changes a bit, even more antimilitaristically. In *Art Libre* the resurrection of *Haro!* was announced as follows: 'We signal the birth – or better the resurrection – of the sympathetic libertarian journal *Haro!*, which, under the direction of our confrère Daenens vigorously undertakes the good fight.'[33]

The first issues contained mainly illustrations by Daenens, with an exception for the second issue with two drawings by the still unidentified F. E. and the third issue with a satirical drawing by his old friend Charles Counhaye on the involvement of two big industrial players in the war, Schneider and Krupp, and issue five with two more illustrations by Counhaye. While the previous imagery was a continuation of the slightly Brabant impressionist-fauvist pre-war style, Daenens now used a more contrasted way of drawing. It must be noted that he, evidently influenced by the material he had to work with, which now was linoleum as a cheap replacement for wood, already preferred a more clear-cut style from the first issue of the second series, but only for the full-page covers. With number six, published in November 1919, things really changed. And thus artistically this second series of *Haro!* became the most interesting, because next to the aforementioned illustrators, graphical work by Jozef Cantré, Frans Masereel, Frits Van den Berghe and Paul Joostens was published.[34] I could identify two other contributors living then in Blaricum, writing under the pseudonyms Vesa and Nele for the second series of *Haro!*, as Dr. Victor Cnop and his future wife, the art historian Juliane Gabriel.[35] And then for several months, Daenens seemed to have not enough money to publish and it took until 1 May 1920 before the next issue saw the light, thanks to donations and efforts of friends of the journal and its cause. The biting full-page cover by Daenens showed the Belgian king, scared, hiding behind a window curtain, and overlooking workers' demonstrations, saying: "What would I do without socialist ministers?". But this issue is important for something else: an extract of Clément Pansaers' *Apologie de la Paresse* was published for the first time.[36] Written in 1917, but only printed in 1921 by the Antwerp editor *Ça Ira*, this proved that *Haro!* was open to new artistic tendencies, in this case Dadaism. But the new start lasted for only three numbers and in June 1920 the second series really ended.

Recently another interesting contact of Albert Daenens was revealed. His archive holds a lost radical anti-militarist and anti-religion play by Theo van Doesburg, handed over to Daenens to translate into French and to publish in *Haro!* The translation was indeed made, but the publication never took place.[37]

Rupture or continuity? "The family" (1918 vs 1926)

In 1926 Manuel Devaldès[38] asked Daenens for illustrations to a new forthcoming anthology *Anthologie des écrivains réfractaires*.[39] Conscientious objector by principle during World War I, Devaldès had fled to England, where he was imprisoned for a while due to a so-called illegal stay. He did not return to France until years later, when persecution was lifted for draft resisters. This is someone who already had a long career in anarchist and antimilitarist, but also artists' circles. And he was one of the few people who were published in the three series of *Haro!*[40] For this anthology Devaldès brought together writers from different angles, who were "excluded" from publishing because they dared to write pacifist, anti-militarist or even just questioning-war texts. But what is important here is that one of the illustrations resembled an older scene created in (or for) a completely different context. While in the drawing for *De Toorts* (fig. 11.2) there is a criticism of the war, this more general message partly disappears because of the reference to a very specific situation, namely the bombing of Flanders at the end of the war, clarified by the title and legend of the drawing: "Aeroplane attacks by the Entente-liberators in Flanders" and "The long-promised liberation and the end of their misery".[41] The illustration for Devaldès' anthology some years later gains depth and importance by the universality of its expression (fig. 11.3). It is no longer a specific situation in a war, it is the general rejection of the atrocities of all wars. The subtitle reads "The family, at the back".[42] Not only is the publication environment different, also the style seems like a complete makeover. As seen during the war, but not always reflected in the commissioned work for Flemish activist newspapers, Daenens seemed to have evolved from a loose drawing style to a more expressionist one, playing with the possibilities of relative hard contrasts which wood and linoleum offered. This reflects an evolution of Daenens as an artist. While we see a continuity in the subject, although the message conveyed differs, there is a clear rupture in style, and this also shows that he followed contemporary avant-garde expressions.

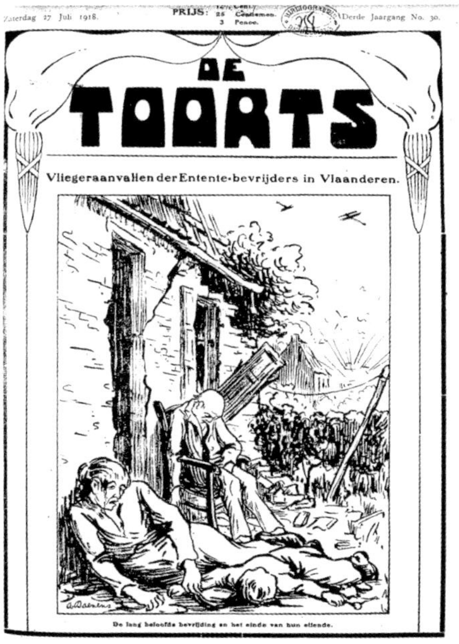

11.2. Albert Daenens, *De lang beloofde bevrijding en het einde van hun ellende*, 1918, in *De Toorts*, 3(30), p. 1 (27 July 1918).

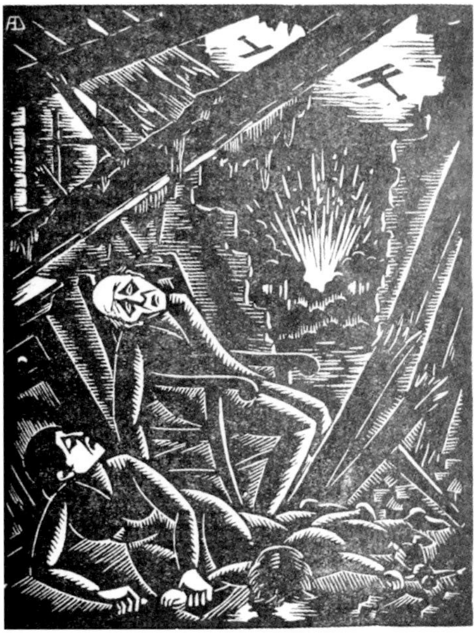

11.3. Albert Daenens, *La famille, à l'arrière*, 1926, in Manuel Devaldès, *Anthologie des écrivains réfractaires. Les Humbles, Revue Littéraire des Primaires*, 12, 1927, p. 13.

Indeed, between the second and third series of *Haro!* a few words need to be said about his artistic career. Probably through the contacts with Theo van Doesburg and *De Stijl*, he started experimenting with abstraction. In the French neo-plasticist magazine *Vouloir* (Lille, 1924-1927) Daenens had some of his work reproduced. In September 1924 he contributed an undated abstract linocut. In the following year, some of his more figurative linocuts were published. The most intriguing mention of his work is by late 1926, for the *Lyrisme?* issue of *Vouloir*, in which he has two abstract linocuts, one dated 1924, and one which he seems to have made in 1919. In his archives this work bears the date "1919-1924" in pencil, and written over it "191?-1924" in black ink, so it cannot be guaranteed it was indeed made solely in 1919. It would not be the first time an artist had pre-dated work to look more avant-garde. But then again, given the contacts he had with Theo van Doesburg right after the war, this could indeed be a very early abstract work.[43]

Another person from the north of France, and collaborator of *Vouloir*, is Maurice Wullens, who for many years edited the pacifist artistic-literary journal *Les Humbles*. Daenens made several contributions to it. Wullens will defend Daenens when Maurice Casteels, in a 1924 article for *Mercure de Flandre* about linocut as a revolutionary art in Belgium, did not even mention Daenens, except with a deliberately vague "one of them":

> "This *one of them* is our comrade Albert Daenens, the illustrator of the *Kraskreml*, by Henri Guilbeaux .... But back to Casteels. Why does he not mention Daenens? Does he not know him? ... They conducted together the beautiful magazine *Haro!* before and after the war: Casteels dealing with the literary part, Daenens with the artistic programme. *Haro!* was among the first Belgian magazines to publish linocuts. Better than that: Daenens illustrated Casteels' prose collection *Banalités* with five linocuts, and in *Esthétique* (both of them editions of the Pot d'Étain in Brussels) the only modern lino (and awfully reduced!) was by Albert Daenens. Come on, another little hatred, some jealousy! So much pettiness among these writers!"[44]

In 1927, from London, then still exiled, Devaldès contacted Daenens for more illustrations to a new book he was preparing. Even though subscriptions were asked for in *Les Humbles* not enough money was raised and the book was never published.

Haro! third series (1927-1928), WW II and aftermath

From 1927 to 1928 the third series of *Haro!* was published. This time the political programme was again more libertarian and pacifist, with among others Manuel Devaldès, Ernestan and Mil Zankin. For the literary criticism, a certain Babylas signed, who was none other than the famous writer Michel de Ghelderode.[45] There were no more illustrations running along the text, but the full-page front cover was, as always, by Daenens.

A highlight of Daenens' career is the publication in 1929 of *20 linos pamphletaires*.[46] This album chronologically lists his best linocuts from 1919 to 1929. The foreword was written by his friend René Baert.[47] This album was even sent to Gandhi.[48] Indeed Daenens became in that period more and more involved in the international pacifist movement. His work appeared in antimilitarist magazines and journals all over the world, but his artistic career seemed over. Word War II again brought misery and once more he had to beg his friends for work, but some of these friends were now collaborating with the Nazi occupiers. Daenens' view on the world became very bleak.[49] By 1937, he had moved to the small village of Drogenbos, not far from Brussels but close to his lifelong friend Felix De Boeck. He did occasionally work with the local amateur theatre group for some plays, as well as director and designer. His social situation steadily worsened, and by the end of his life he was living in real poverty. Felix De Boeck's wife brought him a daily bowl of soup.[50] On 25 August 1952 he died in a hospital in nearby Uccle. And then for many years, Albert Daenens was forgotten by most. It is only by digging in his archive that the role he played in as well local as international artistic and anti-militarist circles comes to light. It's about time Albert Daenens gets his rightful place in Belgian art history.

Notes

1 Archive of Albert Daenens, D1175, Letterenhuis, Antwerp.

2 To be understood in the context of Flemish dialect.

3 "Les Théâtres. Au Palais des Arts. Le Théâtre national d'art et d'application", *Le Thyrse* 13, no. 5 (1911), 192. "Les décors nouveaux de M. Daenens sont vraiment très réussis".

4 Erik Buelinckx, "Enkele anarchistisch gezinde kunstenaars rond Emile Verhaeren" in *Anarchisten rond Emile Verhaeren*, ed. David Gullentops and Hans Vandevoorde, Tekst en Tijd (Brussel: VUBPress, 2005), 71-109; David Gullentops, *Émile Verhaeren inédit* (Brussel: VUBPress, 2015).

5 Archives of the City of Brussels, Archives of the Police, Bureau des Étrangers, dossier 76065 : Rapport mai 1913. "Le prénommé a fait mutation de Molenbeek St. Jean avec sa maîtresse, une nommée Lebègue, Alice Jeanne, née à Bruxelles, le 26 mars 1886, célibataire, laquelle est décédée, rue Rittweger, 27, le 21 novembre 1912."

6 Daphné de Marneffe, "Entre modernisme et avant-garde. Le réseau des revues littéraires de l'immédiat

après-guerre en Belgique (1919-1922)" (Thèse de Doctorat en Langues et Lettres, Université de Liège, 2007).

7 "La Foi nouvelle", La Foi nouvelle 1, no. 1 (1912), 1. "Oh! Petits Dieux de bois et petits saints de pierre, / Que de crimes pour vous en cette ère amassés ! / Le peuple ne croit plus. Tes beaux jours sont passés ; / Pleure en ton Vatican, successeur de Saint-Pierre / Le Tout-Puissant, hélas, ce n'est qu'une chimère / Que nos sens abusés s'en sont chercher au ciel / En des vapeurs d'encens qu'un rite artificiel / Berce, mystérieux, tel un rêve éphémère."

8 *Ibid.*

9 Abel Gerbaud (1888-1954) was a French painter, with an interest in applied arts, who stayed in Brussels before WWI to avoid conscription, where he met Daenens. They stayed friends for a long time and worked together with another French artist and friend, Marcel Bouraine, his Belgian friend Frédéric Denis, and the Dutch artist Theo van Doesburg for the great exhibition of Modern Art in Genève (23/12/1920-25/01/1921).

10 Albert Daenens, "A propos d'Art appliqué," *La Foi nouvelle* 1, no. 4 (1912), 7: "Aux vrais artistes à se révolter, il ne nous reste plus rien à attendre de l'état social d'aujourd'hui, le salut nous viendra du peuple, source inépuisable d'énergie nouvelle. Préparons avec lui la révolution qui balayera cette bourgeoisie sans idéal, sans âme et sans cerveau."

11 Pierre Kropotkine, "Aux jeunes gens" in *Paroles d'un révolté. Ouvrage publié, annoté et accompagné d'une préface par Elisée Reclus* (Paris: Flammarion, 1885), 43-75; Henry van de Velde, "Déblaiement de l'Art" *La Société Nouvelle* 10, no. 112 (1894), 444-456.

12 Paul Ruscart (1893-1946?): after a rather short anarchist period Paul Ruscart would become a collaborator of the pro-German journal *La Belgique* and evolved towards Walloon activism during the first World War. From 1940 to 1944 he worked for the collaborating journal *Le Soir* and was editor in chief of the Nazi journal *Les Hommes au Travail*. At the end of the war he managed to escape and in 1946 he was sentenced in absentia to the death penalty.

13 Léon De Roos was also manager of *Le Revolté* in 1912. Later he would adhere to the Flemish movement.

14 René Bianco, "Un siècle de presse anarchiste d'expression française, 1880-1983. Répertoire des périodiques anarchistes de langue française" (Université de Provence, 1987): fiche 893: 'En Marge'.

15 Archives of the City of Brussels, Archives of the Police, Bureau des Étrangers, dossier 76065: Rapport mai 1913. "Daenens, Louis Albert répond au signalement suivant : / taille 1m55 à 1m57 / figure maigre et osseuse / teint plutôt jaunâtre / cheveux blond-roux, assez longs / barbe blond-roux, carrée / Boite fortement de la jambe droite et de ce chef est tout à fait défranché / Porte toujours un grand chapeau feutre mou à larges bords et une cravate genre « La Vallière »".

16 Raphaël Dubois (1888-1960?) was a Belgian artist, who lived in Brussels before WWI, and was afterwards active in France and Belgium.

17 Archives of the City of Brussels, Archives de la Police, Bureau des Étrangers, dossier 76065: Rapport mai 1913. "J'ai appris que, presque journellement, Daenens, Dubois et consorts, se rendent rue Paepenkasteel, 3, chez Gerbaud et y tiennent, très probablement leur réunion de la presse anarchiste, car il paraitrait qu'une machine à imprimer existe suscite adresse et que la publication « En Marge » s'y imprimerait ainsi que la nouvelle édition du journal anarchiste « Le Révolté » publié sous la direction de Daenens, Louis Albert."

18 Maurice Casteels (1890-1962): Belgian writer who before WWI frequented anarchist circles, for instance in *Le Diable au Corps*. After the war, he aligned himself with the pacifist movement around Romain Rolland, which costs him his job at the city of Brussels. He wrote on art and architecture. In 1920, he co-organised in Brussels a conference where Theo van Doesburg spoke, for the first time in Belgium, about his ideas on abstract art. Selected bibliography: Maurice Casteels, "Pour l'art

moderne" *Haro!* 1e série, no. 2 (1913), 12-14; "Pour l'art moderne" *Haro!* 1e série, no. 3 (1913), 20-21; *Banalités. Avec 5 linos par Albert Daenens* (Bruxelles: Édition du Pot d'etain, 1921); *Esthétique* (Bruxelles: Édition du Pot d'etain, 1921); *Die Sachlichkeit in der Modernen Kunst. Vorwort: Henri van de Velde* (Paris und Leipzig: Henri Jonquières, 1930).

19 About Marsile Armigny and Louis Fel I couldn't find biographical information. René Schmickrath was a Belgian poet and was published, among others, in the bilingual Luxemburg magazine *Floréal. Revue libre d'art et de littérature – Freie Rundschau für Kunst und Literatur* (1907-1908).

20 Véronique Waterlot-Jottrand and Daniel Lefebvre, eds., *Haro! Une revue belge d'avant-garde 1913-1928* (Mons: Renard Découvert / Mundaneum, 1995). This is the only, but very interesting, study on *Haro!*, created for an exhibition in Mundaneum (Mons, Belgium), with a very practical index of most articles and contributors.

21 La Rédaction, "HARO ! paraît au moins une fois par mois..." *Haro!* 1e série, no. 1 (1913): 2: "HARO ! ne groupe que les littérateurs et artistes d'avant-garde. / HARO ! est en Belgique, le premier journal d'action d'art moderne dans son acceptation le plus intransigeante. / Les collaborateurs de HARO ! s'occuperont, en même temps que de littérature et d'art, des faits d'actualité. Car si la mission de l'artiste exige la solitude muette, il doit néanmoins prêter l'oreille à tout ce qui peut intéresser les autres hommes et s'il se mêle de leurs actes il leur démontrera l'héroïsme."

22 Albert Daenens, "Ni fleurs, ni couronnes" *ibid.*, 8: "Rik Wouters, sculpteur, a cette fois la lourde tâche de montrer aux peintres les tendances nouvelles en peinture. Il s'en tire d'une façon admirable. [...] J. Ensor a fait mieux."

23 Charles Counhaye (1884-1971) was a Belgian engaged multidisciplinary artist, who had contact with Romain Rolland, Philippe Soupault and Henri Barbusse in Paris.

24 Depicted by Ary Delen, one of the members of the group, as follows: "Where once the altar stood, Steinlen's poster *L'Aurore* was hung, depicting a woman stretching longingly her arms towards the flaming dawn of the future. Right under it a long table with journals and magazines, such as *Van Nu & Straks*, *La Société Nouvelle* and *Les Temps Nouveaux*." Cited in Stijn Vanclooster, Jan Moulaert, and Erwin Joos, *De Kapel tussen droom en daad. Anarchie en artistieke heropleving in Antwerpen rond 1900* (Antwerpen: VZW Eugeen Van Mieghem, 2013), 91.

25 For more on the relation between Daenens and Gijssels see: Erik Buelinckx, "Albert Daenens & Willem Gijssels. Een Brusselse anarchistische kunstenaar en een Vlaamse dichter", *Zuurvrij*, no. 21 (2011), 50-57.

26 Stijn Streuvels (1871-1969): Flemish naturalist writer.

27 Maurice Roelants (1895-1966): Flemish "psychological" writer.

28 Maurice Roelants, *De driedubbele verrassing* (Brussel: De Nieuwe Boekhandel, 1917). "Albert Daenens sneed de platen en de bandversiering in perelaarhout terwijl de schrijver leerde om dit te zetten de edele drukkunst."

29 Willem Gijssels, ed. *Zomertentoonstelling 1918. Tweede Reeks. Kataloog* (Brussel: Kunstkring Doe Stil Voort, 1918).

30 Draft letter of Albert Daenens to Willem Gijssels, 31 July 1918 [Archive of Albert Daenens, D1175, Letterenhuis, Antwerp]. "Het is hoog tijd dat er een einde kome aan een toestand waardoor de pogingen tot maatschappelijke beschaving dreigen schipbreuk te lijden. Het Vlaamsche volk is reeds achterlijk genoeg. Met dergelijke kritiek helpt men zijn geest verstompen in plaats van het voor te lichten. Dat is ellendig en misdadig werk."

31 Joos Florquin and Felix De Boeck, "Ten huize van... Felix De Boeck" in *Ten huize van...* ed. Joos Florquin (Leuven / Brugge: Davidsfonds / Orion-Desclé De Brouwer, 1971), 185-86. "In de lente van 1918 is hij met Albert Daenens bij mij geweest en toen heeft Daenens voor Van den Berghe een vals paspoort gemaakt, waarmee Frits naar Holland is kunnen gaan."

32 La Rédaction, "HARO !", *Haro!* 2e série, no. 1 (1919), 2. "Le plus abominable des crimes que des gouvernements aient ourdi contre des peuples vient de se commettre. La plus horrible des guerres vient de finir. Au nom de vieilles et mensongères conventions, dix millions d'hommes, les plus jeunes, les plus ayant droit à ta vie, viennent d'être fauchés, abattus à jamais. (...) Camarades, aidez-nous à renverser la vieille bâtisse pourrie ! Aidez-nous à faire la révolution, à chasser les indésirables et les méchants. (...) Alors, d'un dernier et unanime coup de pioche, nous enfoncerons les portes qui cachaient le soleil ; nous ferons crouler à nos pieds et pour toujours le vieux monde moisi, décrépit, sans vie."

33 "Notes et nouvelles", *L'art libre*, 10 (1919), 112: "Nous signalons la naissance — ou plutôt la résurrection — du sympathique journal libertaire « Haro », qui, sous la direction de notre confrère Daenens, entreprend vigoureusement le bon combat."

34 The contacts with these graphic artists explains the title of a small exhibition in 2003 in Drogenbos: Jan D'Haese, *"De Vijf + Één". Jan-Frans Cantré, Jozef Cantré, Frans Masereel, Joris Minne, Henri Van Straten + Albert Daenens*, ed. Jan De Kelver, Ontmoeting met Felix (Drogenbos: Stichting Felix De Boeck en v.z.w. Museum Felix De Boeck, 2003).

35 Letter from Frits van den Berghe to Albert Daenens (probably in September 1919). [Archive of Albert Daenens, D1175, Letterenhuis, Antwerp].

36 Clément Pansaers, "L'Apologie de la Paresse", *Haro!*, 2e série, no. 10 (1920), 6-7.

37 Sjoerd van Faassen, Hans Renders, and Erik Buelinckx, "'De stem uit de diepte': een onuitgegeven 'simultanéistisch spel' van Theo van Doesburg", *Zacht Lawijd. Literair-historisch tijdschrift*, no. 15-3 (2016), 4-55.

38 Manuel Devaldès (Évreux 1875 – Paris 1956) was a well-known individualist anarchist, neo-Malthusian, pacifist and very productive contributor to numerous libertarian journals. He was the founder in 1895 of *La Revue rouge*, which had Félix Fénéon, Zo d'Axa and Paul Verlaine as collaborators, and of *L'Action d'Art* in 1912, with Gérard de Lacaze-Duthiers. The anarchist and pacifist writer Gérard de Lacaze-Duthiers was the inventor of the term *Artistocratie*. See Erik Buelinckx, "Mauer – film préhistorique. Gérard de Lacaze-Duthiers et l'esthétique libertaire," in *Cinémas libertaires. Au service des forces de transgression et de révolte* ed. Nicole Brenez and Isabelle Marinone, Arts du spectacle – Images et sons (Paris: Presses Universitaires du Septentrion, 2015), 151-162.

39 *Anthologie des écrivains réfractaires*, ed. Maurice Wullens, Revue Littéraire des Primaires "Les Humbles" [Douzième série] (Paris: Les Humbles, 1927). An original linocut is kept in Letterenhuis under the title "Zij die te huis bleven. La famille du combatant" (Those who stayed at home. The family of the combatant.). D 1175 / I (Box 3)

40 A selection: Manuel Devaldès, "Le salvateur néo-malthusianisme," *Haro!* 1e série, no. 3 (1913); "Bonhomme," *Haro!* 2e série, no. 11 (1920); "Les Réfractaires," *Haro!* 3e série, no. 5 (1928).

41 De Toorts, derde jaargang, no. 30, 1 (27 juli 1918): "Vliegeraanvallen der Entente-bevrijders in Vlaanderen" / "De lang beloofde bevrijding en het einde van hun ellende".

42 Devaldès, *Anthologie des écrivains réfractaires*, (1927), 13. 'La famille, à l'arrière'.

43 Sylvie Férey, ed. *Vouloir 1924-1927. Collection complète de 26 numéros*, Temps, espace et société. Collection « Histoire de l'art » (Villeneuve d'Ascq: Presses Universitaires du Septentrion, 2006).

44 Maurice Wullens, "Revue des revues," *La Revue Anarchiste* 3, no. 26 (1924). "Cet *un d'eux* est notre camarade Albert Daenens, l'illustrateur du *Kraskreml*, d'Henri Guilbeaux (...). Mais revenons à Casteels. Pourquoi ne nomme-t-il pas Daenens ? Ne le connait-il pas ? Disons donc ! Ils dirigèrent ensemble la belle revue *Haro!* avant et après la guerre : Casteels s'occupant de la partie littéraire, Daenens du programme artistique. *Haro!* fut des premières, parmi les revues belges, à publier des linos. Mieux que ça : Daenens illustra de cinq linos gravés *Banalités* au recueil de prose de Casteels, et dans l'*Esthétique*, du même (ces deux plaquettes aux éditions du Pot d'Étain, à Bruxelles) le seul

lino moderne (d'ailleurs fâcheusement rapetissé !) est d'Albert Daenens. Allons, encore une petite haine, une jalousie quelconque ! Que de mesquineries parmi ces littérateurs !"

45 Roland Beyen, ed. *Correspondance de Michel de Ghelderode 1919-1927*, 9 vols., Archives du Futur (Bruxelles: Labor / AML, 1991).

46 Albert Daenens, *20 linos pamphletaires. 20 pamphlet-linos* (Brussels: Éditions du Repos Bien Mérité, 1929).

47 René Baert (1903-1945): Belgian writer and poet. In the 1930s he becomes more and more interested in Nazi mysticism and ends up as an adherent of Hitler. He was killed in Germany by Belgian soldiers at the end of the war.

48 Letter from the Belgian peace activist Marcel Van Diest to the then imprisoned pacifist Mohandas Karamchand Gandhi, 1930, in N. R. Phatak, ed. *Mahatma Gandhi Part III (1930-1931)*, Source material for a history of the freedom movement in India (Bombay, Maharashta State: Direcrorate of Printing and Stationery, 1969), 597-98. "P. S.—At the reception of your card I sent you the album of our friend Albert Daenens, we suppose that it duly reached you."

49 "Albert Daenens, een "obscuur" leven in dienst van de kunst", in *"De Vijf + Één". Jan-Frans Cantré, Jozef Cantré, Frans Masereel, Joris Minne, Henri Van Straten + Albert Daenens*, ed. Jan De Kelver (Drogenbos: Stichting Felix De Boeck en v.z.w. Museum Felix De Boeck, 2003).

50 Joos Florquin and Pol Jacquemyns, "Ten huize van... Pol Jacquemyns (1967)" in *Ten huize van...* ed. Joos Florquin (Leuven: Davidsfonds, 1980), 137.

Belgian Art and the International Avant-garde of the 1920's-Networks

Modernist Generations in Belgium: United and Divided by Community Art

Hans Vandevoorde

"Our generation is lost, it may be, but it is more blameless than those earlier ones."[1] (Franz Kafka)

"I can only see decline everywhere, in saying which, however, I do not mean that earlier generations were essentially better than ours, but only younger; that was their great advantage, their memory was not so overburdened as ours today ..." Those are the words of the first-person narrator in Kafka's short story *Investigations of a Dog* (*Forschungen eines Hundes*). Then he takes it a step further: "[n]o, whatever objection I may have to my age, former generations were not better, indeed in a sense they were far worse, far weaker."[2] The dog is thus making two salient points: 1) that the memory of earlier generations was less overwhelmed than that of his; and 2) that those generations were somehow wanting compared to the newer one.

The main dynamic in this Kafka story, however, revolves around not so much the conflict between generations as that between the individual subject and the community of which he is part. Dogs are faithful beings who band together, but this one wants to set himself apart, thinking himself better than the rest of the pack, even though his actions are repeatedly determined by his fellows. These two conflicts – old versus new and individual versus community – constitute the primary themes of this article. I will be exploring their occurrence in the generations of artists from before, during and after the First World War. More specifically, I place these conflicts in the context of the discussions about geometric abstraction waged everywhere in the avant-garde world, which acquired a specific meaning in Belgium in terms of the debate about community art. In doing so, I intend to show how a model of generations can reflect the continuity between various succeeding modernist generations, while also demonstrating the specificity of the art that evolved after the war—from both a national and an international perspective.

"Generation" as a concept is currently used to denote both the particular time period in which a group of people was born and the point in time at which they came into prominence (around the age of thirty, according to Robert Wohl).[3] I use both of these perspectives, but adopt the latter in defining my generations; accordingly I term the generations of artists born between 1875 and 1890 and 1890 and 1905, respectively, the Generations of 1910 and 1920. In the historical account later created, the artists I attribute to the first generation were the heirs to the subjectivist, individualist movements of previous generations (in art this refers predominantly to impressionism), whereas those of the second generation (belonging to the radical, "historical avant-garde") tended to valorise community, culminating in the objectivist, geometric trend of the early 1920s. We will ascertain if this is anything more than self-positioning on the part of that younger generation and whether there is a need to further differentiate those generations.

Although approaching things from the standpoint of generations is largely frowned upon in literary and art history, I will reintroduce it here – not in the naïve, unthinking manner so common in our daily language, but by evoking the theories of Karl Mannheim and Henk Becker. Thinking in terms of generations in my opinion still yields undeniable benefits.[4] It allows us, among other things, to adopt both a transnational and national perspective; to look beyond social class; to examine older and younger groups (from different "generations") together at a single point in time and thus take into account both what is established and what is "fresh and new"; and to integrate various smaller formations (which I call "families") into larger wholes. I will therefore attempt to study the diverse constructivist movements that originated around 1920 (Russian constructivism, Bauhaus, purism, Dutch neo-plasticism and the Belgian "Modern Art" group) as a unified whole so as to compare their ideas and forms with those of other currents of thought among the same generation of avant-garde artists. Another advantage of viewing things through the lens of generations is that it allows us to include both visual and performing arts and literature in our examination.

The ultimate benefit of this exercise would be to answer the question whether there was a break between the radical avant-garde youth and older artists. The 1920s generation in particular was forever citing the war as an element that solidified its unity and distinguished it from the previous generation. It propagated community art in two distinct senses of the term which, although related (and often used interchangeably), still differ substantially. I call them "art for the community" and "communal art".[5] The first concerns art produced for the community as a whole, while the second involves the integration of all forms of art (in the tradition of Wagner's *Gesamtkunstwerk*).

Taking this dual notion of community art as a premise, I will therefore examine whether the First World War brought about a break with previous generations, some of whose members also championed a form of community art, with examples ranging from H.P. Berlage (1856-1934)[6] and Henry van de Velde (1863-1957) in architecture to the individualistic generation associated with the journal *Van Nu en Straks* in the literature of the late 19th century.[7]

I will take Flanders as my case study, where the situation is further complicated by the fact that the "art for the community" becomes caught up in the struggle on the part of some young intellectuals and artists against French as the dominant cultural language.[8] In 1916 Paul van Ostaijen published his *Music-Hall* collection there, which is considered the first work of the "historical avant-garde" in literature and has traces of experimentation and the sense of brotherhood inspired by French unanimism that would soon lead him to humanitarian expressionism. Could it be then that 1916 – historically seen as the year in which not only radical modernism burst onto the scene in Dutch-language literature, but also abstractionism took hold in Belgian art – was a breaking point; or was it more a case of continuity, readily evident when considered from the point of view of community art (in both senses of the term)?

A generational model

The First World War can obviously be viewed as a "major event", the concept so central to the thinking about generations derived from the seminal essay "The Problem of Generations" by Karl Mannheim from 1928. The Great War is one of those formative collective experiences (*entscheidende Kollektivereignisse*) that underlie generational identity formation, or at least a belief in a common fate (*Schicksal*), in Western European countries. Mannheim did not think that such formative experiences were strictly necessary for defining a generation, but some of his successors, such as the Dutch sociologist Henk Becker, believe they are essential. Becker defines a generation as "a class of contemporaries whose behaviour reflects the effects of one or more discontinuous changes experienced during their formative years."[9] Becker goes on to specify that these formative years occur during the ages of 10 to 25 and, according to him, the effect of the major event must last for at least ten years.

That theory would imply that artists born between 1889 and 1904 (who were between 10 and 24 years old in 1914) were most affected by the First World War, whereas their younger colleagues were less aware of the war and older individuals were already too set in their ways, personally developed or socialised to still be determinatively influenced by it. Artistic development, moreover, often occurs under the influence of older artists teaching at art academies, whereby the younger artists inevitably need time to wrest themselves free of their schooling and early socialisation. The defining moment comes when the members of a new generation, generally educated in the manner of a previous one, start generating attention through a journal, for example, or an influential exhibition.

We will return to Mannheim for help in further defining generations. Mannheim combines the positivist vision of generations (French) with the idealistic one (German). The primary significance of his article derives from the three concepts underlying this synthesis: "generation status" (*Generationslagerung*), "generation as actuality" (*Generationszusammenhang*) and "generation unit" (*Generationseinheit*). The generation status, or "social location" of a generation, is the potential created by the biological rhythms of life and death (the *Geburtsjahrgang*, or "age group"). This develops, however, primarily as a result of non-biological factors (economic and spiritual), and it is these extra-biological factors that determine Mannheim's two other concepts. A "generation as actuality" occurs when people are subjected to a common fate, with all that that implies.[10] What matters here is not the vital (physical) "location" or temporal definition, but the sociohistorical context. Much more concrete is Mannheim's "generation unit" produced by socialising forces, the "fundamental integrative attitudes" (*Grundintentionen*), such as attitudes to life or schools of thought, and "formative principles" (*Gestaltungsprinzipien*)[11] that members of a generation have in common. Mannheim draws a distinction between a generation unit and a "concrete group" (*konkrete Gruppe*), in which fundamental integrative attitudes form naturally, such that the group then forms the core of a generation unit.[12]

Mannheim has been criticised for his presentism, or horizontal notion of generation,[13] for failing sufficiently to take the vertical, genealogical dimension of generations into account. Although in my view this criticism is somewhat unfounded,[14] I have aspired to avoid such concerns by emphasising both vertical and horizontal axes in my model. Since impressionism was followed by a series of successive other modernist generations, all these generations constitute the *vertical axis* in my generational model for art history. While I am aware of the arbitrary nature of the so-called age cohorts of which scholars such as Pierre Nora have spoken so disparagingly, they are the norm in sociology, and I find them a useful device.[15] So, I use the age cohort divisions here as a heuristic device,[16] a conceptual model and not a categorical fact. I also tentatively link the various generations to certain movements in an attempt to reconcile the generational model with periodisation. A vertical interpretation of age cohorts as related to the history of modernism in the visual arts yields in broad outlines the following overview (diagram 1).[17]

1830-1845: first impressionist generation	Edouard Manet (1832-1883) Edgar Degas (1834-1917) Paul Cézanne (1839-1906) Claude Monet (1840-1926) Auguste Renoir (1841-1919)
1845-1860: post-impressionism, e.g. Les Nabis Cf. R. Wohl: 1840-1855 = generation 1875	Paul Gauguin (1848-1903) Vincent van Gogh (1853-1890)
1860-1875: neo-impressionism Cf. R. Wohl : 1855-1870 = generation 1890	Georges Seurat (1859-1891) Paul Signac ((1863-1935)
1875-1890: e.g. 'Les Fauves' Cf. R. Wohl: 1870-1885) = generation 1905	Henri Matisse (1869-1954) Maurice de Vlaminck (1876-1954) Kees van Dongen (1877-1968)
1890-1905: historical avant-garde Cf. R. Wohl: 1885-1900 = generation 1914	Cf. infra

Diagram 1: Modernist generations ('age cohorts')

I would add two important restrictions. On the one hand different generations can continue to operate side by side (Wilhelm Pinder's "unsimultaneity of the simultaneous" (*Ungleichzeitigkeit des Gleichzeitigen*) and influence one another. On the other the generations themselves are comprised of synchronic groups sharing different "thematic coherencies"; alongside the modernist generation there were of course also groups of artists still working intensively in the academic spirit whom you could just as well designate a generation (with various successive vertical age cohorts) and members of that generation that stand apart (although critical of impressionism, Fantin-Latour would certainly not be considered an academici painter either). That leads to my *horizontal axis*. Every expression of generational coherence such as modernism consists in turn of conservative, moderate and radical factions operating simultaneously (in the literature of the early 20th century, for instance, the moderate faction was identified with the modernism of Marcel Proust and Thomas Mann), which we can call generation units, adopting Mannheim.

One of the major segments within the modernist generation of the First World War is the historical avant-garde, as defined by Peter Bürger.[18] We clearly see the international imprint of this generation unit from around the First World War shortly before, during and especially after the war in at least two different age cohorts (the age groups of 1875-1890 and 1890-1905), as well as in different families (constructivists, expressionists, futurists, cubists, Dadaists) and concrete groups (e.g. Die Brücke, Der Blaue Reiter and Der Sturm among the expressionists). We will discuss what that means for Belgium below. Here I will briefly show (diagram 2) how Mannheim's theory is applicable to the modernist generation of the war (already the fifth in the row of modernist generations) as a whole, that is a more comprehensive generation of more or less modern artists who at one point were all subjected to the same fate: World War One.

Generation status (*Generationslagerung*)	Three generations that made the experience of the First World War: ca. 1860-1875; 1875-1890; 1890-1905
Generation als actuality (*Generations-zusammenhang*)	For the 1890-1905 generation: World War 1 as *major event*
Generation unit (*Generationseinheit*): - Unit 1: historical avant-garde - Unit 2: more moderate modernism - Unit 3: conservative art movements	→ The **historical avant-garde unit** has the following * fundamental integrative attitudes (*Grundintentionen*): a) opposition against art as an institution b) integration of art and life * formative principles (*Gestaltungsprinzipien*): anti-mimesis (from deformation unto abstraction)
Families - family 1: constructivists → different 'groups' - family 2: expressionists - family 3: futurists ...	→ E.g. the constructivist family (cf. infra)

Diagram 2: Modernist generations and World War 1

The historical avant-garde thus constitutes a generation unit within the more comprehensive modernist generation, with a horizontal (synchronic) and vertical (diachronic) dimension of its own. The vertical dimension of different age groups allows for the standard adoption of the term "avant-garde" to describe progressive movement such as art nouveau in the visual arts and the individualists in literature at the end of the 19th century.[19] From among the successive vertical or diachronic avant-garde generations, then, I will be examining here the horizontal, synchronic dimension of the radical, historical avant-garde generation from around the First World War.

The constructivist family

I will start by developing my theory in greater depth for constructivism as a *family*. On my horizontal, synchronic level, that family is part of the generation unit of the historical avant-garde, which in turn is part of the broader modernist generation. This radical avant-garde of constructivists working primarily after the war, however, has an initial age group, when considered vertically, of founders who were older. The artists we call constructivist can consequently be subdivided into at least three sequential age groups that I will call the "founding fathers" (born around 1860-1875), the "first generation" (born around 1875-1890) and the "second generation" (born around 1890-1905 and emerging only after the war). Diagram 3 clearly shows how the path toward innovation was primarily forged by the older artists.

1. Founding fathers (1860-1875)	Wassily Kandinsky (1866-1944), Russia and Germany Piet Mondriaan (1872-1944), Netherlands
2. First generation constructivists (1875-1890) [Cf. also the family of German expressionists]	Kasimir Malevich (1879-1935), Ukraine Fernand Léger (1881-1955), France Théo van Doesburg (1883-1931), Netherlands Walter Gropius (1883-1969), Germany Vladimir Tatlin (1885-1953), Russia Robert Delaunay (1885-1941), France Antoine Pevsner (1886-1962), Russia & France Amédée Ozenfant (1886-1966), France Georges Vantongerloo (1886-1965), Belgium Le Corbusier (1887-1965), France Lajos Kassák (1887-1967), Hungary Willi Baumeister (1889-1955), Germany El Lissitzky (1890-1941), Russia Konstantin Stepanowitsch Melnikow (1890–1974), Russia
3. Second generation constructivists (1890-1905)	Naum Gabo (1890-1977), Russia & US Alexander Michailowitsch Rodtschenko (1891-1956), Russia László Moholy-Nagy (1895-1946), Hungary Jozef Peeters (1895-1960), Belgium Marcel-Louis Baugniet (1896-1995), Belgium Marcel Janco (1895-1984), Romenia Victor Servranckx (1897-1965), Belgium Karel Maes (1900-1974), Belgium Pierre-Louis Flouquet (1900-1967), Belgium Michel Seuphor (1901-1999), Belgium & France

Diagram 3: Age cohorts within the constructivist family

With this classification, moreover, we can then designate the various major, essentially national, movements as separate *groups* for placement in our overview. The constructivists (in the broadest sense of the word) sometimes saw themselves as a generation,[20] but their thinking – as evident from their many manifestos – ran more along the lines of a group. Constructivist groups and movements include the French purists, Dutch De Stijl and neo-plasticism, the Belgian "Modern Art" group of Jozef Peeters and others, German Bauhaus, and the Russian,[21] Romanian, Polish, Serbo-Croatian and Czechoslovakian constructivists.

With regard to the national character of these groups, it is important to add the following caveats: 1) they all had a very international profile or were at least internationally oriented (as reflected in the Bauhaus and De Stijl movements); and 2) different groups could co-exist in a single country, such as in Russia, where one had the anti-metaphysical, object-oriented art associated with Tatlin side-by-side with the "non-objective" school of Malevich. Belgium was also home to different groups, such as those associated with the bi-weekly, French-language modernist magazine *7 Arts* (1922-1929) and the Dutch-language review *Het Overzicht* (1920-1925),[22] which became increasingly international in its scope. Berlin and, to a lesser degree, Paris served as points of reference for these two magazines.

In addition to referring to generations and groups, I will thus also refer to that intermediate stage I called "the family", which allows us to view the various constructivist schools as a whole (diagram 4).

We can identify the following concepts as *fundamental integrative attitudes* of the entire constructivist school family: the integration of art, science and technology (machines);[23] the conjoining of different art genres such as painting, sculpture and design; and the utopian ideal of a new world in which art and life converge. The associated *formative principles* would be the concept of abstraction (in its various gradations) and the principles of clarity, precision, rationality and objectivity, as formally expressed in "hard-edged geometric forms, which serve to emphasize the flatness of the picture plane and the expressive qualities of form and colour".[24] Through a certain social dynamic, the fundamental integrative attitudes and formative principles – elements, that is, of the socialisation process – can lead to a new *generation style* (*Generationstil*), or so-called *generation entelechy*.[25]

Generation status (*Generationslagerung*)	Three generations of modernists cf. supra
Generation als actuality (*Generations-zusammenhang*)	For the second generation: World War 1 as *major event*
Generation unit (*Generationseinheit*)	Historical avant-garde unit around 1920 (cf. supra)
Concrete 'groups': Purists, De Stijl & Neo-Plasticism, Belgian "Modern Art" group of Jozef Peeters, Bauhaus, Russian, Romanian, Polish, Serbo-Croatian and Czechoslovakian constructivists	**Constructivist family** around 1920: * fundamental integrative attitudes: a) integration of art, science and technology → machines b) the conjoining of different art genres such as painting, sculpture and design → interior design c) the utopian ideal of a new world in which art and life converge → art for the community * formative principles: a) geometrical abstraction; clarity, precision, rationality & objectivity; b) form: flatness of the pictures plane and the expressive qualities of form and colour

Diagram 4: The constructivist 'family' (ca. 1920)

I believe generation style is a useful concept to apply in art and literary history.[26] The fundamental integrative attitudes and formative principles – Mannheim also refers to "interpretive formative principles" (*Formungs- und Gestaltungsintentionen*)[27] – constitute everything that makes an artwork continuable (*fortsetzbar*).[28] When someone affiliates with a group, Mannheim says, he will "absorb those interpretative formative principles which enable the individual to deal with new impressions and events in a fashion broadly pre-determined by the group".[29] In other words an artist belonging to a particular group will adopt the new creative models being formed or used by that group. That is why Mannheim also talks about the genres (*Gattungen*) that dominate a given generation.[30] In addition to generation style, then, a *generation genre* (in other words the genre preferred by a generation) seems to me also a useful concept when writing about art and literary history.

How, then, are generation style and generation genre reflected in the avant-garde from after the First World War? The generation style can be found in the prevailing geometric abstraction, with its specific use of abstraction as a formative principle. And we can identify a generation genre in painting, where abstraction, with all its geometric forms and crystal precision, melds as a formative principle with the fundamental integrative attitudes based on an integration of the arts, which is what I call the community art ideal. Even more interesting than this abstract generation genre, because it is more closely associated with the generation in question than painting, are the decorative arts: many painters tried their hand at ceramics (even Malevich) and furniture design at some point. The defining elements of this anti-decorative, inexpensive-to-produce interior design were simplicity and lightness.[31]

The Belgian context

The generations of prominent artists and authors in Belgium from around 1910 and 1920 have not received much attention in art criticism as *generations* as such (in the sense of generational coherence and generation units). Part of the reason for that stems from the fact, as mentioned earlier, that for a long time the generational concept was maligned theoretically. At the same time it can be difficult to identify the first generation, in particular, as a generation. That is directly attributable to the war, which caused a delay in the emergence of an entire generation of Belgians. The so-called lost generation[32] includes members of both my generations, those of 1910 (born 1875-1890) and 1920 (born 1890-1905): people born between 1885 and 1900 who primarily came into prominence as artists in the 1920s.[33]

The Generation of 1910 was decimated around the world by the war. In Belgium, too, it was largely truncated, if not on the battlefields of the First World War, then elsewhere (see the artists Rik Wouters and Jules Schmalzigaug, who died during the war but not in Flanders' fields). It is important here to see that war artists such as Maurice Langaskens (1884-1946) and Achiel Van Sassenbrouck (1886-1971) are – in contrast to many of their contemporaries abroad – far from radical avant-gardists. Similarly, in the literary arts the generation that emerged before 1914 would hardly be considered avant-garde.[34] Nevertheless, the fact is that later, during and after the war, they would play an essential role as "mentors" to the younger generation, a primary example being the writer, critic and art-dealer Paul-Gustave (Gust) van Hecke (1887-1967).[35] In the lead-up to the war and during it, the somewhat older Brabant fauvists dominated the visual arts (diagram 5). It was only Schmalzigaug who so immediately aligned with futurism and was one of the first painters to produce abstract works, along with other members of this generation (Marthe Donas, Paul Joostens, Georges Vantongerloo) who were starting to experiment with geometric abstraction during the war. Prosper de Troyer makes a first appearance only after the war, as a mentor to young painters such as Floris Jespers.[36]

(1860-1875)	Auguste Oleffe (1867-1931) Ferdinand Schirren (1872-1944) Louis Thevenet (1874-1930)
(1875-1890) GENERATION 1910	Willem Paerels (1878-1972) Edgar Tytgat (1879-1957) *Prosper De Troyer (1880-1961)* Rik Wouters (1882-1916) *Jules Schmalzigaug (1882-1917)* Jean Brusselmans (1884-1953) *Marthe Donas (1885-1967)* *Georges Vantongerloo (1886-1965)* *[Oscar Jespers (1887-1970); Floris Jespers (1889-1965)]* *Paul Joostens (1889-1960)*
(1890-1905) GENERATION 1920	*Jan Cockx (1891-1976)* *Jozef Peeters (1895-1960)* *Marcel-Louis Baugniet (1896-1995)* *Edmond Van Dooren (1896-1965)* *Victor Servranckx (1897-1965)* *Felix De Boeck (1898-1995)* *Karel Maes (1900-1974)* *Pierre-Louis Flouquet (1900-1967)* *Michel Seuphor (1901-1999)*

Diagram 5: Brabant fauvists (roman) versus Belgian abstract painters (italic)

The members of the second generation, my Generation of 1920, engaged in a wide variety of movements and were also partially compromised – in Flanders – by their "activism" (as the collaboration of primarily young people with the Germans is called). This generation was marked by the front or the occupation. In painting, it is the generation with the most abstract painters, at a time – in the early 1920s – when the older expressionists at Sélection and elsewhere had the greatest influence. In literature, meanwhile, we had a younger generation (e.g. Paul van Ostaijen and Gaston Burssens writing in Dutch and René Verboom and Maurice Van Essche writing in French) that primarily aligned itself with German humanitarian expressionism or French unanimism, and it is not until the organic expressionism of Van Ostaijen that we see a derivation of the constructivism of Victor Servranckx et al., although the former never fully embraced geometricism.[37]

An interesting element in the transition in literature, in particular, from the first to the second generation – which thus coincides with the political activism – is a new, scarcely studied journal called *De Tijd*, established in 1913 and published in Antwerp, with drawings by Edmond van Offel on the front and back covers. The editors were veterans of the old *Van Nu en Straks*, Victor de Meyere (1873-1938) and Lode Baekelmans (1879-1965), along with two old-timers from the journal *De Boom-gaard* (1909-1911), the artist and writer Edmond van Offel (1971-1959) and Van Hecke. You might expect that this epigonal journal would continue in the tradition of trumpeting new sounds. It lacked cosmopolitanism, however, and the young contributors were anything but trendsetters. Of note is that it introduced a couple of new authors who ended up in the war a year later. With the exception of the somewhat older Berto van Kalderkerke (1885-1961) (the pseudonym of Albert Jan Van Driessche) and Leo van Goethem (1887-1931),[38] they belong to the second generation: Franz de Backer (1891-1961), Daan Boens (1893-1977), Fritz Francken (1893-1969) and M.B. Ledegouwer (1895-1914).[39] Here we have some members of Robert Wohl's "lost generation".

Despite the fact that the expressionist representatives of the newest generation in literature (in addition to Burssens, Victor Brunclair in particular) were especially keen after the war to position themselves in opposition to the older generation, whom they accused of being individualistic and having an ivory tower mentality, their ideas did not fundamentally differ from those of their predecessors who came of age in the 1890s, the *Van Nu en Straks* generation of Van de Velde and August Vermeylen.[40] Members of the Generation of 1910 who had debuted after 1900, including the writer-art critics Van Hecke and André De Ridder (1888-1961), presumably helped bridge the gap in this regard. Both shifted their sites from literature to painting and from the Dutch linguistic to the French linguistic field, but we know that in terms of painting, they remained adherents of figurative art.[41]

The Flemish expressionism that they promoted was practised by painters who had come of age before the First World War and originally still painted frequently in a post-impressionist style but came into contact with more radical movements, such as cubism, futurism and the like, during or shortly after the war. They belong to an older generation than the Belgian constructivist artists who emerged after the First World War and are peers of the rarely abstract-minded artists already working before the First World War (Schmalzigaug). As in literature, that generation in painting included transitional figures who mentored the younger artists of the second generation. Often, they were in turn influenced by the art of their mentees. But regarded in a more general way, while the war certainly also left its mark on all the members of that expressionist family, they never fully opened themselves to the experimentation of cubism and futurism.[42]

Results from taking a generational perspective

Thinking in terms of generations brings to the fore certain traits that are common: a generation style, a generation genre. It is in these areas that we see the innovation, instead of in utopian ideas, which tended to more strongly accentuate pre-war ideas such as the notion of community, as primarily evidenced by songs of fraternity, for instance. Among the constructivist-leaning adherents of the notion of community (Peeters, Servranckx and others), community art quickly starts to become what I have termed "communal art" – which confusingly enough has also been called "community art" but in fact aims at a synthesis of the arts. Elsewhere I have described manifestations of the work of *Het Overzicht*, the *7 Arts* group (including Pierre Bourgeois, Pierre-Louis Flouquet and Karel Maes) and their associates in the different branches of art.[43] I examined various forms of integration between the arts: first between literature, visual art and music; then between dance, music, theatre and film; and finally between structural design, interior design and even sculpture in architecture.

A focus on generations makes it easier to compare all those arts. More specifically, for the visual arts we can group several smaller formations ("groups") under the larger family of constructivism between 1920 and 1925. This also allows us to see how older and younger artists (from different "generations") were working together at a given point in time and reveals how the less well-off, young Flemish artists broke through on the international stage somewhat later than their more elite, generally French-educated compatriots (Donas, Vantongerlo), all while an older generation of Flemish expressionists remained in charge. If we expand our perspective to the transnational level – yet another advantage of the generational concept – we see that what was happening in Belgium was also occurring in other countries.

One of the objections to viewing things through the lens of generations is that it erases individual differences among artists or fails to accommodate the aesthetic or emotional impact of individual artworks. While such reservations are certainly justified, my generational model does not rule out individual examination of the artists or their works. In fact it shines more light on individuals at risk of being overlooked because they are not associated with any particular group (e.g. Vantongerlo, Donas or Joostens, who were already producing their earliest abstract works during the war). These benefits come on top of those listed above.

I will now summarise some more results of adopting that generational perspective to study the art from around 1920. First we see – as we already knew[44] – that abstraction evolved later in Belgium and had fewer women artists working in it than, for example, Russia. Viewed in terms of generations we can attribute that delay to the lack of a pioneer from the generation born between 1860 and 1875 (or earlier). Perhaps it was the late emergence of impressionism and the impact of someone like Ensor (born somewhere on the cusp between old and new) that had a negative effect. The lack of women avant-garde artists is probably related to the low level of (artistic) education among women, a factor we also see at work in the written arts. Sociologically the formative years of these artists were between 1870 and 1885 for the oldest and 1885 and 1900 for the youngest. The youngest of them, those born in 1875, were able to benefit from *Les XX* and *La Libre Esthétique*, as was the subsequent generation.

Second we can determine that the second generation of abstract-constructivists, who theoretically constitute a "family" and should have been the most strongly impacted by the war, did indeed place the greatest emphasis on community art, but with their own specific interpretation; they pursued not only "art for the community", but also a "communal art". That singular interpretation resulted in a distinct generation style and generation genre. The generation style was highly geometric and the defining generation genre was interior design. While we may not necessarily need the generational concept to identify that generation style and genre, the model does confer legitimacy for studying them more as a unit, something which has to date been largely neglected.[45] This further allows us to view the Exposition Internationale des Arts Décoratifs et Industriels Modernes of 1925 as a sort of crowning achievement – and the beginning of the end.

Moreover, by combining the development of a communal art with the utopian ideal of "art for the community" from a transnational perspective, it becomes possible to highlight the difference between the more politically motivated trends (expressionists and revolutionary constructivists) and the more autonomy-oriented ones (such as suprematism and purism). All of this is further inflected with the opposition of individualism and collectivism, whereby it should be noted that aspiring to an un-individualised art did not necessarily imply engagement on the part of the members of the Generation of 1920 on behalf of the masses.

Finally the question remains whether 1916 can truly be seen as a watershed (*Wendepunkt*). From a purely historical perspective, it is indeed in 1916, or shortly thereafter, that we see the first signs of radical avant-gardism in Belgian literature (Van Ostaijen) and art (Donas, Vantongerlo), which can only be explained by exposure to foreign examples. The limited reach of that avant-gardism, however, forces us to push the true turning point to after the war. The avant-garde only truly breaks through with the Generation of 1920, who attempt – full of utopian ideals – to achieve the reconstruction of a community.

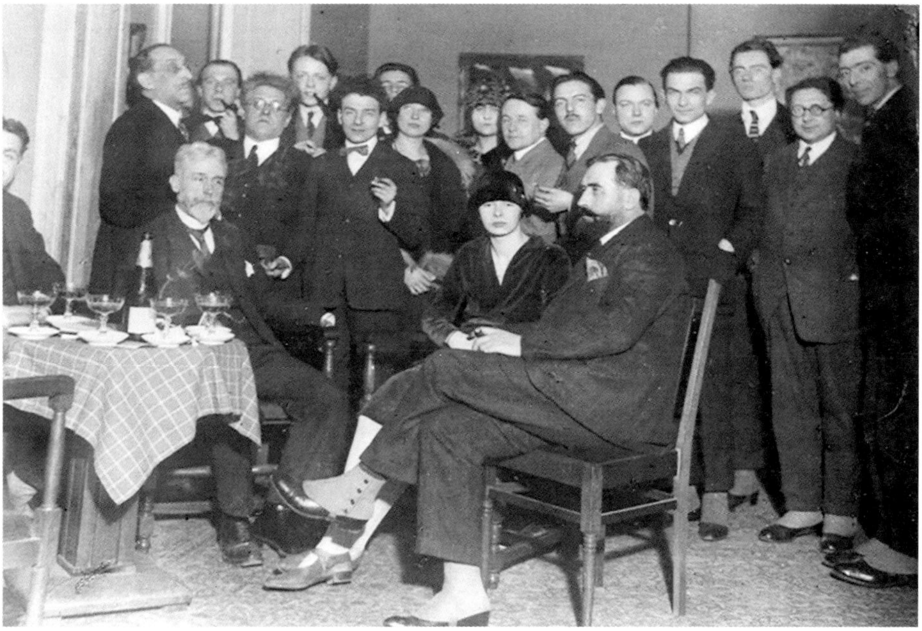

12.1. Two generations at the Vlaamsche Club in 1926. (Unknown source)

There is a photo from 1926 that provides evidence of how both a national and supra-national perspective and a diachronic and synchronic perspective can meld together (fig. 12.1).[46] The photo, often erroneously dated as 1923, shows Belgian and Dutch luminaries coming together at the Vlaamsche Club to celebrate Piet van Wijngaerdt (1873-1964), a Dutch painter who introduced expressionism to the Netherlands together with Henri Le Fauconnier and was having an exhibition at La Vierge poupine, the gallery run by Van Ostaijen and Geert Van Bruaene. The French-speaking members of the L'Assaut and La Lanterne Sourde circles stand side by side with the Flemish Vermeylen, Van Bruaene, Jef Mennekens and Frantz Alofs. At the same time the photo is a wonderful depiction of generational dynamics. Van Wijngaerdt and Vermeylen are part of the older generation, but they both played a prominent role in the literary and art world of their time: Vermeylen was a negative reference point for the youngest generation; Van Wijngaerdt a positive one. In any event, the two generations met,[47] exchanged ideas, competed against each other and celebrated one another.

Notes

1 Franz Kafka, "Investigations of a Dog," in *The Complete Stories*, trans. Willa and Edwin Muir (New York: Schocken Books Inc., 1988), 331.

2 *Ibid.*, 330-331.

3 Robert Wohl, "The Generation of 1914 and Modernism," in *Modernism: Challenges and Perspectives*, ed. Monique Chefdor, Ricardo Quinones and Albert Wachtel (Urbana and Chicago: University of Illinois Press, 1986), 69.

4 See Hans Vandevoorde, "Over 'generaties' in de literatuurgeschiedenis. Een revisie," in *Breuken en bruggen. Moderne Nederlandse literatuur / Hedendaagse perspectieven,* ed. Lars Bernaerts, Carl de Strycker and Bart Vervaeck (Ghent: Academia Press, 2011), 23-24.

5 See Hans Vandevoorde, "L'art communautaire au début des années 1920: de l'expressionisme au constructivisme," in *Modernisme. L'art abstrait belge et l'Europe*, ed. Johan De Smet (Ghent: Museum voor Schone Kunsten/Fonds Mercator, 2013), 223–247.

6 See Caroline Boot and Marijke van der Heijden, "Gemeenschapskunst," in *Kunstenaren der idee. Symbolistische tendenzen in Nederland, ca. 1880-1930*, ed. Carel Blotkamp et al. (The Hague: Staatsuitgeverij, 1978), 36-47.

7 For more on Van de Velde see my unpublished lecture "Henry van de Velde en de Gemeenschapskunst" on his early years and involvement in community art, prepared for a workshop given on 5 December 2013 at Letterenhuis, Antwerp.

8 See Kurt De Boodt and Paul Dujardin, "Committing Sacrilege in the 'Cubist and Flemish Nationalist Church'. On the rise and fall of community art in Belgium," in *The Power of the Avant Garde. Now and Then*, ed. Ulrich Bischoff and Jürgen Müller (Tielt: Lannoo, 2016), 30-39.

9 H.A. Becker, *De toekomst van de Verloren Generatie* (Amsterdam: Meulenhoff, 1997), 17.

10 Karl Mannheim, "Das Problem der Generationen," in Karl Mannheim, *Wissenssoziologie. Auswahl aus dem Werk*, ed. Kurt H. Wolff (Luchterhand: Neuwied/Berlin 1964), 547) (English terms from Karl Mannheim, "The Problem of Generations," in Karl Mannheim, *Essays*, ed. Paul Kecskemeti [London: Routledge, 1952]), 302).

11 *Ibid.*, 545.

12 *Ibid.*, 547.

13 Sigrid Weigel, *Genea-Logik. Generation, Tradition und Evolution zwischen Kultur- und Naturwissenschaften* (Munich: Wilhelm Fink Verlag, 2006).

14 Mannheim attempted to reconcile a more biological (vertical) vision of the 19th century with his own sociohistorical vision of a generation as a group of people of the same age with a specific historical and social identity, thereby at least implicitly incorporating the diachronic dimension.

15 The starting and ending points of such age groups are frequently subject to discussion (see Pierre Nora, "Generation", in *Realms of Memory*: *Rethinking the French Past*, Vol. I, ed. Pierre Nora [New York: Columbia University Press, 1996], 499-531). Mannheim believed that it was at the age of 17 that a person gained full consciousness (Karl Mannheim, "The Problem of Generations," in Karl Mannheim, *Essays*, ed. Paul Kecskemeti [London: Routledge, 1952], 300).

16 Robert Wohl, "The Generation of 1914 and Modernism," in *Modernism: Challenges and Perspectives*, ed. Monique Chefdor, Ricardo Quinones and Albert Wachtel (Urbana and Chicago: University of Illinois Press, 1986), 68.

17 My classification differs by five years from that of Wohl. On the one hand this is useful in terms of demonstrating the arbitrary nature of any generational classification; on the other it is advantageous for my case in that I can have the first age group start ten years earlier, which accords a place to important figures such as Manet and Degas.

18 Peter Bürger, *Theorie der Avantgarde* (Frankfurt am Main: Suhrkamp, 1982).

19 In Belgium the groups associated with the French-language literary society and journal *La Jeune Belgique* (1881-1897) and the Dutch-language journal *Van Nu en Straks* (1893-1894; 1896-1901) were seen as the avant-garde movements of the 1880s and 1890s (see Francis Mus and Hans Vandevoorde, "'Streetscape of new districts permeated by the fresh scent of cement': Brussels, the avant-garde, and internationalism," in *The Oxford Critical and Cultural History of Modernist Magazines. Volume III: Europe 1880-1940*, ed. Peter Brooker, Sascha Bru, Andrew Thacker and Christian Weikop [Oxford: Oxford University Press, 2013], 336-360). Each of those groups is also often referred to as a generation.

20 See for example José de Almada-Negreiros: "Ich gehöre keiner der revolutionären Generationen an. Ich gehöre einer konstruktiven Generation an" ("I don't belong to any revolutionary generation; I belong to the constructivist generation"); *Manifeste und Proklamationen der europäischen Avantgarde (1909–1938)*, ed. Wolfgang Asholt and Walther Fähnders (Stuttgart/Weimar: Metzler, 1995), 128. Cf. "Das Realistische Manifest" signed by Naum Gabo and Noton Pevsner (1920): "Aber das Leben wartet nicht und die Folge der Generationen hält nicht an" ("But life doesn't wait and the march of generations never stops") (*ibid.*, 207).

21 Russian constructivism only truly emerged in 1921, ultimately being codified in 1922 in the constructivist manifesto by Alexeï Gran (fragments in Camilla Gray, *L'avant-garde russe dans l'art moderne, 1863–1922* [Lausanne: La Cité des Arts, 1968], 272-276; John E. Bowlt, *Russian Art of the Avant-Garde: Theory and Criticism 1902–1934.* Revised and enlarged edition. [London: Thames and Hudson, 1988], 214-225). It was comprised of the objectivist group of Tatlin and Rodchenko and the more spiritualistic group of Malevich (Camilla Gray, *L'avant-garde russe dans l'art moderne, 1863–1922* [Lausanne: La Cité des Arts, 1968], 233), which included the Pevsner brothers, who emigrated to the West in 1922.

22 For more on *7 Arts* see Serge Goyens de Heusch, *7 Arts. Bruxelles 1922–1929. Un front de jeunesse pour la révolution artistique* (Brussels: Ministère de la culture française de Belgique, 1976). For more on *Het Overzicht* see Sjoerd van Faassen and August Hans den Boef, eds., *Het pseudo moderne nevens het ware. De briefwisseling van de architect J.J.P. Oud met Jozef Peeters en Michel Seuphor, redacteuren van het constructivistische tijdschrift* Het Overzicht*, 1921-1925* (Antwerp: Zacht Lawijd/Garant, 2007); and Frederik Leen, "*Het Overzicht* en de Brusselse avant-garde van de jaren twintig", in *Michel Seuphor 1901-1999. Grensverkenner van de avant-garde*, special issue of *Zacht Lawijd* 8 (2009), 100-113.

23 Cf. Doris Wintgens Hötte, "Utopia 1900-1940. Visions of a New World: An Introduction", in *Utopia 1900-1940. Visions of a New World* (Rotterdam: nai010, 2013), 8-19. Van Doesburg however opposed any "machinisme en art" ("technologism in art"). See Theo van Doesburg, "Vers une Construction collective," *Punct. Revista de arte constructivista internationala*, no. 8 (9 January 1925).

24 Christina Lodder, "Constructivist Visions of Utopia," in *Utopia 1900–1940: Visions of a New World* (Rotterdam: nai010, 2013), 95.

25 Karl Mannheim, "Das Problem der Generationen," in Karl Mannheim, *Wissenssoziologie. Auswahl aus dem Werk*, ed. Kurt H. Wolff (Luchterhand: Neuwied/Berlin 1964), 550 (English terms from Karl Mannheim, "The Problem of Generations," in Karl Mannheim, *Essays*, ed. Paul Kecskemeti [London: Routledge, 1952]), 309).

26 See Hans Vandevoorde, "Generatie Schierbeek. Lyricisering in de jaren vijftig," in 'Een eeuw lyrisch

proza", ed. Lars Bernaerts, Hans Vandevoorde and Bart Vervaeck, ed., *Belgisch Tijdschrift voor Filologie en Geschiedenis/Revue Belge de Philologie et d'Histoire* 91, no. 3 (2013), 1129–1146.

27 Karl Mannheim, "Das Problem der Generationen," in Karl Mannheim, *Wissenssoziologie. Auswahl aus dem Werk*, ed. Kurt H. Wolff (Luchterhand: Neuwied/Berlin 1964) (English terms from Karl Mannheim, "The Problem of Generations," in Karl Mannheim, *Essays*, ed. Paul Kecskemeti [London: Routledge, 1952]), 546. (English terms from Karl Mannheim, "The Problem of Generations," in Karl Mannheim, *Essays*, ed. Paul Kecskemeti [London: Routledge, 1952]), 306).

28 *Ibid.*, 544.

29 *Ibid.*, 546.

30 *Ibid.*, 564.

31 Christina Lodder, "Constructivist Visions of Utopia," in *Utopia 1900–1940: Visions of a New World* (Rotterdam: nai010, 2013), 98.

32 See Robert Wohl, *The Generation of 1914* (Cambridge: Harvard University Press, 1979).

33 Note then that I do not consider this "lost generation" a separate generation but a collective term for members of two generations engaged in European modernism.

34 It is interesting to note that the writers of that generation took primarily to poetry, especially the Dutch ones (which contributed to their being misunderstood as a generation); many of the Flemish ones debuted either in the theatre or with an urban novel. They met in the (anarchist-inspired) Flemish journal *Ontwaking*:
- Willem Elsschot (1882-1960): book debut *Villa des Roses* (1913) – urban novel
- Jan van Nijlen (1884-1965): *Verzen* (1906), *Het licht* (1909), *Naar 't geluk* (1911) – poetry
- Gerard Ceunis (1884-1964): *De gevangene princes* (1909) – play
- Firmin Van Hecke (1884-1961): *Verzen* (1912) – poetry
- Paul Kenis (1885-1934): *De roman van een jeugd. Een ondergang in Parijs* (1914) – urban novel
- J.C. Bloem (1887-1966): he first debuted in 1910 in *De beweging* (cf. *Ontwaking*) and with a book in 1921 – poetry
- P.N. van Eyck (1887-1954): *De getooide doolhof* (1909) – poetry
- Paul-Gustave van Hecke (1887-1967): *De schoone droom* (1911) – drama
- André De Ridder (1888-1961): *Gesprekken met den wijzen jongeling* (1910) – roman
- Jan Greshoff (1888-1971): *Lumen* (1909), *Aan den verlaten vijver* (1909) and *Door mijn open venster...* (1910) – poetry
- Adriaan Roland Holst (1888-1976): *Verzen* (1911); *De belijdenis van de stilte* (1913) – poetry

35 See Hans Vandevoorde and Christophe Verbruggen, "*Transgenerational Brokering*. The case for Symbolism and Surrealism in Flanders," *Belgisch Tijdschrift voor Filologie en Geschiedenis/Revue Belge de Philologie et d'Histoire* 92, no. 4 (2014), 1343-1358.

36 Kurt De Boodt, *Prosper De Troyer. Schilder in beweging* (Mechelen: Stedelijke Musea Mechelen, 2013), 23.

37 For more on Van Ostaijen versus Peeters see Paul Hadermann, "Peeters en Joostens: twee problematische gevallen in Van Ostaijens kunstkritiek," in *Paul van Ostaijen en de kunst van zijn tijd 1896-1996*, ed. Michel Bartosik, Michel Dupuis and Jean Weisgerber (Ghent: Koninklijke Academie voor Nederlandse Taal- en Letterkunde, 1997), 381-395.

38 For more on Van Goethem, see Jan Lampo, "Vuile manieren in Vlaamsche Arbeid. Karel van den Oever wordt het slachtoffer van een mystificatie," *Zuurvrij* 22 (2012), 34-41.

39 For more on Ledegouwer, see Matthijs De Ridder, "De kleine garnaal. M.B. Ledegouwer," *Zacht Lawijd* 6, no. 4 (2006-2007), 20-37.

40 See Hans Vandevoorde, "L'art communautaire au début des années 1920: de l'expressionisme au constructivisme," in *Modernisme. L'art abstrait belge et l'Europe*, ed. Johan De Smet (Ghent: Museum

voor Schone Kunsten/Fonds Mercator, 2013), 223–247.

41 For more on Van Hecke see among others Virginie Devillez, Michel Draguet and Manu Van der Aa, eds., *Kunstpromotor Paul-Gustave Van Hecke (1887-1967) en de avant-garde* (Brussels/Ghent-Kortrijk: Koninklijke Musea voor Schone Kunsten van België-Uitgeverij Snoeck, 2012). On the activities of Van Hecke and De Ridder in the arts, see among others An Paenhuysen, *De nieuwe wereld. De wonderjaren van de Belgische avant-garde (1918–1939)* (Antwerp: Meulenhoff/Manteau, 2010), and the recent biography by Van der Aa on Van Hecke: *Tatave! Paul-Gustave van Hecke. Kunstpaus – modekoning – salonsocialist* (Tielt: Lannoo, 2017).

42 See for this tentative attitude, the limited futurist influences on Flemish art from 1918 Phil Mertens, *Jules Schmalzigaug 1882-1917* (Brussels: R. and J. Van de Velde/I.C.S.A.C., 1984), 157-159, and the exhibition catalogue *Jules Schmalzigaug en het kookboek van het futurisme*, Mu.ZEE, Ostend, 2016.

43 Hans Vandevoorde, "L'art communautaire au début des années 1920: de l'expressionisme au constructivisme," in Johan De Smet, ed., *Modernisme. L'art abstrait belge et l'Europe* (Ghent: Museum voor Schone Kunsten/Fonds Mercator, 2013), 223–247.

44 This notion of a late breakthrough is not a new observation, see e.g. Eric Pil, "Verschuivingen binnen de avant-garde. Evoluties in de plastische kunsten in België, 1917-1929," in *Avant-garde in België 1917-1929* (Brussels/Antwerp: Gemeentekrediet, 1992), 59.

45 One exception is Philippe Roberts-Jones, *La peinture abstraite en Belgique. 1920-1970* (Ghent: Snoeck-Ducaju/ Brussels: Crédit Cummunal, 1996).

46 See Hans Vandevoorde, "De vete Van Ostaijen-Vermeylen," in *Arduin* 11, no. 22 (2017), 47-57.

47 Vermeylen introduced Van Ostaijen at a reading on 8 December 1925 at the Vlaamsche Club in Brussels.

The Originality of the 7 Arts' Constructivism: The Connections to The Belgian Pre-War Art Scene

EVA FRANCIOLI

Amidst the International Avant-Garde Movements

The present essay aims to reconsider the history of the weekly *7 Arts*, which challenged itself with Belgium's political, social and cultural changes in the aftermath of the First World War. This famous magazine, which was published in Brussels from 1922 to 1928, was founded by the brothers Pierre and Victor Bourgeois, Pierre-Louis Flouquet, Karel Maes and Georges Monier: a group of progressive artists, architects, musicians and writers who promoted a radical update of the traditional artistic production and fruition systems.[1]

The five founders and their "comrades" (who also included René Magritte,[2] at the very beginning) were deeply concerned with the search for innovative plastics, graphical and architectonical solution. They aimed at combining a formalist approach with a more pragmatic attitude, as also revealed by the choice of publishing their review in a gazette format, which seemed to be more in touch with the necessities of a modern society.

The intent of "the five" was explicitly declared in the "Numéro-Manifeste" of *7 Arts*. In the "Périodicité, prix, durée" section, in particular, they announced the technical aspects of the publication and stated that every organ could be viable if it responded to a need. The editors also asserted that a cultural weekly of minimal price was missing in Brussels' artistic life, and for that reason they decided to get it into print. According to them, both the newspaper format and the moderate price would increase the circulation of the periodical, and that was the only way to make an artistic fight which would give concrete answers to modernity's quest for the new.[3]

Their collective work was therefore devoted to promoting modern art, which was characterised – in accordance with their own words – by the interconnection among different disciplines, and by a new relationship between man and the surrounding environment. As also declared in the second paragraph of the manifesto, entitled "Objet, principes, tactique", the integration of all the artistic expressions was in fact an indispensable condition for art's penetration into society.

Therefore, the aesthetic principles of *7 Arts* seem to be essentially in line with those of the international avant-garde, revealing several points of contact with French Post-Cubism, Dutch Neo-Plasticism and Russian Constructivism. After all, Brussels had intercepted the new European art trajectories since the 1910s, as testified, for example, by the activity of the Galerie Georges Giroux, which hosted the first Futurist exhibition in Belgium (May-June 1912), and the first show of Kandinsky's paintings (between the end of 1912 and the beginning of 1913). Furthermore, the connections with abroad widely increased after the "break" of the First World War. For example, the contacts with Theo van Doesburg, who held a conference at the Centre d'Art[4] in rue de Coudenberg in 1920, should be mentioned.

The Sélection group, founded this same year by Paul-Gustave van Hecke and André De Ridder, also contributed to the debate on modern art from other countries, as revealed by the magazine published until 1927 and by the shows organised at the homonymous gallery in rue des Colonies, which was active between 1920 and 1922. As regards its activity, an undated letter of Magritte to Flouquet can be recalled, where the artist mentioned a Cubist exhibition in a "nouvelle boite, Sélection" which included works by Picasso, Survage, Metzinger and Léger, among others. What is most interesting is the letter's closure, in that Magritte ended his missive by saying that they were "stronger" than the Cubists.[5]

In those crucial months the connections with the Russian avant-garde intensified, too. That period was marked by the early political and social effects of the Soviet Revolution and by the growing knowledge of architectonic and artistic experimentations in R.S.F.S.R.

In this regard, it is worth recalling the presence of the Russian writer I'lija Ehrenburg in Brussels from May to October 1921.[6] He arrived from Paris, from where he was exiled, and thanks to the friendship with Franz Hellens[7] he published some articles about the revolutionary art in Soviet Russia.[8] While he was in Belgium, Ehrenburg also worked on the book *A vse-taki ona vertitsja* (*Et pourtant elle tourne*!), which contained important references to the constructivist theories he would develop with El Lissitzky in the famous review *Vešč'/Objet/Gegenstand*, which was published by Skythen-*Verlag* in Berlin, between March/April and May 1922. This magazine, characterised by an innovative layout, was meant as a bridge between European and Russian culture (the articles were in Russian, French or German). Franz Hellens, too, was one of its contributors,[9] together with Gino Severini, Fernand Léger, Theo van Doesburg and many others.

The Belgian intellectuals' first journeys to post-revolutionary Russia should also be taken into account. This was the case with War Van Overstraeten: a co-founder of the Groupe Communiste de Bruxelles and a contributor to magazines such as *Au Volant* (which was published by the Bourgeois brothers) and *Le Geste* (a magazine derived from the fusion of *Au Volant* and *Demain littéraire et social*, founded by Aimé Declercq and Léon Chenoy), who first went to Russia in 1920. This was also the case with Jacques Mesnil (Jean-Jacques Dwelshauvers's *nom de plume*), who held a conference on Soviet art at the Galerie Georges Giroux in December 1921.[10]

Therefore, the publication of the weekly *7 Arts* can be placed in the wake of all those events that marked, together with other significant episodes, the spread of the so-called International Constructivism throughout Europe. That is even more true if we assume that the "Numéro-Manifeste" was probably published not in late spring, as commonly assumed,[11] but in October 1922, as suggested by some documentary evidence.[12] In this case, in fact, *7 Arts* would have been published after the Congress of Progressive Artists in Düsseldorf (29-30 May 1922), as well as after the Dadaist and Constructivist Congress in Weimar (25 September 1922), where the "Manifesto of the International Union of Neoplasticist Constructors", signed by Theo van Doesburg, El Lissitzky, Hans Richter, Max Burchartz and Karel Maes, was presented.

However, the magazine's connection with other artistic movements, which were certainly important and fruitful, needs to be put into a new perspective. The hypothesis of a deep influence of the international avant-garde on *7 Arts* and its "Constructivist" aesthetics merits being reconsidered, since its principles and artistic actions do not seem to be directly derived from those experiences. In this regard, it is perhaps significant to note that part of the group was already working at the creation of a magazine the title of which should have been *Construction*, in late 1920 – early 1921.[13]

"Continuity or rupture?": Looking for '7 Arts' origin in the Belgian artistic tradition

On closer inspection, *7 Arts*' aim, strictly connected to the need of the material and cultural reconstruction after the Great War, seems to be firmly rooted in the Belgian artistic and architectural "milieu" of the late 19th and the early 20th centuries. The creation of a new visual vocabulary and the exploration of modern production systems in fact reveal the relationship with the Belgian recent pictorial tradition (with Symbolism, in particular), as well as with Art Nouveau's functionalist principles (fostered by masters such as Victor Horta and Henri van de Velde) and with the cultural and political struggles promoted by magazines such as *L'Art Moderne* and by the Section d'Art of the Parti Ouvrier Belge.

As regards the connection with Symbolism, it is perhaps interesting to note that a first nucleus of the upcoming *7 Arts* group was possibly created in the mid-1910s within the Académie Royale des Beaux-Arts in Brussels, where the teaching was geared to the symbolist theories supported by Constant Montald and Jean Delville. This group, composed by Pierre-Louis Flouquet, René Magritte, Victor Servranckx and Victor Bourgeois, among others, was later joined by Karel Maes, who attended the academy courses for only a short period, then favouring a self-taught training. The painting of those young artists would become extremely different from that of their teachers, in that after a few years, in connection with the research of artists such as Paul Joostens and Jozef Peeters.[14] their works would be characterised by a shared interest in abstraction. Anyway, Symbolism may have represented a theoretical model for their research into an original sign system, made of geometrical forms and pure colours, which was commonly defined as "Plastique Pure". Symbolist painting, freed from the narration of phenomenological reality, may have been a conceptual premise for their self-referential style, whose evolution was then probably partly encouraged by the knowledge of Post-Cubist and Futurist experiences.

Regarding Art Nouveau's legacy, it seems noteworthy to recall the aforementioned review *Au Volant*, whose fourth and last issue appears to be largely devoted to the defence of Victor Horta's artistic education reform. Horta's proposal was aimed at integrating artistic creation and industrial production, thus opening the way to a radical transformation of the relationship between manual and intellectual work. According to Victor Horta and the editors of *Au Volant*, only through a conscious and integrated teaching of both theoretical and practical subjects could the academic institutions respond to modern society's rhythms and needs in a proper manner. In that perspective, the combination of creativity with the artisanal and industrial production would constitute the expression of real progress by the community. Victor Bourgeois had proposed to publish an inquiry about Horta's reform also in the magazine *La Cité*,[15] where *7 Arts* would be publicised in 1922.[16] As one of its contributors since 1919, he supported the architectonical renewal fostered by this periodical, which was also engaged in the cultural battle against the Ypres reconstruction according to the traditional principles of a stylistic restoration. This was an important fight for the *7 Arts*' editors, too,[17] whose functionalist aesthetics were deeply influenced by the discussion on housing emergency caused by the First World War.

Henry van de Velde's work, too, had a strong and lasting impact on this generation of Belgian artists and architects. Although in the 1970s Pierre Bourgeois firmly opposed a common conviction concerning his and his brother's derivation from van de Velde's theories,[18] in those years he still recognised his pivotal role for the evolution of both art and architecture in the early 20th century. The artist Marcel-Louis Baugniet, who studied alongside Flouquet, Magritte and Servranckx at the Royal Academy of Fine Arts in Brussels and collaborated with *7 Arts* from 1923 onward (since he was in Paris when the review was first published), still recalled in 1960 that both his generation and the following one underwent the powerful influence of this master. According to Baugniet, his work was important not only on the architectural level, since van de Velde was above all a notable theorist and a great educator in the field of modern art. His extraordinary revolution – which was based on his graphic research – was considered as decisive for both architects like Victor Bourgeois and painters like Flouquet, Peeters and Servranckx.[19]

After all, van de Velde's work was the subject of an intensive propaganda campaign on *7 Arts* between 1923 and 1924. At the end of the second season, for example, he was designated amongst "les precurseurs" in the first special issue of a series dedicated to the history of Modern Style (fig. 13.1). Furthermore, in 1923 the Coopérative Editrice L'Equerre (that also had in charge the publishing of *7 Arts*) published *Formules de l'esthétique moderne*, a new edition of his *Formules de la beauté architectonique* with a preface by Victor Bourgeois. In a long article dedicated to the forthcoming publication of this book, the editors of *7 Arts* underlined the scientific value of his author's theories, that were considered as the most complete conceptual premise for modern plastic research.[20] More notably, in a letter to Charles Rochat dated 10 November 1923, Victor Bourgeois alluded to van de Velde's role within the international avant-garde, pointing out that, when the Modern Movement in Germany was at its early stage, the Germans used to call that style "style belge". According to Bourgeois, this could solely mean that the new style was not only German, as commonly thought, but European instead.[21]

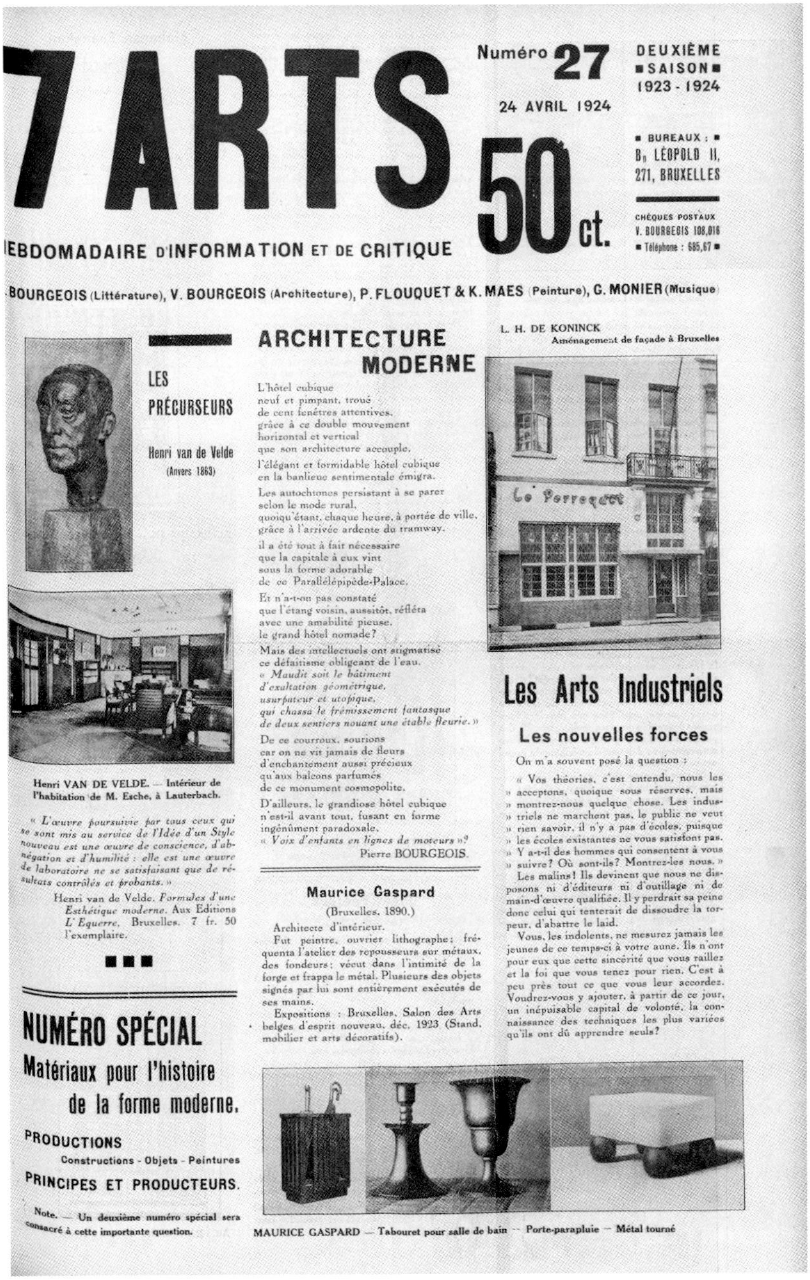

7 ARTS

Numéro 27

24 AVRIL 1924

DEUXIÈME SAISON 1923 - 1924

50 ct.

BUREAUX : B^d LÉOPOLD II, 271, BRUXELLES

CHÈQUES POSTAUX V. BOURGEOIS 108,016

Téléphone : 685,67

EBDOMADAIRE D'INFORMATION ET DE CRITIQUE

BOURGEOIS (Littérature), V. BOURGEOIS (Architecture), P. FLOUQUET & K. MAES (Peinture), G. MONIER (Musique)

LES PRÉCURSEURS

Henri van de Velde (Anvers 1863)

Henri VAN DE VELDE. — Intérieur de l'habitation de M. Esche, à Lauterbach.

« L'œuvre poursuivie par tous ceux qui se sont mis au service de l'Idée d'un Style nouveau est une œuvre de conscience, d'abnégation et d'humilité : elle est une œuvre de laboratoire ne se satisfaisant que de résultats contrôlés et probants. »

Henri van de Velde. *Formules d'une Esthétique moderne.* Aux Editions *L'Equerre*, Bruxelles. 7 fr. 50 l'exemplaire.

NUMÉRO SPÉCIAL

Matériaux pour l'histoire de la forme moderne.

PRODUCTIONS

Constructions - Objets - Peintures

PRINCIPES ET PRODUCTEURS.

Note. — Un deuxième numéro spécial sera consacré à cette importante question.

ARCHITECTURE MODERNE

L'hôtel cubique
neuf et pimpant, troué
de cent fenêtres attentives,
grâce à ce double mouvement
horizontal et vertical
que son architecture accouple,
l'élégant et formidable hôtel cubique
en la banlieue sentimentale émigra.

Les autochtones persistant à se parer
selon le mode rural,
quoiqu'étant, chaque heure, à portée de ville,
grâce à l'arrivée ardente du tramway,

il a été tout à fait nécessaire
que la capitale à eux vint
sous la forme adorable
de ce Parallélépipède-Palace.

Et n'a-t-on pas constaté
que l'étang voisin, aussitôt, refléta
avec une amabilité pieuse,
le grand hôtel nomade?

Mais des intellectuels ont stigmatisé
ce défaitisme obligeant de l'eau.
« Maudit soit le bâtiment
d'exaltation géométrique,
usurpateur et utopique,
qui chassa le frémissement fantasque
de deux sentiers nouant une étable fleurie. »

De ce courroux, sourions
car on ne vit jamais de fleurs
d'enchantement aussi précieux
qu'aux balcons parfumés
de ce monument cosmopolite.

D'ailleurs, le grandiose hôtel cubique
n'est-il avant tout, fusant en forme
ingénûment paradoxale,
« Voix d'enfants en lignes de moteurs »?

Pierre BOURGEOIS.

Maurice Gaspard

(Bruxelles, 1890.)

Architecte d'intérieur.

Fut peintre, ouvrier lithographe; fréquenta l'atelier des repousseurs sur métaux, des fondeurs; vécut dans l'intimité de la forge et frappa le métal. Plusieurs des objets signés par lui sont entièrement exécutés de ses mains.

Expositions : Bruxelles, Salon des Arts belges d'esprit nouveau, déc. 1923 (Stand, mobilier et arts décoratifs).

L. H. DE KONINCK
Aménagement de façade à Bruxelles

Les Arts Industriels

Les nouvelles forces

On m'a souvent posé la question :

« Vos théories, c'est entendu, nous les » acceptons, quoique sous réserves, mais » montrez-nous quelque chose. Les indus- » triels ne marchent pas, le public ne veut » rien savoir, il n'y a pas d'écoles, puisque » les écoles existantes ne vous satisfont pas. » Y a-t-il des hommes qui consentent à vous » suivre? Où sont-ils? Montrez-les nous. »

Les malins! Ils devinent que nous ne disposons ni d'éditeurs ni d'outillage ni de main-d'œuvre qualifiée. Il y perdrait sa peine donc celui qui tenterait de dissoudre la torpeur, d'abattre le laid.

Vous, les indolents, ne mesurez jamais les jeunes de ce temps-ci à votre aune. Ils n'ont pour eux que cette sincérité que vous raillez et la foi que vous tenez pour rien. C'est à peu près tout ce que vous leur accordez. Voudrez-vous y ajouter, à partir de ce jour, un inépuisable capital de volonté, la connaissance des techniques les plus variées qu'ils ont dû apprendre seuls?

MAURICE GASPARD — Tabouret pour salle de bain — Porte-parapluie — Métal tourné

13.1. Cover of *7 Arts*, n. 27, 24 avril 1924, deuxième saison 1923-1924, Archives de la Ville de Bruxelles, AVB J 215.

The social value of art

As for the cultural and political struggles that were at the core of the *7 Arts* action, it is finally important to recall the possible reference to the ideal of the social function of art that was promoted by some magazines dating back to the end of the 19th century. That was the case, for example, of the weekly *L'Art Moderne*, which was founded by Edmond Picard and Octave Maus in March 1881. At first this magazine, which supported the artwork's social and educative value, significantly consisted of only unsigned articles. This choice, which was pursued at least until 1898, would then be continued by the five editors of *7 Arts*, who stated that they would not sign their articles because they had collective responsibility for what was written.[22]

The hiding of the author in a collective production is a highly modern concept which was largely reintroduced by artistic groups in the 1960s-1970s. Nonetheless, the idea of an anonymous creation was also part of van de Velde's *Première Prédication d'art*, which was published in the magazine *L'Art Moderne* between the end of 1893 and the beginning of 1894. In this text, which focused on art as an agent of social renewal, van de Velde was alluding to the need to counter the end-of-century decadence. According to him, that specific trend was partially caused by the myths of the author, and it could be contrasted with the anonymous artistic creation, as well as with the integration between art and craft, which would lead to serially produced objects for a large public: an essential condition for being modern.

The defence of the social value of art, promoted through the pages of *L'Art Moderne*, was in line with the developing links with the intellectual circles of the Parti Ouvrier Belge and with the activity of the Section d'Art et d'Enseignement de la Maison du Peuple, which was founded in 1891 and then re-founded by the editors of *7 Arts* in 1924. The Section d'Art was originally supported by a group of intellectuals including, among others, Emile Vandervelde, the founders of *L'Art Moderne* and Jules Destrée.[23] This last, in his essay "Le Socialisme en Belgique" published with Vandervelde in 1896, defended the ideal of a collective sharing of beauty in accordance with the needs of the new era, that was marked by the mechanisation of the production process, as well as by the progressive affirmation of a mass society.[24]

In conjunction with the work of the Section d'Art, a new magazine called *L'art social* was founded in 1892. It also included articles by Lemonnier, Eekhoud, Verhaeren and Vandervelde, whose thought inspired the members of *7 Arts*, and in particular Pierre Bourgeois, who attended not only Edmond Picard's lessons of right, but also Georges Eekhoud's lessons of literature at the Université Nouvelle.[25] More significantly, the third and final issue of *Le Geste*, which was published under the direction of the Bourgeois brothers together with Aimé Declercq and Léon Chenoy, was entirely dedicated to Eekhoud's life and work, with the delicate Flemish question in its background.[26]

Among the contributors to *Le Geste* there was also Maurice Casteels, who then became one of the most important authors of *7 Arts* (the only one, together with Léon Chenoy, who signed his articles from the beginning).[27] In the first series of the weekly, in particular, Casteels inaugurated the "Les arts industriels" section, where he gave his personal definition of social art, combining formalist request and pragmatic needs.[28] According to Casteels, art could be authentically modern only if it had a social connotation. Since it was conceived for the greatest number of people, the better way to achieve it was through a mechanical creation process. Therefore Casteels declared that either a stamp or an aeroplane, a public building or a chair could be social artworks, because those objects could be produced from a unique and original model and enjoyed by many individuals at the same time. Their beauty was derived from the harmony between their form and the necessity for which they were designed. Art had to be useful. In this perspective, an easel painting with realist subjects could not be considered either modern or social art. Casteels criticised the Socialist Realism and its uselessness and decorative value, because they were not in accordance with the society's necessities. The modern ideal of beauty would combine a new style with the utility and with a technological creation of the artwork. Thus, beyond the reduction of both the purchase and the production costs and the increase of the buying power, the production in series would lead to new aesthetic categories.

Conclusion

In conclusion, following up from what Maurice Casteels asserted in *7 Arts*, a magazine – which is a useful item, as well as a serially produced object destined for a large public – can also be conceived as an expression of social art. All this may lead to re-examining the history of *7 Arts* as the progressive affirmation of an autonomous Constructivist movement that promoted, first of all, an original aesthetic of the review (fig. 13.2), which can be considered as a multiple artwork made through a collective process.

However, its action no longer seems to be based on a radical refusal of the past. The revaluation of the relationship with the previous generation's masters (with particular reference to some of the most important protagonists of the Belgian pre-war movements) finally allows one to shed new light on *7 Arts*' aesthetics and its origin. Its innovative strength lay within the recent artistic tradition: the group followed the renovation of art, literature and architecture that started at the end of the 19th aveugles, cauchemar du vieux — qui portent le film à son niveau véritable, niveau vite abandonné. l'œuvre évite toute puissance de drame et de prise de vue. Règne un parti-pris de caricature (discrète, certes) en contradiction avec le thème et qui réduit le film à la valeur d'une « composition ».

Bref, *film confortable* : utilisant lumière, décors, costumes, virages, photos de qualité, et science de l'effet, prouvant également une connaissance parfaite des procédés intensifs, mais n'en faisant qu'un prudent usage.

Ainsi donc, produit de révolution et missionnaire, le *Maître de Poste* vaut par la richesse des sous-moyens techniques et se refuse à toute intensité d'inspiration.

C'est le droit de l'Art russe de vouloir reconquérir sur le marché européen, une place qu'il n'a d'ailleurs jamais perdue : Dostoïewsky règne seulement : n'était-ce le nôtre, artistes révolutionnaires, d'escompter une plus hautaine affirmation — et plus créatrice?

PAUL WERRIE.

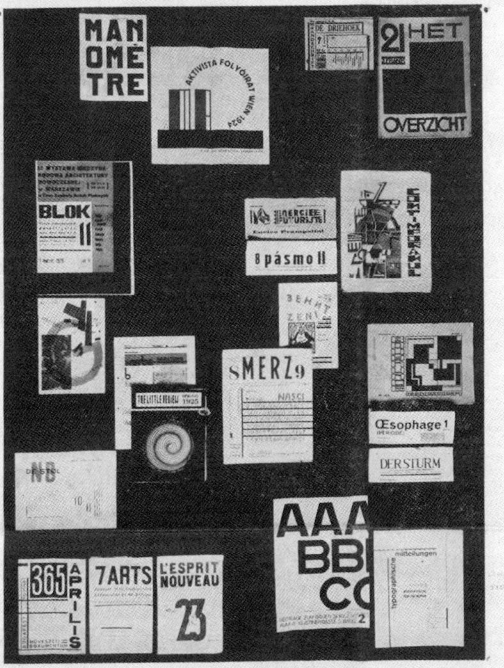

Quelques revues modernistes. — Extrait de Hannes Meyer, « Die Neue Welt ». (Cliché Werk.)

Matériaux pour une histoire de l'Architecture nouvelle

Forme et Fonction

II.

Nul doute que l'esprit du modernisme ne soit contenu dans la machine et dans les édifices industriels; leur signification étant d'ailleurs incontestable, leur forme influe déjà sur le style contemporain: surfaces unies, lignes et angles nets.

Ainsi, *Peter Behrens* conçoit des usines qui, faites de fer, béton et verre, n'ont plus le caractère des hangars ou d'habitations.

Or, c'est *Henri Van de Velde* qui magnifie la beauté nouvelle. La révolution est donc marquée de son signe.

Mais fonction, mouvement, expression, symbolisme, romantisme, individualisme, anthropomorphisme, toutes influences inspirées par ce génial animateur, conduisent parfois à des errements fort nuisibles chez un

Mendelssohn, qui pousse l'expressionnisme à l'extrême dans sa tour d'Einstein, et chez un

Hugo Haring, représentant du fonctionalisme, pour qui les lignes géométriques étant formes mécaniques, l'emploi des courbes est seule admissible.

flexibilité de pensée s'unit à la rigidité de la forme. L'individualisme fonctionaliste ne saurait évidemment le concevoir, par contre le collectivisme de la *Russie* nouvelle le devrait. Mais si la voix la plus certaine conduisant aux réalisations d'expression collective, peut se trouver dans les possibilités techniques, cela signifie-t-il que l'idéal constructif soit celui préconisé au pays de la révolution? Bâtir du mouvement, c'est-à-dire concevoir dynamiquement des projets montés et assemblés comme des ponts roulants ou comme des décors de théâtre, fait songer à certain romantisme frère du futurisme italien qui défend également le mouvement dramatique et lyrique en architecture. Erreur de faire toujours primer l'élévation sur le plan, oubli de la loi interne qui anime les masses!

Mieux vaut la tendance occidentale qui, avec le théoricien *Le Corbusier*, se réclame d'un idéal collectif et d'un machinisme entièrement soumis à l'esprit créateur. Tout s'y révèle synthèse et son idéal proclame les vertus de la standardisation: le principe du plan : pure abstraction, généralité, paraît surtout prôné: sans plan point de rythme, de jeux de volumes, de satisfaction, d'esprit et de plaisir des yeux. Car Le Corbusier admet le jeu et il considère que l'architecture doit tendre à d'autres tâches que de remplir uniquement des fonctions matérielles.

Il revient donc à Le Corbusier d'avoir su expr mer clairement les idées que partagent les architect modernes français tels que Mallet-Stevens, Gevr kian, Dufour, Jourdain, dont les aînés furent Perr et Tony Garnier.

La personnalité de ces deux précurseurs domi encore réellement l'architecture française. Mais ta dis que *Perret*, animé de l'esprit d'un Eiffel, en ploie le béton avec une force inventive formidabl s'avérant ainsi comme le constructeur-né. *Tony Ga nier* peut être considéré comme appartenant à cet lignée de maîtres-architectes qui surent périodiqu ment s'arracher à la tradition pour créer des form viriles. Rien de plus raisonnable pourtant que conception de la forme :

Elle n'est, pour lui, que la conséquence de ra ports d'homme à homme: pour l'homme isolé poi de forme, elle se présente là où il y a société; q admet celle-ci admet celle-là.

Ainsi, sans qu'on tombe dans la tyrannie de fonction, extrême opposé de la forme classique, de l'utilité, ni du dynamisme, ni de l'intelligen pure, on peut admettre *la norme, la volonté, le je la forme et surtout la fonction sociale de l'arch tecture.* Peut-être que, dans cette voie, se trouvera vérité qui ne peut être, évidemment, celle des tem révolus: de l'art grec qui n'a pas hésité à sacrif la logique pure à l'harmonie formelle; de l'art r main, si impressionnant dans ses compositions c lossales, ses systèmes nouveaux de construction, audaces, mais à la contre-partie décorative menso gère; de l'art classique d'esprit si équilibré mais roné lorsqu'opposé aux lois de l'évolution.

L'architecture, pour être de son temps, doit soumettre aux exigences nouvelles et adopter matériaux nouveaux (Viollet-le-Duc). Son esser étant jeu de forces en équilibre, charge et app traction et compression, elle ne peut se former q leur image. Actuellement, le béton armé, arme l'étonnant aujourd'hui, affirme une telle supérior qu'il vaincra tous les scrupules traditionnalistes.

A. BRUNFAUT.

Une Création au Théatre Flamand

La Révolution au Village

Ce n'est pas une pièce banale, la pièce de *W Schouteden*, que M. Poot nous a réservée pour dernière *Kunstvertooning* mensuelle du Thé royal flamand. Et il serait injuste de n'en po parler. Mais soyons prudents, après avoir résolu nous prononcer favorablement. L'auteur ne profi t-il de circonstances tellement propices qu'il lui f peu démontrer pour mériter l'acquittement? En monde où triomphe le relatif, comme les pièces théâtre se mesurent aux autres pièces de théâtre, critique est obligé de dire : c'est bon, quand c seulement mieux.

M. Schouteden, après l'escamotage politique « dictateur » de Romains qui paraît parfaitem raisonnable à celui qui prend au sérieux un guide chemins de fer (comme base sociale), et parfai ment ridicule à celui chez qui ce guide, au co traire, déclanche le grotesque.

M. Schouteden, dis-je, escamote les dimensi d'une révolution mondiale en la conduisant au lage. Cette solution moins grave, même un peu ri cule, permet à l'artisan de la scène de simplifier compliqué, de grossir les traits essentiels, de sau la révolution universelle en la réduisant à une p originalement flamande. Oui, *cette révolution* très grande parce qu'elle se passe chez des petit

Jézabel, tel est le titre de l'œuvre dont le p sonnage principal cumule les emplois de servante curé, échevin des travaux publics, organiste et gr dictateur du petit village de Hoxelaer. Combien dictature de Jézabel est tyrannique! C'est un sans sexe, qui a simultanément l'importance d' idée philosophique et celle d'une maîtresse d'éc Dans les moments les plus critiques de son règ quand le peuple s'agite en pleine révolution, Jéza frappe dans ses mains. Alors tout le monde sait la récréation est terminée.

Mais, dans le village, vit un petit orphelin cheveux sont rouges, comme ceux de Thyl, Spa cus et Liebknecht. Sa mission semble d'aller cherc les marrons dans le feu. Quelqu'un lui ayant conté l'histoire de Samson et Dalila, il décide

13.2. *7 Arts*, n. 10, 23 janvier 1926 (1927 ?), cinquième saison, p. 2, Archives de la Ville de Bruxelles, AVB J 215.

century and gave it new life, thanks to both new communication strategies and an original visual lexicon. This tradition was therefore reduced to the essential: *7 Arts* opened up to new constructive possibilities that intended to convey modern aesthetic (and social) principles and tended towards an extreme functionalism. Maybe the war, together with the changes it entailed, influenced their research and oriented it towards an original economy of means of expression.

In the end, *7 Arts* editors' position within the European culture of the 1920s can also be redefined. Since their work was deeply rooted in the past but firmly pointed toward the future, they can now be considered as having acted as protagonists (and not as epigones) within the international artistic scene,[29] where they created fruitful and equal contacts with other exponents of both Constructivism and the Modern Movement.

Notes

1 The composer Georges Monier contributed to the weekly *7 Arts* until 1926. From the fifth season on, he was substituted by Paul Werrie. For further information about the other four editors please see André Doms, *Pierre Bourgeois. Une lecture de soixante ans de poésie* (Brussels : Maison internationale de la poésie, 1976); *Victor Bourgeois, 1897-1962* (Brussels : Archives d'Architecture Moderne, 1971); Serge Goyens de Heusch, *Pierre-Louis Flouquet* (Brussels : Fonds pour l'Art Belge Contemporain, 1993); *Karel Maes*, ed. V. Verhack et al. (Drogenbos: Musée Felix De Boeck, 2007).

2 Magritte, who was one of the Bourgeois and Flouquet's best friends at that time, collaborated with them mostly between 1919 and 1922. Nonetheless he never gave his direct contribution to *7 Arts* and, some years later, he would become one of their greatest opponents. For more details please see René Magritte's correspondence with Pierre-Louis Flouquet now conserved in Los Angeles at the Getty Research Institute (henceforth GRI), Research Library, Special Collections, *René Magritte Correspondence*, Call Number 870435, box 1, folder 1; *René Magritte, catalogue raisonné. I : Oil Paintings 1916-1930*, ed. by David Sylvester and Sarah Whitfield (Huston: Menil Foundation; Milano: Electa; London: Fonds Mercator, 1992), 15-37.

3 Please see "Périodicité, prix, durée", *7 Arts* Numéro-Manifeste, October (?) 1922, 1.

4 This Centre, which can be considered as a kind of "artist-run space" *ante litteram*, was directed by a group of young artists and men of letters including Pierre and Victor Bourgeois.

5 René Magritte, Letter to Pierre-Louis Flouquet, s.d., Los Angeles, GRI Research Library, Special Collections, *René Magritte Correspondence*, Call Number 870435, box 1, folder 1, 1 *f. ms. r.*

6 For more details please see I'lija Ehrenburg, *Uomini, anni, vita*, vol. 2 (Roma: Editori Riuniti, 1961-1963), 226-229.

7 Franz Hellens, Frédéric van Ermengen's *nom de plume*, was the editor of magazines such as *Signaux de France et de Belgique* and *Le Disque Vert*. For more information about his relation with the Russian culture please see Franz Hellens, *Documents secrets, 1905-1956. Histoire sentimentale de mes livres et de mes quelques amitiés* (Paris: Editions Albin Michel, 1958), 73-85.

8 Cf. I'lija Ehrenburg, "La poésie russe et la révolution. Lettre inédite", *Signaux de France et de Belgique* 4 (1921), 178-191; I'lija Ehrenburg, "La littérature russe en 1922. Lettre inédite", *Le Disque Vert* 3 (1922), 63-68.

9 Franz Hellens, "Literature i kinematograf" [Literature and cinema], *Vešč'/Objet/Gegenstand* 1-2 (March-April 1922), 11-12.

10 In this regard please see Jacques Mesnil, "L'art dans la Russie des Soviets", *L'Art Libre* 1 (1922), 3-8; Jacques Mesnil, "L'art dans la Russie des Soviets", *Bulletin Communiste* 10 (1922), 193-196; Frederik Leen, *Cercles et coteries*, in *L'avant-garde en Belgique, 1917-1929*, ed. Anne Adriaens-Pannier (Brussels: Crédit Communal, 1992), 24; D. de Marneffe, "Entre modernisme et avant-garde. Le réseau des revues littéraires de l'immédiat après-guerre en Belgique (1919-1922) " (PhD diss., Université de Liège, 2007), 214. Mesnil probably had the opportunity to participate in the exhibition that was organised during Comintern's Third Congress, in summer 1921. According to El Lisickij's memories, Lisickij himself gave his contribution to the setup of the exhibition for foreign delegates. Please see El Lisickij, "Nuova arte russa", in *El Lisitskij: pittore, architetto, tipografo, fotografo. Ricordi, lettere e scritti*, ed. Sophie Lisitskij-Küppers (Rome: Editori Riuniti, 1967), 333

11 On this subject please see, for example, Serge Goyens de Heusch, *7 Arts, Bruxelles 1922-1929. Un front de jeunesse pour la révolution artistique* (Brussels: Ministère de la Culture Francophone de Belgique, 1976). The date commonly accepted by the critics is remembered in a letter from Pierre Bourgeois to Serge Goyens de Heusch, dated 8 September 1972, that was conserved in Brussels at the Archives et Musée de la Littérature (henceforth AML), Boite FS XVIII 18 7 ARTS at the time of our research. This same letter, anyway, contains some incorrect information, as those, for example, concerning the exhibition *Les Constructeurs* (Marcel-Louis Baugniet, Pierre-Louis Flouquet, Jean-Jacques Galliard, Sta Jasinsky, Victor Servranckx and Maurice Xhrouet, Brussels, Cabinet Maldoror, November 1925). Bourgeois asserted, in fact, that the exhibition's catalogue was no longer published, while it was actually made (a copy is still conserved in Los Angeles, GRI Research Library, Special Collections, Call Number ND668.5.C64 L36 1925).

12 For this new dating hypothesis, please see also the correspondence between Pierre Bourgeois and Pierre-Louis Flouquet dating to the August 1922, when Bourgeois was settling in Genève and asked his friend if he was still thinking about the weekly (cited here as 'l'hebdomadaire'). Therefore, at that time, the review seemed to be still a project, since no title or other specific elements about it were mentioned. Moreover, many references to that specific issue have been published in *7 Arts*. For example, in the last issue of the first year (dated 19 April 1923) it is cited as having been put to bed in autumn, while at the end of the third year (issue of 19 March 1925), the editors remembered of having "announced" (not started) the publishing of a modernist weekly in October 1922.

13 Some references to that plan are contained in the correspondence between Pierre Bourgeois and Pierre-Louis Flouquet probably dated to those months. Please see, in particular, a letter from Pierre Bourgeois to Pierre-Louis Flouquet s.d. (2 *ff. mss. r., v.*), which was conserved in Brussels at the AML, Boite FS XVIII 18 7 ARTS, at the time of our research. A document that is perhaps related to that project is the printed sheet called *Construire*, which can be dated to the end of 1920 or the beginning of 1921, thanks to some Bourgeois' letters and to the stamps on a group's printed invitation. Cf. *Construire*, Archives d'Art Contemporain de Bruxelles – Musées Royaux des Beaux-Arts, Brussels (henceforth MRBAB-AACB), n. inv. 12.734; Pierre Bourgeois, Letter to Pierre-Louis Flouquet, 14 November 1920, Brussels, AML, Fonds Pierre-Louis Flouquet, n. inv. M.L. 7508/17/5, 1 f. *ms. r., v.*; Pierre Bourgeois, Letter to Karel Maes' family, 13 July 1974, Brussels, AML, Fonds Pierre Bourgeois, Lettres de Pierre Bourgeois, n. inv. FS XVIII 1/784, 1 *f. ds. r.*; *Construire – Invitation*, Bruxelles, MRBAB-AACB, n. inv. 45.491.

14 It is interesting to recall that, between 1920 and 1922, some of the artists that were next to *7 Arts* took part in some of the activities organised by the Kring Moderne Kunst, which was founded in Antwerp in late 1918.

[15] Please see Victor Bourgeois, "Un programme d'enseignement", *La Cité* 7 (1920), 127-129. For any further specification on the correspondence prior to the publication of the article, please see: Raphaël Verwilghen, Letter to Victor Bourgeois, 19 September 1919, Bruxelles, MRBAB-AACB, Fonds Victor Bourgeois, n. inv. 45.384, 1 *f. ms. r.*; Raphaël Verwilghen, Letter to Victor Bourgeois, 5 October 1919, Brussels, MRBAB-AACB, Fonds Victor Bourgeois, n. inv. 45.385, 1 *f. ms. r.*

[16] "7 Arts", *La Cité* 7 (1922), 147-148.

[17] Welcoming Raphaël Verwilghen's invitation, Victor Bourgeois wrote an article on that specific topic, that was at the centre of the public debate in those years. In this regard, it is also important to recall that a copy of the pamphlet *Ypres. Essai sur la formation et sur la reconstruction*, published by Jean de Ligne in 1918, is still part of the Fonds Pierre Bourgeois now conserved in Brussels at the AML, Fonds Pierre Bourgeois, n. inv. FS XVIII 20000/852.

[18] Please see Pierre Bourgeois, Letter to 'Monsieur Léonard' about Serge Goyens de Heusch's book, s. d. Bruxelles, AML, Fonds Pierre Bourgeois, FS XVIII 1/733, 1 *f. ds. r.*

[19] Marcel-Louis Baugniet, "L'esthétique industrielle", *Synthèse* 174 (1960), in Marcel-Louis Baugniet, *Vers une synthèse esthétique et sociale* (Brussels: Editions Labor, 1986), 77-95.

[20] "Formules d'une esthétique moderne par Henry Van de Velde", *7 Arts*, 22 February 1923, 1.

[21] Victor Bourgeois, Draft of a letter to Charles Rochat, 10 November 1923. Brussels, MRBAB-AACB, Fonds Victor Bourgeois, n. inv. 45.558, 1 *f. ds. r.*

[22] *7 Arts* Numéro-Manifeste, October (?) 1922, 1.

[23] For further details on the history of this organisation, please see Paul Aron, *Les écrivains belges et le socialisme (1880-1913). L'expérience de l'art social: d'Edmond Picard à Emile Verhaeren* (Brussels: Editions Labor, 1985), 65-125.

[24] One of the main topics of Destrée's theory was the artwork's utility: if art penetrated into every sector of society, it could contribute to the abolition of class distinctions, typical of the bourgeois culture. Therefore, the art of the future should tend toward the idea and descend to the common objects of everyday life. Cf. Jules Destrée, *Art et Socialisme* (Brussels: Le Peuple, 1896) : 1; Jules Destrée and Emile Vandervelde, *Le socialisme en Belgique* (Paris: V. Giard & E. Brière, 1903^2), 395.

[25] Cf. Iwan Strauven, *Les frères Bourgeois. Architecture et plastique pure* (Brussels: Editions Archives d'Architecture Moderne, 2005), 124.

[26] Please see "L'Ecrivain", *Le Geste* 3 (1920), 18.

[27] Maurice Casteels, who was also the author of a small volume entitled *Esthétique*, defended a modern idea of beauty, which was strictly related to both its rationalist origin and its useful aim. Cf. Maurice Casteels, *Esthétique* (Brussels: Edition du Pot d'Etain, 1921).

[28] Maurice Casteels, "Les arts industriels", *7 Arts*, 30 November 1922, 3.

[29] In this regard, please see what Aleksandr Lavrentiev suggested about the relationship between Soviet Constructivism and the art nouveau movement: Aleksandr Lavrentiev, "The Three Constructivisms of Aleksander Rodchenko, in Constructivism and the Art of Everyday Life," Tate Modern, 28 March 2009. http://www.tate.org.uk/context-comment/video/constructivism-and-art-everyday-life-part-4 (accessed 2 December 2012).

Réseaux d'artistes avant et après la guerre : le cas exemplaire de la Section d'or

Françoise Lucbert

La réflexion qui suit émane d'une recherche en cours dont l'objectif est de mieux connaître les expositions tardives de la Section d'or.[1] Celles-ci furent présentées entre 1920 et 1922 dans huit villes européennes – Paris, Rotterdam, La Haye, Arnhem, Amsterdam, Bruxelles, Genève, Rome – sous la bannière d'une association portant expressément le nom de « Section d'or » (ill. 14.1). À ce jour plutôt méconnues, ces expositions itinérantes, dont la liste des exposants et des œuvres varia au gré de ses différentes étapes, comprenaient les travaux d'une trentaine d'artistes associés à de multiples formes d'expression de l'art moderne international au début des années 1920. Outre quelques représentants du cubisme parisien d'avant-guerre, dont Albert Gleizes, Fernand Léger, Louis Marcoussis et Jacques Villon, s'y croisèrent plusieurs tendances artistiques contemporaines. Le tiers des exposants environ appartenait à des mouvements organisés, comme le cubisme, le néoplasticisme hollandais (Piet Mondrian, Vilmos Huszár et surtout Theo van Doesburg) ou le futurisme italien (Giacomo Balla, Umberto Boccioni [à titre posthume], Luigi Russolo et, le plus jeune d'entre eux, Enrico Prampolini). En revanche, la majorité des participants restent difficiles à rattacher à un courant portant un nom en « isme ». Ces personnalités assez disparates, mais toutes liées à des cercles d'avant-garde ou à tout le moins progressistes, demeurent en quelque sorte orphelines au regard d'une vision canonique de l'histoire de l'art du XXe siècle puisqu'elles ne se réclamaient, ni officiellement ni officieusement, d'une mouvance esthétique délimitée. La plupart de ces créateurs, dont un nombre important était d'origine russe ou ukrainienne, étaient venus des quatre coins de l'Europe pour grossir, avant, pendant ou après la Première Guerre mondiale, les rangs d'une École de Paris de plus en plus cosmopolite.[2] À cet égard, la série d'expositions à l'étude constitue un cas exemplaire pour aborder les deux questions énoncées dans le titre du colloque dont le présent ouvrage collectif se fait l'écho.[3]

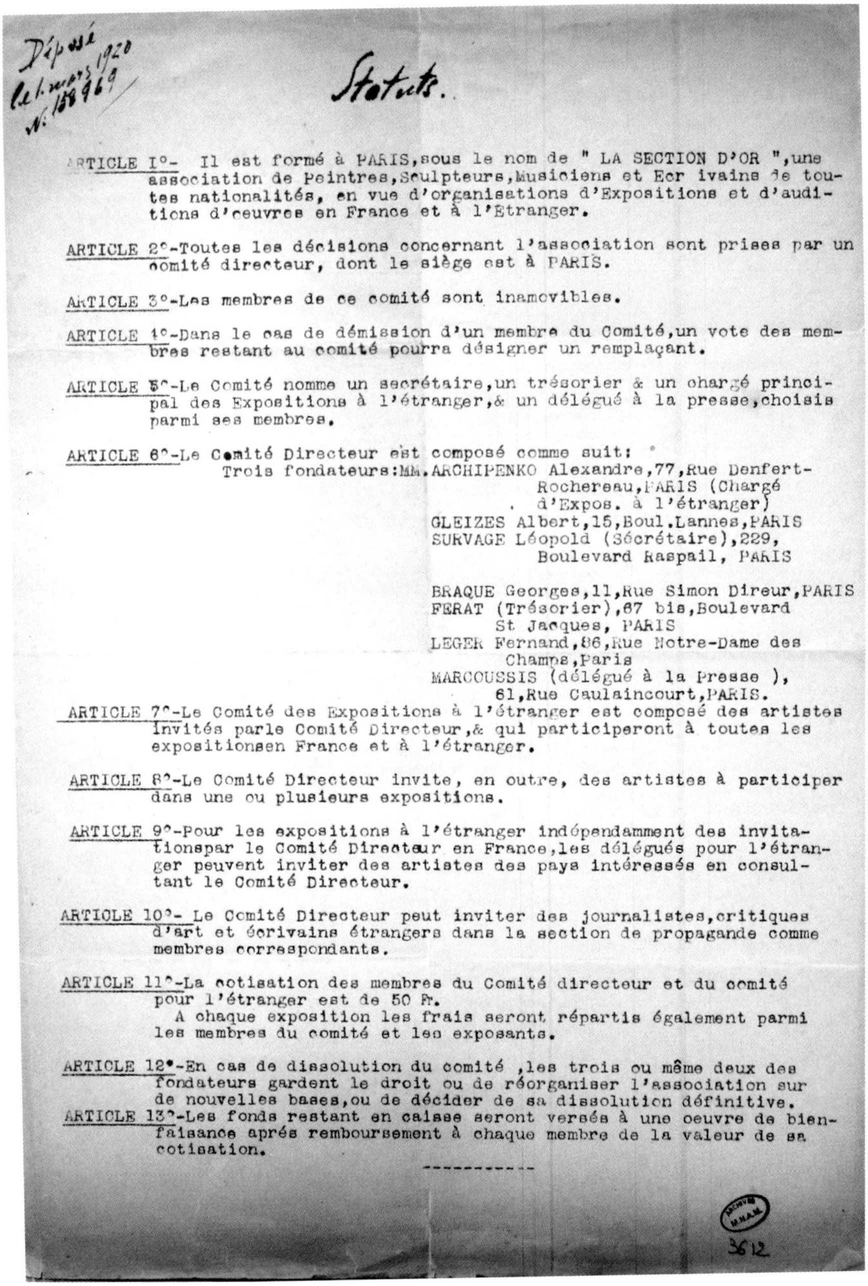

Déposé le 1 mars 1920 N. 158969

Statuts.

ARTICLE I°- Il est formé à PARIS, sous le nom de " LA SECTION D'OR ", une association de Peintres, Sculpteurs, Musiciens et Ecr ivains de toutes nationalités, en vue d'organisations d'Expositions et d'auditions d'ceuvres en France et à l'Etranger.

ARTICLE 2°-Toutes les décisions concernant l'association sont prises par un comité directeur, dont le siège est à PARIS.

ARTICLE 3°-Les membres de ce comité sont inamovibles.

ARTICLE 4°-Dans le cas de démission d'un membre du Comité, un vote des membres restant au comité pourra désigner un remplaçant.

ARTICLE 5°-Le Comité nomme un secrétaire, un trésorier & un chargé principal des Expositions à l'étranger, & un délégué à la presse, choisis parmi ses membres.

ARTICLE 6°-Le Comité Directeur est composé comme suit:
Trois fondateurs: MM. ARCHIPENKO Alexandre, 77, Rue Denfert-Rochereau, PARIS (Chargé d'Expos. à l'étranger)
GLEIZES Albert, 15, Boul. Lannes, PARIS
SURVAGE Léopold (Sécrétaire), 229, Boulevard Raspail, PARIS

BRAQUE Georges, 11, Rue Simon Direur, PARIS
FERAT (Trésorier), 67 bis, Boulevard St Jacques, PARIS
LEGER Fernand, 86, Rue Notre-Dame des Champs, Paris
MARCOUSSIS (délégué à la Presse), 61, Rue Caulaincourt, PARIS.

ARTICLE 7°-Le Comité des Expositions à l'étranger est composé des artistes invités parle Comité Directeur, & qui participeront à toutes les expositionsen France et à l'étranger.

ARTICLE 8°-Le Comité Directeur invite, en outre, des artistes à participer dans une ou plusieurs expositions.

ARTICLE 9°-Pour les expositions à l'étranger indépendamment des invitationspar le Comité Directeur en France, les délégués pour l'étranger peuvent inviter des artistes des pays intéressés en consultant le Comité Directeur.

ARTICLE 10°- Le Comité Directeur peut inviter des journalistes, critiques d'art et écrivains étrangers dans la section de propagande comme membres correspondants.

ARTICLE 11°-La cotisation des membres du Comité directeur et du comité pour l'étranger est de 50 Fr.
A chaque exposition les frais seront répartis également parmi les membres du comité et les exposants.

ARTICLE 12°-En cas de dissolution du comité, les trois ou même deux des fondateurs gardent le droit ou de réorganiser l'association sur de nouvelles bases, ou de décider de sa dissolution définitive.

ARTICLE 13°-Les fonds restant en caisse seront versés à une oeuvre de bienfaisance aprés remboursement à chaque membre de la valeur de sa cotisation.

14.1. Statuts de l'association "La Section d'or", déposés en mars 1920. Paris, Bibliothèque Kandinsky (Centre Pompidou), Fonds Survage.

Se pose en premier lieu avec acuité la question de l'avant et de l'après, ne serait-ce que parce que les expositions de la Section d'or se tinrent effectivement en deux périodes distinctes : tout d'abord à la veille de la Première Guerre mondiale, c'est-à-dire de façon tout à fait ponctuelle en octobre 1912, et exclusivement à Paris ; puis, à l'issue du conflit mondial, à partir de mars 1920, sur un laps de temps assez long (jusqu'en mai 1922) et à une échelle bien plus vaste que pour la première édition. Il est en soi intéressant de comparer les œuvres exposées lors de ces deux moments et de s'attacher à leur mode de circulation, autant qu'à leurs conditions de présentation, qui diffèrent nécessairement. Mais dans la perspective développée ici, il est fondamental de comprendre comment ont pu se mettre en place, évoluer et s'entrecroiser plusieurs groupes autour d'un ambitieux projet transnational, imaginé sur les ruines d'une Europe artistique malmenée par la guerre. Dans quelle mesure le cosmopolitisme affirmé de la deuxième Section d'or est-il lié aux transformations que la guerre a infligées au milieu de l'art parisien – en envoyant les artistes, marchands et critiques sous les drapeaux, dans les camps de prisonniers ou en les contraignant à l'exil ?

En second lieu, la reprise après 1918 d'un nom déjà utilisé avant 1914 incite le chercheur à s'interroger sur le problème des continuités et/ou des ruptures au sein des réseaux artistiques de l'époque. S'agissait-il des mêmes groupes, des mêmes enjeux ? Qu'impliquait exactement cette renaissance de l'idée de Section d'or aux plans artistique, esthétique, stratégique ? Y eut-il véritablement continuité avec le cubisme d'avant-guerre ? Si oui, dans quel contexte et sur quels fondements ? Et comment la gloire associée, dès le lendemain de la guerre, à des années déjà perçues comme « héroïques »,[4] a-t-elle pu rejaillir sur les tentatives de régénérer, sinon le projet du cubisme, alors ébranlé,[5] du moins l'idéalisme moderniste à l'origine de la première Section d'or ?

La Section d'or, avant 1914 et après 1918 : un renouvellement cosmopolite

Faute d'espace, je ne pourrai détailler les différentes étapes de l'exposition de la Section d'or ni analyser le rôle des organisateurs de celles-ci.[6] Je n'insisterai que sur quelques éléments saillants qui aideront à replacer ce groupe d'artistes et de médiateurs à l'intérieur d'un vaste réseau européen aux visées internationales. Définir la Section d'or comme un réseau international et internationaliste, partiellement mis en place avant la guerre puis réactivé après celle-ci, ouvre des pistes stimulantes pour analyser la résurgence des initiatives promotionnelles d'artistes dès la fin de la guerre. Plus encore, aborder le problème en utilisant certains outils de l'histoire transnationale

– en particulier la perspective « horizontale »[7] et la méthode qui consiste à penser l'interaction des acteurs de la médiation artistique « entre » et à « travers »[8] les instances organisationnelles de divers pays – aide à caractériser les relations que la cinquantaine d'exposants de la Section d'or entre 1912 et 1922 entretenaient entre eux et avec les animateurs des milieux culturels (dont les directeurs de revues, les critiques, les galeristes, les conservateurs), tant en Belgique qu'à l'échelle européenne et internationale.

Présenté à Paris en octobre 1912, le Salon de la Section d'or reste un jalon majeur dans l'histoire du cubisme. Avec la salle des cubistes au Salon d'Automne de la même année, cette exposition collective suscita une véritable onde de choc. Elle contribua à mettre le cubisme à l'avant-plan, non seulement au sein des milieux culturels, mais aussi sur la scène politique et, par voie de conséquence, dans la sphère médiatique. Cette exposition a été relativement bien étudiée et surtout beaucoup commentée par les contemporains de l'événement[9]. Or, la renaissance du groupe autour de 1920 fut négligée des spécialistes, y compris par l'auteure de la plus récente étude sur la Section d'or.[10] Fondée en octobre 1919 par le sculpteur Alexandre Archipenko, le peintre Albert Gleizes (tous deux présents en 1912) et Léopold Survage (un nouveau venu), l'association La Section d'or prépara une exposition itinérante à géométrie variable. Après son inauguration parisienne (Galerie La Boëtie, 3-16 mars 1920), sur laquelle nous savons encore peu de choses (ill. 14.2), l'exposition s'arrêta à Rotterdam (Rotterdamsche Kunstkring, 20 juin-4 juillet 1920), La Haye (Haagsche Kunstkring, 10-31 juillet 1920), Arnhem (Korenbeurs, août-septembre ? 1920), Amsterdam (Stedelijk Museum, 23 octobre-7 novembre 1920), Bruxelles (Sélection, 4-18 décembre 1920), Genève (Palais Électoral, 26 décembre 1920-25 janvier 1921) et, après une longue interruption, Rome (Galleria del Arte moderna italiana, 17 avril-2 mai 1922).

Un relevé statistique des exposants de la Section d'or avant et après la guerre permet de conclure à un renouvellement très important du groupe. En effet, seulement sept artistes de la « première Section d'or » (en comptant Kupka),[11] dont l'un à titre posthume (Duchamp-Villon), exposèrent à la Section d'or des années 1920. Au total donc, 26 « nouveaux » ont remplacé 24 des exposants de 1912 ; les nouveaux venus représentaient en définitive 75 % de l'ensemble. Ce profond renouvellement pose bien sûr la question des continuités et/ou ruptures par rapport aux enjeux d'avant-guerre, d'abord sur le plan esthétique puisque la plupart des exposants ne s'inscrivaient ni dans le cubisme « orthodoxe » défendu par le marchand Henry Kahnweiler avant la guerre, ni même dans le prolongement esthétique du « cubisme écartelé » propre à la première Section d'or.[12] La comparaison des groupes avant et après la guerre démontre également l'ampleur du cosmopolitisme au sein du réseau étudié. Sur l'ensemble des 33 exposants des années 1920, neuf seulement (soit 27 %) étaient nés en France, tandis que 24 (soit 73 %) étaient d'origine autre. Notons que les Français, qui étaient majoritaires à 72 % en 1912, ne représentaient plus que 27 % des exposants de 1920. Les proportions s'étaient ainsi pratiquement inversées. S'y trouvaient en fait un nombre élevé d'artistes nés dans l'Empire russien (Archipenko, Survage, Serge Férat, Natalia Gontcharova, Michel Larionov, la baronne d'Oettingen, Marie Vassilieff),[13] sans oublier les ressortissants du nord ou de l'est de l'Europe : Bohème (Kupka), Pologne (Marcoussis, Hayden, Lambert-Rucki), Hongrie (Csaky, Huszár, Miklos), Roumanie (Brâncuşi), Norvège (Hellesen), mais aussi Belgique (Donas), Pays-Bas (le groupe De Stijl), Suisse (Buchet) et Italie (plusieurs futuristes).

Comment interpréter ce phénomène : doit-on le considérer « négativement » comme une « désertion » des Français ou, à l'inverse, « positivement » comme un élément constitutif d'une École de Paris par essence cosmopolite ? À un autre niveau, cette forte représentation « étrangère » dans les expositions tardives de la Section d'or indique-t-elle une meilleure diffusion du cubisme (en outre grâce aux initiatives des membres du réseau) ou au contraire sa dilution ? La guerre aurait-elle eu comme conséquence de faire éclater définitivement le cubisme déjà « écartelé » d'avant 1914 en une nébuleuse néo-cubiste sans consistance ? En réalité, l'antenne parisienne de la Section d'or, elle-même très cosmopolite, fonctionnait comme un réseau paneuropéen qui s'efforçait de tisser des contacts avec des personnalités influentes en art moderne dans d'autres grands centres urbains. Au fil de l'itinérance, les exposants nouèrent à leur tour des relations avec les organisateurs ou exposants des étapes suivantes. Les échanges peu connus entre le Hollandais Van Doesburg et l'Italien Prampolini[14], ou encore avec les Belges Marthe Donas et André De Ridder en sont de bonnes illustrations.

La Belgique au cœur d'un réseau artistique transnational

Situons à présent dans un environnement transnational l'évolution de l'art et l'interpénétration des canaux artistiques, tels que les sociétés d'artistes, les galeries, les revues, dans le Royaume de Belgique juste après la guerre. À l'aide des concepts de cosmopolitisme, d'internationalisme, de transnationalisme, tels que (re) définis par la recherche récente,[15] l'exemple choisi permet de se pencher sur certains créateurs originaires de ce pays, telle Marthe Donas (alias Tour-Donas),[16] exposante assidue aux salons organisés, depuis Paris, par l'association La Section d'or ; ou le graveur et animateur de revues Albert Daenens, lié au groupe à sa façon lorsqu'il aida les Français Marcel Bouraine et Abel Gerbaud à préparer l'Exposition internationale d'art moderne de Genève, à laquelle les exposants de la Section d'or de Paris firent un envoi groupé en janvier 1921.[17] Donas, résidant à Anvers avant la Première Guerre mondiale, n'avait pas été impliquée à la Section d'or de 1912. S'installant à Paris fin 1916, elle fréquenta brièvement l'atelier d'André Lhote, un exposant de la première Section d'or. Selon son témoignage, « une exposition de ce dernier l'avait tout à fait conquise au cubisme »,[18] ce qui l'incita à réaliser des toiles inspirées par cette mouvance. Mais étant donné l'absence de Lhote à la seconde Section d'or, ce furent plutôt les liens étroits qu'elle noua avec Archipenko, déjà présent en 1912 et désormais « chargé d'Expositions à l'étranger » – voir les statuts de l'association La Section d'or déposés en mars 1920 (ill. 14.1) – qui lui permirent de se joindre au groupe que nous étudions. Quant à Daenens, il n'était pas personnellement lié aux organisateurs de la Section d'or de 1912 ; c'est en fait son amitié d'avant-guerre avec le peintre Gerbaud, installé à Bruxelles en 1908 et proche du cercle de la revue *La Foi nouvelle*, qui le mit indirectement en rapport avec certains des membres de la Section d'or de 1920.[19]

Sur un autre plan, considérer séparément l'étape belge de cette tournée d'expositions éclaire de manière inédite l'apport de Sélection. Ce lieu plutôt atypique de diffusion de l'art moderne, sis au 62 rue des Colonies à Bruxelles, accueillit l'exposition de la Section d'or en décembre 1920 grâce à l'ouverture d'esprit de ses deux fondateurs, André De Ridder et Paul-Gustave van Hecke. Sans pouvoir développer ce point ici, précisons qu'il n'était pas forcément évident de présenter une telle manifestation dans la Belgique de l'immédiat après-guerre. Si un certain public en quête de nouveauté avait fini par accepter le langage synthétique des cubistes d'avant-guerre, il fallut aux propriétaires de Sélection une certaine audace pour recevoir cette exposition dans leur jeune galerie. Ils avaient aussi été d'excellents stratèges, en la situant au sein d'un programme cohérent « d'expositions collectives et personnelles de Peintres et de Sculpteurs représentant les *tendances modernes internationales* ».[20] L'exposition de la Section d'or avait non seulement été annoncée et expliquée par une série d'articles publiés dans *Sélection*, la revue homonyme créée par leurs soins pour soutenir leurs activités ; elle avait en quelque sorte été « préparée » par deux expositions au cours des mois précédents. La première, tenue pendant l'été 1920 à Anvers,[21] ralliait stratégiquement vingt artistes belges – un nombre rappelant les fameux Vingt du siècle précédent – à une trentaine d'invités, nommément libellés « Exposants étrangers » (dix, dont Dufy, Le Fauconnier, Modigliani et Zadkine), et surtout « Les cubistes » (vingt en tout, autant français qu'étrangers : dont Braque, Csaky, Derain, Gris, Lhote, Rivera, etc., et hormis Picasso). Au lendemain de l'armistice, une telle liste constituait en elle-même un manifeste en faveur de la libre circulation des œuvres d'art par-delà les pays et les courants artistiques. La deuxième, présentée dans les locaux bruxellois de Sélection sous le titre éloquent de "Cubistes français et belges",[22] préfigurait de manière encore plus évidente la venue du groupe de la Section d'or. Le parti des animateurs de Sélection ne pouvait être plus clair : associer les jeunes cubistes belges à leurs prestigieux « aînés » résidant en France.

Plus globalement, s'il faut tenir compte de la réalité propre au milieu de l'art belge à l'aube des années vingt pour entrevoir la spécificité du cas étudié, il importe de l'intégrer dans un ensemble qui dépasse largement la limite des frontières nationales, culturelles ou linguistiques. En l'occurrence, la nature volontairement internationale du réseau de la Section d'or dans cinq pays différents – France, Hollande, Belgique, Suisse, Italie – incite le chercheur à réfléchir sur la dimension européenne, voire transnationale, des interactions en jeu[23]. Le réseau étudié comprend trois ensembles : les membres en titre de l'association éponyme, les artistes qui ont participé aux activités de diffusion de leurs œuvres (expositions, concerts, conférences), de même que les « amis » ou intermédiaires ayant directement contribué à l'organisation de ces activités. Cerner un tel réseau suppose de s'arrêter aux relations, multiples et complexes, entre les individus et groupes qui le composent. Il convient également de s'interroger sur les conditions de possibilité de ces interrelations, ainsi que sur les convergences artistiques, sociales et politiques entre les acteurs du réseau, malgré les divergences d'opinions qui pouvaient aussi les diviser.

La plupart de ces personnages étaient très marqués par une idéologie internationaliste particulièrement militante au cours des mois qui suivirent l'armistice de novembre 1918. On doit souligner la communauté d'idées qui, par exemple, liait plusieurs sociétaires ou amis de la Section d'or à des membres du groupe Clarté. Une franche camaraderie unissait ainsi Paul Colin, représentant du mouvement Clarté pour la Belgique et animateur de l'organe bruxellois *L'Art Libre*, et l'écrivain Florent Fels, qui rejoignit les rangs de l'association La Section d'or à l'époque où il fonda à Paris le mensuel *Action* (février 1920-mars/avril 1922). Un rédacteur anonyme de *L'Art Libre* (sans doute Colin) appelait d'ailleurs Fels « notre camarade »[24] ou encore « notre collaborateur »,[25] avant de déplorer le retrait du commerce, du fait de la censure française, du premier numéro d'*Action*, « vaillante et belle revue »[26] qui, toujours selon ce point de vue élogieux, n'en continuerait pas moins à « défendre la cause de l'art moderne et de l'internationale de la Pensée ».[27] Une telle formule montre à quel point internationalisme et idéalisme se rencontraient dans le dessein de reconstruire les mondes de l'art sur les bases d'une « Pensée » (noter l'usage révélateur de la capitale) à même de transcender les frontières de tous ordres. Ce sont des convictions similaires qui expliquent les liens significatifs entre Gleizes, cofondateur de la deuxième Section d'or, et les milieux internationalistes et pacifistes ravivés au sortir de la Grande Guerre. L'amitié ancienne de ce peintre avec les poètes René Arcos, Georges Duhamel, Alexandre Mercereau, tous « artisans » de la défunte Abbaye de Créteil (1906-1909), doit être prise en compte pour décrire le substrat intellectuel qui incita un groupe d'artistes et d'écrivains à s'unir, dès octobre 1919, sous la bannière d'une Section d'or renouvelée (ill. 14.2).[28] On ne s'étonnera guère, dès lors, que Mercereau, ami de plusieurs exposants de la Section d'or de 1912, et Fels, membre de celle de 1920, aient collaboré à *Sélection*. Signalons enfin que d'autres noms associés à l'histoire du cubisme émaillaient les sommaires de cette revue : les peintres Le Fauconnier et Lhote, le critique André Salmon, le marchand Léonce Rosenberg, etc.

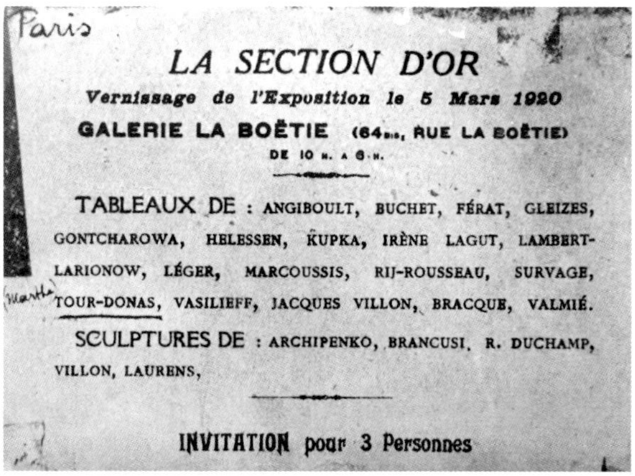
Paris
LA SECTION D'OR
Vernissage de l'Exposition le 5 Mars 1920
GALERIE LA BOËTIE (64 bis, RUE LA BOËTIE)
DE 10 H. A 6 H.

TABLEAUX DE : ANGIBOULT, BUCHET, FÉRAT, GLEIZES, GONTCHAROWA, HELESSEN, KUPKA, IRÈNE LAGUT, LAMBERT-LARIONOW, LÉGER, MARCOUSSIS, RIJ-ROUSSEAU, SURVAGE, TOUR-DONAS, VASILIEFF, JACQUES VILLON, BRACQUE, VALMIÉ.

SCULPTURES DE : ARCHIPENKO, BRANCUSI, R. DUCHAMP, VILLON, LAURENS,

INVITATION pour 3 Personnes

14.2. Reproduction photographique du carton d'invitation de l'exposition La Section d'or, Paris, Galerie La Boëtie, 5 mars 1920. Bruxelles, Musées royaux des Beaux-Arts de Belgique, Archives de l'Art contemporain en Belgique.

Le milieu associatif comme complément au système marchand-critique

Une réflexion sur la dimension associative du groupe[29] permet de s'intéresser aux rapports complexes, parfois contradictoires, d'une petite association de créateurs résolument modernes avec d'importantes sociétés d'artistes établis, des marchands professionnels et, plus généralement encore, des structures (officielles ou non) de diffusion de l'art. La tentative de fédérer en association un groupe déjà en partie formé avant la guerre résultait d'une méfiance bien ancrée à l'endroit du marché de l'art. Loin d'être nouvelles, ces réticences paraissaient plus fermes en raison de la professionnalisation grandissante du métier de galeriste (techniques commerciales modernisées, côté systématique des interventions et des transactions, etc.), contre laquelle les marchands amateurs ne pouvaient guère lutter. De nombreux peintres et sculpteurs tâchaient de profiter des bienfaits de ce système ; en même temps, leur désir d'indépendance se trouvait contraint par les lois du marché, et au premier chef par les contrats d'exclusivité de plus en plus souvent imposés par les propriétaires de galeries.[30] L'association apportait potentiellement une certaine protection contre les pressions et les aléas de ce marché.

Une société se constituait le plus souvent dans un esprit de continuité avec les corporations plus anciennes, qui avaient réuni les artistes en fonction de leur technique (pastellistes, graveurs, aquarellistes, etc.), leur sujet (paysagistes, orientalistes, etc.), leur esthétique (p. ex. impressionnisme), leur genre – au sens de « *gender* » (p. ex. l'Union des femmes peintres et sculpteurs). Ce pouvait aussi être des « unions » regroupant, de façon beaucoup plus large, tous les praticiens en arts plastiques d'une même commune, sans égard pour leur orientation artistique, sur le modèle des « cercles artistiques » nés au XIXe siècle. Les sociétaires de la Section d'or appartenaient, pour leur part, à un regroupement associatif moins normé, qui demeurait souple et laissait une grande liberté aux artistes, mais qui se révélait précaire puisque la viabilité de l'association reposait entièrement sur l'activisme et la bonne volonté de son comité organisateur.

Les expositions de la Section d'or, qui eurent toutes directement ou indirectement à voir avec le marché de l'art, furent en ce sens soumises aux lois de ce marché. Parfois présentées dans des galeries d'une certaine notoriété, comme la galerie La Boëtie, siège des expositions parisiennes de 1912 et de 1920, elles furent le plus souvent montrées dans des lieux moins habituels. À Bruxelles, Sélection fit, pour une courte durée (1920-1922), office de « galerie » d'art actuel, sans pour autant en avoir le statut ni même le nom.[31] La singularité de cet « Atelier d'art contemporain » (c'était son enseigne) tenait d'abord à la personnalité de ses directeurs, les Anversois De Ridder et Van Hecke. Ni l'un ni l'autre n'étaient galeristes à l'instar de professionnels tels que Georges Giroux à Bruxelles, Léonce Rosenberg à Paris ou Max Moos à Genève. Ces « animateurs d'art », selon l'heureuse manière de désigner ce type d'intervenants du milieu de l'art,[32] se distinguaient par leur polyvalence et leur originalité. Auteurs, fondateurs de revues, amis des artistes, ces médiateurs exerçaient, parallèlement au commerce de l'art, d'autres métiers pour assurer leur pain quotidien : essayiste, romancier, De Ridder gagnait sa vie comme professeur de sciences financières et statistiques dans plusieurs établissements d'éducation supérieure,[33] tandis que l'inclassable Van Hecke écrivait, créait des objets d'art décoratif, avant de devenir, grâce à sa femme Norine, une figure influente de la haute couture en Belgique.[34]

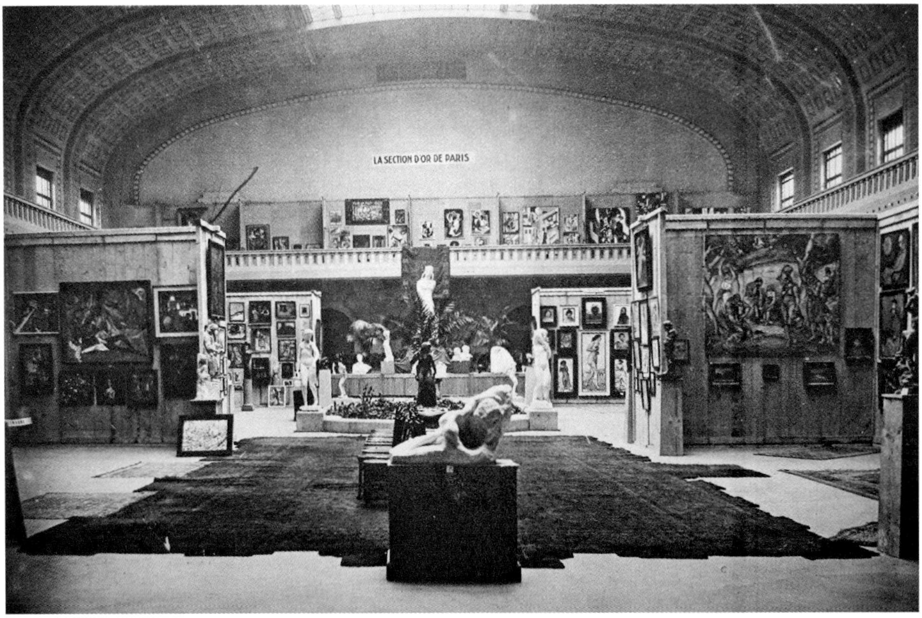

14.3. Exposition internationale d'art moderne, Genève, Palais électoral, 26 décembre 1920-25 janvier 1921. Photographie parue dans *La Patrie suisse* (Genève), janvier 1921, n° 713, p. 24.

Une association comme La Section d'or pouvait représenter une alternative, ou au moins un complément, au marché de l'art. Parmi d'autres avantages, elle permettait d'éviter certaines contraintes de celui-ci. Mais le mode associatif présentait aussi des défauts. Le type de rassemblement choisi semblait, dès le départ, vouer l'association à une existence aussi brève qu'exaltante. L'exposition de la Section d'or s'agrégea ainsi à des sociétés plus grandes qu'elle, au sein desquelles elle s'intégrait assez mal, comme lors de son passage à Rotterdam ou à La Haye ; avec le recul, il semble certain que les propositions plastiques de ses participants pouvaient paraître radicales, en particulier les toiles extrêmement épurées de Donas ou les expérimentations abstraites de Van Doesburg et de Mondrian, comparées aux propositions nettement plus conventionnelles des membres des cercles artistiques (*kunstkringen*) de ces villes. À d'autres occasions, l'exposition risqua même d'être engloutie dans un ensemble trop vaste. Ce fut un peu le cas à Genève, lorsque l'association La Section d'or fit un envoi groupé à l'Exposition internationale d'art moderne. Cette participation en bloc eut beau avoir été conçue pour faire connaître mondialement le groupe, cette ambitieuse manifestation ne lui donna que partiellement la tribune espérée. Si « La Section d'or de Paris » – c'est sous ce nom qu'elle exposa – parvint à se faire remarquer dans un accrochage distinct (à la différence du groupe « Sélection », également invité, mais moins remarqué),[35] bien en vue à l'étage du Palais Électoral (ill. 14.3), cet isolement lui donna finalement peu de visibilité, du moins dans la presse. Il est vrai que le catalogue de l'exposition ne maintint pas la séparation qui existait sur les cimaises ; les exposants y figuraient par pays d'origine (et encore, pas forcément !) et non par « esthétique » ou regroupement.[36] Logiquement, les éventuels commentateurs de l'exposition suivirent les entrées du catalogue, en ignorant ou en omettant de mentionner l'existence de ce groupe délibérément constitué.[37]

La figure de l'artiste « entrepreneur »

La difficulté de se faire reconnaître en tant qu'artiste moderne dans un marché plutôt saturé, et bientôt perturbé par la venue de la guerre, encouragea plusieurs créateurs à devenir eux-mêmes des promoteurs de leurs œuvres. La Section d'or favorisa le développement d'un modèle spécial d'artiste « entrepreneur » qui, pour les motifs évoqués plus haut, refusait de confier uniquement la promotion de son art aux marchands ayant pignon sur rue, aux corporations traditionnelles ou aux instances artistiques officielles. Van Doesburg et Prampolini s'y illustrèrent par leur dynamisme et par l'inventivité de leurs initiatives. L'implication de Van Doesburg au sein de maints réseaux artistiques de son temps, notamment grâce aux innombrables échos et ramifications du périodique *De Stijl*, qu'il avait fondé aux Pays-Bas en pleine guerre, puis diffusé à travers le monde entier avec une infatigable énergie par la suite, en faisait réellement un artiste « international », dont les ambitions internationalistes étaient notoires.[38] Internationaliste, l'était aussi Prampolini qui, tel son aîné Van Doesburg, avait créé une revue d'art moderne au beau milieu de la guerre, *Noi*, dont le joli nom, qui signifie « nous » en langue italienne, sonnait comme un cri de ralliement pour des artistes de plusieurs générations et obédiences, mais réunis autour d'une conception commune de la modernité. En 1920, ce jeune homme avide d'affirmer sa position sur la place de l'art contemporain entrait en contact avec Archipenko et Survage ; il leur proposait de devenir le représentant de la Section d'or pour l'Italie – ce que Van Doesburg avait fait pour la Hollande quelques mois auparavant.

Les démarches de ces « nouvelles » figures d'entrepreneurs[39] mènent à une interrogation de fond sur le rôle des artistes dans la diffusion de leur art. Plusieurs membres de la Section d'or furent non seulement des praticiens et des théoriciens de l'art ; ces sortes d'hommes-orchestres brillèrent aussi comme critiques d'art, fondateurs de revues, directeurs de cercles ou de centres d'art, organisateurs d'expositions, etc. On décèlera à juste titre de l'opportunisme dans leur attitude, comme l'ont montré les travaux de Marguerite Tuijn sur les stratégies autopromotionnelles de Van Doesburg, Archipenko, Tristan Tzara, ou encore Marthe Donas – quoique dans une moindre mesure pour cette dernière.[40] Toutefois, il serait abusif de réduire à cet unique aspect les multiples actions initiées par ces artistes entreprenants et habiles. Que Van Doesburg, Archipenko, Prampolini ou même Survage, dévoué secrétaire de l'association La Section d'or, aient excellé à mettre en valeur leurs productions, voire leur propre personne (aspect qui me semble cependant secondaire), grâce au tremplin que constitua, pour une courte période, le réseau transnational de la Section d'or, ne veut pas dire qu'ils n'eurent pas à cœur de promouvoir sincèrement l'art de leurs amis et/ou alliés. Certes ils ne furent pas « désintéressés » en se lançant dans une telle aventure ; un désintéressement qui, selon une vision idéalisée de l'artiste[41], eût pu conférer à leur entreprise une plus-value morale. Rappelons que la Section d'or était bel et bien une association de *promotion* artistique, dont la mission première consistait en l'organisation d'activités destinées à diffuser les œuvres de ses sociétaires. Par conséquent, le fait même d'avoir été « intéressés », au sens propre comme au sens figuré, colora l'engagement des membres les plus militants de la Section d'or. Car il ne leur suffisait pas d'appartenir à une association fondée à Paris, capitale culturelle jouissant encore à leurs yeux d'un prestige inégalé. La situation allait changer peu après, et Paris serait pour eux, avec Londres, Berlin, Bruxelles, Anvers, Rome, Vienne, Prague et New York, l'*un* des centres à partir duquel ils pourraient rayonner[42]. Encore fallait-il pouvoir s'y *impliquer*, et le plus activement possible. Cette forte implication, en partie motivée par un désir de reconnaissance dans leur pays autant qu'à l'étranger, découlait aussi de la simple nécessité d'exister comme artistes.

Au-delà des considérations esthétiques : la logique du regroupement stratégique

Finalement, le cas de la Section d'or montre que la logique du regroupement dépasse le cadre artistique et esthétique. Dans l'état actuel des connaissances, le contenu de ces expositions[43] frappe l'historien par ce qui pourrait aisément apparaître comme de l'éclectisme. L'impression de disparité, au départ suscitée par la présence de plusieurs formes esthétiques, dont bon nombre paraissent aujourd'hui difficilement conciliables, est accentuée par le fait que la majorité des exposants ne souhaitaient pas se voir rattacher à un mouvement proclamé. Le nom « Section d'or » n'avait pas vraiment de définition précise : à quoi cela correspondait-il exactement ? Manifestement, cette appellation ne signalait ni un « style » connu ni une esthétique partagée, ce qui lui conférait peut-être un intérêt supplémentaire... Insistons de surcroît sur l'absence d'un contenu d'ordre esthétique ou stylistique dans les statuts mêmes de l'association. En d'autres termes, il valait mieux s'associer sans aucun projet artistique commun que rester isolé dans un milieu de l'art de plus en plus compétitif. De telles considérations éclairent aussi sous un jour neuf les relations pour le moins improbables entre les militants les plus modernistes de cette association et leurs homologues des galeries ou des sociétés d'artistes plus conventionnelles.

Il convenait en définitive de rallier autour d'une idée fédératrice une série de personnalités œuvrant à la création et à la diffusion de l'art moderne dans plusieurs pays européens, tantôt selon une logique de rassemblement stratégique, tantôt parce qu'elles partageaient des affinités personnelles, politiques ou esthétiques. La dimension stratégique d'une telle association offre des arguments convaincants pour interpréter, au-delà des questions de style, l'hétérogénéité du groupe. Il est dès lors pertinent d'envisager sous cet angle les rapports entre le cubisme, écartelé ou non, et les autres mouvances artistiques. De toute évidence, les cubistes « français » d'avant-guerre durent s'accommoder de leurs nombreux confrères, à la fois cosmopolites et « néo-cubistes », pour parvenir à conserver leur identité. Dans le monde de l'art aussi ouvertement international qu'était devenue l'Europe avant-gardiste d'après 1918 coexistaient des formes d'expression très variables, y compris les plus incompatibles. À l'échelle de la Belgique, l'idée d'un regroupement stratégique permet de mieux comprendre comment et pourquoi Sélection, un lieu d'art éphémère qui s'attacha beaucoup à la promotion de l'art expressionniste belge – après tout, Gustave de Smet en avait cofondé le bulletin de promotion, *Sélection* – put temporairement embrasser la noble cause universaliste de la Section d'or.

Notes

1 Entrepris en janvier 2015 grâce au programme d'Année d'étude et de recherche de l'Université Laval, le projet intitulé « Les expositions de la section d'or entre 1920 et 1922 : contribution à l'étude des prolongements du cubisme en Europe » est subventionné jusqu'en 2021 par le Conseil de recherches en Sciences humaines du Canada.

2 Employé par l'écrivain Roger Allard dès 1923, le nom de l'École de Paris a généralement été attribué au critique d'art André Warnod, dont l'ouvrage *Les Berceaux de la jeune peinture. L'école de Paris* (Paris : Albin Michel, 1925) a marqué un tournant dans la conceptualisation d'une telle École. Voir notamment le catalogue de l'exposition *L'École de Paris 1904-1929, la part de l'Autre* (Paris : Musée d'Art moderne de la Ville de Paris/Paris musées, 2000).

3 Le colloque *Avant et après ? Continuité ou rupture ? L'art belge au temps de la Grande Guerre* a eu lieu aux Musées royaux des Beaux-Arts de Belgique les 24 et 25 novembre 2016. J'en remercie vivement les instigatrices, Laura Kollwelter et Inga Rossi-Schrimpf, pour la richesse des questions soumises aux participants, pour la qualité de leur accueil et pour l'intérêt des débats qu'elles ont su susciter.

4 Si l'expression ne s'imposera qu'après coup, par exemple dans les écrits tardifs du marchand Kahnweiler (*Les Années héroïques du cubisme*, Paris : Braun, 1950) et par plusieurs expositions des années cinquante et soixante, dont celle portant le titre *Évocation de l'époque héroïque* (Paris : Galerie de l'Institut, 18 mars-13 avril 1955, préface au catalogue par Waldemar-George), la notion d'héroïsme était déjà sous-jacente dans l'essai fondateur du célèbre galeriste : *Der Weg zum Kubismus*, publié à Munich en 1920 et traduit en français par Denise Naville sous le titre « La Montée du cubisme », dans Daniel-Henry Kahnweiler, *Confessions esthétiques* (Paris : Gallimard, 1963, 13-60).

5 Voir sur ce plan la magistrale étude de Christopher Green, *Cubism and its Enemies : Modern Movements and Reaction in French Art, 1916-1928* (New Haven et Londres : Yale University Press, 1987).

6 Ces aspects seront développés dans l'ouvrage de synthèse que je prépare sur la Section d'or des années 1920.

7 Celle développée par l'historien de l'art polonais Piotr Piotrowski enrichit indéniablement l'étude des réseaux artistiques. Voir en particulier son texte programmatique « Toward a Horizontal History of European Avant-Garde », dans *European Avant-Garde and Modernism Studies*, dir. Sacha Bru et Peter Nichols, vol. 1 (Berlin : De Gruyter, 2009), 49-58.

8 Pierre-Yves Saunier insiste sur cette manière transversale de penser « entre et à travers » chez certains historiens qui, comme lui, « (...) adoptent une perspective dite "transnationale" (...) une telle perspective permet de contribuer à historiciser les phénomènes d'interdépendance, d'interconnexion, de relations entre et à travers les sociétés et les entités qui structurent les sociétés modernes. » (Saunier, « Les régimes circulatoires du domaine social 1800-1940 : projets et ingénierie de la convergence et de la différence », *Genèses*, 2008/2, n° 71, 4.)

9 J'ai pu analyser une partie de ces commentaires : « Du succès de scandale au désenchantement. La réception contrastée de la Section d'or », dans Cécile Debray et Françoise Lucbert, dir., *La Section d'or 1912-1920-1925* (Paris : Éditions Cercle d'art, 2000), 43-61.

10 Lisa Werner, *Der Kubismus stellt aus. Der Salon de la Section d'Or, Paris 1912* (Berlin : Reimer, 2011).

11 La présence de Kupka à la Section d'or fait pour l'instant débat. Le spécialiste Pierre Brullé s'est penché sur la question dans l'essai « La création de Kupka et le cubisme "écartelé" de la Section d'or : un rapprochement problématique », dans Debray et Lucbert 2000, 85-95. Werner 2011 estime que Kupka n'a pas participé au Salon de la Section d'or en 1912. Quant aux manifestations des années 1920, seule sa présence à l'étape parisienne de l'exposition est attestée par quelques sources, dont le carton d'invitation au vernissage du 5 mars 1920 à la Galerie La Boëtie. Une reproduction photographique de ce rare document (ill. 14.2), dont je n'ai pas pu retracer l'original, est conservée aux Archives de l'art contemporain en Belgique (Bruxelles, MRBAB). Je remercie Véronique Cardon de m'avoir facilité l'accès à maintes pièces d'archives et de m'avoir permis de reproduire celle-ci.

12 Dans la conférence qu'il prononça à la Galerie La Boëtie le lendemain du vernissage de la Section d'or d'octobre 1912 en ces mêmes lieux, le poète Guillaume Apollinaire perçut comme un « écartèlement du cubisme » (titre qu'il donna à sa conférence), la diversité stylistique déjà à l'œuvre parmi les exposants.

13 Voir Jean-Claude Marcadé, « Les artistes de Russie et d'Ukraine à la Section d'or (1912-1925) » dans Debray et Lucbert 2000, 111-117 ; Françoise Lucbert, « L'amitié artistique franco-russe, le cas exemplaire de la Section d'or », dans *Paris-Russe 1910-1960*, cat. exp., Saint-Pétersbourg, Musée national russe, 28 avril-30 juillet 2003 ; Wuppertal, Von der Heydt-Museum, 10 août-26 octobre 2003 ; Bordeaux, Musée des Beaux-Arts, 7 novembre 2003-1er février 2004 (Moscou : Palace Editions, 2003, 24-27).

14 Marguerite Tuijn, « Archipenko and Theo van Doesburg », dans *Alexander Archipenko Revisited : An International Perspective. Proceedings from the Archipenko Symposium* (Cooper Union, New York

City, 17 septembre 2005), dir. Deborah Goldberg et Alexandra Keiser (Bearsville: Archipenko Foundation, 2008, 42-56).

15 Akira Iriye, *Cultural Internationalism and World Order* (Baltimore et Londres : Johns Hopkins University Press, 1997); Pheng Cheah et Bruce Robbins, dir., *Cosmopolitics : Thinking and Feeling beyond the Nation* (Minneapolis et Londres : University of Minnesota Press, 1998); Akira Iriye et Pierre-Yves Saunier, dir., *The Palgrave Dictionary of Transnational History from the mid-19th Century to the Present Day* (Basingstoke et New York : Palgrave Macmillan, 2009); Grace Brockington, dir., *Internationalism and the Arts* (Oxford, etc. : Peter Lang, 2009); Daniel Laqua, dir., *Internationalism Reconfigured : Transnational Ideas and Movements Between the World Wars* (Londres : I.B. Tauris, 2011); Daniel Laqua, *The Age of Internationalism and Belgium, 1880-1930: Peace, Progress and Prestige* (Manchester : Manchester University Press, 2013); Pierre-Yves Saunier, *Transnational History* (Basingstoke et New York : Palgrave Macmillan, 2013).

16 Voir ma notice sur Donas dans *La Section d'or 1912-1920-1925,* dir. Cécile Debray et Françoise Lucbert (Paris : Éditions Cercle d'art, 2000, 258). Les rapports de l'artiste avec le groupe de la Section d'or ont aussi été étudiés par mes soins sous le titre « L'internationalisme de "Tour-Donas" à l'époque des expositions européennes de la Section d'or », dans le catalogue de l'exposition *Marthe Donas et l'avant-garde parisienne (1916-1921)* (Ittre : Musée Marthe Donas, 8 octobre-20 novembre 2016), 25-26. Je salue les organisateurs de cette exposition, Marcel Daloze et Jean-Marie Aendekerk, de m'avoir donné l'occasion de formuler un premier état de cette réflexion. Plus généralement sur Donas, voir la monographie de Peter J. H. Pauwels, *Marthe Donas : A Woman Artist in the Avant-Garde* (Anvers : Ludion, 2016), ainsi que l'article de ce dernier dans le présent ouvrage.

17 Daenens, remarquable figure de médiateur, fut au cœur d'un réseau transnational, à la fois artistique et politique, dont Erik Buelinckx retrace les contours dans une des contributions de ce volume.

18 Marthe Donas, « Biographie de Marthe Donas », premier de trois feuillets manuscrits non datés, Archives de la Fondation Marthe Donas. Donas put voir sept œuvres de Lhote lors d'une exposition collective de Lyre et Palette, 28 janvier-11 février 1917. Voir Jean-Marie Aendekerk dans *Marthe Donas et l'avant-garde parisienne (1916-1921)* (Ittre : Musée Marthe Donas, 8 octobre-20 novembre 2016), 9.

19 Voir en outre la correspondance de Gerbaud à Daenens conservée à la *Letterenhuis* d'Anvers – dont je remercie l'aimable personnel, en particulier Danielle Palmans.

20 Je souligne ces mots. *Sélection. Bulletin de la vie artistique* (Bruxelles), n° 1, 1er août 1920, s.p. Ce programme inaugural, ouvrant le premier numéro de ce « bulletin », sous-titré « chronique » dès le deuxième numéro, était signé des trois noms : P. Gustave van Hecke, André De Ridder et Gustave de Smet.

21 Exposition du groupe « Sélection », Anvers, Cercle royal artistique et littéraire, 24 juillet-12 août 1920. Le catalogue est inclus dans la livraison de *Sélection* citée à la note précédente.

22 Les Cubistes français et belges, Bruxelles, Sélection, 18 septembre-8 octobre 1920. Le catalogue, publié dans *Sélection*, n° 2, 15 septembre 1920, s.p., distinguait la vingtaine d'exposants « français » [*sic*], dont Blanchard, Braque, Csaky, Derain, Férat, Picasso, Survage, etc., des cinq Belges (Counhaye, De Troyer, Jespers, Joostens, Peeters).

23 Une telle approche fait écho à celle de Béatrice Joyeux-Prunel, dont l'ouvrage *« Nul n'est prophète en son pays » ? L'internationalisation de la peinture avant-gardiste parisienne (1855-1914)* (Paris : Musée d'Orsay/Nicolas Chaudun, 2009) a lancé la méthode quantitative et transnationale qui informe ses plus récents travaux. Pour le domaine littéraire, notamment en Belgique, je retiens l'utile synthèse par Daphné de Marneffe et Benoît Denis, dir., *Les Réseaux littéraires* (Bruxelles : Le Cri/Ciel-ULB-Ulg, 2006), ainsi que la thèse de Marneffe sur la période au centre de mon projet actuel : « Entre modernisme et avant-garde. Le réseau des revues littéraires de l'immédiat après-guerre en

Belgique (1919-1922) » (Université de Liège : 2007).

24 « Notes et nouvelles », *L'Art libre* (Bruxelles), 15 septembre 1919, 148.

25 « Les revues de la quinzaine », *L'Art libre* (Bruxelles), 1er avril 1920, 83.

26 « Revues du mois », *L'Art libre* (Bruxelles), 2e année, n° 16, décembre 1920, 224.

27 *Ibid.*

28 Selon Fels, la Section d'or fut fondée dès octobre 1919 par Archipenko, Gleizes et Survage. Voir Florent Fels, « La Section d'or », *Sélection. Chronique de la vie artistique* (Bruxelles), n° 5, 15 décembre 1920, s.p. Toutefois, les statuts de l'association ne furent déposés qu'en mars 1920. Un exemplaire de ces statuts (ill. 14.1) est conservé dans le fonds Survage, Bibliothèque Kandinsky, Centre Pompidou, Paris. J'adresse mes chaleureux remerciements à Didier Schulmann, ainsi qu'à l'équipe de la Bibliothèque Kandinsky, pour leur aide précieuse.

29 J'exprime ma gratitude à Gayle Zachmann, Richard Shryock et Sophie Lucet, organisateurs de l'atelier *Cultural Production in the 19 th Century*, sur le thème Alterities/Altérités (Paris : Université Paris-Diderot, Paris 7, 20-21 juin 2016), qui m'ont permis de présenter mes premières observations à ce sujet sous l'intitulé « L'association de la Section d'or en 1920 : rupture ou continuité par rapport aux sociétés d'artistes du XIXe siècle ? ».

30 Se reporter aux publications connues de Malcom Gee, Raymonde Moulin, Paul-André Jaccard pour la Suisse, etc.

31 Il est à noter que les activités de promotion de la salle d'exposition et de vente Sélection se prolongèrent dans le périodique éponyme qui lui survécut plusieurs années (1920-1927).

32 La notion d'animateur d'art, utilisée depuis une vingtaine d'années, a dernièrement fait l'objet de définitions plus précises, entre autres par Ingrid Goddeeris et Noémie Goldman, dir., *Animateur d'art : marchand, collectionneur, critique, éditeur... L'animateur d'art et ses multiples rôles. Étude pluridisciplinaire de ces intermédiaires culturels méconnus des XIXe et XXe siècles* (Bruxelles, Musées royaux des Beaux-Arts de Belgique, 2015).

33 Institut supérieur de Commerce, Anvers, 1920-1921 ; Université coloniale, 1921-1922 ; Université de Gand, 1923-1959. Les archives De Ridder, de même que celles de Van Hecke, sont conservées à la *Letterenhuis* d'Anvers.

34 Voir les travaux de Manu van Aa, dont la récente biographie *Tatave ! Paul-Gustave van Hecke. Kunstpaus, modekoning en salonsocialist* (Tielt : Lannoo, 2017), ainsi que Virginie Devillez et Peter J.H. Pauwels, dir., *L'Animateur d'art : Paul-Gustave van Hecke (1887-1967) et l'avant-garde* (Bruxelles : Musées royaux des Beaux-Arts de Belgique ; Gand-Courtrai : Snoeck, 2012).

35 Deux lettres de De Ridder à Daenens, datées 10 et 23 novembre 1920 (Anvers, *Letterenhuis*, fonds Albert Daenens), expriment la volonté de leur auteur de voir les peintres de Sélection présents à l'exposition de Genève.

36 Avec des conséquences inattendues ou amusantes, comme des ressortissants russes avec un pseudonyme à consonance francophone, par exemple Angiboult (c'est-à-dire la baronne d'Oettingen), exposante de la Section d'or, classés parmi les artistes français...

37 Cela fut le cas de la majorité des comptes rendus de l'exposition, dont celui, pourtant substantiel, publié par Élie Moroy, « L'Art à l'étranger. La première exposition internationale d'art moderne à Genève », *Mercure de France* (Paris), 1er février 1921, 793-797.

38 Voir la thèse doctorale de Marguerite Tuijn : « Mon cher ami... Lieber Does... Theo van Doesburg en de praktijk van de internationale avant-garde » (Université d'Amsterdam, 2003), ainsi que, parmi d'autres, les textes de Gladys Fabre dans les catalogues des expositions *Van Doesburg and the International Avant-Garde. Constructing a New World*, Leyde, Stedelijk Museum De Lakenhal, 20 octobre 2009-3 janvier 2010; Londres, Tate Modern, 4 février 2009-16 mai 2010 et *Theo van Doesburg. Une nouvelle expression de la vie, de l'art et de la technologie*, Bruxelles, Bozar, 26 février-29

mai 2016 (Bruxelles : Fonds Mercator/Bozar, 2016).

39 Étaient-elles, au reste, si neuves que cela ? La question mériterait d'être approfondie, avec comme point de comparaison, des initiatives antérieures d'artistes eux-mêmes « promoteurs », en particulier celles liées aux mouvements sécessionnistes de la fin du XIXe siècle.

40 Tuijn a publié et analysé une belle lettre de Donas à Van Doesburg dans « "C'est donc partout la même chose." Marthe Donas en Theo van Doesburg », *Jong Holland* 15 (1999) 1, 32-41. Cet article a été traduit en français par Jean-Marie Aendekerk, « "C'est donc partout la même chose." Marthe Donas explore le monde de l'art anglais pour Theo van Doesburg », dans une publication du Musée Marthe Donas (Ittre : février 2015).

41 Plusieurs sociologues, dont Pierre Bourdieu et Nathalie Heinich, ont mis au jour les contradictions et les apories d'une telle idéalisation, et montré les limites de cette conception surannée, mais tenace, de l'artiste.

42 Christophe Charle et Daniel Roche, dir., *Capitales culturelles, capitales symboliques : Paris et les expériences européennes, XVIIIe–XXe siècles* (Paris : Publications de la Sorbonne, 2002). Sur la « perte de vitesse » de Paris par rapport aux autres capitales culturelles européennes, voir le 2e volume de la synthèse de Béatrice Joyeux-Prunel, *Les Avant-gardes artistiques 1918-1945. Une histoire transnationale* (Paris : Gallimard, 2017).

43 Dans la mesure où l'on peut le restituer… car les sources restent malheureusement imparfaites et lacunaires.

Belgian Art and the International Avant-gardes of the 1920's – Case Studies

From Avant-garde to Arrière-garde? – Henry van de Velde's Architectural Oeuvre Before and After World War I

Ole W. Fischer

After Art Nouveau? – Years of search and crisis (1906–14)

The years prior to World War I were a time of personal and artistic crisis for the Flemish artist, architect, designer, theoretician and educator Henry van de Velde (1863–1957).[1] Trained as a painter in the Academy of Antwerp, his native city, he had studied the emerging artistic tendencies in Paris in 1884, practised open air painting of the social disadvantaged peasants in the footsteps of Millet and Barbizon after his return to Belgium, and then became a member of the Brussels' avant-garde group Les XX. The annual exhibition of this secessionist circle staged many controversial artists of the time, including Toulouse-Lautrec, Pissarro, Monet, Seurat, Gauguin, Cézanne and van Gogh. In close contact with international avant-gardes, van de Velde was able to test his artistic stance between symbolism and neo-impressionism.

Yet, despite some early success, he turned away from painting and embraced theoretic reflection and applied arts instead, an artistic reorientation informed by Viollet-le-Duc, Ruskin and Morris, but also Nietzsche as well as socialist-anarchist critique. This change materialised in the textile application *La Veillée des Anges* of 1892–93, and with the help of his wife to be Maria Sèthe, van de Velde soon designed furniture, interiors and their own house *Bloemenwerf* in Uccle near Brussels in 1895, which he, despite being an autodidact, authored from inside out as a synthesis of arts. The same year, the art dealer Samuel Bing invited van de Velde to furnish two rooms in his gallery "L'Art Nouveau" in Paris for the inaugural exhibition of December, which were rejected by critics as "barbaric". Nevertheless, the event marks one of the beginnings of Art Nouveau, since interest grew among a group of German collectors and critics, all involved with the literary-artistic magazine *Pan*. The same Parisian interiors marked his break-through at the Arts and Crafts section of the Art Exposition Dresden of 1897. Overnight, van de Velde had become a "star" in the German Empire, where his call for a "New Style" fell in line with the work of many other applied artists, and German Jugendstil was born. Various commissions in Germany and financial difficulties of his craft workshops in Brussels made a move to Berlin necessary in 1900, where he was only to find himself trapped in an unhappy collaboration with a local gallerist. With the help of his patrons Harry Count Kessler and Eberhard von Bodenhausen, van de Velde was appointed by the young Grand-Duke Wilhelm-Ernst of Saxony-Weimar-Eisenach as artistic advisor for the arts and craft industries in late 1901, a position which gave high hopes for a "New Weimar" – after the "golden age" of Goethe and Schiller and the "silver age" of Franz Liszt – to revive the small, but culturally rich town and turn it into a centre of international avant-gardes under the seal of Nietzsche's philosophy. If his acclaimed work between *Bloemenwerf* and Berlin has been characterised by a linear-graphic style and a forced dynamisation of space, which derived clearly from his ornamental work ("the line is a force"), the Weimar phase marks a shift towards a more sculptural and organic oeuvre, exemplified in the Nietzsche Archive Weimar (1902–04) or the Grand-Ducal School of Applied Arts (1906–08).[2]

Jugendstil in general, and van de Velde explicitly, have been attacked as "fashionable", "graphical" or "superficial" from the beginning, as for example by Adolf Loos or Hermann Muthesius, to name the most famous critics, both initially united with him in their rejection of eclectic historicism.[3] In addition, many critics in the Wilhelmine Empire degraded it as "foreign" with nationalistic undertones. Starting in 1900 with the *Exhibition Universelle de Paris* and again in 1901 with the opening exhibition of the Darmstadt artists' colony Mathildenhöhe entitled "A Document of German Art", van de Velde distanced himself from the tendencies of Art Nouveau, Secession or Jugendstil. He grasped the danger of success that his "New Style" had become a fashionable trend much copied by others, undermining his reformist intentions. But despite a noticeable turn towards objectivity after 1902, he did not live up to his vows to leave ornamentation behind and concentrate merely on form, material and use. He saw his fears that Art Nouveau would not be "new" any longer, but out of fashion, come true at the Arts and Crafts Exhibition in Dresden in 1906.[4] Here, where van de Velde had celebrated his first international success in 1897, he had to acknowledge the dawn of his "New Style", replaced by Neo-Biedermeier, Neo-Classicism and Regionalism ("Heimatschutz"). Originally, the Dresden exhibition was initiated as a convention of the reformers against historic eclecticism, but many of the early modernists, like Peter Behrens, Joseph Maria Olbrich, Richard Riemerschmid, Bruno Paul or Josef Hoffmann practised now in classicist tendencies. To make things worse, van de Velde faced staunch criticism of his contribution of a hall for the Museum of Fine and Applied Arts Weimar (*Museumshalle*), then under the director Count Kessler. Critics noted the unresolved discrepancies between van de Velde's rationalist theory of functional form and material honesty versus an extravagant design that featured a romantic synthesis of arts by integrating large-scale "ornamental" paintings by Ludwig von Hoffmann, which was received as flamboyant, irrational, deformed and above all as old-fashioned – read: as Jugendstil.

In the following years, van de Velde searched for alternatives. He experimented with regionalism, as for example the *Hohenhof* for Karl Ernst Osthaus in Hagen (1906–08), a spiraling land-house worked with local stone, deep slate roofs, and other details from the Bergische Land. Or the later *Villa Theodor Springmann*, also in Hagen (1914–16), a massive volumetric block of stone quarried on site. Even his own house *Hohe Pappeln* at Ehringsdorf near Weimar (1907–08) showed elements drawn from a local Thuringian vernacular. (fig. 15.1). In an alternative trait, van de Velde explored cyclopean neo-classicism, which recalled his travels to archaeological sites in Sicily, Greece and the Orient in 1903. This body of works includes the Monument

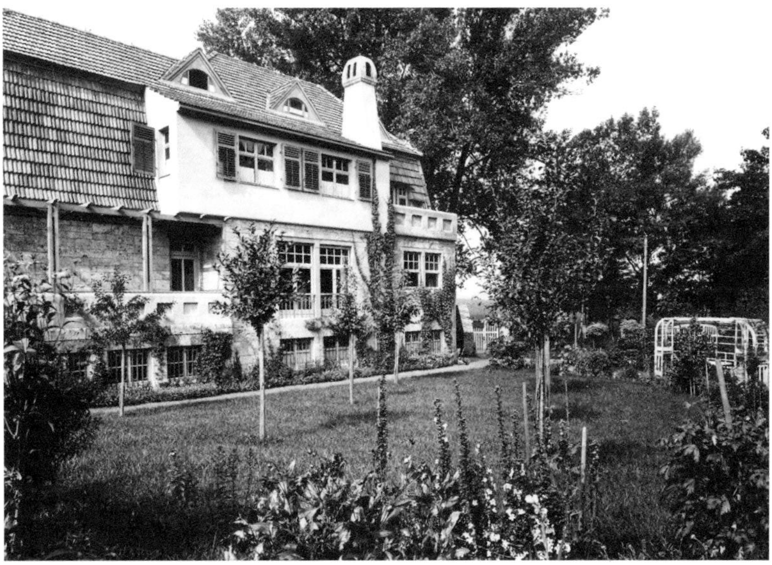

15.1. Henry van de Velde's own house "Hohe Pappeln", Ehringsdorf, Germany, 1907–08, view from the garden.

for Ernst Abbe in Jena (1908–11) designed as a modern temple and expressive in its symmetry and tectonic language of limestone and concrete, as well as the family tomb for Karl Kötschau in Weimar (1908–10) with its archaic piling of monumental blocks of stone. Also, the Nietzsche Stadium and Monument for Weimar (planned 1911–13) speaks volumes about his gigantic ambitions to compete with the nationalist Monument of the Battle of Nations in Leipzig by Bruno Schmitz (finished 1913), hence breaking with rational-organic form-giving and material honesty of the "New Style".[5] This is even more true for the third design strategy employed before 1914: a retreat into Neo-Rococo aestheticism, such as the over refined Palais Dürckheim in Weimar (1912–13) or the pasty plan for the Universal Museum Erfurt (1913–14),[6] even if van de Velde designed the latter in ferro-concrete.

All of these approaches seemed to be unsatisfactory and far away from his avant-garde designs of around 1900. For van de Velde, a new, modern era had begun, one that was calling for a radical break with history and a contemporary artistic expression (*Zeitgeist*), but despite his theoretic calls for a "New Style" based on rational conception and modern sensuality, the translation into design and build reality remained problematic. In addition, he felt isolated in the provincialism of Weimar, ridden by sorrows over the underfinanced Grand-Ducal School of Applied Arts, which he had served as founding director since 1908, and offended by the intrigues at the Grand-Ducal court. 1911 seemed to offer an opportunity: thanks to Count Kessler the Parisian impresario Gabriel Astruc commissioned van de Velde to design a modern stage, the Théâtre des Champs-Élysées. Previously van de Velde had worked on several theatre designs: together with Edward Gordon Craig for the actress Louise Dumont in Weimar (1903–05), for Max Reinhardt in Berlin (1905–06), and a study for the replacement of the Grand-Ducal Theatre in Weimar of the Goethe era (1907) – all in vain.[7] Eagerly, he embraced this chance to realise his vision of new stage design, and since this commission coincided with a residential project in Paris (for Victor de Golubeff), van de Velde hoped to leave Weimar behind, move to the thriving French metropolis, and reconnect with the current artistic avant-gardes (Nabis, etc.). He rented a studio in Paris, asked for a sabbatical at the School of Applied Arts (which was denied), and immersed himself in the project – which turned into another failure. Due to the restricted site at Avenue Montaigne, he wanted to stack vestibule, theatre auditorium and the smaller stages above each other, supported by a structure in ferro-concrete. Following recommendations, he invited the Perret brothers as specialists in concrete construction, but they pushed van de Velde out of the project with nationalist arguments. Disillusioned by the chauvinism he faced in Paris as well as his experiences at the World's Fair in Ghent 1913, where he as a

Belgian citizen practising in Germany could neither exhibit with his home country nor with his host nation, he withdrew to internationalist dreams. In reality, however, he was under constant attack in Germany as a suspicious "foreigner" by conservative traditionalists as well as nationalist reformers, such as Muthesius or Schultze-Naumburg, not to mention the local press of Weimar.

The Werkbund Theatre in Cologne 1914: A late break-through and first victim of the war

Under these circumstances, the theatre built for the first German "Werkbund" exhibition of 1914 in Cologne seems miraculous: van de Velde returned to his earlier ability to combine functional considerations and new technologies with plastic form-giving and merged them into an organic synthesis of the arts. He was next to Bruno Taut and his glass pavilion and Walter Gropius and Adolf Meyer and their factory, amongst the few architects who did not fall prey to Neo-Classicism or *Neo-Biedermeier*, as noted already by critics of the time (fig. 15.2).

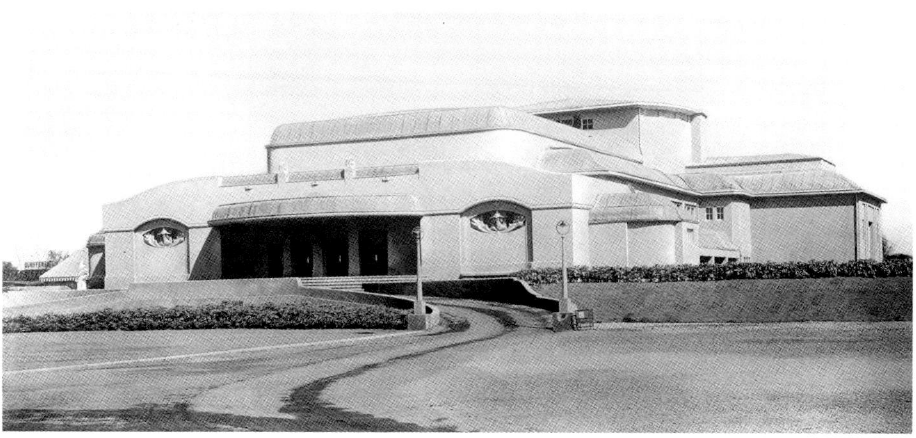

15.2. Henry van de Velde Werkbund Theater Cologne, Germany, 1914, view from South-West.

The theatre, however, is only one part of van de Velde's contribution to the Cologne "Werkbund" exhibition. The other is the infamous "Werkbund" debate, taking place at the annual congress on 2-6 July 1914.[8] Here, the positions of Muthesius and van de Velde clashed furiously, leading almost to the break-up of the organisation. The group of "individualists" interpreted the circulation of the 10 theses by Muthesius as an affront. They gathered around Karl Ernst Osthaus and decided that van de Velde should present 10 anti-theses, which were discussed and spelled out the very same night. Despite what has been written on the "Werkbund" debate by modernist protagonists of the next generation, van de Velde actually achieved a considerable points win within the institution. After a hefty debate, Muthesius had to withdraw his theses, since he had manoeuvred the institution to breaking point, while Gropius, Taut and Osthaus launched a motion of no confidence against him, even calling for van de Velde as the new "dictator" of the "Werkbund" – a truly avant-garde move, if one recalls the original martial meaning of the word as spearhead of an army, and the secondary political meaning of a conspiratorial cadre party.

Today, the neo-classicism supported by Muthesius is all but forgotten, while the contributions by the "individualists" exerted a long-term influence on the architecture of the 20th century: van de Velde's plastic, sculptural architecture echoes in organic tendencies from Erich Mendelsohn to Alvar Aalto, Taut's early crystalline fractals reemerged in German expressionism and the Dutch "Wendingen" group, if not as deconstructivist architecture of the 1980s, and the industrial design of Gropius & Meyer led to high modernism, though even its protagonists acknowledged van de Velde's Werkbund Theatre.[9]

All of this hope was destroyed with the outbreak of World War I in August 1914 due to general mobilisation of 28 July in Austria-Hungary, and on 1 August in the German Empire. The exhibition closed early, the theatre was in operation for only six weeks (instead of the planned-for three months) and never reached its full potential staging the avant-garde pieces van de Velde had hoped for. Despite the respect and support he had gained during the "Werkbund" debate, van de Velde could not execute his leadership role as the voice of internationalist modernism within the institution to take a different direction. Instead the "Werkbund" immersed in war economy, dedicated its energies to standardisation, like the German Institute for Norming DIN, which was created out of the need for war rationalisation. Van de Velde, deprived of the fruits of his success, became a hostage to Grand-Ducal war bureaucracy, treated as an "enemy alien". The imposed house detention and absence of work led to severe depression ("neurasthenia") and hospitalisation in various sanatoria, while his Belgian passport was confiscated. It was not until 1917 that Count Kessler arranged permission for van de Velde to leave for neutral Switzerland with a vague mandate to report on exiled German artists and cultural activities. Once there, he connected swiftly with pacifists and internationalists like René Schickele and Ernst Ludwig Kirchner, while his family had to wait until the armistice to receive permission to follow.

After the War: A new start in the Netherlands (1920–25)

After a first attempt to resettle in Switzerland on Lake Constance, which materialised neither in architectural work, nor a new private art school, van de Velde in 1919 accepted the position as in-house architect of the Kröller-Müller family in the Netherlands, succeeding H. P. Berlage. Van de Velde's designs during his Dutch period (1920–25) can be categorised mainly into two formal lines: on the one hand a return to regionalist vocabulary already present in his pre-War German villae, yet now adapted to the post-war economic and social realities. With the design of prefabricated wood single family houses, including his own *De Tent* in Wassenaar (1920–21), he explores the possibilities of rationalisation, cost savings, and shortened construction times (fig. 15.3). The layout of the house combines middle-class comfort (detached car garage, central heating, spaciousness around a central hall, and his in-house atelier with separate bedroom), while it features on the symmetrical outside traditional "low land" features such as a steep thatched roof and wood panelling. This searched-for "primitivism" can be paralleled to similar tendencies of Dutch and German expressionism, as for example within the "Wendingen" group in Amsterdam or the Sommerfeld House near Berlin, the first building erected by the Bauhaus workshops under van de Velde's successor Walter Gropius in the same year 1920–21. The second tendency surfaces in the various folios for a new museum for Anton and Helene Kröller-Müller: after a first concept for a spiraling land house in combination with gallery wings for a site in Wassenaar was quickly set aside (1920),[10] van de Velde designed several stages for a Museum on the "Franse Berg" in the "Hoge Veluwe" park near Otterlo (1921–29),[11] independent of a residential programme, but in proximity to their hunting lodge Sint Hubertus by Berlage (1914–20) (fig. 15.4). The plans show a massive East-West axial arrangement around a central octagonal core, expanding into the landscape of the hillside with embedded terraces, while a cour d'honneur-like configuration with rows of severe pylons marks the counter-axis to the north entrance. The strong symmetrical layout with only minimal differentiation, palace-like triple-run staircases, few low and heavy horizontal openings (if not all reduced to skylights) and ashlar stone detailing returns formally to a cyclopean monumentalism already present in the pre-war commemorative works for Abbé (Jena, 1908–11) and Nietzsche (Temple and Stadium Weimar, 1911–13). In addition, van de Velde seems to have taken into account inspirations from his predecessor Berlage's design for the museum (1916–18), as well as restrained references to French Art Déco, which evolved in parallel and would be codified with L'Exposition internationale des arts décoratifs et industriels modernes, Paris of 1925. Yet while van de Velde was executing a number of smaller works for Kröller-Müller (offices, interiors, peripheral structures, monuments, etc.)

the large museum project was stalled, finally begun after he had left the Netherlands, and then aborted again because of first signs of the economic depression of 1929. Years later, when during the Great Depression the private collection was offered to the Dutch state, a smaller, much humbler single-story edifice in brick with top-lit galleries around a geometrical courtyard was executed as a "temporary museum" (1935–38) on a site close by – a provisory that still exists today, expanded in several stages, as the Rijksmuseum Kröller-Müller.

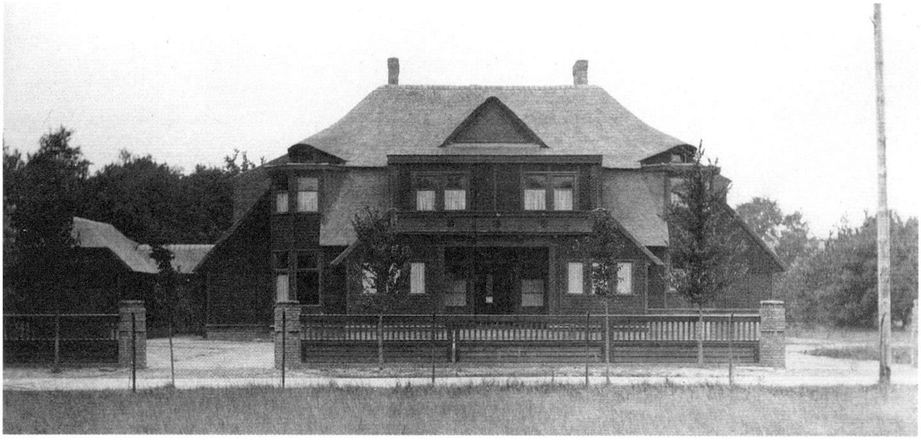

15.3. Henry van de Velde, own house "De Tent", Wassenaar, The Netherlands, 1920–21. AML (Archives et Musée de la Littérature).

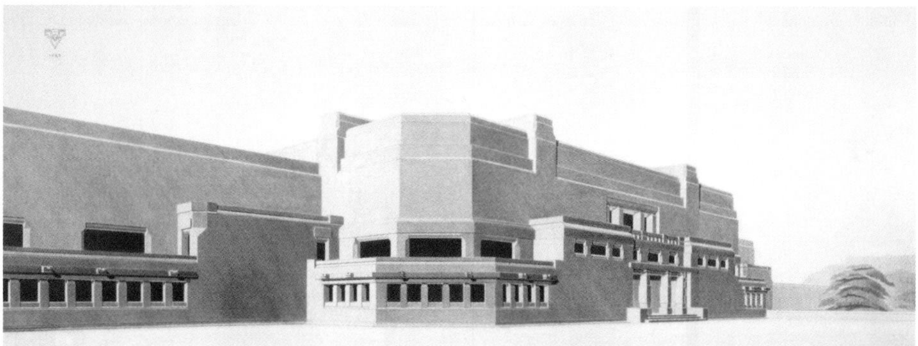

15.4. Henry van de Velde, Museum on the Franse Berg, park Hoge Veluwe, Otterlo, The Netherlands, perspectival drawing from South-West. Collection Kröller-Müller Museum, Otterlo, The Netherlands.

Outlook: 1925 Return to Belgium – Towards a humanist modernism?

As the brief overview of postwar designs demonstrates, van de Velde did not continue the evolutionary line of the Werkbund theatre; rather he explored a pathetic style with heavy handed historic references or the vernacular respectively, while a younger generation of architects experimented with the possibilities of abstraction, purism, technology, industrial materials and rational functionalism. Van de Velde felt the need to reinvent himself once more, this time not at the forefront of the movement, but as a commentator and keeper of modern values. This turn is exemplified by a series of reviews of the Parisian Art Déco exhibition in 1925: still an outspoken critic against eclectic historicism and the neo-classical tendencies of the 1920s, he celebrated the pavilions by Bob Mallet-Stevens, Josef Gočár and Konstantin Melnikov as achievements of a new international architecture in continuation of the German, Austrian and Belgian "New Styles" before World War I. But now he expands his criticism towards the tendency of "extreme abstraction" and "perverse mechanisation" he saw represented in the everyday objects of the radical avant-gardes of Soviet Russia[12] an accusation of "fatalism" and "lack of humanism" that in later iterations of the argument he directed against other avant-gardists such as Le Corbusier, Bauhaus or *De Stijl*.[13]

With the sought-after return to Belgium in 1925/26 van de Velde tried to reposition himself along the lines he had called for theoretically: in continuity of a pre-war modernism which he helped to bring about, and in creative reaction to but also distanced from the new tendencies, he built an alternative practice of moderate modern buildings. Van de Velde's designs of the Belgian interwar period sport cubic massing, flat roofs, horizontal steel windows, are often in brick and concrete, and – important in his case – almost devoid of any ornament, but with distinct detailing enhancing the materiality and individual distinction of spaces and buildings, as realised for example in his own La Nouvelle Maison in Tervuren near Brussels (1927–28) (fig. 15.5). This moderate modern approach concludes his search for a new architectural expression *after* his avant-gardism described above, but does not fall under the abstraction of purist white render, primary colours and tubular furniture. Instead of the excursions into regionalism and monumentalism of the years directly following the war, van de Velde arrived at a "humanist modernism" that eschewed "newness for newness' sake", as a critique of the extreme positions of the younger avant-garde movements. Symptomatic of his interwar position is his insistence that there would be no "New Style", but only a "true style" as the timeless way of designing in response to function, logic, material and artistic sensibility. His position now sprang from live-long

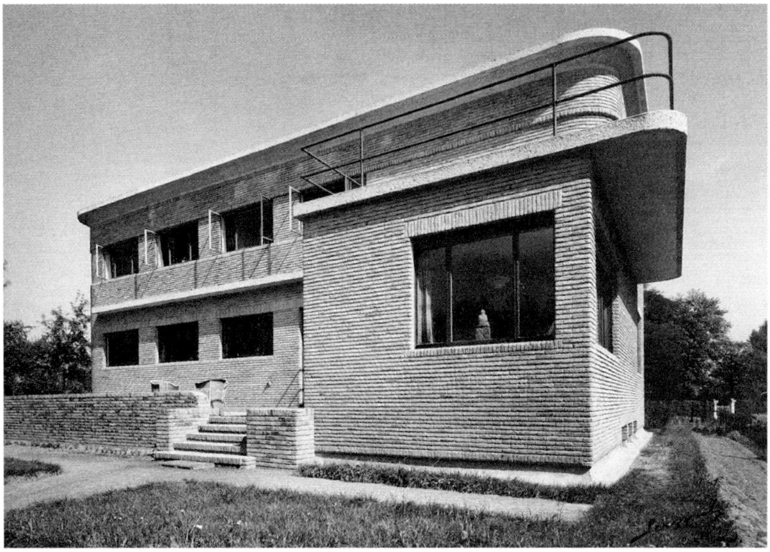

15.5. Henry van de Velde, own house "La Nouvelle Maison", Tervuren, Belgium, 1927–28.

experience as well as from creative and fruitful reaction to the new avant-gardes, that is, an arrière-garde position, not unlike Frank Lloyd Wright in the USA: that is, as a predecessor to the new avant-gardes, as a "pioneer of the modern movement",[14] but still one to be reckoned with!

Notes

1 Henry van de Velde, *Récit de ma vie. Berlin – Weimar – Paris – Bruxelles. II. 1900–1917*, ed. by Anne van Loo and Fabrice van de Kerckhove (Brussels; Paris: Flammarion; Versa,1995), 369; the following stations of his life are based on this critical edition of his memoirs as well as on the two catalogues: Klaus-Jürgen Sembach, Birgit Schulte (eds.), *Henry van de Velde: Ein europäischer Künstler seiner Zeit* (Cologne: Wienand, 1992); Thomas Föhl, Sabine Walter (eds.), *Leidenschaft, Funktion und Schönheit: Henry van de Velde und sein Beitrag zur europäischen Moderne* (Weimar: Weimarer Verlagsgesellschaft, 2013); in English: Werner Adriaenssens, Thomas Föhl, Sabine Walter (eds.) *Henry van de Velde: Passion, Function, Beauty 1863–1957* (Brussels: Lannoo Publishers, 2014).

2 For a general overview of the architectural work of van de Velde see Léon Ploegaerts, Pierre Puttemans, *L'Œuvre Architecturale de Henry van de Velde* (Brussels, Québec: Atelier Vokaer, Les Presses de l'Université Laval, 1987).

3 On Loos and van de Velde see Ole W. Fischer, "Objected into the void – The polemics of Adolf Loos against Henry van de Velde: a cultural-psychological analysis of Modernism," *Umení/Art. Journal of the Institute for Art History of the Academy of Sciences of the Czech Republic*, 55, No. 4 (2007), 294–315; see also Christopher Long, "The Origins and Context of Adolf Loos's 'Ornament and Crime'," *Journal of the Society of Architectural Historians*, 68, No. 2 (June 2009), 200–223; on

Muthesius and van de Velde see Ole W. Fischer, "The Veil of Truth? – Van de Velde, Muthesius, and the Battle over Ornament in Modern Architecture," in Loretta Vandi (ed.), *Ornament and European Modernism: From Art Practice to Art History* (London: Routledge, 2017), 104–136.

4 Fritz Schumacher (ed.), *Das Deutsche Kunstgewerbe 1906: 3. Deutsche Kunstgewerbeausstellung Dresden 1906* (Munich: F. Bruckmann, 1906).

5 Cf. Günther Stamm, "Monumental Architecture and Ideology: Henry Van de Velde's and Harry Graf Kessler's Project for a Nietzsche Monument at Weimar, 1910–1914," *Gentse Bijdragen tot de Kunstgeschiedenis*, 23, (1973–75), 303–342; cf. Jürgen Krause, *»Märtyrer« und »Prophet«: Studien zum Nietzsche-Kult in der bildenden Kunst der Jahrhundertwende* (Berlin; New York: Walter de Gruyter, 1984, in the series: Behler; Montinari; Müller-Lauter; Wenzel (eds.), *Monographien und Texte zur Nietzsche-Forschung. 14*), here: chapter 4.5 "Das Projekt eines Nietzsche-Tempels und -Stadions für Weimar," 199–210; cf. Thomas Föhl (ed.), *ihr Kinderlein kommet... – Henry van de Velde: ein vergessenes Projekt für Friedrich Nietzsche* (Ostfildern: Hatje Cantz, 2000); see as well: Ole W. Fischer, *Nietzsches Schatten: Henry van de Velde – von Philosophie zu Form* (Berlin: Gebr. Mann, 2012), here: chapter 3.10 "Der neue Stil," 340–73.

6 Cf. Ole W. Fischer, "Museen für Nietzsches Neuen Menschen? Henry van de Veldes Planung zum »Universalmuseum« Erfurt zwischen Krise und Wille zum Stil," in Miriam Krautwurst, Kai Uwe Schierz (eds.), *Henry van de Velde. Ein Universalmuseum für Erfurt* (Berlin: Kerber Art, 2013, catalogue for the Angermuseum Erfurt), 57–79 (in German).

7 Cf. Dennis Sharp (ed.), *Henri van de Velde: Theatre designs 1904–1914 = Projets du théâtre 1904–1914* (London: Architectural Association, 1974).

8 Hermann Muthesius, *Die Werkbund-Arbeit der Zukunft; und Aussprache darüber von Ferdinand Avenarius Peter Behrens, Rudolf Bosselt, Robert Breuer, Peter Bruckmann, August Endell, von Engelhardt, Karl Groß, Hermann Obrist, Karl Ernst Osthaus, Wilhelm Ostwald, Erich Pistor, C. A. Reichel, Richard Riemerschmid, Walter Riezler, Karl Schäfer, Bruno Taut, Joszef Vago, van der Velde. Friedrich Naumann: Werkbund und Weltwirtschaft. Der Werkbund-Gedanke in den germanischen Ländern: Österreich-Ungarn, Schweiz, Holland, Dänemark, Schweden, Norwegen* (Jena: Eugen Diederichs, 1914), 32–3; Henry van de Velde, "Gegen-Leitsätze," in Muthesius, *Die Werkbund-Arbeit der Zukunft* (1914), 49–51; for an English translation of the "Theses" and "Anti-Theses" see John V. Maciuika, *Before the Bauhaus. Architecture, Politics and the German State, 1890–1920* (Cambridge UK: Cambridge University Press, 2005), 300–4.

9 Walter Gropius, *Internationale Architektur* (Munich: Langen, 1925, in the series: *Bauhaus Bücher 1*); Gustav Adolf Platz, *Die Baukunst der neuesten Zeit* (Berlin: Propyläen-Verlag, 1927, 1930).

10 Cf. Léon Ploegaerts, Pierre Puttemans, *L'Œuvre Architecturale de Henry van de Velde* (Brussels, Québec: Atelier Vokaer, Les Presses de l'Université Laval, 1987), project 97 "Maison Kröller-Müller »Groothaesebroek« à Wassenaar," 342–3.

11 Cf. Léon Ploegaerts, Pierre Puttemans, *L'Œuvre Architecturale de Henry van de Velde* (Brussels, Québec: Atelier Vokaer, Les Presses de l'Université Laval, 1987), project 108 "Grande musée d'Hoenderloo," 350–3.

12 Henry van de Velde, "Die Pariser Kunstgewerbeausstellung," *Europäische Revue,* 1, No. 7 (October 1925), 41–52, here, 48–9.

13 Henry van de Velde, "De heilige Weg," *Kunst*, No. 10/11/12 (1933), 327–342, here: 338, in French: idem: *La Voie Sacrée* (Brussels: Institut Supérier des Arts Décoratives, 1933).

14 Taking up the phrase employed even by the post-WWII-generation see Alfred Roth, *Begegnung mit Pionieren: Le Corbusier, Piet Mondrian, Adolf Loos, Josef Hoffmann, Auguste Perret, Henry van de Velde* (Basel: Birkhäuser, 1973), which, of course, refers to Nikolaus Pevsner, *Pioneers of the Modern Movement from William Morris to Walter Gropius* (London: Faber & Faber, 1936).

'Votre lettre m'a bien intéressée': Marthe "Tour" Donas and the Belgian Art Scene Around 1920

Peter J.H. Pauwels

In recent years the artist Marthe Donas has been gradually being rediscovered both in her own country and internationally.[1] A major exhibition in the spring of 2016 at the Museum of Fine Arts in Gent was the first ever in Belgium focussing entirely on her early cubist and abstract production. Her works were included in an important exhibition about "La Société Anonyme", organised by the Yale University Art Gallery, which toured the United States from 2006 until 2013. She was represented in "Amazonas del arte nuevo" in Madrid in 2008 and also featured in "Constructing the New World", an exhibition on the network of Theo van Doesburg, which opened in Leiden in 2009 before moving to Tate Modern in London the following year. Germany too has revived its interest in Donas. Six of her paintings and six drawings were among the revelations at a large-scale *Der Sturm* exhibition at the von der Heydt Museum in Wuppertal in 2012. An entire section, reuniting 21 works, was devoted to her work in "Sturm-Frauen", a pioneering exhibition on female artists of that legendary gallery at the Schirn-Kunsthalle in Frankfurt in the autumn and winter of 2015-2016.

This international rediscovery echoes the interest several artists and art critics had already taken in her work immediately after the First World War. Her paintings and collages, enigmatically signed "Tour Donas" hung at the time alongside the leading names of the avant-garde in London, Geneva, Berlin, Paris, Amsterdam, Brussels and Rome and toured in exhibitions in the Scandinavian countries and the United States. It was via Paris rather than Belgium however that Donas came to be part of an international network that included key figures like Alexander Archipenko, Amedeo Modigliani, Tristan Tzara, Piet Mondrian, the Sitwells, Theo van Doesburg, Enrico Prampolini and Herwarth Walden. She was the first Belgian modern artist to do so and one of the very few whose work appeared early on in major avant-garde reviews such as *De Stijl*, *Noi*, *Der Sturm* and *Mécano*.

This essay will discuss Donas' early work and network and also focus on her presence on the Belgian art scene around 1920, especially on her contacts with two prominent art promoters, André De Ridder and Jozef Peeters.

Donas was born in Antwerp in 1885 into an upper-class family. Already as a child her natural artistic talent attracted attention, so she attended lessons at a small private drawing-school for girls of the bourgeoisie. Defying the fierce resistance of her environment, she managed to enrol at the Antwerp Academy, first briefly in 1902 and then from 1912 until the outbreak of the war in 1914. After a brief stay in The Netherlands, she travelled to Dublin where in December 1915 she joined An Tur Gloine, the studio the artist Sarah Purser had founded to breathe new life into the old Irish stained-glass tradition.

Donas left Ireland after the Easter Rising. After a stay in Eastbourne, she crossed the Channel to settle in Paris. There she took classes at the "Académie de la Grande Chaumière and the Académie Ranson". The exciting atmosphere in Montparnasse and the discovery of Cubism at the second salon of Lyre et Palette in January 1917 proved to be transformative for her art. The lessons she immediately started taking with André Lhote, especially his insistence on "plastic rhymes", the echoing of undulating lines or forms to create a balanced composition, would have a lasting influence.

During a stay on the French Riviera in the Spring of 1917 she met the Ukrainian Alexander Archipenko, one of the leading avant-garde sculptors of the time, who suggested that she come to work with him. Donas' surviving work from this period shows how quickly she assimilated, in a nonetheless highly personal way, elements of his famous sculpto-paintings, as the intertwining of convex and concave forms, the curves and the lustre of metal, in her own art. While Archipenko included materials like wood, nickel and glass in his constructions, so as to melt together different materials and combine colour and form, she experimented in her collages with fabrics and wallpaper and sometimes integrated sand into her paint to lend greater texture to her work. The female figure became one of her favourite themes: standing or sitting, washing or dancing. Working wholly in the cubist line, Donas disassembled the human body before putting it back together, simplified and reduced to basic cylindrical and conical forms, viewed from different angles. Archipenko considered Donas his most talented pupil. She was certainly inspired by his revolutionary work, but the dazzling colours, dreamlike mother-of-pearl sheens and the exquisite gradients are entirely her own and show that she was without doubt the better painter of the two. (fig. 16.1).

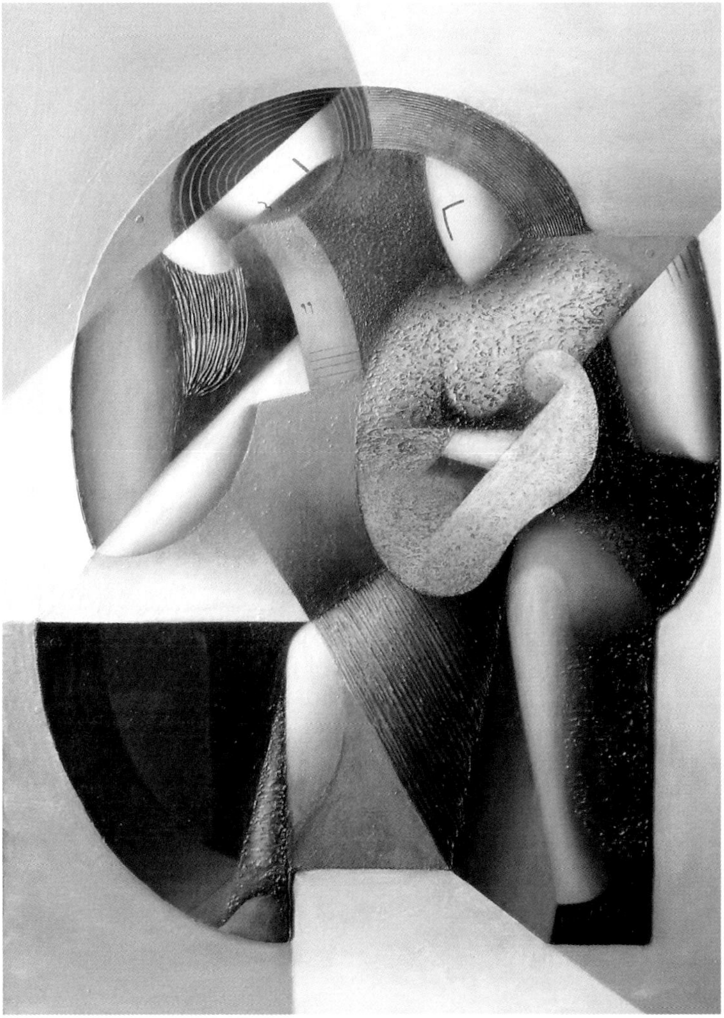

16.1. Marthe Donas, *The Music*, 1918-19, oil and mixed material on board, 77 x 52,5 cm. Private collection. Courtesy Roberto Polo Gallery, Brussels.

Their intense collaboration in the hills above Nice led to an amorous relationship which, though vague for lack of surviving correspondence, is attested to by several of their acquaintances, including Mondrian, Van Doesburg and Peeters.

After the Armistice Donas took a new studio in Montparnasse, 26 Rue du Départ, in a complex where Mondrian, Diego Rivera and Jan Sluijters had lived before the war.

From the beginning of 1919 on Archipenko started to promote Donas' career

intensively. In February he sent an article and photographs of her paintings to the art promoters Prampolini and Van Doesburg. The article, by an otherwise mysterious Roger Biron, praising "Tour d'Onasky's" work for its perfect use of colour, its almost architectural structure and powerful synthesis in the expression of movement was printed with a reproduction of a *Nature morte* in the April 1919 issue of *De Stijl.* A photograph of *Danseuse* was included two issues later, accompanied by a glowing text by Van Doesburg with appreciation for the tightening of elements, the tension in the line, the violent onslaught of the organic form, and most of all the deliberate and distinct stance against Impressionism. The article and the photograph of the *Nature morte* also appeared in Prampolini's magazine *Noi* in January 1920.
Archipenko wrote to Van Doesburg again in the spring. The letter contained an intriguing passage, in which "Tour d'Onasky", now simplified to "Tour Donas" conveyed her regards:

> "Tour Donas sends his sincere admiration for your magazine; he is very happy to participate in your artististic project. Should you need it, his adress is Tour Donas, 26 Rue du Départ, Paris XIV."[2]

When Mondrian returned to the Rue du Départ in July 1919 the concierge informed him that the "Tour Donas" who was now working in Rivera's old studio was not a man but a woman. "Precisely the kind of intrigue they go in for here" he commented in a letter to Van Doesburg. He had gathered from Rivera that Archipenko had launched her as a man in order to make "a better impression". "[Rivera] said that the response would be less good if it were known she was a woman. Although Mondrian felt that Archipenko was being dishonest", he added tellingly. "And that is probably correct."[3]

Although a striking number of women artists were active in Paris[4] and participated in the artistic gatherings, it remained hard for them to make a genuine breakthrough. There was a prevailing attitude at the time: true artistic genius was the preserve of men. Even though many women were active in Cubist and Abstract circles, they appear to have suffered from the sexist theory that this kind of art belonged firmly to the male domain. It was supposedly too intellectual and rational for women, who were simultaneously seen as more sensitive and as more practical and realistic. If women insisted on engaging in fine art, their alleged lack of "imagination" meant they were better off restricting themselves to academic and figurative art, ideally portraits and floral paintings. Modigliani's dealer Zborowski was prepared to take on an artist like Marevna only if she adopted the masculine pseudonym "Stebel".[5] Marie Blanchard signed her work "R.G.B" to mask her identity. Tamara de Lempicka started her career using the male variant of her name "Lempitzky", while even the energetic baroness d'Oettingen, who was at the centre of Apollinaire's *Les Soirées de Paris* and a good friend of Archipenko and Donas, painted under the pseudonym François Angiboult. Adopting a male pseudonym meant potentially more respect and a greater likelihood of promotion and hence of sales. "… because certain artists had told her" Donas wrote herself long afterwards "that she herself was too much of an artist to have a female name".[6] The mysterious, sophisticated and French-sounding "Tour" neatly disguised the artist's gender, while "d'Onasky" sounded noble and cosmopolitan and very "École de Paris". She quickly dropped the "sky" suffix however, finding it over the top.

The network Donas had built up through Archipenko in Nice and Paris bore its first fruit in her participation, with seven paintings, in the Exhibition of French Art 1914-1919, in London in the late summer of 1919. Organised by the Sitwell brothers and Zborowski, whom Donas had met in Nice through Modigliani, it was the first of its kind in post-war London and brought together works by amongst others Derain, Matisse, Picasso, Modigliani, Valadon, Utrillo, Archipenko and Zadkine.

In December 1919 Donas had a first solo exhibition at the avant-garde Librairie Kundig in Geneva, immediately following an exhibition of Archipenko's work. Through Tristan Tzara, with whom Donas had already been in correspondence since January 1919, Archipenko also tried to have a joint exhibition in Zürich in January 1920. Tzara swiftly replied that the Kunsthaus was receptive to an exhibition of his work, but that one featuring Donas was proving more difficult.[7]

Archipenko had introduced Donas to Herwarth Walden in August 1919 as his best pupil, worth showing in his gallery Der Sturm. Due however to Archipenko's participation at the Biennale in Venice, a joint exhibition proved impossible and Donas shared in Berlin in June 1920 the bill with Nell Walden, Herwarth's second wife.[8] The famous critic Adolph Behne was enchanted by her refined colour palette, describing her paintings as "extraordinary appealing, buoyantly playful and easy to fall in love with."[9]

With Archipenko, Albert Gleizes and Léopold Survage, Donas devoted herself in Paris to the reorganisation of the artist's circle La Section d'or.[10] Donas was given a place on the board as one of the members of the Foreign Exhibitions Committee. The opening of the group's first exhibition in March 1920 was a large scale event at the Galerie La Boétie, featuring amongst others paintings by Donas, Angiboult, Gleizes, Braque, Férat, Larionov and Goncharova and sculpture by Archipenko, Brancusi and Laurens.

It was around this period that Donas made the personal acquaintance of Van Doesburg, who visited the exhibition, staying with his friend Mondrian. Although Van Doesburg felt that the artists of De Stijl had made further strides towards abstraction, he viewed an alliance with the internationally orientated Section d'or as a useful move in the battle for modernism. He wasted no time in reporting on the important Paris exhibition, proudly revealing that in the months to come a touring exhibition would be organised in several Dutch cities under De Stijl's auspices.[11]

Transport remained a problem right up to the opening of the first exhibition in Rotterdam. A relieved Van Doesburg informed his friend J.J.P. Oud that the last works had finally arrived thanks to the intervention of Donas, who accompanied the convoy and had much trouble getting them through customs.[12] Donas stayed three days with Van Doesburg in Leiden and the two talked and worked together.[13] A very emotional letter, written three months later from London, in which Donas poured out her ideals and doubts proves how connected these two artists became.[14]

After Rotterdam, the Section d'or exhibition moved to The Hague and Arnhem, and finally to the Stedelijk Museum in Amsterdam, where it closed on 7 November 1920. Van Doesburg was personally involved in the packing of the works, sending most of them to their next destination: Brussels.[15] A Section d'or exhibition in Belgium had been planned for some time. (fig. 16.2).

Letters written by or to Donas before the Second World War are extremely rare. The recent reappearance of two of them in an American private archive throws an interesting new light on her role in the organisation of the exhibition in Belgium and on her contact with the Belgian art critic and art promoter André De Ridder.

Donas seems from the start to have played an active part in the negotiations. These had begun as early as the winter of 1920, during or perhaps even before the opening of the initial Section d'or exhibition in Paris. In an undated letter to Van Doesburg, probably written immediately after his return to Leiden in March 1920, Archipenko mentions:

> "Mademoiselle Donas already informed you that at the moment of your trip negotiations were already in progress about exhibitions of La Section d'Or in Belgium. These are not yet finished. I will let you know more in a short while and also communicate to you the name of the person with whom to confer on the exhibition dates in Belgium, so that these can correspond as favourably as possible with those in your country."[16]

The original intention was for the exhibition to be staged at several venues in Belgium before moving on to The Netherlands. Preliminary discussions were held with the Gallery Giroux in Brussels, which had already organised important international exhibitions featuring cubist and futurist art before the War. Giroux apparently agreed to make its exhibition space available in May. According to an early report in *De Stijl*, the art circle Moderne Kunst in Antwerp, whose chairman was the artist Jozef Peeters, had also been contacted.[17]

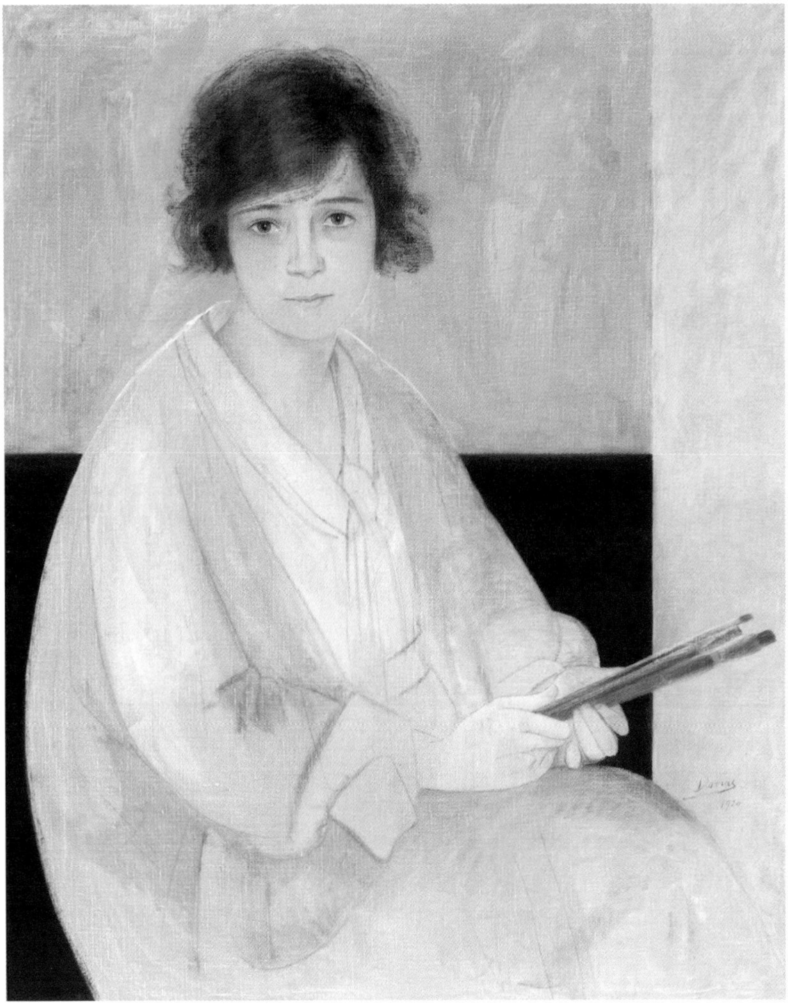

16.2. Marthe Donas, *Selfportrait*, 1920, oil on canvas, 92 x 71,5 cm. Ittre, Collection Marthe Donas Foundation.

Final agreement still had not been reached at the beginning of April 1920. At the end of the same month Van Doesburg was still struggling to find appropriate locations in Rotterdam and Amsterdam for the Dutch part of the tour.[18]

Donas seems to have been exploring at the same time the possibility of venues in Belgium, in Antwerp and Ostend. The exhibitions needed to follow in quick succession to avoid racking up storage costs. She however soon came to the conclusion that all the interesting exhibition spaces had already been taken.[19]

Instead of returning immediately to Paris after her visit to Van Doesburg in Leiden, Donas spent several weeks in Antwerp at her parents' house. There she painted the important *Composition abstraite no. 6*, based on her drawings *d'après deux femmes*. Staying a couple of days with friends at the Château des Hautes Bruyères in Arendonk near Turnhout, on 23 June she received a letter from André De Ridder.

From the start of 1920 De Ridder and his business partner Paul-Gustave van Hecke had been regular visitors to Paris. The dynamic Van Hecke together with his wife Norine ran a successful *maison de couture* in Brussels, but had already befriended several artists in Sint-Martens-Latem before the war. De Ridder, less flamboyant, had moved in artistic circles in The Netherlands during the war and already had a serious reputation as art critic. They were planning to open a new gallery in Brussels, Sélection, that would bring the best of the international art movements to Belgium and confront it with the work of advanced local artists. A new art review, also called *Sélection*, would accompany the exhibitions and offer more in-depth information as well as literary contributions by "en vogue" authors. Both soon had their entries in the Parisian artistic milieus, looking for contacts with art dealers and artists. De Ridder must have been the mysterious man from Antwerp,[20] who had visited the Section d'or exhibition in Paris.

De Ridder wrote to Donas to discuss with her the possibility of an exhibition of the Section d'or, if possible as early as in July 1920. It is unclear whether he had in mind an exhibition at the new gallery in Brussels, which was almost ready – and would in fact open on 18 September 1920 – or if his plans were connected with the Salon des cubistes, the inaugural exhibition of the Sélection group, which ran at the Cercle artistique in Antwerp between 24 July and 2 August 1920. This impressive show confronted artists working in Paris such as Foujita, Modigliani, Zadkine, Braque, Laurens, Lipchitz, Severini and several others with Belgian artists such as Cantre, Cockx, De Troyer, Ensor, the Jespers and the De Smet brothers, Joostens, Permeke and Spilliaert.

July was obviously too early for Donas. Van Doesburg had already secured the Kunstkring in The Hague between 11 July and 1 August. The summer months of August and September did not seem to her propitious for exhibitions, except perhaps in Ostend, where the summer season was on. Perhaps De Ridder could organise something in Antwerp in September, if he had a hall. The exhibition could then continue in October or November in Brussels. She agreed to see De Ridder immediately after her return from the country the following week. "As soon as I will get your answer I will ask the artists in Paris if it suits them. But I have to inform you that they will not contribute to the costs. You will have to take the publicity, catalogues and shipping at your own expense."[21]

On 2 July she had an answer from Paris. The "artists in Paris" were clearly not overwhelmed by the initiative:

> "The artists of the cercle in Paris of which I am a member write me they will not send pictures for an exhibition only to be held in Brussels. There should be exhibitions in two or three cities. Moreover, they cannot exhibit in Belgium before winter, as we have already confirmed several exhibitions abroad." [22]

Donas preferred to postpone the meeting for a couple of weeks, until after her return from London.[23] On 11 August 1920 De Ridder confirmed to Van Doesburg that Sélection had been selected to take care of the Belgian leg of the Section d'or tour.[24] In the meantime Van Doesburg had already managed to secure the Stedelijk Museum between 23 October and 7 November 1920 for a final stop in Amsterdam; so the idea of exhibitions in three Belgian cities had to be reduced to one in the capital alone.

The exhibition at Sélection eventually opened on 4 December and ran until 17 December 1920. There were a few changes in the works on show. Huszar and Mondrian were replaced by Joseph Czaky and Henri Hayden. Donas supplied three different paintings: *Femme et accessoires*, *Femme assise* and *Toits*. This was the first time her work was included in an exhibition in her native country. Although she was the only Belgian member of La Section d'or this got no special mention in *Sélection*, The catalogue at the back of the issue even identified her as a Parisian artist.

The three works have disappeared, but a drawing of *Femme assise* (Private collection, Chantilly) and a contemporary photograph of *Toits* show that she preferred not to send to Brussels some of the abstract works she had been painting that year. Probably she thought these would not be in harmony with the other paintings in the exhibition, or else she had doubts about the new direction her art had taken. The 15 December 1920 issue of *Sélection* included an illustration of yet another painting, *Carrousel*, an imposing work which she had shown at the Salon des Indépendants in Paris and which was to reappear a few weeks later, with her *Danse d'Arlequin et de Colombine*, *Deux femmes*, *La Femme* and *Poterie* at the grand *Exposition d'art moderne* in Geneva.

In January 1921 Der Sturm again exhibited twenty-four of Donas' paintings in a joint exhibition featuring work by Albert Gleizes, Jacques Villon, Louis Marcoussis, Julio Evola and Sonia Delaunay. The machine-like character of many of her figures was noted to a much greater degree than it had been the previous year. Yet it was her colour palette that drew the most interest.[25] Donas is presented in the catalogue, which featured an introduction by Waldemar George, for the first time as an Antwerp artist, rather than a Parisian. She had indeed visited her family several times in 1920 and she might have send her more recent drawings to Berlin from there. One of those, an *Abstract composition with red circle*, was bought in 1922 by Katherine Dreier, who had already bought four of her canvasses before. It is possible that Donas was distancing herself somewhat from Paris. Alternatively, the reference to Antwerp might have been part of Walden's efforts to bolster his European credentials. By emphasising Donas' Flemish origins, he was in a sense laying claim to Belgium as part of his sphere of influence. The January exhibition thus featured work by artists from Antwerp, Paris (Gleizes, Villon and Marcoussis), Rome (Evola) and Madrid, where Delaunay was based at the time. This was at any rate the interpretation of the Flemish poet and art critic Paul van Ostaijen. Van Ostaijen lived at the time in Berlin, having fled post-war Belgium for fear of possible reprisals for his activist past. In the catalogue, which he sent as a new year's gift to Floris and Oscar Jespers, his artist friends living in Antwerp, he placed a large question mark after the words "Tour Donas (Antwerpen)" making it clear that the name did not mean anything to him:

> "Der Sturm always acts like it represents the whole world. It is how it advertises itself. Tour Donas is a pupil of Archipenko and lives in Paris and Nice, etc. But Walden wants it all, so he claims she comes from Antwerp, perhaps because she happened to be born there (her name is d'Onaski = Polish!)."[26]

In the summer of 1921, back in Paris, Donas received a visit from Jozef Peeters. Peeters had organised a First Congress for Modern Art in Antwerp in October 1920. He was already thinking of a second, more internationally orientated Congress and had come to strengthen his contacts with artists like Léger, Gleizes, Vantongerloo and Mondrian.

Peeters had known Donas at the academy in Antwerp. Recalling his Parisian stay in autobiographical notes written more than thirty years later, he recalled that Donas "was known in the whole of Paris for her capricious childish behaviour".[27] He did not get along with Mondrian either, and the feeling was mutual. Peeters also mentioned that Donas introduced him to Archipenko, with whom she lived and whose work he knew from *De Stijl* and *Der Sturm*, but which did not really strike him as new. In the end Cubism did not attract him.[28] However it is highly unlikely that Peeters met Archipenko in Paris at that moment, as in a letter sent to Van Doesburg at the beginning of September 1921 from his Berlin address he stated that he had been in Germany for months, coordinating his various exhibitions.[29] Maybe Peeters had met Archipenko a year earlier as one of his ink drawings, dated "Antwerp, 4 june 1920" (Private collection) shows the sculptor in profile.

Donas fell gravely ill at the end of the summer of 1921. Lack of money and this severe setback persuaded her to return to Antwerp and leave her studio in the Rue du Départ to Willem and Tonia Stieltjes. They in turn would rent it out to Mondrian from the end of October 1922.[30]

Peeters organised his Second Congress for Modern Art in Antwerp in January 1922, which featured a whole series of lectures by Hoste, Oud, Collaer, Huszar and himself on every aspect of contemporary art. In parallel with the congress a large-scale exhibition was held, assembling an impressive survey of modernist international trends. The exhibition at El Bardo was the first ambitious avant-garde event in post-war Belgium. In addition to painting and sculpture, it featured prints and drawings, books, magazines, architectural designs and even musical scores. Most of the Belgian modernists were represented: De Troyer, Flouquet, Leonard, Maes, Magritte, Peeters, Servranckx and Vantongerloo, who with Donas had featured prominently in *De Stijl*.

There were works by Italian Futurists through connections with Marinetti. Peeters also arranged via Walden for numerous Sturm artists to be included: Archipenko, Balla, Bauer, Campendonk, Klee, Puni and Schwitters.

It was most likely at this exhibition that Fernand Berckelaers who, under the name Michel Seuphor, became a leading art critic on abstract art first discovered Donas' work. During a visit to the then elderly artist forty years later, Seuphor recalled the air of mystery that had surrounded her at the time. "Am I truly in the presence of the woman who so captured our imagination in Antwerp in the early 1920s?" She was referred to back then as "Tour Donas" (in *Der Sturm*) and "Tour D'Onasky" (in *De Stijl*). It was said she came from Antwerp, that she lived in Paris, in Berlin too, and in Nice and, what's more, that no one had ever actually seen her.'[31]

He was mistaken, however, when he claimed that Donas' works were among the consignment that Walden sent to Antwerp. The catalogue of the exhibition does not describe her as a Sturm member, as it does with other artists shown at the Berlin Gallery. None of her works at the exhibition belonged to the ensemble in Walden's possession. This means that she must have been in direct contact with Peeters again during her stay in Antwerp. She was a prominent presence, with twelve paintings and – according to the catalogue, at least – a portfolio of linocuts. No trace of the latter has ever been found, not even a reference in her notebooks, prompting the question whether these linocuts were in fact not the powerful pen and ink drawings she produced in 1920.

In Antwerp Donas made a point by submitting – and this for the first time – her most abstract developments. Already by the end of 1919 the sense of the sculptural that Donas, under the influence of Archipenko, sought to convey in her work had gradually disappeared. Creating increasingly rational constructions, she aligned herself with the development towards a purer and more organised form of cubism that Ozenfant and Jeanneret were calling for. Donas was one of the first subscribers to their revue *L'Esprit Nouveau*. Her steadily increasing focus on compositions of planes, arranged almost like painted paper collages on top or alongside one another, also reflects her close contact with Gleizes, like her a member of La Section d'Or. Under the influence of Van Doesburg she radically simplified her earlier work, reducing the human figure, a landscape or a city view to an ensemble of geometric planes. The dynamism of her Cubist work gave way to a more static character. However she rarely abandoned the undulating line, which tempered the new-found austerity of the composition. "You and Mondrian are the ones I most admire in modern art, because you achieved the greatest degree of simplicity and purity, unity and infinity", she wrote to Van Doesburg from London in September 1920.[32] But she seldom went as far as in *Construction*, (KMSKB, Brussels), restricted to the horizontals and verticals Mondrian called for, its rigid composition however softened by the use of entirely personal shades of pink and grey.

In addition to *Tête*, *La cible*, *Verreries*, *Les tulipes* and *Le profète*, Donas showed seven *Compositions* in Antwerp. Where she had continued in the period 1917-1919 to identify even her most abstract paintings with the term *Nature morte*, she now gave these seven works the title *Composition*, which for the catalogue had been translated into Dutch as *Samenstelling*. In so doing, she clearly associated herself with international Constructivism. (fig. 16.3)

On 4 January 1922 Donas married Henri Franke and moved back to Paris, where Franke was studying philosophy at the Sorbonne. The marriage offered her an escape from her parents and the opportunity to reintegrate her place in the Parisian artistic world. Donas' second stay in Paris was marred by ill health. The couple moved in April 1922 to Fontenay-aux-Roses, a village in the *banlieue* which was popular with artists. A highly refined portrait in oils, *Jeune fille au ruban rouge* (Ittre, Musée Marthe Donas), shows how Donas was moving away from geometric abstraction and developing in a new figurative direction. Donas had already expressed her doubts – as did many other modernist painters at the time – in 1920 in her letter to Van Doesburg: this abstract, intellectualised art was a wonderful ideal, but was the world ready for it? "... because afterwards... What will we do? Virtually no more progress, no more change, is possible. Is it not going too far?"[33]

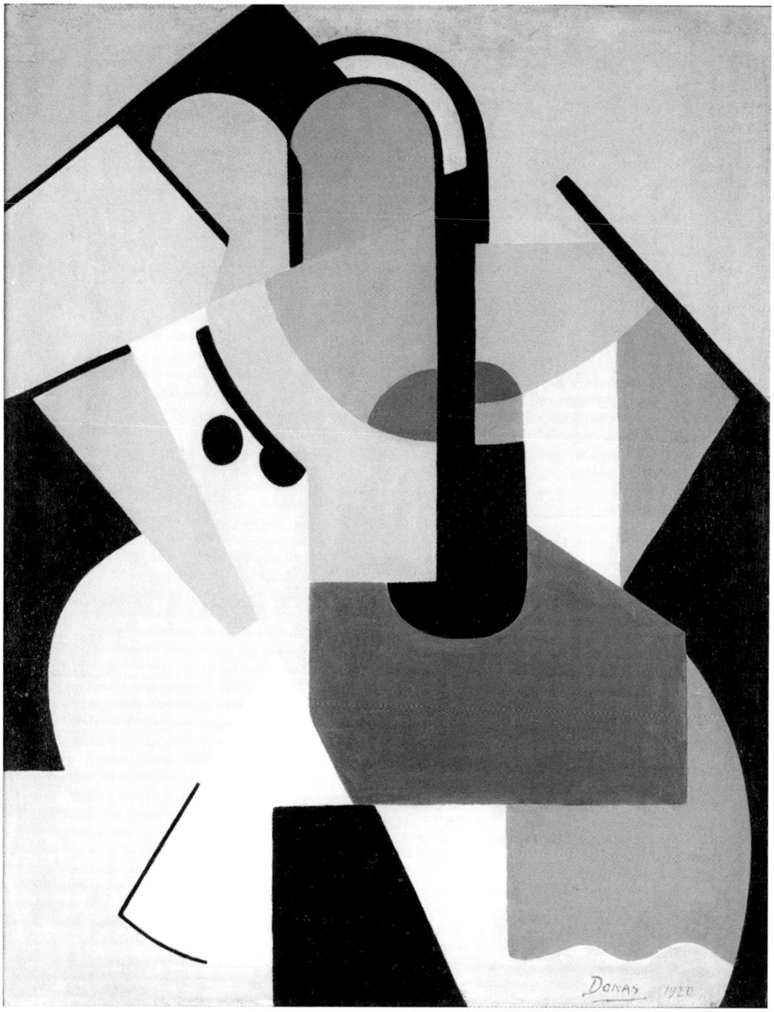

16.3. Marthe Donas, *Abstract Composition no. 6*, 1920, oil on wood, 63 x 48 cm. Private collection.

Returning to Paris deprived Donas of the role she might otherwise perhaps have played within the Antwerp avant-garde. Although he was not himself a member of the group, Rudolf Belling was involved in the organisation of the "Erste Internationale Kunstausstellung" organised by "Das Junge Reinland" in Düsseldorf in the late spring of 1922. Belling had asked Peeters to send exhibition applications to artists of his acquaintance. Peeters submitted three paintings. He was probably also responsible for the inclusion of five paintings by Hubert Wolfs. We do not know if he also informed Donas of the impending manifestation, in which she participated with five paintings: *Le bouquet de violettes*, *Femme avec miroir*, *Le baiser*, *Nature morte* and *Maternité*. In the Düsseldorf catalogue she is clearly identified as a Sturm artist and all five paintings had previously been shown in Berlin, so it must have been Walden who sent them.

However Peeters certainly contacted Donas again for his next project. Berckelaers, whom Peeters had met at the Second Congress in Antwerp, had asked him to join him at the head of his review *Het Overzicht* and transform it from a more politically orientated into a contemporary art magazine. Peeters and Berckelaers were keen to raise the magazine's international profile, so they wrote to a number of European artists, including Marinetti, Schwitters, Archipenko and Donas. She replied to Peeters on 6 October 1922, expressing her interest and asking for some more information.[34] Although Donas' future collaboration was announced from the March-April 1923 issue – alongside that of Archipenko, Kassak, Marinetti and Schwitters – none of her paintings or drawings were ever ultimately reproduced or discussed in the magazine. She did not become one of the artists associated with *Het Overzicht*, which is also evident from the fact that when Peeters and Berckelaers compiled a special "Flemish issue" for *Der Sturm*, none of Donas' works were included, unlike those of Leonard, Maes, De Boeck, Joostens and Peeters himself.

In the spring of 1923 Donas collapsed both physically and mentally. She returned to Belgium, where she settled in Ittre. The quiet beauty of the surroundings had a positive influence, and after a while she started to paint again. Her new work showed a clear return to figuration, however markedly simplified and retaining traces of cubism. Though it remained consistently refined it was notably less bold than her pioneering work around 1917-1920.

In 1926 Donas had a big exhibition at La Vierge Poupine, Geert Van Bruaene's Brussels' art gallery. It offered a survey of her whole production in seventy works. De Ridder missed the exhibition of this "cubiste répentie", albeit much to his regret, as he reported in an article in *Sélection*, having heard lots of good things about it.[35] Though his gallery had already closed in 1922, he continued to promote Belgian and French contemporary art in his magazine, however neglecting the abstract movement.

The exhibition revived Donas' desire to live in Brussels. Her renewed contact with an urban artistic milieu gave her a fresh boost. It resulted in a return to neo-cubism and remarked participation in 1928 in the exhibitions of the L'Assaut group in Brussels and Paris, where she shared the bill with Baugniet, De Boeck, Gailliard, Flouquet and Servranckx, artists associated with the review *7 Arts* and the lesser known Van Der Cammen and Wolfs. However by the end of the 1920s the abstract movement in

Belgium seemed as good as dead. It was not supported by major galleries, museums, collectors or patrons. Newspapers considered the phenomenon too unimportant for more than cursory coverage. *Het Overzicht* had already ceased appearing in 1925, as had Peeters' new art review *De Driehoek*. The final edition of *7 Arts* was published in 1928. In the same year a disheartened Donas stopped painting for twenty years. In 1948 she picked up her brushes, but her work never re-attained the level of achievement, nor the international recognition of the years around 1920.

It was only in 1959, after a gap of thirty-six years, that Donas came into contact with Peeters again. At the end of the 1950s there was at last a renewal of interest in the pioneers of abstraction. Young artists associated with the recently founded G58 group in Antwerp enjoyed good contacts with Peeters. During meetings at the Middelheim, which were also attended by critics like Maurits Bilcke and Marc Callewaert the idea arose of paying tribute to all the more or less forgotten artists who had been painting abstract works at the start of the 1920s. The exhibition Bilcke and Callewaert brought together in October-November 1959 with the painter Jo Delahaut was ground breaking and pivotal in the reappreciation of early Belgian abstract art. Donas provided not only what she had left of her early work, but also a large amount of documentation from her own archive. She thought the project, which reunited all those who had fought for a new art, very successful as she wrote to Peeters, whom she sincerely thanked for all his efforts.[36]

Notes

1 See: Peter J.H. Pauwels, *Marthe Donas, a Woman-artist in the Avant-garde* (Antwerp: Ludion, 2015).

2 "Tour Donas vous envoie l'expression de sa profonde sympathie pour votre revue, il est très heureux de participer dans votre manifestation d'art. En cas ou vous en auriez besoin voici son adresse Tour Donas, 26 Rue du Départ, Paris XIV," Letter from A. Archipenko to T. Van Doesburg, spring 1919, RKD, The Hague.

3 "Echt zooals ze hier meer intriges gebruiken (...) Hij zei als men hoort dat 't een vrouw is vertrouwt men 't minder. En dat zal ook wel zoo zijn." Letter from P. Mondrian to T. Van Doesburg, 1 August 1919, RKD, The Hague.

4 See Fabienne De Meulemeester, *Vrouwelijke kunstenaars in de marge van de Parijse avant-garde* (Master's thesis, Leuven University, 2004).

5 Marevna, *Life with the painters of La Ruche* (London, 1962), 22.

6 "(...) car des artistes lui avaient dit qu'elle était trop artiste pour garder un nom féminin." Autobiographic notes, 1961, Donas Archives, Ghent.

7 Letter from A. Archipenko to T. Tzara, 21 November 1919, in Raoul Schrott, *Dada 15/25* (Innsbruck: DuMont, 1992), 247.

8 See Peter Pauwels, "Die Belgische Künstlerin Marthe Donas und Der Sturm," in *Der Sturm. Zentrum der Avantgarde*, ed. Andrea von Hülsen-Esch and Gerhard Finckh (Wuppertal: von der Heydt-Museum, 2012), 359-376.

9 "ausserordentlich reizvolle, heitere Spielereien in die man sich leicht verliebt" unidentified newspaper cutting, Donas Archives, Ghent.

10 See Françoise Lucbert's essay on La Section d'Or in this volume.

11 *De Stijl*, III, 5, 1920.

12 Postcard from T. Van Doesburg to J.J.P. Oud, 17 June 1920, Frits Lugt Collection, Institut Néerlandais, Paris.

13 Letter from T. Van Doesburg to A. Kok, 24 June 1920, in Alied Ottevanger, *De Stijl overal absolute leiding* (Bussum: Thoth, 2008), 296.

14 Letter from M. Donas to T. Van Doesburg, 16 September 2009.1920, RKD, The Hague.

15 Letter from T. Van Doesburg to A. Kok, 5 November 1920, in Alied Ottevanger, *ibid.*, 304.

16 "Mademoiselle Donas vous a communiqué qu'au moment de votre voyage nous avons engagé des pourparlers pour les expositions de la Section d'or en Belgique. Ces pourparlers ne sont pas encore terminés. D'ici peu je vous communiquerai des nouvelles et à l'adresse par laquelle vous saurez vous entendre de façon que les dates des expositions en Belgique puisent correspondre à des conditions favorables pour les expositions dans votre pays." Letter from A. Archipenko to T. Van Doesburg, Spring 1920, RKD, The Hague.

17 *De Stijl*, III, 5, 1920.

18 Letter from T. Van Doesburg to A. Kok, 25 April 1920, in Alied Ottevanger, *ibid.*, 290.

19 Letter from M. Donas to A. De Ridder, 23 June 1920. Private Archives, Washington.

20 Van Doesburg suspected wrongly that this mysterious man was the Antwerp artist Jozef Peeters. Peeters however could not have been in Paris at the time as he was serving in the Belgian army. Letter from T. Van Doesburg to P. Pruym (Peeters' wife), 24 March 1920. Letterenhuis, Antwerp.

21 "Aussitôt votre réponse je demanderai aux artistes à Paris si celà leur convient. Mais je dois vous avertir qu'ils ne veulent pas de frais à leurs charge. Vous devez vous occuper à vos frais des réclames, catalogues, expéditions." Letter from M. Donas to A. De Ridder, 23 June 1920. Private Archives, Washington.

22 "Les artistes de la société dont je fais parti à Paris m'écrivent qu'ils n'enverront pas des toiles pour une exposition à Bruxelles seul. Qu'il faudrait pouvoir exposer dans deux ou trois villes. Qu'en plus, avant l'hiver ils ne pourront pas exposer en Belgique, car nous avons déjà arrêté plusieures expositions à l'étranger." Letter from M. Donas to A. De Ridder, 2 July 1920. Private Archives, Washington.

23 Letter from M. Donas to A. De Ridder, 2 July 1920. Private Archives, Washington.

24 Letter from A. De Ridder to T. Van Doesburg, 11 August 1920. RKD, The Hague.

25 Unidentified newspaper cutting. Donas Archives, Ghent.

26 "Der Sturm wil steeds doen of hij den al vertegenwoordigt. Dat is zo zijn reklame. Tour Donas is een leerlinge van Archipenko en woont te Parijs, te Nizza, enz. Maar Walden wil alles hebben en daarom zet hij Antwerpen, omdat zij misschien te Antwerpen geboren is (zij heet d'Onaski = Polen!." Paul Borgers, *Paul van Ostaijen, een documentatie* (The Hague: B. Backer, 1971), 419.

27 "... was over heel Parijs bekend voor haar nukkige kinderstreken", J. Peeters Autobiographical notes, [1958], Private archive.

28 J. Peeters, Autobiographical notes, [1958], Private archive. With thanks to S. Servellon.

29 Letter from A. Archipenko to T. Van Doesburg, 17 September 1921. RKD, The Hague.

30 See Peter Pauwels, *Marthe Donas* (Antwerp: Ludion, 2015), 202.

31 "Ben ik werkelijk bij de persoon die ons in 't begin der jaren twintig in de Antwerpse kringen zo fel geïntrigeerd heeft? Ze heette toen Tour Donas (in Der Sturm) en Tour d'Onasky (in De Stijl). Er werd verteld dat zij een Antwerpse was, te Parijs leefde, ook te Berlijn en te Nice, en wat nog, maar niemand had ze ooit gezien." Michel Seuphor, *De abstracte kunst in Vlaanderen* (Brussels: Arcade, 1963), 77.

32 "Dans l'art moderne c'est Mondriaan et vous que j'approuve le plus, car vous avez atteint le degré le plus élevé de la simplicité et pureté, de l'unité et de l'infini." Letter from M. Donas to T. Van Doesburg, 16 September 1920, RKD, The Hague.

33 "(...) car après ... que ferons nous? Il n'y a presque plus de progret [sic] ni de changement possible. N'est-ce pas aller trop vite?" Letter from M. Donas to T. Van Doesburg, 16 September 1920, RKD, The Hague.

34 Photocopy of letter from J. Peeters to M. Donas, 6 October 1922, AHKB, Brussels.

35 André de Ridder, "Les expositions," *Sélection*, 6 (1926), 328.

36 Letter from M. Donas to J. Peeters, 11 December 1959. Donas Archives.

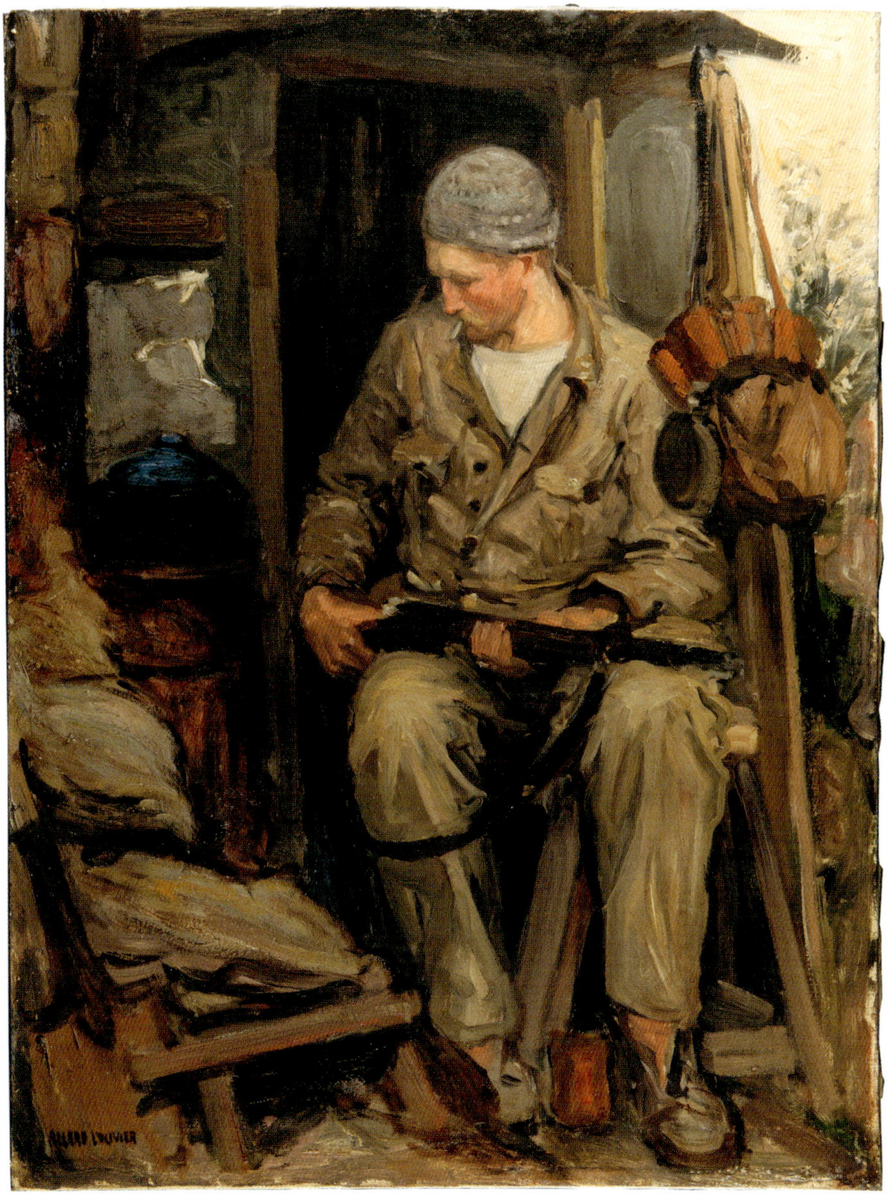

4.1. Fernand Allard l'Olivier, « Fantassin au repos dans la tranchée », s.d., huile sur toile, 73 x 54 cm. Bruxelles, Musée royal de l'Armée et d'Histoire militaire. Inv. n° 201000112.

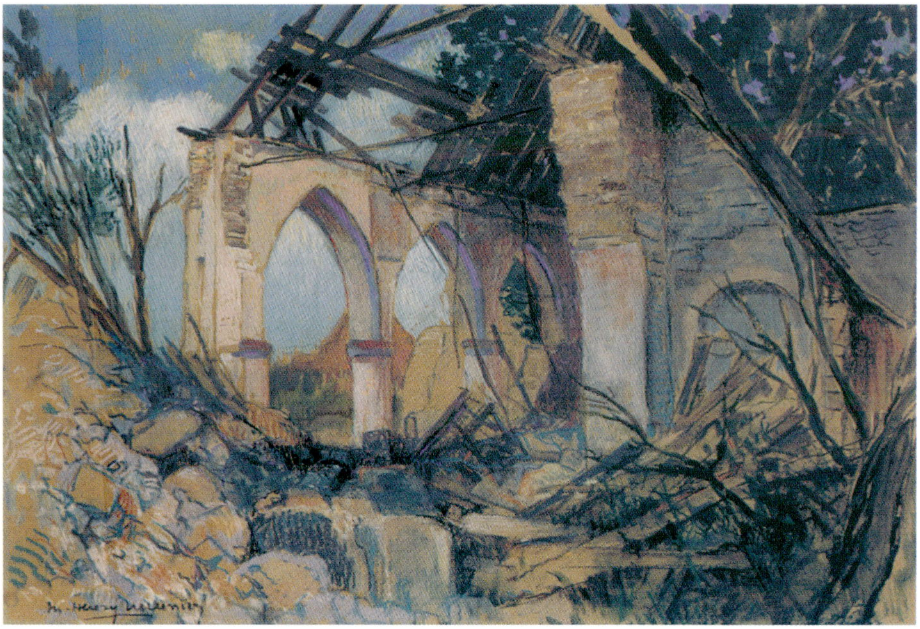

4.2. Marc-Henry Meunier, « Ruines de l'église de Saint-Jacques-Capelle », 1917, fusain, gouache et pastel sur papier, 51,6 x 74,4 cm. Bruxelles, Musée royal de l'Armée et d'Histoire militaire. Inv. n° 88100021.

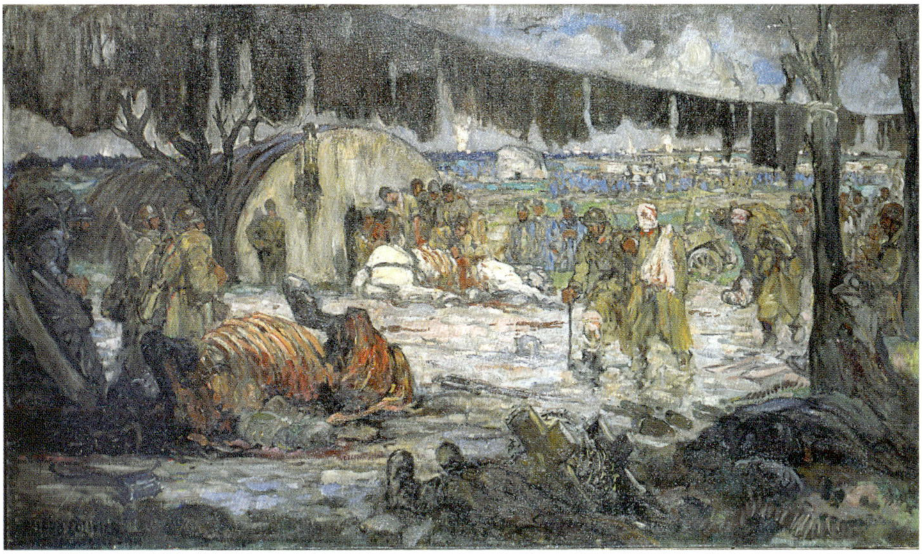

4.3. Fernand Allard l'Olivier, « Le chemin de la victoire à Westrozebeke », 1918, huile sur toile, 98 x 162 cm. Bruxelles, Musées royaux des Beaux-Arts de Belgique (en dépôt au MRA). Inv. n°10076/54.

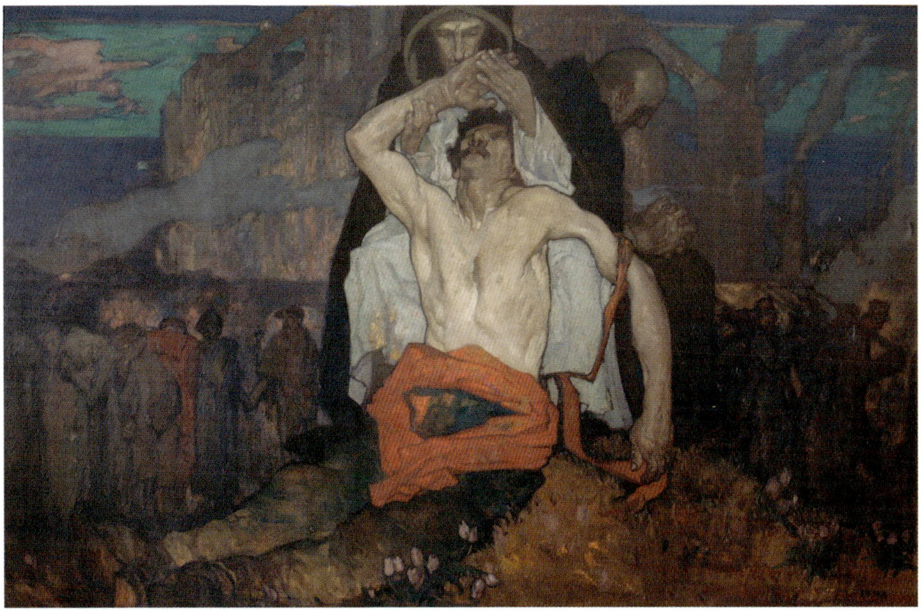

5.1. Frank Brangwyn, *Mater Dolorosa Belgica*, 1915, oil on canvas, 159 x 234 cm. William Morris Gallery, London Borough of Waltham Forest, BrO3.

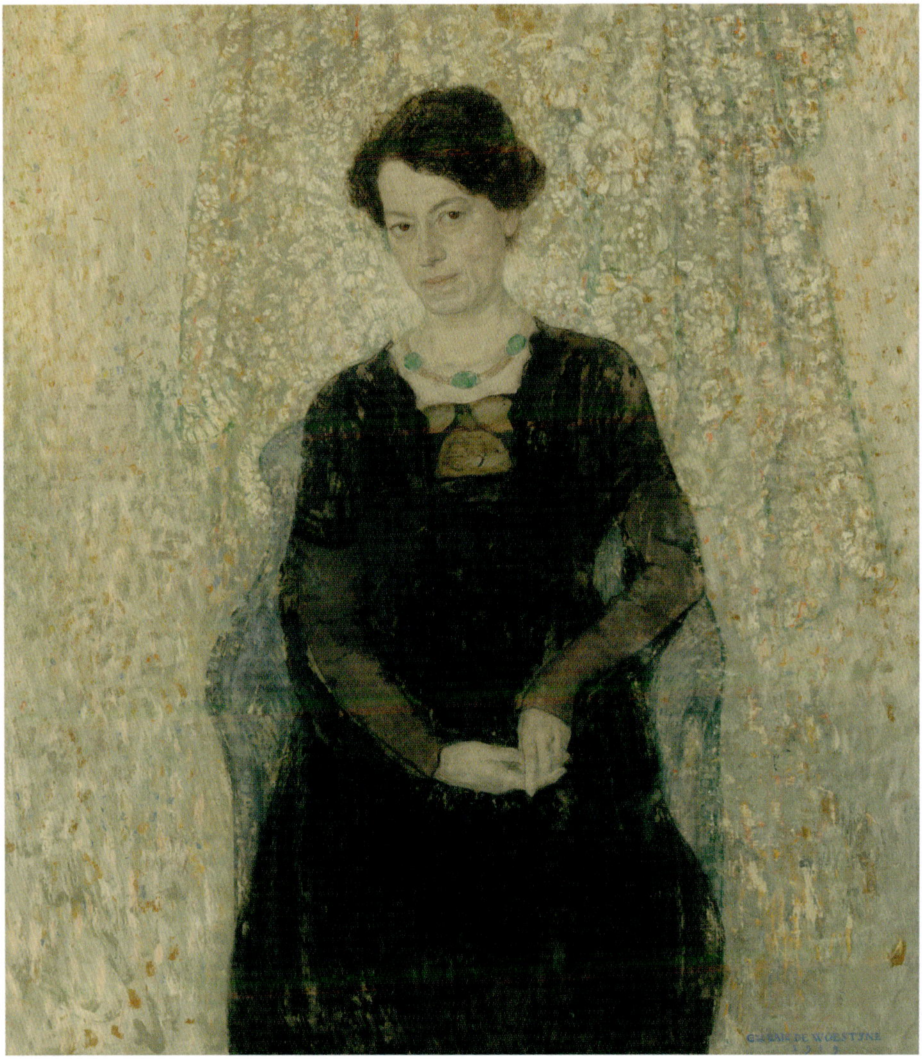

6.3. Gustave van de Woestyne, *Portrait de madame Louise de Graaff*, 1919, oil on canvas, 122 x 107 cm. Brussels, Royal Museums of Fine Arts of Belgium, Inv. 6520.

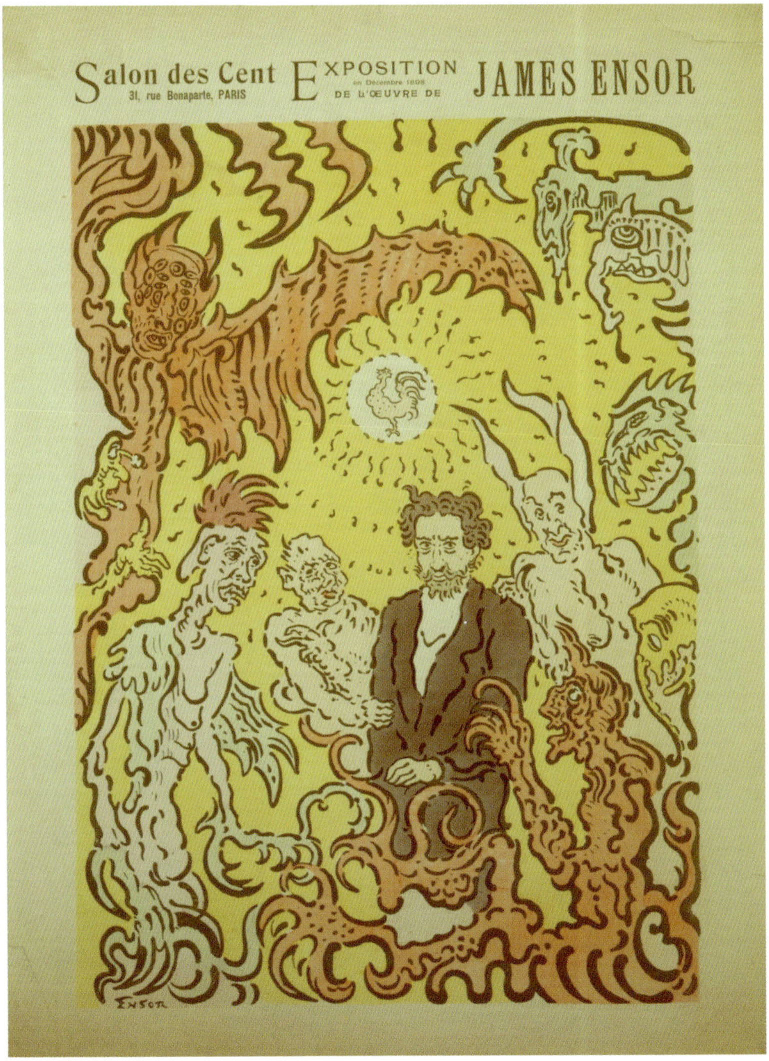

9.4. James Ensor, *Salon des Cent. 31, rue Bonaparte, Paris. Exposition en décembre 1898 de l'oeuvre de James Ensor/* Démons me turlupinant,1898, colour lithograph, 649 x 468 mm, Brussels, Royal Museums of Fine Arts of Belgium, inv. 7526.

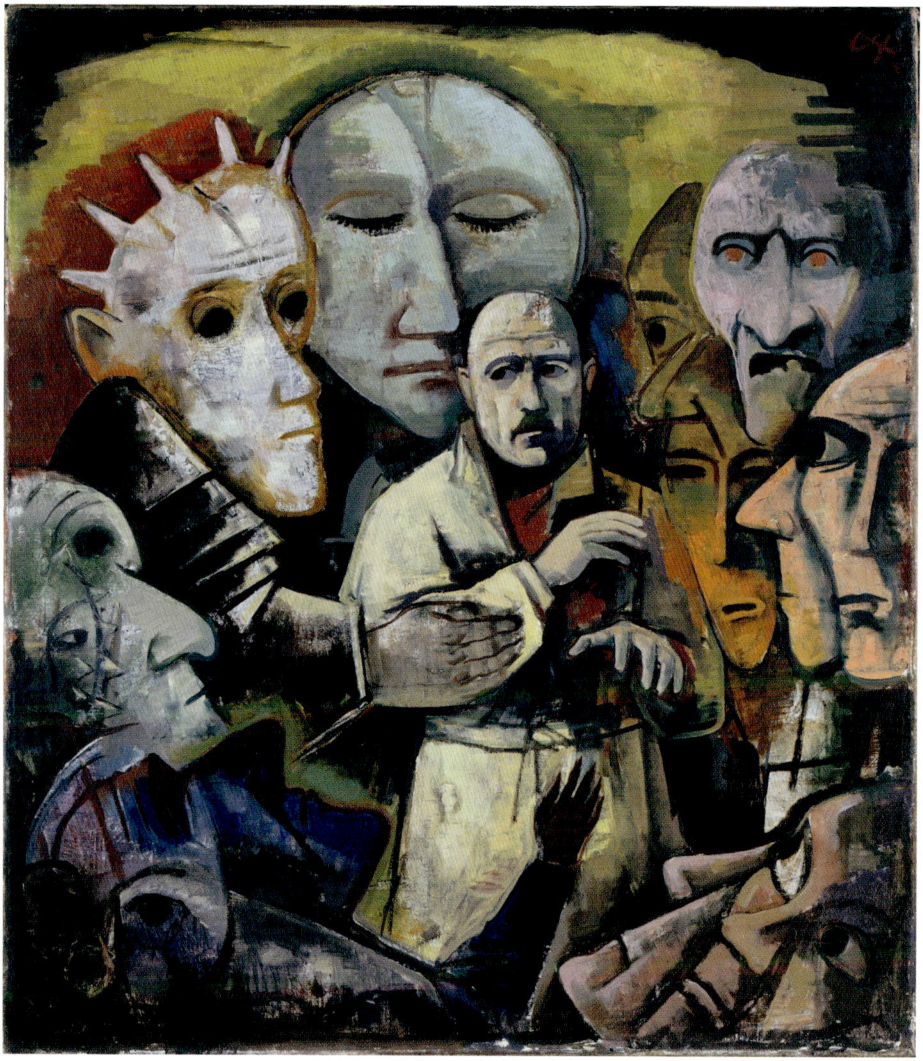

9.5. Karl Hofer, *Selbstbildnis mit Dämonen* (ca. 1928), oil on canvas, 147 × 124 cm, Ettlingen, Schloßmuseum (Dauerleihgabe Nachlaß Hofer Nr. 381).

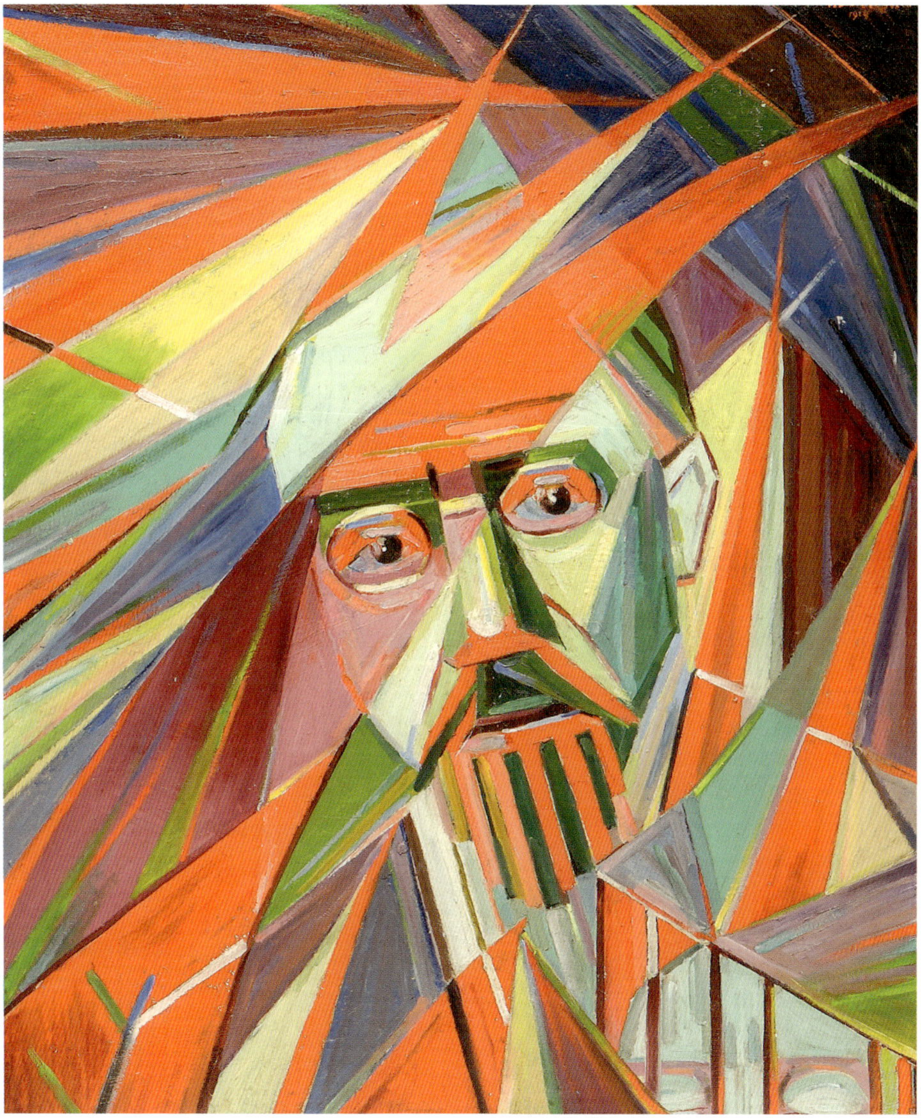

10.2. Felix De Boeck, *Portrait of Borms*, 1919, oil on cardboard, 88 x 71 cm. Collectie Vlaamse Gemeenschap, BK6271a.

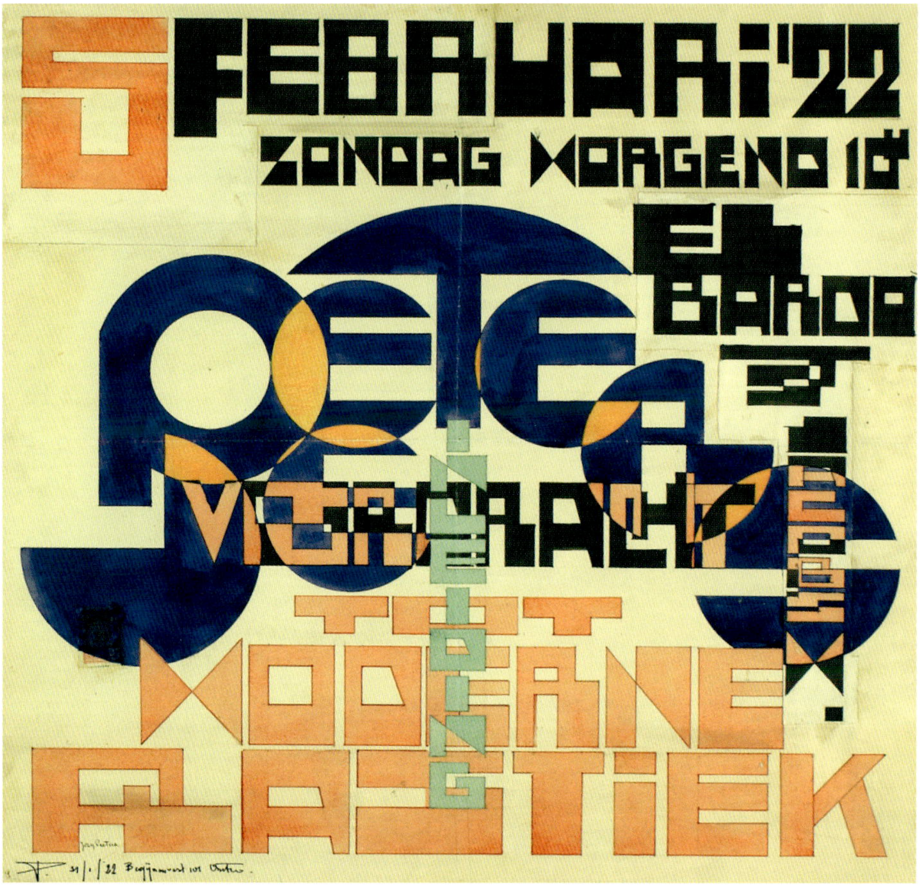

10.3. Poster Jozef Peeters, *Voordracht. Inleiding tot modern plastiek* [Introduction to modern plasticism], 1922. Letterenhuis, Antwerpen.

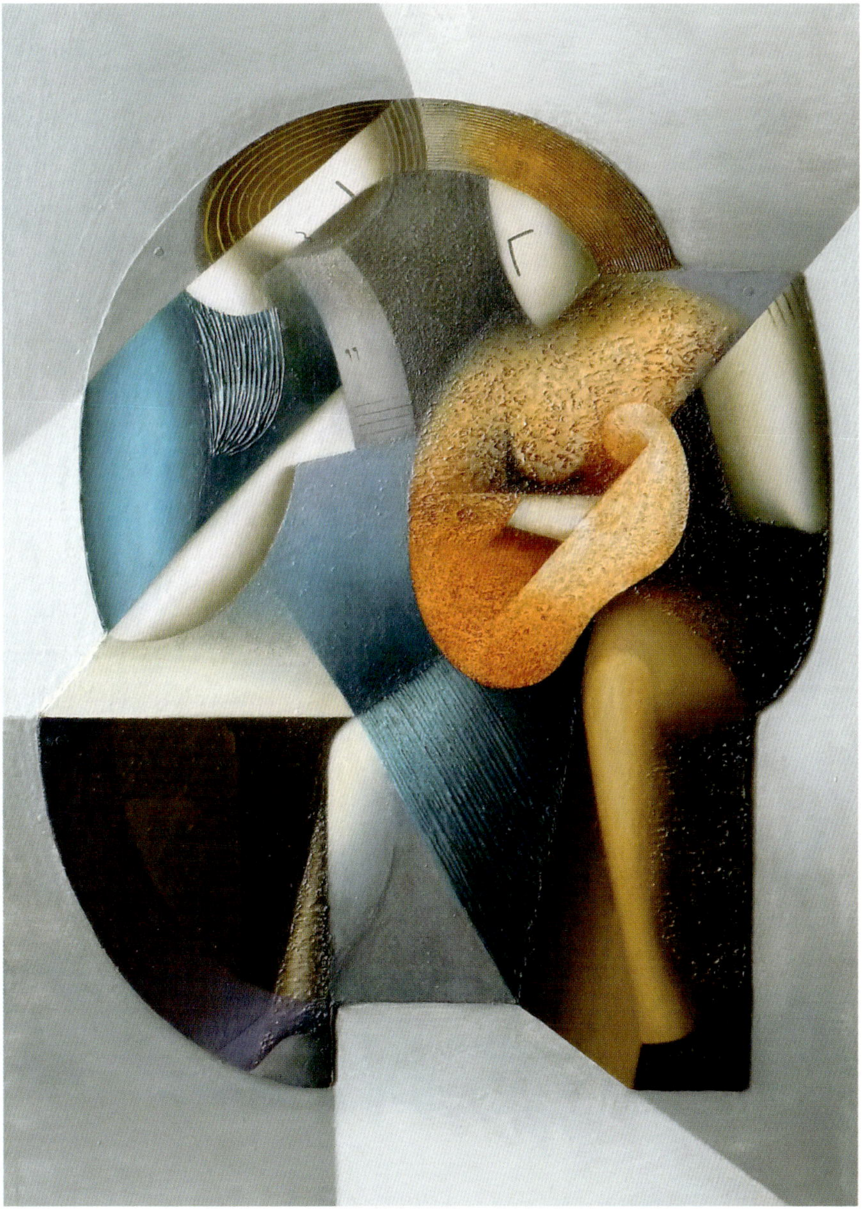

16.1. Marthe Donas, *The Music*, 1918-19, oil and mixed material on board, 77 x 52,2 cm. Private collection. Courtesy Roberto Polo Gallery, Brussels.

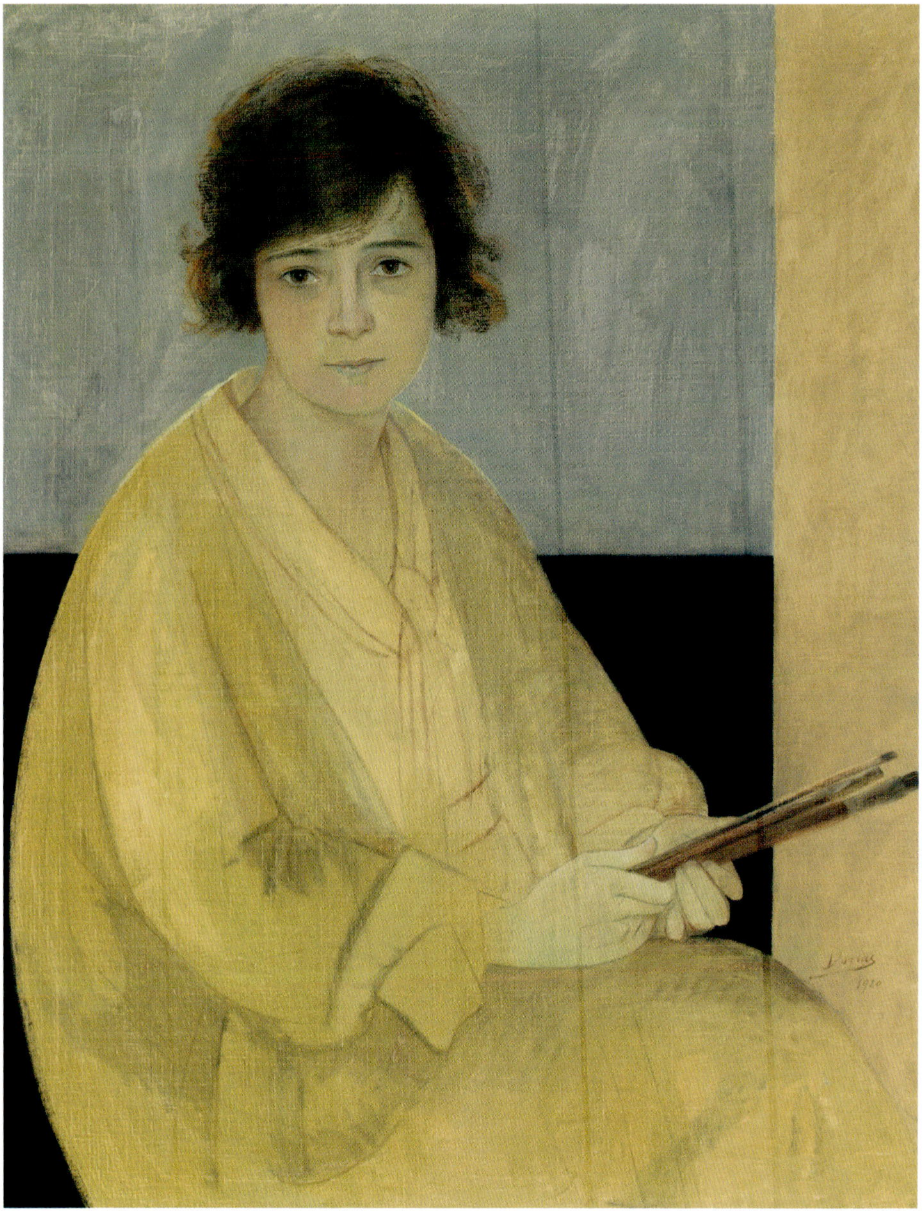

16.2. Marthe Donas, *Selfportrait*, 1920, oil on canvas, 92 x 71,5 cm. Ittre, Collection Fondation Marthe Donas.

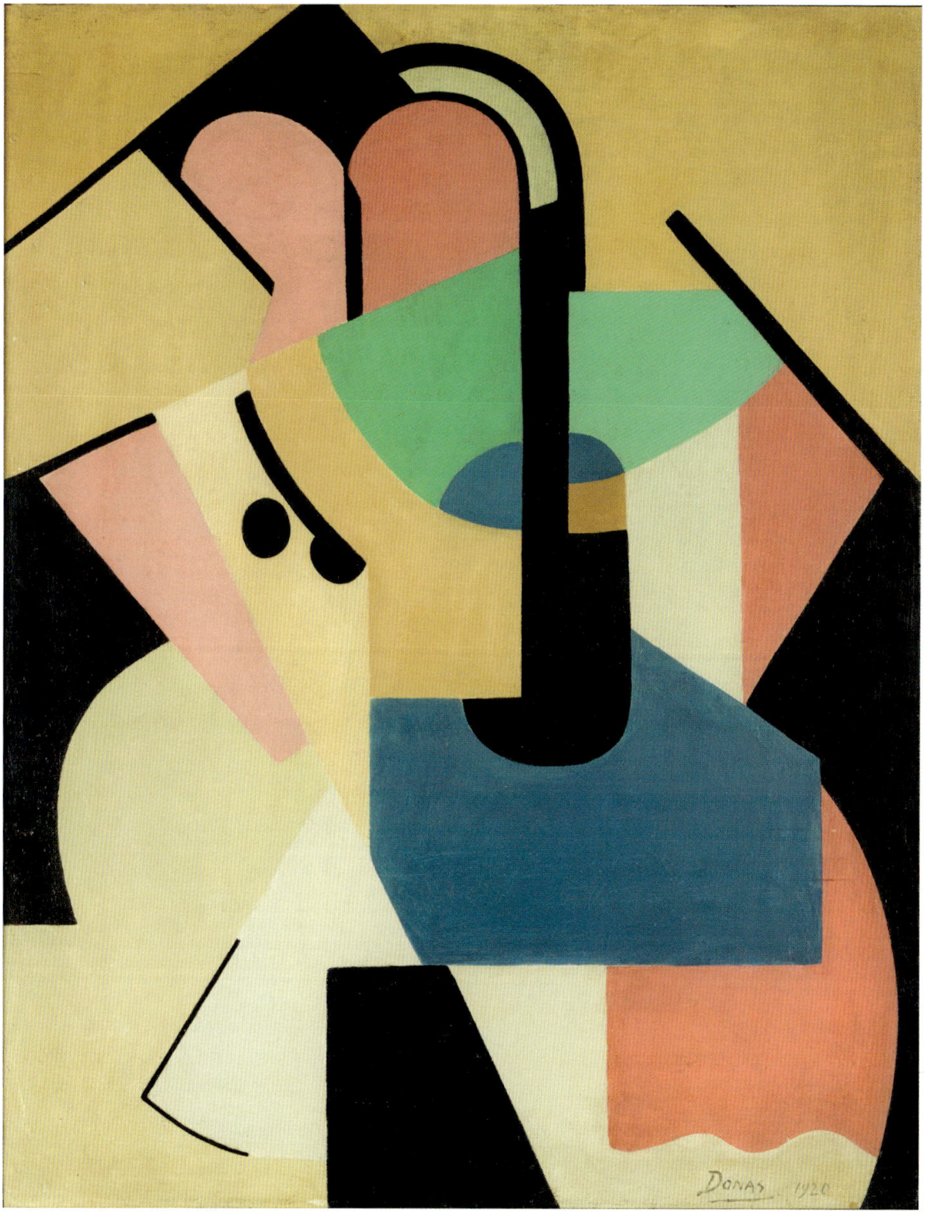

16.3. Marthe Donas, *Abstract Composition no. 6*, 1920, oil on wood, 63 x 48 cm. Private collection.

Abstracts

Former l'expérience de l'occupation militaire : dix images

SOPHIE DE SCHAEPDRIJVER

Les historiens culturels de la Première Guerre mondiale définissent la « culture » au sens large : ils cherchent à retracer comment les gens qui ont vécu la guerre, donnaient un sens à leur expérience, aussi bien pendant qu'après le conflit. Cette approche est particulièrement fructueuse en ce qui concerne le théâtre de guerre que fut l'occupation militaire. L'Europe occupée, pendant la Première Guerre mondiale, forma un espace liminal, qui n'était ni front ni front intérieur. L'occupation militaire était une expérience déroutante, aussi bien pour les occupés que pour les occupants.

Cette contribution se concentre sur la Belgique occupée par l'Allemagne et étudie la façon dont aussi bien les occupés que les occupants ont essayé de donner un sens à leur expérience et de définir leur rôle. La contribution évoque cette problématique à l'aide de dix images (photographies, bande dessinée, œuvres d'art). Chacune de ces images, à sa façon, illustre la recherche d'un sens d'intention (par les civiles occupés ou par les membres de la force occupante), tout comme les paradoxes inhérents à cet effort.

14/18 : Rupture ou continuité ? L'art belge aux environs de la Première Guerre mondiale au sein des collections des Musées royaux des Beaux-Arts

LAURA KOLLWELTER ET INGA ROSSI-SCHRIMPF

Jusqu'en 1925, les Musées royaux des Beaux-Arts de Belgique ne présentent dans leurs collections que très peu d'œuvres d'artistes belges de la génération née après 1882. L'application de politiques administratives restrictives, de même que la présence d'une majorité de membres conservateurs dans les instances de direction expliquent cette absence. Les artistes belges de cette génération restaient pour leur part plus fortement influencés par des courants artistiques tels que le postimpressionnisme ou le luminisme, au contraire de nouvelles formes d'expression telles que le futurisme ou le cubisme, qui ne trouvaient que peu d'ancrage dans ce pays. La Première Guerre mondiale modifia profondément cet équilibre, soit par le chemin de l'exil que prirent certains artistes, les obligeant à se confronter à d'autres formes artistiques, soit par la confrontation à la vie sous l'occupation allemande.

Cet article présente cinq aspects de l'art belge aux environs de cette période charnière, avec tout d'abord Wouters et Schirren qui représentent une nouvelle génération de l'art belge d'avant-guerre, toujours fortement influencé par le postimpressionnisme. Schmalzigaug, que certains considèrent comme le seul futuriste belge d'avant-guerre, un courant artistique qu'il découvrit à l'occasion d'un exil volontaire mû par des considérations artistiques, préféra s'ôter la vie après avoir fui la Belgique en direction des Pays-Bas lors de la Première Guerre mondiale, un évènement qui le traumatisera. Néanmoins, ce courant futuriste connaitra un plus grand succès après la guerre, notamment grâce à des artistes tels que Paul Joostens ou encore Prosper De Troyer. Ce nouvel intérêt se traduit également dans la création de cercles d'artistes en Belgique, comme le Bond Zonder Gezegeld Papier en 1917 ou encore le Kring Moderne Kunst après la guerre, qui se nourrissent de la modernité artistique présente en France avec le cubisme, en Italie avec le futurisme ou encore en Allemagne avec l'expressionnisme. Les noms de Jozef Peeters, figure centrale du renouveau artistique de cette époque, et de Marthe Donas, célèbre artiste, sont essentiels à la compréhension de cette époque.

L'expressionisme flamand est un courant artistique prépondérant dans la Belgique d'après-guerre. Les artistes s'y rattachant se nourrissent pour la plupart de leur expérience d'exil durant la guerre, à la manière de Gustave De Smet ou de Frits Van den Berghe, qui cherchent par cette forme d'expression à renouveler la création dans leur pays par l'apport de nouvelles techniques. Néanmoins, une généralisation de cette situation serait fallacieuse : des artistes comme Albert Servaes, resté en Belgique, ou George Minne participent aussi à ce courant. La représentation de la guerre elle-même s'est faite selon deux grands axes. Premièrement par la mise en place de la Section artistique de l'Armée belge en Campagne, adoptant un style luministe à l'exception d'Achille Van Sassenbrouck et dépeignant le plus souvent des ruines, plutôt que les champs de bataille eux-mêmes. Deuxièmement, et plus paradoxalement, cette guerre est aussi présentée par le regard porté par des artistes ne l'ayant pas directement expérimentée mais cherchant à la représenter souvent dans ses travers les plus spectaculaires.

Art at war! The Belgium state as patron of combatting artists: benevolent politics or imperious necessity?

Sandrine Smets

With the invasion of Belgium by German troops in August 1914, the Kingdom's artistic community was forcefully dispersed. Young men were mobilised, others joined the army on a voluntary basis, some remained in Belgium and yet others sought refuge in the neighbouring countries.

Starting in the autumn of 1914, the Belgian State set up relief funds for artists, at the beginning mainly for those exiled, trying to rebuild their lives abroad. In London, a committee was created, which would organise charity exhibitions as well as lectures on Belgian art and literature throughout the country. In 1915, Queen Elisabeth eventually granted a large subsidy of which 80% would go to the artists who remained in Belgium.

Meanwhile at the front, artists often grabbed their pencil or brush in order to capture what they saw and felt. Furthermore, artistic practices were being utilised in a more pragmatic way by the military. Precise drawings show the whereabouts of the enemies and camouflage techniques are perfected by able artistic craftsmanship. Exhibitions and contests by artists at war were also taking place. In May or June of 1916 the importance and utility of artists at the front was officially recognised and the "Artistic Section of the Belgian Army on the Field" was founded. Its goal was to document the war but also to shake off the image of "Poor Little Belgium" and reinforces the propaganda. The preference for painting and drawing over photography was noticeable. Painting was being considered as the medium which could more easily transfer emotions. The members of the "Artistic Section" stemmed from different artistic currents but all remain in the realm of figuration. Most of them do not experiment stylistically between 1914 and 1918. Some exceptions would be Achile Van Sassenbrouck and Maurice Caneel.

The paintings mostly show the consequences of battle in land- and cityscapes, as well as the day to day life of the troops. Through self-censorship death is almost entirely omitted from this official art.

The lack of battlefield images carries the idea of a non-aggressive soldier, putting the blame on the attacking enemy. Showing a well fed and healthy soldier also allows the spectator to imagine a strong army that is holding up well and is worth supporting. By depicting the enemy's use of toxic gases the barbarism of this last one is accentuated. In a more symbolic way, the ruin is a recurring motive in the paintings of the "Artistic Section". The destruction of national heritage shows the disrespect of the enemy and stresses the violation of a nation's neutrality.

After the war the artists of the "Section" stop representing war scenes and return to their artistic pre-war affiliations. The works of the Artistic Section were regularly exhibited in war memorial shows in the interbellum but have since fallen into oblivion.

« My heart is sore about brave Belgium » Exode artistique : Artistes belges réfugiés en Grande-Bretagne pendant la Grande Guerre

Caterina Verdickt

L'invasion allemande oblige environ 250 000 Belges à s'exiler en Grande-Bretagne. Parmi eux, de nombreux artistes s'installent sur les îles britanniques. L'accueil des artistes belges est chaleureux. La cause belge tout comme le patrimoine, la culture et les arts belges sont d'un intérêt majeur pour la population autochtone accueillant les réfugiés. Ainsi, des expositions d'art et d'arts appliqués sont organisées dans tout le pays, la plupart du temps au profit d'une œuvre de bienfaisance.

Outre les expositions apparaissent également des publications sur l'art, l'architecture et l'histoire des villes belges. De plus, des conférences sont organisées, dont notamment celles d'Émile Verhaeren, Émile Vandervelde et Émile Claus qui font une tournée du pays afin de propager les vertus de leur patrie.

Ces événements doivent être compris dans le contexte de propagande et de charité. Les innovations artistiques ne sont pas prioritaires dans ces circonstances. En effet, le caractère conservateur de ces manifestations, desquelles les artistes modernes restent presque entièrement absents, est remarquable. L'art belge exposé est de caractère rural, traditionnel et conformiste. Cette tendance de s'attacher à un art moins novateur est établie dès le début de la guerre et aide à souligner que l'identité nationale est ancrée dans l'histoire de l'art belge.

Afin de coordonner ces expositions, différents comités d'artistes réfugiées en Grande-Bretagne sont formés. Le directeur du ministère belge des Arts et Sciences, Paul Lambotte joue un rôle prépondérant dans ces comités. Personnage énigmatique, Lambotte avait déjà établi un certain réseau en Grande-Bretagne avant 1914 qu'il étend et diversifie pendant la guerre. Les membres de ce réseau proviennent majoritairement d'institutions traditionnelles aux esthétiques victoriennes. Il utilise son réseau pour introduire des artistes belges sur la scène artistique britannique. Ainsi il présente Albert Baertson à John Singer Sargent qui permet au peintre belge d'utiliser son atelier lors des années de guerre.

L'art non conventionnel et controverse est évité par Paul Lambotte. Premièrement il se méfie de toute introduction novatrice au niveau stylistique et thématique. De plus, il écarte tout artiste ayant un lien artistique ou commercial avec l'Allemagne de l'avant-guerre. Ainsi George Minne qui jouissait d'un certain succès en Allemagne est exclu de toute exposition organisée par Lambotte. De manière stratégique, ce rejet de tout art qui pourrait impliquer la moindre controverse veut préserver la bienveillance du public britannique envers les réfugiés belges.

Jacob et Louise de Graaff – Mécènes d'artistes modernes belges en exil

Laura Kollwelter

L'homme d'affaires néerlandais Jacob De Graaff et sa femme Louise Bachiene-De Graaff sont les plus importants mécènes d'art belge pendant la guerre 14-18. Le couple déménage à Londres en 1900. Pendant les années de guerre, Jacob De Graaff rencontre trois artistes belges qui l'introduisent à l'art moderne. Il s'agit de Gustave Van de Woestyne, Léon de Smet et Edgard Tytgat, artistes exilés, ayant fui l'occupation allemande. Ces trois artistes introduisent De Graaff auprès de toute une série d'autres artistes belges résidant au Royaume-Uni. La plupart de ces artistes viennent de la colonie d'artistes de Laethem-Saint-Martin. En Grande-Bretagne, leur art n'est que rarement exposé dans des institutions publiques ou des galeries. De plus, ils sont presque entièrement écartés de l'organisation belge d'expositions de charité. Le mécénat privé de De Graaff est donc indispensable pour ces artistes, leur permettant de continuer à produire et à gagner leur vie.

La plupart des artistes soutenus par De Graaf se connaissent déjà avant la guerre. Ils forment un réseau bien rodé et promeuvent leur art et l'art de leurs collègues et amis auprès de De Graaff. Dans de multiples lettres ils mettent en avant l'art de leurs collègues et de manière plus pratique organisent des visites d'atelier pour De Graaff afin qu'il puisse lui-même s'assurer de la valeur artistique de ces Belges exilés.

Après la guerre les artistes retournent en Belgique. Des doutes s'installent quant à ce retour : la Belgique semble provinciale comparée à la capitale anglaise. En même temps, on doit accepter qu'à Londres, on ne va pas pouvoir s'établir et entamer une carrière. Le retour est facilité par le succès que l'expressionnisme flamand trouve en Belgique et par le soutien de certaines nouvelles galeries. Jacob De Graaff continue à acheter les œuvres des artistes rencontrés en Angleterre. Il ne s'intéresse néanmoins pas à d'autres artistes belges vivants. Son intérêt se porte plutôt sur les artistes parisiens dont il fait la connaissance par le biais du marché belge. Ses amis artistes l'introduisent ainsi dans les plus importantes galeries bruxelloises. Plusieurs des artistes deviennent même ses conseillers et commencent à acheter de l'art pour lui à Bruxelles ou à Paris. De Graaff semble faire entièrement confiance à ces artistes et avec leur aide commence à développer une importante collection d'œuvres modernes françaises et belges.

La dynamique entre artistes et mécène change donc après la guerre. Le couple De Graaff agit comme mécène et protecteur pendant la guerre, aidant les artistes belges à prendre pied en Angleterre. Après la guerre ces mêmes artistes ne dépendent plus du couple. Au contraire, c'est De Graaff qui maintenant demande de l'aide à ces anciens protégés, faisant appel à leur expertise artistique pour élargir sa collection d'art.

L'art belge pendant la Première Guerre mondiale. Expositions et Salons à Bruxelles

Werner Adriaenssens

Pendant la Première Guerre mondiale et contrairement à ce que l'on peut croire et à ce qui a été longtemps présumé, la vie artistique à Bruxelles continue sans relâche, malgré les conflits internationaux. Les occupants mènent une politique culturelle active, le marché de l'art est florissant et les expositions institutionnelles et privées sont nombreuses. Vu la lacune complète dans l'histoire des expositions en zone occupée, cette contribution propose un premier compte-rendu des activités à Bruxelles.

En 1914 à l'aube du conflit, Bruxelles a une saison d'expositions à succès jusqu'à l'invasion de l'armée allemande en Belgique. Le 1er août, les musées bruxellois ferment leurs portes, pour être rouverts plus tard dans l'année par le gouverneur général allemand Moritz von Bissing. Les activités d'exposition et de marché d'art vont reprendre également et le Salon des Beaux-Arts est alors la première grande exposition organisée pendant la Grande Guerre. Une partie des collectes de cette exposition vont à la Fédération professionnelle des Beaux-Arts, une association qui aide les artistes qui sont sans revenus depuis l'occupation allemande. Les expositions d'art belge organisées sous l'occupation et en exil sont certes souvent à but charitable, mais diffèrent les unes des autres, notamment par la sélection d'artistes. Ainsi, Paul Lambotte, exilé à Londres pendant la guerre, organise des événements de charité introduisant la capitale britannique à l'art belge. Beaucoup d'artistes accuseront Lambotte de désertion et d'un choix trop subjectif des œuvres montrées, pas représentatif des artistes les plus renommés de Belgique.

En 1915 rouvrent aussi bien les espaces d'exposition officiels que les galeries privées. La première exposition de galerie à ouvrir ses portes pendant l'occupation se tient à la Salle Studio, gérée par Isy Brachot. Contrairement aux institutions publiques, l'accent est ici mis sur la qualité plutôt que sur la quantité. À la galerie Georges Giroux, un nombre important d'expositions thématiques et d'expositions de groupe ont lieu. Le fait que tant d'expositions sont organisées dans ces galeries privées indique que le pouvoir d'achat est élevé. Une raison pour ceci peut être que pendant cette période de guerre, les œuvres d'art étaient un investissement prudent. Ce raisonnement purement économique n'a pas aidé à la promotion des jeunes artistes émergents.

Par ailleurs, pendant l'occupation, on investit plus vite dans des peintures que dans des sculptures ou dans l'art appliqué. Les expositions montrent surtout des peintures, non seulement à cause des préférences du public, mais aussi parce que certains matériaux, avant tout le bronze deviennent rares. Par ailleurs, les œuvres vendues ne représentent pas de scènes de destruction et de conflit, mais au contraire ont un aspect joyeux et idyllique. Ceci n'est pas dû à la censure. En effet, le gouvernement allemand n'a pas dû intervenir vu le caractère prosaïque de ces expositions. Il n'y avait simplement pas d'acheteurs pour de tels sujets moroses.

"Intercultural encounters" and occupation : a new momentum for the Belgo-German artistic transfers after 1918

Hubert Roland & Christina Kott

During the German occupation of Belgium in 1914-1918, the intercultural encounters intensified. A recent thesis by Hans-Jürgen Lüsebrink stipulates that war or occupation can indeed reinforce contacts and the curiosity in getting to know the other country, thus increasing cultural transfers. This contribution tries to analyse the impact of these transfers and their repercussions on the modification of collective identity schemes in the context of the active cultural propaganda of the *Flamenpolitik*.

The first part of the text concerns the project of the creation of a Flemish literary heritage, the *flämische Serie,* created by the director of the Insel-*Verlag*, Anton Kippenberg publishing house. This series gives an overview of the Flemish works throughout history, from the Middle Ages to the great classics of the 19th century, while at the same time allowing contemporary authors to have an international breakthrough.

This promotion of Flemish literature in Germany is not the sole result of the occupation and the *Flamenpolitik* but is inscribed in a long tradition of mutual interest that dates back to the Belgian revolution. Paradoxically, Kippenberg will publish many Flemish authors writing in French, contradicting the objective of the *Flamenpolitik* which seeks the Flemish emancipation of the French cultural model. This contradiction will prevail even when Kippenberg extends his publishing programme of Flemish literature during the Third Reich.

The second part of this contribution looks at the photographic inventory of the artistic heritage of Belgium assembled by German art historians, architects and photographers during the years of occupation. Here again, the role of the *Flamenpolitik* is obvious. The idea of exploring the Flemish territory and historic heritage with expansionist intentions is palpable. On closer inspection however, one realises that the political implications of this project are secondary. It is firstly a scientific project exploring the ancestral links between Germany and Belgium that could be found in the artistic styles and productions, while at the same time putting Germany on the map as experts in the field of photographic inventory, not only in Germany or Belgium but on an international level. After the heavy destruction in Louvain and Reims by German troops, this project was a way of rehabilitating the German supremacy when it came to preserving and valorising artistic heritage. During the occupation, the Belgian authorities are suspicious of and mainly reject this inventory and its authors. After the war and the repatriation of the photographs to Germany, Belgium considers this to be theft of a national good and a long chain of negotiations with Germany ensues in order to get the inventory back. In 1927, the Belgian state retrieves the inventory of over 10,000 plates.

The photographic inventory as well as the series of Flemish literature can, in the short term, be considered a nationalistic and expansionist enterprise. In the long term, however, one can consider both of them as a transnational transfer having repercussions up to today.

Précurseurs ou « Follower » ? Hannes Meyer, la scène artistique allemande et le rôle et l'image de l'art belge au temps de la Grande Guerre

Inga Rossi-Schrimpf

Les relations culturelles et littéraires entre la Belgique et le monde germanophone de l'art nouveau et du symbolisme, tout comme celles de l'avant-garde de l'entre-deux-guerres, ont été traitées dans la recherche récente. Dans cette contribution, l'attention est placée sur la relation entre image et image de soi de l'art belge dans la perception germanophone, ainsi que sur le facteur clé de la notion de terre-entre-deux.

Le point de départ de la contribution est l'article « Junge Kunst in Belgien » de l'architecte suisse Hannes Meyer publié en 1925 dans la revue *Das Werk*. En 1924, Meyer a collaboré à l'Exposition internationale des coopératives à Gand, où il fait connaissance d'acteurs importants de l'avant-garde belge tels que Paul-Gustave van Hecke, Victor Bourgeois et Jozef Peeters.

L'article de Meyer, de par la diversité des positions esthétiques belges présentées, peut être considéré comme le plus exhaustif de l'entre-deux-guerres en langue allemande. Meyer se sert également de l'image de la Belgique comme État tampon et pays de contradictions. Ces idées s'inscrivent dans une recherche d'identité qui date de la fin du XIXe siècle et sont renforcées lors de l'invasion et l'occupation allemande pendant la guerre. Ainsi Meyer évoque les concepts d'avant-guerre d'une Flandre mystique et d'une Wallonie industrialisée, tout en essayant de réconcilier Bruxelles et Anvers, en introduisant le nouvel internationalisme à travers *7 Arts* et *Het Overzicht*.

À partir de 1890, l'art belge et surtout la sculpture belge étaient très présents dans les Sécessions allemandes (et autrichiennes) et dans les cercles soutenant la réforme culturelle. Ainsi James Ensor, George Minne et d'autres connaissent un certain succès dans l'Allemagne de l'avant-guerre. Ces relations vont être perturbées par la guerre. Après l'occupation, les relations restent troublées. En même temps se développe un réseau d'artistes internationalistes et pacifistes favorisant le rapprochement d'artistes allemands et belges, autour de l'avant-garde abstraite ou de la revue *L'Art Libre* qui s'inscrit dans le mouvement Clarté. De son côté, l'expressionnisme flamand connaît une relation ambiguë avec son homonyme allemand.

En tenant compte de tous ces développements, on peut constater que l'art belge et son lien avec le monde germanophone se placent plutôt dans la continuité que dans la rupture, le mouvement de l'avant-garde internationale pouvant être considéré comme un interlude. Les artistes d'avant-guerre connaissent un nouvel apogée et l'identité double de l'art belge continue à être exploitée en réaction à la domination artistique française.

Lorsque Nationalisme flamand, progressivité et avant-garde coïncidaient (1917-1922)

Sergio Servellón

Tout comme dans d'autres pays européens, l'art abstrait apparaît en Belgique pendant les deux premières décennies du XXe siècle. Dans le contexte belge, cet art abstrait et constructiviste se lie au nationalisme flamand. C'est surtout à Anvers que se rassemblent de jeunes artistes qui veulent fusionner ces deux points pour créer une nouvelle société plus juste.

Les liens entre la jeune génération d'artistes et le mouvement flamand se tissent lors de la Première Guerre mondiale par la fondation de nombreuses associations et cercles artistiques, comme Doe Stil Voort. En 1918 est organisée une exposition où ce groupe de pionniers autour de Jozef Peeters, Felix de Boeck, Edmond Van Dooren et Prosper De Troyer expose leurs œuvres qui rompent radicalement avec les normes de la peinture. Willem Gijsels, initiateur de Doe Stil Voort, demande le soutien au Conseil de Flandre et inscrit ainsi le cercle dans un contexte politique. Ce rapprochement politique se manifeste aussi dans certains tableaux. L'activisme anversois date de la même période. Herman Vos, sociologue et journaliste, ensemble avec ses collègues Marten Rudelsheim, Anton Jacob ou Paul van Ostaijen, est à la base de celui-ci. Lors de son enfermement en prison après la guerre, il correspond avec son ami Eugeen De Bock. Se consolident alors les idées que l'art est une manière de protestation qui peut mener à une meilleure société. L'antidote à l'art individuel doit être un nouvel art « éthique ». Ces idées seront explorées dans la revue *Ruimte,* dont De Bock est l'éditeur. C'est ici qu'en 1920 est introduit pour la première fois le terme « art communautaire » (*'gemeenschapskunst'*) par Herman Vos. Il associe les idées de John Ruskin ou William Morris d'un art réconciliant l'esthétique et le social à la lutte de l'émancipation flamande.

Un des premiers acteurs à vouloir réunir art et politique est Paul van Ostaijen. Il considère qu'un art non individualiste ne peut pas émerger dans une société bourgeoise. Dans le contexte activiste, ses motivations socialistes prévalent sur la question de langue. Ainsi, lors de son exil à Berlin, il est en contact avec le *Spartakusbund* et reconnaît un lien entre la lutte flamande et la lutte socialiste des classes opprimées en Allemagne. Jozef Peeters lui aussi s'inscrit dans le réseau d'artistes manifestant de nouvelles revendications artistiques au sein de cercles activistes. Il organise les premières expositions du Kring Moderne Kunst, des lectures et des congrès dans des endroits emblématiques du mouvement flamand. De Bock et Vos y jouent également un rôle important. Ils donnent des conférences aux congrès et publient des articles sur les événements dans *Ruimte*.

Il est remarquable que *Ruimte* soit encore souvent considéré comme un événement marginal dans l'histoire de l'art de l'entre-deux-guerres. Il s'agit pourtant d'une plateforme au beau milieu entre engagement social et renouvellement de la forme, d'où partent des impulsions pour examiner le rôle de l'art au sein de la société.

Albert Daenens (1882-1952) : Artiste belge de Bruxelles, activiste flamand, publiciste français, anarchiste international et antimilitariste, avant, pendant et après la Première Guerre mondiale

Erik Buelinckx

L'artiste, anarchiste, antimilitariste et activiste flamand Albert Daenens est encore peu connu, malgré ou peut-être à cause de ses activités disparates. L'examen de son énorme fonds d'archives permet de mettre en valeur cet artiste qui mérite sa place dans le discours artistique belge et international.

Daenens appartient à des cercles anarchistes et révolutionnaires bruxellois. Il fait la découverte de ces cercles probablement dans des cafés et cabarets alternatifs et commence à collaborer à plusieurs revues radicales. Dans *La Foi nouvelle*, il est mentionné en tant que contributeur dès le premier numéro. Il dessine la couverture et est responsable des articles sur les arts appliqués. La participation de Maurice Casteels, écrivain belge, à *La Foi Nouvelle* à partir de 1912 est vraisemblablement à la base de la rencontre des deux artistes qui mènera à la fondation de la revue *Haro !* en 1913. Encore une fois, Daenens s'occupe de l'illustration de la couverture. À l'intérieur de la revue sont reprises des œuvres d'Abel Gerbaud, de Marcel Bouraine et de Ferdinand Schirren, artistes ayant déjà contribué à *La Foi Nouvelle*. Des œuvres de Rik Wouters et Léon Spilliaert trouveront également leur place dans *Haro !*. La première série de *Haro !* s'arrête soudainement en janvier 1914 suite à l'accroissement tangible d'une rhétorique de guerre dans la société belge et internationale. Le discours radical et pacifiste de *Haro !* atteint de moins en moins de lecteurs, même au sein de l'avant-garde.

Il est difficile de retracer les pas de Daenens pendant les années de guerre. Toujours à court d'argent, il travaille en tant qu'illustrateur pour la revue *Vlaamsch Leven*, publiée par son ami Willem Gijssels. Tandis que ces illustrations tout comme d'autres commandes ne témoignent pas d'audace artistique, son œuvre personnelle devient plus expérimentale, explorant la gravure sur bois aux contrastes achromes. Ces gravures sont montrées à l'exposition *Doe Stil Voort* à Bruxelles en été 1918. Après la guerre Daenens réinstalle sa revue *Haro !* en 1919. Le ton de la revue reste sévère et radical mettant l'accent sur l'antimilitarisme d'après-guerre. Les illustrations de Daenens dominent, mais il introduit également des œuvres de l'exposition *Doe Stil Voort* tout comme des gravures de Frans Masereel, pacifiste belge internationalement reconnu. *Haro !* ouvre ses pages aux nouveaux courants artistiques tels le dadaïsme de Clément Pansaers et Paul Joostens, l'art abstrait, dans lequel Daenens lui-même s'exprime, et la nouvelle technique de la linogravure.

En 1927 apparaît la troisième et dernière série de *Haro !*. Le travail de Daenens s'inscrit de plus en plus dans le mouvement pacifiste international et son œuvre est publiée dans multiples revues et ouvrages à travers le monde.

Génération 1910 et 1920 : perdue et unifiée dans l'art communautaire

Hans Vandevoorde

Les tensions entre vieux et jeunes et entre individus et communautés forment les sujets capitaux de cet article. Ils sont projetés sur les générations ayant vécu avant, pendant et après la Première Guerre mondiale, à savoir la génération 1910 et la génération 1920. Les deux générations se distinguent par leur style. La première se compose des descendants de l'art subjectif de l'impressionnisme, la deuxième se tourne vers l'avant-garde historique et sa revendication d'art communautaire qui se manifeste dans un art objectif et abstrait.

La notion de génération peut selon le sociologue et philosophe Karl Mannheim être divisée en trois parties (*Generationslagerung, Generationszusammenhang* et *Generationseinheit*). Le travail essaye de placer l'avant-garde radicale dans ses trois parties en relation avec les courants simultanés et les générations précédentes et antécédentes. La classification en générations permet une lecture transnationale et sociale.

Les générations d'artistes et d'auteurs d'environ 1910 et 1920 en Belgique n'ont pas encore reçu beaucoup d'attention. Ceci en partie parce que l'idée théorique de génération n'est plus courante. La première génération, la « lost generation » de la Grande Guerre est réduite fortement par la guerre. La génération de 1920, dont nombreux sont ceux qui s'engagent dans l'activisme pendant la guerre, se tourne vers l'abstraction et le constructivisme au moment où leurs collègues plus âgés découvrent l'expressionnisme. Dans la première génération, nous trouvons néanmoins des figures intermédiaires comme Prosper de Troyer qui prennent le rôle de mentor pour la génération suivante.

Ce point de départ des générations permet d'observer que l'abstraction se manifeste plus tard et a moins de membres féminins en Belgique que par exemple en Russie. Le manque d'un précurseur de ce courant dans la première génération est certainement une raison de ce retard. Les deux générations s'inscrivent encore dans l'héritage de James Ensor, des XX et de la Libre Esthétique. En même temps, la deuxième génération arrive à créer un style générationnel : l'abstraction géométrique, ainsi qu'un genre générationnel : l'architecture d'intérieur (*interieurkunst*).

D'un point de vue transnational, on constate que le développement de la deuxième génération belge est similaire aux développements internationaux avec une dissociation entre l'art aux motivations politiques (expressionnisme et constructivisme révolutionnaire) et l'art aux tendances plus autonomes (suprématisme et abstraction géométrique). Enfin, en Belgique comme ailleurs, les deux générations, bien que différentes, se rencontrent, échangent des idées, rivalisent et se célèbrent.

L'originalité du constructivisme de '7 Arts' : la connexion avec la scène belge d'avant-guerre

EVA FRANCIOLI

La revue *7 Arts* est fondée en 1922 par Victor et Pierre Bourgeois, Pierre-Louis Flouquet, Karel Maes et Georges Monier avec le but premier de promouvoir l'art moderne et l'interdisciplinarité des arts, condition indispensable pour sa pénétration dans la société. Les principes esthétiques de *7 Arts* s'alignent sur ceux de l'avant-garde internationale. Cette avant-garde est introduite à Bruxelles entre autres par Théo van Doesburg en 1920, par la fondation du groupe Sélection en 1920 ou encore par l'écrivain russe Ilya Ehrenbourg qui séjourne à Bruxelles en 1921.

L'objectif de *7 Arts* de créer un nouveau vocabulaire visuel est ancré dans la tradition belge de l'avant-guerre avec notamment le symbolisme et l'art nouveau comme exemples de créations inédites. En effet, certains fondateurs de *7 Arts* connaissent très bien les propos symbolistes, ayant été éduqués à l'Académie Royale des Beaux-Arts par des professeurs symbolistes. Dans l'art nouveau, ils apprécient la fusion de la création artistique et de la production industrielle. Ces propos sont abordés à plusieurs reprises dans la revue à travers l'œuvre de Victor Horta et de Henry van de Velde. Ce dernier sera même considéré par *7 Arts* comme un des précurseurs du style moderne.

Pour ce qui est des luttes culturelles et politiques centrales pour *7 Arts*, il est important de renvoyer aux fonctionnements sociétaux promus dans des revues du XIXe siècle tel *L'Art Moderne*. Cette revue, qui souligne les aspects sociaux et éducatifs que peut avoir une œuvre d'art, publie ses articles sans qu'ils soient signés. *7 Arts* va faire de même. Les intérêts sociaux de *7 Arts* sont également liés à la Section d'Art et d'Enseignement de la Maison du Peuple, fondée en 1891 par le Parti ouvrier belge et réanimée en 1924 par *7 Arts*. Parallèlement à la fondation de la Section d'Art apparaît en 1892 la revue *L'Art Social* qui publie des contributions de Camille Lemonnier, Georges Eekhoud, Émile Verhaeren et Émile Vandervelde, auteurs qui jouent un rôle prépondérant dans les réflexions de *7 Arts*.

Selon Maurice Casteels, contributeur régulier de *7 Arts*, l'art ne peut être moderne que s'il a une connotation sociale. Un objet usuel, produit à grande échelle, comme la revue *7 Arts*, peut également s'inscrire dans ce cadre et peut être considéré comme une expression d'art social à part entière. *7 Arts* puise donc dans les mouvements belges de l'avant-guerre tout en étant tourné vers l'avenir.

Artists' networks before and after the war: the exemplary case of the Section d'or

FRANÇOISE LUCBERT

Since the history of the Section d'or can be divided into two distinct periods, one before and one after World War I, the question of a before and after as suggested by the symposium can also be analysed. The paper tries to understand to what degree the new cosmopolitanism of the second Section d'or is linked to the changes that the First World War brings about. At the same time it acknowledges the fact that the post-war group still works under the same name and is thus imbedded in a certain continuity.

Only seven artists of the pre-war Section d'or are still showing at the post-war Section d'or. The group thus undergoes an important renewal that is also determined by the diverse origins of the exhibiting artists. Of the 33 artists showing in the exhibitions of the 1920s only nine are French, a considerable change compared to the exhibition in 1912 and either reflecting the new importance of a cosmopolitan opening in avant-garde art or rather the desertion of the group by French artists.

One of these foreign artists is the Belgian Marthe Donas. She works in Paris and through her connections with Alexander Archipenko is joining the Section d'Or. The artist Albert Daenens, through his friendship with Abel Gerbaud, had some less direct contacts with certain members of the group.

In December 1920, the Section d'or will hold an exhibition in Brussels. They did so at Sélection, an atypical exhibition space founded by André De Ridder and Paul-Gustave van Hecke. The avant-garde style of the Section d'or was not widely recognised In Brussels and thus the show in Sélection required a certain audacity by its organisers. The show falls into a bigger exhibition programme of de Ridder and Van Hecke promoting "modern international tendencies" in Brussels and Antwerp.

Most of the actors in and around the Section d'or are marked by internationalist ideologies. Many of them had some kind of affiliation to the *Clarté* movement. Thus the writer Florent Fels is developing a friendship with the Belgian representative of *Clarté*, Paul Colin. Fels, a member of the Section d'or, as well as Alexandre Mercreau, a friend of many of its members, also collaborate with Sélection's eponymous magazine.

The Section d'or is not isolated from the art market of the time. With the gallery system becoming more and more professionalised and exclusive contracts becoming more normal, the associative character of the Section d'or forms a certain protection against the mercantile pressures of the art world. This association grants the artist liberties while at the same time being precarious as it relies exclusively on the goodwill of its organising committee.

A couple of artists of the Section d'or can be considered real businessmen. This promotion of one's own art in the context of the Section d'or does not mean the negation of the promotion of the art of others. It has thus an active implication in the art world, promoting the art of all its members.

At the Section d'or exhibitions many different esthetics coexist. The association never shared a common "style" but rather understood itself as a way of assembling people from different aesthetic horizons and giving them a chance to come together rather than to be isolated in an art world that becomes more and more competitive.

De l'avant-garde à l'arrière-garde ? – L'œuvre architecturale d'Henry van de Velde avant et après la Première Guerre mondiale

OLE W. FISCHER

La période de l'avant-guerre représente pour l'artiste, architecte, théoricien et enseignant flamand Henry van de Velde, des années de crise personnelle et artistique. Étant un des fondateurs de l'art nouveau – étiquette qu'il a toujours rejetée – il doit reconnaître que l'époque de ce courant a définitivement pris fin après l'exposition de Dresde en 1906. Sa recherche d'alternatives inclut le régionalisme (Villa T. Spinger 1914-16), le néoclassicisme (Monument Nietzsche à Weimar 1911-1913) et le retrait vers l'esthétisme néo-rococo (Palais Dürckheim 1912-1913). Toutes ces conceptions ne sont pas satisfaisantes et loin de ses plans avant-gardistes et de ses appels théoriques à une rupture radicale avec l'histoire de la fin de siècle. De plus, il se sent isolé dans la ville provinciale de Weimar, déchiré par le chagrin du sous-financement de l'école des arts appliqués, offensé par les intrigues de la cour grand-ducale et désillusionné par le chauvinisme qu'il affronte à Paris avec son projet du Théâtre des Champs-Élysées (1911-1913), à Gand à l'exposition universelle de 1913 ou en Allemagne où on le traite avec méfiance parce qu'il est étranger.

Avec la construction du théâtre de l'exposition du *Werkbund* à Cologne en 1914 il semble avoir retrouvé sa force antérieure et combine les considérations fonctionnelles avec la nouvelle technologie. À côté de Bruno Taut et de Walter Gropius, il est un des seuls architectes à ne pas devenir victime du néoclassicisme ou du néo-Biedermeier. Van de Velde sortira également victorieux d'un débat ardent avec l'architecte Hermann Muthesius qui se termine à peu de choses près par la dissolution du *Werkbund*.

Ce développement de Van de Velde au sein du *Werkbund* s'arrête brusquement avec le déclenchement de la Grande Guerre en août 1914. À cause de la mobilisation militaire, l'exposition du *Werkbund* doit fermer avant l'heure. Le théâtre de Van de Velde n'atteint jamais son potentiel et ne produit pas les pièces avant-gardistes que l'architecte espérait. De plus il ne peut pas exécuter son rôle de leader au *Werkbund* qui aurait dû renouveler l'institution. Le *Werkbund* est immergé dans l'économie de guerre et Van de Velde, dénué des récoltes de ses succès, est pris en otage par la bureaucratie de guerre du Grand-Duché de Weimar avant de trouver exil en Suisse en 1917.

Après la guerre et une première tentative de s'établir au lac de Constance, Van de Velde accepte la position d'architecte de la famille Kröller-Müller aux Pays-Bas. Son style d'après-guerre ne suit néanmoins pas la ligne évolutionnaire du théâtre du *Werkbund*. Van de Velde travaille dans un style pathétique avec des références historiques maladroites, pendant qu'une jeune génération d'architectes explore les possibilités d'abstraction, de purisme, de technologie et de fonctionnalisme rationnel. Il ressent de nouveau le besoin de se réinventer, cette fois-ci en tant que moderniste humaniste, non pas à la tête d'un mouvement, mais plutôt en tant que commentateur et gardien des valeurs modernes.

« Votre lettre m'a bien intéressée », Marthe « Tour » Donas et la scène artistique vers 1920

PETER J.H. PAUWELS

Ces dernières années, l'œuvre de Marthe Donas a été redécouverte à travers plusieurs expositions importantes. Artiste belge, c'est à Paris, où elle séjourne pendant la guerre, qu'elle s'inscrit dans un réseau d'avant-garde internationale. Élève d'André Lhote et d'Alexander Archipenko, elle explore le collage et la simplification des formes. La figure féminine devient un de ses thèmes de prédilection.

Marthe Donas, comme beaucoup d'autres femmes artistes de l'époque est victime de son sexe. La notion que le vrai génie artistique, et avant tout celui du cubisme et de l'art abstrait, ne peut être que masculin, est encore courante. Elle décide donc, sous le conseil d'Archipenko, de signer ses œuvres Tour Donas, nom neutre et donc présumé masculin. Le réseau que Donas a su se construire pendant et après la guerre porte ses fruits. Elle expose en 1919 aux côtés d'entre autres Matisse, Picasso et Zadkine à Londres. La même année, elle a sa première exposition monographique à Genève. En 1920, elle montre ses œuvres dans la galerie Der Sturm à Berlin. Marthe Donas est également membre du cercle artistique La Section d'or qui organise de multiples expositions en France et dans les pays voisins. Après des expositions aux Pays-Bas, la Section d'or veut exposer à Bruxelles. Après de nombreuses négociations avec des galeries bruxelloises, c'est en 1920 que Donas est contactée par Andrée De Ridder, qui lui propose d'exposer avec la Section d'or dans sa toute nouvelle galerie Sélection. En décembre, De Ridder, Donas et Van Doesburg organisent ensemble l'exposition dans la capitale belge. C'est la première fois que Donas expose dans son pays natal.

Marthe Donas est reprise dans les expositions de groupe organisées par Herwarth Walden dans sa galerie Der Sturm. En 1921, Donas est visitée par Jozef Peeters qui l'invite à présenter pas moins de 12 peintures au Deuxième Congrès d'Art Moderne à Anvers qu'il organise en 1922. Ici, elle expose ses recherches abstraites. Cependant, avec son retour en Belgique en 1923, Donas commence à réintégrer la figuration dans son œuvre.

Suite au manque de reconnaissance de l'avant-garde abstraite en Belgique des années 20, Donas s'arrête de peindre en 1928. Ce n'est qu'après la Deuxième Guerre mondiale et la relance des premiers abstraits que Marthe Donas reprend son pinceau en main. Néanmoins, son art n'atteint plus jamais le niveau extraordinaire des années 20.

About the Authors

WERNER ADRIAENSSENS - Professor of Decorative Arts at the Vrije Universiteit Brussel / Conservator of the– 20th century Collection at the Royal Museums of Art and History, Brussels, Belgium

Werner Adriaenssens has a PhD in Archeology and Sciences of Art (Vrije Universiteit Brussel). Since 2000, he is curator of the department Decorative Arts of the 20th century of the Royals Museums of Arts and History (Brussels). His policy is characterized on the one hand by well-though purchases for the widening of the collections and on the other hand by renewed studies of subjects about the Belgian Art-nouveau and Art-déco periods which are published regularly. He is curator of different exhibitions, such as De Wolfer Dynastie (Design museum Gent, 2006-2007), Royal tables (BEL-Vue, 2012) and of the large retrospective Henry van de Velde Passion, Function, Beauty (Royal Museums of Art and History, 2013-2014). He is besides professor of applied arts at the Vrije Universiteit Brussel. He was associated as researcher to the Royal Institute for Cultural Heritage from 2014 to 2016.

ERIK BUELINCKX - Scientific assistant at the Royal Institute of artistic heritage, Brussels, Belgium

Erik Buelinckx (°1959) is an art historian working as scientific assistant at the Royal Institute of Cultural Heritage (KIK-IRPA) in Brussels. He's responsible at the documentation department for digitization, databases, thesauri and terminologies, and for regional, national and international projects in these domains. He's currently finishing a PhD at the Vrije Universiteit Brussel (VUB) on the subject of *Anarchist influences in Belgian art from 1850 to 1940*. He has published on *Henry van de Velde, Art Nouveau and intellectual anarchism*, on digitizing photographic archives, on the 1783 pages long film scenario *Mauer* by the French libertarian 'artistocrat' Gérard de Lacaze-Duthiers, and most recently on the once lost but now rediscovered theatre play *De Stem uit de Diepte (1914-15)* by Theo van Doesburg, found in the archives of and translated into French by Albert Daenens. The anarchist antimilitarist artist Daenens, and his surprising network, is currently at the centre of his research.

OLE W. FISCHER - Assistant Professor History and Theory of Architecture at the School of Architecture at the University of Utah, United States of America

Dr. Ole W. Fischer studied architecture at the Bauhaus University Weimar and the Eidgenössische Technische Hochschule (ETH) Zurich. Between 2002-08 he taught at the Institute of History and Theory of Architecture (gta) of ETH Zurich, where he also obtained his PhD In his thesis he analyzed the programmatic transcription of the philosophy of Friedrich Nietzsche into theory and work of Henry van de Velde In summer 2004 and 2005 he was a research fellow of Klassik Stiftung Weimar, in spring 2005 a visiting PhD fellow at Harvard GSD, and in 2008–09 fellow in residence of Akademie Schloss Solitude, Stuttgart. In spring 2009 he returned as postdoc research fellow to Harvard GSD to work on the history of critical theory in architecture. In fall 2009 he was an visiting adjunct professor for history and theory of architecture at RISD Providence, in spring 2010 a visiting assistant professor at the HTC program of MIT school of architecture and planning and co-curator & general commissioner of the German pavilion themed "Sehnsucht" at the Biennale di Venezia 2010. In summer 2010 he was appointed as assistant professor for history & theory of architecture at the School of Architecture at the University of Utah, Salt Lake City, where he continues to research and teach since spring 2011. In summer 2015 he served as visiting professor for architectural theory at the Technical University of Vienna.

EVA FRANCIOLI - Editor at the Museo Novecento, Florence / Teaching assistant at the University of Florence, Italy

Eva Francioli got a PhD at the Graduate School of Architecture, Design and Art History of the University of Florence, where she discussed a thesis on the network of Constructivist reviews in the interwar period, under the direction of Prof. Alessandro Nigro. She's "cultore della materia" at the University of Florence and currently works at the Museo Novecento of Florence. She held lessons at the University of Florence and participated as a teacher at the didactic project "Arte per tutti (Art for All)", promoted by Centro per l'Arte Contemporanea Luigi Pecci Prato, in 2014-2015. She has worked as a tutor in History of Contemporary Art at the Middlebury College School in Italy, Florence and participated as Contemporary art mediator at the project "Open Studios", promoted by Centro di Cultura Contemporanea Strozzina, Fondazione Palazzo Strozzi Firenze.

LAURA KOLLWELTER - Scientific researcher at the Royal Museums of Fine Arts of Belgium, Brussels, Belgium

Studied Art History at the Université Libre de Bruxelles and La Sapienza – Università di Roma. As an independent researcher, she has contributed to several publications on the cultural transfers of Belgian and German art in the beginning of the 20th century. From 2016 to 2018 she was a scientific researcher at the Royal Museums of Fine Arts of Belgium where she works on the Project "14-18, Continuity or Rupture". Research fields: Reception of abstract art in Belgium (interbellum), Belgian and German cultural transfers, Patronage during World War I.

CHRISTINA KOTT - Maitre de conférence à l'Université du Panthéon-Assas, Université Paris 2, France

Née à Karlsruhe en Allemagne, elle a étudié l'histoire et la philologie allemande à Düsseldorf et à Paris, où elle est par ailleurs docteure en histoire de l'École des Hautes Études en Science sociales. Sa thèse de doctorat avait pour thème « Protéger, confisquer, déplacer. Le service allemand de préservation d'œuvres d'art (Kunstschutz) en Belgique et en France occupées pendant la Première Guerre mondiale (1914-1924) » (publiée en 2006, cf. publications). Depuis 2005, elle est maître de conférences auprès de l'Université Panthéon-Assas à Paris. Elle a été membre non-résidente de l'Association Paul J. Getty en 2008-2009 et devient la curatrice scientifique de l'exposition « Sauve qui veut. Des archéologues et des musées mobilisés, 1914-1918 à Douai et Bavay (dans le Nord de la France) » entre 2012 et 2014. En 2016 et 2017, elle fait partie du projet de recherche auprès de l'IRPA à Bruxelles consacré aux « clichés allemands ». Ses sujets de recherches sont : l'histoire de l'héritage culturel, les European transfer studies, l'historiographie de l'art, la muséologie, l'histoire de la photographie de monuments.

FRANÇOISE LUCBERT - Professeure d'histoire de l'art à l'Université Laval, Québec, Canada

Françoise Lucbert est professeure d'histoire de l'art au Département des Sciences historiques de l'Université Laval, à Québec. Spécialiste de l'époque du symbolisme et du cubisme, elle s'intéresse plus particulièrement à la critique d'art, à l'histoire des expositions, aux rapports entre la littérature et les autres arts, aux écrits d'artistes, de même qu'aux relations artistiques entre la France et les autres pays européens. Elle a publié la synthèse Entre le voir et le dire. La critique d'art dans la presse symboliste en France de 1882 à 1906 (2005) et dirige une collection sur la critique d'art aux Presses universitaires de Rennes. Elle a réalisé plusieurs expositions en collaboration avec des musées en France, en Espagne et en Chine : La Section d'or 1912-1920-1925 (2000), Roger de La Fresnaye (1885-1925). Cubisme et tradition (2005), Gustave Kahn (1859-1936), écrivain symboliste et critique d'art (2006) et Avion, aviateur, aviation. Cent ans de fascination pour la conquête de l'air (2008). Ses travaux actuels portent sur les prolongements européens du cubisme au cours des années 1920.

PETER PAUWELS - Independent researcher

Peter J.H. Pauwels (°1963), Honorary Notary Public, Master at Law and Notarial Studies (Universities of Antwerp and Ghent), Master in Art History (University of Ghent) is an independant researcher. He collaborated on several publications and/or exhibitions on Belgian art in the Interwar period (e.g. P.-G. van Hecke (MRBAB, Brussels), Modernism (MSK, Ghent), E.L.T. Mesens (MuZee, Ostend), Saverys (Mudel, Deinze), ...) He published several articles and a monograph on Marthe Donas, advised the Von der Heydt Museum in Wuppertal (Der Sturm, 2012) and Schirn Halle in Frankfurt (Sturm-Frauen) in the selection of her work and curated a Donas-exhibition at the MSK in Ghent (2016). He currently works on a monograph on the sculptor Jozef Cantré.

HUBERT ROLAND - Professeur à l'Université Catholique de Louvain (UCL), Louvain-la-Neuve, Belgique.

Hubert Roland est Maître de Recherches du Fonds de la Recherche Scientifique-FNRS belge et professeur à l'Université catholique de Louvain (UCL). Il est boursier de la Fondation Alexander von Humboldt, a séjourné et enseigné aux universités de Marburg (1999-2001), de Münster (2009) et de La Réunion (2010). Ses centres d'intérêt principaux portent sur l'histoire des transferts culturels et littéraires entre la Belgique et les pays de langue allemande, le réalisme magique / *magischer Realismus* dans la littérature allemande et européenne et l'historiographie comparée des avant-gardes (guerre et littérature, primitivisme littéraire). Il est directeur de la collection « comparatisme et société » (P.I.E.-Peter Lang).

INGA ROSSI-SCHRIMPF - Curator of works on paper modern art at the Royal Museums of Fine Arts of Belgium and Coordinating Curator of the Fin-de-Siècle Museum, Brussels, Belgium

Ph.D. (Dr. phil.), Dissertation: The early work of George Minne and its reception in Germany and Austria; she studied History of Art, French literature and Applied Cultural Studies/ Cultural Management in Münster (Germany) and Louvain-la-Neuve (Belgium). Since 2000 at the Royal Museums of Fine Arts of Belgium and currently curator of modern works on paper as well as Coordinating Curator of the Fin-de-Siècle Museum, she is promotor of the project '14-18, Continuity or Rupture' within the RMFAB. Most recent publications or conference papers include "'Terribly modern'. Belgian artists and the Secessionist battle for Modern Art", "Der Rembrandtdeutsche. George Minne, Gothicism and German Rootedness", "L'âme des choses!: Aspects of Belgian-Nordic affinities in Fin-de-Siècle". Research fields: Belgian art of the turn of the century until the Interbellum; reception studies; artistic and cultural transfers between Belgium and Germanic countries; history of Belgian drawing.

SOPHIE DE SCHAEPDRIJVER - Professor at The Pennsylvania State University, Pennsylvania, United States of America

Sophie De Schaepdrijver, professor of modern European history at The Pennsylvania State University (USA), is a historian of the First World War with a special interest in gender, class, the uses of language, and military occupations. Her most recent books are Military Occupations in the First World War (edited, 2014); Bastion: Occupied Bruges in the First World War (2014); Gabrielle Petit: The Death and Life of a Female Spy in the First World War (2015); and An English Governess in the Great War: The Secret Brussels Diary of Mary Thorp (with Tammy Proctor; 2017). In 2016-2017, she held a Leverhulme Visiting Professorship at the University of Kent (UK), where she delivered a series of lectures on the military occupations of the First World War.

SERGIO SERVELLÓN - General and artistic director of the FeliXart Museum, Drogenbos, Belgium

Studied at the Royal Academy of Fine Arts Antwerp and Cultural Management at Antwerp University. Since 2005, he has been director of FeliXart Museum, which he has reoriented from a monographic to a thematic museum with a focus on the Belgian historical avant-garde movement in the inter-war period. In 2012, the museum brought the surprising reconstruction *Grenoble 1927, a panorama of Belgian art*. In connection with abstract art, he has organised retrospective exhibitions of pioneers like Karel Maes, Paul Joosten, Maurice Carlier, and second generation abstract artists like Paul Van Hoeydonck and Jan Yoors. In 2012, he published a catalogue raisonné of the drawings of Felix De Boeck and in 2013 a monograph on the author-artist Michel Seuphor. He also worked as program coordinator of the Conservation and Restoration Studies of the Artesis Hogeschool Antwerp from to 2009-2011. He is currently preparing the site theme 'Abstract Modernism' for the Flemish Art Collection.

Sandrine SMETS - Chef du Service Projets / Assistante Collections Première Guerre mondiale au Musée royal de l'Armée et d'Histoire militaire, Bruxelles

Licenciée en Histoire de l'Art et Archéologie (Université Libre de Bruxelles 1995), Sandrine Smets est également titulaire d'un Diplôme d'Etudes approfondies à l'Ecole doctorale Histoire, Cultures et Sociétés (ULB 2006). Elle a entrepris une thèse de doctorat ayant pour thème Les artistes belges face à la Grande Guerre (ULB). Depuis 2003, elle travaille au Musée royal de l'Armée et d'Histoire militaire à Bruxelles en qualité d'Assistante Collections Première Guerre mondiale. Elle a assuré le commissariat scientifique de plusieurs expositions Le pinceau au fusil. La guerre 1914-1918 en peinture ; Wilchar, un artiste dans la résistance ; Chienne de guerre ! Les animaux dans la Grande Guerre 1914-1918 ; 14-18, c'est notre histoire. En 2011, elle prend la direction du service scientifique qui gère les collections de 1914 à nos jours. Dans la perspective du centenaire, elle a mis sur pied un cycle d'expositions temporaires Reflet(s) de la Grande Guerre. Actuellement, elle dirige le Service Projets et coordonne le groupe de travail chargé de l'élaboration de la nouvelle scénographie de la +salle 1914-1918 dans le cadre des commémorations de 2014-2018.

Hans VANDEVOORDE - Coordinator of the Study Centre Experimental Literature (CEL/SEL) at the Vrije Universiteit Brussel / Chief editor of the *Cahier voor Literatuurwetenschap* (CLW), Brussels, Belgium

Hans Vandevoorde is associated to the Vrije Universiteit Brussels as professor of Dutch literature. He publishes over literature and culture of the 19th and 20th century and over contemporary poetry. He is editor in chief of the Cahier voor Literatuurwetenschap and he coordinate the group of research CEL (Study Centre Experimental Literature) in collaboration with Lars Bernaerts & Bart Vervaeck.

Caterina VERDICKT - Researcher and lecturer of History of Interior Architecture 1850 – 1950 at the Faculty of Design Sciences at the Antwerp University, Antwerp, Belgium

Caterina Verdickt graduated magna cum laude from KU Leuven in 1999. Her master thesis "*Belgische kunstenaars in Groot-Brittannië tijdens de Eerste Wereldoorlog. 1914-1918*" examined Belgian artists in exile. In 2002 she was co-curator of the international exhibition *'Art in Exile. Flanders, Wales and the Great War'* with Robert Hoozee and Oliver Fairclough, which had venues in Belgium, the Netherlands and Great Britain. Caterina Verdickt also researched the opportunities of a partnership between the Museums of Fine Arts in Flanders. This resulted in the set-up and founding of the *Vlaamsekunstcollectie*, for which she was the first liaison-officer. Currently she teaches the history of interior design at the University of Antwerp where she is finalizing her PhD entitled "*The Realm of Silence. Consequences of the Belgian artistic migration towards Great Britain during the Great War on post war Belgian interior design*". She has lectured widely on the Belgian Artistic Exile Community during the Great War, most recently at the University of Cardiff, the University of Aberystwyth and the University of Stirling in Scotland. In 2014 she provided the keynote lecture at the 2014 'International Arts Festival - War' in Wales, and her research has been published in *The British Art Journal*.

Bibliography

Adams, Myrah. *Julius Baum. Museumsdirektor zwischen Tradition und Moderne.* Ulm: Ulmer Museum, 2005.

Adriaens-Pannier, Anne, ed. *L'avant-garde en Belgique, 1917–1929.* Bruxelles: Crédit Communal, 1992.

Amara, Michaël. "Une icône... des propagandes au cœur du conflit. Les grands défis de la propagande belge durant la Première Guerre mondiale." In *La petite Belgique dans la Grande Guerre. Une icône, des images. Actes du colloque de Namur 24-27/11/2010*, edited by Bénédicte Rochet and Axel Tixhon. Namur: Presses universitaires de Namur, 2012: 21–35.

Amara, Michäel. *Des Belges à l'épreuve de l'exil: Les réfugiés de la Première guerre mondiale / France, Grande-Bretagne, Pays-Bas, 1914–1918.* 2e tirage. Histoire 1. Bruxelles, Paris, Le Plessis-Pâté: Éditions de l'Université de Bruxelles; diff. Sodis; diff. ToThèmes, 2014.

Ameskamp, Simone. "On Fire: Cremation in Germany, 1870s–1934." PhD diss. Georgetown University, 2006.

———. "Fanning the Flames: Cremation in late imperial and Weimar Germany." In *Between Mass Death And Individual Loss: The Place of the Dead in Twentieth-Century Germany*, edited by Alon Confino, Paul Betts and Dirk Schuman. Berghahn Books, 2013: 93–112.

Anonymous. "7 Arts." *La Cité* 7 (1922): 147–148.

Anonymous. "À Anvers." *Le Progrès,* 12 avril, 1915.

Anonymous. *A Book of Belgium's Gratitude.* London, 1916.

Anonymous. "À Bruxelles. L'exposition de 1914." *L'Indépendance belge*, 20 juin, 1918.

Anonymous. "À la Fédération Professionnelle des Beaux-Arts." *Le Bruxellois*, 17 septembre, 1915.

Anonymous. "À la Salle Giroux." *Le Messager de Bruxelles,* 16 mai, 1915.

Anonymous. "À la Salle Studio." *L'Écho de la presse internationale*, 17 décembre 1914.

Anonymous. "À la Salle Studio." *La Belgique*, 27 décembre, 1914.

Anonymous. "À la Salle Studio." *Le Quotidien*, 18 décembre, 1914.

Anonymous. "À la Salle Studio." *Le Quotidien*, 1 janvier, 1915.

Anonymous. "À travers les ventes publiques." *Le Messager de Bruxelles*, 20 décembre, 1916.

Anonymous. "Albert Daenens, een "obscuur" leven in dienst van de kunst." In *"De Vijf + Één". Jan-Frans Cantré, Jozef Cantré, Frans Masereel, Joris Minne, Henri Van Straten + Albert Daenens*, edited by Jan De Kelver. Drogenbos: Stichting Felix De Boeck en v.z.w. Museum Felix De Boeck, 2003: 20–21.

Anonymous. "Arts and Crafts." *Journal of the Royal Society of Arts*, Vol. 63, No. 3251, March, (1915): 379–381.

Anonymous. "Au Studio." *Le Bruxellois*, 15 août, 1915.

Anonymous. "Autumn Exhibition at the Goupil Gallery." *The Connoisseur*, Vol. 41, No. 161, January 1915: 54.

Anonymous. "Chronique artistique. Le Salon d'Automne de 1915." *Le Messager de Bruxelles*, 21 octobre, 1915.

Anonymous. "Dernières dépêches." *Le Messager de Bruxelles*, 3 janvier, 1915.

Anonymous. "Exposition de la Galerie Giroux." *La Belgique*, 13 mai, 1915.

Anonymous. "Flandern" Special issue, *Der Sturm: Monatsschrift für Kultur und die Künste* 15, 1 (März) (1924).

Anonymous. "Important vol au Salon Triennal." *Le Quotidien*, 15 mai, 1915.

Anonymous. "L'Art et les Boches." *L'Étoile Belge*, 1 décembre, 1918.

Anonymous. "L'Ecrivain", *Le Geste* 3 (1920): 18.

Anonymous. "L'Exposition Nationale." *Le Messager de Bruxelles*, 2 septembre, 1916.

Anonymous. "L'Ouverture du Salon d'Automne." *Le Progrès*, 5 octobre, 1915.

Anonymous. "La détresse des artistes." *Le Quotidien*, 18 novembre, 1914.

Anonymous. "La Foi nouvelle." *La Foi nouvelle* 1, no. 1, 20 février, 1912: 1.

Anonymous. "La tombola du Salon." *Le Quotidien*, 04 avril, 1915.

Anonymous. "Le 'Labor'." *Le Quotidien*, 12 novembre, 1914.

Anonymous. "Le dernier Salon." *Le Vingtième Siècle*, 21 janvier, 1915.

Anonymous. "Le Diable Boiteux, Un plaidoyer." *Le Quotidien*, 9 avril, 1916.

Anonymous. "Le Salon d'Automne." *Le Quotidien*, 24 octobre, 1915.

Anonymous. "Le Salon d'Automne." *Le Quotidien*, 7 novembre, 1915.

Anonymous. "Le Salon d'automne." *Le Quotidien*, 13 novembre, 1915.

Anonymous. "Le Salon d'automne. Statuaires." *L'Écho de la Presse Internationale*, 13 octobre, 1915.

Anonymous. "Les artistes." *La Belgique*, 26 novembre, 1914.

Anonymous. "Les expositions." *L'indépendance Belge*, 26 septembre, 1918.

Anonymous. "Les Théâtres. Au Palais des Arts. Le Théâtre national d'art et d'application." *Le Thyrse* 13, no. 5 (1911): 192–93.

Anonymous. "Périodicité, prix, durée", *7 Arts Numéro programme*, october (?), 1922: 1.

Anonymous. "Notes et nouvelles." *L'art libre*, 1 août, 1919: 112.

Anonymous. "Notes of the Month." *The Welsh Outlook*, November, 1914.

Anonymous. "Notes of the Month." *The Welsh Outlook*, December, 1914.

Anonymous. "Constant Montald inaugure la Galerie Sneyers." *L'Événement illustré* 145 (1917): 840–841.

Anonymous. "Membres abonnés aux expositions de la Salle 'Studio'." In *Studio Noël-Salon*. Bruxelles: I. Brachot, 1916.

Anonymous. "Membres du Cercle Artistique du Studio." In *Studio Noël 1917*. Bruxelles: I. Brachot, 1917.

Anonymous. "Mise au point." *La Belgique*, 22 novembre, 1914.

Anonymous. "Nos artistes peintres." *La Belgique*, 20 novembre, 1914.

Anonymous. "Nos Peintres." *Le Temps Présent*, 34 (1915): 503.

Anonymous. "Pour les 'Éprouvés des temps présents'." *La Belgique*, 18 février, 1915.

Anonymous. "Pour les artistes." *Le Bien Public*, 27 novembre, 1915.

Anonymous. "Pour les artistes." *Le Quotidien*, 07 février, 1915.

Anonymous. "Pour les artistes." *Le Quotidien*, 15 août, 1915.

Anonymous. "Pour nos artistes." *L'Indépendance belge* (édité en Angleterre), 11 novembre, 1914.

Anonymous. "Rapport critiques sur l'action du comité Aide et Protection aux Artistes." *Le Bruxellois*, 12 juin, 1916.

Anonymous. "Salle Studio." *Le Quotidien*, 9 décembre, 1914.

Anonymous. "The War Relief Exhibition at the Royal Academy." *The Connoisseur*, Vol. 41, No. 162, February, 1915: 110–112.

Anonymous."Une exposition d'art à Bruxelles." *L'information de Bruxelles*, 13 décembre, 1914.

Anonymous. "Une exposition d'oeuvres belges." *L'Indépendance belge* (édité en Angleterre), 18 novembre, 1914.

Arndt, Ernst Moritz. *Belgien und was daran hängt*. Leipzig, Weidmann'sche Buchhandlung, 1834.

———. *Um Flandern und Brabant. Die Frage über die Niederlande und die Rheinlande, Belgien und was daran hängt*. Im Auftrage d. Freiwilligen Aufklärungskorps zur See u. zur Luft, Reichsverband E.V. von 1913, herausgegeben von K.H.L. Walter van der Bleek, mit einer Erklärung d. Bevollmächtigten d. Rates von Flandern Achilles Brijs-Schouppe, Berlin: Boll und Pickardt, 1918.

Arnout, Anneleen. "Archimedes achterna: De Belgische musea tijdens de Eerste Wereldoorlog." *Bijdragen tot de Eigentijdse Geschiedenis* 22 (2010): 55–92.

Aron, Paul. *Les écrivains belges et le socialisme (1880–1913). L'expérience de l'art social: d'Edmond Picard à Emile Verhaeren*. Bruxelles: Editions Labor, 1985.

Audouin-Rouzeau, Stéphane, Aldo Battaglia, Marine Branland et al. ed. *Vu du front: représenter la Grande Guerre*. Paris: Somogy - Musée de l'Armée - Bibliothèque de documentation contemporaine, 2014.

Audoin-Rouzeau, Becker and Smith, *France and the Great War 1914–1918*. Cambridge: Cambridge University Press, 2003.

Asholt, Wolfgang, and Walther Fähnders ed. *Manifeste und Proklamationen der europäischen Avantgarde (1909–1938)*. Stuttgart/Weimar: Metzler, 1995.

Ausstellung belgischer Kunst 15. März bis 5. April 1925. cat. [Basel]: [Kunsthalle Basel], 1925. Aendekerk, Jean-Marie, *Marthe Donas et l'avant-garde parisienne (1916–1921)*, Ittre: Musée Marthe Donas, 2016.

Aust, Martin and Daniel Schönpflug ed. *Vom Gegner lernen. Feindschaften und Kulturtransfers im Europa des 19. und 20. Jahrhundert*. Francfort/New York: Campus, 2007.

Baum, Julius. *Brüssel als Kunststätte*. Strasbourg: Heitz 1915.

B.-O.-N. “Á la Salle Giroux.” *Le Messager de Bruxelles*, 16 mai, 1915.

Bajkay, Eva. “L’avant-garde hongroise et ses relations avec la Belgique et les Pays-Bas de 1915 à 1925 / De Hongaarse Avant-garde en de relaties met België en Nederland van 1915 tot 1925.” In *Avant-garde hongroise / Hongaarse Avant-garde: 1915–1925*, edited by Eva Bajkay et al. Europalia 99 Hungaria. Bruxelles: BBL; Brepols, 1999–2000: 17–67.

Barchan. “Anto-Carte: Brüssel.” *Deutsche Kunst und Dekoration* (1928/29): 177.

Baugniet, Marcel-Louis. *Vers une synthèse esthétique et sociale*. Bruxelles: Editions Labor, 1986.

Baumann, Roland. “Visions allemandes de l’art belge (1891–1944).” In *Deutsch-belgische Beziehungen im kulturellen und literarischen Bereich 1890–1940: Les relations culturelles et littéraires belgo-allemandes 1890–1940*. Studien und Dokumente zur Geschichte der romanischen Literaturen 36, edited by Leonardy, Ernst, and Hubert Roland. Frankfurt am Main, Berlin, Bern, New York, Paris, Wien: Peter Lang; Lang, 1999: 191–207.

Behne, Adolph. “Pierre Flouquet.” *Welt am Abend*, 19.05.

Bennet, Phillippa and Rosie Miles. *William Morris in the Twenty-first Century*. Bern: Peter Lang, 2010.

Becker, H.A. *De toekomst van de Verloren Generatie*. Amsterdam: Meulenhoff, 1997.

Berg, Bettina and Ernst van Raaij, ed. *George Minne: Ein Anfang der Moderne*; *George Minne: voorbode van de moderne kunst.* Köln: Wienand, 2013.

Bertrand, Olivier, *Rik Wouters. Visies op een levensloop. Nel Wouters onuitgegeven herinneringen*. Brussels: Belgian Art Research Institute, 2000.

Beyen, Roland, ed. *Correspondance de Michel de Ghelderode 1919–1927*. 9 vols., Archives du Futur, vol. I. Bruxelles: Labor / AML, 1991.

Bianco, René. “Un siècle de presse anarchiste d’expression française, 1880–1983. Répertoire des périodiques anarchistes de langue française.” Université de Provence, 1987.

Bex, Flor. *Jozef Peeters 1895–1960*. Antwerp: International Cultural Centre, 1973.

Blomme, Françoise. *À la rencontre d’Adrien Blomme.* Brussels: CIVA, 2016.

Boon, Kristien. *Marthe Donas*, Oostkamp: Stichting Kunstboek, 2004.

Boot, Caroline and Marijke van der Heijden, “Gemeenschapskunst.” In *Kunstenaren der idee. Symbolistische tendenzen in Nederland, ca. 1880–1930*, edited by Carel Blotkamp et al. Den Haag: Staatsuitgeverij, 1978: 36–47.

Borgers, Gerrit. *Paul Van Ostaijen: Een documentatie*. 2nd ed. Amsterdam: Uitgeverij Bert Bakker, 1996.

Bourgeois, Pierre. “L’Effort belge et l’Etranger: La Revue allemande ‘Bauwelt’ consacre un article aux modernistes belges.” *7 Arts* 3, 5 (4.12.1924) (1924/25).

Bourgeois, Victor. “Un programme d’enseignement”, *La Cité* 7 (1920): 127–129.

Bowlt, John E. *Russian Art of the Avant-Garde: Theory and Criticism 1902–1934*. Revised and enlarged edition. London: Thames and Hudson, 1988.

Boyens, Piet. *L’Art flamand: Du symbolisme à l’expressionnisme à Laethem-Saint-Martin*. Tielt, Sint-Martens-Latem: Lannoo; Art Book Company, 1992.

———. *De Passage: Vlaamse kunstenaars in Nederland 1914–1922*. Kranenburgh Cahiers 10, Bergen: Museum Kranenburgh, 2000.

Brachot, Isy. "Cercle artistique du Studio." In *Studio Noël* 1917. Bruxelles: I. Brachot, 1917.

Brandon, Laura. *Art & War*. London: I.B. Tauris, 2009.

———. *Art or memorial ? The forgotten history of Canada's war art*. Calgary: University of Calgary Press, 2006.

Branland, Marine ed. *1914 – Guerre et avant-gardes,* Paris: Presses universitaires Paris Ouest, 2016.

Branland, Marine. "La gravure en Grande Guerre: donner corps à son experience (France, Belgique, Angleterre)." PhD diss. Paris X Nanterre, 2013.

Breton, André, Georges Henein, Marcel Martinet, Maurice Parijanine, Magdeleine Paz, Jean-Paul Samson, Victor Serge, and Maurice Wullens. *Dossier des fusilleurs. Après le 30 Juin de Staline. Illustrations d'Albert Daenens et de Vladi. Revue Littéraire des Primaires "Les Humbles"* [Vingt-et-unième série], edited by Maurice Wullens. 2d ed. Paris: Les Humbles, 1936.

Brockington, Grace dir. *Internationalism and the Arts*. Oxford etc.: Peter Lang, 2009.

Buelens, Geert. "Een avant-gardist is (g)een groep. Over de wankele avantgardestatus van de flaminganten tijdens het interbellum" In *Avantgarde! Voorhoede? Vernieuwingsbewegingen in Noord en Zuid opnieuw beschouwd*, edited by Hubert F. van den Berg and Gillis J. Dorleijn. Nijmegen: Vantilt, 2002: 93–102.

Buelinckx, Erik. "Enkele anarchistisch gezinde kunstenaars rond Emile Verhaeren." In *Anarchisten rond Emile Verhaeren*, edited by David Gullentops and Hans Vandevoorde. Tekst en Tijd. Brussel: VUBPress, 2005: 71–109.

———. "Albert Daenens & Willem Gijssels. Een Brusselse anarchistische kunstenaar en een Vlaamse dichter." *Zuurvrij*, no. 21 (december 2011): 50–57.

———. "Henry Van de Velde, Art Nouveau and Intellectual Anarchism." *Uncommon Culture* 4, 7/8 (Art Nouveau) (2013): 33–43.

———. "Mauer – film préhistorique. Gérard de Lacaze-Duthiers et l'esthétique libertaire." In *Cinémas libertaires. Au service des forces de transgression et de révolte,* edited by Nicole Brenez and Isabelle Marinone. Arts du spectacle - Images et sons. Paris: Presses Universitaires du Septentrion, 2015.

Bürger, Peter. *Theorie der Avantgarde*. Frankfurt am Main: Suhrkamp, 1982 (1974).

Buschmann, Paul. "Belgian artists in England." *The Studio*, Vol. 65, No. 261, December, 1914: 182–210.

Buschmann, Paul. "Belgian Artists in England," *The Studio*, Vol. 67, No. 263, February, 1915: 43–48.

Buschmann, Paul. "Belgian Artists in England" *The Studio* Vol. 68, No. 264, April, 1915: 260–270.

C. D. "L'Exposition des Beaux-Arts." *Le Messager de Bruxelles*, 03 mars, 1915.

C. H. "A Travers les Ventes publiques. A la Galerie Giroux – La vente des tableaux Marlier. – Á la salle Aeolian – La vente de la collection dépendant de la succession Théo Hannon." *Le Messager de Bruxelles*, 12 janvier, 1917.

Cahalan, Peter. *Belgian Refugee Relief in England during the Great War.* London – New York: Garland, 1982.

Casteels, Maurice. "Pour l'art moderne." *Haro!* 1e série, no. 2 (juillet 1913): 12–14.

———. "Pour l'art moderne." *Haro!* 1e série, no. 3 (août 1913): 20–21.

———. "Pour l'art moderne." *Haro!* 1e série, no. 5 (décembre 1913): 37–38.

———. *Banalités. Avec 5 linos par Albert Daenens.* Bruxelles: Édition du Pot d'etain, 1921.

———. *Esthétique.* Bruxelles: Édition du Pot d'etain, 1921.

———. "Les arts industriels", *7 Arts* 5 (1922–1923): 3.

———. *Die Sachlichkeit in der Modernen Kunst.* Vorwort: Henri van de Velde. Paris und Leipzig: Henri Jonquières, 1930.

Ceuppens, Jan. "De Germaanse leeuw. Consciences Leeuw van Vlaenderen als inzet van Duits-Vlaamse betrekkingen 1840–1918." In *Verslagen & Mededelingen van de Koninklijke Akademie voor Nederlandse Taal- en Letterkunde*, vol. 123, nr. 2–3 (2013): 233–247.

Cheah, Pheng, and Bruce Robbins dir. *Cosmopolitics: Thinking and Feeling beyond the Nation.* Minneapolis and London: University of Minnesota Press, 1998.

Claes, Marie-Christine. "Un héritage bénéfique des deux guerres mondiales. Le concept et les collections de l'IRPA." *Bruxelles Patrimoines 011–012 (numéro spécial – septembre 2014),* Journées du Patrimoine Région de Bruxelles-Capitale: 61–73.

Claisse, Stéphanie. "Du soldat inconnu aux monuments commémoratifs belges de la guerre 14–18." Mémoire de la classe des lettres et des sciences morales et politiques 1. Bruxelles: Académie Royale des Sciences, 2013.

Clerbois, Sébastien, ed. *Artistes belges en 1914–18: 80ème anniversaire de l'Armistice du 11 novembre.* La Louvière: Musée Ianchelevici, 1998.

Collins, Judith. *The Omega Workshops.* Chicago: The University of Chicago Press, 1984.

Connelly, Mark. "Visualization of Violence." *1914–1918 online. International Encyclopedia of the First World War*, https://encyclopedia.1914-1918 online.net/article/visualization_of_violence?version=1.0

Cork, Richard. *A Bitter Truth: Avant-Garde Art and the Great War*, New Haven: Yale University Press, 1994.

Daenens, Albert. "A propos d'Art appliqué." *La Foi nouvelle 1,* no. 4 (1 juin 1912): 4–7.

———. "Ni fleurs, ni couronnes." *Haro!* 1e série, no. 1 (juin 1913): 8.

———. *20 linos pamphletaires. 20 pamphlet-linos.* Bruxelles: Éditions du Repos Bien Mérité, 1929.

Dagen, Philippe. *Le silence des peintres: Les artistes face à la Grande Guerre.* Paris: Fayard, 1996.

Dascher, Ottfried. *Alfred Flechtheim: Sammler, Kunsthändler, Verleger.* With the assistance of Rudolf Schmitt-Föller and Rico Quaschny. 2. Aufl. Quellenstudien zur Kunst Bd. 6. Wädenswil: Nimbus, 2013.

D'Haese, Jan. *"De Vijf + Één". Jan-Frans Cantré, Jozef Cantré, Frans Masereel, Joris Minne, Henri Van Straten + Albert Daenens,* edited by Jan De Kelver Drogenbos: Stichting Felix De Boeck en v.z.w. Museum Felix De Boeck, 2003.

De Bock, Eugène. *Een uitgever herinnert zich.* Antwerp: De Sikkel, 1979.

De Boodt, Kurt. *Prosper De Troyer. Schilder in beweging.* Antwerp: Pandora, 2013.

De collectie De Graaff - Bachiene: Schilderijen, Beeldhouwwerken, Tekeningen en Grafiek. Heino/Wijhe, Gent: 1992.

De Geest, Joost, et De Gryse, Piet. *Couleurs au front 1914–1918. Les peintres au front belge.* Bruxelles: Crédit communal de Belgique, 1999.

De Jastrzebski, T.T.S. "The Register of Belgian Refugees." *Journal of the Royal Statistical Society,* Vol. LXXIX, II, March, 1916: 133–158.

De Man, R. "Pour les Artistes. Une idée du 'Quotidien'." *Le Quotidien,* 22 novembre, 1914.

De Marneffe, Daphné, and Benoît Denis dir. *Les Réseaux littéraires.* Bruxelles: Le Cri /Ciel-ULB-Ulg, 2006.

De Marneffe, Daphné. "Entre modernisme et avant-garde. Le réseau des revues littéraires de l'immédiat après-guerre en Belgique (1919–1922)." PhD diss., Université de Liège, 2007.

De Meulemeester, Fabienne. "Vrouwelijke kunstenaars in de marge van de Parijse avant-garde. Een case-studie Marthe Donas." Master's thesis, Katholieke Universiteit Leuven, 2004.

De Ridder, André. "Les expositions." *Sélection* (june 1926): 328.

———. "James Ensor." *Der Querschnitt* 7 (1927): 115–18.

———. "L'école belge contemporaine." *Cahiers de la Belgique,* 4me année, avril–mai, n°4–5, (1930).

De Ridder, Matthijs. "De kleine garnaal. M.B. Ledegouwer," *Zacht Lawijd* 6, no. 4 (2006–2007): 20–37. http://www.dbnl.org/tekst/_zl_001200601_01/_zl_001200601_01_0028.php

De Schaepdrijver, Sophie. "Occupation, Propaganda, and the Idea of Belgium." In *European Culture in the Great War: the Arts, Entertainment, and Propaganda, 1914–1918,* edited by Aviel Roshwald and Richard Stites. Cambridge University Press, 1999: 267–294.

———. "Polichinelles dans la ville: la vision de l'Allemand dans les caricatures." In *L'humour s'en va-t-en guerre. Bruxelles et la caricature en 14–18,* edited by Serge Jaumain and Valérie Piette. Bruxelles: Archives de la Ville series *Fontes Bruxellae,* 2, 2005: 101–107.

———. "Antimémoire d'une antimémoire: les occupations d'un écrivain belge." In *Mémoires et antimémoires littéraires: la première guerre mondiale,* edited by Annamaria Laserra, Nicole Leclercq and Marc Quaghebeur. Frankfurt, Brussels: P.I.E.-Peter Lang, 2008 Vol. I: 19–32.

———. "*Ô faiseuse de crépuscule.* Deutschlandbilder in Belgien im Großen Krieg." In *Deutschlandbilder in Belgien 1830–1940,* edited by Hubert Roland, Marnix Beyen and Greet Draye. Münster: Waxmann, 2011: 292–310.

———. *Gabrielle Petit: The Death and Life of a Female Spy in the First World War.* London: Bloomsbury Academic, 2015.

———. "New Research on First World War Belgium." *Revue belge d'Histoire contemporaine* XLVI, 3/4 (2016): 206–210.

———. "Measuring lost time: civilian diaries under military occupation." In *Inside World War One? Ego-documents and the Experience of War,* edited by Richard Bessel and Dorothee Wierling. Oxford: Oxford University Press, 2018: 57–81.

———. "No country for young men: patriotism and its paradoxes in German-occupied Belgium, 1914–1918." In *Breaking Empires, Making Nations: The First World War and the Reforging of Europe*, edited by Richard Butterwick-Pawlikowski, Quincy Cloet and Alex Dowdall. Warsaw: The College of Europe at Natolin, 2018: 124–153.

———. "Patriotic Distance." *1914–1918-online. International Encyclopedia of the First World War*, https://encyclopedia.1914-1918-online.net/article/patriotic_distance?version=1.0.

De Schaepdrijver, Sophie, and Emmanuel Debruyne. "Sursum Corda: The Underground Press in Occupied Belgium, 1914–1918." *First World War Studies* 4:1 (March 2013): 23–38.

De Schaepdrijver, Sophie, and Tammy Proctor. *An English Governess in the Great War: The Secret Brussels Diary of Mary Thorp*. New York: Oxford University Press, 2017.

De Smedt, Marcel. "Philologische Kontakte zwischen Deutschland und Flandern in der ersten Hälfte des 19. Jahrhunderts." In *Deutschlandbilder in Belgien 1830–1940*, edited by Hubert Roland, Marnix Beyen, Greet Draye. Münster: Waxmann, 2011.

De Smet, Johan ed. *Modernisme: L'art abstrait belge et l'Europe*; [paraît à l'occasion de l'Exposition Modernisme. L'Art Abstrait Belge et l'Europe 1912–1930, Museum voor Schone Kunsten Gent, Gand, 2 mars – 30 juin 2013]. With the assistance of Peter J.H. Pauwels. Bruxelles, Gent: Fonds Mercator; Museum voor Schone Kunsten Gent, 2013.

Debonnets, Charles. "Galerie Sneyer: L'Art Décoratif." *Le Messager de Bruxelles*, 26 mai, 1918.

Debray, Cécile, and Françoise Lucbert ed. *La Section d'or 1912–1920–1925. Le cubisme écartelé*, (exh.cat.) Châteauroux, Musée, 21 September – 3 December 2000, Montpellier: Musée Fabre, 15 December 2000 – 18 March 2001, Editions Cercle d'art, 2000.

Defraeye Piet, Helga Mitterbauer, and Chris Reyns ed., *Vienna : 1900 : Brussels*, Amsterdam: Rodopi, to be published in 2018/2019.

Dekoster, Marcel. "Salle Studio." *Le Temps Présent* 33 (1915): 477.

Deshoulières, Valérie, Hans-Jürgen Lüsebrink, and Christoph Vatter ed. *Europa zwischen Text und Ort – L'Europe entre Texte et Lieu / Interkulturalität in Kriegszeiten (1914–1954) – Interculturalités en temps de guerre (1914–1954)*. Jahrbuch des Frankreichzentrums der Universität des Saarlandes (2013), Bd. 12. Bielefeld: transcript Verlag, 2013.

Destrée, Jules. *Art et Socialisme*. Bruxelles: Le Peuple, 1896.

Destrée, Jules, and Emile Vandervelde. *Le socialisme en Belgique*. Paris: V. Giard & E. Brière, 1932.

Devaldès, Manuel. "Le salvateur néo-malthusianisme." *Haro!* 1e série, no. 3 (août 1913): 18–19.

———. "Bonhomme." *Haro!* 2e série, no. 11 (20 mai 1920): 4–5.

———. *Anthologie des écrivains réfractaires. Revue Littéraire des Primaires "Les Humbles"*. [Douzième série]. Edited by Maurice Wullens. Paris: Les Humbles, 1927.

———. "Les Réfractaires." *Haro!* 3e série, no. 5 (mars 1928): 2.

Devillez, Virginie, Michel Draguet, and Manu Van der Aa, ed. *Kunstpromotor Paul-Gustave Van Hecke (1887–1967) en de avant-garde*. Brussel/Gent-Kortrijk: Koninklijke Musea voor Schone Kunsten van België; Uitgeverij Snoeck, 2012.

Devillez, Virginie. *Le retour à l'ordre: Art et politique en Belgique 1918–1945*. Bruxelles: Dexia, 2003.

———. "Les arts en crise: la Belgique dans le contexte européen (1918–1940)." *Textyles. Revue des lettres belges de langue française* 24 (2004): 52–62.

———. "1920–1940 Entre animisme et modernité, l'énigme Schirren," In *Ferdinand Schirren*, Cahiers des Musées royaux des beaux-Arts de Belgique, vol. 11 (2011): 95–107.

———. "Paul-Gustave Van Hecke, Max Ernst & Co.: die Wahlverwandtschaften der deutsch-belgischen Avantgarde 1918–1940." In *Deutschlandbilder in Belgien 1830–1940*, edited by Hubert Roland, Marnix Beyen, Greet Draye. Münster: Waxmann, 2011: 424–455.

Dewilde, Jan and Thomas Schlesser. *Henry De Groux. Oorlogsgetuige / Témoin de guerre 1866–1930*, Ieper: In Flanders Fields Museum vzw, 2008.

Doherty, Charles E. "Nevinson's Elegy: Paths of Glory." *Art Journal* 51/1 (1992): 64–71.

Doms, André, and Pierre Bourgeois. *Une lecture de soixante ans de poésie*. Bruxelles: Maison internationale de la poésie, 1976.

Edschmid, Kasimir. "Appel à la jeunesse intellectuelles français. Manifeste des intellectuels allemands." *L'Art Libre*, Bruxelles, 1919–1922. MRBAB, Bibl., Kopien. 1, no. 15 (1.11.1919): 173–75.

Ehrenburg, I'lija. "La littérature russe en 1922. Lettre inédite." *Le Disque Vert* 3 (1922): 63–68.

———. "La poésie russe et la révolution. Lettre inédite." *Signaux de France et de Belgique* 4 (1921): 178–191.

———. *Uomini, anni, vita*. Vol. 2. Roma: Editori Riuniti, 1961–1963.

Eickmans, Heinz. "Ehrengast der Frankfurter Buchmesse 2016. Flandern und die Niederlande: Was sie teilen und was sie teilt." *literaturkritik.de, Nr. 10*, Oktober 2016, http://literaturkritik.de/id/22567 (accessed 29.10.2017).

Elslander, Jean-François. *Figures et Souvenirs d'une Belle époque*. Bruxelles: La Renaissance du Livre, 1944.

Engelen, Leen. "Film/ Cinéma (Belgium)." *1914–1918-online. International Encyclopedia of the First World War*, no. 85 (2017), https://encyclopedia.1914-1918-online.net/article/filmcinema_belgium?version=1.0 (accessed 15.10.2017)

Espagne, Michel, and Michael Werner. *Transferts les relations interculturelles dans l'espace Franco-Allemand (XVIIIe et XIXe siècles)*. Paris: Ed. Recherche sur les Civilisations, 1988.

Exhibition of Works given by Belgian Artists, cat. London: Goupil Gallery, s.d.

Exposition Générale des Beaux-Arts (Salon Triennal). Cat. Bruxelles: Palais du Cinquantenaire, 1914.

Fletcher, Pamela, and Anne Helmreich ed. *The Rise of the Modern Art Market in London 1850–1939*. Manchester: Manchester University Press, 2011.

Férey, Sylvie ed. *Vouloir 1924–1927. Collection complète de 26 numéros Temps, espace et société. Collection « Histoire de l'art »*, vol. 923. Villeneuve d'Ascq: Presses Universitaires du Septentrion, 2006.

Ferré, Fernand. *Luzia. Nouvelle, illustrée de sept linos gravés par Albert Daenens. Revue Littéraire des Primaires "Les Humbles"* [Onzième série], edited by Maurice Wullens. Paris: Éditions de la Brochure Mensuelle, 1926.

Fierens, Paul. "Die junge Kunst in Belgien." *Der Cicerone: Halbmonatsschrift für die Interessen des Kunstforschers & Sammlers* 17, 7 (April) (1925): 363–72.

Finckh, Gerhard, ed. *Das Menschenschlachthaus: Der Erste Weltkrieg in der französischen und deutschen Kunst.* Wuppertal: Von der Heydt-Museum, 2014.

Fischer, Ole W. "Objected into the void – The polemics of Adolf Loos against Henry van de Velde: a cultural-psychological analysis of Modernism." *Umení/Art. Journal of the Institute for Art History of the Academy of Sciences of the Czech Republic* 55, 4 (2007): 294–315.

———. *Nietzsches Schatten: Henry van de Velde – von Philosophie zu Form.* Berlin: Gebr. Mann, 2012.

———. "Museen für Nietzsches Neuen Menschen? Henry van de Veldes Planung zum »Universalmuseum« Erfurt zwischen Krise und Wille zum Stil." In *Henry van de Velde. Ein Universalmuseum für Erfurt*, edited by Miriam Krautwurst and Kai Uwe Schierz. Berlin: Kerber Art, 2013, catalogue for the Angermuseum Erfurt: 57–79.

———. "The Veil of Truth? – Van de Velde, Muthesius, and the Battle over Ornament in Modern Architecture." In *Ornament and European Modernism: From Art Practice to Art History*, edited by Loretta Vandi. London: Routledge, 2017: 104–136.

Florquin, Joos, and Felix De Boeck. "Ten huize van... Felix De Boeck." In *Ten huize van...*, edited by Joos Florquin. Leuven / Brugge: Davidsfonds / Orion-Desclé De Brouwer, 1971.

Florquin, Joos, and Pol Jacquemyns. "Ten huize van... Pol Jacquemyns (1967)." In *Ten huize van...*, edited by Joos Florquin. Leuven: Davidsfonds, 1980.

Flouquet, Pierre. "Cabinet graphique: Otto Dix. Série: 'La Guerre'", *7 Arts*, 3 (1924/25).

Föhl, Thomas ed. *Ihr Kinderlein kommet... – Henry van de Velde: ein vergessenes Projekt für Friedrich Nietzsche.* Ostfildern: Hatje Cantz, 2000.

Föhl, Thomas, and Sabine Walter ed. *Henry van de Velde: Leidenschaft, Funktion und Schönheit und sein Beitrag zur europäischen Moderne.* [Neues Museum Weimar 24. März bis 23. Juni 2013; eine Ausstellung der Klassik-Stiftung Weimar in Kooperation mit den Musées Royaux d'Art et d'Histoire, Brüssel]. With the assistance of Werner Adriaenssens. Weimar: Weimarer Verl.-Ges, 2013.

Foster, Stephen C. "World War I: The Grand Illusion, the Avant-Garde and the Formal Revolution." In *The Ideological crisis of expressionism. The literary and artistic German War colony in Belgium 1914–1918,* edited by Rumold, Rainer and Otto Karl Werckmeister. Columbia: Camden House, 1990.

Germain, G. "Les Salons du 'Studio'." In *Studio-Noël-Salon*. Bruxelles: I. Brachot, 1916.

Gijssels, Willem ed. *Zomertentoonstelling 1918. Tweede Reeks.* cat. Brussel: Kunstkring Doe Stil Voort, 1918.

Goddeeris, Ingrid, and Noémie Goldman, dir. *Animateur d'art: marchand, collectionneur, critique, éditeur... L'animateur d'art et ses multiples rôles. Étude pluridisciplinaire de ces intermédiaires culturels méconnus des XIXe et XXe siècles*. Bruxelles: Musées royaux des Beaux-Arts de Belgique, 2015.

Gonnissen, Adriaan, ed. *Schmalzigaug en het kookboek van het futurisme*. Oostende: Mu.ZEE, 2016.

Goyens de Heusch, Serge. *7 Arts, Bruxelles 1922–1929. Un front de jeunesse pour la révolution artistique*. Bruxelles: Ministère de la Culture Francophone de Belgique, 1976.

———. *Pierre-Louis Flouquet*. Bruxelles: Fonds pour l'Art Belge Contemporain, 1993.

Graul, Richard. *Alt-Flandern. Brabant, Artois, Hennegau, Lüttich, Namur*. Dachau/Munich: Roland-Verlag, 1915.

Gray, Camilla, *L'avant-garde russe dans l'art moderne, 1863–1922*. Lausanne: La Cité des Arts, 1968.

Green, Christopher. *Cubism and its Enemies: Modern Movements and Reaction in French Art, 1916–1928*. New Haven and London: Yale University Press, 1987.

Groot, Marjan. *Vrouwen in de vormgeving in Nederland 1880–1940*. Rotterdam: uitg. 010, 2007.

Gropius, Walter. *Internationale Architektur*. Bauhaus Bücher 1. Munich: Langen, 1925.

Guilbeaux, Henri. *Kraskreml et Autres Poèmes. Revue Littéraire des Primaires "Les Humbles"* [Septième série], edited by Maurice Wullens. Paris: Les Humbles, 1922.

Gullentops, David. *Émile Verhaeren inédit*. Brussel: VUBPress, 2015.

Hadermann, Paul. "Echanges belgo-berlinois de l'Art Nouveau aux années vingt." In *Expressionisme à Berlin, 1910–1920*: Palais des beaux-arts, Bruxelles, 22 septembre-4 novembre 1984. Bruxelles: Société des expositions du Palais des beaux-arts de Bruxelles, 1984: 33–37.

———. "Belgo-German Relations in the Arts, 1890–1918." In *The Ideological crisis of expressionism: The literary and artistic German War colony in Belgium 1914–1918*, edited by Rainer Rumold and Otto K. Werckmeister. Studies in German literature, linguistics, and culture 51. Columbia, SC: Camden House, 1990: 19–39.

———. "Les métamorphoses de *Sélection* et la propagation de l'expressionnisme en Belgique." In *Les Avant-gardes littéraires en Belgique. Au confluent des arts et des langues (1880–1950)*, edited by Jean Weisgerber. Brussels: Labor, 1991, (Archives du Futur): 241–276.

———. "Peeters en Joostens: twee problematische gevallen in Van Ostaijens kunstkritiek." In *Paul van Ostaijen en de kunst van zijn tijd 1896–1996*, edited by Michel Bartosik, Michel Dupuis and Jean Weisgerber. Gent: Koninklijke Academie voor Nederlandse Taal- en Letterkunde, 1997: 381–395.

Hausenstein, Wilhelm. *Der Bauern-Bruegel. Mit einem Vorwort zur neuen Ausgabe über Bruegel den Belgier. Mit sechsundsechzig Abbildungen nach Gemälden, Kupferstichen und Zeichnungen*, München: Piper Verlag, 1916.

Hellens, Franz. "Literature i kinematograf." [Letteratura e cinema], *Vešč'/Objet/Gegenstand* 1-2 (March-April 1922): 11–12.

———. *Documents secrets, 1905–1956. Histoire sentimentale de mes livres et de mes quelques amitiés*. Paris: Editions Albin Michel, 1958.

Heusinger von Waldegg, Joachim. "Ensor und Deutschland: Die Wirkung des Flamen auf die Künstler des Nachbarlandes." *Kunst & Antiquitäten*, no. 4 (1988): 84–96.

Hochschild, Adam. *To End all Wars, A story of loyalty and rebellion, 1914 – 1918*. New York: Houghton Mifflin, 2011.

Hopkinson, Martin. "Belgian Prints in Britain during World War I." *Print Quarterly*, XXXIII, 2016, 4: 416–427.

Hoozee, Robert. *George Minne en de kunst rond 1900*, cat. Gent,1982.

Hoozee, Robert, and Piet Boyens. *Vlaams expressionisme in Europese context, 1900–1930*. Gent: Snoeck-Ducaju; Ludion, 1990.

Hoozee, Robert et. al., *L'art moderne en Belgique. 1900–1945*. Antwerp, Mercator Fonds,1992.

Hoozee, Robert and Verdickt, Caterina, et.al. *Kunst in Ballingschap. Vlaanderen, Wales en de Eerste Wereldoorlog*. Cat., Gent, 2002.

Huijbrechts, Jan. *Vlaams bewegen in Antwerpen, Een stadsgids met 5 cultuurhistorische wandelingen*. Brussel: Uitgeverij Egmont, 2011.

Humbeek, Kris. "God geve dat wij Staatsgevaarlijk wezen! Mijn kleine oorlog en de retoriek van het linkse activisme." In *Avantgarde! Voorhoede? Vernieuwingsbewegingen in Noord en Zuid opnieuw beschouwd*, edited by Hubert F. van den Berg and Gillis J. Dorleijn. Nijmegem: Vantilt, 2002: 103–112.

Iriye, Akira. *Cultural Internationalism and World Order*. Baltimore and London: Johns Hopkins University Press, 1997.

Iriye, Akira, and Pierre-Yves Saunier, dir. *The Palgrave Dictionary of Transnational History from the mid-19th Century to the Present Day*. Basingstoke and New York: Palgrave Macmillan, 2009.

Jespers, Henri-Floris. *Floris Jespers, and the Gay Twenties*, Antwerp: Deus Ex Machina The Private Press, 1989.

Joffe, Helene. "Le pouvoir de l'image: persuasion, émotion et identification." *Diogène* 217 (2007/1): 102–115.

Joyeux-Prunel, Béatrice. *Les Avant-gardes artistiques 1918–1945. Une histoire transnationale*. Paris: Gallimard, 2017.

Kafka, Franz. "Investigations of a Dog" ("Forschungen eines Hundes", 1922). In *The Complete Stories*, transl. Willa and Edwin Muir. New York: Schocken Books Inc., 1988 (1971): 310–386.

Kähler, Susanne. "Belgische Bildhauer im Berlin der Jahrhundertwende." *MuseumsJournal. Berichte aus den Museen, Schlössern und Sammlungen in Berlin und Potsdam* 8, 4 (Oktober) (1994): 12–14.

Keiser, Alexandra. "Alexander Archipenko in an International Network of Cultural Exchange (1920–23)." In *Alexander Archipenko Revisited: An International Perspective*, edited by David Goldberg, and Alexandra Keiser. Bearsville: The Archipenko Foundation, 2008: 57–69.

Kollwelter, Laura. "Ein Spiel in drei Akten. Entwicklungsstufen der Zeitschriften *Der Sturm* und *Die Aktion* am Beispiel belgischer Kunstbeiträge." *Expressionismus. Der Sturm und Die Aktion* 5, 2017: 77–86.

Kott, Christina. *Préserver l'art de l'ennemi? Le patrimoine artistique en Belgique et en France occupées, 1914–1918*. Comparatisme et société No. 4. Bruxelles, Bern, Berlin, Frankfurt am Main, New York, Oxford, Wien: PIE Lang, 2006.

———. "'Inventorier pour mieux contrôler ?' L'inventaire photographique allemand du patrimoine culturel belge entre recherche historique et politique d'occupation." In *Une guerre totale ? La Belgique dans la Première Guerre mondiale. Nouvelles tendances de la recherche historique*, edited by Serge Jaumain, Michaël Amara, Benoît Majerus et Antoon Vrints, 283 sq. Bruxelles, 2004, Archives Générales du Royaume (Actes du colloque international organisé à l'ULB du 15 au 17 janvier 2003), (Etudes sur la Première Guerre mondiale/ Studie over de Eerste Wereldoorlog, n° 11).

———. "Photographier l'art de l'ennemi: les inventaires photographiques allemands en Belgique, 1917–18 et 1940–44." *citygraphy 1* (2006): 53–65.

Krause, Jürgen. *»Märtyrer« und »Prophet«: Studien zum Nietzsche-Kult in der bildenden Kunst der Jahrhundertwende.* Monographien und Texte zur Nietzsche-Forschung. 14, edited by Behler; Montinari; Müller-Lauter; Wenzel. Berlin; New York: Walter de Gruyter, 1984.

Krautwurst, Miriam, and Kai Uwe Schierz, ed., *Henry van de Velde. Ein Universalmuseum für Erfurt*. Berlin: Kerber Art, 2013, catalogue for the Angermuseum Erfurt.

Kropotkine, Pierre. "Aux jeunes gens." In *Paroles d'un révolté*. Ouvrage publié, annoté et accompagné d'une préface par Elisée Reclus, 43–75. Paris: Flammarion, 1885.

Küster, Bernd ed., *Der Erste Weltkrieg und die Kunst: Von der Propaganda zum Widerstand*, Gifkendorf: Merlin Verlag, 2008.

Lambotte, Paul. "Belgian Artists in England." *The Connoisseur*, Vol. 50, No. 200, April 1918: 183–193.

———. "L'Evolution de l'Ecole Belge de Peinture (1830–1900)." *Journal of The Royal Society of Arts*, Vol. 63, No. 3255, 9 April 1915: 469–479.

Lampo, Jan. "Vuile manieren in Vlaamsche Arbeid. Karel van den Oever wordt het slachtoffer van een mystificatie." *Zuurvrij* 22 (2012): 34–41.

Lanneau, Catherine. "DEBATE - DÉBAT. Les commémorations du centenaire de la Première Guerre mondiale: réflexion à mi-terme." *Revue belge d'Histoire contemporaine* XLVI, 3/4 (2016): 206–10.

Laqua, Daniel. *The Age of Internationalism and Belgium, 1880–1930: Peace, Progress and Prestige.* Manchester: Manchester University Press, 2013.

———. dir. *Internationalism Reconfigured: Transnational Ideas and Movements Between the World Wars*. Londres: I.B. Tauris, 2011.

Lavrentiev, Aleksandr. "The Three Constructivisms of Aleksander Rodchenko, in Constructivism and the Art of Everyday Life." *Tate Modern*, March 28, 2009.

Le Naour, Jean-Yves. *1916. L'enfer.* Paris: Perrin, 2014.

Le Vieil Hibou. "Le Salon des Beaux-Arts." *Le Messager de Bruxelles*, 28 avril, 1915.

———. "Un comble." *Le Messager de Bruxelles*, 28 janvier, 1915.

Les clichés allemands (1917–1918). Le patrimoine artistique belge à travers l'objectif de l'occupant / De Duitse negatieven (1917–1918). Het Belgisch artistiek erfgoed door de lens van de bezetter, Parc de Bruxelles, Brussels, 15.06.2017–17.09.2017, organized by KIK-IRPA.

Lechien-Durant, Françoise, and Paul Eeckhout. *Musée David et Alice Van Buuren: Maison de mémoire*. Bruxelles: Racine, 1995.

Leclerc, Georges-Louis, comte de Buffon, *Discours sur le style*, discours prononcé à l'Académie française le jour de sa réception, le 25 août 1753.

Lefèvre, Patrick, and Richard Boijen. *14–18: Regards d'artistes*. Bruxelles: Musée royal de l'Armée et d'Histoire militaire, 1993.

Leonardy, Ernst, and Hubert Roland, ed. *Deutsch-belgische Beziehungen im kulturellen und literarischen Bereich 1890–1940: Les relations culturelles et littéraires belgo-allemandes 1890–1940*. Studien und Dokumente zur Geschichte der romanischen Literaturen 36. Frankfurt am Main, Berlin, Bern, New York, Paris, ·Wien: Peter Lang; Lang, 1999.

Levitas, Ruth. "After Morris: Warwick Herbert Draper and the pursuit of Utopia." In *William Morris in the Twenty-first Century*, edited by Phillippa Bennet and Rosie Miles. Bern, 2010: 32–33.

Lisitskij-Küppers, Sophie ed. *El Lisitskij: pittore, architetto, tipografo, fotografo. Ricordi, lettere e scritti*. Roma: Editori Riuniti, 1967.

Lodder, Christina. "Constructivist Visions of Utopia." In *Utopia 1900–1940: Visions of a New World*. Rotterdam: nai010, 2013: 92–105.

Long, Christopher. "The Origins and Context of Adolf Loos's »Ornament and Crime«." *Journal of the Society of Architectural Historians*, 68, No. 2 (June 2009): 200–223.

Lorette, Jean ed. *14–18: Kunstenaarsvisie,* Brussel: Koninklijk Museum van het Leger en van Krijgsgeschiedenis, 1993.

Lucbert, Françoise. "L'internationalisme de 'Tour-Donas' à l'époque des expositions européennes de la Section d'or." In *Marthe Donas et l'avant-garde parisienne (1916–1921)*. Ittre: Musée Marthe Donas, 8 octobre–20 novembre 2016: 25–26.

Lukas. "Kunstkroniek." *Gazet van Brussel,* 19 mars 1918.

Lust for Life, Mechelen, Hof van Busleyden, 26.08 2016 – 11.12 2016; Antwerpen, MoMu - ModeMuseum Provincie Antwerpen, 17.09 2016 – 26.02 2017

Lutgarde, Dusar. "Doorheen het leven van Felix De Boeck: zijn vormingsjaren en deelname aan de modernistische kunststrekkingen van de twintiger jaren, geplaatst in het kader van de Europese en Belgische kunstevolutie" unpublished thesis Katholieke Universiteit Leuven, Leuven 1973.

Lüthgen, Eugen. *Belgische Baudenkmäler,* Leipzig: Insel-Verlag, 1915.

Maciuika, John V. *Before the Bauhaus. Architecture, Politics and the German State, 1890–1920*. Cambridge UK: Cambridge University Press, 2005.

Maingon, Claire. *L'art face à la guerre*. Vincennes: éd. PUV, 2015.

———. *Modern art, Britain and the Great War*. New Haven: The Paul Mellon Centre for Studies in British Art, 2004.

Malvern, Sue. "Art." *1914–1918 online. International Encyclopedia of the First World War*, https://encyclopedia.1914-1918-online.net/article/art?version=1.0

Mannheim, Karl. "The Problem of Generations." In Karl Mannheim, *Essays*. London: Routledge, edited by Paul Kecskemeti. 1952 (repr. 1972): 276–322.

———. “Das Problem der Generationen.“ In Karl Mannheim, *Wissenssoziologie. Auswahl aus dem Werk*, edited by Kurt H. Wolff. Luchterhand: Neuwied/Berlin, 1964: 509–565. (Originally published as Karl Mannheim. “Das Problem der Generationen,” *Kölner Vierteljahreshefte für Soziologie* 7 (1928/29): 157–184).

Mario. “Le Salon du Studio.” *Le Bruxellois*, 21 mars 1915.

Maus, Octave. “Lettre de Lausanne. La Peinture en Belgique.” *L’Indépendance belge*, 13 juin, 1918.

Melders, Robert. *Jozef Peeters (1895–1960)*. Antwerp/Amsterdam: Uitgeverij Nederlandsche Boekhandel, 1978.

Mertens, Phil. *Jules Schmalzigaug 1882–1917*. Brussel: R. en J. Van de Velde/I.C.S.A.C., 1984.

Mesnil, Jacques. “L’art dans la Russie des Soviets.” *Bulletin Communiste* 10 (1922): 193–196.

———. “L’art dans la Russie des Soviets.” *L’Art Libre* 1 (1922): 3–8.

Meyer, Hannes. “Junge Kunst in Belgien.” *Das Werk: Architektur und Kunst / L’oeuvre: architecture et art 12*, no. 9 (1925): 257–76.

———. “Junge Kunst in Belgien.” *Das Werk: Architektur und Kunst / L’oeuvre: architecture et art* 12, no. 10 (1925): 304–305.

Mommsen, Wolfgang, *Max Weber und die Deutsche Politik 1890–1920*. 2nd revised ed. Tübingen, 1974.

Muls, Francis, Hubert Roland, and Dennis van Mol. “Discours internationaliste et conscience identitatire des échanges culturels: l’exemple belgo-allemand.” In *Europa! Europa? The avant-garde, modernism, and the fate of a continent*, edited by Sascha Bru and Jan Baetens. European avant-garde and modernism studies 1. New York: Walter de Gruyter, 2009: 267–82.

Muls, Francis and Hans Vandevoorde, “‘Streetscape of new districts permeated by the fresh scent of cement’: Brussels, The avant-garde, and internationalism.” In *The Oxford Critical and Cultural History of Modernist Magazines. Volume III: Europe 1880–1940*, edited by Peter Brooker, Sascha Bru, Andrew Thacker, and Christian Weikop. Oxford: Oxford University Press, 2013: 336–360.

Musée d’Art moderne de la Ville de Paris. L’École de Paris 1904–1929, la part de l’Autre, cat.Paris: Paris musées, 2000.

Muthesius, Hermann. *Die Werkbund-Arbeit der Zukunft; und Aussprache darüber von Ferdinand Avenarius Peter Behrens, Rudolf Bosselt, Robert Breuer, Peter Bruckmann, August Endell, von Engelhardt, Karl Groß, Hermann Obrist, Karl Ernst Osthaus, Wilhelm Ostwald, Erich Pistor, C. A. Reichel, Richard Riemerschmid, Walter Riezler, Karl Schäfer, Bruno Taut, Joszef Vago, van der Velde. Friedrich Naumann: Werkbund und Weltwirtschaft. Der Werkbund-Gedanke in den germanischen Ländern: Österreich-Ungarn, Schweiz, Holland, Dänemark, Schweden, Norwegen*. Jena: Eugen Diederichs, 1914.

Nohl, Herman. *Ein Landsturmmann im Himmel: Flandern und der Erste Weltkrieg in den Briefen von Herman Nohl an seine Frau*, edited by Walter Thys. Leipzig: Leipziger Univ.-Verl., 2005.

Nora, Pierre. “Generation.” *Realms of Memory. Rethinking the French Past*, Vol I. New York: Columbia University Press, 1996: 499–531.

Ottevanger, Alied ed. *'De Stijl overal absolute leiding' De briefwisseling tussen Theo van Doesburg en Anthony Kok*. Bussem: Thoth, 2008.

Paenhuysen, An. "Berlin am Sonntag: Die belgische Avantgarde über das Chicago an der Spree." In *Deutschlandbilder in Belgien 1830–1940*, edited by Hubert Roland, Marnix Beyen, Greet Draye. Münster: Waxmann, 2011: 311–331.

———. *De nieuwe wereld: De wonderjaren van de Belgische avant-garde (1918–1939)*. Antwerpen: Meulenhoff/Manteau, 2010.

Pansaers, Clément. "L'Aplogie de la Paresse." *Haro!* 2e série, no. 10 (1 mai 1920): 6–7.

Pauwels, Peter J.H. "Die Belgische Künstlerin Marthe Donas und Der Sturm." In *Der Sturm*, edited by Andrea von Hëlsen-Esch and Gerhard Flinckh. Wuppertal: von der Heydt Museum, 2012: 359–376.

———. "'Trop artiste pour garder un nom féminin', Marthe 'Tour' Donas. Eine belgische Avantgarde Künstlerin und Der Sturm." In *Sturm-Frauen. Künstlerinnen der Avant-Garde in Berlin,* edited by Ingrid Pfeiffer and Max Hollein. Cologne: Wienand, 2015: 72–93.

Pauwels, Peter J. H. *Marthe Donas: A Woman Artist in the Avant-Garde*. Anvers: Ludion, 2016.

Peeters, Jozef. "Die flämische Kunst der Avantgarde." *Der Sturm: Monatsschrift für Kultur und die Künste* 15, 1 (März) (1924): 4–6.

Peeters, Natasja, and Sandrine Smets. "Face au portrait militaire: conventions et renouveau d'un genre de Waterloo à l' Yser." In *Actes du 8e Congrès de l'Association des Cercles francophones d'Histoire et d'Archéologie de Belgique – LVe Congrès de la Fédération des Cercles d'Archéologie et d'Histoire de Belgique, Namur 28–31 août 2008*. Namur, Société archéologique de Namur, 2011: 1219–1229 et 1401–1403.

Pevsner, Nikolaus. *Pioneers of the Modern Movement from William Morris to Walter Gropius*. London: Faber & Faber, 1936.

Phatak, N. R. ed. *Mahatma Gandhi Part III (1930–1931): Source material for a history of the freedom movement in India*, vol. III. Bombay, Maharashta State: Direcrorate of Printing and Stationary, 1969.

Picard, Leo. "The Flemish movement in a new world." In *Het Leven in de jaren 20*, Documentation brochure, NDJ Stage for advanced students at Genval, 20–29 August 1963, Brussels: Ministry of Education, National department for youth, 1963.

Pinney, Thomas, ed. *The Letters of Rudyard Kipling*. Volume 4, Iowa: University of Iowa, 1999: 1911 – 1919.

Piron, Christophe. "Le rôle des Services photographiques et du Laboratoire des Musées royaux d'Art et d'Histoire dans la sauvegarde du patrimoine artistique belge durant la Seconde Guerre mondiale." *Bulletin de l'IRPA (Institut Royal du patrimoine artistique/Koninklijk Instituut voor het kunstpatrimonium)* 33, (2009–2012), 2013: 257–287.

Piotrowski, Piotr. "Toward a Horizontal History of European Avant-Garde." In *European Avant-Garde and Modernism Studies*, directed by Sacha Bru and Peter Nichols, vol. 1. Berlin: De Gruyter, 2009: 49–58.

Platz, Gustav Adolf. *Die Baukunst der neuesten Zeit.* Berlin: Propyläen-Verlag, 1927, 1930.

Ploegaerts, Léon, and Pierre Puttemans. *L'Œuvre Architecturale de Henry van de Velde*. Brussels, Québec: Atelier Vokaer, Les Presses de l'Université Laval, 1987.

Pound, Ezra. "Emile Verhaeren." *Poetry*, Vol. 9, No. 5, February 1917, 257.

Purseigle, Pierre. "'A Wave on to Our Shores'; The Exile and Resettlement of Refugees from the Western Front, 1914 – 1918." *Contemporary European History*, 16, 4, 2007: 427–444.

Rainbird, Sean, ed. *Kollwitz - Beckmann - Dix - Grosz: Kriegszeit*. Tübingen/ Berlin: Ernst Wasmuth Verlag, 2011.

Rédaction, La. "HARO! paraît au moins une fois par mois...". *Haro!* 1e série, no. 1 (juin 1913): 2.

———. "HARO !." *Haro!* 2e série, no. 1 (5 Juillet 1919): 2.

Roberts-Jones, Philippe. *Du Réalisme au Surréalisme, Belgique art du temps*, Brussels, Laconti, 1969.

Robichon, François, ed. *La France et la Belgique occupies (1914–1918): Regards croisés*, Cahiers de l'IRHiS n° 7, Lille, 2009.

Roelants, Maurice. *De driedubbele verrassing*. Brussel: De Nieuwe Boekhandel, 1917.

Roland, Hubert. "*Résurrection*, Clément Pansaers et Carl Sternheim: 'comment rendre une revue intéressante.'" *Les Lettres romanes* XLVIII, 3–4 (1994): 259–275.

———. *Die deutsche literarische « Kriegskolonie » in Belgien 1914–1918. Beitrag zur Geschichte der deutsch-belgischen Literaturbeziehungen 1900–1920*. Bern: Peter Lang, 1999.

———. *La 'colonie' littéraire belgo-allemande 1914–1918*. Bruxelles: Archives et Musée de la Littérature, 2003.

———. "Construction identitaire et regard de l'autre. Récits de voyage allemands et français en Belgique 1830–1850." In *Literaire belgitude littéraire. Bruggen en beelden. Vues du Nord. Hommage aan Sonja Vanderlinden*, edited by Stéphanie Vanasten and Matthieu Sergier. Louvain-la-neuve: Presses Universitaires de Louvain, 2011: 133–152.

———. "Jean Delville et la Première Guerre Mondiale." In *Jean Delville (1867–1953): Maître de l'idéal*, edited by Jean Delville and Denis Laoureux. Paris: Somogy Editions, 2014: 96–102.

———. "Un Verhaeren expressionniste. La traduction allemande des Blés mouvants (Die wogende Saat, 1914/1917) par Paul Zech." In *Verhaeren en son temps*, directed by Paul Aron and Jean-Pierre Bertrand. n° 50–51/2016 of *Textyles. Revue des lettres belges de langue française*: 89–102.

Roland, Hubert, Marnix Beyen, and Marnix Draye, ed. *Deutschlandbilder in Belgien 1830–1940.* Studien zur Geschichte und Kultur Nordwesteuropas, 22. Münster, New York, München, Berlin: Waxmann, 2011.

Rossi-Schrimpf, Inga. "Terribly modern. Belgian artists and the Secessionist battle for Modern Art." In *Vienna : 1900 : Brussels*, edited by Piet Defraeye, Helga Mitterbauer, Chris Reyns. Amsterdam: Rodopi (to be published in 2018/19).

———. "From Art Nouveau to New Objectivity. Relations and interactions between the German and Belgian art milieux." In *The New Berlin. 1912-1932*, edited by Inga Rossi-Schrimpf, Tielt: Lannoo; Brussels: Royal Museums of Fine Arts of Belgium, 2018: 15-31.

Rost, Nico. "À propos du festival des Lettres flamandes." *Combat*, 4 décembre 1937.

Roth, Alfred, *Begegnung mit Pionieren: Le Corbusier, Piet Mondrian, Adolf Loos, Josef Hoffmann, Auguste Perret, Henry van de Velde*. Basel: Birkhäuser, 1973.

Salon d'Automne 1915, cat. Bruxelles: Musée Moderne, 1915.

Salon des Beaux-Arts 1915, cat. Bruxelles: Musée Moderne, 1915.

Sarkowski, Heinz. *Der Insel-Verlag 1899–1999.* Eingeleitet von Siegfried Unseld, Frankfurt/M.-Leipzig: Insel, 1999.

Saunier, Pierre-Yves. *Transnational History*. Basingstoke and New York: Palgrave Macmillan, 2013.

Scaldis. "L'Actualité. L'Art à Bruxelles. L'Exposition au Musée Moderne." *Le Bruxellois*, 26 février 1915.

Schneede, Uwe M. "Vorwort. " In *Die zwanziger Jahre. Manifeste und Dokumente deutscher Künstler*, edited by Uwe M. Schneede. Köln: DuMont, 1979.

Schneede, Uwe M., ed. *1914: the Avant-Gardes at war*. Köln: Snoeck – Kunst- und Ausstellungshalle der Bundesrepublik Deutschland, 2013.

Schultz, Joachim. "Mysterium, soziale Revolution, Menschenseele: Das Bild Belgiens in deutschen Literatur- und Kulturzeitschriften zwischen 1900 und 1930. Anmerkungen zu ausgewahlten Beispielen." In *Deutsch-belgische Beziehungen im kulturellen und literarischen Bereich 1890–1940: Les relations culturelles et littéraires belgo-allemandes 1890–1940*. Studien und Dokumente zur Geschichte der romanischen Literaturen 36, edited by Leonardy, Ernst, and Hubert Roland. Frankfurt am Main, Berlin, Bern, New York, Paris, Wien: Peter Lang; Lang, 1999: 108–122.

Schumacher, Fritz, ed. *Das Deutsche Kunstgewerbe 1906: 3. Deutsche Kunstgewerbeausstellung Dresden 1906.* Munich: F. Bruckmann, 1906.

Section artistique de l'Armée. 2e Exposition (La Panne, 15–31 mars 1917), cat.

Sembach, Klaus-Jürgen, and Birgit Schulte, eds. *Henry van de Velde: Ein europäischer Künstler seiner Zeit*. Cologne: Wienand, 1992.

Servellón, Sergio. *Karel Maes 1900–1974*. Drogenbos: Museum Felix De Boeck, 2007.

———. "Gemeenschapskunst en Zuivere Beelding: twee kanten van dezelfde constructivistische medaille, Victor Servranckx in de jaren 1922–23." In *Victor Servranckx, de jaren twintig*. Ostend: Mu.ZEE- AsaMER, 2012: 36-57.

———. "Een ontbolsterende avant-garde. Felix De Boeck tijdens WO I." In *De Groote Oorlog in Vlaams-Brabant*. Themanummer van Openbaar Kunstbezit Vlaanderen, edited by M. Vervaeck, 18–21. Ghent: Openbaar Kunstbezit Vlaanderen, 2014: 18-21.

Seuphor, Michel et al. *Abstract Painting in Flanders*. Brussels: Arcade, 1963

Sharp, Dennis, ed. *Henri van de Velde: Theatre designs 1904–1914 = Projets du théâtre 1904–1914*. London: Architectural Association, 1974.

Simoens, Tom. "De operaties van het Belgische leger tijdens de stellingsoorlog (1914–1917)." In *14–18 Oorlog in België*, edited by Luc Devos et al. Leuven: Davidsfonds, 2014: 245–64.

Smets, Marcel. *RESURGAM, De Belgische wederopbouw na 1914*. Brussel: Gemeentekrediet van België, 1985.

Smets, Sandrine. "Les artistes belges face à la Grande Guerre." Mémoire de Diplôme d'Etudes approfondies en Philosophie et Lettres, Université Libre de Bruxelles, 2006.

———. "Paysage de ruines ou ruine du patrimoine. Topos de la vision apocalyptique des artistes belges et français de la Grande Guerre." In *Actes de la Journée d'étude France-Belgique "La France et la Belgique occupées (1914–1918): regards croisés" 25 avril 2008 – Cahier de l'IRHiS* n° 7. Lille, Université Charles-de-Gaulle – Lille 3, 2009: 46–57.

———. "Section artistique de l'armée belge." In *1917*, edited by Laurent Le Bon et Claire Garnier. Metz, Centre Pompidou-Metz, 2012: 264.

———. "Achille Van Sassenbrouck. A Wounded Body, a Healing Oeuvre." In *War & Trauma*, edited by Patrick Allegaert, Georgina Boyes et al. Ieper - Gent, Hannibal: In Flanders Fields Museum - Museum Dr. Guislain, 2013: 114–119.

———. "Créer sous le feu. Origines et organisation de la section artistique de l'armée belge." *Bulletin du Musée royal de l'Armée et d'Histoire militaire. Contributions à l'étude du patrimoine militaire* 3 (2014): 124–43.

———. "André Lynen, observateur d'artillerie. L'œil de l'artiste au service de la tactique militaire pendant la Grande Guerre." In *Un milliard d'obus, des millions d'hommes*, edited by Gilles Aubagnac, Johanne Berlemont, Marjolaine Boutet et al. Paris - Meaux: Liénart - Musée de la Grande Guerre du Pays de Meaux, 2016: 38–47.

Sonderausstellung der belgischen Kunstvereinigung L'Art Contemporain. 1914.

Stamm, Günther. "Monumental Architecture and Ideology: Henry Van de Velde's and Harry Graf Kessler's Project for a Nietzsche Monument at Weimar, 1910–1914." *Gentse Bijdragen tot de Kunstgeschiedenis*, 23, (1973–75): 303–342.

Storr, Katherine. *Excluded from the Record. Women, Refugees and Relief. 1914–1929*, Oxford: Peter Lang, 2009.

Strauven, Iwan. *Les frères Bourgeois. Architecture et plastique pure*. Bruxelles: Editions Archives d'Architecture Moderne, 2005.

Sylvester, D. and Whitfield S., ed. *René Magritte, catalogue raisonné. I: Oil Paintings 1916–1930*. Houston: Menil Foundation; Milano: Electa; London: Fonds Mercator, 1992.

http://www.tate.org.uk/context-comment/video/constructivism-and-art-everyday-life-part-4 (accessed December 2, 2012).

Tiedau, Ulrich. "De Duitse cultuurpolitiek in België tijdens de Eerste Wereldoorlog." *Cahiers d'Histoire du Temps présent*, no. 11 (2003): 21–45.

Toussaint, Nathalie. "Contacts des peintres et graphistes belges avec Ia revue Der Sturm." In *Deutsch-belgische Beziehungen im kulturellen und literarischen Bereich 1890–1940: Les relations culturelles et littéraires belgo-allemandes 1890–1940*. Studien und Dokumente zur Geschichte der romanischen Literaturen 36, edited by Leonardy, Ernst, and Hubert Roland. Frankfurt am Main, Berlin, Bern, New York, Paris, ·Wien: Peter Lang; Lang, 1999: 221–245.

———. "Interconnexions des avant-gardes picturales entre la Belgique, l'Allemagne et les Pays-Bas de 1914 à 1924: Une exemplification." PhD diss. Université Catholique de Louvain, 2000. Accessed March 11, 2018.

Tuijn, Marguerite. "'C'est donc partout la même chose'. Marthe Donas verkent de Engelse kunstwereld voor Theo van Doesburg." *Jong Holland*, 1999, no. 1: 32–41.

———. "Mon cher ami... Lieber Does... Theo van Doesburg en de praktijk van de international avant-garde" Doctoral thesis, University of Amsterdam, 2003

———. "Archipenko and Theo van Doesburg". In *Alexander Archipenko Revisited: An International Perspective. Proceedings from the Archipenko Symposium* (Cooper Union, New York City, 17 septembre 2005), directed by Deborah Goldberg et Alexandra Keiser. Bearsville: Archipenko Foundation, 2008: 42–56.

Uyttenhove, Pieter. "Internationale inspanningen voor een modern België." In *RESURGAM De Belgische wederopbouw na 1914,* edited by Marcel Smets. Brussels: 1985: 33–68.

Van Causenbroeck, Bernard. *Herman Vos. Van Vlaams-nationalisme naar socialisme.* Antwerp-Ghent: 1997.

Van de Kerckhove, Fabrice, ed. *Bruxelles, Vienne 1890–1938.* Bruxelles: CFC, 1987.

Van de Velde, Henry. "Déblaiement de l'Art." *La Société Nouvelle* 10, no. 112 (avril 1894): 444–56.

———. "Gegen-Leitsätze." In Muthesius. *Die Werkbund-Arbeit der Zukunft* (1914): 49–51

———. "Die Pariser Kunstgewerbeausstellung." *Europäische Revue,* 1, No. 7 (october 1925): 41–52.

———. "De heilige Weg." *Kunst,* No. 10/11/12 (1933): 327–342; in French: idem: *La Voie Sacrée.* Brussels: Institut Supérier des Arts Décoratives, 1933.

———. *Récit de ma vie. Berlin – Weimar – Paris – Bruxelles. II. 1900–1917,* edited by Anne van Loo and Fabrice van de Kerckhove. Brussels; Paris: Flammarion; Versa,1995.

Van Doesburg, Theo. "Vers une Construction collective." *Punct. Revista de arte constructivista internationala,* no. 8 (9 januari 1925).

Van Fassen, Sjoerd and August H. den Boef. *Het pseudo moderne nevens het ware. De briefwisseling van de architect J.J.P. Oud met Jozef Peeters en Michel Seuphor, redacteuren van het constructivistische tijdschrift Het Overzicht, 1921 – 1925.* Antwerp: Zacht Lawijd / Garant Uitgevers, 2008.

Van Faassen, Sjoerd, Hans Renders, and Erik Buelinckx. "'De stem uit de diepte': een onuitgegeven 'simultanéistisch spel' van Theo van Doesburg." *Zacht Lawijd. Literair-historisch tijdschrift,* no. 15–3 (2016): 4–55.

Van Kalck, Michèle, ed. *Les Musés royaux des Beaux-Arts de Belgique. Deux siècles d'histoire, vol. 1.* Brussels: Dexia Banque/ Racine, 2003.

Van Ostaijen, Paul. "Open letter to Mr Camille Huijsmans." *De Toorts* (24 April 1920).

———. *Verzameld werk. IV. Proza: Besprekingen en beschouwingen,* Amsterdam: Bakker, 1979.

Van Peteghem, Sylvia. "Hoe staat het nu toch met Onze Kunst? Een briefwisseling tussen L.J Veen en Paul Buschmann sr. en jr. (1900–1919)." *Jaarboek Letterkundig Museum* 3. Nederlands Letterkundig Museum en Documentatiecentrum: Den Haag 1994: 11–22.

Van Uffelen, Herbert. *Moderne niederländische Literatur im deutschen Sprachraum 1830–1990.* Münster: Zentrum für Niederlande-Studien, 1993.

Van Ypersele, Laurence. "Propagandes de guerre et consentements des populations." In *Questions d'histoire contemporaine. Conflits, mémoires et identités*, edited by Laurence van Ypersele. Paris: Presses Universitaires de France, 2006: 186.

Vanclooster, Stijn, Moulaert, Jan and Joos, Erwin. *De Kapel tussen droom en daad. Anarchie en artistieke heropleving in Antwerpen rond 1900.* Antwerpen: VZW Eugeen Van Mieghem, 2013.

Vandenbroucke, Dieter. *Dansen op een vulkaan. Victor J. Brunclair, schrijver in een bewogen tijd.* Antwerp: De Bezige Bij, 2013.

Vanderleenen, Albert, and Gheysens, Godwin. "Daenens, Albert." In *Nieuwe Encyclopedie van de Vlaamse Beweging*, edited by Reginald de Schryver, Bruno de Wever, Gaston Durnez, Lieve Gevers, Pieter van Hees and Machteld de Metsenaere. Tielt: Lannoo, 1998: 841.

Vandevoorde, Hans. "L'art communautaire au début des années 1920: de l'expressionisme au constructivisme." In *Modernisme. L'art abstrait belge et l'Europe*, edited by Johan De Smet. Gent: Museum voor Schone Kunsten/Fonds Mercator, 2013: 223–247.

———. "Generatie Schierbeek. Lyricisering in de jaren vijftig," *"Een eeuw lyrisch proza." Belgisch Tijdschrift voor Filologie en Geschiedenis/Revue Belge de Philologie et d'Histoire* 91, no. 3 (2013): 1129–1146.

Vandevoorde, Hans, and Christophe Verbruggen. "*Transgenerational Brokering*. The case for Symbolism and Surrealism in Flanders." *Belgisch Tijdschrift voor Filologie en Geschiedenis/ Revue Belge de Philologie et d'Histoire* 92, no. 4 (2014): 1343–1358.

Vandeweyer, Luc. *De eerste wereldoorlog. Koning Albert en zijn soldaten*. Anvers: Standaard Uitgeverij, 2005.

Vandi, Loretta, ed. *Ornament and European Modernism: From Art Practice to Art History*. London: Routledge, 2017.

Varlez, Armand. *Les Belges en Exil*, London: Librairie Moderne, 1917.

Venema, Adriaan. *De ballingen: Frits van den Berghe, Gustave De Smet en Rik Wouters in Nerderland 1914–1921*. Baarn: Het Wereldvenster, 1979.

Verhack, Valérie et al. ed. *Karel Maes*. Drogenbos: Musée Felix De Boeck, 2007.

Verhack, Valérie, Giovanni Lista, and Willard Bohn, *Jules Schmalzigaug: Un futuriste belge*. Cahiers des Musées royaux des Beaux-Arts de Belgique, vol. 8 (2010).

Verdickt, Caterina. "Belgische kunstenaars in Groot-Brittannië tijdens de Eerste Wereldoorlog 1914 – 1918." Lic. Verh., Katholieke Universiteit Leuven, 1999.

———. "The case of Elisabeth De Saedeleer (1902–1972): The influence of Welsh hospitality in the Great War on Belgian Modernist interior design." *The British Art Journal* 3, vol XV, 2015.

Vermeylen, Auguste. "Vlaamsche en Europese Beweging." *Van Nu en Straks*, new series 4 (november 1900), No. 5/6: 310.

Vinzent, Jutta. *Identity and Image. Refugee artists from Nazi Germany in Britain (1933–1945).* Weimar: VDG, Verlag und Datenbank für Geisteswissenschaften, 2006.

Vogt, Sébastien. "La dévotion des combattants à la « petite Soeur » Thérèse de Lisieux pendant la Première Guerre mondiale. " Master's Thesis, Université de Strasbourg, 2012.

Von der Lancken-Wakenitz, Oscar. *Gouverner en Belgique occupée. Oscar von der Lancken-Wakenitz – Rapports d'activité 1915–1918*, edited by Michael Amara et Hubert Roland, directed by Michel Dumoulin et José Gotovitch. Bruxelles: P.I.E.-Peter Lang, 2004.

Von Garvens, Herbert. *James Ensor: Maler, Radierer, Komponist; Ein Hinweis mit d. vollst. Katalog s. radierten Werkes als Anh.* Hannover: Ey, 1913.

Von Ploennies, Luise. *Reise-Erinnerungen aus Belgien*. Berlin: Verlag von Duncker & Humblot, 1845.

Vos, Herman, "Ter inleiding." *Ruimte* volume I, no. 1-2 (March 1920): 1–4.

Watelet, Jacques G., and de Ville, Annick. "La première rencontre de Hannes Meyer et de Victor Bourgeois." *ICSAC* 6/7, Februrar (1987): 297–315.

Waterlot-Jottrand, Véronique, and Lefebvre, Daniel ed. *Haro! Une revue belge d'avant-garde 1913–1928*. Mons: Renard Découvert / Mundaneum, 1995.

Weigel, Sigrid. *Genea-Logik. Generation, Tradition und Evolution zwischen Kultur- und Naturwissenschaften*. München: Wilhelm Fink Verlag, 2006.

Wendland, Ulrike. *Biographisches Handbuch deutschsprachiger Kunsthistoriker im Exil. Leben und Werk der unter dem Nationalsozialismus verfolgten und vertriebenen Wissenschaftler*. Vol. 1. München: Saur, 1999.

Werner, Lisa. *Der Kubismus stellt aus. Der Salon de la Section d'Or.* Paris 1912. Berlin: Reimer, 2011.

Whitley, W.T. "Notes. Belgian Art." *The Burlington Magazine for Connoisseurs*. Vol. 26, No. 144, March 1915: 255–261.

Winskell, Kate. "The Art of Propaganda: Herwarth Walden and ‚Der Sturm' 1914–1919." *Art History* 18, 3 (1995): 329.

Wintgens Hötte, Doris. "Utopia 1900–1940. Visions of a New World: An Introduction." In *Utopia 1900–1940. Visions of a New World*. Rotterdam: nai010, 2013.

Wohl, Robert. *The Generation of 1914*. Cambridge: Harvard University Press, 1979.

———. "The Generation of 1914 and Modernism." In Monique Chefdor, Ricardo Quinones and Albert Wachtel. *Modernism. Challenges and Perspectives*. Urbana and Chicago: University of Illinois Press, 1986: 66–78.

Wullens, Maurice. "Revue des revues." *La Revue Anarchiste* 3, no. 26 (avril 1924).

———. *Eroïnes. Proses. Ballades à travers la vieille Carte du Tendre en compagnie d'éroïques héroïnes modernes*, edited by Valentin Bresle Lille: Mercure de Flandre, 1925.

Zacharias, Kylikki. "Surreale Sachlichkeit." In *Surreale Sachlichkeit: Werke der 1920er- und 1930er Jahre aus der Nationalgalerie*, edited by Kylikki Zacharias. Berlin, Dresden: Neue Nationalgalerie - Staatliche Museen zu Berlin; Sandstein Verlag, 2016: 8-23.

Zweig, Stefan. *The World of Yesterday. An Autobiography*. London, Toronto, Melbourne, Sidney: Cassell and Company Ltd. 1947.

Illustration Credits

akg-images, Paris : 9.5
Archives de la ville de Bruxelles : 2.5 ; 2.6 ; 13.1-2
Archives Général du Royaume, Belgique : 2.4
Atelier Louis Held, Weimar : 15.1
Bibliothèque Kandinsky (Centre Pompidou), Fonds Survage, Paris : 14.1
Bildarchiv Foto Marburg: 15.2
CegeSoma, Brussels: 2.2
Coll. IHOES, Seraing : 2.3a-b
Felix De Boeckarchief, FeliXart Museum, Drogenbos: 10.1
FeliXart Museum, Drogenbos: 10.2
KIK-IRPA, Brussels : 2.1 ; 8.1-3; p. 378, inv. 4682/ p. 380, inv. 4680
Lauric Beugnies: 1.1
Letterenhuis, Antwerpen: 10.3
National Portrait Gallery, London: 5.2
Private collection : 2.7; 11.1-3; 12.1; 16.1-3
Rijksmuseum Kröller-Müller, Otterlo: 15.4
Royal Library, Archives and French Literature Museum, Brussels: 15.3; 15.5 (© Photo Sergysels)
Royal Museum of the Armed Forces and Military History, Belgium: 2.10; 4.1-3; p. 380, inv. 70076/53; p. 381, inv. 10076/17
Royal Museum of Fine Arts of Belgium: 3.2; 3.6; 3.10; 3.12
Royal Museum of Fine Arts of Belgium/ ACAB: 6.1-2; 14.2
Royal Museum of Fine Arts of Belgium/ photo: ACL: 3.1
Royal Museum of Fine Arts of Belgium/ photo : Guy Cussac, Bruxelles: 9.4
Royal Museum of Fine Arts of Belgium/ photo: Grafisch Buro Lefevre, Heule: p. 375, inv. 10538
Royal Museum of Fine Arts of Belgium/ photo : J. Geleyns - Art Photography: 3.3; 3.5; 3.9; 3.13; 3.15; 3.16; 6.3 and p. 369-381
Royal Museum of Fine Arts of Belgium/ photo: F. Maes (RMFAB): p. 370, inv. 7557
Staatsbibliothek zu Berlin : 2.8
Stadsarchief Aalst: 2.9
William Morris Gallery: 5.1

The publishers have made every effort to trace all relevant copyright holders and apologise for omissions that may have been made.

List of works shown in the exhibition 14-18. Rupture or Continuity – Belgian Art around World War I

All following works are from the collection of the Royal Museums of Fine Arts of Belgium, Brussels.

14-18. Rupture or Continuity?

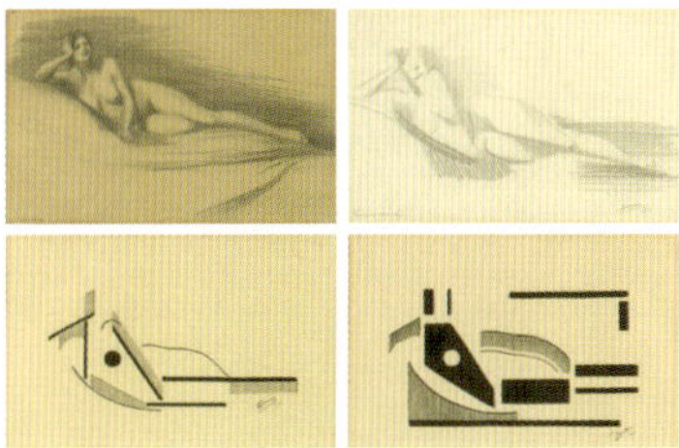

Marthe Donas (1885 – 1967)
Lying nude n° 1-4
Nu couché n° 1-4
Liggend naakt nr. 1-4
(1915) l 1917 l 1920
Lead pencil on paper l Mine de plomb sur papier | Loodpotlood op papier
Indian ink on paper l Encre de chine sur papier | Oost-Indische inkt op papier
16 x 24,4 cm l 15 x 23 cm l 18 x 24,5 cm
Inv. 6958 - 6961
Date of acquisition 1962

Rik Wouters and Ferdinand Schirren: Beyond Ensor

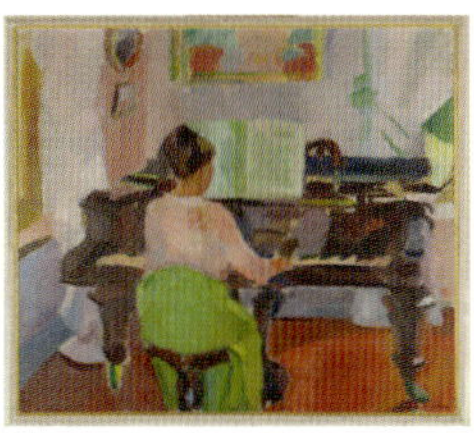

Ferdinand Schirren (1872 – 1944)
The woman at the piano
La femme au piano
De vrouw aan de piano
(ca. 1915-1917)
Oil on canvas l Huile sur toile | Olieverf op doek
136 x 151 cm
Inv. 8955
Date of acquisition 1977

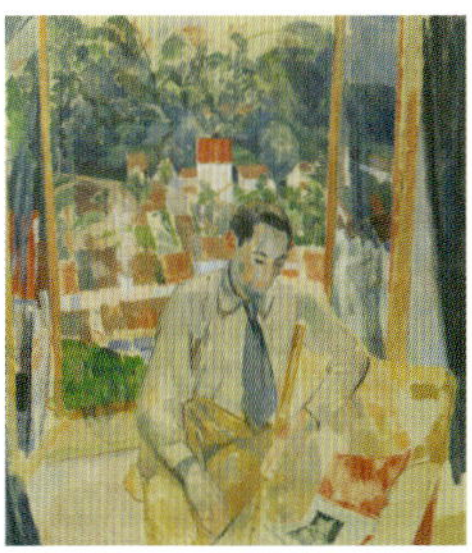

Rik Wouters (1882 – 1916)
The flautist
Le flûtiste
De fluitspeler
(1914)
Oil on canvas l Huile sur toile | Olieverf op doek
133,5 x 115 cm
Inv. 4742
Date of acquisition 1928

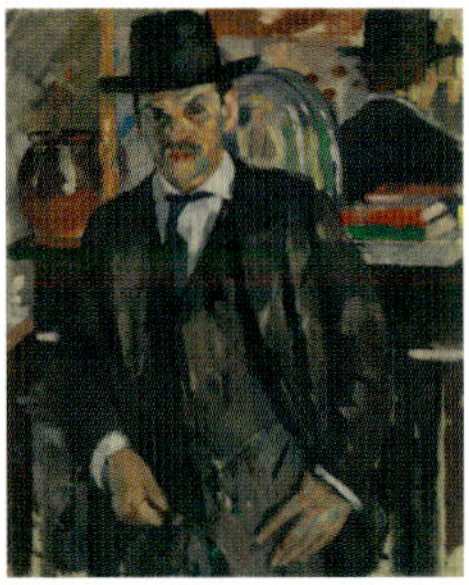

Rik Wouters (1882 – 1916)
Portrait of Simon Lévy
Portrait de Simon Lévy
Portret van Simon Lévy
(1913)
Oil on canvas l Huile sur toile | Olieverf op doek
100,5 x 80,2 cm
Inv. 4744
Date of acquisition 1928

Jules Schmalzigaug: a new world

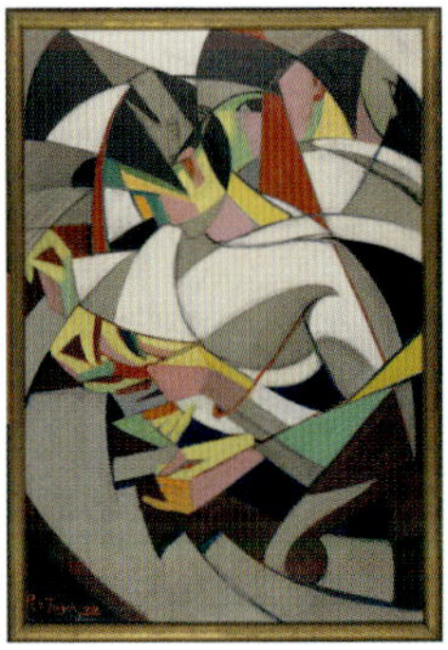

Prosper de Troyer (1888 – 1961)
The seamstress
La couturière
De naaister
1920
Oil on wood l Huile sur bois | Olieverf op hout
150 x 99 cm
Inv. 7939
Date of acquisition 1971

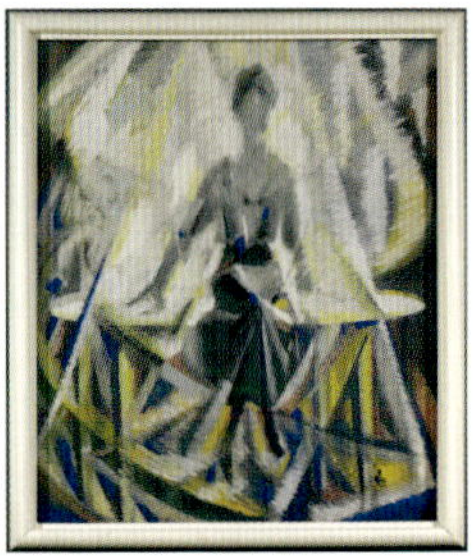

Jules Schmalzigaug (1882 – 1917)
Mrs Nelly Hurrelbrinck
Madame Nelly Hurrelbrinck
Mevrouw Nelly Hurrelbrinck
(ca. 1917)
Distemper on triplex panel l Peinture à la colle sur triplex |
Lijmverf op triplexplaat
120 x 101 cm
Inv. 7557
Date of acquisition 1968

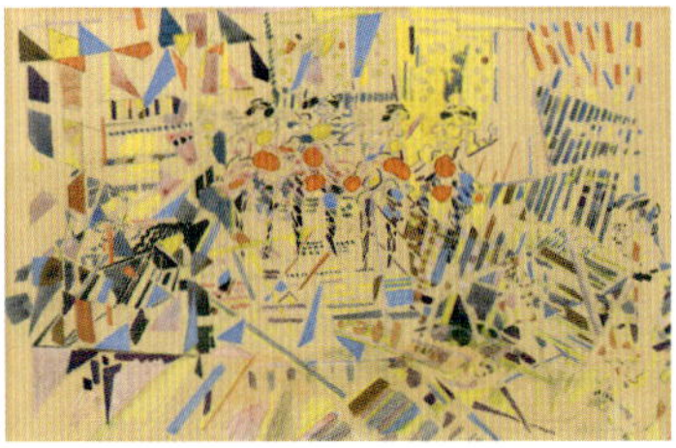

Jules Schmalzigaug (1882 – 1917)
The dancers
Les danseuses
De danseressen
(1914-1915)
Black chalk, watercolour on paper l Craie noire, aquarelle sur papier | Zwart krijt, aquarelle op papier
33,9 x 50,6 cm
Inv. 10046
Date of acquisition 1983

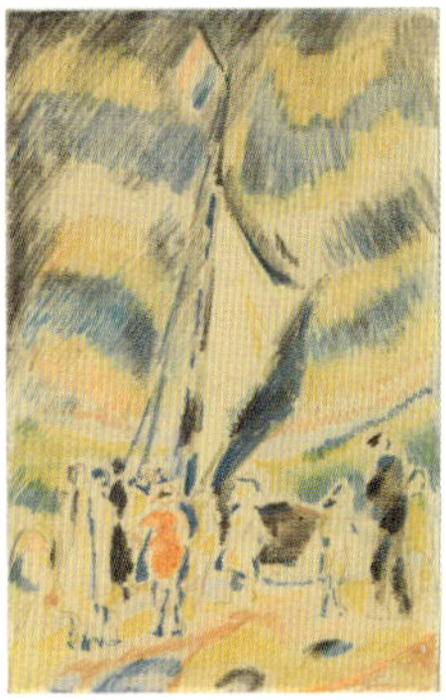

Jules Schmalzigaug (1882 – 1917)
Scheveningen
(1914 - 1915)
Colour chalk and pastel on paper, glued on cardboard l Craie de couleur et pastel sur papier, collé sur carton | Kleurkrijt en pastel op papier, gekleefd op karton
33 x 20,6 cm
Inv. 10047
Date of acquisition 1983

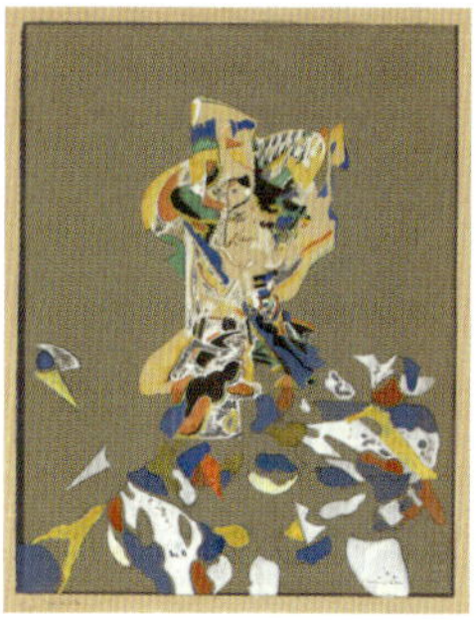

Jules Schmalzigaug (1882 – 1917)
Revolving door
Porte tournante
Draaideur
(1915-1917)
Black chalk, gouache, collage on gray paper l Craie noire, gouache, collage sur papier gris | Zwart krijt, gouache, collage op grijs papier
32,3 x 24,5 cm
Inv. 10052
Date of acquisition 1983

Abstraction, avant-garde and the community

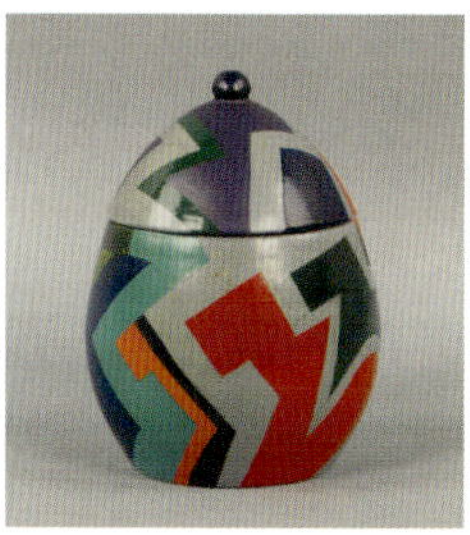

Jan Cockx (1891 – 1976)
Small painted vase, with lid
Petit vase peint, avec couvercle
Beschilderd potje, met deksel
(ca. 1920-1922)
Oil on terra cotta l Huile sur terre cuite | Olieverf op terracotta
9,5 x 10,5 cm, ø 8,5 cm
Inv. 10374
Date of acquisition 1985

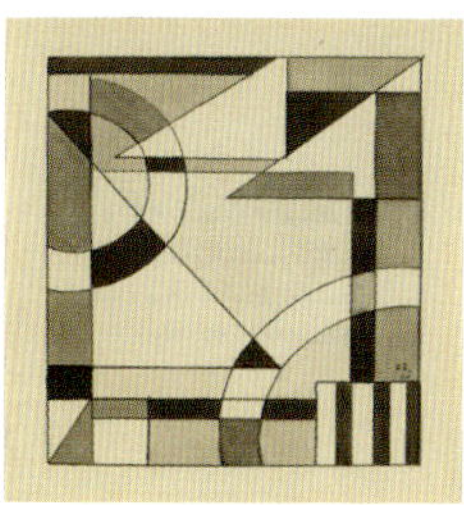

Félix De Boeck (1898 – 1995)
Geometrical composition
Composition géométrique
Geometrische compositie
1920
Indian ink, washing on paper l Encre de Chine, lavis sur papier | Oost-indische inkt, gewassen op papier
14,7 x 13,7 cm
Inv. 7834
Date of acquisition 1971

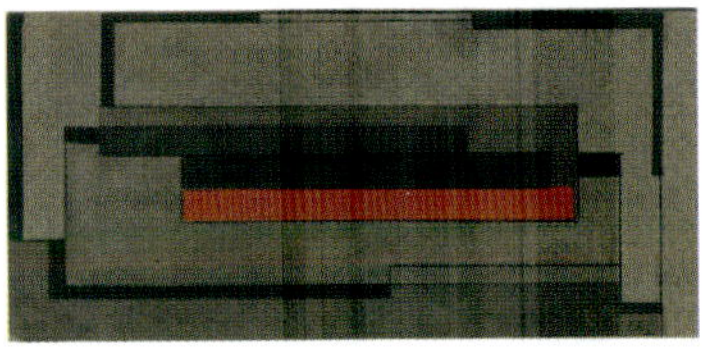

Félix De Boeck (1898 – 1995)
Abstract collage
Collage abstrait
Abstracte collage
1920
Indian ink, washing on red glazed paper l Encre de Chine et lavis, sur papier glacé rouge | Oost-indische inkt, gewassen, op rood glanspapier 10 x 20,8 cm
Inv. 7837
Date of acquisition 1971

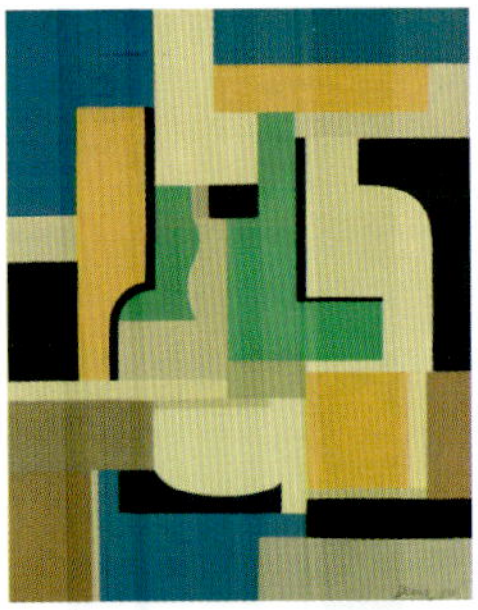

Marthe Donas (1885 – 1967)
Abstract composition n° 5
Composition abstraite n° 5
Abstracte compositie nr. 5
1920
Oil on cardboard l Huile sur carton | Olieverf op karton
63,4 x 49,4 cm
Inv. 8579
Date of acquisition 1976

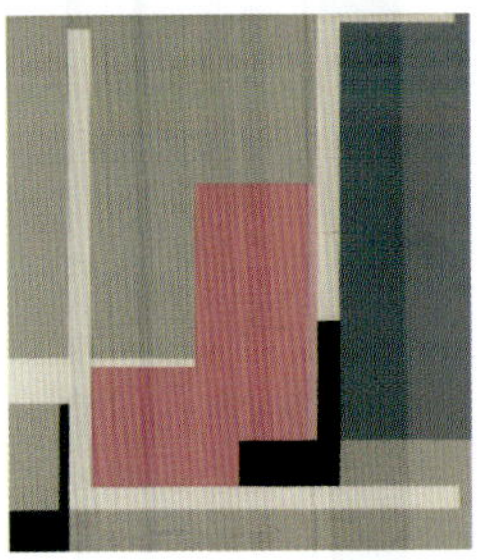

Marthe Donas (1885 – 1967)
Construction
Construction
Constructie
(1920)
Oil on wood l Huile sur bois | Olieverf op hout
48 x 42 cm
Inv. 12035
Date of acquisition 1998

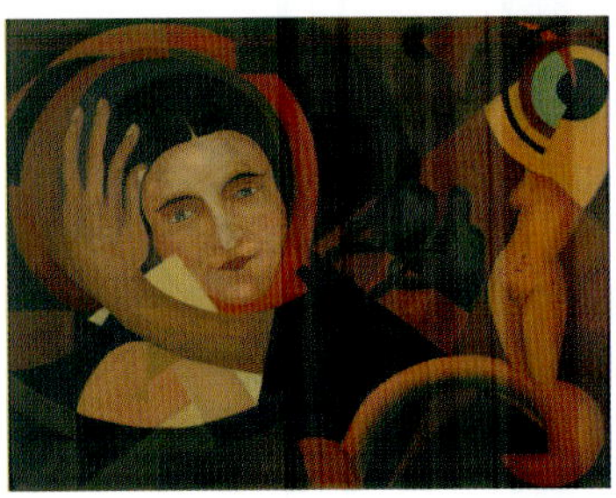

Marc Eemans (1907 – 1998)
Opus 26
1926
Oil on wood l Huile sur bois | Olieverf op hout
57,5 x 73 cm
Inv. 11858
Date of acquisition 1996

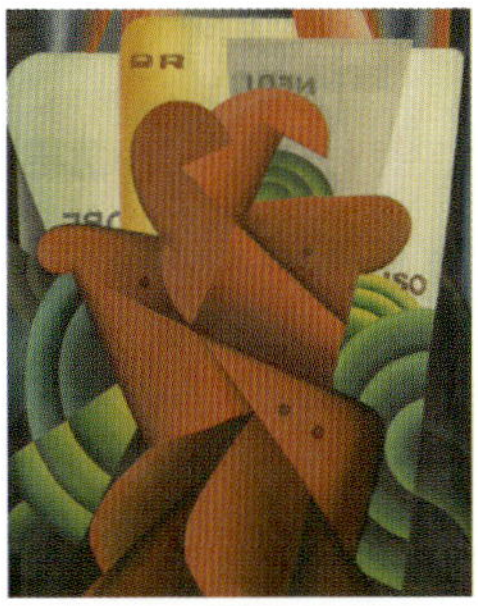

Pierre-Louis Flouquet (1900 – 1967)
Composition
Composition
Compositie
(1921)
Oil on triplex panel l Huile sur triplex | Olieverf op triplex
71,5 x 56,5 cm
Inv. 7645
Date of acquisition 1969

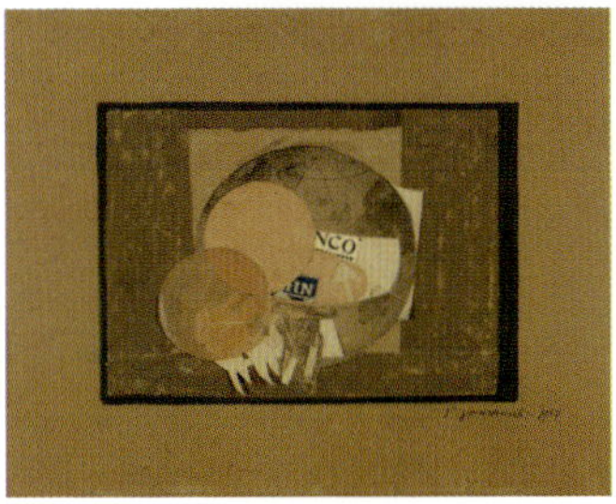

Paul Joostens (1889 – 1960)
Collage
1917
Coloured paper, printed paper glued on cardboard, rim in Indian ink l Papier de couleur, papier imprimé collés sur carton, bord à l'encre de Chine | Gekleurd papier, bedrukt papier gekleefd op karton, boord in Oost-Indische inkt
27,5 x 33,6 cm
Inv. 6886
Date of acquisition 1960

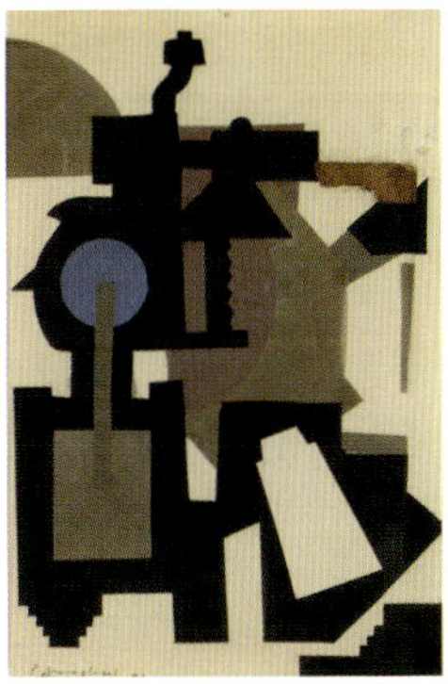

Paul Joostens (1889 – 1960)
Collage
1920
Coloured paper glued on cardboard l Papier de couleur collé sur carton | Gekleurd papier gekleefd op karton
42,4 x 28,8 cm
Inv. 6887
Date of acquisition 1960

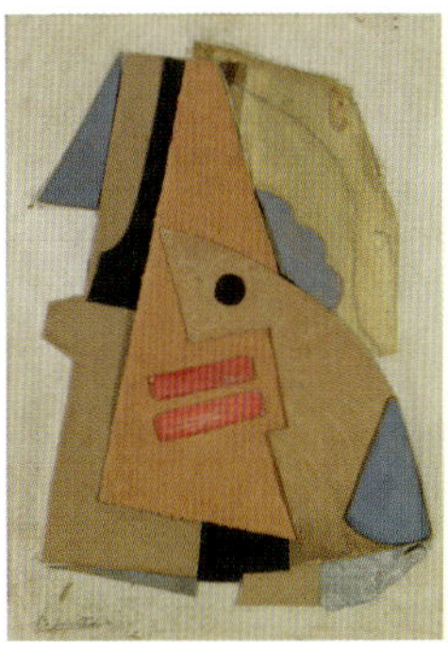

Paul Joostens (1889 – 1960)
Collage
1922
Coloured paper and silver paper glued on cardboard l Papier de couleur et papier d'argent collés sur carton | Gekleurd papier en zilverpapier gekleefd op karton
38,4 x 28 cm
Inv. 6888
Date of acquisition 1960

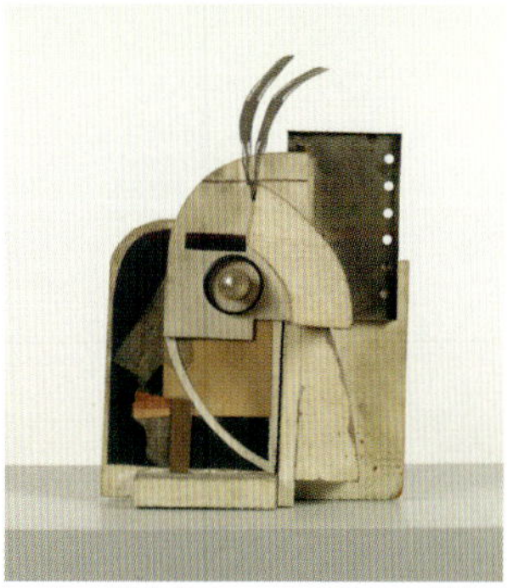

Paul Joostens (1889 – 1960)
Object – collage
Objet – collage
Object – collage
1922
Assemblage of painted wood, metal, gas, coloured paper, cardboard and nacre ball l Assemblage de bois peint, métal, gaze, papier de couleur, carton et boule en nacre | Assemblage van beschilderd hout, metaal, gaas, gekleurd papier, karton en parelmoeren bol
48 x 31,3 x 24,5 cm
Inv. 6885
Date of acquisition 1960

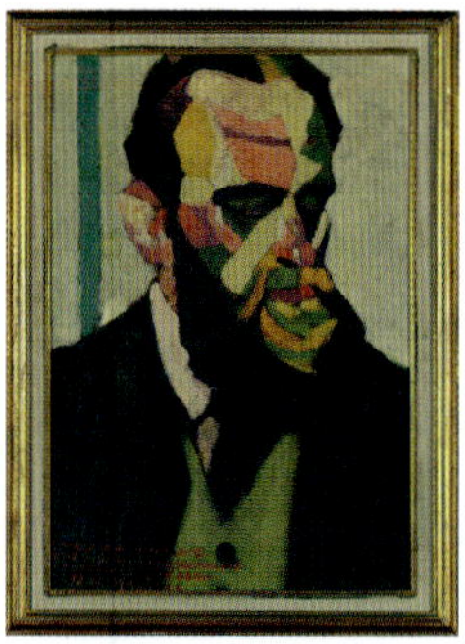

René Magritte (1898 – 1967)
Portrait of the writer Pierre Broodcorens
Portrait de l'écrivain Pierre Broodcoorens
Portret van de schrijver Pierre Broodcoorens
1921
Oil on canvas mounted on unalit panel l Huile sur toile marouflée sur unalit | Olieverf op doek voluit gekleefd op unalit
59,5 x 37,5 cm
Inv. 7801
Date of acquisition 1972

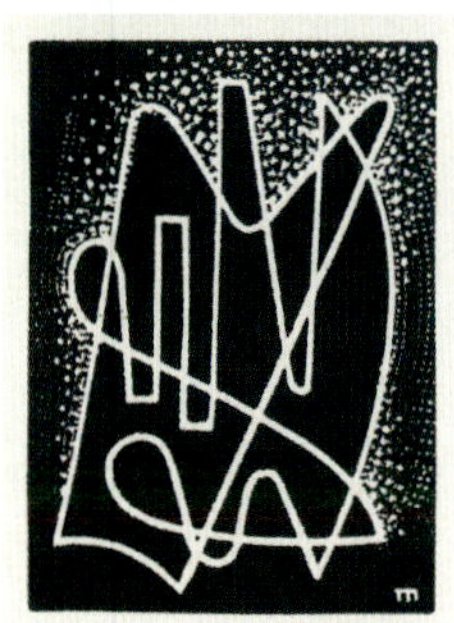

Karel Maes (1900 – 1974)
Lino block (1); Lino print (2)
Bloc de lino (1) ; lino (2)
Linoblok (1) ; Linodruk (2)
(1919)
Linoleum on wood (1), Printing ink on paper (2) l Linoléum sur bois (1), Encre d'impression sur papier (2) | Linoleum op hout (1), Drukinkt op papier (2)
8,5 x 6 cm
Inv. 10369/1-2
Date of acquisition 1985

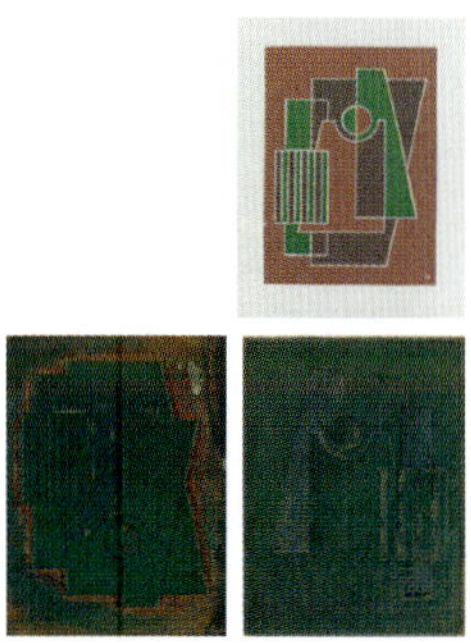

Karel Maes (1900 – 1974)
Lino block (1); Lino block (2); Lino print (3)
Bloc de lino (1) ; Bloc de lino (2) ; Lino (3)
Linoblok (1); Linoblok (2); Linodruk (3)
(1921)
Linoleum on wood (1; 2); Coloured printing ink on paper (3) l Linoléum sur bois (1; 2) ; Encre d'impression de couleur sur papier (3) | Linoleum op hout (1; 2) ; Gekleurde drukinkt op papier (3)
14,9 x 11,3 cm l 18 x 13 cm l 18,1 x 13 cm
Inv. 10372/1-3
Date of acquisition 1985

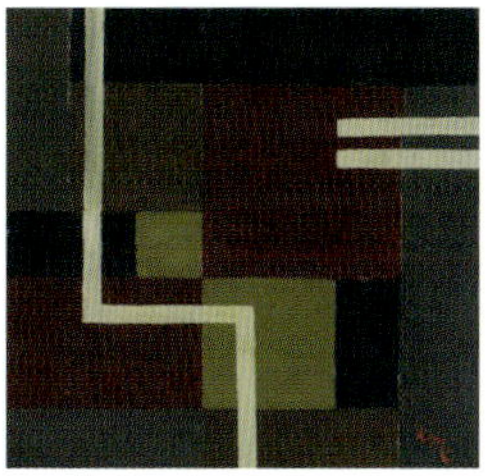

Karel Maes (1900 – 1974)
Painting
Peinture
Schilderij
(1922)
Oil on cardboard l Huile sur carton | Olieverf op karton
36,8 x 36,4 cm
Inv. 10538
Date of acquisition 1986

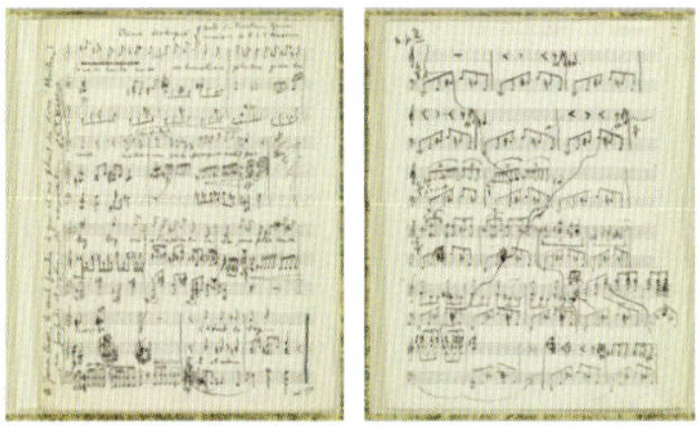

E.L.T. Mesens (1903 – 1971)
Crime distingué
(1924)
Indian ink on paper l Encre de Chine sur papier | Oost-Indische inkt op papier
31,2 x 23,5 cm
Inv. 8614
Date of acquisition 1976

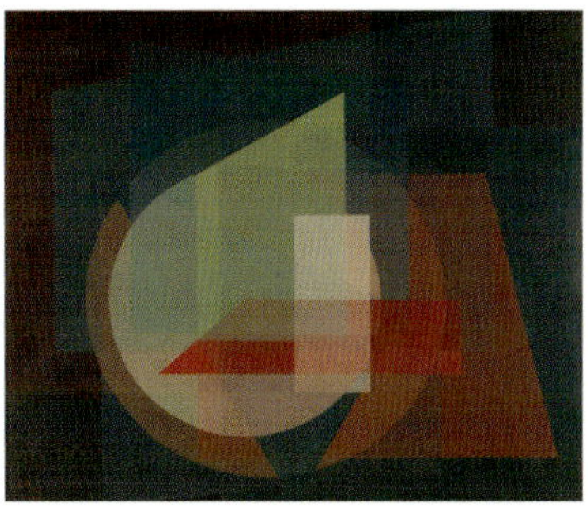

Jozef Peeters (1895 – 1960)
Oil n° 21
Huile n° 21
Olieverf nr. 21
(1924)
Oil on canvas l Huile sur toile | Olieverf op doek
144 x 166,5 cm
Inv. 6892
Date of acquisition 1960

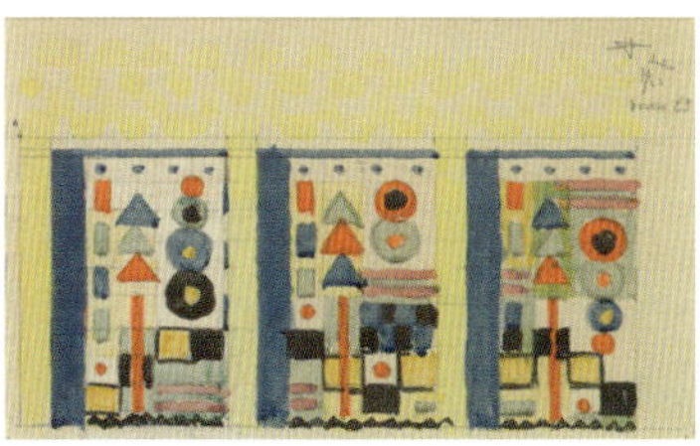

Jozef Peeters (1895 – 1960)
Project for a vase n° 23
Projet pour un vase n° 23
Ontwerp voor een vaas nr. 23
1923
Pencil, watercolour on paper l Crayon, aquarelle, collage sur papier | Potlood, aquarel, collage op papier
16,9 x 27,3 cm (jour)
Inv. 10336
Date of acquisition 1985

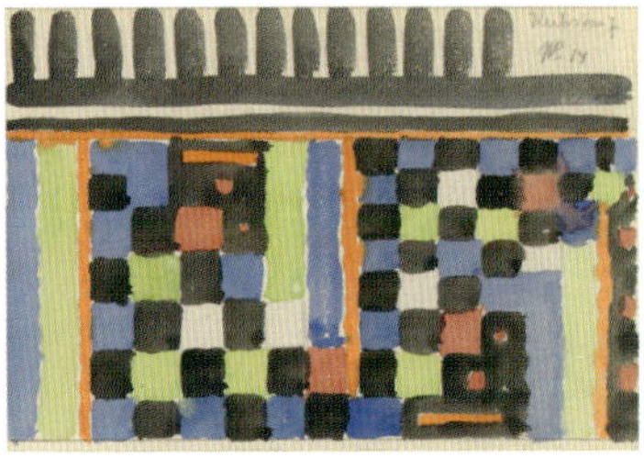

Jozef Peeters (1895 – 1960)
Typographical composition : Wensen aan Pelleke. 19 mei 1922
Composition typographique : Wensen aan Pelleke. 19 mei 1922
Typografische compositie : Wensen aan Pelleke. 19 mei 1922
1922
Pencil, Indian ink, plume, brush, watercolour on paper l Crayon, encre de Chine, plume, pinceau, aquarelle sur papier | Potlood, Oost-Indische inkt, pen, penseel, aquarel op papier
47,6 x 37,1 cm
Inv. 10330
Date of acquisition 1985

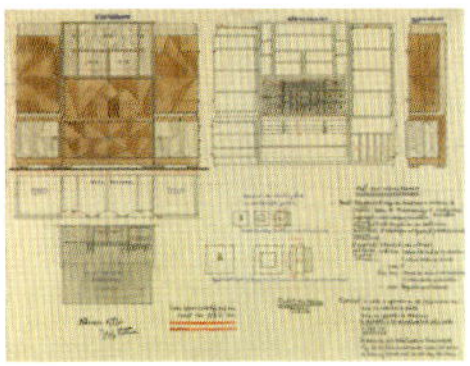

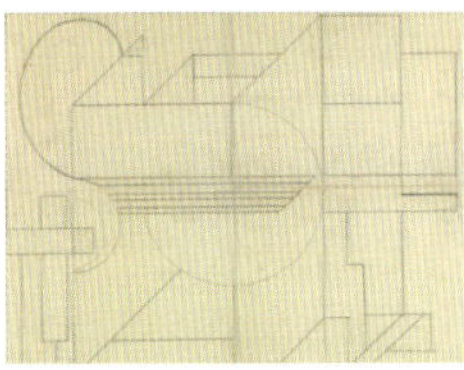

Jozef Peeters (1895 – 1960)
Project for wardrobe in a living room
Projet pour armoire pour salle de séjour
Ontwerp voor kast voor woonkamer
1924
Pencil, Indian ink, plume, watercolour, green ink on paper l Crayon, encre de Chine, plume, aquarelle, encre verte sur papier | Potlood, Oost-Indische inkt, pen, aquarel, groene inkt op papier
50,1 x 65,1 cm
Inv. 10345
Date of acquisition 1985

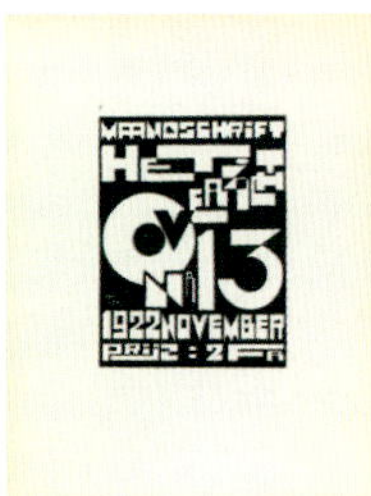

Jozef Peeters (1895 – 1960)
Cover of l Couverture de | Titelblad van "Het Overzicht" in l dans |in Album with l de | met | XVII lino cuts l lino-gravures | linos
1920 - 1925
Print ink on paper l Encre d'impression sur papier | Drukinkt op papier
64,7 x 48,7 cm
Inv. 11411
Date of acquisition 1985

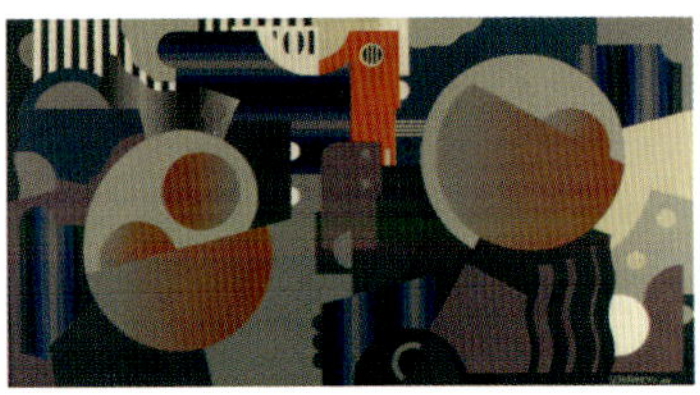

Victor Servranckx (1897 – 1965)
Opus 47. Glorification of the machinery
Opus 47. Exaltation du machinisme
Opus 47. Verheerlijking van de machinerie
1923
Oil on canvas l Huile sur toile | Olieverf op doek
113 x 210,5 cm
Inv. 6859
Date of acquisition 1959

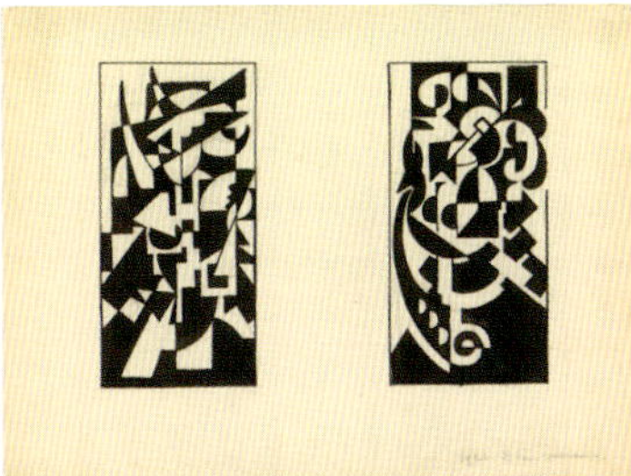

Edmond van Dooren (1896 – 1965)
Two constructivist compositions
Deux compositions constructivistes
Twee constructivistische composities
1920
Indian ink on paper l Encre de Chine sur papier | Oost-Indische inkt op papier
25 x 32,5 cm
Inv. 7935Date of acquisition 1971

Flemish Expressionism at large

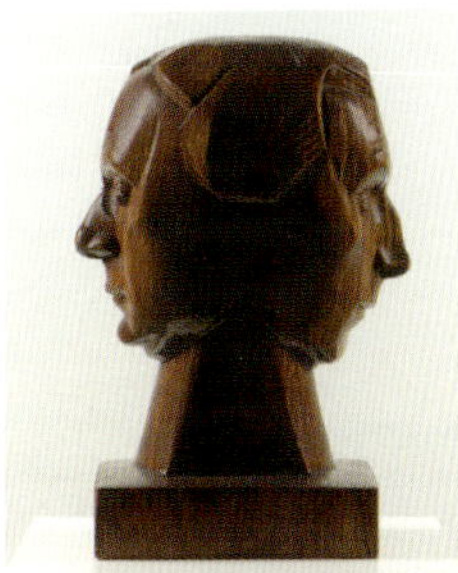

Jozef Cantré (1890 – 1957)
Double portrait of Gustave de Smet and Frits van den Berghe
Double portrait de Gustave de Smet et Frits van den Berghe
Dubbel portret van Gustave de Smet en Frits van den Berghe
(1921)
Wood l Bois | Hout
35,8 x 23 x 16,1 cm
Inv. 6805
Date of acquisition 1958

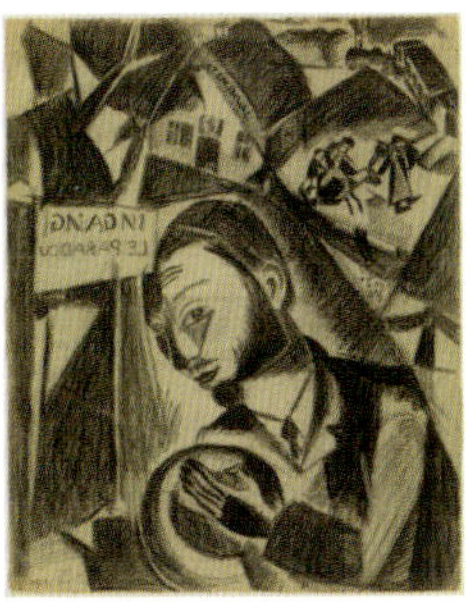

Jozef Cantré (1890 – 1957)
The visit
La visite
Het visite
1921
Black chalk on paper l Craie noire sur papier | Zwart krijt op papier
Inv. 9995
Date of acquisition 1983

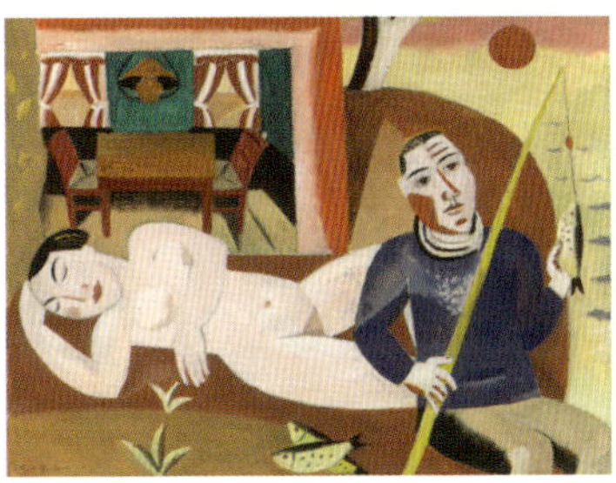

Gustave De Smet (1877 – 1943)
The summer
L'été
De zomer
(ca. 1925)
Gouache, oil on paper glued on cardboard l Gouache, huile sur papier collé sur carton | Gouache, olieverf op papier gekleefd op karton
51,2 x 66,7 cm
Inv. 12004
Date of acquisition 1997

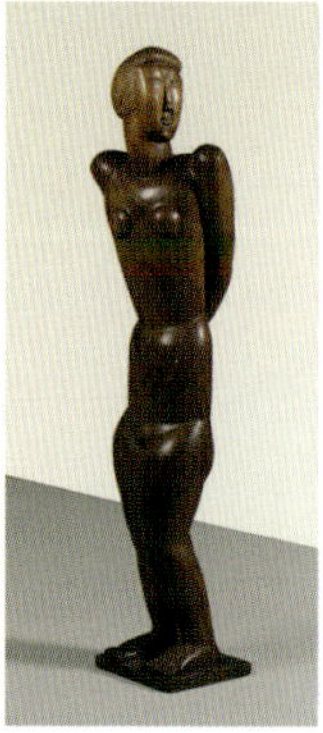

Oscar Jespers (1887 – 1970)
Young woman
Jeune femme
Jonge vrouw
(1930)
Wood (Limba) l Bois (Limba) | Hout (Limba)
167 x 39,5 x 35 cm
Inv. 7228
Date of acquisition 1965

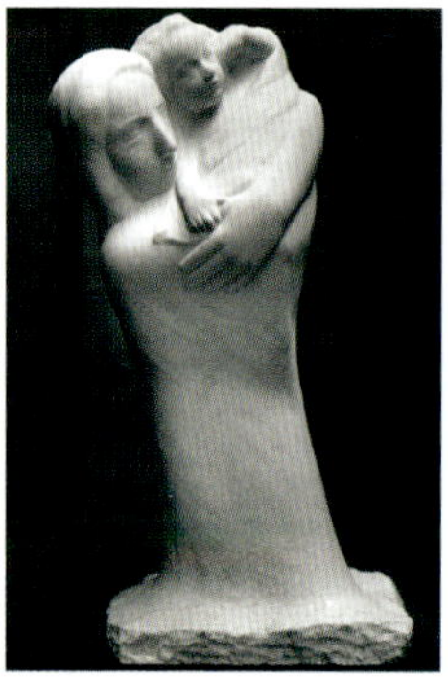

George Minne (1866 – 1941)
Mother and child IV
Mère et enfant IV
Moeder en kind IV
(ca. 1922)
Marble l Marbre | Marmer
68 x 37,5 x 37 cm
Inv. 4682
Date of acquisition 1927

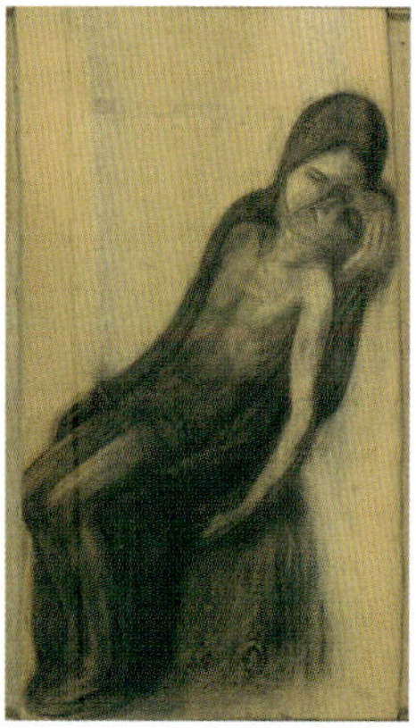

George Minne (1866 – 1941)
Pietà
Pietà
Piëta
(1921)
Charcoal on wood (lime) l Fusain sur bois (tilleul) |
Houtskool op hout (linde)
107 x 54 cm (jour)
Inv. 4330
Date of acquisition 1921

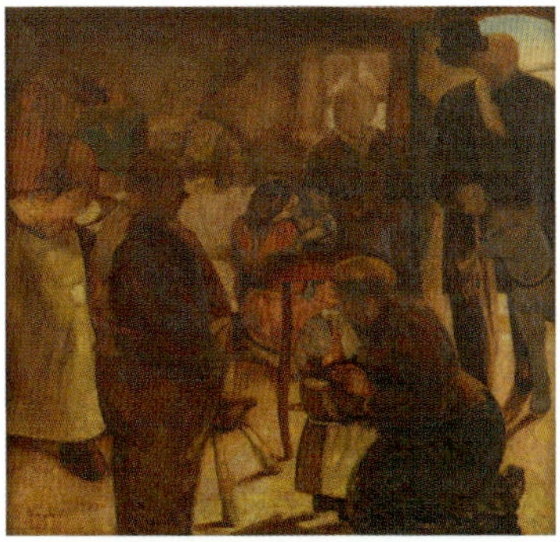

Constant Permeke (1886 – 1952)
The stranger
L'étranger
De vreemdeling
1916
Oil on canvas l Huile sur toile | Olieverf op doek
173 x 180 cm
Inv. 4655
Date of acquisition 1927

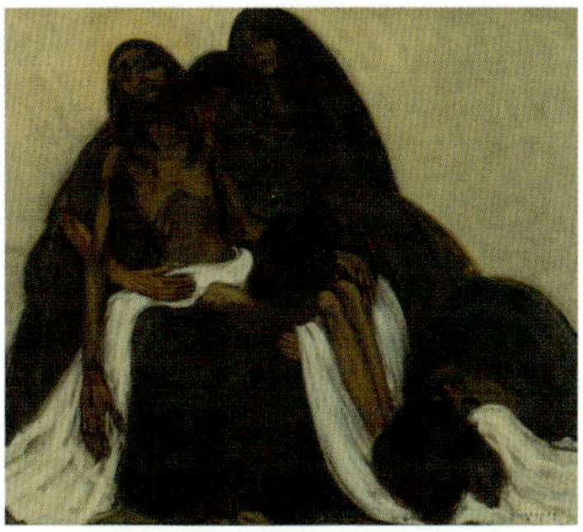

Albert Servaes (1883 – 1966)
Pietà
Pietà
Piëta
1920
Oil on canvas l Huile sur toile | Olieverf op doek
88 x 96 cm
Inv. 4183
Date of acquisition 1920

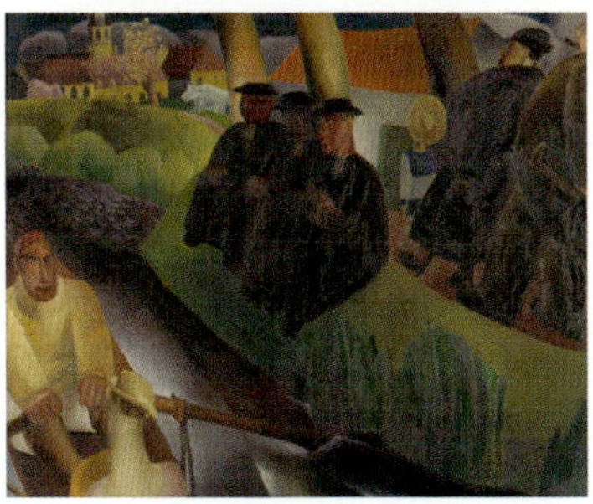

Frits Van den Berghe (1883 – 1939)
Sunday
Dimanche
Zondag
(1924)
Oil on canvas l Huile sur toile | Olieverf op doek
138,5 x 163 cm
Inv. 4697
Date of acquisition 1927

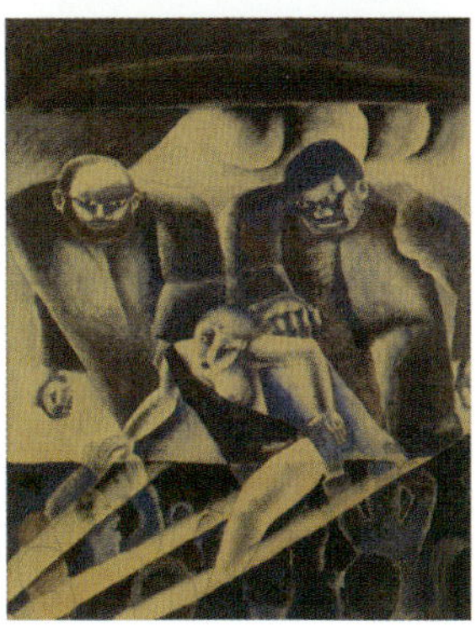

Frits van den Berghe (1883 – 1939)
The cinema
Le cinéma
De film
Gouache on paper glued on unalit panel l Gouache sur papier, collé sur unalit | Gouache op papier, gelijmd op unalit
62 x 47 cm
Inv. 7625
Date of acquisition 1969

Artists at war

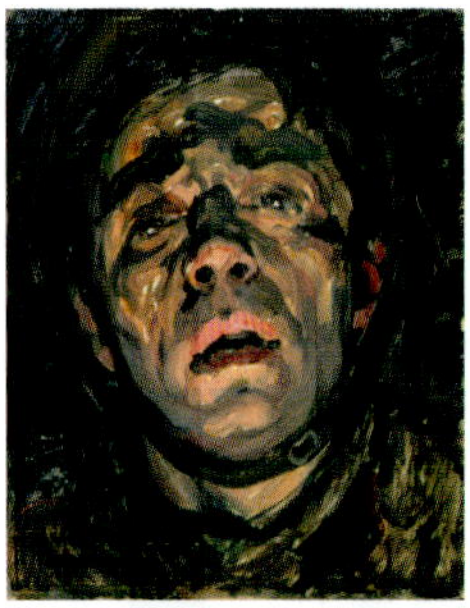

Fernand Allard l'Olivier (1883 – 1933)
Soldier surprised by the glow of a flare
Type de soldat surpris par la lueur d'une fusée
Soldaat opgeschrikt door het schijnsel van een vuurpijl
(1914-1918)
Oil on canvas l Huile sur carton | Olieverf op karton
35 x 27 cm
Inv. 10076/53
Date of acquisition 1920. On permanent loan in the Royal Museum of the Armed Forces and Military History, Brussels

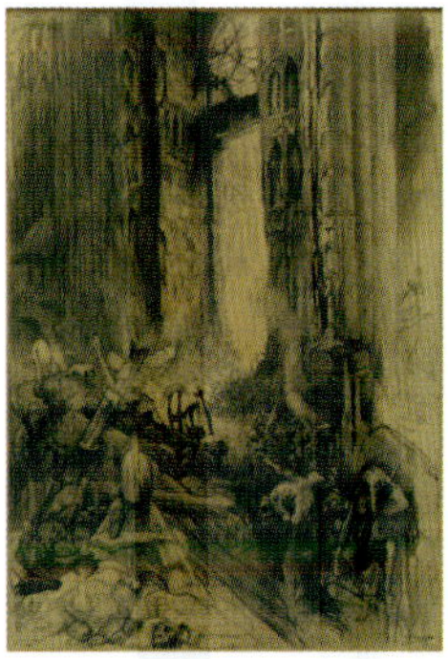

Jules De Bruycker (1870 – 1945)
The cathedral of Reims
La cathédrale de Reims
De kathedraal van Reims
1918
Black pencil on paper l Crayon noir sur papier | Zwart potlood op papier
99,5 x 67 cm
Inv. 4488
Date of acquisition 1923

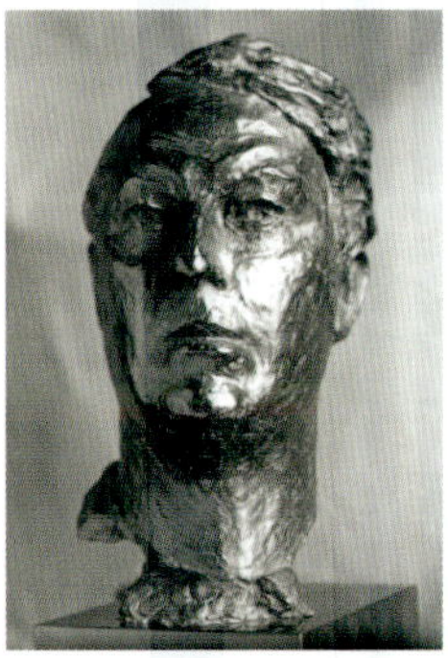

Gustave Fontaine (1877 – 1952)
Hippolyte Fierens-Gevaert, curator of the Royal Fine Arts Museum of Belgium
Hippolyte Fierens-Gevaert, conservateur du Musée royal des Beaux-Arts de Belgique
Hippolyte Fierens-Gevaert, conservator van het Koninklijk Museum voor
Schone Kunsten van België
1923
Bronze l Bronze | Brons
39,5 x 24,5 x 29 cm
Inv. 4680
Date of acquisition 1927

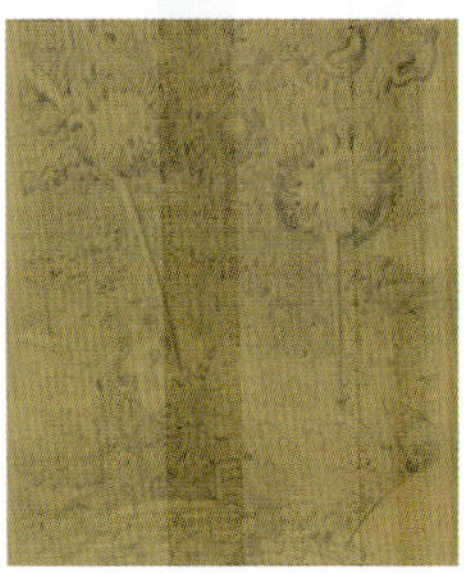

Paul Joostens (1889 – 1960)
Composition (The war)
Composition (La guerre)
Compositie (De oorlog)
Pencil on paper l Crayon sur papier | Potlood op papier
59,2 x 48 cm
Inv. 7933
Date of acquisition 1971

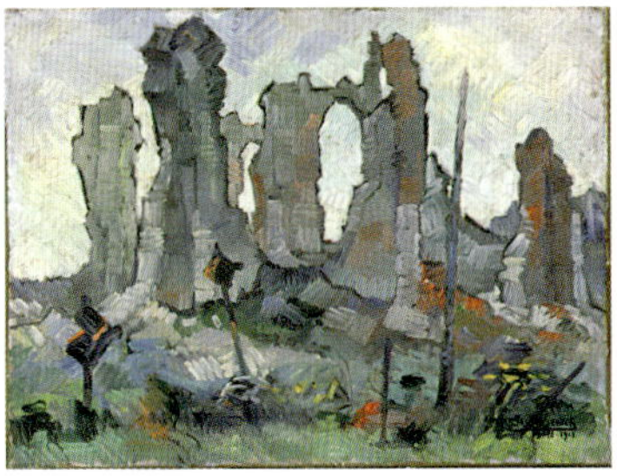

Achille Van Sassenbrouck (1886 – 1979)
Ruins of the church of Nieuwpoort
Ruines de l'église de Nieuport
Ruïnes van de kerk te Nieuwpoort
1918.
Oil on canvas l Huile sur toile | Olieverf op doek
54,2 x 69,6 cm
Inv. 10076/17
Date of acquisition 1920. On permanent loan in the Royal Museum of the Armed Forces and Military History, Brussels

Colophon

This book is the result of the research project and international symposium *14/18. Before and After? Rupture or Continuity? Belgian art around the First World War*, organized by the Royal Museums of Fine Arts of Belgium, Brussels, in collaboration with the Université Catholique de Louvain.

Exhibition 14/18. Rupture or Continuity? Royal Museums of Fine Arts of Belgium, Brussels: September 29, 2016 – January 22, 2017.
Symposium, Royal Museums of Fine Arts of Belgium / Bozar, Brussels: November 25/26, 2016.

General Management
Michel Draguet

Promotor & Curator
Inga Rossi-Schrimpf

Scientific researcher
Laura Kollwelter

COLLECTION RESEARCH AND EXHIBITION

Documentation and Collection Assessment
Laura Kollwelter, Inga Rossi-Schrimpf, Veronique Cardon,
with the collaboration of Sandrine Smets (RMAF)
Secretary: Charles Fumunjere

Production
Exhibition management: Sophie Van Vliet, Valérie Haerden
Collection management: Ludovic Godfrin, Yvon Lespagne, Stéphane Vandemaele, Jean-Marie Schoumaekers
Conservation: Inga Rossi-Schrimpf and Femke Segers
Graphic Design: Piet Bodyn, Vladimir Tanghe
Set design: Thu-Maï Dang, Inga Rossi-Schrimpf
Digital Museum: Pierre-Yves Desaive, Karine Lasaracina, Lies Van de Cappelle
Content Digital Experience: Laura Kollwelter, Géraldine Barbery (time line)
Stagiaire Online Collection: Aimée Auguin
Photographic service: Ward Verheyen, Johan Geleyns
Support service management: Colette Janssen
Financial management: Vinciane de Brouwer, Rik Snauwaert
IT service: Jack Claeys
Security & Facility management: Maarten Lousbergh in collaboration with Thu-Maï Dang, Yves Vandeven and Joachim Meert, assisted by the technical staff, the maintenance team and the security and dispatch staff
Public Service Management: Isabelle Vanhoonacker
Communication & Press: Isabelle Bastaits, Samir Al-Haddad, Gladys Vercammen-Grandjean
Public activities: Isabelle Vanhoonacker and team
Time Line: Géraldine Barbery
Conferences: Jean-Philippe Theyskens
Front Office: Koenraad Reynaert, Laurence Ryckaert

INTERNATIONAL SYMPOSIUM

Organisation
Inga Rossi-Schrimpf, assisted by Laura Kollwelter
Stagiaire: Alexandra Mönkemöller

Scientific committee
Véronique Cardon (MRBAB | KMSKB), Christina Kott (Université Panthéon-Assas Paris 2 | Institut d'histoire du temps présent IHTP), Hubert Roland (Université Catholique de Louvain | FNRS), Inga Rossi-Schrimpf (MRBAB | KMSKB), Lara Schrijver (Universiteit Antwerpen), Axel Tixhon (Facultés Universitaires de Namur), Rudi Van Doorslaer (CEGESOMA | Universiteit Gent), Michèle Van Kalck (MRBAB | KMSKB), Francisca Vandepitte (MRBAB | KMSKB), Caterina Verdickt (Universiteit Antwerpen)

Contributors
Werner Adriaenssens (Royal Museums of Art and History, Brussels), Erik Buelinckx (Royal Institute for Cultural Heritage, Brussels), Pierre Dejemeppe (Independent writer, Brussels), Ole W. Fischer (University of Utah, Salt Lake City), Eva Francioli (Università degli Studi di Firenze), Laura Kollwelter (Royal Museum of Fine Arts of Belgium, Brussels), Christina Kott (Université Panthéon-Assas Paris 2), Françoise Lucbert (Université Laval, Québec), Peter Pauwels (Independant at historian, Antwerp),Hubert Roland (F.R.S. – FNRS / Université Catholique de Louvain), Inga Rossi-Schrimpf (Royal Museum of Fine Arts of Belgium, Brussels), Sophie de Schaepdrijver (Pennsylvania State University), Sergio Servellón (FeliXart Museum, Drogenbos), Sandrine Smets (Royal Museum of Armed Forces and Military History, Brussels), Hans Vandevoorde (Vrije Universiteit Brussel), Caterina Verdickt (Universiteit Antwerpen)

Chairs
Laura Kollwelter (MRBAB | KMSKB), Hubert Roland (Université Catholique de Louvain | FNRS), Inga Rossi-Schrimpf (MRBAB | KMSKB), Sophie de Schaepdrijver (Pennsylvania State University), Lara Schrijver (Universiteit Antwerpen), Francisca Vandepitte (MRBAB | KMSKB)

Public service management
Isabelle Vanhoonacker
Secretary: Katrien De Geest
Events: Caroline Haraké
Press, communications and public relations: Isabelle Bastaits, Samir Al-Haddad, Gladys Vercammen-Grandjean
Graphics: Piet Bodyn, Vladimir Tanghe

PROCEEDINGS

General coordination for the Royal Museums of Fine Arts of Belgium: Inga Rossi-Schrimpf, Laura Kollwelter and Laurent Germeau, with the cooperation of Vincent Ladang

Editorial control: Kate Elliott, Luc Lontie, Inga Rossi-Schrimpf, Laura Kollwelter

Funding of the research project, symposium and publication
Belgian Federal Science Policy Office
Gouvernement de la région de Bruxelles-Capitale | Visit Brussels
Fonds National de la Recherche Scientifique

Fundraising
Inga Rossi-Schrimpf, Hubert Roland

Partners
Université Catholique de Louvain, BOZAR

Thanks to
Ulrich Bischoff, Adriaan Gonnissen, Musée Marthe Donas, Sub Rosa, Maïté Smeyers, Friends of the Royal Museums of Fine Arts

Royal Museums of Fine Arts of Belgium
9 rue du Musée / Museumstraat
1000 Brussels, Belgium
Tel.: + 32 (0) 2 508 32 09
www.fine-arts-museum.be
info@fine-arts-museum.be